THE GOSPEL OF MARK

Sacra Pagina Series

Volume 2

The Gospel of Mark

John R. Donahue, S.J.
and
Daniel J. Harrington, S.J.

Daniel J. Harrington, S.J.
Editor

A Michael Glazier Book

THE LITURGICAL PRESS
Collegeville, Minnesota

www.litpress.org

A Michael Glazier Book published by The Liturgical Press.

Cover design by Don Bruno.

2	3	4	5	6	7	8

Library of Congress Cataloging-in-Publication Data

Donahue, John R.
    The Gospel of Mark / John R. Donahue and Daniel J. Harrington ; Daniel J. Harrington, editor.
        p. cm. — (Sacra pagina series ; v. 2)
    Includes bibliographical references and index.
    ISBN 0-8146-5804-0 (alk. paper)
    1. Bible. N.T. Mark—Commentaries.   I. Harrington, Daniel J.   II. Title.
III. Sacra pagina series ; 2.

BS2585.53 .D66   2002
226.3'077—dc21
                                                        2001038722

In Memory of

Norman Perrin (1920–1976) and George W. MacRae (1928–1985)

Mentors and Friends

CONTENTS

The Gospel of Mark

Translation, Notes, Interpretation

Indexes

EDITOR'S PREFACE

Sacra Pagina is a multi-volume commentary on the books of the New Testament. The expression *Sacra Pagina* ("Sacred Page") originally referred to the text of Scripture. In the Middle Ages it also described the study of Scripture to which the interpreter brought the tools of grammar, rhetoric, dialectic, and philosophy. Thus Sacra Pagina encompasses both the text to be studied and the activity of interpretation.

This series presents fresh translations and modern expositions of all the books of the New Testament. Written by an international team of Catholic biblical scholars, it is intended for biblical professionals, graduate students, theologians, clergy, and religious educators. The volumes present basic introductory information and close exposition. They self-consciously adopt specific methodological perspectives, but maintain a focus on the issues raised by the New Testament compositions themselves. The goal of Sacra Pagina is to provide sound critical analysis without any loss of sensitivity to religious meaning. This series is therefore catholic in two senses of the word: inclusive in its methods and perspectives, and shaped by the context of the Catholic tradition.

The Second Vatican Council described the study of the "sacred page" as the "very soul of sacred theology" (*Dei Verbum* 24). The volumes in this series illustrate how Catholic scholars contribute to the council's call to provide access to Sacred Scripture for all the Christian faithful. Rather than pretending to say the final word on any text, these volumes seek to open up the riches of the New Testament and to invite as many people as possible to study seriously the "sacred page."

DANIEL J. HARRINGTON, S.J.

ABBREVIATIONS

Biblical Books and Apocrypha

Gen	Nah	1-2-3-4 Kgdms	John
Exod	Hab	Add Esth	Acts
Lev	Zeph	Bar	Rom
Num	Hag	Bel	1-2 Cor
Deut	Zech	1-2 Esdr	Gal
Josh	Mal	4 Ezra	Eph
Judg	Ps (*pl.*: Pss)	Jdt	Phil
1-2 Sam	Job	Ep Jer	Col
1-2 Kgs	Prov	1-2-3-4 Macc	1-2 Thess
Isa	Ruth	Pr Azar	1-2 Tim
Jer	Cant	Pr Man	Titus
Ezek	Eccl (*or* Qoh)	Sir	Phlm
Hos	Lam	Sus	Heb
Joel	Esth	Tob	Jas
Amos	Dan	Wis	1-2 Pet
Obad	Ezra	Matt	1-2-3 John
Jonah	Neh	Mark	Jude
Mic	1-2 Chr	Luke	Rev

Other Ancient Texts

Ant.	Josephus, *Antiquities of the Jews*
Apoc. Abr.	*Apocalypse of Abraham*
b.	Babylonian Talmud
B. Qamma	*Baba Qamma*
2–3 Bar	Syriac, Greek *Apocalypse of Baruch*
CD	Cairo Genizah copy of the *Damascus Document*
Eccl. Hist.	Eusebius, *Ecclesiastical History*
Gos. Thom.	*Gospel of Thomas*
Ḥag.	*Ḥagiga*
Ign., *Eph.*	Ignatius, *Letter to the Ephesians*
Jub	*Jubilees*

Ketub.	*Ketubot*
LXX	Septuagint
m.	Mishnah
MT	Masoretic Text
Ned.	*Nedarim*
NT	New Testament
OT	Old Testament
P. Oxy.	Papyrus Oxyrhynchus
Q	Sayings Source Q
1QapGen	Qumran Cave 1 *Genesis Apocryphon*
1QM	*War Scroll*
1QpHab	*Pesher Habakkuk*
1QH	*Hodayot*
1QS	*Rule of the Community*
1QSa	*Rule of the Community (Appendix)*
4Q	Qumran Cave 4
Spec. Leg.	Philo, *Special Laws*
T. Levi	*Testament of Levi*
Test. Sol.	*Testament of Solomon*
Toh.	*Toharot*
Vit. Mos.	Philo, *Life of Moses*
Yad.	*Yadayim*

Periodicals, Reference Works, and Serials

AB	Anchor Bible
ABD	*Anchor Bible Dictionary,* ed. David N. Freedman et al.
BAGD	Walter Bauer, W. F. Arndt, F. W. Gingrich, and F. W. Danker, *A Greek-English Lexicon of the New Testament and Other Early Christian Literature* (2nd ed.)
BDAG	F. W. Danker, reviser and editor, *A Greek-English Lexicon of the New Testament and Other Early Christian Literature* (3rd ed.)
BDF	Friedrich Blass, Albert Debrunner, and R. W. Funk, *A Greek Grammar of the New Testament*
Bib	*Biblica*
BTB	*Biblical Theology Bulletin*
BZ	*Biblische Zeitschrift*
CBQ	*Catholic Biblical Quarterly*
EKKNT	Evangelisch-katholisches Kommentar zum Neuen Testament
ETL	*Ephemerides theologicae Lovanienses*
ExpTim	*Expository Times*
HNT	Handbuch zum Neuen Testament
HTKNT	Herders theologischer Kommentar zum Neuen Testament
HTR	*Harvard Theological Review*
ICC	International Critical Commentary
IDB	*Interpreter's Dictionary of the Bible*

Int	*Interpretation*
JAAR	*Journal of the American Academy of Religion*
JBL	*Journal of Biblical Literature*
JES	*Journal of Ecumenical Studies*
JR	*Journal of Religion*
JSNT	*Journal for the Study of the New Testament*
JSP	*Journal for the Study of Pseudepigrapha*
JSS	*Journal of Semitic Studies*
JTS	*Journal of Theological Studies*
MPL	Patrologia Latina, ed. J. Migne
NAB	New American Bible
NCE	*New Catholic Encyclopedia*
NIV	New International Version
NovT	*Novum Testamentum*
NRSV	New Revised Standard Version
NTS	*New Testament Studies*
OTP	*Old Testament Pseudepigrapha*, ed. J. H. Charlesworth
RB	*Revue Biblique*
RQ	*Revue de Qumran*
SBLDS	SBL Dissertation Series
SBLMS	SBL Monograph Series
SJT	*Scottish Journal of Theology*
Str-B	Hermann Strack and Paul Billerbeck, *Kommentar zum Neuen Testament aus Talmud und Midrasch*
TDNT	*Theological Dictionary of the New Testament*, ed. Gerhard Kittel and Gerhard Friedrich
TS	*Theological Studies*
USQR	*Union Seminary Quarterly Review*
WBC	Word Biblical Commentary
ZNW	*Zeitschrift für die neutestamentliche Wissenschaft*

INTRODUCTION

1. *AN INTRATEXTUAL AND INTERTEXTUAL COMMENTARY*

One of the most striking developments in biblical studies in recent years has been the dramatic expansion of methods used in interpreting the text. From its inception the Sacra Pagina series has encouraged its authors to use those methods that are most appropriate and most fruitful for bringing out the distinctive character of the various writings that comprise the New Testament. The approach taken to Mark's Gospel in this volume can be expressed by two terms currently used in literary criticism: intratextuality and intertextuality.

Since these terms may be new to many readers and can have several meanings, we need to define carefully what we mean by them in this commentary. By "intratextuality" we mean reading Mark as Mark and by Mark. In reading Mark as Mark we express our interest in the final form of the gospel (not its sources or literary history) and in its words and images, literary devices, literary forms, structures, characterization, and plot. In reading Mark by Mark we want to give particular attention to the distinctive vocabulary and themes that run throughout the gospel and serve to hold it together as a unified literary production.

Since "intertextuality" is a protean term, comprising the relation between texts and a textual tradition and also referring to contextual materials not usually classified as texts (e.g., archaeological data), we use "intertextuality" to note the links of the text of Mark's Gospel to other texts (especially the Old Testament) and to the life of the Markan community and of the Christian community today. From the very beginning (Mark 1:2-3) the evangelist tells us that the Old Testament is an authoritative text and is being fulfilled in the story of Jesus. Moreover, Mark seems to have written to respond to the needs of a Christian community that was suffering persecution (most likely at Rome around 70 C.E.) in the hope that his text (his story of Jesus) would become their "text" too. Not only did it become the text of one community but it soon became the text of Matthew and Luke (who revised and expanded it) and the text of the whole church (when it became part of the Christian canon of Scripture). And Mark's text has continued to have theological and pastoral significance into the third Christian millennium.

Our decision to attempt an intratextual and intertextual reading of Mark's Gospel has implications for what one can expect to find (and not find) in this volume. While our introduction does take up the customary topics (author, date, place, genre, themes, purpose), its main goal is to provide the information necessary to appreciate the literary character of Mark's Gospel, its setting in life, and its distinctive approaches to the Old Testament, Jesus, and early Christian theology.

In keeping with the format of the Sacra Pagina series we present for each pericope in Mark's Gospel a translation, notes on the text, and an interpretation. The translation is based on the Greek text in *Novum Testamentum Graece* (27th ed. 1993)/*Greek New Testament* (4th ed. 1994). In rendering Mark's Greek we have tried to be straightforward and simple but not slavishly literal. Our goal is to capture the vividness and flow of Mark's narrative without necessarily translating every Greek participle as a participle or every case of the "historical present" in the present tense when the past makes better sense in English.

The notes deal with problems encountered in the text, supply necessary background information, and make links to other parts of Mark's Gospel. Some notes concern important textual variants and matters of philology and syntax while others explain and defend our translations. With respect to background, we have tried to supply the information—Old Testament terms and concepts, parallels in contemporary Jewish and Greco-Roman texts, customs and sociological assumptions, comparisons with Matthew and Luke, etc.—that is needed by readers in the twenty-first century to understand a first-century Christian text. A very important category of notes calls attention to verbal and conceptual links with other passages in Mark's Gospel. We have sought to be very concise in these notes; further information can be found in the standard Bible dictionaries and encyclopedias.

Another way to describe what we try to provide in the notes is to say that they proceed on three levels: contextual (the information that twenty-first-century readers need in order to understand the text of Mark's Gospel), intratextual (reading a Markan text in the light of other Markan texts), and intertextual (the relationship of Mark to the Old Testament and to other pertinent ancient texts).

The interpretations take as their focus the place of the passage in Mark's narrative and theology. Our concern is the Markan meaning, not the historical Jesus or the pre-Markan tradition (though in some cases we do make observations on those topics). To bring out the Markan meaning of a passage we consider its context, literary structure, and contributions to understanding Markan theology and the Markan community. Our basic principle is to interpret Mark as Mark and by Mark. Each interpretation contains some reflection on the significance of the passage for Christian theology in general and for preaching, teaching, and other forms of "actualization." A short list of books and articles for reference and further study is provided for each passage. In many cases we have included items that present different approaches and interpretations from the ones offered in our commentary, though we have not given much space to interacting with other Markan specialists.

We are aware that today no biblical commentary can do everything. We have tried to do a few things that we regard as very important: interpreting Mark as Mark and by Mark, noting the links between Mark's Gospel and the Old Testament, and exploring the meaning of Mark's Gospel for its first readers and for Christians today.

We regard the notes as the most important part of our commentary because they provide the basic information for appreciating the literary, historical, and theological significance of each passage. Readers may find it useful to read the interpretation immediately after the translation in order to get an overview, but a careful reading of the notes at some point is essential to using this commentary as we intend it and for understanding the richness of Mark's Gospel.

The authors, both American Jesuit priests, first met in the summer of 1966 in Jerusalem at the Pontifical Biblical Institute. We have independently pursued research on Mark for many years, and we are glad to have had the opportunity to join forces in explicating a text we both love. Donahue took primary responsibility for Mark 1:1–8:21 (and 14:1-31), and Harrington for the rest. Each contributed parts to the Introduction. And each criticized and revised the other's work.

2. MARK AMONG THE GOSPELS

For the bulk of church history the Gospel according to Mark, often called the Second Gospel (because of its frequent listing after Matthew), was of little independent significance. The famous statement of Augustine (354–430 C.E.) that Mark was primarily a follower, lackey, and digester of Matthew (*De consensu evangelistarum* 1.2.4) both crystallized much patristic thought and shaped opinion on Mark well into the nineteenth century. Greater authority was given to gospels thought to be by apostles (Matthew, John) than those by *apostolici viri* ("apostolic men"), Luke and Mark. Moreover, since ninety percent of Mark appears in Matthew there seemed to be little need to comment on Mark. Though there were *catenae* (collections) of Markan texts (e.g., by Victor of Antioch in the patristic period), no commentary appeared until the early Middle Ages. Michael Cahill has argued that the earliest commentary (which was thought to be from Jerome) is most likely by an unknown seventh-century Irish monk. Cahill contends that this work predates that of Venerable Bede (673–735 C.E.), who was thought to be the author of the first independent commentary on Mark. See Michael Cahill, *The First Commentary on Mark;* and idem, "The First Markan Commentary," *RB* 101 (1994) 258–68.

Since the rise of historical criticism the situation could not be more different. Virtually every major movement in the modern study of the Gospels has emerged in dialogue with Mark. Of particular importance was the development of the still-debated "Two-Source" hypothesis regarding the Synoptic Gospels. Though full discussion of the Synoptic Problem is beyond the scope of this commentary, and excellent discussions are found in most New Testament introductions (especially that of Raymond E. Brown), some review of the issues pertaining to Mark might be helpful here.

Basically the Two-Source hypothesis argues that Matthew and Luke used as written sources the Gospel of Mark and another source called Q (from the German *Quelle* meaning "source"). This latter source consists of roughly 335 verses, mostly sayings of Jesus, that *Matthew and Luke share in common* but that are not found in Mark. Many considerations have been adduced and debated, consisting of literary observations, logic of usage, and theological concerns, to argue that Mark is thus the earliest gospel so that, in effect, Matthew and Luke remain its earliest commentaries.

Most New Testament scholars favor the priority of Mark on the basis of certain ways in which Matthew and Luke are related to Mark. Generally Matthew and Luke follow the Markan order of events and actual wording, and when they diverge from Mark they rarely agree in their divergences. This suggests that Matthew and Luke must not have known each other, and that they used Mark and Q independently.

Though the literary arguments are endlessly debated and repackaged, the logic of usage and the theological arguments are much stronger. It seems more logical that Matthew and Luke would, as they constantly do, alter Mark's negative portrait of the disciples than that Mark would add this theme in a "digest." Also Matthew and Luke constantly soften some of the "realistic" or human aspects of Jesus' actions and reactions and so present a Jesus more in line with their "higher" christology. On the assumption of Markan use of Matthew and/or Luke some omissions would seem strange, most notably the absence of any resurrection appearance or infancy narrative as well as the Sermon on the Mount/Plain. It seems odd that the Markan Jesus would exhort his disciples to "pray that you may not enter temptation" and omit the Lord's Prayer, which concludes with such a petition. If Mark were offering a digest or summary of Matthew or Luke the presence of so many doublets and duplicate expressions would seem strange, as would Mark's tendency to have more detailed accounts of incidents contained in all three gospels.

While this commentary will proceed from the assumption of the priority of Mark, we recognize that the Two-Source hypothesis does not resolve all problems and that the relationships among the Synoptic Gospels should not be conceived in a wooden fashion. The so-called "minor agreements" (those places where Matthew and Luke agree against Mark) have been the major weapon in the arsenal of those who defend the priority of Matthew. Though many of these objections can be answered in terms of stylistic changes that may occur coincidentally (for example, two editors today could independently change "ain't" to "are not" without knowing each other), a mechanistic defense of the priority of Mark need not be maintained. Due to the persistence and even preference for the oral tradition among certain early Christian groups, Matthew and/or Luke may conceivably have had an earlier version of a particular narrative or saying found in Mark, which they retained even as they edited and incorporated Mark's Gospel.

Another area of intensive debate on Mark that bears mention here is its relation to the Gospel of John. Three positions emerge: John does not know Mark or the traditions found in Mark; John knows the Gospel of Mark; and John and Mark share some common traditions, even though each uses them in distinctive ways. Again this is a very complex issue due to the debates about the status of both pre-Markan and pre-Johannine material, and it is important mainly for reconstructing the currents and directions in the development of first-century Christianity, which was always a combination of shared traditions and distinct perspectives.

The major theological contribution associated with the priority of Mark emerged in the nineteenth century as "the Markan hypothesis." Mark was viewed as the earliest of the gospels and the closest to eyewitness recollections of Jesus' earthly ministry, and hence one less influenced by the post-Easter faith of the community. The author of Mark was viewed primarily as a *Sammler*, a collector of undigested traditions, and any theology in the work was seen as the theology of the traditions. The Markan hypothesis also had major impact on the original "Quest for the Historical Jesus," so ably catalogued in Albert Schweitzer's landmark work, *The Quest of the Historical Jesus: A Critical Study of Its Progress from Reimarus to Wrede* (London: A. & C. Black, 1910; German original, *Von Reimarus zu Wrede*, 1906), which culminated in Adolf von Harnack's *What is Christianity?* (London: E. Benn, 1958; German original, *Das Wesen des Christentums*, 1900), a monumental bestseller in its day. Here Jesus' life and teaching were summarized as concern for "the fatherhood of God" and "the brotherhood of man." Not only was Harnack's vision of Jesus shattered during the mutual Christian slaughter of World War I ("the

Great War"), but it was given its farewell commendation by George Tyrrell's famous statement: "The Christ that Harnack sees, looking back through nineteen centuries of Catholic darkness, is only the reflection of a Liberal Protestant face, seen at the bottom of a deep well" (from D. G. Schultenover, *George Tyrrell: In Search of Catholicism* [Shepherdstown, W. Va.: Patmos, 1981] 432, quoting from Tyrrell, *Christianity at the Crossroads* [London and New York: Longmans, Green, 1909] 44).

3. MARK BEFORE THE GOSPELS

Along with the emergence of historical and source criticism in the nineteenth century, "form criticism" dominated New Testament studies from the early decades of the twentieth century until after World War II, and it, too, found in Mark a fertile field for its investigation. Richard Soulen offers this helpful description: "Form criticism may be loosely defined as the analysis of the typical forms by which human existence is expressed linguistically; traditionally this referred particularly to their oral pre-literary state, such as legends, hymns, curses, and laments" (*Handbook of Biblical Criticism* [Atlanta: John Knox, 1981] s.v.). Form criticism also argues that each form has a distinct social and cultural setting, the *Sitz im Leben*, so that the religious and social lives of communities can be described through a study of the forms and genres of literature that they use. Form criticism also stresses the stages in the development of the form and of traditional material, so that it becomes a tool for finding the earliest traditions behind our extant texts.

Though rooted in the work of classicists and Old Testament scholars, New Testament form criticism is most prominently associated with Martin Dibelius (1883–1947) and Rudolf Bultmann (1884–1976). Dibelius' foundational work, *Die Formgeschichte des Evangeliums*, was first published in 1919 (English: *From Tradition to Gospel* [New York: Scribner's, 1965]). He stressed that the evangelists were compilers of pre-existing material and he studied the forms of pre-gospel materials and their settings (*Sitze im Leben*) defined as "the historical and social stratum in which precisely these literary forms were developed" (*From Tradition to Gospel* 7). Dibelius's famous adage was "in the beginning was the sermon" (his father was a pastor and preacher). His method has been called "constructive" in that he stressed how literary forms evolved according to the needs of the early communities (e.g., in preaching or religious practice).

Shortly afterward, Rudolf Bultmann published *Die Geschichte der synoptischen Tradition* (1st ed. Göttingen: Vandenhoek & Ruprecht, 1921; English: *The History of the Synoptic Tradition* [New York: Harper and Row, 1968]). This was one of the most influential works of the twentieth century in New Testament studies. Bultmann worked "inductively" (that is, from a careful analysis of the material in the Synoptic tradition), and then postulated a *Sitz im Leben* for the material. He also studied the laws of the transmission of oral and written material. This work became the foundation of Bultmann's later studies on the historical Jesus and on New Testament theology.

Both Dibelius and Bultmann distinguished between forms proper to narrative and those proper to discourse, but Bultmann's categories won the day. Narrative material falls into the categories of miracle stories and legends (that is, stories with no historical value and whose sole purpose was religious edification). His major influence may have been in his category of apophthegms (sometimes spelled simply apothegms), from the Greek *apophtheggomai* meaning "speak out plainly." The noun is used for a terse pointed saying and often for anecdotes with a narrative frame but where the narrative culminates in and is subservient to a specific saying. Bultmann distinguished three types of apophthegms: controversy dialogues, scholastic dialogues, and biographical apophthegms. The "radical" aspect of Bultmann's work initially for most Protestant scholars and continually for many Catholic scholars was the assumption that these apophthegms did not capture recollections of the historical Jesus but were created by the early church in the service of its proclamation about Jesus. Likewise, Bultmann described "dominical sayings" which he further subdivided into *logia* or "wisdom sayings" (e.g., Matt 6:19-34), prophetic and apocalyptic sayings (Matt 5:3-9; Mark 13), legal sayings and community rules (Matt 18:15-22), similes and parables (Mark 4:1-34), and "I" sayings (Matt 10:34-36; 11:25-30).

Though the emphasis was to shift away from form criticism and its quest for the earliest traditions and their subsequent modification, there has been a great deal of research since Bultmann on a form from antiquity similar to the apophthegm called the *chreia* (also spelled *chria*), a technical term in ancient rhetoric to denote a literary form containing an epigram or a "sharp pointed saying" of general significance, or "a concise statement or action attributed with aptness to some specified character or to something analogous to a character" (James R. Butts, "The *Chreia* in the Synoptic Gospels," *BTB* 16 [1986] 132–38; also Vernon Robbins, "The *Chreia*," in David E. Aune, ed., *Greco-Roman Literature and the New Testament* [Atlanta: Scholars, 1988] 21–33). The importance of the *chreiae* is that they were used extensively in the rhetorical exercises called *progymnasmata* which were part of basic Greco-Roman education. Like apophthegms, they call into question the historicity of certain sayings and events. Since they were also used extensively by Cynic philosophers they have become a fertile field for finding major Cynic influence everywhere from Jesus through the Gospels and in Paul.

Movements in New Testament studies rarely die out but often merge into other movements or arise like a phoenix from the ashes. Form criticism still remains important for research into the life of Jesus (for example, see the careful discussion of the development of the miracle traditions by John P. Meier in *A Marginal Jew* 2:617–1038) and for the history of the early church. Also, as more knowledge of ancient rhetorical modes of composition emerges, the question of the classification and life-setting of different blocks of literature remains acute.

4. REDACTION CRITICISM: MARK AS "AUTHOR" AND THEOLOGIAN

In 1969 Norman Perrin described redaction criticism (from the German *Redaktor*, "editor") as "concerned with studying the theological motivation of an author as this is revealed in the collection, arrangement, editing and modification of traditional material and in the composition of new material or the creation of new forms within the traditions of early Christianity" (*What is Redaction Criticism?* [Philadelphia: Fortress, 1969] 1). As Perrin's description indicates, redaction criticism describes a complex of approaches to the text rather than a single unified method. The term is subsequently used in a double, and often confusing, sense. Narrowly conceived it means "editorial criticism." The more widely-used sense comprises "composition criticism" in which other activities, such as the arrangement of material and the creation of new material, are attributed to the evangelist.

As heir to form criticism in Germany, redaction criticism developed with a strong stress on the history of the traditions that lay behind a given work—Mark and Q in the case of Matthew and Luke, and reconstructed traditions in the case of Mark. (The vast majority of redaction critics have held the Two-Source theory.) In Germany the emphasis was predominantly on the separation of tradition and redaction. For the sake of convenience we can describe this as "strict editorial criticism." Willi Marxsen stated that "we depend on literary-critical analysis for separating tradition from redaction" (*Mark the Evangelist* 26), and Rudolf Pesch in his influential study of Mark 13 wrote: "The division of tradition from redaction must be undertaken on a verse-by-verse basis, and occasionally word by word. Only in this fashion does one attain a foundation for a complete understanding of the tradition and of the redaction by the evangelist" (*Naherwartungen* [Düsseldorf: Patmos, 1968] 47). Robert Fortna comments that "the redaction critic pays closest attention to what distinguishes the work before him from the earlier material on which it is based" ("Redaction Criticism, NT," *IDBSup* 733–35).

An internal tension characterized many important early "editorial-critical" studies. On the one hand the Gospel of Mark became an area of intensive investigation. On the other hand there was no agreed-upon received tradition *(Vorlage)* for Mark. Yet during the first decades of redaction criticism, in individual studies (Quentin Quesnell, *The Mind of Mark*, AnBib 38 [Rome: Biblical Institute Press, 1969] 39–57; Detlef Dormeyer, *Die Passion Jesu als Verhaltensmodell*, NTAbh, n.s. 11 [Münster: Aschendorff, 1974] 24–33; Pesch, *Naherwartungen*) and in more explicit methodological statements such as those by Robert Stein, a number of procedures and implicit criteria were developed for distinguishing between tradition and redaction (see Stein, "What is Redaktionsgeschichte?" *JBL* 88 [1969] 45–56; "The 'Redaktionsgeschichtlich' Investigation of a Markan Seam (Mc 1.21f)," *ZNW* 61 [1970] 70–94; and "The Proper Methodology for Ascertaining a Markan Redaction History," *NovT* 13 [1971] 181–98).

A brief summary of these procedures and criteria would include the following items:

1. Use of form criticism and tradition history to uncover possible oral traditions or blocks of tradition behind the Markan text; for example, an earlier apocalyptic pamphlet *(Flugblatt)* as the basis of Mark 13.

2. Study of characteristic Markan vocabulary and stylistic features (see E. J. Pryke, *Redactional Style in the Marcan Gospel: A Study of Syntax and Vocabulary as Guides to Redaction in Mark*; Frans Neirynck, *Duality in Mark: Contributions to the Study of the Markan Redaction*; idem, "The Redactional Text of Mark" *ETL* 57 [1981] 144–62, reprinted in Frans van Segbroeck, ed., *Evangelica I: Gospel Studies: Collected Essays by Frans Neirynck*. BETL 60 [Leuven: Leuven University Press, 1982] 618–36; and Max Zerwick, *Untersuchungen zum Markus-Stil* [Rome: Biblical Institute Press, 1937]).

3. Examination of compositional devices such as intercalation (or sandwiching) of one pericope within another (for example, Mark 14:3-9 within 14:1-2 and 14:10-11; see John R. Donahue, *Are you the Christ? The Trial Narrative in the Gospel of Mark* 58–59, 240–43), and fondness for duplication (Neirynck, *Duality*). Crucial to this aspect of the method was study of the Markan seams and introductions to pericopes, which were thought most to reveal the hand of the author (Kendrick Grobel, "Idiosyncrasies of the Synoptists in their Pericope Introductions," *JBL* 59 [1940] 405–10).

4. Determination of the extent of a given pericope and analysis of "tensions" that would suggest the joining of sections not originally joined (e.g., Mark 2:1-12, which seems to combine a miracle story and a controversy story), as well as the study of duplicates within

the same gospel, which might suggest different traditions (see Paul J. Achtemeier, "The Origin and Function of the Pre-Marcan Miracle Catenae," *JBL* 91 [1972] 198–221). Quesnell (*Mind of Mark* 51) describes one of the ways in which the study of tensions discloses redaction: "redactional by nature is that which shows signs of having been written in the light of a larger whole than the pericope or speech in which it stands, or at least from a different viewpoint and/or giving form to the pericope in which it stands."

5. Examination of parallel material in Matthew and Luke to speculate about whether the ways in which Matthew and Luke edited Mark might reveal the distinctive characteristics of Mark.

6. Study of the postulated literary activity of "Mark" in a given pericope in comparison with "Markan" editing of other places in the gospel to find if a consistent pattern emerges; for example, the tendency of Mark to universalize scenes by the frequent addition of "all" or "very many" (Donahue, *Trial* 66–67).

From an examination of the editorial activity of Mark, hypotheses were then formed about the intention—most often described as the "theological intention"—of the author. As redaction criticism has evolved, three elements have come to characterize it: (1) study of the editorial or compositional activity of an "author" (2) as a key to his theological intention, or in more neutral literary terms, his ideology, (3) which is in response to questions or issues alive in a particular community within the last decades of the first century C.E.

The separation of tradition from redaction results in a view of the evangelist as in either dialogic or dialectical relationship with the tradition. For example, in his study of the Markan miracle tradition Karl Kertelge concluded that miracles traditionally functioned primarily as divine epiphanies. Mark, according to Kertelge, does not deny this primary focus but subsumes the miracles into his gospel as epiphanies of the crucified and risen one. Ludger Schenke conversely states that in the pre-Markan tradition the miracles functioned as props for an incorrect *theios anēr* ("divine man") christology. Mark is thought to oppose the proponents of this christology and by his redaction to refute their use of miracles. By inserting them into a temporal and geographical structure Mark deprives the miracles of their power as isolated epiphanies and reduces them to episodes of the life of Jesus. They are subordinated to teaching, and the motif of secrecy deprives them of their revelatory power. This dialectical relation of Mark to the tradition has been postulated in respect to Mark 13 (Pesch, *Naherwartungen*), the picture of discipleship (Theodore J. Weeden, *Mark—Traditions in Conflict;* Tagawa), and the Passion narrative

(Ludger Schenke, Wolfgang Schenk). See Karl Kertelge, *Die Wunder Jesu im Markusevangelium: Eine redaktionsgeschichtliche Untersuchung.* SANT 23 (Munich: Kösel, 1970); Ludger Schenke, *Die Wundererzählungen des Markusevangeliums.* SBB 5 (Stuttgart: Katholisches Bibelwerk, 1974); Wolfgang Schenk, *Der Passionsbericht nach Markus: Untersuchungen z. Überlieferungsgeschichte d. Passionstraditionen* (Gütersloh: Gerd Mohn, 1974); Kenzo Tagawa, *Miracles et Évangile: La pensée personnelle de l'évangile Marc.* Études d'histoire et de philosophie religieuses 62 (Paris: Presses Universitaires de France, 1966).

In addition to "strict editorial criticism," redaction criticism (as a generic term) also developed into "composition criticism." In his commentary on Mark and its synoptic parallels Ernst Haenchen stresses that he is interested in the Markan material in its *Sitz im Leben der Evangelist selbst;* that is, primarily in the location of a given block of material in the gospel in relation to its immediate and larger context as an index of the intention of the author (*Der Weg Jesu: Eine Erklärung des Markus-Evangeliums und der kanonischen Parallelen* [Berlin: de Gruyter, 1968] 23–24). Composition criticism, which directed attention to the setting of a given pericope in the larger context of a particular gospel, quickly gave birth to a great number of studies on the themes or motifs of each gospel.

The term "composition criticism" itself conveys a certain ambiguity since it can be used for describing the *creation* or composing of new material or for the *putting together* of pre-existing material in a new arrangement. Thus composition criticism came to describe a method employed by two major groups of scholars with distinct views of the relation of Mark to tradition. One group views virtually everything in Mark's Gospel as tradition and sees Mark at work as "author" only in brief introductory sentences and occasional editorial additions. Ernest Best suggests that rather than referring to Mark as author one should think of him as an artist creating a collage ("Mark's Preservation of the Tradition," in M. Sabbe, ed., *L'Évangile selon Marc.* BETL 34 [Leuven: Leuven University Press, 1974] 21–34; reprinted in William Telford, ed., *The Interpretation of Mark* [Philadelphia: Fortress, 1985] 119–33). Another group of scholars who practice composition criticism are willing to admit that Mark may be the actual author (composer) of large parts of the text and are ready to abandon the attempt to distinguish tradition from redaction.

The shift from "editorial criticism" to "composition criticism" can be seen most dramatically in the career of Rudolf Pesch. His first work, *Naherwartungen* (1968), was a model of careful attention to the text of Mark 13 in order to distinguish the extent of Markan editing of an earlier reconstructed tradition. Mark's purpose in this was to deflect attention of the Markan community shortly after the destruction of Jerusalem away from an expectation that the tragic events of 70 C.E. were the immediate prelude to the return of Jesus. Rather, according to Pesch, Mark substitutes a "near expectation," which does not identify the *parousia* with any particular event and redacts the apocalyptic tradition in the direction of paraenesis by warning the community against false messianic claimants (especially Mark 13:21-22). However, by the time Pesch published his two-volume commentary on Mark in 1976–77 he held that the bulk of Mark's text is tradition and that Mark was a "conservative redactor" whose creativity is manifest primarily in his *arrangement* of material. The Gospel of Mark presents something of a paradox. It is virtually all "tradition" in the sense that no final editor or author "composed" the narrative as a modern author might; at the same time it is all "composition" in the sense that the final editor created a narrative tapestry where the different parts are woven together to present a coherent and complex story that is greater than the sum of its parts.

Though the attempt to distinguish tradition from redaction in Mark has remained problematic, composition criticism of Mark has proved to be one of the most fruitful approaches to this gospel as important studies have appeared on Mark's distinctive theological perspectives in areas such as christology, discipleship, and eschatology. These studies have underscored the distinctive contribution of Mark to an understanding of the theological pluralism alive in the first century. But the same Norman Perrin who welcomed and fostered redaction criticism commented shortly before his death in 1976 that redaction criticism had developed in its own special way in the United States and had mutated into a "genuine literary criticism" ("The Interpretation of the Gospel of Mark," *Int* 30 [1976] 115–24).

5. MARK AS "LITERATURE"

One of the obstacles to viewing Mark as literature was a certain sociological bias that Mark was basically an unlettered religious enthusiast who wrote in simple Greek; this judgment is resonant of the late-nineteenth-century view of the Gospels as artless writings *(Kleinliteratur)*. An early objection to this view was voiced by the distinguished Oxford literary critic Helen Gardner, who spoke of the "poetry of St. Mark": "Reading the Gospel is like reading a poem. It is an imaginative experience. It presents us with a sequence of events and sayings which combine to create in our minds a single complex and powerful symbol, a pattern of meaning. Reading St. Mark is quite unlike reading a series of entries made by a compiler of annals, or a collection of separate anecdotes" ("The Poetry of St. Mark," in her *The Business of Criticism* [Oxford: Clarendon Press, 1959] 103).

The mid-1970s witnessed a flowering of literary critical studies of the Gospels, understood not in the traditional New Testament sense as detection of literary sources but with the meaning employed in general literary criticism (often prefaced with the misnomer "secular," as if there is a distinct "religious" literary criticism). Apropos of Mark, but with implications for the other gospels, Mary Ann Tolbert sketched the fundamental assumptions of such an approach: "The first and most important of these assumptions . . . is that Mark is a self-consciously crafted narrative, a fiction, resulting from literary imagination, not from photographic detail" (*Sowing the Gospel* 30). After pointing out that its status as fiction does not mean that Mark has no connection with history, but rather that the author has "made" the narrative, Tolbert articulates a second assumption: "a narrative is unified and coherent" (ibid. 38). Stephen Moore noted another important assumption of the literary turn that distinguishes it from redaction or composition criticism: "For composition critics, the meaning resides in the text's theological (or ideational) content. The content is separable in principle from the narrative form; narrative is the vehicle of theology. Narrative criticism, in contrast, is a *formalist* criticism; the meaning of the biblical text is located in the details of its structure" (Stephen Moore, *Literary Criticism and the Gospels: The Theoretical Challenge* [New Haven: Yale University Press, 1989]).

To better appreciate the literary turn in Mark, two topics deserve more attention: the genre of Mark and its "narrative artistry."

6. *THE GENRE OF MARK*

A fundamental principle for reading any text is to understand its "genre" or what kind of literature it represents (e.g., history or legend, exhortation or law). A current reference work describes genre in this way: "Genre classification implies that there are groups of formal or technical characteristics among works of the same generic kind regardless of time or place of composition, author, or subject matter; and that these characteristics when they define a particular group of works are of basic significance in talking about literary art" (C. Hugh Holman and William Harmon, *A Handbook to Literature* [6th ed. New York: Macmillan, 1992] 212). Mark seems unique in describing the genre in the first verse of the gospel: "The beginning of the good news (*euangelion*, also "gospel") about Jesus, Messiah" (1:1). This has led some authors to think of Mark as creating a distinct genre "gospel," which was then imitated by Matthew, Luke, and writers of subsequent apocryphal gospels.

Although Mark is the only evangelist to use the noun *euangelion* (1:1, 14, 15; 8:35; 10:29; 13:10; 14:9), the term does not originate with him. In secular Greek it describes the public proclamation of a significant event, as shown in an inscription dated to 9 B.C.E. and discovered at Priene in Asia Minor (near Miletus) that celebrates the birthday of Augustus: "the birthday of the god [= emperor] was for the world the beginning of joyful tidings *(euangelia)* which have been proclaimed on his account." In the Septuagint the singular use of the noun is found only three times (2 Kgdms 4:10; 18:22, 25 = 2 Sam 4:10; 18:19-20), while the verbal form *euangelizesthai* ("to announce good news") appears in the context of a joyful or important message delivered by a designated messenger, especially in significant contexts in Deutero-Isaiah (Isa 40:9; 52:7, "How beautiful upon the mountains are the feet of the messenger who proclaims peace, who announces salvation, who says to Zion, 'Your God reigns,'" cf. Mark 1:15; Isa 60:6; 61:1, cf. Luke 4:18-19).

The distinctive Christian use of *euangelion* is found in the Pauline writings where the term appears over sixty times as a virtual recapitulation of the Christ-event; that is, the meaning of the life, death, and resurrection/exaltation of Jesus (select examples: 1 Thess 1:2-9; 1 Cor 15:1-11; 1 Cor 1:17-25; Rom 1:1, 9, 16-17; 10:14-21; Rom 15:14-21; see Joseph A. Fitzmyer, "Gospel"). If, as is highly likely, Mark knew the Pauline tradition, then theologically Mark's Gospel can be understood as the proclamation of the Christ event in narrative form.

Still, the questions of literary genre and models for the Markan composition remain highly debated. Many different models and influences on Mark have been proposed. "Biography" is one of the leading contenders, not in the modern sense of the exhaustive study of the personal history, social interaction, and psychological development of a person, but as a narrative influenced by the numerous and diverse Greco-Roman *bioi*. These works are variously described: "ancient biography is prose narration about a person's life, presenting supposedly historical facts which are selected to reveal the character or essence of the individual, often with the purpose of affecting the behavior of the reader" (Charles H. Talbert, *What is a Gospel? The Genre of the Canonical Gospels* [Philadelphia: Fortress, 1977] 17). Or biography is "a discrete prose narrative devoted exclusively to the portrayal of the whole life of a particular individual perceived as historical" (David Aune, *The New Testament in Its Literary Environment* [Philadelphia: Westminster, 1987] 29). Various ancient works and authors have been proposed as embodying the type of writing that might have influenced Mark; even though some were composed later than Mark, these works involved set conventions (see Aune, "Greco-Roman Biography," *Greco-Roman Literature* 107–26; Adela Yarbro Collins, "Is Mark's Gospel a Life of Jesus?" in her *The Beginning of the Gospel. Probings of Mark in Context* [Minneapolis: Fortress, 1992] 1–38; Christopher Bryan, *A Preface to Mark. Notes on the Gospel in Its Literary and Cultural Settings* [New York and Oxford: Oxford University Press, 1993] 1–64). Examples would be Suetonius (born ca. 69 C.E.), *Lives of the Caesars;* Plutarch (ca. 50–120 C.E.), *Parallel Lives;* Philo of Alexandria (ca. 20 B.C.E. to 50 C.E.), *On the Life of Moses;* and the various accounts of Socrates, especially of his death: Plato (429–347 B.C.E.), *Apology,* and Xenophon (428–354 B.C.E.), *Memorabilia.* A constant yet debated claim for influence on the Gospels, especially in the narration of the miracles, is Flavius Philostratus (born ca. 170 C.E.), who studied at Athens and later joined the philosophical circle patronized by Septimus Severus and his wife Julia Domna, and wrote at her insistence a life of Apollonius of Tyana (a city in Cappadocia). Apollonius was a wandering Pythagorean sage and wonder worker in the late first century C.E. who had disciples and suffered persecution under Nero and Domitian (see *Philostratus: The Life of Apollonius of Tyana,* 2 vols. LCL 16, 17 [Cambridge, Mass.: Harvard University Press; London: W. Heinemann, 1912–50] 121–22).

Other more intriguing proposals for an influence on Mark include the suggestions that it imitates popular Hellenistic novels and romances (Tolbert, *Sowing the Gospel*), Greek tragedy (Gilbert G. Bilezikian, *The Liberated Gospel: A Comparison of the Gospel of Mark and Greek Tragedy* [Grand Rapids: Baker Book House, 1977]), or Greco-Roman rhetorical forms, particularly encomiastic or expository speeches (Benoît H. M. G. M. Standaert, *L'évangile selon Marc: Composition et genre littéraire* [Brugge: Zevenkerken, 1978]). Recently Dennis R. MacDonald has argued strongly and interestingly for the direct influence of the Homeric epics on Mark (*The Homeric Epics and the Gospel of Mark* [New Haven: Yale University Press, 2000]).

In a fine survey of these proposals Adela Yarbro Collins contests the view that various Hellenistic lives were generic models for Mark ("Is Mark's Gospel a Life of Jesus?"). She argues that Mark did not intend to present Jesus as a model, or to authenticate his life as the source of a tradition (as in the case of the lives of philosophers), or to synthesize diverse traditions about his life. She states clearly: "the primary intention of Mark was to write history." Yet this "history" is not simply the depiction of the events from the life of Jesus, but "a particular kind of history . . . a narration of the course of the eschatological events," not history in the "rational, empirical sense of Thucydides, or in the modern critical sense, but . . . history in an eschatological or apocalyptic sense" (p. 27). The background for this history is found in Jewish apocalyptic literature such as Daniel (where eschatological events are put in a narrative frame of the career of Daniel) and in *1 Enoch.* Interpretation of Mark today demands an appreciation for "the broad scope of the vision of the Gospel," as depicting Jesus caught up in the events of the end time. Collins acknowledges that her proposal is similar to that of Norman Perrin who described Mark as an "apocalyptic drama" (Norman Perrin and Dennis C. Duling, *The*

New Testament: An Introduction [2nd ed. New York: Harcourt Brace Jovanovich, 1982]).

If awareness of genre is a necessary entree to proper interpretation, then potential readers of Mark may be lost in the welter of proposals. Even if there may have been no single model that Mark followed, his work is most at home in the realm of biblical narrative. Both in its simple but vivid language and in its style of rapid narrative with frequent changes of scene it resonates with the Old Testament cycles of prophetic narratives and with the stories of the lives of biblical heroes like Moses and David. Despite the claims for various influences of Greco-Roman literature on Mark (and elsewhere), the gospel contains no quotation of any Greco-Roman author and no allusion to any significant public figure apart from Herod and Pilate. Mark's "pre-texts" are the Jewish Scriptures, which he generally cites in Greek. The authentication of his story comes "from above," as is clear in the prologue in 1:1-13 (see the Commentary). Although study of the proposed Greco-Roman models is intrinsically interesting and helpful for a broader understanding of the world that may have been confronted by early Christian preaching, it is more fruitful to view Mark as a "gospel," not a unique but at least a *distinctive* genre of literature, which presents the Pauline Christ-event (also called "gospel") in a narrative form, and which weaves together diverse traditions (including the Old Testament) to create a unified story of saving significance of the public life, death, and raising up of Jesus of Nazareth.

7. THE LITERARY ARTISTRY OF MARK

The English term "text" is derived from the Latin word "weave" *(texere)*, so that every text is an interwoven tapestry. "Close reading," with its attention to a wide spectrum of literary issues, is as essential for Mark as for any ancient text. Though "tapestry" is an apt metaphor for a text, Mark shares many characteristics with the oral literature of antiquity (Bryan, *Preface*). In this sense Mark is similar to a symphony, which is "composed" and often draws on motifs from earlier traditions and integrates different themes. Here we highlight some aspects of Mark's manner of composition:

A. Vivid and Detailed Narratives

Mark often conveys a "you are there" quality. Some examples would be the accounts of the Gerasene demoniac (Mark 5:1-20 = Matt 8:28-34), Jairus' daughter and the woman's faith (Mark 5:21-43 = Matt 9:18-26), and the epileptic boy (Mark 9:14-29, shortened by both Matt 17:14-21 and Luke 9:37-45a). The attempts to bind the Gerasene demoniac are vividly described, as are his cries and self-inflicted wounds; the dire medical condition of the bleeding woman is detailed, and in the narratives of the epileptic boy both Matthew and Luke omit the vivid descriptions of his convulsions, foaming at the mouth, and the cry of the father, "I believe; help my unbelief" (Mark 9:24). Matthew condenses virtually every narrative taken over from Mark, and Luke, though following Mark more closely, often omits the most realistic and vivid details. Even in the Passion narratives (Mark 14–15; Matthew 26–27; Luke 22–23), where the agreements tend to be closest among the Synoptics, Matthew omits "realistic" details such as the description of the upper room (Mark 14:13), the young man at the arrest (Mark 14:51-52), the fuller description of Barabbas (Mark 15:5), and the mocking of Jesus as a "royal figure" (Mark 15:20). Luke softens even more the details of the Passion such as the scourging and mocking by Pilate's soldiers (Mark 15:15-20), and omits Mark's "cry of dereliction" (15:24, "My God, my God, why have you forsaken me?") while substituting a prayer of resignation (Luke 22:46).

Mark writes about Jesus with a great human realism that Matthew and Luke often omit or tone down; see, for example, 1:41 (his compassion); 1:43 (strong displeasure); 6:5 (surprise at disbelief); 8:12 (deep sigh); 10:14 (indignation); and 10:21 (love). Likewise Matthew and Luke omit or play down Mark's realistic pictures of the disciples' faults; e.g., in 1:36 they "track him down"; in 3:21 they try to seize him, for they think he is mad; in 4:40 Jesus asks them, "Have you no faith?" while in 6:52 their "hearts are hardened"; in 8:18-19 they have "eyes that do not see and ears that do not hear"; and in 8:33, Peter is called "Satan" (cf. Matt 16:23).

B. Rapid Movements and Changes of Scene

Very characteristic of Mark's style is *kai* parataxis, a sequence of sentences and clauses joined by a simple "and," which Matthew and Luke regularly edit out. Of roughly eighty-eight sections (or pericopes) in Mark, eighty begin with the simple conjunction "and." Such narration not only reflects popular storytelling but also is found in works such as Homer's epics and certain historical books of the Old Testament. Allied to this usage is the characteristic adverb *euthys* ("immediately," "right away") to join sections or describe transitions (forty-two times in Mark versus seven in Matthew and one in Luke).

This narrative style creates a sense of urgency in the narrative. The Markan Jesus appears as a person in a hurry, moving somewhat breathlessly from place to place, taking the lead and determining the direction of the narrative. Yet the pace of the narrative slows as the Passion approaches.

During the bulk of the Galilean ministry and the journey narrative (Mark 1–10) the time designations are general, e.g., 1:9 and 8:1 ("in those days"); 2:1 ("after some days"); 9:1 ("after six days"), or they indicate simply the morning or evening of particular days (1:32, 35; 4:35; 6:47). This creates a rapid-paced narrative that corresponds to Jesus as a figure of power who shapes the world around him, both the world of humans by calling disciples and by conquering illness and evil spirits, and the world of nature by calming the seas and by producing miraculous food. After Jesus enters Jerusalem (11:1), the time is designated in carefully designated days (11:11-12, 19; 14:1, 12, 17; 15:1, 42; 16:2), and the final day of Jesus' life is carefully demarcated by hours (15:1, 25, 33, 34). The temporal pace reflects the narrative development. Jesus as a figure of power and strength initially moves rapidly from place to place dictating the location and tempo of the narrative. At Jerusalem the pace slows as opposition grows and as Jesus becomes more passive, unable to move from place to place while his life is being slowed to a halt; the time is carefully marked, like the execution watches in U.S. prisons.

C. Repetition

This is one of the most noticeable literary features of Mark (see Neirynck, *Duality*, who has catalogued this phenomenon). Examples include the following: (1) repetition of key words to establish verbal threads throughout the narrative: "gospel" (1:1, 14-15; 8:35; 10:29; 13:10); *exousia* (1:22, 27; 2:10; 3:15; 6:7; 11:28-33; 13:34). Allied to this is "catchword" composition, e.g., 9:37-40, and (2) repetition of phrases or sentences to call attention to important material (also called interpositions or insertions), e.g., 2:9b, 11a; 3:14, 16; 5:29, 34; 8:17, 21; 14:56, 59 (for a complete list see Donahue, *Trial* 241–43).

D. Framing or Bracketing

1. In the Markan "sandwiches" or intercalations a narrative is begun, interrupted, and then resumed, e.g., 3:20-21 [22-30], 31-35; 5:21-24 [25-34], 35-43; 6:7-13 [14-29], 30-32; 11:12-14 [15-19], 20-26; 14:1-2 [3-9], 10-11; 14:10-11 [12-16], 17-21 [22-25]; 14:54 [55-65], 66-72. This technique serves to create suspense and also either to contrast one narrative with another (e.g., the trials of Jesus and of Peter in 14:54-72) or to interpret one narrative by another (e.g., the cursing of the fig tree and the cleansing of the Temple in 11:12-26).

2. Mark also frames large blocks of material by similar incidents: e.g., 8:22-26 [8:27–10:45], 10:46-52, where two healings of blind people frame and contrast the gift of sight with the progressive blindness of the dis-

ciples as they face the mystery of Jesus' suffering, and 14:3-9 [14:11–15:39], 15:40–16:8, which highlights the devotion of the women disciples during the Passion of Jesus. See J. R. Edwards, "Markan Sandwiches: The Significance of Interpolations in Markan Narratives," *NovT* 31 (1989) 193–216.

E. Other Narrative Patterns

1. Chiasms in the ABB'A' pattern; e.g., "the Sabbath was made for humankind, and not humankind for the Sabbath" (2:27). Allied to this device is the use of the ABCB'A' "concentric pattern" (for a full discussion see Joanna Dewey, *Markan Public Debate: Literary Technique, Concentric Structure and Theology in Mark 2:1–3:6.* SBLDS 48 [Chico: Scholars, 1980]).

2. There is also a fondness for a threefold pattern with progressive heightening, e.g., three calls or commissionings of the disciples (1:16-20; 3:13-19; 6:7-13); three Passion predictions (8:31; 9:31; 10:33-34); Jesus comes three times to his disciples in Gethsemane (14:32-42); and the three denials by Peter (14:66-72).

F. Foreshadowings and Echoes

That these are important characteristics of oral narratives even in a work as "literary" as Sophocles' *Oedipus Tyrannus* was underscored by Eric Havelock ("Oral Composition in the *Oedipus Tyrannus* of Sophocles," *New Literary History* 16 [1984] 183): "All oral narrative is in structure continually both prophetic and retrospective. . . . Though the narrative syntax is paratactic—the basic conjunction being 'and then,' 'and next'— the narrative is not linear but turns back on itself in order to assist the memory to reach the end by having it anticipated somehow in the beginning."

Joanna Dewey and Elizabeth Struthers Malbon have noted extensive use of this technique by Mark (see Dewey, "Mark as Interwoven Tapestry: Forecasts and Echoes for a Listening Audience," *CBQ* 53 [1991] 221–36, and "Oral Methods of Structuring Narrative in Mark," *Int* 43 [1989] 32–44, and Malbon, "Echoes and Foreshadowings in Mark 4–8: Reading and Rereading," *JBL* 112 [1993] 211–30). Examples would be the "handing over" of John the Baptist in 1:14 as foreshadowing his death in 6:14-29 and also the "handing over" of Jesus (14:1-11) and of his disciples (13:9-13), and the frequent references to lethal opposition to Jesus as foreshadowing his death (3:6; 11:18; 12:12; 14:1). Mark constantly echoes Old Testament texts and motifs as will be shown in the Commentary, and within the gospel, sections echo earlier texts (e.g., the parable of Jesus as the strong one in 3:27 echoes John's prediction of a stronger one who would follow him in 1:7).

8. NARRATIVE CRITICISM AND THE GOSPEL OF MARK

Contemporary biblical scholars have adopted the term "narrative criticism" to describe a way of reading biblical materials that centers on the "how" of the story, on its component parts and how they contribute to meaning. This approach is in debt to nonbiblical literary criticism and combines both the "close reading" of the New Critics and the formalistic thrust of structuralism. Though having become a virtual sub-discipline highlighting certain elements, narrative criticism allows readers to look at Mark as through a prism that discloses rich dimensions of the story. See David Rhoads, Joanna Dewey, and Donald Michie, *Mark as Story* (2nd ed. Minneapolis: Fortress, 1999) and Mark Allan Powell, *What is Narrative Criticism?* (Minneapolis: Fortress, 1990).

A. Mark as Narrator and Implied Author

Contemporary literary critics make three distinctions that influence the reading of Mark: between the author, the implied author, and the narrator.

1. The "author" is the actual person who wrote or composed the story. Authors of contemporary literary works are more easily known, while ancient authors, especially in the case of the Gospels, would be the final editors or composers who gathered the different traditions and gave them shape. Both contemporary literary critics and biblical critics have moved away from the study of the actual author as key to the meaning of a text.

2. The term "implied author" designates the author as constructed from the narrative itself, as the one who is responsible for the shape of the narrative. The implied author is not a real flesh and blood person but serves as a way of describing or even personifying the text and is a summary of the kinds of things that the text itself reveals. For example, the implied author of Mark knows the Jewish Scriptures but explains Jewish customs to non-Jews; the implied author uses all the literary devices described above. The concept of the implied author focuses on the "intention" of the text rather than on the conscious intent of the flesh-and-blood author or composer. In this commentary "Mark" generally designates the implied author and narrator rather than the historical composer of the gospel, and functions as a virtual personification of the text.

3. The narrator is not simply the voice that tells the story. The narrator of the Gospel of Mark is anonymous, writes as an eyewitness to those events that even the followers of Jesus do not know about (e.g., at the trial of Jesus), and knows the inner thoughts of both Jesus and others in the gospel. The narrator gives "asides" to readers that communicate important information (2:10; 7:3-4; 7:19; 13:14), and the narrator controls the "point of view" or "perspective" (see 8:23). These characteristics of the

narrator establish rapport with the reader and also increase the authority of the narrative.

B. *The Implied Reader and Reader Response Criticism*

A counterpart to the implied author is the "implied reader," or the sum of the different ways in which the text speaks to a given reader and how he or she is supposed to react to the text. This has in turn led to another virtual subdiscipline known as "reader response" criticism, which studies the ways in which the text involves the reader or evokes a particular response. Throughout this commentary we will indicate ways in which the text may guide or challenge the reader, especially since the narrator gives the readers more information than is possessed by the characters.

C. *Other Aspects of Narrative Criticism*

1. Settings: These are settings internal to the narrative, not the historical setting of the gospel or of the traditions embodied in it. They include the background, the locale, and the context of the narrative action. The settings in Mark are an important key to the meaning of the text (see especially Elizabeth Struthers Malbon, *Narrative Space and Mythic Meaning in Mark*). The major settings are the following:

(a) Geopolitical Settings: Galilee and Jerusalem are not simply the two major locales of Jesus' ministry but also have theological import that is communicated early in the gospel. Galilee is the place of the initial proclamation of the kingdom and of the manifestation of Jesus as a figure of power. From the arrival of the scribes from Jerusalem who accuse Jesus of demonic possession (3:22) until the end of the gospel Jerusalem functions as the place of opposition where Jesus predicts the destruction of the Temple and where he himself becomes progressively more powerless. The Markan Jesus also travels outside of Jewish areas into the Transjordan, the Decapolis, and the regions around Tyre, symbolizing the future mission of the disciples to the Gentiles. The journey to Jerusalem (8:22–10:52) provides the bridge between these locales as Jesus speaks of his suffering in Jerusalem. Galilee returns then as the place of the awaited manifestation of the risen Jesus (see 14:28; 16:7).

(b) Topographical Settings: These often recall events of Israel's past, e.g., "the Jordan" (1:5, 9; 3:8, 10:1; cf. Josh 3:14-17), the "desert" (1:3, 4, 12, 13, 35, 45; 6:31, 32, 35), and the "sea" (1:16; 2:13; 4:1; 4:39-41; 5:13; 6:47-49; 9:42). Jesus frequently crosses the Sea of Galilee, which represents the barrier between Jewish and Gentile territory, and works similar miracles in both territories, especially the two feedings that symbolize the bread

given to both Israel and the Gentiles (see the Commentary on 6:30-44 and 8:1-10).

(c) Architectural Settings: Mark contrasts the actions of Jesus in the "house" (too numerous to list; e.g., 1:29; 2:15; 5:19; 7:17; 9:33; 14:3, 14-15) with those in the synagogue where he most often meets opposition, reflecting perhaps the emerging conflict between the Markan "house churches" and the synagogues (1:21-28; 1:29, 39; 3:1; 12:39; 13:9).

2. Plot: Aristotle called plot the "arrangement of incidents" (*Poetics* 1450a), and M. H. Abrams defined plot as the "structure of actions" ordered to achieving effects on the readers (*A Glossary of Literary Terms* [5th ed. New York: Holt, Rinehart, and Winston, 1985] 139). Plot dynamics emerge either from conflict or from the resolution of an initial tension. Plot elements in Mark include the early conflict between Jesus and authorities (3:6), the mounting misunderstanding between Jesus and disciples (1:36), the frequent question about Jesus' identity: "Who is this?" (1:27; 2:7; 4:41; 6:2, 14; 8:27; 11:27; 14:61-62; 15:2; 15:31-32), and the suspense that arises from the early enthusiastic reception of Jesus by the crowds along with intimation of lethal opposition.

3. Characters: A character is etymologically a "stamp" that an author gives to persons in the narrative. Literary critics distinguish between "rounded" characters, those with memorable and often complex traits who resist easy description, and "flat" or one-dimensional characters. In Mark the principal rounded character is Jesus, and to a certain extent the disciples, especially Peter. Other characters such as the crowds or the opponents of Jesus are flat and seem to be performing roles rather than acting as persons. Yet some of the more interesting characters in Mark are "the little ones who who believe in Jesus" (9:42)—such figures as the Gerasene demoniac (5:1-20), the hemorrhaging woman (5:24-34), the Syrophoenician woman (7:25-30), and Bartimaeus (10:46-52). See below under Discipleship for a larger list.

D. Summary on Narrative/Literary Criticism of Mark

With the increasing specialization of gospel study no one commentary can embody all the contemporary approaches to Mark. There are narrative commentaries, reader-response commentaries, feminist commentaries, and now calls for post-colonial commentaries. This present commentary embodies certain aspects of the literary turn by focusing on Mark as Mark, as we call attention to a close reading of the text, to the structure, and to the web of connections that echo through the text. As with any ancient text historical information from the context will be presented, but as an aid for reading the text and not as an end in itself.

9. *MARK'S PICTURE OF JESUS*

A. Mark's Narrative Christology

Mark's Gospel is a narrative mainly about Jesus of Nazareth. In the prologue (1:1-13) the evangelist tells the reader that John the Baptist prepared the way for Jesus (thus fulfilling OT prophecies), that a voice from heaven declared Jesus to be "my beloved Son" (1:11), and that Jesus withstood testing by Satan (1:12-13). The prologue has the effect of identifying Jesus as the Son of God (1:1, 11) and placing him and his public ministry in the context of a cosmic battle with Satan.

In his first major section (1:14–8:21) Mark describes how Jesus the anointed Son of God proclaims in Galilee and environs the imminence of God's reign through his teachings and actions. At the same time, Mark shows that Jesus encounters misunderstanding and opposition from many groups. The scene of Jesus' activity in 1:14–8:26 is Galilee and environs, which in Mark's theological geography is the place for the revelation or manifestation of Jesus as a powerful teacher and healer. The summary statement in 1:14-15 places everything that Jesus says and does in the context of his proclamation of God's kingdom: "Now is the time of fulfillment; the kingdom of God is at hand."

In 1:16–3:6 the Markan Jesus hurries about (an impression fostered by Mark's frequent uses of the adverb *euthys,* "immediately"), calls disciples, teaches, and heals people suffering from demonic possession and physical illnesses (1:16-45). In 2:1–3:6 he engages in debates with various opponents and shows wisdom and even brilliance in eluding their various traps, though in 3:6 we find the first notice of an organized plot against Jesus.

In 3:7–8:22 we learn more about Jesus as a teacher and healer, and more about the misunderstanding and opposition he encounters. As Jesus gains a popular following (3:7-12) and chooses the Twelve as his inner circle of disciples (3:13-19), he is called "mad" by family members and accused by the scribes of acting out of demonic power (3:20-35). With his parables of God's kingdom in 4:1-34 Jesus explains the dimensions of the mystery of God's kingdom—its presence, future fullness, and growth, along with the dispositions necessary to receive it properly.

That Jesus who is mighty in word (as his teaching shows) is also mighty in deed is illustrated by a series of miracle stories in 4:35–5:43. Here Jesus displays his power over the storm at sea (4:35-41), demons (5:1-20), and sickness and death (5:21-43). Nevertheless, in his home area Jesus meets unbelief (6:1-6).

To extend his mission Jesus empowers his disciples to do what he does: preach and heal (6:7-13). The story of the death of John the Baptist in 6:14-

29 anticipates the death of Jesus and reminds prospective disciples about the suffering that may befall them. As the shepherd of Israel (6:30-56) Jesus feeds the 5000, walks on the waters, and performs many healings. But as the authoritative interpreter of the Torah Jesus breaks down barriers between Jews and Gentiles (7:1-23), accedes to a request for healing from a Gentile woman (7:24-30), heals a man in Gentile territory (7:31-37), and feeds a crowd of 4000, also in Gentile territory (8:1-10). Nevertheless, the Pharisees demand further "signs" (8:11-13), and with a series of harsh questions in 8:14-21 Jesus exposes his disciples' failure to understand him.

The second major section (8:22–10:52) is introduced and concluded by narratives in which blind men come to see (8:22-26 and 10:46-52). Throughout the journey from Caesarea Philippi in northern Galilee to Jerusalem the Markan Jesus instructs his disciples (and Mark's readers) about Jesus' identity as the Son of Man who must suffer, die, and rise and about what it means to follow him. The three units each feature a Passion-resurrection prediction (8:31; 9:31; 10:33-34), a misunderstanding on the disciples' part (8:32-33; 9:32; 10:35-41), and further instructions by Jesus (8:34–9:1; 9:33-50; 10:42-45) along with related material in two "interludes" (9:2-29; 10:1-31). The theological climax of the journey narrative is Jesus' statement that the Son of Man came "to give his life as a ransom for many" (10:45). Nevertheless, Jesus' own disciples seem obtuse to his clear teachings, and remain so throughout the Passion narrative.

The third major section in Mark's narrative (11:1–16:8) takes place in Jerusalem, which in Mark's theological geography is primarily the place where Jesus is rejected. After his provocative symbolic actions in entering the city and "cleansing" the Temple (11:1-25), Jesus enters into debate with various Jewish groups (11:27–12:44). By his superior wisdom Jesus infuriates the chief priests, elders, and scribes—the Jewish leaders in Jerusalem who eventually hand him over for execution under Pontius Pilate. When asked about the destruction of the Jerusalem Temple, Jesus in his farewell discourse (or testament) in 13:1-37 moves to the cosmic level and looks forward to the coming of the Son of Man in glory as the sign of the fullness of God's kingdom.

In the events leading up to Jesus' arrest (14:1-52) Jesus remains very much in command (even though the Gethsemane episode shows that he struggles to accept death on the cross as his Father's will) in that he knows what is going to happen and is confident that the Scriptures are being fulfilled. In the trials before the Sanhedrin and Pilate (14:53–15:20) Jesus appears as Messiah/Son of God and as the Suffering Servant of Isaiah 53. In the crucifixion narrative (15:21-41) Jesus is the embodiment of Psalm 22, the psalm of the suffering righteous person. The confession by the Roman centurion at the moment of Jesus' death ("Truly this man was the Son of God") in 15:39 is the first recognition by a human character in Mark's

Gospel (and by a Gentile no less!) of Jesus' real identity—something that Mark's readers have known since the beginning of the story (1:1, 11).

The women disciples, who are introduced only at 15:40-41, witness the death of Jesus (15:40-41) and his burial (15:47), and they discover his tomb to be empty on Easter Sunday morning (16:1-8). The explanation offered by the "young man" at the tomb is that "he has been raised" (16:6). Jesus the suffering Son of Man, who personifies the suffering righteous person of Psalm 22 and the Suffering Servant of Isaiah 53, has been vindicated in his resurrection from the dead.

B. The Names and Titles of Jesus

1. Son of God (and Beloved Son). In the OT the title "Son of God" is applied to Israel as God's people (Hos 11:1), the king at his coronation (Ps 2:7), the angels (Job 38:7), and the suffering righteous person (Wis 2:18). In Mark's Gospel "Son of God" is a very prominent title for Jesus. Most manuscripts include this title as part of Mark 1:1: "The beginning of the gospel of Jesus Christ, the Son of God." At Jesus' baptism (1:11) a voice from heaven proclaims: "You are my Son, the Beloved." Demons or "unclean spirits" recognize Jesus as "the Son of God" (3:11) and as the "Son of the Most High God" (5:7). At Jesus' transfiguration (9:7) a voice from heaven proclaims: "This is my Son, the Beloved." In Jesus' parable of the vineyard (12:1-12) it is hard to escape the implication that the son ("a beloved son . . . my son," 12:6) is Jesus. In claiming that only the Father knows "that day or hour" (13:32), Jesus seems to refer to himself as the Son of God. When at the Sanhedrin trial the chief priest asks whether Jesus is "the Son of the Blessed One" (14:61), Jesus answers "I am" (14:62). Finally, at the moment of Jesus' death on the cross the Roman centurion proclaims: "Truly this man was the Son of God" (15:39). The first time that a human character (who happens to be a Gentile) in Mark's narrative recognizes Jesus' true identity is at the time of his death!

2. Messiah (and Son of David). The Hebrew word for "anointed one" is *mašiaḥ*. In the OT priests, prophets, and kings are anointed. In NT times there was no single Jewish concept of Messiah, and much depends on the context in which the term appears.

Mark employs the Greek word *christos* ("anointed") for Hebrew *mašiaḥ*. In 1:1 Mark uses "Christ" as a surname for Jesus ("the gospel of Jesus Christ"), a practice that is common in the Pauline epistles. In 9:41 Jesus speaks about one who bears "the name of Christ"; in 12:35-37 he relates "Christ" and "Son of David"; and in 13:21 he warns about those who might say: "Look! Here is the Messiah."

The most distinctive and theologically important Markan occurrences of *christos* appear in the context of Jesus' suffering and death. When Peter confesses that Jesus is the Messiah/Christ in 8:29, almost immediately Jesus utters his first Passion prediction: "the Son of Man must suffer many things . . ." (8:31). At the trial before the Sanhedrin the chief priest asks Jesus: "Are you the Messiah/Christ . . . ?" (14:61). And as Jesus is lifted up on the cross the chief priests and scribes taunt him: "Let the Messiah/Christ, the King of Israel, come down . . ." (15:32). The appearance of the title "Messiah/Christ" in the context of Jesus' suffering and death— in three of the most significant passages in the gospel—suggests that Mark is deliberately redefining the title with reference to Jesus. Mark's point seems to be that Jesus' messiahship involves suffering, and that Jesus cannot be understood as the Messiah/Christ apart from the mystery of the cross.

Two variants of "Messiah/Christ" are "Son of David" and "King of the Jews." The former title is used twice by Bartimaeus: "Son of David, have mercy on me!" (10:47-48), and "Son of David" appears in the controversy about the interpretation of Ps 110:1, when Jesus asks: "How can the scribes say that the Messiah/Christ is the Son of David?" (12:35). "King of the Jews" is the "outsider" Roman translation of "Messiah/ Christ," and it occurs exclusively in ch. 15 (vv. 2, 9, 12, 18, 26).

3. Son of Man. In the OT the prophet Ezekiel is frequently addressed by God as "son of man" (*ben ʾadam* in Hebrew) and told to prophesy (see 2:1, 3, 6, 8; 3:1, 3, etc.). In Daniel 7:13 a figure described as "one like a son of man" (*bar ʾenash* in Aramaic) receives from the "Ancient of Days" dominion and glory and kingship. In 1 *Enoch* 48 "the Son of Man" is a pre-existent heavenly being who passes judgment upon all human and angelic beings.

In Mark's gospel "Son of Man" is a prominent title for Jesus. The most distinctive and theologically important uses of "Son of Man" (*ho huios tou anthrōpou*) appear in the context of Jesus' Passion, death, and resurrection. This title is part of the three Passion predictions (8:31; 9:31; 10:33-34). It occurs twice more in the conversation about Jesus' death and resurrection after the transfiguration (9:9, 12). It also appears in the pivotal declaration of Jesus toward the end of the journey narrative: "For the Son of Man came . . . to give his life as a ransom for many" (10:45).

A second category of "Son of Man" sayings in Mark is akin to the "son of man" in Ezekiel. In several places Jesus uses "Son of Man" to refer to himself in his authority to forgive sins (2:10) and in his role as Lord of the Sabbath (2:28). At the Last Supper Jesus remarks that "the Son of Man goes as it is written of him" (14:21), and at his arrest he observes that "the Son of Man is betrayed into the hands of sinners" (14:41). In all these cases one gets the sense that more is meant than "I." There is a solemnity to these sayings and a suggestion that Jesus is a very significant "son of man/Adam."

The third category of Markan "Son of Man" sayings is more in line with Daniel 7 and *1 Enoch* 48. In 8:38 Jesus warns that the Son of Man will be ashamed of those who in turn are ashamed of him and his words "when he comes in the glory of his Father with the holy angels." The apocalyptic scenario developed in Mark 13 reaches its climax in 13:26 with the vision of "the Son of Man coming in clouds," which is a clear allusion to Dan 7:13. At the trial before the Sanhedrin, Jesus again alludes to Dan 7:13 when he promises "you will see the Son of Man seated at the right hand of the Power and coming with the clouds of heaven." In all three cases there can be little doubt that Mark identifies the glorious eschatological Son of Man as Jesus.

4. Other Titles. In the Markan context John the Baptist's preaching about "the stronger one" (1:7) makes this phrase function as a title for Jesus. In 1:24 the demon being exorcised correctly identifies Jesus as "the Holy One of God." Mark does not do much with "prophet" as a title for Jesus (compare Luke–Acts). While Jesus explains his rejection at Nazareth as due to his identity as a prophet ("prophets are not without honor . . . ," 6:4), elsewhere the title is reserved for Isaiah (1:2) and John the Baptist (11:32) or is cited as one of the popular (but inadequate) perceptions of Jesus (6:15; 8:28). Likewise "Lord" *(kyrios)* is not a prominent title for Jesus in Mark (compare Matthew). The term is generally used as a title for God the Father of Jesus (see 11:9; 12:11; 12:29-30; 12:36-37; 13:20) as in the Greek OT. In 5:19 and 11:3 Jesus uses *kyrios* to refer to himself, and there it may not have much theological significance ("the Master"). In the Markan context of 1:3 ("Prepare the way of the Lord"), its occurrence in Isaiah 40:3 is assumed to refer to Jesus. In the debate about interpreting Ps 110:1 ("The Lord said to my Lord") in 12:35-37, the second "Lord" is taken to imply the superiority of this title to "Messiah/Christ" and "Son of David." See the survey article by J. C. Naluparayil, "Jesus of the Gospel of Mark: Present State of Research," *Currents in Research: Biblical Studies* 8 (2000) 191–226.

C. The Messianic Secret

The term "messianic secret" has become a prominent part of Markan scholarship since the publication of William Wrede's *Das Messiasgeheimnis in den Evangelien* in 1901 (English: *The Messianic Secret,* 1971). The clearest and most important example of the "messianic secret" comes immediately after Peter's confession of Jesus as the Messiah/Christ when Mark adds in 8:30: "But he forbade them to tell anyone about him." This is the only case where the title "Messiah" applied to Jesus and a command to be silent about it are joined.

There are other Markan texts in which Jesus' commands to be silent are linked to his exorcisms and healings. When an "unclean spirit" identifies Jesus as "the Holy One of God," Jesus in 1:25 tells it to be silent. In 1:34 Jesus does not allow the demons to speak "because they knew him." When unclean spirits call him "the Son of God," Jesus in 3:12 orders them not to make it known. Likewise, in several instances Jesus instructs those whom he has healed not to tell anyone about it: the man with leprosy (1:44), those who witnessed the restoration of Jairus' daughter to life (5:43), and the man whose hearing and speech were restored (7:36). Note, however, that Jesus tells the Gerasene demoniac to go home and tell his friends "how much the Lord has done for you" (5:19; see also 8:26).

There are also Markan texts in which Jesus promotes an atmosphere of secrecy. He offers private instructions to his disciples about the parables (4:10, 34), ritual purity (7:17), exorcism (9:28), his Passion and other issues (9:31-50), and the last things (13:3). He tells Peter, James, and John not to mention what they observed at his transfiguration "until the Son of Man had risen from the dead" (9:9). At several points Jesus goes into hiding to escape the crowds he had attracted (6:31; 7:24; 9:30). However, Jesus' efforts at maintaining secrecy are not successful. In some cases those who have been sworn to secrecy seem unable to contain their enthusiasm for Jesus and what he has done (see 1:45; 7:36), and his attempts to avoid the crowds end in failure (see 6:33-34; 7:24-25; 10:1).

What are often lumped together under the heading "messianic secret" are quite disparate phenomena: the one clear case of the "messianic secret" in 8:30, the injunctions to silence in miracle stories, Jesus' private instructions for his disciples, and his unsuccessful efforts at hiding from the public. But if they are thus combined, the problem of interpreting the data still remains.

One traditional approach to the issue is to say that the historical Jesus feared that if he revealed himself as the Messiah many segments among his people might use it as the occasion for a military revolt. At the other end of the spectrum, Wrede attributed the motif to Mark's effort to explain the tension between the early church's belief in Jesus as the Messiah and the fact (as Wrede assumed) that Jesus did not present himself as the Messiah during his public ministry. A better and more widely accepted explanation is that Mark sought to redefine the term "Messiah" and other christological titles in the light of Jesus' death and resurrection, and so he puts off revealing Jesus' true identity until his death (see 15:39) and his resurrection (see 9:9). This interpretation takes its lead from the one clear instance of the messianic secret in Peter's confession of Jesus as the Messiah, with Jesus' command to be silent and his Passion prediction (8:27-33).

Ultimately the term "messianic secret" is a misnomer. It arises from Mark 4:11: "to you has been given *to mystērion* of the kingdom of God."

Some translations render *mystērion* as "secret." But "mystery" is a term with apocalyptic overtones connoting the disclosure by God of a truth hidden until a certain decisive point in the divine plan is reached (see Rom 11:25; 1 Cor 15:51; Col 1:26). From the opening of the gospel, readers know that *Jesus* is the "Messiah." What awaits full disclosure is *the kind of* Messiah Jesus is. The mystery is that of a suffering Messiah who is also God's chosen Son. The full unveiling of this secret comes at the cross when the centurion cries out: "This was truly the Son of God" (15:39), and the dramatic challenge of Mark's Gospel is whether the followers of Jesus can accept Jesus' own revelation that he is such a Messiah, and whether they are ready to follow him to the cross (8:31-38).

10. DISCIPLESHIP IN MARK

One of the most intense areas in the recent discussion of Mark has been the role of the disciples. Though Mark is primarily the "good news" of Jesus, it also tells the story of what it means to be involved with Jesus. Since Mark looks to a period after the death and resurrection of Jesus and before the return of Jesus when the gospel will be proclaimed (13:10; 14:9), the stories of the disciples are not simply about the past of Jesus but function as both paradigms for and warnings to the Markan community.

A. Language of Discipleship in Mark

Mark's primary term for the disciples is *mathētēs* (46 times from *man-thanein*, "learn"), with overtones of being a "learner" or "apprentice." It is never used in the NT outside of the gospels and Acts; e.g., Paul does not have "disciples." Although there is no abstract term for "discipleship," the verb *akolouthein*, "follow" (Mark 1:17-18; 2:14-15; 8:34; 10:21, 28; 15:41) and the related phrase "come after" (1:17, 20; 8:34) capture the meaning of what it means to be a disciple. In the Hellenistic world they suggest "following" in an intellectual, moral, or religious sense (e.g., the disciples of Socrates), and involve personal relationship to the one who is followed, adopting the pattern of his life and not simply coming after that person. Though Mark uses the verb *apostellein* ("send out" with the authority of the sender) to describe commissions given by Jesus to the disciples (3:14; 6:7; 11:1; 14:13), the noun *apostolos* is found only in a textually disputed comment of 3:14 where Jesus calls the Twelve "apostles."

B. Background to Discipleship in Mark

Although the Old Testament rarely uses the terminology associated with discipleship, similarities to Jesus' call of the disciples can be found in the call of Elisha by Elijah (1 Kgs 19:19-21; see the Commentary on Mark 1:16-20) and in the relationship between Moses and Joshua. The closest parallel to the NT picture of Jesus and his followers is the Jewish institution of a rabbi with his students *(talmidim)* who spend time with the teacher and learn from him. The major difference, however, between the NT picture and that of the rabbis is that a student seeks out a rabbi and petitions to sit at his feet, while Jesus takes the initiative in calling disciples without any previous contact (see 1:16-20). The Markan picture seems to represent a merger of different traditions: prophetic call, Jewish practice, and the custom of Hellenistic teachers and their followers.

C. The "Twelve" in Mark

Along with a wider circle of the "disciples," the Markan Jesus appoints a group named "the Twelve" (3:14-16) who seem to form an inner circle around him (4:10; 6:7; 9:35; 10:32; 11:11; 14:17), one of whom (Judas) is instrumental in handing Jesus over (3:19; 14:10, 20, 43). Unlike the Q saying (Matt 19:28; Luke 22:28-29) where Jesus promises the Twelve that they will be the eschatological nucleus of a renewed people of God, Mark attaches little theological or symbolic importance to the Twelve. Though at times the Twelve and the disciples seem interchangeable, Mark pictures others who are close to Jesus at crucial times or are the audience for his important teaching (4:10; 8:34); and he often highlights groupings of two (10:35; 11:1), three (5:37; 9:2-9; 13:3; 14:33), or four disciples (1:16-20) from among the Twelve, more for dramatic effect than for theological significance. Mark seems to have inherited the "Twelve" from tradition, but his main focus is on the "disciples" and their responses to the challenges and pitfalls of following Jesus.

D. Positive Aspects of Discipleship in Mark

Mark presents the disciples as ambivalent figures with both positive and negative features. The major positive aspects include the following:

1. The importance of disciples to the structure and content of Mark: Every major section begins with a discipleship pericope (see the Outline). The mission of the disciples is parallel to that of Jesus (3:13-19; 6:7-13). They are recipients of private instruction from Jesus (4:10-34; 7:1-23; the bulk of 8:27–10:45; 13:1-37), and are privileged witnesses to the deeds of Jesus (4:35-41; 5:37-43; 6:45-52; 9:2-8). They assist Jesus in the feeding of the multitudes (6:30-44; 8:1-10) and share a final meal with Jesus (14:12-26). Jesus promises that he will go before them into Galilee (14:28), and the women are instructed to tell the disciples that Jesus will see them in Galilee (16:7).

2. The call/commissioning narratives as paradigms of discipleship (1:16-20; 3:13-19; 6:6b-13): The first act of Jesus after summoning people to conversion and faith is the calling of disciples. The call in 1:16-20 (also 2:14) has the following characteristics: (i) an initiative from Jesus; (ii) those who are called are engaged in ordinary work; (iii) the call is in the form of a clear summons ("Follow me"); (iv) the call is to share in the mission or activity of the one calling; (v) the response to the call is immediate and un-reflective, and there is a "leaving" of former occupations; and (vi) re-sponding to the call is not a private choice, but an entry into a group that has responded to the call. Subsequent calls repeat and elaborate the initial call, with more stress on the mission. In 3:13-19 the disciples are to "be with Jesus" and are sent out to preach and *to have authority* over demons. In 6:6-13 they are explicitly commissioned as itinerant missionaries and are to preach repentance (see 1:4, 15), to exorcise demons, and to heal the sick. The two essential elements of the call to discipleship are "being with" Jesus and doing the things of Jesus. These elements also provide dramatic tension in the gospel: whether the disciples will "be with" Jesus at all stages, and whether they will take up their cross as Jesus did (see 8:31-38, which is a "call narrative" inaugurating the second major part of the gospel).

3. "Other" disciples in Mark: In Mark there are significant indications of other persons functioning as "disciples" in their own ways: 1:31, Peter's mother-in-law rises up and serves *(diēkonei)*; 1:45, the leper goes out and begins to proclaim and spread the word; 2:15, tax collectors and sinners follow *(ēkolouthoun)*; 3:35, "whoever" does the will of God is a member of Jesus' family; 5:20, the healed demoniac goes out and begins to proclaim; 7:36, witnesses to a healing proclaim what Jesus has done; 8:34-38 contains gnomic sayings (i.e., "if anyone") on discipleship; 9:38, one explicitly described as not following the disciples casts out demons, and Jesus says "Whoever is not against us is 'on our side'" (9:40); 10:29-31, "whoever" leaves family, etc. will receive the hundredfold; 10:52, the healed Bartimaeus "follows Jesus on the way"; 11:23, "whoever" prays with faith will be heard; 12:34, the scribe who articulates the love com-mand is not far from the kingdom; 12:44, the widow gives her whole life; 13:13, the one who endures to the end will be saved; 13:37, Jesus' state-ments are meant for all; 14:9, an unnamed woman anoints Jesus; 15:21, a "passer-by" carries Jesus' cross; 15:39, the centurion confesses Jesus; 15:41, the women who had followed him and ministered to him *(ēkolouthoun kai diēkonoun)* in Galilee are at the cross; 15:43-47, Joseph of Arimathea, who was waiting for the kingdom of God, performs the burial ritual (cf. 6:29, where John's "disciples" do this); and 16:1-8, the women come to the tomb and hear the resurrection proclamation. This phenomenon of "other disciples" supports the position that Mark's readers are given multiple

and diverse models to imitate in their own attempt to have a change of
heart and believe in the gospel (1:14-15).

E. The Negative Picture of the Disciples in Mark

One of the more startling phenomena in Mark is the negative portrait
of disciples, especially the chosen Twelve. They seem to move through a
negative progression from lack of perception of Jesus through rejection of
the way of suffering that he predicts to flight and outright denial of him.
The principal texts are these: 1:36, they "track down" Jesus; 3:21, those
"around him" (most likely his relatives but possibly his disciples) think
that Jesus is insane; 4:13-20, the word will fail in different kinds of "soils"
(hearers) among whom will be the disciples themselves; 4:40, after a
manifestation of his power Jesus rebukes the disciples, saying: "Have you
no faith?"; 5:31, the disciples seem to make fun of Jesus by saying that he is
surrounded by crowds and yet says, "Who touched me?"; 6:50-52, after
the miracle of the loaves their hearts are hardened because of lack of
understanding, perspectives that are repeated in 7:18 ("Are you without
understanding?") and 8:4; and 8:16-21, at the end of the bread section
where the earlier judgment on outsiders (4:10-12) is uttered against them:
"Are your hearts hardened? Having eyes do you not see, and having ears
do you not hear?"

After Jesus predicts his suffering, death, and resurrection, Peter rebukes him and Jesus responds in 8:33: "Get behind me, Satan, for you
think human thoughts, not the thoughts of God." After each Passion prediction the disciples misunderstand, and in two of the three cases they are
concerned for their own power and precedence (9:32; 10:35-45). Judas, one
of the Twelve, betrays Jesus (14:10, 42); in 14:33-41 the chosen three disciples sleep when Jesus comes to them in Gethsemane; and in 14:50 at his
arrest all flee. In 14:66-72 Peter denies knowing Jesus, so that the last
words spoken by the first one of the Twelve to be called and the one who
first called Jesus "Messiah" are "I do not know the man of whom you
speak" (see 8:38–9:1). It is disputed whether the women who followed
Jesus to the cross, prepared his body for burial, and received the first
proclamation of the resurrection are positive examples of faithful discipleship or are failures for not delivering the message about the resurrection
(16:7-8).

There have been many interpretations of this aspect of Mark's Gospel.
Some contend that Mark uses the disciples simply as literary foils for a
"corrective christology" to counter certain views alive in his community
that are represented in the gospel by the failing disciples. Theodore Weeden
(*Mark: Traditions in Conflict*) argued that they represent those in the
Markan community who were fascinated by a theology of glory or power

and could not cope with a suffering Jesus. Werner Kelber *(The Kingdom in Mark)* argued that they represent the resistance of the Jerusalem church to the extension of the gospel to the Gentiles. Other proposals center on a literary reading where the failure of the disciples is intended to mirror the readers' own experience of initial enthusiasm for the gospel followed by a growing realization of the necessity of suffering (Donahue, *The Theology and Setting of Discipleship in the Gospel of Mark*). Similarly Ernest Best *(Disciples and Discipleship: Studies in the Gospel According to Mark)* argued that the disciples reflect the progress of recently baptized Christians from an enthusiastic faith to the challenge of following Jesus on the way of the cross.

Two other alternatives may be considered:

1. Intertextually two very strong Old Testament themes merge in the Gospel of Mark. One is that Jesus is the "suffering just one" who is "tested" by God (see Mark 1:12-13), suffers opposition from enemies, and is abandoned by friends and companions. Jeremiah (20:6-11) and Job (12:2-3; 16:20; 19:14) may be the oldest examples of this motif, which appears strongly in the Psalms; e.g., Ps 38:11-12, "my friends and companions stand aloof from my afflictions, and my neighbors stand far off"; Ps 41:9-10, "my bosom friend in whom I have trusted, who ate of my bread, has lifted the heel against me," (see Mark 14:1-11); also Pss 31:11 and 88:19. L. Ruppert, who has studied this motif extensively, subsumes under it the sufferings of the Servant in Isaiah 52:13–53:12, and argues that the motif persists through the Wisdom of Solomon (2:10-20; 5:1-8) and in the *Hodayot* of Qumran (1QH 10[formerly col. 2]:9-13, 16; 10[2]:31-36; 11[3]:5-10; 19[11]:22-25). The failure of Jesus' disciples, who are most often the chosen "Twelve," does not arise from moral or psychological failures, or because they are exemplars of a wrong theology; it simply continues the motif of the suffering just one who is abandoned even by friends and companions.

A second motif that may influence the failure of disciples and of the crowds in Mark is the pervasive rhythm of the Old Testament in which God's love is met by infidelity and failure, but only to be renewed by God. This theme appears in the early narratives of Israel's rebellions in the wilderness, where the people reject Moses' leadership and their own deliverance from Egypt. It is dramatically found in Exodus 32–34 where Israel breaks the covenant just made with the twelve tribes in Exod 24:4. The Deuteronomic historian views the period of Judges as a cycle of apostasy and divine punishment, followed by the plea of the people and divine forgiveness (see Judges 2:6–3:6). This cycle pervades the retelling of the Exodus narratives in Psalm 78 and characterizes the calls to repentance or return in the prophetic writings (Isa 1:17-19; 40:2; 44:21-23; 59:13; Lam 4:12-14; 21-23). Another instance of this motif is Mark's use of Isa 6:9-

10 in 4:12 ("so that they may look and see, but not perceive, and that they may hear and listen, but not understand; lest they convert, and be forgiven") to describe the lack of understanding by outsiders and in 8:17-18 to describe the obtuseness of the disciples. The almost universal failure of those associated with Jesus in Mark continues the theme of human failure in the face of God's self-disclosure. The promise of resurrection and renewed contact with the disciples (Mark 16:7-8) is an instance of the offer of forgiveness that concludes the cycle of human infidelity and divine gift.

2. Contextually the Gospel of Mark is clearly written with memories of persecution vivid in the minds of its readers (see below under "Date and Audience"). If this is, as we suggest, the brutal persecution following the great fire of Rome under Nero, during which some Christians failed under persecution and under torture betrayed other Christians (as Tacitus attests), the figure of failing disciples and even Peter who denied so much as knowing Jesus would be a powerful symbol of hope to those who failed, especially since Peter most likely died a martyr during this persecution. Others in the community could use the rehabilitation of Peter by the risen Jesus as a motive to be reconciled with those who had even betrayed loved ones. G.W.H. Lampe has argued that the narratives of Peter's denial served this function in the early church; see "St. Peter's Denial and the Treatment of the *Lapsi*," in David Neiman and Margaret Schatkin, eds., *The Heritage of the Early Church. Essays in Honor of Georges Vasilievich Florovsky on the Occasion of his Eightieth Birthday.* Orientalia Christiana Analecta 195 (Rome: Pontifical Oriental Institute, 1973) 114–30. The failure of the disciples thus paradoxically becomes good news for a community struggling with failure and apostasy while called to repentance, forgiveness, and reconciliation.

11. *MARK AND THE OLD TESTAMENT AND JUDAISM*

Mark's Gospel is sometimes called anti-Jewish or anti-Semitic, and is described as proclaiming the end of Judaism as a religion. Such claims are much too broad and (as history shows) very dangerous. A careful reading of Mark's Gospel and a sober appreciation of what the text does and does not say can contribute greatly to progress in relations between Christians and Jews.

A. Mark's Use of the Old Testament

That Mark respected the Jewish Scriptures (the OT) and regarded them as authoritative is clear from 1:2-3 where he uses a quotation from "Isaiah the prophet" to explain the relationship between John the Baptist ("the voice") and Jesus ("the Lord"). His failure to note that the first part of this quotation came not from Isaiah but from Exod 3:20 and Mal 3:1 suggests that Mark may have used a collection of biblical *testimonia,* or at least that he was not as conversant with the OT as Matthew was (see Matt 3:3). Another mistake in Mark's use of the OT occurs at 2:26 where he says that Abiathar (rather than Ahimelech) was the priest when David demanded the bread of the presence (1 Sam 21:1-6). Nevertheless, at many pivotal points in his story of Jesus, Mark appeals to OT texts and appears to assume that his readers know these texts and receive them as authoritative.

After 1:2-3 there is an impresssive number of explicit OT quotations in Mark's account of Jesus' public ministry, especially from the book of Isaiah. Jesus appeals to Isa 6:9-10 ("that they may indeed look, but not perceive . . .") to explain why outsiders (4:12) and even his own disciples (8:18) fail to understand his preaching about God's kingdom. In his critique of the Pharisees' traditions about ritual defilement Jesus in 7:6-7 quotes Isa 29:13: "This people honors me with their lips . . . teaching human precepts as doctrines." The crowd's acclamation of Jesus in 7:37 ("He has done everything well; he even makes the deaf to hear and the mute to speak") is an echo of Isa 35:5-6.

When Jesus enters Jerusalem he is greeted in 11:9-10 with words from Ps 118:25-26: "Blessed is the one who comes in the name of the Lord." His symbolic action in "cleansing" the Temple is justified in 11:17 by an appeal to the combination of Isa 56:7 and Jer 7:11: "My house shall be called a house of prayer for all the nations. But you have made it a cave for bandits." His parable of the wicked tenants (12:1-12) ends with a quotation of Ps 118:22-23: "The stone that the builders rejected—this has become the cornerstone." He presents in 12:35-37 an interpretation of Ps 110:1 ("the Lord said to my Lord") designed to show the superiority of the title "Lord" to "Messiah" and "Son of David." In the apocalyptic discourse in Mark 13 many of the major terms and concepts—the great tribulation, the abomination of desolation, the glorious Son of Man, and the resurrection of the dead—come from the book of Daniel.

One of the great themes of the Markan Passion narrative is expressed by Jesus in 14:49: "Let the Scriptures be fulfilled." On the Mount of Olives Jesus quotes Zech 13:7 ("I will strike the shepherd, and the sheep will be scattered") as a prophecy that his disciples would soon desert him. At his trial before the Sanhedrin, Jesus identifies himself as the glorious Son of Man with words taken from Dan 7:13, and in ch. 15 there are enough quotations and allusions to Isaiah 53 and Psalm 22 to describe Jesus as the personification of the Suffering Servant and the Suffering Righteous One (see also Wis 2:12-20).

B. Mark's Treatment of Jews and Judaism

It is customary to cite the parenthetical comment about Jewish traditions regarding ritual purity in 7:3-4 as evidence that Mark wrote for a
predominantly non-Jewish audience. This may be so. But if Mark expected
his first readers to understand most of his story of Jesus, he assumed that
they knew something about "things Jewish" and were interested in them.
He tells the story of Jesus as a Jewish teacher and healer who gathered
Jewish disciples, worked in Galilee and Judea, and died with the words of
Ps 22:1 on his lips ("My God, my God, why have you abandoned me?").
Jesus' debates with various Jewish groups deal almost entirely with Jewish
topics, and his positions on these matters are generally within the range of
opinions represented by other first-century Jewish teachers.

While Mark's Jesus is clearly Jewish, Mark also presents his hero as
superior to other Jewish teachers and healers and as possessing significance for non-Jews too (see 7:24–8:10). During his Galilean ministry Jesus
engages fellow Jews in debate, and his success results in a plot against
him by Pharisees and Herodians (3:6). During his ministry in Jerusalem
Jesus has more controversies with various Jewish groups in 11:27–12:44,
and wins the envy and hostility of the chief priests, elders, and scribes
there. While these Jewish officials take the initiative in getting Jesus arrested and condemned to death, it is the Roman prefect Pontius Pilate
who is ultimately responsible for Jesus' execution.

From his entry into Jerusalem at the beginning of Mark 11 Jesus is critical of the Jerusalem Temple and those who are responsible for it. His action in the Temple complex in 11:15-19 is sandwiched between sections
about the withered fig tree (11:12-14, 20-21). Jesus' symbolic action and his
prophecy about the destruction of the Temple (see 13:2) are major issues
in the trial before the Sanhedrin (14:58) and at the crucifixion (15:29), and
those who plot Jesus' arrest and execution (most obviously the chief
priests) stand to lose the most if Jesus' prophecies about the Temple come
to pass.

The Markan Jesus has conflicts with other Jews and Jewish groups. He
is critical of the Jerusalem Temple and the Jewish leaders associated with
it. But these facts hardly set Jesus outside the boundaries of Judaism in the
first century. As the Dead Sea scrolls have shown, Judaism in Jesus' time
was both diverse and contentious, and there was strong opposition to the
Jerusalem Temple and its officials from Jews other than Jesus.

Furthermore, there are several texts in Mark's Gospel in which Jews
who do not belong to Jesus' followers are treated with tolerance and respect. When an outsider (presumably a Jew) has success in casting out
demons in Jesus' name, Jesus counsels his disciples to be tolerant: "Whoever is not against us is for us" (9:40). When a rich man inquires about

what he must do to inherit eternal life, Jesus tells him to keep the commandments set forth in the Torah (10:19). When a scribe agrees with Jesus about the centrality of the love commandment(s) in the Torah, Jesus pronounces him "not far from the kingdom of God" (12:34). And Mark gives no indication in 15:43-46 that he regards Joseph of Arimathea as a disciple of Jesus (though Matthew and John do). Rather, Mark gives the impression that Joseph tended to Jesus' burial out of respect for the OT commandment in Deut 21:22-23 to bury someone who had been hanged upon a tree on "that same day," in this case before the Sabbath began. These examples suggest that, in Mark's view, there are righteous Jews outside of Jesus' circle.

12. *THE ESCHATOLOGY OF MARK*

Mark 1:15 is the evangelist's summary of Jesus' preaching: "Now is the time of fulfillment; and the kingdom of God is at hand. Reform your lives and place your faith in the good news." This summary situates Mark's story of Jesus in an eschatological context. The main topic is the kingdom of God, that moment when all creation will acknowledge the sovereignty of God and proceed according to God's original plan. While the kingdom's fullness is future, the teaching and healing activity of Jesus represent its anticipated or inaugurated dimension most dramatically. Jesus' proclamation of the future and present dimensions of God's kingdom demands an appropriate response by way of conversion and faith in the good news that Jesus brings.

The testing of Jesus by Satan (1:12-13) alerts the reader to Mark's conception of Jesus' ministry as a struggle against the cosmic forces of evil. An eschatological dualism familiar from the Dead Sea scrolls (the Prince of Light with the children of light versus the Prince of Darkness with the children of darkness; see 1QS 3–4) is an assumption that underlies Mark's narrative. Jesus' first public activities in 2:1–3:6—his exorcisms, healings, and debates with hostile opponents—are decisive moments in the struggle against the forces of the Evil One. The debate with the scribes in 3:22-30 makes clear that the origin of Jesus' power as a teacher and healer is the Holy Spirit, and that he stands over against the one who is called Satan/Beelzebul/Prince of Demons.

The parables in 4:1-34 impart some basic teachings about the kingdom of God. It is God's kingdom to bring about; there is a huge contrast between its small beginnings in the present and its future fullness; something decisive is happening in Jesus' ministry; and Jesus' proclamation of God's kingdom deserves an enthusiastic and fruitful response. The power of Jesus as the herald of God's kingdom is illustrated by his deeds in 4:35–5:43 when he shows himself to be the master of those forces that in Jewish and Ancient Near Eastern traditions appear to be under the dominion of Satan: the storm at sea, the demons, sickness and the suffering it brings, and death.

Having placed Jesus' ministry in the context of a cosmic and eschatological struggle against the forces of evil, Mark from ch. 6 onward pits Jesus against misunderstanding and hostility from human opponents: the people of Nazareth (6:1-6), his own disciples in 8:14-21 and throughout the journey and Passion narratives, and the chief priests, elders, and scribes of Jerusalem from ch. 11 onward. In the midst of this narrative we are given in the transfiguration account (9:2-8) an insight into and an anticipation of the true nature of Jesus as the glorious Son of Man, and in Jesus' apocalyptic discourse (13:1-37) the climax of the scenario of end-time events is the manifestation of "the Son of Man coming in clouds with much power and glory" (13:26). Since these events are to take place in "this generation" (13:30)—though the precise time remains unknown (see 13:32)—the appropriate religious and ethical stance is constant vigilance (13:33-37).

In Jewish theology of Jesus' time, resurrection was understood to be an eschatological event (see Dan 12:1-3). In Mark 12:18-27 Jesus stands with the Pharisees against the Sadducees, and argues that resurrection is in the Torah (Exod 3:6, 15-16) and within the power of God. In Mark's narrative Jesus is the first example or case of resurrection. According to 16:6 the reason why Jesus' tomb was found empty was that "he is risen." In the resurrection of Jesus a decisive event in the eschatological scenario has already taken place in "this generation."

13. *MARK IN RELATION TO PAUL AND TO PETER*

A. The Identity of "Mark"

What we call the Gospel of Mark is technically an anonymous composition. At no point does the evangelist identify himself by name or claim to be a participant in or an eyewitness to the events described in the work (compare John 21:24). The heading "According to Mark" was not part of the original text; rather, it was a later addition reflecting the early church's custom of ascribing this gospel to Mark.

Fifty years ago the great British commentator Vincent Taylor asserted that "there can be no doubt that the author of the Gospel was Mark the attendant of Peter." He went on to state that the view that Mark was the John Mark of Acts and the companion of Paul "is held almost with complete unanimity and it may be accepted as sound" (*The Gospel According to St Mark* 26). Scholars since Taylor do not generally share his certitude, nor do they regard these matters to be as important as he did. The focus of more recent scholars is the evangelist's literary artistry, the complexity of the process by which the gospel came to be, and the distinctive theological voice expressed in it.

The Pauline epistles mention someone named "Mark" (a common name in the Greco-Roman world) in three places. In the list of Paul's coworkers (*synergoi*) in Philemon 24 there is mention of "Mark." In Col 4:10 there is a reference to "Mark the cousin of Barnabas." In 2 Tim 4:11 Paul instructs Timothy to "get Mark and bring him with you, for he is useful in my ministry." If all these "prison letters" were composed by Paul in Rome their testimony would firmly link Mark both to Paul and to Rome. But since Paul was imprisoned more than once and since the direct Pauline authorship of Colossians and 2 Timothy is dubious, the evidence is less compelling than it may seem at first glance.

There are also three mentions of "John Mark" in the Acts of the Apostles. According to Acts 12:12 the "house of Mary, the mother of John whose other name was Mark" was a center for the Christian community in Jerusalem in its early days. According to Acts 12:25 "John whose other name was Mark" returned to Jerusalem with Paul and Barnabas after completing their apostolic mission to Antioch, and Acts 15:37-39 describes a bitter disagreement between Paul and Barnabas over "John called Mark." Paul refused to take John Mark along on their next apostolic mission on the grounds that he "had deserted them in Pamphylia and had not accompanied them in the work" (15:38). The result was that Barnabas and Mark went off to Cyprus while Paul and Silas went through Syria and Cilicia.

The figure called Mark or John Mark that emerges from these NT passages is the son of a prominent Jerusalem Christian woman, an early coworker of Paul and Barnabas (and Barnabas' nephew), and the occasion of a split between Paul and Barnabas. It is unlikely that this Mark was the author of the gospel for a number of reasons. For a "Jerusalemite" he seems far less Jewish than, for example, Matthew. The Old Testament is most often cited in a form closer to the Old Greek version than according to the Hebrew text. His knowledge of Palestinian customs and geography is sometimes faulty, and the gospel seems more destined as "good news for the nations" with some distancing from Judaism implied.

B. Relation to the Pauline Tradition

Mark's Gospel and the Pauline letters have different vocabulary and theological concerns. Since Mark's primary interest is the public ministry and Passion of Jesus, while Paul focuses on the significance of Jesus' death and resurrection for early Christians, we should not expect much overlap. Yet there are some intriguing contacts between Mark and Paul or the Pauline tradition, especially as they are present in the letter to the Romans. These were noted by B. W. Bacon early in the twentieth century (*Is Mark A Roman Gospel?* [Cambridge, Mass.: Harvard University Press, 1919]; *The Gospel of Mark: Its Composition and Date* [New Haven: Yale University Press, 1925]). See now Joel Marcus, "Mark—Interpreter of Paul," *NTS* 46 (2000) 473–87.

1. Similarities in Terminology and Theology: The major verbal and thematic similiarities include the term "gospel of God" (Mark 1:14; Rom 1:1; 15:16; also used in 1 Thess 2:2, 9; 1 Pet 4:17), a similar view of OT as "written" (Mark 1:1-3; Rom 1:20), the "cultic" language used for ministry (Mark 10:45; Rom 1:9; 15:16), the saying in Mark 7:27 ("let the children *first* be fed") and Rom 1:16 ("to the Jews *first*"), the catalogues of vices in Mark 7:21 and Rom 1:29, the emphasis on "hardness of heart" in Rom 2:5 and Mark 10:5, Mark's teaching on a woman's right to divorce as mirroring Roman law (10:10-12), the virtue of *hypomonē* prior to the end-time (Rom 2:7; Mark 13:13), the stress on the difference between hidden and revealed (Mark 4:21-25; Rom 2:28), mention of Rufus (Mark 15:21; Rom 16:13), and a similar soteriology (Mark 10:45; Rom 3:24).

2. Similar Community Concerns: The teaching of Jesus about clean and unclean in Mark 7:14-23 could continue to address the kind of dispute mirrored by Rom 14:1-23. The view of the state in Rom 13:1-7 is similar to that in Mark 12:13-17, and both passages are closely related to the love command (Rom 13:8-10; Mark 12:28-34). If Mark was written soon after the disastrous Jewish War of 66–74 C.E., "rendering to Caesar" could simply be a counter to the path of violent revolution.

3. Structures: There is also significant affinity between the structures of the community as reflected in Paul's letter to the Romans and in the Gospel of Mark. Both documents are similar in not using the word *ekklēsia* for the community's self-identification. In Mark, Jesus promises his disciples that they will have "houses" (10:3), and the communities at Rome are organized as house churches (Rom 16:1-16). Likewise, the absence of a central authority at Rome is mirrored in Mark's view of communities without a single dominant authority or "father" (10:29-30).

C. Relation to Peter

There is also a reference to Mark in 1 Pet 5:13: "Your sister church in Babylon . . . sends you greetings; and so does my son Mark." As in the book of Revelation, "Babylon" is a code-name for Rome. Thus 1 Pet 5:13 links Mark with Peter and with Rome. As with the Pauline references to

Mark, the critical problem is whether 1 Peter was directly composed by Peter or originated in a Petrine circle at Rome after Peter's death (as most scholars today hold).

The earliest patristic evidence regarding the authorship of Mark's Gospel comes from "the Elder" as quoted by Papias (early 2nd c.) as quoted by Eusebius (*Hist. eccl.* 3.39.15): "Mark, having become the interpreter *(hermēneutēs)* of Peter, wrote down accurately whatever he remembered of what was said or done by the Lord, but not in order." This description raises questions about the meaning of *hermēneutēs* ("interpreter, translator, secretary," or what?) and about the qualification "not in order" (compared to what?). But it does affirm Mark's relationship to Peter.

The tradition of Mark as Peter's "interpreter" is often repeated by early Christian writers: "the interpreter of Peter" (Anti-Marcionite Prologue); "Mark the disciple and interpreter of Peter" (Irenaeus); "Peter . . . sought out Mark . . . to record his words" and "Mark the follower of Peter" (Clement of Alexandria); "Mark who did as Peter instructed him" (Origen); and "Mark the interpreter of the apostle Peter" (Jerome). The tradition about the link between Mark and Peter and about Mark as the author of the gospel that bears his name is impressive. One can object, however, that this tradition may have arisen from an effort in the early second century to relate the four Gospels to apostolic figures. But why Mark rather than Peter himself?

In our commentary we neither reject this solid tradition nor rely very heavily on it. Our interests are more with the author we can come to know through careful literary analysis of his work as it stands and with the distinctive theological perspectives that emerge out of his story of Jesus' public ministry and Passion. But we are much impressed by the tradition's link of Mark's Gospel to Rome and the experience of the Christian community there, and regard it as the most likely life-setting for the composition of Mark's Gospel.

14. *THE DATE AND AUDIENCE OF MARK*

In surveying the ancient evidence and modern scholarship about the date and audience for Mark's Gospel, Vincent Taylor again represented traditional scholarly wisdom when he contended that it "is generally agreed that Mark wrote during the decade A.D. 60–70" (*Gospel* 31), and that "the Gospel was probably written for the use of the Church in Rome" (p. 32). These positions go back to the earliest sources. The Anti-Marcionite prologue states that "after the death of Peter himself, he [Mark] wrote down this same Gospel in the regions of Italy." And according to Irenaeus

(*Adv. haer.* 3.1.2) Mark wrote down his gospel "after the death of these [i.e., Peter and Paul]." Since Peter and Paul are generally believed to have suffered martyrdom in the persecution after the great fire of 64 C.E. these patristic testimonies place the composition of the gospel in the late 60s or early 70s of the first century C.E. That Mark wrote primarily (though not exclusively) for the church at Rome seems likely (as we will see) in light of the content of his gospel, which appears to address a community that has suffered persecution from the outside and division from the inside.

While Mark wrote his gospel to encourage and challenge his readers to reflect on their own lives in light of the story of Jesus, it can also be used as a "window" onto the circumstances in which the gospel was written. See John R. Donahue, "Windows and Mirrors: The Setting of Mark's Gospel," *CBQ* 57 (1995) 1–26.

The theme of the cross can be compared to a magnet that attracts the other motifs that appear throughout the gospel. The cross casts its shadow even over the opening of the gospel in 1:1-15, especially in the scene of the testing of Jesus by Satan (1:12-13). Here the reader learns that what will unfold in Jesus' public ministry and in his Passion is part of a cosmic struggle between good and evil that is waged by Jesus as God's righteous one (see Wis 2:12-20; 5:1-7). Before the summary of Jesus' preaching in 1:14-15 we are told that John the Baptist was "handed over" (*paradidonai*). John preaches and is handed over (1:2-15); Jesus preaches and is handed over (9:31; 10:33); and Christians preach and are handed over (13:9-13). In the Passion narrative Jesus is handed over to sinners by Judas (14:41-42), and is eventually handed over by the chief priests with the elders and scribes to the Roman prefect Pontius Pilate for execution (15:2, 10, 15).

As Mark's narrative of Jesus unfolds, there are other intimations of Jesus' Passion and foreshadowings of the crisis that will bring suffering to Jesus' followers. His healing of a paralyzed man in 2:1-12 evokes the charge that his talk about forgiving sins is blasphemy (2:7)—a charge repeated at Jesus' trial before the Sanhedrin in 14:64. At the center of the first block of controversy stories (2:1–3:6) we are told that the bridegroom will be taken away (2:19-20), and at the end we hear about a plot between Pharisees and Herodians to destroy Jesus (3:6).

At three crucial points in Jesus' ministry in Jerusalem there are further hints about Jesus' death. After his prophetic action in the Temple the chief priests are prevented from destroying Jesus only by their fear of the crowd (11:18). When they perceive that Jesus' parable of the vineyard (12:1-11) is about them, they again are prevented from arresting him only out of fear of the crowd (12:12). And the starting point of the Passion narrative is their desire to arrest Jesus and put him to death (14:1).

Besides the motifs of the shadow of the cross and opposition to Jesus by powerful leaders, the theme of division among Jesus' followers runs through the gospel. As Jesus begins to gather disciples we learn that one of the Twelve is "Judas Iscariot who betrayed him" (3:19; see 14:10, 17-21, 43). Jesus meets suspicion from his own family (who think that he is "out of his mind," 3:20-21) and disbelief from the people of his hometown (6:1-6). His own disciples move from imperceptiveness in 1:1–8:26 (see 6:52; 8:4, 16-21), through misconceptions about the nature of Jesus' messiahship in 8:27–10:52 (8:32-33; 9:32; 10:35-45), to betrayal, abandonment, and denial of Jesus (see 14:10, 37-41, 50, 66-72).

Persecution is also a prominent theme in Mark's Gospel. The interpretation of the fate of the seeds sown on rocky ground (see 4:5, 16 *petrōdes*—perhaps an allusion to Peter) as falling away because of "trouble" *(thlipsis)* or "persecution" *(diōgmos)* foreshadows the "trouble" *(thlipsis)* prior to the coming of the Son of Man (see 13:19, 24) and the "persecutions" *(diōgmoi)* promised to those who leave everything to follow Jesus (see 10:30). In the eschatological discourse in 13:9-13 Jesus warns his disciples that persecutions and trials will be part of the process by which the gospel will be preached to all nations.

In the same passage Jesus warns about betrayals: "Brother will hand over brother to death, and a father his child, and children will rise up against parents and have them put to death" (13:12). And Peter in 14:66-72 denies Jesus three times and so becomes the symbol for all those who betray Jesus and their fellow Christians.

The shadow of the cross, opposition from powerful leaders, divisions among Jesus' followers, persecutions, and betrayals—all these themes in Mark's Gospel would have been especially meaningful to an early Christian community that had suffered for the name of Jesus and was expecting even more suffering. These themes fit well with the experience of Christians at Rome in the late 60s of the first century C.E. There is solid historical evidence that the Christian community at Rome faced persecutions, brutal executions, and intrafamilial betrayals some time after the great fire of 64 C.E. under Nero. According to the Roman historian Cornelius Tacitus, who wrote around 115 C.E., the emperor Nero in order to shift blame for the fire from himself fixed the guilt on the Roman Christians (*Ann.* 15.44). Tacitus described the procedure used in arresting the Christians as follows: "First, then, the confessed members of the sect were arrested; next, on evidence furnished by them a huge multitude was convicted not so much on the count of arson as hatred of the human race." Tacitus goes on to recount the horrible punishments inflicted on them: "they were covered with wild beasts' skins and torn to death by dogs; or they were fastened on crosses, and when daylight failed were burned to serve as lamps by night."

The persecution of the Roman Christians that Tacitus describes took place after the great fire of 64 and probably lasted into the late 60s and even early 70s. It is in this atmosphere that Mark's Gospel very likely took shape. This setting fits remarkably well with Jesus' "prophecies" to his disciples in Mark 13:9-13. In the context of proclaiming the gospel in a predominantly Gentile milieu the Roman Christians were forced to bear witness before Roman officials (see 13:9-11). There were intrafamilial betrayals (see 13:12), and they were "hated by all for my sake" (13:13).

Along the same lines, Clement the bishop of Rome in writing to the Corinthian Christians in the late first century C.E. states that "by reason of jealousy and envy the greatest and most righteous pillars of the church were persecuted and contended even unto death" (1 Clem. 5:2). He goes on to recount the deaths of Peter and Paul, and notes that a "great multitude" was also persecuted. He suggests that the deaths of the Christians at Rome were due to the same *zēlos* that was destroying the unity of the Christian community at Corinth.

Both Tacitus and Clement indicate that apostasy and betrayal were byproducts of the persecutions under Nero. However, Clement's praise of Peter's heroism in the face of suffering ("having borne his testimony, he went to his appointed place of glory") also suggests that Peter was rehabilitated after his denials of Jesus (see 14:66-72). And if Peter could be forgiven his apostasy and betrayal, so others who had given up their fellow Christians could be forgiven.

So the early patristic tradition, the content of Mark's Gospel, and events at Rome in the late 60s of the first century C.E. all point to Rome around 70 C.E. as the historical setting for the origin of Mark's Gospel. Whether it was composed shortly before or shortly after the destruction of the Jerusalem Temple in 70 C.E. is not clear. At any rate, since Christianity was perceived by the Romans as either a Jewish sect or an offshoot from Judaism the negative feelings that Romans had toward Jews (and vice versa) at the time were very likely a factor in the persecution of Christians.

This confluence of evidence is impressive, and the commentary that follows reads Mark's Gospel as having been composed originally for Roman Christians around 70 C.E. But we acknowledge that since the late 1950s there have been tendencies to move the composition of Mark's Gospel toward the East and to give more attention to events in Palestine during the First Jewish Revolt (66–73 C.E.). See John R. Donahue, "The Quest for the Community of Mark's Gospel," in Frans van Segbroeck et al., eds., *The Four Gospels, 1992: Festschrift Frans Neirynck*. 3 vols. (Leuven: Leuven University Press, 1992) 2:819–34.

About the same time (1956) that Vincent Taylor affirmed the consensus about the place and date of Mark's Gospel as Rome between 60 and 70 C.E., Willi Marxsen in *Der Evangelist Markus* (English: *Mark the Evangelist* [Philadelphia: Fortress, 1969]) located its composition in Galilee (the place of Jesus' first manifestation) in a Christian community that had escaped the horrors of the First Jewish War and was expecting the return of Jesus in Galilee (see 14:28; 16:7). Howard Clark Kee in *The Community of the New Age* (Philadelphia: Westminster, 1977) traced the gospel's origin to a sectarian community strongly influenced by apocalypticism (especially the book of Daniel) and suggested a location near Palestine, most likely in southern Syria. On the basis of the "local coloring" in Mark's Gospel, Gerd Theissen in *Lokalkolorit und Zeitgeschichte in den Evangelien* (1989; English: *The Gospels in Context* [Minneapolis: Fortress, 1991]) argued for a provenance in southern Syria near the border of Palestine, and contended that Mark 13 reflects the evangelist's adaptation of apocalyptic material to his own situation after the destruction of the Jerusalem Temple in 70 C.E. Joel Marcus ("The Jewish War and the Sitz im Leben of Mark," *JBL* 111 [1992] 441–62; see also his *Mark 1–8*) maintains that Mark's Gospel reflects the pervasive influence of the First Jewish Revolt (66–74 C.E.), an event to which the Markan community stood in both geographical and temporal proximity. He appeals to the *ex eventu* prophecies in Mark 13, the description of the Temple as "a den of brigands" (11:17), and the treatment of Davidic messianism (see 10:46-52; 11:10-11; 12:35-37). Marcus concludes that Mark's Gospel was written shortly after 70 C.E., perhaps in one of the Hellenistic cities of Palestine.

This survey of the views of four distinguished Markan scholars (and the list could be expanded) establishes at the very least that the old "consensus" among scholars for the origin of Mark's Gospel at Rome before 70 C.E. no longer holds. The new approaches are valuable in explaining the "local coloring" and the apocalyptic features that are so prominent in Mark's Gospel. They also serve to make certain elements in the text come alive (e.g., the prominence of Galilee, the Jerusalem Temple as "a cave for bandits"). But their reliance on Mark 13 as clearly conveying *ex eventu* prophecies and their appeal to the character and experiences of early Christian communities in Palestine and Syria (about which we know little or nothing) do call for caution.

Two other (well publicized but highly dubious) proposals related to the origin of Mark's Gospel that emerged in the early 1970s have won few supporters over the long haul. Jose O'Callaghan (in "¿Papiros neotestamentarios en la cueva 7 de Qumran?" *Bib* 53 [1972] 91–100) identified two Greek papryus fragments from Qumran Cave 7—7Q5 and 7Q6—as Mark 6:52-53 and 4:28, respectively. These identifications, if correct, would place a Greek copy of Mark's Gospel in an Essene Jewish community in Palestine before 50 C.E. But even O'Callaghan's parade example 7Q5 = Mark 6:52-53 requires several Greek textual emendations and is better identified as a text from the Greek OT or from the Greek *1 Enoch*. For a recent critique see Robert H. Gundry, "No *NU* in Line 2 of 7Q5: A Final Disidentification of 7Q5 with Mark 6:52-53," *JBL* 118 (1999) 698–707.

In *Clement of Alexandria and a Secret Gospel of Mark* (Cambridge, Mass.: Harvard University Press, 1973) Morton Smith published what he claimed to be a copy of a letter from Clement of Alexandria to Theodore that he found in 1958 at the Mar Saba monastery in Palestine. In it Clement provides quotations from a "secret Gospel" or a "more spiritual Gospel" attributed to Mark in which there is reference to a nocturnal meeting between a young man and Jesus as a rite of erotic magic. But Smith's work has raised many questions. Was the letter really written by Clement of Alexandria, or was it an ancient or modern forgery? Does the "secret Gospel" have a claim to be an early edition of Mark, or is it at best a second-century C.E. harmonization of Mark with other gospel texts (especially John 11)? For critical discussions see Herbert Musurillo, "Morton Smith's Secret Gospel," *Thought* 48 (1973) 327–31; Quentin Quesnell, "The Mar Saba Clementine: A Question of Evidence," *CBQ* 37 (1975) 48–67; and recently D. H. Akenson, *Saint Saul: A Skeleton Key to the Historical Jesus* (Oxford: Oxford University Press, 2000) 84–89. For critical assessments of both 7Q5 and "Secret Mark" see Graham Stanton, *Gospel Truth? New Light on Jesus and the Gospels* (Valley Forge, Penn.: Trinity Press International, 1995).

In this commentary we opt for a date around 70 C.E. and for an original audience among the persecuted Christians at Rome. We are proposing the ca. 70 C.E. Roman setting for the final composition of the gospel, while realizing that it bears the imprint of earlier stages of composition. We are also aware of more recent studies that question whether gospels as such were directed to particular communities or rather were meant to be texts circulated throughout the Christian mission as Matthew and Luke's use of Mark would seem to suggest. See Richard Bauckham, ed., *The Gospels for All Christians. Rethinking the Gospel Audiences* (Grand Rapids: Eerdmans, 1998). Still a gospel could both reflect the setting of its final composition and be used in a wider context. For reservations about specific contextual readings of Mark see Tolbert, *Sowing the Gospel,* and Richard A. Burridge, *What are the Gospels? A Comparison with Greco-Roman Bibliography.* MSSNTS 70 (Cambridge and New York: Cambridge University Press, 1992) and idem, *Four Gospels, One Jesus?: A Symbolic Reading* (Grand Rapids: Eerdmans, 1994).

15. THE OUTLINE OF MARK'S GOSPEL

Although there are many outlines proposed for Mark, the one used for this commentary reflects a growing consensus at least in its major divisions and subdivisions. Virtually all commentators agree that there is a major difference between the Galilean section (1:1–8:21) and the Jerusalem ministry and Passion (11:1–16:8), with the central section 8:22–10:52 organized around the motif of a journey to Jerusalem that is punctuated by the three Passion predictions followed by misunderstanding and further teaching. The journey section is a clearly organized unit comprising the midpoint and theological centerpiece of the gospel, culminating in Jesus' self-affirmation in 10:45 that he has come "not to be served but to serve, and to give his life as a ransom for many." While this outline presents an overview for readers today it does not exhaust the many ways in which Mark through foreshadowings and echoes relates different parts of the gospel, or other ways by which material is grouped (e.g., collections of miracle stories and controversies, the structure of the sea voyages, and the bread section in 6:8–8:16). It might be best to think of Mark as a series of overlays that comprise multiple structures and modes of composition; see F. G. Lang, "Kompositionsanalyse des Markusevangeliums," *ZThK* 74 (1977) 1–24.

A DESCRIPTIVE OUTLINE OF THE GOSPEL OF MARK

*(Numbers in **bold italics** refer to sections of Commentary)*

MAJOR SECTION ONE:
JESUS AS THE ANOINTED SON OF GOD PROCLAIMS
IN GALILEE THE IMMINENCE OF GOD'S REIGN IN
POWERFUL WORDS AND DEEDS (1:16–8:22 [26])

I. PROLOGUE: THE BEGINNING OF THE GOOD NEWS (1:1-13) *[1]*
   A. Superscript and Preparation for Ministry of Jesus (1:1-8) by God (1:2-3) and by John (1:4-8)
   B. Messianic Preparation of Jesus (1:9-13):
      1. Baptism (1:9-11)
      2. Temptation (1:12-13)

II. AUTHORITY AND POWER *(exousia)* OF JESUS IN
   WORD AND DEED (1:14–3:6)
   A. Transition to Ministry of Jesus and Proclamation of the Kingdom (1:14-15) *[2]*
   B. Beginning of Jesus' Powerful Works (1:16-34):
      1. The Call of the First Disciples (1:16-20) *[3]*
      2. Paradigmatic "Day" Begins Ministry of Jesus (1:21-34) *[4]*
   C. Highpoints of Jesus' Work in Galilee (1:35-45): retreat to desert and preaching (1:35-39); healing of leper, return to desert (1:40-45) *[5]*

D. Vindication of Authority of Jesus in Word by Controversies with
     Opponents (2:1–3:6):
  1. Healing of Paralyzed Man (2:1-12) *[6]*
  2. Call of Levi and Meals with Tax Collectors and Sinners (2:13-17) *[7]*
  3. Fasting, Torn Garments, and New Wineskins (2:18-22) *[8]*
  4. Plucking Grain on the Sabbath (2:23-28) *[9]*
  5. Healing on Sabbath and Plan to Kill Jesus (3:1-6) *[10]*

III. ACTIVITY OF JESUS AROUND THE SEA OF GALILEE (3:7–8:26)
  A. Transitional Markan Summary: Healing Beside the Sea (3:7-12) *[11]*
  B. Choosing and Naming of the Twelve (3:13-19) *[12]*
  C. The Beelzebul Controversy and the True Family of Jesus (3:20-35) *[13]*
    1. Charges of "madness" by those around him and of possession by
       scribes (3:21-30)
    2. Division within family of Jesus, and his true family (3:31-35)
  D. Parables and Sayings (4:1-34)
    1. Parable of the Sower; Sayings on the Mystery of the Kingdom of
       God; and the Allegory of the Seeds (4:1-20) *[14]*
    2. Four sayings on Revelation and Two Kingdom Parables (4:21-34)
       [15]
  E. Culmination of Jesus' Mighty Works (4:35–5:43)
    1. Jesus' Power over the Wind and the Waves (4:35-41) *[16]*
    2. Jesus' Mighty Works are Extended to Gentile Territory;
       exorcism of Gerasene Demoniac (5:1-20) *[17]*
    3. Two Intercalated Miracles: Jairus' Daughter (5:21-24, 35-43), and the
       Woman Who Touched Jesus' Garment (5:25-34) *[18]*
    4. The Rejection at Nazareth (6:1-6a) *[19]*
  F. Mission Charge to the Twelve (6:6b-13) *[20]*
  G. Interlude: Identity of Jesus and Execution of
     John the Baptist (6:14-29) *[21]*
  H. First Feeding Cycle: 6:30-56 *(Note that the same sequence appears in John 6
     and how the motif of "bread" appears in this section.)*
    1. The Feeding of the 5000 by the Sea of Galilee (6:31-44) *[22]*
    2. Jesus Walks on Water and Astounds the Disciples (6:45-52) *[23]*
    3. Markan Summary about the Healing Power of Jesus (6:53-56) *[24]*
  I. Dispute over Clean and Unclean (7:1-23) *[25]*
  J. Jesus Turns to Gentiles (7:24-37)
    1. The Faith of the Syrophoenician Woman (7:24-30) *[26]*
    2. Jesus Restores Hearing and Speech to a Suffering Man (7:31-37) *[27]*
  K. Second Feeding Cycle (8:1-21)
    1. Second Feeding Narrative: The 4000 (8:1-9) *[28]*
    2. Crossing of Sea (8:10)
    3. Pharisees and Scribes Seek a Sign (8:11-12) *[29]*
    4. Crossing of Sea; Further Misunderstanding; and
       Conclusion of Bread Discourse (8:13-21) *[30]*

MAJOR SECTION TWO:
JOURNEY TO JERUSALEM WHERE JESUS, AS GOD'S SON,
IS THE SON OF MAN WHO MUST SUFFER, DIE, AND RISE AGAIN.
HIS LIFE IS A RANSOM FOR MANY (8:27–10:45)

Transitional Giving of Sight Story:
Gradual Healing of Blind Man: (8:22-26) *[31]*

IV. CHRISTOLOGY AND DISCIPLESHIP ON THE WAY (8:27–10:45)
  A. First Passion Prediction Unit (8:27–9:1) *[32]*
      1. Question to Disciples; Confession of Peter (8:27-30)
      2. Passion Prediction (8:31); Misunderstanding (8:32-33); Instruction
         on Discipleship (8:34–9:1)
  B. Interlude: Transfiguration and Appended Material (9:2-29) *(Within A and B,
     8:27-30 and 9:2-9 provide contrasting christological panels, one stressing what
     humans think of Jesus, the other the perspective "from above," cf. 1:11.)*
      1. Transfiguration and Appended Material (9:1-13) *[33]*
      2. Healing of a Possessed Boy *[34]*
  C. Second Passion Prediction Unit and More Instruction for the Disciples
     (9:30-50): (i) instruction (9:30-31a); (ii) Passion prediction (9:31b);
     (iii) misunderstanding (9:32); and further instruction (9:33-50) *[35]*
  D. Interlude: Teaching to Crowds "Across the Jordan" (10:1-31)
      1. Marriage and Divorce (10:1-12) *[36]*
      2. Jesus Receives and Blesses Children (10:13-16) *[37]*
      3. Riches and Poverty (10:17-27), and Rewards of Discipleship
         (10:28-31) *[38]*
  E. Third Passion Prediction Unit (10:32-45): (i) instruction (10:32);
     (ii) Passion prediction (10:33-34); (iii) misunderstanding (10:35-41);
     instruction (10:42-44), *Son of Man came to give his life as a ransom for
     many* (10:45) *[39]*

Transitional Giving of Sight Story:
Healing of Blind Bartimaeus (10:46-52) *[40]*

MAJOR SECTION THREE:
JESUS IN JERUSALEM:
CONFLICT OF KINGDOMS; FAREWELL ADDRESS OF JESUS;
PASSION, DEATH, AND RESURRECTION (11:1–16:8)

V. MINISTRY OF JESUS IN JERUSALEM;
   CONFLICT OF KINGDOMS (11:1–12:44)
  A. Entry into Jerusalem: Jesus and Disciples (11:1-11) *[41]*
  B. The Fig Tree and the Temple (11:12-25) *[42]*

16. GENERAL BIBLIOGRAPHY

1. Commentaries

Achtemeier, Paul. *Mark*. Proclamation Commentaries. Philadelphia: Fortress,
    1986.
Cahill, Michael, editor and translator. *The First Commentary on Mark: An Annotated
    Translation*. New York: Oxford University Press, 1998.
Carrington, Philip. *According to Mark: A Running Commentary on the Oldest Gospel*.
    Cambridge and New York: Cambridge University Press, 1960.
Cranfield, C. E. B. *The Gospel according to St Mark: An Introduction and Commentary*.
    Cambridge Greek Testament Commentary. Cambridge and New York:
    Cambridge University Press, 1963.
Donahue, John R. "Mark," in James L. Mays, ed., *HarperCollins Bible Commentary*.
    San Francisco: Harper San Francisco, 2000, 901–24.

Dowd, Sharyn E. *Reading Mark: A Literary and Theological Commentary*. Macon, Ga.: Smyth & Helwys, 2000.

Evans, Craig A. *Mark 8:27–16:20*. WBC34b. Dallas: Word Books, 2001.

Garland, David E. *Mark*. NIV Application Commentary. Grand Rapids: Zondervan, 1996.

Gnilka, Joachim. *Das Evangelium nach Markus*. 2 vols. EKKNT 2. Zürich: Benziger; Neukirchen-Vluyn: Neukirchener Verlag, 1978–79.

Gould, Ezra P. *A Critical and Exegetical Commentary on the Gospel According to Mark*. ICC 27. 3rd. ed. New York: Scribner's, 1901.

Guelich, Robert A. *Mark 1–8:26*. WBC 34a. Dallas: Word Books, 1989.

Gundry, Robert H. *Mark: A Commentary on His Apology for the Cross*. Grand Rapids: Eerdmans, 1993.

Haenchen, Ernst. *Der Weg Jesu: Eine Erklärung des Markus-Evangeliums und der kanonischen Parallelen*. Berlin: Walter de Gruyter, 1968.

Hare, Douglas R. A. *Mark*. Westminster Bible Companion. Louisville: Westminster, 1996.

Harrington, Daniel J. "The Gospel According to Mark," in Raymond E. Brown, Joseph A. Fitzmyer, and Roland E. Murphy, eds., *New Jerome Biblical Commentary*. Englewood Cliffs, N.J.: Prentice-Hall, 1990, 596–629.

Harrington, Wilfrid J. *Mark*. New Testament Message 4. Wilmington, Del.: Michael Glazier, 1979.

Heil, John P. *The Gospel of Mark as a Model for Action*. New York: Paulist, 1992.

Hooker, Morna D. *The Gospel According to St Mark*. Black's New Testament Commentary. Peabody, Mass.: Hendrickson, 1991.

Hurtado, Larry. *Mark*. New International Bible Commentary 2. Peabody, Mass.: Hendrickson, 1989.

Iersel, Bas M. F. van. *Mark: A Reader-Response Commentary*. Sheffield: Sheffield Academic Press, 1998.

Johnson, Sherman. *A Commentary on the Gospel According to St Mark*. Black's/ Harper's New Testament Commentary. 2nd. ed. London: A & C Black, 1977.

Juel, Donald H. *Mark*. Augsburg Commentary on the New Testament. Minneapolis: Augsburg, 1990.

Kertelge, Karl. *Markusevangelium*. Die Neue Echter Bibel, NT 2. Würzburg: Echter, 1994.

Lachs, Samuel T. *A Rabbinic Commentary on the New Testament: The Gospels of Matthew, Mark and Luke*. Hoboken, N.J.: Ktav, 1987.

Lagrange, Marie-Joseph. *Évangile selon Saint Marc*. Études Bibliques. Paris: Gabalda, 1929.

Lane, William. *Commentary on the Gospel of Mark*. New International Commentary on the New Testament. Grand Rapids: Eerdmans, 1974.

LaVerdiere, Eugene. *The Beginning of the Gospel: Introducing the Gospel According to Mark*. 2 vols. Collegeville: The Liturgical Press, 1999.

Légasse, Simon. *L'Évangile de Marc*. Lectio Divina, Commentaires 5. 2 vols. Paris: Cerf, 1997.

Lohmeyer, Ernst. *Das Evangelium nach Markus*. Meyer Kommentar. 11th. ed. Göttingen: Vandenhoeck & Ruprecht, 1951.

Lührmann, Dieter. *Das Markusevangelium*. HNT 3. Tübingen: J.C.B. Mohr [Paul Siebeck], 1987.

Mann, Charles S. *Mark*. AB 27. Garden City, N.Y.: Doubleday, 1986.

Marcus, Joel. *Mark 1–8*. AB 27A. New York: Doubleday, 2000.

Moule, C. F. D. *The Gospel According to Mark*. Cambridge Bible Commentary on the New English Bible. Cambridge: Cambridge University Press, 1965.

Nineham, Dennis E. *Saint Mark*. Pelican Gospel Commentary. Harmondsworth: Penguin, 1964.

Oden, Thomas C., and Christopher A. Hall, eds. *Mark*. Ancient Commentary on Scripture. New Testament 2. Downers Grove, Ill.: InterVarsity, 1998.

Painter, John. *Mark's Gospel: Worlds in Conflict*. New Testament Readings. London and New York: Routledge, 1997.

Perkins, Pheme. "Mark." *The New Interpreter's Bible* 8. Nashville: Abingdon, 1995, 507–733.

Pesch, Rudolf. *Das Markusevangelium*. 2 Vols. HTKNT 2. Freiburg: Herder, 1976.

Rawlinson, A. E. J. *St Mark: With Introduction, Commentary and Additional Notes*. Westminster Commentaries. London: Methuen, 1925.

Schweizer, Eduard. *The Good News According to Mark*. Atlanta: John Knox, 1977.

Standaert, Benoit. *L Évangile selon Marc*. Paris: Cerf, 1997.

Swete, Henry B. *The Gospel According to St Mark: The Greek Text with Introduction, Notes and Commentary*. 3rd ed. London: Macmillan, 1920.

Taylor, Vincent. *The Gospel According to St Mark*. 2nd. ed. London: Macmillan, 1966.

Trocmé, Etienne. *L Évangile selon Saint Marc*. Commentaire du Nouveau Testament 2. Paris: Labor et Fides, 2000.

Williamson, Lamar. *Mark*. Interpretation. Atlanta: John Knox, 1983.

Witherington, Ben. *The Gospel of Mark. A Socio-Rhetorical Commentary*. Grand Rapids: Eerdmans, 2001.

(Commentaries will generally be referred to simply by the name of the author.)

2. Bibliographies

Humphrey, Hugh M. *A Bibliography for the Gospel of Mark 1954–1980*. New York: Mellen, 1981.

Mills, Watson E. *The Gospel of Mark*. Lewiston, N.Y.: Mellen, 1994.

Neirynck, Frans, et al., *The Gospel of Mark. A Cumulative Bibliography, 1950–1990*. Leuven: Leuven University Press/Peeters, 1992.

3. General Studies

Achtemeier, Paul J. "The Origin and Function of the Pre-Marcan Miracle Catenae," *JBL* 91 (1972) 198–221.

Ambrozic, Aloysius M. *The Hidden Kingdom. A Redaction-Critical Study of the References to the Kingdom of God in Mark's Gospel*. Washington, D.C.: Catholic Biblical Association, 1972.

Anderson, Janice Capel, and Stephen D. Moore, eds. *Mark & Method: New Approaches in Biblical Studies*. Minneapolis: Fortress, 1992.

Barta, Karen. *The Gospel of Mark*. Collegeville: The Liturgical Press, 1988.

Belo, Fernando. *A Materialist Reading of the Gospel of Mark*. Maryknoll, N.Y.: Orbis, 1981.

Best, Ernest. *Disciples and Discipleship: Studies in the Gospel according to Mark*. Edinburgh: T & T Clark, 1986.

_____. *Following Jesus. Discipleship in the Gospel of Mark*. Sheffield: JSOT Press, 1981.

_____. *Mark: The Gospel as Story*. Edinburgh: T & T Clark, 1983.

_____. *The Temptation and the Passion: The Markan Soteriology*. 2nd ed. Cambridge: Cambridge University Press, 1990.

Black, C. Clifton. *Mark: Images of an Apostolic Interpreter*. Columbia, S.C.: University of South Carolina Press, 1994.

Blackburn, Barry. *Theios Aner and the Markan Miracle Traditions*. Tübingen: J.C.B. Mohr [Paul Siebeck], 1991.

Blevins, James L. *The Messianic Secret in Markan Research, 1901–1976*. Washington, D.C.: University Press of America, 1981.

Blount, Brian K. *Go Preach! Mark's Kingdom Message and the Black Church Today*. Maryknoll, N.Y.: Orbis, 1998.

Broadhead, Edwin K. *Teaching with Authority. Miracles and Christology in the Gospel of Mark*. Sheffield: JSOT Press, 1992.

_____. *Naming Jesus. Titular Christology in the Gospel of Mark*. Sheffield: Sheffield Academic Press, 1999.

_____. *Prophet, Son, Messiah. Narrative Forms and Function in Mark 14–16*. Sheffield: JSOT Press, 1994.

Brown, Raymond E. *The Death of the Messiah: From Gethsemane to the Grave. A Commentary on the Passion Narratives in the Four Gospels*. New York: Doubleday, 1994.

Bryan, Christopher. *A Preface to Mark. Notes on the Gospel in Its Literary and Cultural Settings*. New York and Oxford: Oxford University Press, 1993.

Bultmann, Rudolf. *History of the Synoptic Tradition*. New York: Harper & Row, 1963.

Camery-Hoggatt, Jerry. *Irony in Mark's Gospel. Text and Subtext*. Cambridge and New York: Cambridge University Press, 1992.

Casey, Maurice. *Aramaic Sources of Mark's Gospel*. Cambridge: Cambridge University Press, 1998.

Collins, Adela Yarbro. *The Beginning of the Gospel. Probings of Mark in Context*. Minneapolis: Fortress, 1992.

_____. "Mark and His Readers: The Son of God among Greeks and Romans," *HTR* 93 (2000) 85–100.

Cook, John G. *The Structure and Persuasive Power of Mark. A Linguistic Approach*. Atlanta: Scholars, 1995.

Cook, Michael. *Mark's Treatment of the Jewish Leaders*. Leiden: Brill, 1978.

Davidsen, Ole. *The Narrative Jesus. A Semiotic Reading of Mark's Gospel*. Aarhus: Aarhus University Press, 1993.

Dawson, Anne. *Freedom as Liberating Power. A Socio-Political Reading of the Exousia Texts in the Gospel of Mark*. Fribourg: Universitätsverlag; Göttingen: Vandenhoeck & Ruprecht, 2000.

Dewey, Joanna. "Mark as Interwoven Tapestry: Forecasts and Echoes for a Listening Audience," *CBQ* 53 (1991) 221–36.

Dibelius, Martin. *From Tradition to Gospel.* New York: Scribner's, 1965.

Donahue, John R. *Are You the Christ?* SBLDS 10. Missoula: SBL, 1973.

_____. *The Gospel in Parable. Metaphor, Narrative, and Theology in the Synoptic Gospels.* Philadelphia: Fortress, 1988.

_____. "Jesus as the Parable of God in the Gospel of Mark," *Int* 32 (1978) 369–86.

_____. "The Quest for the Community of Mark's Gospel," in Frans van Segbroeck et al., eds., *The Four Gospels 1992: Festscrift Frans Neirynck.* 3 vols. BETL 100. Leuven: Leuven University Presss, 1992, 2:817–38.

_____. "Recent Studies on the Origin of the 'Son of Man' in the Gospels," *CBQ* 48 (1986) 484–98.

_____. *The Theology and Setting of Discipleship in the Gospel of Mark.* Milwaukee: Marquette University Press, 1983.

_____. "Windows and Mirrors: The Setting of Mark's Gospel," *CBQ* 57 (1995) 1–26.

Doudna, John C. *The Greek of the Gospel of Mark.* JBLMS 12. Philadelphia: SBL, 1961.

Dowd, Sharyn E. *Prayer, Power, and the Problem of Suffering: Mark 11:22-25 in the Context of Markan Theology.* SBLDS 105. Atlanta: Scholars, 1988.

Fleddermann, Harry T. *Mark and Q: A Study of the Overlap Texts: With an Assessment by F. Neirynck.* Leuven: Leuven University Press, 1995.

Garrett, Susan R. *The Temptations of Jesus in Mark's Gospel.* Grand Rapids: Eerdmans, 1998.

Geddert, Timothy J. *Watchwords: Mark 13 in Markan Eschatology.* Sheffield: JSOT Press, 1989.

Hamerton-Kelly, Robert G. *The Gospel and the Sacred. Poetics of Violence in Mark.* Minneapolis: Fortress, 1994.

Hanson, James S. *The Endangered Promises. Conflict in Mark.* SBLDS 171. Atlanta: SBL, 2000.

Hengel, Martin. *Studies in the Gospel of Mark.* Philadelphia: Fortress, 1985.

Hooker, Morna D. *The Son of Man in Mark: A Study of the Background of the Term 'Son of Man' and Its Use in St Mark's Gospel.* London: S.P.C.K., 1967.

Horsley, Richard A. *Hearing the Whole Story: The Politics of Plot in Mark's Gospel.* Louisville: Westminster John Knox, 2001.

Humphrey, Hugh M. *He Is Risen! A New Reading of Mark's Gospel.* New York: Paulist, 1992.

Iersel, Bas M. F. van. *Reading Mark.* Collegeville: The Liturgical Press, 1988.

Juel, Donald H. *A Master of Surprise: Mark Interpreted.* Minneapolis: Fortress, 1994.

_____. *Messiah and Temple: The Trial of Jesus in the Gospel of Mark.* SBLDS 31. Missoula: Scholars, 1973.

Kazmierski, Carl R. *Jesus, the Son of God: A Study of the Markan Tradition and Its Redaction by the Evangelist.* Würzburg: Echter, 1979.

Kealy, Sean P. *Mark's Gospel: A History of Its Interpretation from the Beginning until 1979.* New York: Paulist, 1982.

Kee, Howard Clark. *Community of the New Age. Studies in Mark's Gospel.* Philadelphia: Westminster, 1977.

Kelber, Werner. *The Kingdom in Mark: A New Place and a New Time.* Philadelphia: Fortress, 1974.

_____. *Mark's Story of Jesus.* Philadelphia: Fortress, 1979.

_____. *The Oral and the Written Gospel: The Hermeneutics of Speaking and Writing in the Synoptic Tradition, Mark, Paul, and Q.* Philadelphia: Fortress, 1983.

_____, ed. *The Passion in Mark: Studies on Mark 14–16.* Philadelphia: Fortress, 1976.

Kermode, Frank. *The Genesis of Secrecy. On the Interpretation of Narrative.* Cambridge, Mass., and London: Harvard University Press, 1979.

Kingsbury, Jack Dean. *The Christology of Mark's Gospel.* Philadelphia: Fortress, 1983.

_____. *Conflict in Mark. Jesus, Authorities, Disciples.* Minneapolis: Fortress, 1989.

Kinukawa, Hisako. *Women and Jesus in Mark. A Japanese Feminist Perspective.* Maryknoll, N.Y.: Orbis, 1994.

Levine, Amy-Jill, ed. *A Feminist Companion to Mark.* Sheffield: Sheffield Academic Press, 2001.

Lightfoot, R. H. *The Gospel Message of Mark.* Oxford: Clarendon, 1950.

MacDonald, Dennis R. *The Homeric Epics and the Gospel of Mark.* New Haven and London: Yale University Press, 2000.

Mack, Burton. *A Myth of Innocence: Mark and Christian Origins.* Philadelphia: Fortress, 1988.

Malbon, Elizabeth S. *In the Company of Jesus. Characters in Mark's Gospel.* Louisville: Westminster John Knox, 2000.

_____. *Narrative Space and Mythic Meaning in Mark.* San Francisco: Harper & Row, 1986.

Maloney, Elliott C. *Semitic Interference in Marcan Syntax.* SBLDS 51. Chico: Scholars, 1981.

Marcus, Joel. *The Mystery of the Kingdom of God.* SBLDS 90. Atlanta: Scholars, 1986.

_____. *The Way of the Lord. Christological Exegesis of the Old Testament in the Gospel of Mark.* Louisville: Westminster John Knox, 1992.

Marshall, Christopher D. *Faith as a Theme in Mark's Narrative.* Cambridge: Cambridge University Press, 1989.

Matera, Frank J. *The Kingship of Jesus: Composition and Theology in Mark 15.* SBLDS 66. Chico: Scholars, 1982.

_____. *What Are They Saying About Mark?* New York: Paulist, 1987.

Marxsen, Willi. *Mark the Evangelist.* Nashville: Abingdon, 1969.

Meagher, John C. *Clumsy Construction in Mark's Gospel: A Critique of Form- and Redaktionsgeschichte.* New York and Toronto: Mellen, 1979.

Meier, John P. *A Marginal Jew: Rethinking the Historical Jesus.* 3 vols. New York: Doubleday, 1991, 1994, 2001.

Myers, Ched. *Binding the Strong Man: A Political Reading of Mark's Story of Jesus.* Maryknoll, N.Y.: Orbis, 1988.

Neirynck, Frans. *Duality in Mark: Contributions to the Study of the Markan Redaction.* Leuven: Leuven University Press, 1972.

Orton, David E., ed. *The Composition of Mark's Gospel. Selected Studies from Novum Testamentum.* Leiden: Brill, 1999.

Oyen, Geert van. *De studie van de Marcusredactie in de twintigste eeuw.* Leuven: Leuven University Press, 1993.

Perrin, Norman. "The Christology of Mark," *JR* 51 (1971) 173–87.

_____. "The Creative Use of the Son of Man Traditions by Mark," *USQR* 23 (1968) 357–65.

_____. "Historical Criticism, Literary Criticism, and Hermeneutics: The Interpretation of the Parables of Jesus and the Gospel of Mark Today," *JR* 52 (1972) 361–75.

_____. *A Modern Pilgrimage in New Testament Christology.* Philadelphia: Fortress, 1974.

Peterson, Dwight N. *The Origins of Mark. The Markan Community in Current Debate.* Leiden: Brill, 2000.

Pryke, E. J. *Redactional Style in the Marcan Gospel: A Study of Syntax and Vocabulary as Guides to Redaction in Mark.* Cambridge: Cambridge University Press, 1978.

Quesnell, Quentin. *The Mind of Mark. Interpretation and Method through the Exegesis of Mark 6,52.* AB 38. Rome: Biblical Institute Press, 1969.

Räisänen, Heikki. *The 'Messianic Secret' in Mark's Gospel.* Edinburgh: T & T Clark, 1990.

Reiser, William E. *Jesus in Solidarity with His People. A Theologian Looks at Mark.* Collegeville: The Liturgical Press, 2000.

Rhoads, David, Joanna Dewey, and Donald Michie. *Mark as Story: An Introduction to the Narrative of the Gospel.* 2nd ed. Minneapolis: Fortress, 1999.

Robbins, Vernon K. *Jesus the Teacher. A Socio-Rhetorical Interpretation of Mark.* Philadelphia: Fortress, 1984.

_____. *New Boundaries in Old Territory. Form and Social Rhetoric in Mark.* New York: Peter Lang, 1994.

Robinson, James M. *The Problem of History in Mark and Other Marcan Studies.* Philadelphia: Fortress, 1982.

Schenk, Wolfgang. *Der Passionsbericht nach Markus: Untersuchungen z. Überlieferungsgeschichte d. Passionstraditionen.* Gütersloh: Gerd Mohn, 1974.

Schenke, Ludger. *Die Wundererzählungen des Markusevangeliums.* SBB 5. Stuttgart: Katholisches Bibelwerk, 1974.

Senior, Donald P. *The Passion of Jesus in the Gospel of Mark.* Wilmington, Del.: Michael Glazier, 1984.

Shiner, Whitney T. *Follow Me! Disciples in Markan Rhetoric.* SBLDS 145. Atlanta: Scholars, 1995.

Smith, Morton. *Clement of Alexandria and a Secret Gospel of Mark.* Cambridge, Mass.: Harvard University Press, 1973.

Stein, Robert H. "The Proper Methodology for Ascertaining a Markan Redaction History," *NovT* 13 (1971) 181–98.

Stoldt, Hans-Herbert. *History and Criticism of the Marcan Hypothesis.* Edinburgh: T & T Clark, 1980.

Sweetland, Dennis M. *Our Journey with Jesus: Discipleship according to Mark.* Collegeville: The Liturgical Press, 1987.

Tannehill, Robert C. "The Disciples in Mark: The Function of a Narrative Role," *JR* 57 (1977) 386–405.

Telford, William R. *The Theology of the Gospel of Mark.* Cambridge: Cambridge University Press, 1999.

_____, ed. *The Interpretation of Mark.* 2nd ed. Edinburgh: T & T Clark, 1995.

Theissen, Gerd. *The Gospels in Context: Social and Political History in the Synoptic Tra-dition.* Minneapolis: Fortress, 1991.

_____. *The Miracle Stories of the Early Christian Tradition.* Edinburgh: T & T Clark, 1983.

Thurston, Bonnie B. *Preaching Mark.* Minneapolis: Fortress, 2002.

Tolbert, Mary Ann. *Sowing the Gospel: Mark's World in Literary-Historical Perspective.* Minneapolis: Fortress, 1989.

Trainor, Michael F. *The Quest for Home. The Household in Mark's Community.* Collegeville: The Liturgical Press, 2001.

Trocmé, Etienne. *The Formation of the Gospel according to Mark.* Philadelphia: West-minster, 1975.

Tuckett, Christopher M., ed. *The Messianic Secret.* Philadelphia: Fortress, 1983.

Via, Dan Otto. *The Ethics of Mark's Gospel—In the Middle of Time.* Philadelphia: Fortress, 1985.

Waetjen, Herman C. *A Reordering of Power: A Socio-Political Reading of Mark's Gospel.* Minneapolis: Fortress, 1989.

Watts, Rikki. *Isaiah's New Exodus and Mark.* Tübingen: J.C.B. Mohr [Paul Siebeck], 1997; Grand Rapids: Baker Book House, 2000.

Weeden, Theodore J. *Mark: Traditions in Conflict.* Philadelphia: Fortress, 1971.

Wrede, William. *The Messianic Secret.* Cambridge: James Clarke, 1971.

TRANSLATION, NOTES, INTERPRETATION

1. *The Prologue: The Beginning of the Good News* (1:1-13)

1. The beginning of the good news about Jesus, Messiah, Son of God. 2. As it is written in the prophet Isaiah: "Be alert, for I am sending my messenger in advance; he will prepare your way. 3. The voice of one crying out in the wilderness: Make ready a way for the Lord; straighten his beaten tracks." 4. John the baptizer appeared in the wilderness, proclaiming a baptism of repentance for the remission of sins. 5. And there came out to him the whole land of Judea and all the people from Jerusalem, and they were baptized by him in the River Jordan, as they confessed their sins. 6. Now John was clothed in camel's hair with a leather belt around his waist, and he ate locusts and wild honey. 7. And this is what he proclaimed: "The one who is stronger than I is coming after me; I am not worthy to bend down and untie the thongs of his sandals. 8. I baptized you with water; he will baptize you in the Holy Spirit." 9. In those days it came to pass that Jesus came from Nazareth of Galilee and he was baptized in the Jordan by John. 10. And just then when he was coming up from the water, he saw the heavens torn open and the Spirit, like a dove, descending on him. 11. Then came a voice from the heavens: "You are my beloved son; in you I am well pleased." 12. And just then the Spirit drove him out into the wilderness. 13. He was in the wilderness for forty days, tested by Satan. He was among the wild beasts and angels ministered to him.

NOTES

1. *The beginning:* In Greek *archē* can mean "starting point, foundation, origin," and even "rule," or "governing principle." The meaning in Mark 1:1 is linked to whether a period or a comma is placed after "Son of God." In the former case v. 1 is a kind of title or *incipit* to the whole work, whereas in the latter case the beginning is in the fulfillment of the prophecy quoted in vv. 2-3 ("The

beginning . . . as it is written . . ."). Our translation interprets v. 1 as a title for the whole work, so that the faith and proclamation of Mark's community have both their "beginning" and "rule" of interpretation in the story of Jesus about to unfold.

of the good news: The singular noun *euangelion* is not used in the LXX; the plural noun *euangelia* and the verb *euangelizesthai* ("to announce glad tidings") translate the Hebrew root *bsr,* which is used of a joyful or important message delivered by a designated messenger (e.g., 1 Sam 31:9; Nah 1:15; Jer 20:14-15). It is a very important term in Deutero-Isaiah and in the NT; see Isa 52:7 (and Acts 10:36; Rom 10:15; 2 Cor 5:20; Eph 2:17, 6:15); and Isa 61:1-2 (and Luke 4:18-19; 7:22; also Acts 10:38; Matt 5:3). An important secular Greek usage occurs in the inscription from Priene in Asia Minor that celebrates the birthday of the Roman emperor Augustus, 9 B.C.E.: "the birthday of the god [= emperor] was for the world the beginning of joyful tidings which have been proclaimed on his account." It is used by Paul over sixty times as a virtual recapitulation of the Christ event, that is, to describe the meaning of the life, death, and resurrection/exaltation of Jesus (e.g., 1 Thess 1:2-9; 1 Cor 15:1-11; 1 Cor 1:17-25; Rom 1:1, 9, 16-17; 10:14-21; 15:14-21). It is a characteristically Markan term (1:1, 14-15; 8:35; 10:29; 13:10; 14:9; [16:15]). Mark alone among the Synoptic evangelists uses it without modifiers ("the gospel"). Indeed, Mark's "good news" is the narrative presentation of the Christ event.

Jesus, Messiah, Son of God: As the Pauline letters show, by Mark's time "Jesus Christ (= Messiah)" had become virtually a proper name. The word "Messiah" in Hebrew (*Christos* in Greek) means "anointed" and serves as a royal title (with overtones of being appointed). Jesus is called "Messiah" in 8:29; 14:61; and 15:32, and he is alluded to as such in 9:41; 12:35; and 13:21. The title "Son of God" is omitted in some manuscripts (e.g., by the corrector of Sinaiticus), but is attested in Vaticanus and the Western tradition. Redactional and theological considerations favor its inclusion. Mark stresses this title as a description of Jesus, or a variation of it such as "beloved [or only] son" (1:11; 9:7; 12:6), the Son (13:32), Son of God (3:11), Son of the Most High God (5:7), son of the blessed one (14:61), and "a (or "the") Son of God" (15:39). The density of key terms in 1:1 prepares the reader for the dramatic unfolding of the whole work, which revolves around the proper description of Jesus as Messiah and Son of God (see especially 14:61; 15:32, 39). The textually undisputed use of "Son of God" in the centurion's confession at the death of Jesus (15:39) favors its inclusion here since Mark is fond of both foreshadowings and overarching interconnections.

2. *As it is written:* This formula is used by Mark to cite or allude to OT texts; see also 9:13 and 14:21, as well as (with variations) 7:6; 11:17; and 14:27. The formula is attested in Qumran literature (e.g., 1QS 5:17; 8:14; CD 7:19) and is very frequent in Paul (fourteen times in Romans, e.g., Rom 1:17; 2:24; 3:10; 4:17; 8:36; 9:33; also 1 Cor 1:31; 2:9; 2 Cor 8:15; 9:9). This usage and the texts cited show that Mark's audience is familiar with both the content and mode of citation of the OT. It also suggests a high level of literacy among first-century Jews and Jewish Christians. Josephus (*Against Apion* 2.204) states: "The Law orders

that they [children] be taught to read, and shall learn both the laws and deeds of their ancestors."

in the prophet Isaiah: Isaiah and the Psalms were the most popular OT books both at Qumran and in early Christian literature. Since the verses quoted in Mark 1:2-3 are a combination of Exod 23:20 and Mal 3:1 in 1:2 and Isa 40:3 in 1:3, some manuscripts substitute "prophets." The mixed quotation suggests to some scholars the use of a pre-Markan *testimonia* collection of OT texts assembled with reference to the Christ event. Markan redaction may be also responsible for the present text, since his quotations of the OT do not agree exactly with known Hebrew or Greek texts, especially in the substitution of "prepare *your* way" in 1:2 in reference to Jesus for "a way before my face" in Mal 3:1, and of *"his* beaten tracks" in 1:3 for the "beaten tracks of our God" in Isa 40:3 (LXX). Mark thus gives a christological slant to the OT quotation in anticipation of 1:7, where John points to Jesus as the coming "stronger one."

3. *The voice of one crying in the wilderness:* The voice in this context belongs to John the Baptist. In the context of Mark's description of the Baptist, the "wilderness" designates the barren region east of Jerusalem down to the Dead Sea. Whereas in Isa 40:3 the voice cries out "In the wilderness prepare the way of the Lord," in Mark 1:3 John is "the one crying out in the wilderness." The term "wilderness" (*erēmos* in Greek), which is virtually synonymous with "desert," is a word with broad resonance for Jews, recalling the years of wandering between the Exodus and the entry into the land and the covenant at Sinai (Exodus 19–24), as well as the place where God would again deliver the people by bringing them back from exile (Isa 40:3). It has a dual connotation. It is used positively as the place of God's saving acts and betrothal with the people (Jer 2:2-3; Hos 2:14-15; Pss 78:12-53; 105:39-45), and negatively as the site of testing and rebellion (Exodus 16; Numbers 11; Pss 78:17-22, 32-41; 106:6-43). The Qumran community also invoked Isa 40:3 for its location in the wilderness (1QS 8:13-14; 9:19-20). Jesus is tested in the wilderness in Mark 1:12-13, retreats there for prayer in 1:35 and to avoid crowds in 1:45, and feeds the people in the wilderness in 6:31-32.

Make ready a way for the Lord: The "way of the Lord" is a common figure in Second Isaiah (40:3; 42:16; 43:16, 19; 48:17; 49:11; 51:10) for the path by which God will bring back the people from exile. It is also central to Mark, who captures the double meaning of way as a path or journey (2:23; 4:4, 15; 6:8; 8:3; 10:17; 10:46) and as the journey toward discipleship (8:27; 9:33-34; 10:32; 10:52; 11:8; 12:14). In Acts 9:2 early Christians are called those who "belong to the way."

4. *John the baptizer appeared:* John is thus identified as the messenger of Exod 23:20 and Mal 3:1, and as the voice of Isa 40:3. Some manuscripts omit the Greek article *ho,* so that the verse could be translated as "John appeared, baptizing." In favor of our translation is the Markan usage in 6:14, 24, and the use of the noun *ho baptistēs* in the Matthean parallel (3:1).

proclaiming: The participle *kēryssōn* describes the activity of a herald *(kēryx)* in summoning people to immediate response. It will also characterize the activity of Jesus (1:14, 38-39), the disciples (3:14; 6:12), healed demoniacs (1:45; 5:20; 7:36), and the post-resurrection community (13:10; 14:9). It is one of those terms by which Mark links John, Jesus, and the followers of Jesus (see the Note on *paradidonai* in 1:14).

baptism: The translation "baptism" risks anachronistic interpretation as a fixed initiation rite. In Greek *baptein* and *baptizein* mean "dip" or "immerse," and in the middle voice "wash oneself." Mark knows of Jewish ritual washings (7:4) and also uses "baptism" metaphorically as being "drenched" in suffering (10:38-39). Both the origin and meaning of John's baptism are disputed. Two different proposals have emerged: (1) water rituals of purification known from the OT and Qumran (Lev 14:5-6, 50-52; Num 19:13, 20-21), which are symbols of interior purification (Isa 1:16; Ps 51:7; 1QS 3:4-12; 4:20-22; 1QH 7:6-7; 17:26); and (2) proselyte baptism, which was a ritual washing of initiation for converts to Judaism. Problems attend both as a background to John's baptism. Ritual washings are self-administered and repeated frequently, while John is the agent of a baptism that is not repeated, prepares for the eschaton, and implies moral conversion. Proselyte baptism is not clearly attested in the NT period, nor does John seek to form a community of baptized persons only around himself. John Meier (*A Marginal Jew* 2:53–55) suggests that John's practice of baptism should be regarded as original.

of repentance: This is a genitive of description (i.e., a baptism characterized by repentance) followed by the preposition *eis* ("for forgiveness") to express purpose; the phrase "baptism of repentance" describes the nature and purpose of John's action. "Repentance" (Greek *metanoia*) literally means "after thought" or "change of mind," and in the LXX most often translates the Hebrew *niham* ("be sorry about something"). It is virtually synonymous with "convert" (Greek *epistrephein*; Hebrew *šûb* "to turn back"), and recalls the prophetic call for people to "return" to their former relationship with God.

for the remission of sins: "Remission or "forgiveness" (*aphesis* in Greek from the verb *aphiemi*, "dismiss or send away," used also of cancelling a debt) can mean pardon or release from captivity or cancellation of punishment. John's "immersion" or "dipping" of people in the Jordan is an acting out of the recipients' interior disposition and a symbol of the forgiveness they hope to receive. As the end of v. 5 will make clear, "confession" of sins precedes the baptism of repentance.

5. *And there came out to him the whole land of Judea and all the people from Jerusalem:* The Greek has a chiastic structure, literally "the whole (*pasa*) land of Judea and from Jerusalem all (*pantes*)," thus highlighting Judea and Jerusalem where the narrative will culminate (chs. 11–16). Jerusalem is the capital of Judea, which in the first century was part of a Roman province. A characteristic of Mark's style, which is usually altered by Matthew and Luke, is the "universalizing" of scenes by the use of "all." The device normally enhances the figure of Jesus (e.g., 1:32, 37; 2:12, 13; 6:33; 9:15; 11:17), here anticipated by the description of John's activity as the forerunner of Jesus. Although Mark may exaggerate, Josephus also testifies to the broad popularity of John the Baptist (see *Ant.* 18.118).

and they were baptized by him in the River Jordan: This culminates the description of John as baptizer. The people were being baptized in the River Jordan in the sense of their being "immersed" or "dipped into" it. The Jordan runs 124 miles in the great rift valley from the slopes of Mount Hermon into the Sea of Galilee and southward, through the wilderness of Judea, to the Dead Sea (the lowest spot on earth, 2750 feet below sea level). In addition to being the traditional site of John's baptizing it has a symbolic value as the barrier between the wilderness and the land of promise.

as they confessed their sins: Both private and public confession of sin (suggested here by the Greek *exomologoumenoi*) was strong in Judaism (Lev 5:5; Pss 32:5; 38:18; 51:3-5), and in the late OT period public confession became a standard form of prayer (Dan 9:4-19; Bar 2:6-10). The *Prayer of Manasseh*, which was written between 100 B.C.E. and 100 C.E. and attributed to a most evil king in ancient Israel (see 2 Kgs 21:1-18; cf. 2 Chron 33:12-13, 18), is a powerful example of the confession genre. In language similar to Mark 1:4-5, Josephus (*War* 5.415) says that God "is easily reconciled to those such as confess and repent *(exomologoumenois kai metanoousin).*"

6. *John was clothed in camel's hair with a leather belt around his waist:* After the account of the actions of John the physical description of him is almost an afterthought. The clothing suggests a comparison to Elijah in 2 Kgs 1:8. According to Zech 13:4 the "hairy mantle" is a sign of a prophet.

   ate locusts and wild honey: The periphrastic *ēn . . . esthiōn* (lit. "was eating") is used of customary action. In Lev 11:20-23 locusts are among the winged insects that may be eaten, and according to CD 12:14 the people at Qumran ate locusts. "Wild honey" *(meli agrion)* is the honey recovered from among rocks (Deut 32:13), from trees (1 Sam 14:25-26), or even from an animal carcass (Judg 14:8-9).

7. *And this is what he proclaimed:* The solemn introduction (lit. "and he proclaimed, saying") highlights the message as the first words spoken directly by a character in Mark; the imperfect *ekēryssen* suggests continued action. In contrast to the Q tradition (Luke 3:7-9//Matt 3:7-10), the Markan John utters no threats of eschatological judgment (e.g., as in Luke 3:7: "flee from the wrath to come") but is primarily the herald pointing to Jesus. If Mark knew the Q tradition here he has reworked it in terms of his focus on christology (see the Interpretation).

   One who is stronger: "One who" translates the definite article *ho*. The adjective "stronger" echoes the beginning of Deutero-Isaiah where God will come "in strength" (40:10 LXX, *meta ischyos*). Some have suggested that the stronger one is God, but the image of John untying the thongs of God's sandals is inappropriate. Also the description of Jesus as the "stronger one" foreshadows him as a figure of great power (1:22, 27) and as the one who can plunder the house of the strong one, Satan (3:20-27).

   coming after me: The expression *opisō mou* ("after me") is used by Jesus when he summons followers to come after him (see 1:17). On the relationship of John and Jesus in Mark, see the Interpretation.

I am not worthy to bend down and untie the thongs of his sandals: The image evokes the master/slave relationship; compare the saying of Rabbi Joshua ben Levi in the Babylonian Talmud: "All services which a slave does for his master a pupil should do for his teacher, with the exception of undoing his shoes" (*b. Ket.* 96a).

8. *I baptized you with water; he will baptize you in the Holy Spirit:* The expectation of "the stronger one" and the image of the servant pave the way for the heightened contrast between John and Jesus. Since Jesus does not baptize in the Holy Spirit in Mark these words direct the reader beyond the narrative (see 13:11). Only here and in 3:29 and 13:11 is the "Holy Spirit" mentioned in Mark's Gospel. The "Spirit" suggests God as present through power and action. The Holy Spirit is not so much a person, as in later trinitarian theology, as it is God's power and spirit that effect holiness. Matthew 3:11 and Luke 3:16 read "with the Holy Spirit *and fire.*" Either this is a case of a minor agreement of Matthew and Luke against Mark or (more likely) the saying represents a Q version (perhaps understood as "with wind and fire"). The closest OT parallel to Mark 1:8 is Ezek 36:25-26, where God will renew the people by cleansing them with water and putting a new spirit within them (see also Joel 2:28; Isa 44:3; Ezek 39:29). John's baptism was preparation for the more profound renewal of the people that will take place through "the stronger one."

9. *In those days it came to pass that Jesus came:* This first appearance of Jesus in the narrative is marked by the solemn LXX formula *kai egeneto* ("it came to pass"; see Luke 1:5; 2:1) to introduce the pericope about the baptism of Jesus (vv. 9-11), though the emphasis is more on Jesus' inaugural vision than on the baptism itself.

from Nazareth of Galilee: Nazareth was a small village (about 500 people at the beginning of the first century C.E.) located in Lower Galilee, north of the Valley of Jezreel. The Sea of Galilee lies fifteen miles to the east, while the Mediterranean Sea is twenty miles to the west. Mark describes Jesus as a "Nazarene" in 10:47; 14:67; and 16:6. The name "Galilee" has been interpreted to mean "circle" and describes an area roughly forty-five miles from north to south. It is bounded on the north and the west by Phoenicia and Syria, by Samaria on the south, and by the Sea of Galilee and the Jordan River on the east. It is customarily divided into Upper and Lower Galilee. During the ministry of Jesus it was ruled (from 4 B.C.E. to 39 C.E.) by Herod Antipas, a son of Herod the Great. In 6:14 Mark calls him a "king," though technically he was a tetrarch. In Jesus' time Galilee was densely populated and its principal industries were farming and fishing. Herod Antipas rebuilt two major cities on the model of other Hellenistic cities: Sepphoris (three miles north of Nazareth) and Tiberias on the western shore of the lake and the capital after 18 C.E. In the Gospels Jesus visits neither of these cities.

and he was baptized in the Jordan by John: Mark states simply the fact of Jesus' baptism, with no dialogue between John and Jesus (compare Matt 3:13-17). The stress here is on Jesus' vision and the voice from heaven in vv. 10-11. Matthew describes Jesus' departure from Galilee "to be baptized by John," and Luke (3:21-22) does not say explicitly that John baptized Jesus. Since John's baptism was "of repentance" and "in remission of sin," the Markan Jesus is portrayed as being in solidarity with the sinful human condition (see 2 Cor 5:21), which can be altered only through God's power.

10. *And just then when he was coming up from the water, he saw the heavens torn open:* "Just then" translates *euthys* (lit. "immediately"). This or its variant *eutheōs* is used by Mark 47 times, but is avoided by Matthew and Luke. This characteristic of Mark's rapid and popular style frequently has a temporal function, often serves to focus the reader's attention, and may require different translations according to context. In the ancient cosmology the tearing open *(schizomenous)* of the heavens could symbolize the possibility of divine-human communication (Ezek 1:1; John 1:51). It is also an eschatological motif; see Isa 64:1: "O that you would tear open the heavens and come down" (also Isa 24:17-20 and Rev 19:11), and it foreshadows the "tearing open" of the temple veil at the death of Jesus (Mark 15:38), which, as in 1:9-11, precedes the description of Jesus as Son of God (15:39).

    the Spirit, like a dove, descending on him: The second element of Jesus' inaugural vision is described as the descent of a dove-like Spirit, understood adjectivally rather than adverbially: the Spirit descending "like a dove." The dove symbolism is obscure. Suggested OT allusions such as God's spirit hovering over the waters (Gen 1:2) or the dove in Gen 8:2 do not reflect the language or situation of Mark 1:10. The *Targum of the Song of Songs* interprets the voice of the turtledove as the spirit. Suggestions that the dove is associated with divine figures in Hellenistic religions (Heinrich Greeven, "περιστερά, κτλ.," *TDNT* 6:64–67) lack specificity. The key element in this text is the descent of the Spirit, not the dove simile.

11. *Then came a voice from the heavens:* Mark's expression is similar to the rabbinic *bat qôl* (literally "daughter of a voice"), that is, an echo of the heavenly voice that combines divine transcendence and presence. It, too, symbolizes communication between God and humans.

    You are my beloved son; in you I am well pleased. The words of divine acceptance reflect different OT texts: (1) Ps 2:7, "You are my son," a psalm of royal adoption, and (2) Isa 42:1-2, "in whom my soul delights." God's servant is chosen by God; note also Isa 42:1b, "I have put my spirit in him." The adjective "beloved" is thought to translate the Hebrew *yaḥid* (lit. "only" or "unique"), which in the context of family relationships carries the nuance of "beloved" (Gen 22:2, 12, 16, with regard to Isaac). The divine address also foreshadows the heavenly voice of 9:7 in the transfiguration episode, "This is my beloved son." This text contains a "surplus of meaning," combining royal and servant motifs along with language from the tradition of the suffering just person (Wis 2:12-20, especially vv. 13, 18). It also provides an echo of 1:1 where a similar density of titles appears.

12. *And just then the Spirit drove him out into the wilderness:* The temptation account begins with the familiar *kai euthys*, linking it with vv. 10-11. The Markan testing of Jesus is telegraphic in comparison to the elaborate dialogue of the Q version (Matt 4:1-11; Luke 4:1-13). The power of the Spirit is underscored by

the use of the verb "drive out" *(ekballein),* used very frequently of the expulsion of demons (1:34, 39; 3:15, 22, 23; 6:13; 7:26; 9:18, 28, 38) and elsewhere with overtones of coercion (5:40; 9:47; 11:5; 12:8).

13. *He was in the wilderness for forty days:* The "wilderness" recalls the place where Israel was "tested" for forty years (which is often taken as the the background to the forty days and nights) and echoes the beginning of the gospel (see 1:3-4). But the "forty days" more likely alludes to the fast of Moses (Deut 9:18) in the wilderness of Sinai and that of Elijah near Mount Horeb (see 1 Kgs 19:8). The juxtaposition of Jesus' baptism and his sojourn in the wilderness captures the dual aspect of the wilderness as the place of God's revelation and betrothal and as the place of testing.

tested by Satan: The usual translation of *peirazomenos* as "tempted" has the contemporary overtones of inducement to sin. The rendering "tested" better evokes the wider theme of God's testing of the people of Israel and of the suffering just person, who though tested by God through suffering remains faithful rather than sin, and is called a child of God (Wis 2:12-20 and 5:1-23). The term "Satan" means "the adversary." In some OT texts Satan is a member of the heavenly court who tests the fidelity of God's chosen ones (Job 6:6-12; Zech 3:1). By the NT period, however, "Satan" is synonymous with *diabolos,* the devil. In Mark Satan is clearly identified with the "prince of demons" (3:23, 26), opposes the word (4:15), and leads disciples astray (8:33).

He was among the wild beasts, and angels ministered to him: In the OT wild beasts are associated with evil powers (Ps 22:11-21; Ezek 34:5, 8, 25). Psalm 91:11-13 (cited by Q; see Matt 4:6; Luke 4:10; also *TNaph* 8:4) joins care by angels and safety among beasts. Peaceful living with the animals is affirmed of the first creation (Gen 1:28; 2:19-20), and remains the hope of the renewed creation (Isa 11:6-9; 65:24-25; 2 *Bar* 73:6). The angels also minister to Elijah (1 Kgs 19:1-8), and in *Life of Adam and Eve* 4 the first couple lament their loss of the "food of angels" after their expulsion from the Garden. This short sentence may foreshadow the hope of the new creation that emerges in Mark 13:24-27.

INTERPRETATION

The good news of Mark is a narrative proclamation of the Christ event. Like those who received Paul's letters, Mark's readers, living a generation after the death of Jesus, would have either undergone a significant adult conversion or would be possible converts to the Christian movement. They would have learned the lineaments of the life of Jesus that are reflected in early creedal statements such as 1 Cor 11:23-26 and 15:1-11, the kerygmatic sermons of Acts (which, though edited by Luke, contain early traditions; e.g., 2:32-36; 4:10-12; 5:30-32; 10:36-41), and hymnic fragments that may have been used in early Christian worship (e.g., Phil 2:6-11; Col 1:15-20; 1 Tim 3:16; 1 Pet 3:18-22). The function of Mark's Gospel was not to *prove* that Jesus was the "Son of God," nor was it simply to offer biographical information about Jesus. Rather, it was to engage the readers in the unfolding story of Jesus "from Nazareth of Galilee" (1:9), so that they too might be caught up by his message (1:14-15) and be challenged to believe that neither demonic powers nor brutal rulers can ultimately triumph over Jesus or over them.

The prologue in Mark 1:1-13 supplies readers with important "insider" information about Jesus that none of the human characters in the body of the gospel possess. After the superscription (1:1), Mark begins with a scenic prologue (1:2-13 [14-15]), which is dense with intertextual references to and echoes of the Jewish Scriptures that foreshadow future events in the gospel. The prophecy of "Isaiah" promises a new action of God, who will make a victorious way through the wilderness (1:2-3). Mark identifies this action with Jesus' way, his progress through the world, and his movement toward his death and resurrection in Jerusalem. In his preaching and baptismal activity John the Baptist summons people to a change of heart (1:4-6) and points to the stronger one who will exceed his preaching and baptism (1:7-8). Mark then signals the arrival of this stronger one in solemn language ("In those days") and narrates simply the baptism of Jesus in preparation for the opening of the heavens and the divine adoption and commissioning of Jesus (1:9-11). Having been so commissioned, Jesus, like other figures of destiny (e.g., Moses, David, Elijah) and like the people of Israel, is tested in the wilderness (1:12-13), which foreshadows his future testing during the Passion narrative. Jesus survives his trial and is not overcome by the power of evil, so that in the following verses (1:14-15)—which provide a transition from the prologue to the public ministry of Jesus—he arrives proclaiming the good news of God's victorious reign. However, in these brief verses the enduring power of evil is also highlighted. Jesus arrives only after John, who dominated the prologue, has been "handed over," a fate that anticipates the fates of Jesus and of Christian believers.

The OT references and allusions, especially those to Second Isaiah (Isaiah 40–55) and Third Isaiah (Isaiah 56–66) are very significant in Mark's prologue. In discussing the relationships among different groups within post-exilic Judaism, Menachem Mor ("Samaritan History," in A. D. Crown, ed., *The Samaritans* [Tübingen: J.C.B. Mohr (Paul Siebeck), 1989] 18) has argued that post-exilic Judaism was characterized by two dominant ideologies. The first, reflected in the books of Ezra and Nehemiah, represents an ideology of Jews who returned from Babylon and considered themselves to be the "holy seed" or "remnant" (Ezra 9:2, 15) and stood in opposition to intermarriage with those who had remained in Israel and who were thought to be "unclean with the pollutions of the peoples of the lands, with their abominations" (Ezra 9:11). The program of these return-ing reformers involved the rebuilding of the Temple, codification of the

Law, strong prohibitions against intermarriage, and building a wall around Jerusalem. Against the ideology of the "holy seed" was a second group that was interested in bringing together all the different neighboring groups, and whose theology is reflected in texts such as Isaiah 52 and 63, and the books of Jonah, Ruth, and Judith. Characteristic of this period, then, according to Mor, was the conflict among Judean Jews between those who held a separatist ideology and those who held a universalist ideology. This fundamental tension will characterize Jewish thought well into the NT period.

Mark's use of the OT, and especially Second and Third Isaiah, locates him in the "universalist" strain of post-exilic Judaism. In his prologue many citations and allusions to Isaiah 40–66 are found: 1:3 (see Isa 40:3), the voice in the wilderness; 1:7, 14 (see Isa 40:9-10), the herald proclaiming the joyful news of God's coming in strength; 1:10 (see Isa 64:1), the opening of the heavens; 1:10 (see Isa 63:10), the use of *katabainein* to describe the descent of the Spirit; and 1:11 (see Isa 42:1), the Servant in whom God delights. Equally important are the thematic similarities between Isaiah 40–66 and Mark. Both begin with the voice in the wilderness, both promise a new manifestation of divine rule, and both look to the inclusion of Gentiles (or the nations) in God's saving plan (see especially Isa 42:1, 6; 43:9; 49:6; 52:10; 55:5; 56:7 [= Mark 11:17]; 66:18). Both portray a prophetic figure who suffers and is rejected by his own people (Isa 52:13–53:12; Mark 8:31; 9:31; 10:33-34). There are also structural similarities. Second Isaiah begins with the voice of promise in the wilderness and ends with "nations that you do not know" running to join God's people (Isa 55:4-5), while Mark begins with the voice in the wilderness (1:3) and ends with the confession of the Gentile centurion (15:39). The density of references to Isaiah 40–66 in the prologue prepares for other references to Isaiah throughout the gospel (see Notes in specific places). Mark offers a representation of post-exilic Isaiah, seen through the lens of the Christ event, for a Diaspora community living "among the nations."

A second major feature of the prologue is its treatment of the relationship between John the Baptist and Jesus. In all the narrative NT traditions the preaching and baptizing of John precede that of Jesus, but Mark's characterization of John's work and of the relationship between John and Jesus is different. In the Q source (adapted by Matthew and Luke) John is an Elijah-like reformer who preaches repentance in specific terms, in preparation for the day of the Lord (Mal 3:1-4). In Mark he preaches repentance, but this message is subordinated to his preparation for the stronger one. In John the message of repentance is virtually gone, and John the Baptist's main function is that of preparing for Jesus, though John also has the interesting traditions that Jesus' first disciples came from the ranks of John's followers (John 1:35-42), and that Jesus engaged in baptismal ministry simultaneously with John (3:22-23). Though perhaps aware of other traditions about John the Baptist, Mark makes John primarily into the herald of "the stronger one." When this stronger one arrives John moves out of the picture, though throughout his gospel Mark continues to redefine the role of John. Prior to recounting John's death (6:17-29), Mark puts on the lips of Herod confusion about the relation of John and Jesus (6:14-16; see 8:28). Only in the somewhat cryptic reference in 9:11-13 is John identified with Elijah, and Elijah is redefined as the herald not of the day of the Lord but of the Son of Man.

A third element to highlight in interpreting Mark's prologue is that it contains resonances with the experience of Mark's first readers. They too must root their faith in the promises of the OT, which are actualized in their own lives. Their path to faith in the good news led them through change of heart and baptism. And if (as is highly likely) the Pauline theology of baptism was the theology of the Diaspora communities, they received a spirit of adoption at their baptisms (see Gal 3:23–4:7). This gift, however, does not spare them trials and testing, any more than it spared Jesus. The way that Jesus will proclaim and embody in the gospel—from the experience of God's power through suffering and rejection to the victory over death in the resurrection—is the way presented to them.

The initial verses of Mark's Gospel offer many possibilities for preaching and actualization: the rooting of Christian faith in the Jewish Scriptures; joy over the good news; the ambivalence of the wilderness as the place of testing, rebellion, and renewed love; the role of John as one who prepares the way related to the corresponding vocation of the Christian to prepare for the gospel; the presentation of Jesus as the stronger one in a contemporary world which seems fragile and threatening; recollection of baptismal adoption; and the beginning of a journey to renewed discipleship.

FOR REFERENCE AND FURTHER STUDY

Boring, M. Eugene. "Mark 1:1-15 and the Beginning of the Gospel," *Semeia* 52 (1990) 43–81.

Dormeyer, Detlev. "Mk 1,1-15 als Prolog des ersten Idealbiographischen Evangeliums von Jesus Christus," *Biblical Interpretation* 5 (1997) 181–211.

Elliott, John K. "Mark 1.1-3—A Later Addition to the Gospel?" *NTS* 46 (2000) 584–88.

Gero, Stephen. "The Spirit and the Dove at the Baptism of Jesus," *NovT* 18 (1976) 17–35.

Gibson, Jeffrey B. "Jesus' Wilderness Temptation According to Mark," *JSNT* 53 (1994) 3–34.

Guelich, Robert A. "The Beginning of the Gospel," *BR* 27 (1982) 5–15.

Head, Peter M. "A Text-Critical Study of Mark 1.1 'The Beginning of the Gospel of Jesus Christ,'" *NTS* 37 (1991) 621–29.

Henten, Jan Willem van. "The First Testing of Jesus: A Rereading of Mark 1.12-13," *NTS* 45 (1999) 349–66.

Keck, Leander E. "The Introduction to Mark's Gospel," *NTS* 12 (1965–66) 352–70.

Marcus, Joel. "Jesus' Baptismal Vision," *NTS* 41 (1995) 512–21.

Matera, Frank J. "The Prologue as the Interpretative Key to Mark's Gospel," *JSNT* 34 (1988) 3–20.

Ruddick, C. T. "Behold, I Send My Mesenger," *JBL* 88 (1969) 381–417.

2. *Transitional Markan Summary: Proclamation of the Kingdom* (1:14-15)

14. But after John was handed over, Jesus entered Galilee, proclaiming the good news of God: 15. "Now is the time of fulfillment; and the kingdom of God is at hand. Repent and place your faith in the good news."

NOTES

14. *But after John was handed over:* Mark breaks the long stream of sentences introduced by *kai* ("and") with the adversative *de* ("but") to highlight an important transition. Although the Synoptic Gospels demarcate temporally the ministry of John from that of Jesus and never mention Jesus baptizing, in the Gospel of John they overlap, and Jesus himself baptizes (see John 3:22-24, which seems to be countering the Synoptic tradition). "Handed over" translates *paradothēnai,* which is a very significant term with roots in the fourth Servant Song (Isa 52:13–53:12, especially vv. 6, 12). In pre-Pauline formulas (Rom 4:25; 1 Cor 11:23) and in Paul's letters (Rom 8:32; Gal 1:4; 2:20) forms of this verb become a shorthand way of referring to the Passion and death of Jesus. Mark uses the verb to create a parallelism between John the Baptist (1:4, 14), Jesus (1:14; 8:31; 9:31; 10:33-34), and the Christian (13:10-12). In each instance people proclaim (using a form of *kēryssein*) and are handed over (with a form of *paradidonai*).

Jesus entered Galilee, proclaiming the good news of God: In content (the sudden arrival of Jesus similar to that of John) and language, vv. 14-15 contain echoes of vv. 1-4 ("proclaim . . . good news . . . repent") and form an *inclusio* with the beginning of the prologue. In the "good news of God" the genitive *tou theou* has the double nuance of "from" and "about." Apart from 1 Pet 4:17, "the gospel of God" is used only by Mark and Paul (see 1 Thess 2:2, 9 [with "proclaim"]; 3:2; Rom 1:1; 15:16; 2 Cor 11:7).

15. *Now is the time of fulfillment:* No English term captures exactly the meaning of *kairos* ("time"), which has the connotation of "proper" or "opportune" time as

well as a time of crisis (13:33). With the good news rooted in the proclamation of Isaiah, by the arrival of Jesus heralded by the preaching of John, and through the messianic preparation of Jesus (baptism and testing), the opportune time for the good news has arrived.

and the kingdom of God: Translation is a problem here, and not simply because of the androcentric overtones of "king." The word "kingdom" is static and evokes a *place* where a king (or queen) rules. Greek *basileia* is more active and dynamic, with the nuance of the "reigning" of God as well as a setting for that reign. "Kingdom" is maintained here principally because of its important theological history. Though 1:15 may not provide the exact words of Jesus (some of the vocabulary suggests a post-Easter perspective, and Jesus taught in Aramaic in any case), the proclamation of the kingdom of God is generally admitted to be the heart of Jesus' preaching in both word and deed. While the actual phrase "kingdom of God" is infrequent in the OT and early Jewish literature, the image of God as king is strong, both in the course of history (e.g., Exod 15:11-13, 18; Num 23:21-23; Pss 2; 72; 89; 110; 145:11-12 [royal psalms]; Psalms 95–100 [possible enthronement psalms]), and at the consummation of history when God's definitive reign will be established (Mic 2:12-13; 4:5-7; Isa 44:1-8; Zech 9:9-11; Zeph 3:14-20; Dan 2:44; 7:11-14; *Ass. Mos.* 10:1-25; *Pss. Sol.* 17:23-35).

is at hand: The imminence of God's kingdom is the substance of Jesus' proclamation in Mark, where his conflict with the powers of evil is a clash of kingdoms (3:24). Jesus gives to his disciples the "mystery of the kingdom" (4:11) and describes it in parables (4:26-30). It has an ethical dimension since people are summoned to enter it by adopting a new way of living (9:47; 10:14, 15, 23, 24; 12:34). It is also future (9:1; 11:10; 15:43). The tension between the present and future dimensions determines the much-disputed translation of *ēngiken*, the perfect of *engizein* ("draw near"), which in the perfect tense can mean "has drawn near," and therefore virtually "present." Mark's Jesus announces and enacts God's reign as beginning now in his ministry, but as to be perfected only with the return of the Son of Man (see 8:38–9:2; 13:24-27; 14:62).

repent and place your faith in the good news: The call of Jesus for a change of heart *(metanoia)*, which his deeds and words will evoke, is an epitome of Mark's theology. In the Bible "faith" or "belief" *(pistis)* generally suggests not simply intellectual conviction but also trust and personal commitment, often with an orientation toward a threatening future (e.g., Gen 15:6; Exod 4:4-5; Isa 28:16, 43:10). The verb *pisteuein* is frequent in Mark (1:15; 5:36; 9:23, 24, 42; 11:23, 24, 32; 13:21; 15:32), and the noun *pistis* is "saving faith" especially in the miracle stories (2:5; 5:34; 10:52).

INTERPRETATION

These verses along with 1:21, 28, 39, 45; 2:1-2, 13; 3:6; 4:1-2, 33-34; 6:1, 6b, 7, 12-13, 30, 53, 56; 7:1-2, 24, 31; 8:1, 10, 22a, 27; 9:2, 30, 33; 10:1, 32, 46;

11:1, 11, 12, 15, 19, 20, 27; 13:1, 3; 14:1, 3, 12, 16, 32; 15:1 have been called "summary statements" *(Sammelberichte).* They give an overview or summary of various events in Jesus' ministry. Many function also as bridge or transitional verses that recapitulate a previous section while introducing a new section.

In a sense Mark 1:14-15 concludes the prologue while anticipating the initial public ministry of Jesus that begins in 1:16. The arrival of Jesus (1:14-15) looks back to the ministry of John and recalls his origin "from Galilee." Though these verses take up again the theme of proclamation and gospel, and anticipate the struggle over the kingdom, the times of John and Jesus are clearly distinguished. The narrative about to unfold is to evoke faith (not mentioned in the prologue) and is to be understood as the time of fulfillment.

Most commentators hold that Mark in 1:15 presents an accurate summary of the main thrust of Jesus' ministry in word and deed: the proclamation of God's kingdom, and a change of heart and faith as the proper human responses. However, it is not easy to define the "kingdom of God" because it is future in its fullness and transcendent in its origin. The kingdom is ultimately God's project.

Many OT psalms (see the Note on 1:15) celebrate the kingship of God ("the Lord reigns") and God's lordship over all creation, and look forward to all creation confessing that YHWH is king. Among many Jews in Jesus' time, however, there developed the conviction that the fullness of God's reign was still future and the hope that when the fullness of God's kingdom comes ("thy kingdom come!") all creation will join in the eternal chorus of praise ("Holy, holy, holy . . ."). Then there will be the resurrection of the dead, the last judgment, just rewards for the righteous and punishments for the wicked, and a new heaven and a new earth (see the great Jewish apocalypses Daniel, *1 Enoch, 4 Ezra,* and *2 Baruch).*

Jesus shared the belief of his Jewish contemporaries that the fullness of God's kingdom is future, and yet, according to Mark and the other evangelists, Jesus saw in his own person and ministry the beginning or inauguration of God's reign: "Now is the time of fulfillment; and the kingdom of God is at hand" (Mark 1:15a). Whatever Jesus said or did was in the service of God's kingdom.

The recovery of Jesus' vision of the kingdom of God was one of the great achievements of theology in the twentieth century. And along with it comes the recognition that this vision demands a response that involves not only a change in attitude ("place your faith in the good news") but also a change of life ("repent"). Above all it demands hope: the confidence that God is for us, the trust that God cares for us and guides our lives, and the conviction that God wants us to share eternal life with the risen Christ in the fullness of God's kingdom.

For Reference and Further Study

Berkey, Robert F. *"Eggizein, phthanein,* and Realized Eschatology," *JBL* 82 (1963) 177–87.

Dechow, Jens. *Gottessohn und Herrschaft Gottes. Der Theozentrismus des Markusevangeliums.* Neukirchen-Vluyn: Neukirchener Verlag, 2000.

Kelber, Werner H. *The Kingdom in Mark: A New Place and a New Time.* Philadelphia: Fortress, 1974.

Kuthirakkattel, Scaria. *The Beginning of Jesus' Ministry according to Mark's Gospel.* AB 123. Rome: Biblical Institute Press, 1990.

Malina, Bruce J. *The Social Gospel of Jesus. The Kingdom of God in Mediterranean Perspective.* Minneapolis: Fortress, 2001.

Marshall, Christopher D. *Faith as a Theme in Mark's Narrative.* Cambridge and New York: Cambridge University Press, 1989.

Meier, John P. *A Marginal Jew. Rethinking the Historical Jesus.* Vol. 2, *Mentor, Message, and Miracles.* New York: Doubleday, 1994.

Murphy-O'Connor, Jerome. "Why Jesus Went Back to Galilee," *BR* 12/1 (1996) 20–29, 42–43.

Robbins, Vernon K. "Mark 1:14-20: An Interpretation at the Intersection of Jewish and Greco-Roman Traditions," *NTS* 28 (1982) 220–36.

Viviano, Benedict T. *The Kingdom of God in History.* Collegeville: The Liturgical Press, 1991.

3. *The Call of the First Disciples* (1:16-20)

16. Then as he was walking along the shore of the Sea of Galilee, he saw Simon and Andrew, Simon's brother, casting their nets over the sea, for they were fishermen. 17. Then Jesus said to them: "Come after me, and I will turn you into those who fish for humans." 18. And at once they threw aside their nets and followed him. 19. Walking a little farther, he saw James, the son of Zebedee, and John his brother who were in the boat, preparing their nets. 20. And right away he called them. Leaving their father Zebedee still in the boat with the hired workers, they departed to follow him.

Notes

16. *As he was walking along the shore of the Sea of Galilee:* The expression "along the shore" is implicit in the verb *paragōn.* Although Mark uses the term "sea" *(thalassa),* the body of water is an inland lake, described by Josephus *(Life* 153) as 16 by 4.5 miles (today it is 12.5 by 7 miles). In the OT it is called "the sea of Chinnereth" from the Hebrew *kinnôr* (lyre-shaped), and John calls it the "sea of Tiberias" (John 6:1; 21:1). Ancient writers (Strabo, Pliny, Josephus) all mention

the extensive fishing industry there. The shores of the lake were heavily populated. It also served as a boundary between the heavily Hellenized eastern side (the Decapolis: see Mark 5:20; 7:31) and the mainly Jewish western cities. In Mark Jesus will journey frequently from side to side, symbolizing perhaps the mission to both Jews and Gentiles (see 4:35; 5:1, 21; 6:1, 34, 45, 53; 7:24, 31; 8:14, 22).

he saw Simon and Andrew, Simon's brother: Until 3:16, part of the second call of the disciples (3:13-19), Mark uses "Simon" (1:16, 29, 30, 36; 3:16) and subsequently (with the exception of 14:37) "Peter" (3:16; 5:37; 8:29, 32, 33; 9:2, 5; 10:28; 11:21; 13:3; 14:29, 33, 37, 54, 66, 67, 70, 71; 16:7). In the OT Simon is the second son of Jacob and Leah (Gen 29:33). It is a frequent name in Jewish history (Simon Maccabeus) and in Mark in particular in the NT: Simon the Cananaean, one of the Twelve (3:18); one of Jesus' brothers (6:3); the leper at Bethany (14:3-9); and Simon of Cyrene (15:21). Andrew (see also 1:26, 29; 3:18; 13:3) is a Greek name meaning "brave, heroic," which is never found in the Septuagint. According to John, Peter and Andrew were from Bethsaida (1:44), and Andrew was a disciple of John the Baptist (1:40-42) who brought his brother to Jesus.

for they were fishermen: This phrase seems somewhat superfluous following the description of them "casting" their nets. But duplicate expressions and repetitions are characteristic of Mark's style (see Introduction). Also, Mark often uses *gar* ("for") as a seeming afterthought, more to highlight or allude to an important point. This phrase prepares for the call of Simon and Andrew to be "fishers of humans."

17. *Come after me:* "Come" *(deute),* an adverb serving as hortatory particle (similar to English usage "forward!"), highlights the power of the one calling. "After me" (or "him"), an expression used also at 1:20 and 8:33-34, may reflect the Jewish practice of a student walking a few paces behind the teacher. Mark's more frequent usage is "follow" (1:17-18; 2:14-15; 8:34; 10:21, 28; 15:41).

I will turn you into those who fish for humans: The future *poiēsō* ("I will make you into") points forward to the unfolding narrative and to the challenges to discipleship posed by Jesus' teaching and action. "Fishers of humans" is a somewhat enigmatic phrase. In Jer 16:16 the Lord says that he "is sending for many fishermen," in the context of eschatological judgment. Other images of fishing have a similar or negative connotation (Ezek 29:4-5; Amos 4:2; Hab 1:14-15). See also Matt 13:47-50, the parable of the fishing net in the context of judgment. If this were the meaning here it would contradict the other commissions given to the disciples in 3:13-19 and 6:7-13, 30. Those positive commissions give substance to the term "those who fish for humans" here.

18. *And at once they threw aside their nets and followed him.* "And at once," the now familiar *kai euthys,* suggests the power of Jesus' call and his attractiveness. There is no hesitation or reflection on the disciples' part. The verb "threw aside" (literally "leaving," Greek *aphentes*) foreshadows the command to disciples to leave all to follow Jesus (10:28-29). Mark's preferred term for dis-

cipleship is "follow" *(akolouthein)*. In the Hellenistic world it means following in an intellectual, moral, or religious sense (e.g., the disciples of Socrates), and involves personal relationship to the one followed, "imitating the pattern of his life, not just coming after" (Bede, *Homily* 21 in *Corpus Christianorum, Series Latina* [Turnhout: Brepols, 1955–] 122). It is Mark's favorite term for discipleship (2:14-15; 6:1; 8:34; 10:21, 28).

19. *Walking a little farther, he saw James, the son of Zebedee, and his brother John:* The call of the second pair of brothers is similar to the first in describing a physical action of Jesus ("walking"), his sighting of the fishermen, and his unmediated call to them. "James" (Greek *Iakōbos*) derives from the Hebrew name of the patriarch Jacob, the brother of Esau, and the father of twelve sons (tribes) (Gen 25:26; 27:36), whose name is changed to Israel (Gen 32:28; 35:10). James is a very frequent name in the NT period. This James, later with John called a "son of thunder" (3:17), appears at significant times along with Peter and John (5:37; 9:2; 13:3; 14:33). He and John make a request of Jesus to share in his rule and glory (Mark 10:35-45). According to Acts 12:1-3 he was executed by Herod Agrippa. In Christian tradition he is called James the Great and is honored as the patron of Spain. The phrase "son of Zebedee" distinguishes him from three other persons in Mark who are named James: (1) James, son of Alphaeus, one of the Twelve (Mark 3:18); (2) James, listed as first among the brothers of the Lord, presumably as the oldest (Mark 6:3; see Matt 13:55). He receives a vision of the risen Jesus (1 Cor 15:7) and becomes one of the "pillars" of the Jerusalem church (Gal 1:19, 2:9, 12; see also Acts 12:17; 15:13; 21:18). He is often called "James the Just." According to Josephus he was put to death in 62 C.E. (*Ant.* 20.197-203); and (3) James, one of the sons of that Mary who is the mother of James and Joses, who appears at the cross and visits the tomb of Jesus (15:40; 16:1). The name "John" (Greek *Iōannēs*) is a shortened form of the Hebrew names *Yoḥanan* and *Yehoḥanan* ("God shows favor"). Apart from John the Baptist he is the only character named John who is mentioned in Mark. He appears with Peter and James at important points (see above).

in the boat, preparing their nets: Contrary to most translations, *katartizontes* is better translated as "preparing" rather than "mending," since "preparing" is closer to its more frequent Greek usage of "put in order, get ready." "Mending" also suggests that those in the boats have already finished fishing, while "preparing" captures the more dramatic and dynamic aspect of the call. Jesus calls both those who are actually fishing (Peter and Andrew) and those who are setting out to fish (James and John).

20. *And right away he called them:* In parallelism with 1:18, this verse begins with *kai euthys* ("right away"), but here it is used in reference to the call of Jesus rather than the response.

Leaving their father Zebedee still in the boat: The response is immediate, as with Simon and Andrew, but heightened by the explicit mention of leaving their father Zebedee. It is in contrast to Elijah's call of Elisha, who asks to return to kiss his father and mother (1 Kgs 19:20). Such an abrupt departure from a father would be shocking to the cultural values held by Mark's readers (e.g.,

Exod 20:12; Deut 5:16; Prov 23:22-25; Tob 5:1; Sir 3:1-16, especially v. 16, "Whoever forsakes his father is like a blasphemer"). This also prepares for the instructions about discipleship in Mark 10:29-30.

with the hired workers: This detail is omitted in Matt 4:18-22, which otherwise follows Mark closely here. James and John are portrayed as being at a higher economic level than Peter and Andrew. The latter are fishing basically from the shore with leaded nets, whereas the former possess a boat and have hired workers, would fish by the dragnet method, and would harvest a much larger catch (see Luke 5:6, 9; John 21:6-11). This discrepancy may explain why John and James will be those who ask Jesus for seats of honor in the kingdom (see Mark 10:35, where they are again identified as "sons of Zebedee"). Their ownership of the boat and employment of hired workers in a vital industry are contrary to much contemporary description of Jesus' first followers as a band of itinerant peasants. They may be itinerant during Jesus' ministry, but they hardly represent the most economically deprived groups in Galilee.

they departed to follow him: Literally "they went away behind him." The last words of this section ("behind him," *opisō autou*) links the second call to the initial command of Jesus in v. 17, "come after me" *(deute opisō mou).*

INTERPRETATION

After the prologue with its heavy christological thrust, this first public act of Jesus in summoning people to follow him is an indication that Jesus' work as "the stronger one" (1:7) who proclaims the good news of God will involve other people in a most radical sense. This pericope with its location in Galilee, its mention of Peter and other followers, and especially the picture of Jesus "going before" the disciples (1:16-17) provides an arch to the concluding verses of the gospel, "Go, tell Peter and his disciples that he is *going* before you to Galilee" *(proagei,* 16:7).

As noted in the Introduction, all major sections of Mark begin with stories involving disciples. This first call becomes a paradigm for the subsequent call narratives (2:13-15; 3:13-19; 6:6b-13), consisting of the following elements: (1) the initiative is from Jesus; (2) those called are engaged in ordinary work; (3) the call is in the form of a clear summons to "follow me"; (4) the call is to share in the mission or activity of the one calling; (5) the response to the call is immediate and unreflective, with a "leaving" of former occupations; and (6) responding to the call is not a private choice, but means joining others who have responded as well. After this initial call, the subsequent calls develop even more the mission aspect. According to 3:13-19 the disciples are to "be with Jesus" and to be sent out to preach and "to have authority" over demons. In 6:6b-13 they are explicitly itinerant missionaries and, like Jesus, are to preach repentance (see 1:4, 14), to exorcise, and to heal the sick. Two essential elements in the call to discipleship are "being with" Jesus and doing the tasks of Jesus. Dramatic tension in the gospel will arise from whether disciples will "be with" Jesus at all stages and whether they will take up their cross as Jesus did. See 8:31-38, which functions like a "call narrative" inaugurating the second major part of the gospel.

The background and possible exemplars for these call narratives are complex. Mark 1:16-20 resembles the call of Elisha by Elijah, a prophet endowed with God's spirit (1 Kgs 19:19-21). Yet there is a major difference from Mark, since Elisha does not follow immediately. Compelling calls of prophets come without preparation (Isa 6:1-13; Jer 1:14-19; Ezek 1:1-3; see also Moses in Exodus 3–4). Rabbinic teachers had disciples, but their would-be disciples *seek out* a teacher rather than being chosen by him. Diogenes Laertius (first half of the third century C.E.) records the call of Xenophon by Socrates in language similar to that in Mark. Socrates simply says: "Follow, then, and learn," and Xenophon does so (*Lives of Eminent Philosophers* 2.48). As a work with a Palestinian setting and traditions but written for an audience living in the midst of Greco-Roman culture, Mark combines different influences creatively.

Actualization of this pericope might involve reflection on people's contemporary experience of various "callings" to follow Jesus, either through preparation for baptism as adults or through other experiences of "adult conversion." Narratives of conversions from Paul in Gal 1:11-17 and Augustine's *Confessions* to those of Dorothy Day in *The Long Loneliness* or Thomas Merton in *The Seven Storey Mountain*, though not strictly following the pattern listed above, often involve a sudden and profound experience of God that leads a person to a radically different style of life and involves a new level of "being with Jesus" and doing those things that imitate the pattern of Jesus' life.

FOR REFERENCE AND FURTHER STUDY

Donaldson, J. "'Called to Follow': A Twofold Experience of Discipleship in Mark," *BTB* 5 (1975) 67–77.
Fischer, Georg, and Martin Hasitschka. *The Call of the Disciple. The Bible on Following Christ.* New York: Paulist, 1999.
Moloney, Francis J. "The Vocation of the Disciples in the Gospel of Mark," *Salesianum* 43 (1981) 487–516.
Murphy-O'Connor, Jerome. "Fishers of Fish, Fishers of Men," *BR* 15/3 (1999) 22–27, 48–49.
Wuellner, Wilhelm. *The Meaning of "Fishers of Men."* Philadelphia: Westminster, 1967.

4. *A Paradigmatic Day Begins the Ministry of Jesus* (1:21-34)

21. And they journeyed to Capernaum, and right away on the Sabbath he would go into the synagogue and begin to teach. 22. And people were astonished at his teaching, for he was teaching them as a person with authority, and not as the scribes. 23. At that moment in their synagogue was a person with an unclean spirit; he screamed and shouted: 24. "What do we have in common, Jesus, you Nazarene? Have you come to wipe us out? I know you for what you are—the holy one of God." 25. And Jesus subdued him in these words: "Be quiet; leave this man." 26. After throwing him into convulsions and shouting with a shrill voice, the unclean spirit left the man. 27. And everyone there was so astounded that they carried on a lively discussion, asking each other: "What is happening here? It is a new kind of teaching—with authority; he gives orders even to unclean spirits, and they submit to him. 28. And quickly the report of what he did spread far and wide, even to all the territory surrounding Galilee. 29. And immediately they left the synagogue and came into the home of Simon and Andrew with James and John. 30. But Simon's mother-in-law was bedridden with a fever. Right away they informed Jesus of her condition. 31. He went over to her and, taking her by the hand, raised her up, and the fever left her. She then took care of their needs. 32. When evening came, at sunset, people carried to him all those who were ill and those who were possessed. 33. The whole city was assembled at the gate. 34. And he healed the many who were ill with all kinds of diseases and cast out many demons. But he would not allow the demons to speak, for they recognized him.

NOTES

21. *Capernaum:* Capernaum (from the Hebrew, "village of Nahum") is on the northwest side of the Sea of Galilee, about two and a half miles from the source of the Jordan River. Josephus says it was a fertile and prosperous area known also for its fishing industry (*War* 3.516-521). In the gospels it is the center of Jesus' Galilean ministry, and in Mark 2:1 it is the site of the "home" (*oikia*) of Jesus (see Matt 4:13, who mentions explicitly a departure from Nazareth). Jesus first teaches in the synagogue there (1:21), heals Peter's mother-in-law and others at the house of Peter and Andrew (1:29-34), and passes through there on his way to Jerusalem (9:33). In the Q source Jesus heals the centurion's son there (Matt 8:5-17; Luke 7:1-10; cf. John 4:46-54), but ends up cursing the town (Matt 11:23-24; Luke 10:15) for its lack of response to his preaching about God's kingdom and repentance. Extensive excavations in recent years have uncovered an early synagogue (second or third century C.E.) and an octagonal fifth-century church built on the ruins of an earlier house church, which has been claimed to have been the site of Peter's house in the first century.

and then on the Sabbath . . . to teach: Though connected with the following narrative, 1:21-22 also provide an "anticipatory summary" by highlighting both Jesus' customary practice and the reaction to it. "Sabbath" in Greek is in the dative plural; though used for the single day it can also suggest "on Sabbaths." The translation "he would go . . . and begin to teach" attempts to capture the repetition implied by the participle in the context of a summary report and by the inceptive imperfect, *edidasken.*

synagogue: The word "synagogue" (from the Greek *synagōgē,* "assembling") can mean a gathering of people or the place where people gather. As a building it was a place for study of the Law and religious instruction. Sabbath services most likely consisted of readings from Scripture, instruction in the Law and the prophets, prayers, and blessings (see Josephus, *Against Apion* 2.175). In the gospels Jesus teaches in synagogues, as does Paul in Acts 13:14-16. Jesus appears in synagogues early in Mark's Gospel (1:21, 23, 39; 3:1; 6:2), but never enters one after his rejection in the synagogue at Nazareth (6:2). From then on the synagogue symbolizes hostility (12:39; 13:9) and Jesus teaches primarily in houses in which he gives private instruction to the disciples (e.g., 7:17; 9:28, 33-50; 10:10-12). Throughout the gospel Jesus is accessible to the crowds and teaches them in the open (e.g., 2:13; 3:32; 4:1; 10:1). This could also reflect the practices of Mark's community: instruction in the "house churches" for community members and missionary preaching "outside."

22. *were astonished:* One of the salient characteristics of Mark is the motif of surprise, wonder, awe, and fear (appearing over 34 times). Such reactions embrace all aspects of Jesus' ministry: (1) in reaction to his teaching (1:22; 6:2; 10:24, 26; 11:18, 12:17); (2) as a conclusion to miracle stories (1:17; 2:12; 4:41; 5:15, 20, 33, 42; 6:50, 51; 7:37); (3) in narratives of divine epiphanies (4:41; 6:50-51; 9:6; 16:5; 16:8); (4) notices about the fright of the disciples at predictions of the Passion (9:32; 10:33; cf. 14:33, the fright of Jesus); and (5) reactions by opponents, both before and during the Passion of Jesus (11:18; 12:12; 15:5, 44). Though reactions of awe and wonder are a formal element of miracle stories, the emphasis Mark gives to them establishes a rapport with the reader and becomes a symbolic reaction to the whole gospel.

at his teaching: Mark's Gospel presents something of a paradox. Jesus' identity as a teacher is strongly highlighted, but in comparison with the other gospels and apart from 4:1-34 (the parables discourse) and 13:1-37 (the apocalyptic discourse) Mark contains relatively little teaching and is rather a gospel of action. Matthew (in his five great speeches) and Luke (in his greatly expanded journey narrative) make substantial additions to the content of Jesus' teaching.

as a person with authority: Mark continues the theme of Jesus as "the stronger one" from the prologue (1:7) and stresses here his authority (see also 1:27; 2:10; 11:33) and power (3:27; 5:30; 6:14). Another paradox will unfold: The power of Jesus (*hōs exousian echōn*) is expressed not in dominance but in service (10:45).

and not as the scribes: In ancient societies scribes performed a wide variety of tasks from composing documents to holding official administrative positions. The term *grammateus* is as wide as "secretary" is today, ranging from an office worker to a person in high levels of government (*ABD* 5:1012). In Mark the scribes are not necessarily a unified group but comprise teachers, those who interpret Scripture (9:11; 12:35), and even lawyers (12:38-40). They are associated primarily (but not exclusively) with Jerusalem (3:22; 7:1, 5), and are among Jesus' most adamant opponents (2:6, 16; 11:27). The Jerusalem scribes, with the elders and chief priests, are the prime instigators of the process that leads to Jesus' death (8:31; 10:33; 11:18; 14:1, 43, 53; 15:1, 31). Although some scribes are associated with the Pharisees, their opposition to Jesus is far greater (and more fatal) than that of the Pharisees.

23. *a person with an unclean spirit:* "Unclean spirit" (*pneuma akatharton*) is a common Jewish designation for a demon. Though the Greeks preferred the term *daimonion*, Mark uses the words almost interchangeably (see 3:22-30; 7:25-29). In this context "unclean" (*akatharton*) primarily connotes not a moral (even less a sexual) fault, but rather something that is opposed to the "holy." In the OT the command to be "holy" like God (Lev 11:44) implies life, wholeness, and completeness (Lev 21:17-21), whereas "unclean" suggests something that should not be, something out of place (e.g., soil in the farmer's field is productive, but in the middle of a house it is "dirt"). The opposite of the realm of the holy is the realm of the demonic; hence the spirits there are "unclean." Physical defects and psychological aberrations can make a person "unclean" in the sense of incomplete, imperfect, or out of order.

24. *What do we have in common, Jesus, you Nazarene?:* Literally "what is there between us and you?" The same expression appears in Jesus' response to his mother at Cana in John 2:4. See also 1 Kgs 17:18 (LXX), where the widow of Zarephath addresses Elijah in the same words, thinking he has come to indict her of sin and kill her son. The formula occurs again in 2 Kgs 3:13 and Judg 11:12 (with a variation in Hos 14:9). It functions as a "defensive" formula denying communality with the person to whom it is addressed. In Mark 1:24 and 5:7 it serves as the demon's defense against the exorcist. The adjective *Nazarēnos* could also be translated as "of Nazareth." The translation "you Nazarene" attempts to capture the hostile tone of the unclean spirit; for a similar usage see 14:67.

the holy one of God: Jesus is called by this title only here and in Luke 4:34 and John 6:69. The phrase is not found elsewhere in the NT, and rarely in the OT: 2 Kgs 4:9 (Elisha); Judg 16:17 (Samson); and Ps 106:16 (Aaron). The word "holy" suggests consecration to God and distinguishes Jesus who received the Spirit (1:9-11) and will baptize with the Holy Spirit (1:8) from the "unclean spirit." Since the Hebrew term *nazir* also means "consecrated, holy," some have seen a word play here on "Nazarene."

25. *subdued:* The Greek verb *epitimēsen*, often translated "rebuke," is a judicial metaphor meaning "lay a strong charge or penalty on." In the LXX it translates the Hebrew *gāʿar*, and is used in the sense of exorcising or subduing evil powers (Zech 3:2; Pss 68:31; 106:9); see also the Qumran *Genesis Apocryphon* where its Aramaic equivalent is used when Abraham expels an evil spirit that afflicts Pharaoh (1QapGen 20:28-29). Mark uses it of Jesus in 3:12 (to demons);

4:39 (to the wind); to Peter (8:30, 33); and 9:25 (to an unclean spirit). It is used of others in 8:32 (Peter to Jesus); 9:25 (the disciples to people bringing children); and 10:48 (the crowds to blind Bartimaeus). The translation is determined by the context; what is constant is a word with effective power.

Be quiet: Literally "tie shut" or "muzzle." The imperatives "be quiet" and "leave" followed by the immediate departure of the unclean spirit confirm the authoritative word of Jesus. Also this exorcism lacks any of the physical touching or rituals associated with exorcism narratives outside the NT; their absence confirms the power of Jesus' word.

26. *After throwing . . . left the man:* These vivid and dramatic actions characterize both the demon's effect on the person (see also 5:4-5; 9:18) and its departure (5:13).

27. *astounded:* This is a standard reaction to miracles, but one that is enhanced by Mark (see the Note on 1:22).

    What is happening here?: The Greek is simply, "What is this?" The translation tries to underline the dramatic nature of the scene.

    A new kind of teaching—with authority: Many translations punctuate the Greek text differently and understand "with authority" with the following clause, translating the verse: "What is this, a new kind of teaching? With authority he gives orders. . . ." The chief arguments for our translation are the *inclusio* created with 1:21 and the stress that Mark puts on the authoritative teaching of Jesus.

28. *And quickly . . . surrounding Galilee:* The fame of the miracle worker is a conventional motif. Mark is fond of duplicate expressions where the second reference ("all the territory surrounding Galilee") specifies the first ("far and wide"). Also the conclusion of this first incident foreshadows the missionary journeys of Jesus even to those Gentile lands that surround Galilee.

29. *And immediately:* In Mark 1 alone the phrase *kai euthys* is used eight times (1:10, 12, 18, 20, 21, 23, 29, 30), and along with the extraordinary density of *kai* parataxis (used over 25 times in the first 29 verses) the phrase gives a sense of urgency and rapid progress to these initial accounts of Jesus' work.

    home of Simon and Andrew with James and John: The large building claimed to be the house of Peter in recent excavations at Capernaum is typical of the early Roman period, with a cluster of rooms surrounded by two courtyards. Such a house would fit with the picture of a home occupied by two families (those of Simon and Andrew) with Simon's mother-in-law also in residence. The four disciples who were called first (1:16-20) witness Jesus' initial exorcisms and healings. But they appear as a group again only at 13:3, while Peter, James, and John appear at 5:37 (the raising of Jairus's daughter); 9:2 (the transfiguration); and 14:33 (the agony in the garden).

30. *Simon's mother-in-law:* Other than the disciples and the "they" who inform Jesus of her illness, she is the only person identified in the narrative. Simon's spouse is not mentioned, even though she apparently travelled with Peter in his later missionary journeys (see 1 Cor 9:5).

bedridden with a fever: In antiquity the fever itself was regarded as the illness rather than as a symptom. In Luke 4:39 Jesus "rebuked" *(epetimēsen)* the fever, which indicates a lack of clear distinction between illness and invasion by evil spirits.

31. *He went over . . . raised her up:* By the use of participles (literally "coming over to her, having taken her by the hand, he raised her up"), the Greek text highlights the "raising." The verb "raise" *(ēgeiren),* which connotes setting a person upright or restoring someone to health, is characteristic of the Markan healing narratives (2:9, 11; 3:3; 5:41; 9:27; 10:49). It is used prior to Mark in formulaic expressions about the raising of Jesus from the dead (1 Cor 15:4; Gal 1:1; Rom 4:24; see also Acts 3:15; 4:10).

    taking her by the hand: Physical touch, laying on of hands, and grasping by the hand (see 5:23; 5:41; 7:32; 8:22), as well as the desire of the sick simply to touch the healer (5:28; 6:56), are also common in NT and extrabiblical healing narratives. These gestures strengthen the image of Jesus as a Spirit-empowered person whose presence brings wholeness (Hebrew *shalôm* and Greek *eirēnē;* see the command after a healing, "go in peace" (5:43; Luke 8:48; see 7:50).

    took care of their needs: The woman's action also confirms the healing. "Took care of" translates the Greek *diēkonei* (literally "she served them" or "ministered to them"). This verb was used earlier of the angels "ministering" to Jesus in the wilderness (1:13), and it will next be used when Jesus speaks of the ideal of leadership as the humble service of others and his own mission in 10:45: "The Son of Man came not to be served but to serve *(diakonēsai)."*

32. *When evening came, at sunset:* Duplicate time references are characteristic of Mark (e.g., 1:35; 2:20; 4:35; 14:30; 15:42; 16:2). Mark joins this summary report (vv. 32-34) to the healing narrative in 1:29-31. He also picks up the comment on the spreading fame of Jesus from 1:28. By the use of "all" (all the sick, the whole city) and "many" (many sick, many demons), Mark in 1:32-34 continues to enhance the figure of Jesus. "Sunset" designates the official end of the Sabbath (1:21) when people could move about freely and carry burdens (including the sick).

34. *He would not allow the demons to speak, for they recognized him:* Along with the voice from heaven (1:9-11), preternatural spirits (see 1:24) recognize Jesus as a Spirit-empowered figure. Though the silencing of demons (1:25) is a standard feature of exorcisms, it functions here also as the initial instance of Mark's "messianic secret."

INTERPRETATION

After narrating the initial call of companions for his mission of proclaiming the good news of the kingdom, where Jesus appears as one whose word can uproot people's lives, Mark continues his focus on Jesus as the Spirit-endowed stronger one by portraying a "paradigmatic day" that inaugurates his ministry. This day, a Sabbath, involves demonstration of his power as a teacher through confrontation with an unclean spirit (1:21-28), through the healing of Peter's mother-in-law (1:29-31), and by summary statements on healing and exorcism (1:32-34). The day is structured in a pattern of ABA', since it begins and ends with casting out of demons and injunctions of silence to the demons. Some authors have viewed the day as the first of a "new creation," but there is little direct allusion to creation motifs. More likely this day foreshadows the final section of the gospel, another Sabbath (16:1) between the day of Jesus' condemnation and death (which is clearly defined by time indications: 15:1, 25, 33, 34) and the day of his raising up.

The initial narrative (1:21-28) betrays signs of reworking by the evangelist into a concentric pattern (ABA'). It begins with a summary description of Jesus as one who teaches with authority (1:21-22), though he has taught nothing specific. It then moves to a structured exorcism story (1:23-26), but concludes (1:27-28) with a description of people caught up by Jesus the authoritative teacher.

Although Mark uses neither the verb "exorcise" nor the noun "exorcism," the term can be used as shorthand for subduing or casting out demons. The exorcism in 1:23-26 is the first of four in Mark: 1:21-28 (the unclean spirit in the synagogue); 5:1-20 (the Gerasene demoniac); 7:24-30 (the Syrophoenician woman's daughter with an unclean spirit); and 9:14-29 (the boy with an unclean spirit). See also the summary in 1:39, where Jesus goes throughout Galilee casting out demons.

The first exorcism account is most likely a traditional story that the evangelist locates here and refashions to stress the powerful teaching of Jesus. This narrative exhibits a pattern that will appear in the other exorcisms: (1) the meeting of exorcist and demon (1:23); (2) the attempt of the demon to resist divine power (1:24); (3) the powerful response of the exorcist (1:25), usually commanding silence; (4) a command to leave (1:25); (5) the departure of the demon (1:26); and (6) various reactions of amazement or wonder, often with the story being broadcast far and wide (1:27).

Exorcisms (from the Greek *exorkizein*, "I solemnly adjure you") should be viewed in the social and religious context of the NT period. The ancient universe was perceived as being peopled by a wide variety of spirits, most of them threatening; in fact, humans occupied only a small part of this universe. Popular religion (e.g., mystery cults and healing shrines) in the Greco-Roman period was very much concerned with liberation from these malevolent powers. Likewise, apocalyptic Judaism thought of the world as locked in a lethal struggle between God and the power(s) of evil. Therefore exorcism was not uncommon. Solomon, the son of David, was venerated as an exorcist. Josephus lists Solomon's ability to expel demons among his many accomplishments (*Ant.* 8:45), and the *Testament of Solomon* (first or second century C.E.) is filled with stories of Solomon's victories over demons. Josephus also tells the story of a Jewish exorcist named Eleazar who expelled demons in the presence of Vespasian (*Ant.* 8.46-48). The *Genesis Apocryphon* from Qumran tells of an exorcism performed by Abraham (1QapGen 20:28-29). The *Life of Apollonius of Tyana* (set in the first century C.E. but written by Philostratus ca. 200) contains a rather long narrative of an exorcism, similar in many respects to the gospel narratives (4.20). Apollonius, while teaching in Athens, recognizes a young boy's bizarre behavior as demonic possession. The demon utters cries of fear and rage (cf. Mark 1:26). Apollonius addresses the demon with anger and orders him out of the boy; when the demon enters a statue (cf. Mark 5:13) the reaction of the people is one of amazement (cf. Mark 1:27; 5:14). The boy "stripped off his old self and modelled his life on that of Apollonius" (cf. Mark 5:20, where the healed demoniac "begins to proclaim" all that Jesus did). Though it is possible that the legends surrounding Apollonius are influenced by the gospels, the more important element of the similarity with Jesus in the gospels is that in the *Life* Apollonius is primarily a sage and teacher and his wonder-working activity flows from this.

Only Mark makes the story of Jesus' confrontation with evil spirits the initial public act in Jesus' ministry (since the calling of the disciples has no witnesses apart from Zebedee and his hired men). Luke locates it (4:31-37) after the inaugural proclamation and rejection of Jesus at Nazareth (perhaps to illustrate a Jesus who brings good news to captives), and Matthew omits it completely. The narrative has a clear christological function. Jesus' identity, which was announced earlier by a voice from heaven, is now shouted out by a spirit. Transcendent forces recognize him for who he really is. However human Jesus appears throughout the subsequent narrative, he is also a figure of mystery and power. Through this initial conflict with evil, Mark also stresses that Jesus is the stronger one who has withstood Satan's attacks (1:7, 13) and despoiled his household (see 3:23-27). This in turn underscores the authority of Jesus as teacher. Jesus' word is so powerful that people abandon their occupations and follow him; it is more powerful than that of the scribes, and even demonic powers cower before it. It is a word that is to be spread far and wide.

After the initial confrontation with the destructive power of evil, Mark in 1:29-31 places a narrative in which Jesus restores Peter's mother-in-law to health (see Matt 8:16-17; Luke 4:38-39). This juxtaposition may be due to the ancient conception of the close connection between illness and the influence of evil spirits. These initial miracles also reflect the hope expressed in nonbiblical Jewish texts for the messianic age when Satan will be conquered (*T.Mos.* 10:1) and disease will disappear (e.g., "when the time of my Anointed One comes . . . health will descend in dew and illness will vanish," 2 *Bar* 72:2; 73:3).

The healing of Peter's mother-in-law is the first of eight healing narratives (1:29-31, 44-45; 2:1-12; 3:1-5; 5:24-34; 7:31-37; 8:22-26; and 10:46-52; see also the summary statements in 1:32-34, 39; 3:10-12; 6:2). Mark presents something of a paradox. Miracle stories (exorcisms, healings, resuscitations, and nature miracles) occupy over 200 verses (more than the Passion narrative), and form virtually half of the gospel prior to the Jerusalem ministry. Yet they are often accompanied by an injunction to silence and play little part in the second part of the gospel; the only miracles after 8:22-26 are in 9:14-29 (the epileptic boy), 10:46-52 (Bartimaeus), and 11:12-14 (the withered fig tree). Mark calls miracles not "signs" (*sēmeia*), but rather *dynameis* ("works of power," 6:2, 5). Nor do they function as "proof" for the divine status of Jesus (8:11-13). In fact, false messiahs can also perform "mighty works" (13:4, 22; see also *Apocalypse of Elijah* 3:5-10).

Like the exorcisms, healing narratives exhibit a similar pattern that is found in 1:29-31 in concise form: (1) the arrival of the miracle worker at the locale of the sick person (1:29); (2) a description of the illness or problem (1:30); (3) a request for healing, implicit or explicit (1:30b); (4) the healing action either by gesture or by word (1:31); (5) the effecting of the mighty deed (1:31b); and (6) acclamation by the crowd or some external demonstration of the healing (1:31c). This is the first of four Markan narratives that deal with "acts of power" in favor of women (1:29-31; 5:21-24, 35-43; and 5:25-34). It has many similarities with the raising of the daughter of Jairus in 5:21-24, 35-43: Both take place in the presence of the four disciples who were called first (1:29; 5:37); both take place in a house (1:29; 5:39); in both Jesus takes the woman by the hand (1:31; 5:41); and in each case food is served (1:31, implicitly; 5:43, explicitly).

This healing account not only has a christological function, but also stresses discipleship. Those first called to be disciples are mentioned explicitly as witnesses. More importantly, Peter's mother-in-law embodies and foreshadows the ideal of discipleship as service of others which Jesus will address to all the disciples in response to a question from two of those present in this narrative (James and John): The greatest among them should be their servant (*diakonos* [10:43]—the nominal form of *diakonein* [1:31]), an ideal Jesus himself incarnates (10:45). The action of Peter's mother-in-law also foreshadows the presence of the women at the cross in 15:41 who had followed him and ministered to him (*ēkolouthoun kai diēkonoun*) in Galilee.

In 1:32-34 Mark appends to the narratives of a single exorcism and a single healing a panoramic description of many healings and exorcisms that take place amid the waning light of this first day of Jesus' ministry. The summarizing phrase "various illnesses" evokes the overflowing quality of the benefits that accompanied God's saving activity in the past (see Isa 35:4-5; 42:16; 51:14; 53:4; 61:1-4) and are now to flow from the presence of the Spirit-empowered stronger one. Despite the panoramic nature of the healings, Jesus commands the demons to remain silent. In this instance the command is followed, further enhancing Jesus' power.

For Reference and Further Study

Achtemeier, Paul J. "The Ministry of Jesus in the Synoptic Gospels," *Int* 35 (1981) 157–69.

Adinolfi, Marco. "L'esorcismo di Gesù in Mc 1,21-28 e i quattro esorcismi di Apollonio riferiti da Filostrato," *Studii Biblici Franciscani Liber Annuus* 42 (1992) 49–65.

Cook, John G. "In Defence of Ambiguity: Is There a Hidden Demon in Mark 1.29-31?" *NTS* 43 (1997) 184–208.

Dillon, Richard J. "'As One Having Authority' (Mark 1:22): The Controversial Distinction of Jesus' Teaching," *CBQ* 57 (1995) 92–113.

Iwe, John C. *Jesus in the Synagogue of Capernaum: The Pericope and Its Programmatic Character for the Gospel of Mark. An Exegetico-Theological Study of Mk 1:21-28.* Rome: Gregorian University Press, 1999.

Kollmann, Bernd. "Jesu Schweigegebote an die Dämonen," *ZNW* 82 (1991) 267–73.

LaGrand, James. "The First of the Miracle Stories According to Mark (1:21-28)," *Currents in Theology and Mission* 20 (1993) 479–84.

Twelftree, Graham H. *Jesus the Exorcist: A Contribution to the Study of the Historical Jesus.* WUNT 2d ser. 54. Tübingen: J.C.B. Mohr [Paul Siebeck], 1994.

5. *Highpoints of Jesus' Work in Galilee* (1:35-45)

35. Very early the next morning, before dawn, he got up and left the house. He then departed for a deserted place, and there spent time in prayer. 36. And Simon and those with him tracked him down. 37. Upon finding him, they said: "Everyone is searching for you." 38. Jesus answered them: "Let us go in another direction to the neighboring market towns, in order that I might also preach there. For this is the reason that I have come." 39. And he went and preached in their synagogues throughout all of Galilee, and was casting out demons.

40. Then a leper approached Jesus, and falling on his knees, pleaded with him, saying: "If you will, you have the power to make me clean." 41. Deeply moved with compassion, he [Jesus] stretched out his hand and touched him, and stated: "It is my will; be made clean." 42. At once the leprosy departed from him, and he was cleansed. 43. And with a deep groan, Jesus immediately dismissed him, 44. saying to him: "Take

care that you do not mention this to anyone, but go and show yourself to
the priest and make the purification offering that Moses specified as
testimony for them." 45. But he [the man] rushed out and began to proclaim the news constantly and to broadcast what happened far and wide,
so that he [Jesus] could not enter a city openly, but remained outside in
deserted places. Still they came to him from everywhere.

NOTES

35. *Very early the next morning, before dawn:* This is another instance of a duplicate
temporal expression where the second element specifies the first one (see
1:32).

    deserted place: The use of *erēmos* recalls the motif of the desert (or wilderness)
as a privileged place for contact with God (see the Note on 1:3). Mark uses the
adjectival phrase "deserted place" *(erēmos topos)*, since Capernaum (like
Galilee in general) was well populated and distant from the wilderness of
Judea (see 1:12). The verbs of motion ("got up . . . left . . . departed") suggest
that Jesus seeks out this solitude.

    spent time in prayer: The translation captures the imperfect of *proseucheto*. Daily
prayer in the early morning was part of Jewish piety (Pss 5:3; 88:13; 119:147).
Elsewhere in Mark, Jesus is depicted as being at prayer only at 6:46 (in the
evening) and 14:32-42 (in Gethsemane, also at night). Jesus urges his disciples
to pray in 9:29; 11:24-25; and 13:18. But he criticizes the long prayers of the
scribes when used as a pretext for exploitation of widows (12:40).

36. *those with him:* Many translations prefer "companions." Our somewhat cumbersome translation retains the ambiguity as to whether the pursuers are the
four disciples (1:29) or a larger entourage from Simon's household. There is a
similar expression and ambiguity in 3:21 (literally "those around him").

    tracked him down: The Greek *katediōxen* has the overtone of "pursue" in a hos-
tile sense. It is used in the LXX of the pursuit of the Israelites by Pharaoh's
forces (Exod 14:4, 8, 9, 23) and is very frequent in the psalms for the pursuit of
the innocent sufferer by his enemies (Pss 7:5; 18:37; 31:15; 38:20; 69:26; 109:16,
31; 119:84, 86, 150, 161). This is the first intimation of the progressive misunderstanding of Jesus by those closest to him—his family (3:21-35) and his
disciples—that will unfold throughout the narrative.

37. *they said:* Literally "they say." This is a case of Mark's frequent use (see 1:12, 21;
also 1:38, 41) of the historical present; that is, the present tense ("they say") is
used grammatically where one logically expects the past tense ("they said").
The device adds vividness to the narrative, but translating it literally in every
case (see 1:38 "answer," 1:40 "approaches," etc.) soon becomes impossible to
sustain.

    Everyone is searching for you: Though this continues the motif of the fame of
Jesus (vv. 32-34), the verb "search" or "seek" *(zētein)* will increasingly take on
a negative connotation in Mark when people misunderstand Jesus (3:32;

8:11-12) or when opponents seek him (11:18; 12:12; 14:1; cf. 3:6). The idea that "everyone" (lit. "all") is searching for Jesus is another example of Mark's universalizing technique (see the Note on 1:5).

38. *Let us go in another direction:* The hortatory subjunctive ("Let us go") continues the motif of rapid movement that characterizes Jesus' activity in these initial narratives.

    market towns: Kōmopoleis (lit. "village cities"; only here in the NT) were small commercial centers that lacked the constitution of a *polis* ("city").

    that I might also preach there: The mission of proclaiming or preaching *(kēryssein)* recalls the initial arrival of Jesus in Galilee when he came "proclaiming the gospel of God" (1:14), and prepares for 1:39 where the task is fulfilled.

    that I have come: The verb *exēlthon* (lit. "come out"; see 1:35, "left the house") may have the theological overtone of "coming out from God," a usage found explicitly in John's Gospel (8:42; 13:3; 16:27-30; 17:8). Luke clarifies the verb, changing it to *apestalēn* ("I was sent," 4:43).

39. *preached in their synagogues throughout all of Galilee, and was casting out demons:* This verse echoes 1:14 and anticipates the following narratives. Jesus' movements have been centrifugal. He begins in Capernaum, moves beyond to the neighboring villages, and ultimately embraces all of Galilee. The geographical names highlight the spread of the "gospel of God." The use of "their synagogues" reflects terminology later than the ministry of Jesus (this is a characteristic phrase in Matthew's Gospel); the stress on Jesus' synagogue preaching here may also reflect early missionary practice (see Acts 13:5; 14:1; 18:4). Mark's double use of *eis* (into) both with the synagogues and with all of Galilee serves to locate "preaching" clearly in the synagogues, but leaves unclear the location of the expulsion of demons. The expulsions testify to the power of Jesus' proclaimed word.

40. *a leper approached Jesus:* This pericope, along with its synoptic parallels (Matt 8:1-4; Luke 5:12-16) and Luke 17:11-19 (the ten lepers), are the only NT narratives about the healing of leprosy. The term "leprosy" in the Bible, from the Greek *leptein* ("peel off"), is most likely not modern leprosy (Hansen's disease) but refers to a wide variety of skin disorders. The Priestly legislation of Leviticus 13–14 treats this condition extensively. There the Hebrew term *ṣāraʿat* also describes a fungus that affects fabrics and houses (Lev 13:47-58; 14:13-45). In the OT "leprosy" is frequently regarded as a punishment for sin (Num 12:10-15; cf. Deut 28:27, 35; 2 Kgs 5:25-27; 2 Chr 26:16-21). According to Lev 13:45-46 the person with a leprous disease shall wear torn clothes and have disheveled hair, and shall live alone with a dwelling "outside the camp, and cry out 'unclean, unclean.'" Physical contact with such people rendered a person "unclean" too. Leprosy in the strict sense seems to have spread to the Near East from India ca. 300 B.C.E., and so it could have existed in Palestine at the time of Jesus. Leprosy was thought to be like death (most likely because of the pallor of the person and the isolation from community), and a cure of leprosy was considered as marvelous as raising the dead (Num 12:10-12; 2 Kgs 5:7).

and falling on his knees: This participle is omitted in important manuscripts (e.g., Vaticanus and the Western tradition). The main argument for its inclusion is that Matthew has the leper kneel before Jesus (8:2), and Luke has him prostrate himself (5:12).

If you will: Since the healing of leprosy required divine intervention, the wording of the request contains an implicit christology; that is, it assumes that Jesus embodies the power and will of God. See 1:41 where the actual healing occurs at the word and command of Jesus.

you have the power: The second person singular of *dynamai* (*dynasai*, "have power") can be translated also by the simple modal verb "can." Our translation continues the emphasis throughout Mark 1 on Jesus as "the stronger one" (1:7) who embodies a new teaching with power (1:27-28).

41. *Deeply moved with compassion:* This translates the participle *splanchnistheis*, which is one of the more disputed textual readings in Mark. The root of the verb (the noun is *splanchnon*) designates the seat of affective feeling and emotion (our "guts"), and is often translated "heart." Some Western manuscripts read *orgistheis* ("being angered"), and on the principle of *lectio difficilior potior* (the more difficult reading is to be preferred) many commentators translate "being angered." The argument is that copyists (embarrassed at the anger of Jesus) would more likely change "anger" to "compassion" than vice versa. In favor of "moved with compassion," however, are the weight of the best manuscripts and the fact that copyists have not altered other passages that present Jesus as angry (3:5; 10:14). Moreover, Jesus appears as compassionate in two other healing narratives (6:34; 8:2) and in curing the possessed boy (9:22).

stretched out his hand and touched: The verbs are both in the historical present. According to 2 Kgs 5:10-14, Naaman, who is cured of his leprosy by following the command of Elisha to wash in the Jordan seven times, is initially angered because Elisha did not simply wave his hand over his leprosy. By contrast Jesus touches the leper and so bridges the gap between the holy and the unclean.

it is my will: This translates *thelō* ("I will"). The actual healing is accomplished by Jesus' word rather than by the gesture of touching.

42. *At once the leprosy departed from him, and he was cleansed:* The cure is immediate (*kai euthys*) and complete, which is the usual case in Jesus' exorcisms and healings (but see 8:22-26).

43. *And with a deep groan, Jesus immediately dismissed him:* This verse is a nest of problems. The initial participle, *embrimēsamenos*, literally means "snorting" or "growling," and is more suited to exorcisms. The word used for dismissing the healed man (*exebalen*, lit. "cast out") is used most often for "casting out" demons (1:39; 3:15, 22-23; 6:13; 7:26; 9:18, 28) and appears in other places in a negative sense (5:40; 11:15; 12:8). Why would Jesus "cast out" a healed leper whom he had already touched? Also, in the following verse the man who was apparently harshly dismissed here is still present, and Jesus' words to him there are hardly a stern dismissal. Some scholars take the verse as the residue

of an earlier tradition where the healing was an exorcism, based on the close connection between illness and possession (see also 7:24-30; 9:14-29).

44. *do not mention this to anyone:* This somewhat solemn form of a command to secrecy is highlighted by the double negative in Greek, *mēdeni mēden* (lit. "to no one nothing"). This verse also contains a certain tension, since Jesus will send the healed leper to the priest whom he will inform of his former condition and his healing.

    show yourself to the priest: Leviticus 13:47–14:54 contains an elaborate ritual of cleansing, including sacrifices, with special provisions for sacrifices to be offered by the poor. Of itself the mention of a priest does not demand a Jerusalem setting, since priests lived throughout Palestine (see Luke 10:31-32, where a priest and a Levite are journeying from Jerusalem).

    as testimony for them: In the levitical legislation (chs. 13–14) the cleansing itself is for the examining priest evidence of the cure, while the sacrifice is a public sign of the cure.

45. *But he [the man] rushed out . . . from everywhere:* Some authors suggest that the subject (which is not explicit in Greek) of both main verbs is Jesus. If so, then the major problems of the verse disappear, and it functions simply as a summarizing conclusion to the narrative similar to those in 1:32-34, 39. If the healed man is the subject of the first clause (as in our translation), the verse is somewhat paradoxical. After Jesus' solemn injunction to silence and the command to observe the levitical legislation, the man dramatically violates the command by *kēryssein polla* (literally "proclaiming many things") and *diaphēmizein ton logon* (literally "broadcasting the word"), but also in the sense of telling what happened to him. The subject of the second clause is also ambiguous, since it could refer to the healed leper who as yet had no verification of his cure. Virtually all contemporary translations, however, understand "Jesus" as the subject. The verse is another instance of people who are touched by the power of Jesus but disobey his command of silence (see the Introduction under "Messianic Secret"). It also provides a scenic conclusion to Mark's impressive portrayal of the extent and power of the initial appearance of Jesus.

INTERPRETATION

After his day of confrontation with evil and sickness, Jesus in 1:35-39 rises early and retreats to a deserted place, the traditional site of contact with God (see 1:11-12; and cf. Israel in the desert, Moses and Elijah meeting God in the desert, and John the Baptist in the desert). As mentioned in the Notes on 1:36, on this "second" day of Jesus' mission there is already an intimation of the misunderstanding of Jesus that will unfold extensively in the middle section of the gospel (8:22–10:52), and culminate in the flight of the disciples and the denial of Peter (that same Simon who here leads the band of pursuers). Jesus' prompt departure to other villages sustains the rapid action of this first part of the gospel. Such quick changes of scene and constant movement provide the narrative backdrop for the urgency of the message that is proclaimed. The time is fulfilled, and the reigning of God is imminent. What is demanded is swift response.

The healing of the leper (1:40-45), the only such healing in Mark, seems almost like an awkward appendix to the two summaries of healings and exorcisms (1:34, 39). The text would flow very smoothly from 1:39 to 2:1, with Jesus travelling throughout Galilee and then returning to Capernaum. The story lacks the specific location of the other mighty works in this section (in a synagogue, in the house of Simon and Andrew). Yet it is the most vivid of the narratives thus far. In contrast to those healed previously (the demoniac and Simon's mother-in-law), the leper is shown in action by the use of three closely linked participles: beseeching, falling to his knees, and making a request. Moreover, his request ("make me clean") is explicit. The language of requesting and falling on one's knees attributes a virtually divine status to Jesus, as does the statement that through an act of his will he can effect healing. Leprosy, or the various skin diseases included in the term, was the most dreaded of all diseases because it separated people from family and community and thus constituted a "living death." Indeed, rabbinic sayings compare the cure of leprosy to raising the dead (a divine prerogative).

The narrative is also the most vivid so far in portraying the humanity of Jesus. He acts with a deep feeling of compassion, and he touches a leper, thereby affirming his shared humanity and incurring ritual defilement on himself. In a verse (1:43) that Matthew and Luke omit, Jesus "groans deeply." There is another paradox in the next two verses. Though Jesus violates the purity laws by touching the leper, he orders the leper to obey the legal prescriptions on verification and cleansing (1:44). The man who is cleansed in turn violates the command of Jesus to be silent (1:45). Commands and prescriptions seem to have little power in this narrative. Rather, the humanity and compassion of Jesus and the experience of freedom that the healed man enjoys are the main centers of attention.

The evangelist may well have placed this narrative here as a christological paradigm for the subsequent narratives. Jesus, the stronger one predicted by John (1:7), has power over the dreaded leprosy, and yet he is a figure of compassion who, for the sake of a suffering human, will violate ritual laws. Like the healed leper, those in Mark's community who have been touched by the life-giving power of Jesus are to become missionaries proclaiming and broadcasting "the word" far and wide. This narrative also prepares for the controversies of 2:1–3:6, which will end with the first explicit plan to kill Jesus (3:6) precisely because he violated the Sabbath.

By this point in the narrative Mark's readers have been given grounds for that "faith" that is the proper response to the good news (1:14-15), a faith, however, that will be tested as the life and teaching of Jesus unfold in the gospel. It is a faith that will evoke opposition, as the following controversies show. Contemporary readers might ask whether their faith leads them to a confidence that the gospel can confront and surmount the power of evil that makes our world as fragile as that of men and women of the first century, and whether they will take those risks that may bring conflict and division.

FOR REFERENCE AND FURTHER STUDY

Broadhead, Edwin K. "Mk 1,44: The Witness of the Leper," *ZNW* 83 (1992) 257–65.
Cave, C. H. "The Leper: Mark 1:40-45," *NTS* 25 (1978–79) 245–50.
Elliott, John K. "The Conclusion of the Pericope of the Healing of the Leper and Mark i.45," *JTS* 22 (1971) 153–57.
_____. "Is *ho exelthōn* a Title for Jesus in Mark 1:45?" *JTS* 27 (1976) 402–05.
Kazmierski, Carl R. "Evangelist and Leper: A Socio-Cultural Study of Mark 1.40-45," *NTS* (1992) 37–50.
Pilch, John J. "Understanding Biblical Healing: Selecting the Appropriate Model," *BTB* 18 (1988) 60–66.
Swetnam, James. "Some Remarks on the Meaning of *ho de exelthōn* in Mark 1:45," *Bib* 68 (1987) 245–49.
Twelftree, Graham H. *Jesus the Miracle Worker. A Historical & Theological Study.* Downers Grove, Ill.: InterVarsity, 1999.

6. *The Healing of the Paralyzed Man* (2:1-12)

1. After several days he entered Capernaum a second time, and the report spread that he was in the house. 2. Then so many people congregated that there was no room for them, even in front of the doorway; he then began to speak the word to them. 3. Some people arrived, bringing a paralyzed man to him who was carried by four men. 4. Because of the press of people, they could not get near him; and so they tore open the roof over him, and pushing the debris aside, they lowered the mat on which the paralyzed man was lying. 5. But when Jesus saw their faith, he said to the paralyzed man: "My child, forgiven now are your sins." 6. But there were some scribes sitting there, and they were musing to themselves: 7. "Why does this fellow speak like this; he blasphemes. Who has the power to forgive sins except one, God?" 8. Then Jesus, aware right away in his spirit that these were their musings, said to them: "Why are you harboring such thoughts in your hearts? 9. Which is easier: To say to the paralytic, 'forgiven are your sins,' or to say 'rise up, pick up your mat, and walk away?' 10. But that you might realize that the Son of Man has

power on earth to forgive sin," he said to the paralyzed man: 11. "I command you, rise up, pick up your mat, and return to your own home." 12. He immediately rose up and picked up his mat and walked out where everyone could see him. Consequently everyone was astounded and gave glory to God, saying: "We have never witnessed such a thing."

NOTES

1. *After several days he entered:* The Greek allows this phrase to be understood either with reference to the entry into Capernaum or with the report ("after several days the report spread"). Similar language links this pericope with 1:45: e.g., "so that not" *(hōste mēketi)*, "enter," and "the word" used absolutely for Jesus' teaching (2:2). Since opposition to Jesus characterizes the next five pericopes, Mark does not want readers to forget the powerful Jesus of the initial ministry.

   the house: The house of Simon and Andrew (1:29) is the locus for healing and instruction.

2. *no room . . . even in front of the doorway:* This repeats the language of 1:33 and continues the stress on the magnetism and power of Jesus.

   speak the word: The "word" *(logos)* is often a technical term for Christian missionary preaching (Acts 6:4; 8:4; 17:11; Gal 6:6; Col 4:3). In Mark it has the double nuance of the message proclaimed by Jesus (2:2; 4:14-20, 33; 8:32) and the message proclaimed about him (1:45). Other NT passages speak of "the word of the Lord" (Acts 8:25; 1 Thess 1:8; 1 Tim 6:3) and "the word of God" (Luke 5:1; Acts 4:29; Phil 1:14; Heb 13:7).

3. *a paralyzed person:* Paralysis or palsy is mentioned only here in Mark, but see also Matt 4:24 and 8:6 where its painful character is stressed. Paralysis, like many illnesses, was thought to be due to sin (see John 9:2). Mark stresses the dire straits of this person by the note that he is carried by four others. The noun "paralytic" is never used in the OT, but it is closely associated with lameness in the NT (see John 5:2-9; Acts 3:2; 8:7). Lameness constituted a form of impurity in the OT (Lev 21:18), and at Qumran "the lame, the blind, and the crippled" were not eligible for full participation in the life of the community (1QM 7:4-6; 1QSa 2:6-10). In the OT the "lame" *(chōloi)* shall experience the blessings of the restoration of Zion (Isa 35:6; Jer 31:8; Mic 4:7; Zeph 3:19), and in the NT they are to be the beneficiaries of the blessings of the kingdom (e.g., Luke 7:22 = Matt 11:5; Luke 14:13, 21).

4. *they could not get near him:* This heightens the dramatic tension and prepares for the startling and disruptive action of the four litter-bearers.

   they tore open the roof over him, and pushing the debris aside: The Greek, which is obscure here, first says that they literally "unroofed the roof." The second participle *exoryantes* (lit. "dig out") seems superfluous after the first phrase. For our translation see BAGD 277 (ἐξορύσσω), similarly BDAG 352. Mark here provides an accurate description of the roof of an ordinary Palestinian house in the period, which was covered with mud and thatch. Matthew (9:1-8) follows his usual pattern of condensing Mark and omits the description of the entry, while Luke (5:19) speaks of the "tile roofs" that would be more familiar to urban Hellenistic readers.

the mat: The Greek *krabattos* ("mat, pallet, or litter") is the multi-purpose bed of a poor person that can be carried around during the day or used as a begging mat. Luke (5:19) uses a term more familiar to an urban audience, *klinidion*, the dimunitive of *klinē* ("bed" or "dining couch").

5. *their faith:* The faith of the litter bearers, not that of the paralyzed man, is praised. This is the first mention of the noun "faith" *(pistis)* or the verb "believe" *(pisteuein)* since 1:15. The noun or verb appears in five healing narratives (2:1-12; 5:21-24 and 35-43; 5:25-34; 9:14-29; 10:46-52), in the calming of the sea (4:40), and in the saying on faith that can do the impossible (move mountains) in 11:22-23. It connotes not only trust and hope in God or another person but also a relationship of loyalty (faith as fidelity). On the relation of faith and miracles see the Interpretation.

he said to the paralyzed man: Here the narrative shifts from a rather straightforward miracle to a controversy story (2:5b-10). In the normal structure of the miracle story the actual healing and demonstration would now occur, as happens in 2:11. The interruption is noted by the repetition of "he said to the paralyzed man" (2:5b, 11). Such verbal duplication is very characteristic of Mark and often highlights important material within the repeated phrases (e.g., 2:9b-11a; 3:7, 8, 14, 16; 4:31, 32; 5:10, 23, 29, 34; 6:14, 16; 7:20, 23; 8:17, 21; 14:18, 22; 14:56, 59; 15:2, 4). In their rewriting of Mark, Matthew and Luke almost always alter such duplicate expressions.

forgiven now: This translates the present passive of the verb *aphiemi* and, though awkward, reproduces the Greek word order to stress that the first word spoken by Jesus is the declaration of forgiveness of sins. The Greek can be a "divine passive"; that is, the sins "are forgiven [by God]." So it is not clear here whether Jesus actually "forgives" the sins or acts as an agent of divine forgiveness. The reaction of the scribes in 2:8 suggests the former. The narrative is very spare here. Neither Jesus nor the crowd exhibits any reaction to the sudden opening of the roof or the descent of the paralyzed man into their midst. The somewhat elaborate initial description yields to the main focus of forgiveness and the controversy it evokes.

are your sins: The Bible has a pervasive sense of sin; it is a constant and universal reality that enslaves people and mars God's creation (Rom 3:23). The principal Hebrew term *ḥtʾ* and the Greek *hamartia* both convey the sense of "found lacking" or "miss the mark." Other terms suggest rebellion, injustice, and iniquity. After the idyllic creation narrative, sin "crouches at the door" (Gen 4:7) and the reign of sin unfolds through Genesis 11. Both communities (see Exod 20:20; 32:31) and individuals (Lev 4:3; 1 Sam 12:23; 2 Sam 12:13; Pss 32:5; 38:18) can sin. Though sin can be personal rebellion or disobedience, biblical sin is more an objective reality (what should not be or happen) than the modern individualistic and subjective notion of sin. Sin can be inadvertent or result from a cultic trespass (as in Num 6:9-11, where contact with a corpse requires purification by a sin offering). This helps to explain the connection between sin and illness. Both disease and sin mar God's creation.

6. *But there were some scribes sitting there:* Given the crowded conditions, the appearance of the seated scribes seems strange, which might argue for the joining of originally separate narratives (a healing and a controversy). Since "sitting" was the position of authoritative teaching (Mark 13:3; Matt 23:2), and since Mark will later criticize the scribes for taking "the best seats" in the synagogue (12:39), there may be a subtle irony here. Jesus teaches the experts about forgiveness.

   musing to themselves: Literally "debating" or "discussing *(dialogizomenoi)* in their hearts" (see 2:8). Mark uses the verbal and nominal form of "debate" with negative overtones (2:6, 8; 7:21; 8:16-17; 9:33; 11:31). Often in the OT, especially in the Psalms, the heart is the seat of rebellion and evil designs (Pss 5:9; 10:3; 14:1; 17:10; 28:3; 36:1; 53:1).

7. *Why does this fellow speak like this; he blasphemes:* "This fellow" translates the Greek *houtos,* used in a derogatory sense. In secular Greek the verb *blasphēmein* means simply "to insult" or "revile" someone. Plato *(Republic* 2.381E) uses it of profane speech about sacred things. In the NT it is used almost always of a violation of the power or majesty of God (Mark 3:28; Acts 6:11; Rev 13:6; 16:11, 21). Since Leviticus prescribes death by stoning for the one who "blasphemes the name of the Lord" (24:16), Jewish legal experts debated over what exactly constituted blasphemy. According to the Mishnah *(Sanh.* 7:5) the divine name had to be pronounced, but in the Babylonian Talmud *(Sanh.* 56a) Rabbi Meir argues that the person who curses God blasphemes even if the divine name is not used. Mark seems to use *blasphēmein* in the more general sense of "insult" (see 14:64; 15:29), and in this pericope the charge is that Jesus arrogates divine prerogatives to himself.

   Who has the power to forgive sins except one, God: The translation understands "God" in apposition to "one," which recalls the first words of the Shema (see Deut 6:4-5): "Hear, O Israel, the Lord our God, the Lord is One" (see 12:29). There is a subtle irony here. The scribes voice a theology that would be shared by Mark's readers. In the OT only God forgives sin (Pss 51:1-3; 85:2); forgiveness normally requires confession or admission of sin and a change of heart, most often followed by a sacrifice (Lev 4:1–5:13 contains elaborate directions for sin offerings). Against the backdrop of Isa 53:10-12, Mark's Christian readers would understand that Jesus was the agent of forgiveness (Mark 10:45; 14:24; cf. 1 Cor 15:3). The charge of blasphemy against Jesus in the narrative world of Mark may well reflect a similar charge made against the christological claims of the Markan community.

8. *Then Jesus, aware right away in his spirit . . . in your hearts:* Since God is the one who reads hearts and knows the hidden thoughts of humans (1 Sam 16:7; 1 Kgs 8:39, "for only you know what is in every human heart; Ps 7:9; Jer 11:20; Acts 1:24; 15:8; Rom 8:27), there is also an implicit christological claim here.

9. *Which is easier: To say . . . and walk away:* The narrative here shifts. The scribes have questioned Jesus in their hearts; he now questions them publicly. Jesus'

question here is rhetorical rather than real. Since Jesus *de facto* pronounces both the word of forgiveness and the word of healing, the dilemma is argumentative, and serves as in 11:29-33 to silence the scribes and enhance the authority of Jesus, thus recalling the earlier description of a "new teaching with power" (1:27). The dilemma for the scribes is that on the one hand it seems easier to pronounce forgiveness than to cause a lame man to walk, since the latter is immediately verifiable. On the other hand, restoration of the lame is a sign of divine activity (Isa 35:6; Jer 31:8; Mic 4:6, 7; Zeph 3:19). Either answer would cause difficulty for the scribes. They would not want to call the forgiveness of sin easier (which would be an "insult" to God akin to the blasphemy charged to Jesus), nor would they wish to recognize the wonder-working activity of Jesus as a sign of divine approbation. This staged dialogue prepares for the rest of the narrative where, in effect, the healing is a symbol of the forgiveness of sin. It also reflects the apologetic concerns of the Markan community.

10. *But that you might realize that the Son of Man has power on earth to forgive sin:* This verse constitutes an anacolouthon, that is, a departure from the expected structure of the sentence or flow of thought. Verse 11 could follow immediately upon v. 9. Many authors interpret the Son of Man saying here not as a continuation of Jesus' words but as an authorial aside to the reader (see 13:14). Still, though awkward, the text can be read as a saying of Jesus that interprets the following action. The key elements of the saying are the title "Son of Man" and the phrase "has power (or authority) on earth" *(exousian echei . . . epi gēs).*

11. *I command you, rise up . . . return to your own home:* This is the the powerful word of healing. The verb for "rise up" *(egeire)* is repeated in the raising of Jairus' daughter from the dead in 5:41 and (in the passive) with regard to Jesus' own resurrection (16:6). Thus release from paralysis is a form of restoration of life.

12. *He immediately . . . see him:* This constitutes the final phase of the miracle, the demonstration in which the first two actions, "rose up" and "picked up his mat," repeat exactly the command of Jesus, while the third command, "go to your home," is violated, much as in the case of the leper of 1:45.

everyone was astounded and gave glory to God: This acclamation (see 1:28, 45), while part of the structure of a miracle story, adds to the normal reaction of wonder (see 1:22) the note that the people glorify *God.* This subtly counters the charge of blasphemy, for the result of Jesus' forgiveness and healing is that people acknowledge the power and presence of the God of Israel. Jesus is the model for the Markan community in its mission of leading people to God.

INTERPRETATION

After an initial picture (in Mark 1) of Jesus as powerful in word and deed, one who conquers evil spirits and disease, whose presence evokes wonder and who is acclaimed by crowds, the mood shifts dramatically between 2:1 and 3:6a. Here Mark collects five narratives, often classed as "controversy stories," where, in contrast to the enthusiasm of the "crowds," opposition to Jesus mounts from specific groups: the scribes (2:6), the "scribes of the Pharisees" (2:16), the Pharisees (2:24), and the Pharisees and Herodians who plot his destruction (3:6). As Joanna Dewey has noted (see below), the narratives comprise a "ring composition": (A) a healing that takes place inside a house (2:1-12); (B) the calling of a disciple that takes place initially outside, a dispute inside over eating, and a proverb (2:13-17); (C) an unlocalized dispute over fasting, a saying about the removal of the bridegroom, and a discussion of newness (2:18-22); (B') a dispute outside over eating and a christological proverb (2:23-28); (A') a healing inside the synagogue (3:1-6a; see 2:2, "congregated," *synēchthesan* [from *synagagein*, the root of "synagogue"] and Jesus' command to the disabled man, "rise up" [3:3; cf. 2:11]). Moreover, the first two controversies deal with the acceptance of sinners (2:1-12; 2:13-17), while the last two (2:23-28; 3:1-6) treat violation of the Sabbath law. In effect there is a dual structure, one linear in which the opposition mounts and issues in the plan to kill Jesus (3:6a), while at the midpoint of the concentric structure stands Jesus' own prophecy of the bridegroom's removal and comment about the inability of old structures to contain his new teaching (see 1:28). If the collection of controversies is pre-Markan, then the evangelist may well have superimposed the linear structure in the service of his narrative christology.

Since this is the initial salvo in the mounting opposition to Jesus in Mark, and since the picture of Jewish leaders in the Gospels can foster anti-Semitism, certain principles of interpretation must be kept in mind.

1. Though writing in the form of a *bios* (the career) of Jesus, Mark does not try simply to hand on literal history. His presentation of Jesus contains authentic traditions from and about Jesus, but these had been reworked in the four decades since the death of Jesus. The theme of mounting opposition is part of the narrative world of Mark and reflects the growing estrangement forty years after the death of Jesus between Jews and non-Jews who accepted Jesus as Messiah and those who did not.

2. Mark writes from the post-resurrectional perspective that the rejection, death, and resurrection of Jesus were willed by God (8:31; 9:31; 10:33-34). If God willed Jesus' death and vindication, God must also have willed the opposition that led to that death.

3. Certain Jewish leaders were involved in the death of Jesus, but the precise nature and level of involvement requires the kind of careful analysis of all four Gospels that one finds in Raymond E. Brown's *The Death of the Messiah*.

4. Strong opposition existed between religious groups within Judaism in the first centuries B.C.E. and C.E., and such opposition occasionally led to violence.

5. Subsequent Christian history reveals that disturbing religious figures can and do suffer rejection and persecution. Brown notes wryly that "more than likely were Jesus to appear in our time (with the challenge rephrased in terms of contemporary religious stances) and be arrested and tried again, most of those finding him guilty would identify themselves as Christians and think they were rejecting an imposter" (*Death of the Messiah* 393).

Like miracle stories, controversy stories follow a set pattern: (1) an action by Jesus and/or his disciples (2:5); (2) an objection to this action (2:7); (3) a riposte by Jesus, often in the form of a counter-question (2:9); and (4) a saying that is the real point of the dialogue (2:10). Rudolf Bultmann has argued (*History of the Synoptic Tradition* 12–39) that almost all these dialogues are artificially constructed and reflect post-Easter disputes between the followers of Jesus and other Jewish groups, so that the questions are posed by stylized Jewish leaders.

The dispute over forgiveness of sins set in the context of the healing of the paralyzed man in 2:1-12 is the first and longest of the five controversy stories in Mark 2:1–3:6 and provides a grand opening for the collection. The present narrative weaves together two stories, and they serve mutually to interpret one another. The miracle story begins with a dramatic and disturbing action. Jesus is speaking "the word" to an overflowing audience when this quasi-religious service is rudely interrupted. The roof is torn open and a paralyzed body is let down in front of him. On seeing the litter-bearers, Jesus praises their faith and heals the paralyzed man in response to faith. Mark relates faith to miracle in different ways. In 2:1-12; 5:34 ("your faith has made you well"); 9:23; and 10:52 ("your faith has made you well"), faith precedes healing. But in 9:23 Jesus says that all things are possible to the one who believes, and in 11:23 he speaks of the faith that can move mountains. Conversely, when faith is absent as at Nazareth, Jesus can do no mighty work apart from a few healings, and he marvels at the unbelief of the people there (6:5-6). In these Markan miracles faith is not so much a precondition for healing (see 1:34; 6:5-6), but rather it dramatizes the willingness of suffering people to break through physical and social boundaries in order to approach Jesus.

The interweaving of the conflict over forgiveness with the healing of the paralyzed man not only builds on the traditional relationship between illness and sin but gives an added christological thrust to the pericope. Like God, Jesus can read hearts and know interior dispositions. The *Targum of Isaiah,* which may contain traditions from around Jesus' time, interprets Isa 53:4 ("he has borne our infirmities and carried our diseases . . . and was wounded for our transgressions") as "he will beseech concerning our sins, and our iniquities for his sake will be forgiven" and "by his teaching his peace will increase upon us, and in that we attach ourselves to his words our sins will be forgiven" (trans. Bruce D. Chilton). The hoped-for Messiah will not simply suffer for the people but will also bring forgiveness of sin. The attachment to "his words" also sheds light on the relation between faith and forgiveness.

By his placement of the story of the paralyzed man Mark highlights major themes in the unfolding narrative. Faith, as the proper response to Jesus, last mentioned in 1:15, is given flesh and blood. Faith breaks through barriers to bring a person to Jesus. The major theme of 1:16-45—Jesus as powerful in word and work (1:28)—is continued (2:10), and extends to the restoration of health or wholeness and to the forgiveness of sin. At the same time this power now evokes the kind of opposition (the charge of blasphemy) that will ultimately result in the death of Jesus (14:64). As in earlier narratives, despite Jesus' counsel to those healed not to broadcast the event (1:44; 2:12), the one liberated from suffering proclaims what has happened far and wide.

In the interwoven controversy the "Son of Man" saying is crucial for interpretation. In this first major section of the gospel (1:16–3:6) Mark constructs the grand scenario of a powerful Jesus. The two "Son of Man" sayings (2:10, 28) stress his power on earth and prepare the readers for the proper understanding of the authority of Jesus, which will unfold in the middle section (8:22–10:52)—a paradoxical authority given to a "Son of Man" (with its overtone of a "human one") that is not based on dominating power but achieved through suffering, and is to be at the service of others (10:32-45).

This short narrative provides a rich field for contemporary actualization of fundamental Christian themes. In it faith is not simply intellectual conviction but boundary-breaking activity; the faith of the litter bearers who disrupt the assembly is praised. The text also encourages reflection on the relation between sin and "paralysis." Sin can exercise such force that people are unable to move or to change. They may, like the paralyzed man, be dependent on others on the journey to health and restoration. The word of Jesus is restorative and forgiving. The one who acts as the agent of God's forgiveness and liberation may be not only misunderstood but also may evoke lethal opposition. Those touched by God's forgiveness become public witnesses to others so that they in turn can glorify God.

FOR REFERENCE AND FURTHER STUDY

Dewey, Joanna. "The Literary Structure of the Controversy Stories in Mark 2:1–3:6," *JBL* 92 (1973) 394–401.
_____. *Markan Public Debate: Literary Technique, Concentric Structure and Theology in Mark 2:1–3:6*. Chico: Scholars, 1980.

Doughty, D. J. "The Authority of the Son of Man (Mark 2,1–3,6)," *ZNW* 74 (1983) 161–81.

Dunn, James D. G. "Mark 2:1–3:6: A Bridge Between Jesus and Paul on the Question of the Law," *NTS* 30 (1984) 395–415.

Hunter, Faith and Geoffrey. "'Which is easier?' (Mk 2:9)," *ExpTim* 105 (1993) 12–13.

7. The Call of Levi and Meals with Toll Collectors and Sinners (2:13-17)

13. Once more he went out and walked along the shore of the sea; a very large crowd kept coming to him, and he began to teach them. 14. As he walked along he saw Levi the son of Alphaeus seated at the tax office; and he said to him: "Follow me." And he [Levi] stood up and followed him. 15. Then it happened that while he was at dinner in his [Levi's] house, many toll collectors and sinners were also at table with Jesus and his disciples. (They were a large number, and they also were following him.) 16. Then the scribes from the Pharisees, when they saw that he was sharing a meal with sinners and toll collectors, were asking his disciples: "Why does he share his meals with toll collectors and sinners?" 17. When he overheard this, Jesus answered them: "Those who are well do not need a doctor, but those who are sick do; I did not come to call the just, but sinners."

NOTES

13. *he went out:* This verse is transitional from the setting in the house (in 2:1-12) to the shore of the Sea of Galilee. The location "along the shore of the sea" *(para tēn thalassan)* echoes the phrase in 1:16, which is also an introduction to the calling of disciples.

   a very large crowd. . . . he began to teach them: The language here foreshadows Jesus' teaching in parables to a large crowd "beside the sea" in 4:1-2.

14. *As he walked along.* The phrase *kai paragōn* is identical with 1:16 in the first "call narrative." What this adds to the earlier call narrative is the inclusion of tax collectors and sinners, which links it up with the forgiveness of sin in the previous narrative.

   he saw Levi the son of Alphaeus: The story reproduces in condensed form the structure of the first call narrative (see the Interpretation above of 1:16-20). Only Mark calls Levi "the son of Alphaeus." Luke calls him "the tax collector, Levi" (5:27), and Matthew refers to "a man called Matthew" (9:9). Mark does not include Levi in the list of the Twelve but does include Matthew and calls James the "son of Alphaeus" (3:18; see Luke 6:15; Acts 1:13). A number of solutions have been proposed: (1) Since both characters are depicted as sitting at the toll booth, and since there is evidence for people with two Semitic names

(Acts 4:36), some scholars argue that Matthew is simply another name for Levi. (2) Others contend that Mark means to refer to two distinct people, so that Levi is a disciple but not a member of the Twelve. (3) Since both are called "son of Alphaeus," James and Levi are regarded by other scholars as the same person, a view that is weakly attested in some manuscripts. (4) Though the first four names in the list of the Twelve are identical, there is some variation in the order and the names of the final eight so that, while the number is fixed, the names vary in the tradition. Since Levi the son of Jacob and Leah (Gen 29:34) was the eponymous ancestor of the Levites, there may be some irony in so naming a member of a rejected profession, a tax collector (see below).

seated at the tax office: The seaside near Capernaum would be expected to be the location of a tax office or customs booth *(telōnion)*, since the *Via Maris*, the trade route from Damascus to Caesarea Maritima, ran through this area. In Galilee during the ministry of Jesus a wide variety of taxes and tolls were collected. Since Galilee was not under direct Roman rule (in contrast to Judea), these taxes supported Herod Antipas. Galileans (like all Jews) were also subject to the half-shekel Temple tax which goes back to Nehemiah's original one-third shekel tax (Neh 10:32). Josephus *(Ant.* 18.312) and Philo *(Special Laws* 1:77) state that even Jews outside Palestine paid this tax.

Follow me: See 1:16-20, especially v. 18. The verbal forms of "follow" *(akolouthein)* are used frequently in Mark for discipleship; see 5:37; 6:1; 8:34; 10:21; and 10:32.

and he [Levi] stood up and followed him: The immediacy of the response is stressed. The verb "stood up" *(anastas* from *anistēmi)*, while used for the physical action of change from rest to motion, becomes a metaphor for the resurrection of Jesus (see Mark 8:31; 9:31; 10:34; 12:23, 25; and Acts 2:24, 32; 13:32, 34).

15. *Then it happened:* The traditional introductory formula *kai ginetai* ("it happened, came to pass," with the historical present substituting for the normal aorist *egeneto)* suggests an interval of time between the call of Levi and the dinner.

while he was at dinner: Literally "he reclined (at table)." Jews, Greeks, and Romans at larger or festive gatherings ate while reclining on couches, lying on their left elbow. The verb can also simply mean "dine" or "have a meal with." Mark depicts this as a large gathering (with Jesus, his disciples, and many tax collectors and "sinners").

in his [Levi's] house: The Greek simply reads "his house," which could conceivably be the house of Jesus, though this is less likely in terms of vv. 16-17.

toll collectors: Older translations used "publican" for *telōnēs* ("toll collector" or "tax collector"). The classical "publican" system whereby taxes were "farmed out" to rich and often venal collectors was discontinued by Julius Caesar shortly before his death in 44 B.C.E. Under Herod the Great (37–4 B.C.E.) taxes were collected by royal officials. His son Herod Antipas followed this practice in Galilee. The *telōnai* of the Gospels were most likely minor employees of royal officials who collected taxes at customs booths. In Roman and Hellenistic literature they are lumped together with beggars, thieves, and robbers

(Cicero, *De officiis* 15-21; Dio Chrysostom, *Orations* 14.14); and the *Mishnah* links them to robbers, murderers, and sinners (*m. Toh.* 7:6; *B. Qam.* 10:2; *Ned.* 3:4). In the NT they are paired with sinners (*hamartōloi;* see Mark 2:15; Matt 9:10; 11:19; Luke 7:34; 15:1) and with sexually immoral people (*pornai;* see Matt 21:31; Luke 18:11), and are likened to Gentiles (Matt 5:46; 18:17).

and sinners: The adjective *hamartōloi* (lit. "sinful ones") is used as a noun. "Sinners" were not primarily people who committed occasional transgressions, but rather those who lived outside the Law in a constant and fundamental way (e.g., "Gentile sinners" in Gal 2:15).

with Jesus and his disciples: This is the first use of "disciple" *(mathētēs)* for followers of Jesus in Mark. The noun derives from the verb *manthanein* and means literally "a learner."

They were a large number . . . also were following him: This parenthetical sentence functions as an explanatory comment to the reader. Given the use of "follow" in the call of Levi, Mark suggests here that Jesus had a large number of followers and that some of them came from the "toll collectors and sinners."

16. *The scribes from the Pharisees:* About the scribes, see the Note on 1:22. The Pharisees (most likely from the Hebrew word for "separated ones") were a movement of strictly observant and influential Jews that began in the second century B.C.E. Josephus describes them along with the Sadducees, Essenes, and the "Fourth Philosophy" as one of the Jewish "philosophies," that is, a school of thought teaching a way of life (*War* 2.159-66; *Ant.* 13.171-73, 297-98; 18.11-12). They were a lay movement which stressed the sovereignty of God in every area of life. They were popular with the people at large and were noted for their strict observance and creative interpretation of the Law. They valued oral tradition as well as the written Law and believed in divine providence and in life after death. They appear here first in Mark and subsequently in 2:18, 24; 3:6; 7:1, 3, 5; 8:11, 15; 10:2; and 12:13. They are always in conflict with Jesus over his actions or interpretation of the Law. They do not appear in the Passion narrative nor are they mentioned as directly involved in the death of Jesus. Despite the generally negative NT picture of the Pharisees, they "were the real spiritual leaders of the nation, and their ideas were to prove decisive for the future character of Judaism" (see C.E.B. Cranfield, *St Mark* 105), since rabbinic Judaism developed out of their movement. Since scribes were not a movement but a profession, the wording "from the Pharisees" indicates that some Pharisees functioned as scribes.

Why does he share his meals with toll collectors and sinners: In the space of three verses the phrase "toll collectors and sinners" is repeated three times, giving verbal emphasis to the central thrust of the narrative. "Sharing meals" translates the Greek *esthiei* ("he eats"). The present tense suggests customary action. These two groups are symbolic of people who are religiously and socially marginal.

17. *Those who are well do not need a doctor, but those who are sick do:* Hellenistic literature stressed the duty of the physician to be with the sick (Diogenes Laertius, *Lives* 6.6; Plutarch, *Moralia* 230-31), and often portrayed the philosopher as a

physician, with vice as the illness (Dio Chrysostom, *Orations* 32.14-30; Epicte-
tus, *Discourses* 3.23, 30). For a similar Jewish perspective see Sir 38:1-5. Here
the aphorism functions as a defense of Jesus' action. In light of Sir 38:2 ("the
gift of healing comes from the Most High") there could be an implicit christological claim here. Jesus mediates healing as he did forgiveness in the previous narrative.

I did not come: This is one of two Markan sayings (see also 1:38), along with
10:45 ("the Son of Man did not come to be served but to serve"), where Jesus
speaks explicitly of his "coming." Both appear in the context of forgiveness of
sin ("to give his life as a ransom for many," 10:45b).

to call the just, but sinners: "Call" *(kalein)*, or its intensive form "summon"
(proskalein), suggest "a call to be a follower of Jesus" (1:20; 3:13; 6:7; 8:1; 10:42;
12:43).

the just: A common English translation of the Greek adjective *dikaios* is "righteous." The "just" are those whose style of life is "right" with God and with
their fellow humans. Since the Law is the revelation of God's way of justice,
those habitually outside the Law, like toll collectors, are regarded as "not
right" with God or society. Psalm 37 (LXX 36) is a dramatic act of faith that the
righteous will be rewarded and the wicked *(hamartōloi)* will be punished.
Righteousness is a major theme of the Pharisaic *Psalms of Solomon* (first century B.C.E.) as is the hope for a coming "Son of David" who will "expel sinners
from the inheritance" and "reprove sinners by the word of their own hearts"
(Pss. Sol. 17:23, 25). The saying of Jesus here, while not rejecting "the just,"
would challenge the worldview of many of his hearers who expected that
"sinners" must either convert or suffer divine retribution.

INTERPRETATION

The second "controversy" is really a combination of two interrelated
narratives, the calling of Levi the toll collector (2:13-14) and Jesus' table
fellowship with toll collectors and sinners (2:15-17). Both narratives deal
with sin, implicitly in 2:13-14 and explicitly in 2:15-16, and both culminate
in the saying of 2:17.

In handing on this material Mark presents an accurate representation
of the historical Jesus. Not only Mark here but also Q (Luke 7:34; Matt
11:19), as well as the Lukan special material (Luke 15:1-2; 19:1-10), attest to
Jesus' practice of sharing meals with tax collectors and "sinners," a practice that would hardly have been created by the early church since it
served to discredit Jesus. Jesus' association with such persons is an "acted
parable" of God's offer of mercy and forgiveness (Matt 9:13 adds Hos 6:6,
"I desire mercy and not sacrifice," to Mark 2:17).

As E. P. Sanders has observed in *The Historical Figure of Jesus* (London:
Penguin, 1993, 225–33), what is noteworthy about this fellowship with tax
collectors and sinners in Mark and Matthew is the absence of any explicit

exhortation by Jesus that they must repent (in contrast to Luke 5:32, who alters Mark 2:17 to "I have not come to call the just, but sinners *to repentance*"). Other than Levi/Matthew there is no indication that the toll collectors abandoned their profession after contact with Jesus. This practice of Jesus, according to Sanders, amounted to a simple message that God loved these people and that they would be part of the kingdom being inaugurated by Jesus. This was offensive to Jesus' contemporaries on two counts: "Jesus did not try to enforce the commandments of the Jewish law that stipulate how one changes from being wicked to being upright; Jesus regarded himself as having the right to say who would be in the kingdom" (ibid. 236).

Both in the tradition before Mark and in Mark this practice distinguishes Jesus from John the Baptist. In Mark 1:4-5 John preaches a baptism of repentance for the forgiveness of sin, and people publicly confess their sins. In Q John explicitly calls for repentance (Luke 3:7-9; Matt 3:7-10), and while Mark points simply to a "stronger one" who will come after him (1:7), in Q this stronger one will clear the threshing floor, separate the wheat from the chaff, and throw the chaff into the fire (Luke 3:16-17; Matt 3:11-12). The Q expectation is closer to the messianic hopes of *Pss. Sol.* 17.

There is also a radical difference in both Mark and Q between Jesus and John the Baptist. John expects public confession of sin (Mark) and repentance (Q) as a prelude to communion with God. However, Jesus practices communion, which in the case of Luke leads to repentance but in Mark and Matthew simply symbolizes God's presence among the marginal and God's concern for sinners. Though there may be a hint of repentance in the Markan image of the physician who would be expected to heal the sick (that is, sinners), this idea is not developed.

When 2:13-17 is linked to 2:1-12 our understanding of the Markan Jesus is enriched. Jesus is the "Son of Man" who has the authority to forgive sins. But this authority and power are manifest when a "sinner" who is a toll collector follows him and when he joins in table fellowship with many toll collectors and sinners who, like Levi, follow him. Forgiveness is not merely an external or juridical pronouncement but a new relationship and a new community, the community of sinners who yet are followers of Jesus.

It is somewhat surprising that this image of Jesus sharing meals with marginal people ("sinners") handed on by Mark and Q seems to have had little influence in the early church. Some of the most bitter disputes arose precisely over table fellowship with groups who for one reason or another were considered sinners or unworthy (see Gal 2:11-14, where Peter refuses to eat with Gentiles; 1 Corinthians 8–10; Rom 14:1–15:13).

These narratives provide a continuing challenge to Christian churches. Every denomination has both an ethic and an ethos, that is, accepted ways of behavior that embody a life in fidelity to the biblical vision. Though sinners, Christians strive to live "justly" in their relations to God and neighbor. Yet the practice of Jesus depicted here manifests a preference for the marginal (see also the Q parable of the lost sheep in Luke 15:4-7 and Matt 18:12-14). Churches today are challenged to expend their energy and resources not only on the "well" and the strong but also (and especially) on those who need healing and a sense of divine acceptance.

FOR REFERENCE AND FURTHER STUDY

Donahue, John R. "Tax Collectors and Sinners: An Attempt at Identification," *CBQ* 33 (1971) 39–61.

Malbon, Elizabeth Struthers. *"Tę oikią autou:* Mark 2:15 in Context," *NTS* 331 (1985) 282–92.

May, David M. "Mark 2.15: The Home of Jesus or Levi?" *NTS* 39 (1993) 147–49.

8. *Fasting, Torn Garments, and New Wineskins* (2:18-22)

18. And the disciples of John and the Pharisees were accustomed to fast. Some people came forward and said to him: "Why is it that John's disciples and the disciples of the Pharisees fast, but your disciples do not fast?" 19. Then Jesus responded to them: "The wedding guests cannot fast when the groom is with them, can they? As long as they have the groom with them, they cannot fast. 20. But the days will come when the groom will have been taken away from them; then they will fast on that day. 21. No one sews a patch of unshrunken cloth on an old cloak; otherwise the piece that covers the hole will rip off, that is, the new from the old, and the tear will be even worse. 22. Nor does anyone put new wine into old leather wineskins; otherwise the wine will split the skins, and both the wine and the skins will be destroyed; but new wine is for fresh wineskins."

NOTES

18. *The disciples of John:* The geographical location of this pericope on fasting and its appended sayings is unclear. It could be at the house of Levi or at Jesus' house (see 2:15). Also 2:18a could be an editorial explanation for readers outside of Palestine (see 7:3-4). The questioners of 2:18b are most likely not the disciples of John and of the Pharisees, since they would not speak of themselves in the third person (see Matt 9:14, which identifies the questioners as "we"). At this point in the narrative John is in prison (1:14). While no disciples are mentioned at John's initial appearance (1:4-8), in the retrospective narrative

of his execution (6:17-29) his disciples attend to his burial. In John's Gospel the disciples of Jesus come from the ranks of John's disciples (see John 1:35-42), and in Acts some people know only of John's baptism of repentance (see Acts 18:25; 19:3-4). The Baptist movement continued after John's arrest and death in a manner different from the "Jesus movement." After Jesus' death his disciples fasted and proclaimed a baptism like that of John.

and the disciples of the Pharisees: Mark may here simply mean those who learn and follow the Pharisaic way of life (see Matt 23:15). This designation links the pericope with the preceding one ("the scribes of the Pharisees") and prepares for the dispute that follows.

were accustomed to fast: Literally "were fasting," a periphrastic imperfect to express habitual action. Fasting (*nēstuein,* from the negative prefix and a form of the verb "to eat") as total abstention from food and drink (see Esth 4:16) has a long history in Judaism (see John B. Muddiman, "Fast, Fasting," *ABD* 2:773–76). Public fasting is associated with rites of mourning, repentance, and prayers of supplication (see 2 Sam 12:23; 2 Chr 20:3; Joel 1:14; 2:15; Ezra 8:21; Jon 3:5; Jer 36:9; Pss 35:13; 69:10; 109:24). It symbolizes self-effacement and trust in God. Though the Day of Atonement is the only annual national fast prescribed in the OT (Leviticus 16), public fasts could be proclaimed on special occasions (Neh 9:1; Zech 8:19; Joel 2:12-13). Luke 18:12 indicates that the observant Pharisee fasted twice a week, and *Didache* 8:1 implies the same when urging Christians to fast on different days "from the hypocrites" (see Matt 6:16). There is, however, no rabbinic evidence for fasting as a set practice prior to 70 C.E., and no evidence in the NT itself for set days of Christian fasting. The prophets criticized "inauthentic" fasting when not joined to works of justice and love of neighbor (Isa 58:3-9; Jer 14:12; cf. Matt 6:16). Various forms of the verb "to fast" *(nēsteuein)* appear five times in two verses, which suggests "catchword" composition and editorial comments.

some people came forward: Though these are unspecified, the readers may understand the questioners as "the scribes of the Pharisees" in 2:16 who posed the last question about Jesus' eating practices.

but your disciples do not fast: This is the point of the controversy. Since the teacher was responsible for the behavior of his disciples, the challenge is implicitly to Jesus. The Q tradition implies that Jesus himself did not fast, since his practice is contrasted with that of John who came "neither eating nor drinking," while Jesus is called a "glutton and a drunkard, a friend of tax collectors and sinners" (Luke 7:31-35; Matt 11:16-19).

19. *Then Jesus responded:* In a manner reflective of later rabbinic literature the response unfolds in one parabolic counter-question and two further parabolic sayings, which are themselves implicit questions. All of these tease out the answer "no," thereby vindicating Jesus in debate.

The wedding guests: In Greek the sentence begins with *mē,* which expects a negative reply. "Wedding guests" translates the literal "sons of the wedding hall" (see Matt 22:10) and can mean either the wedding guests or the groom's attendants. Arguments exist for either translation. In favor of "wedding guests" is the inclusive nature of Jesus' "feasting" described in 2:13-17 (disciples along with toll collectors and sinners), while the criticism of the disciples in 2:18 would suggest a parallel between them and the groom's attendants.

the groom: In the OT God is metaphorically described as the spouse of Israel (Hos 2:16-20; Isa 54:4-8; 62:4; Jer 2:2; 31:32; Ezek 16:7-14). The NT uses this imagery with regard to Christ and the church (Matt 22:1-14; 25:1-13; 2 Cor 11:2; Eph 5:22-32; Rev 19:7, 9; 22:17). There is no evidence that "bridegroom" was used of an expected messianic figure in pre-Christian Judaism.

As long as . . . cannot fast: The text here shows signs of editing in transmission. The first part of 2:19 could be a simple response to the challenge and would be more effective in forcing the hearers to answer the question themselves. The second half (2:19b), "as long as," which allegorizes the saying and fits better with 2:20, represents Mark's adaptation of the early Christian "spousal" imagery to the situation of his community. Both Matthew and Luke omit Mark 2:19b.

20. *But the days will come:* Elsewhere this phrase suggests an eschatological event (Luke 17:22; 21:6; Jer 16:14; 19:6; 23:5 [LXX]). Verse 20 in Greek is chiastic: (A) days will come; (B) the groom will be removed; (B') they will fast; and (A') on that day. This pattern calls attention to the reason for fasting and shifts the thrust of the saying from a defense of the disciples' practice of not fasting to a Passion prediction.

will have been taken away: The use of the Greek aorist passive subjunctive (*aparthē*) between the two futures "will come" and "will fast" suggests action antecedent to the fasting and heightens the removal of the groom (Guelich, *Mark* 112). Since the groom would normally leave the feast rather than be removed, the allusion is most likely to the violent death of Jesus. The verb, which is never used elsewhere of the violent death or of the "removal" of Jesus, receives this nuance here because of an intertextual echo of the fate of the Servant in Isaiah 53:8 ("his life will be taken from [*airetai*] the earth . . . and he will be led to death" [LXX]).

then they will fast on that day: "That day" stands in tension with "the days will come," and may reflect the practice of Mark's readers to fast on a particular day, perhaps in memory of Jesus' death. *Didache* 8:1 notes that early Christians did fast on Wednesdays and Fridays.

21. *No one sews . . . old cloak:* The next two parabolic statements may have been independent and are joined here by the theme of new versus old, as well as by the association of clothing (Matt 22:11-14) and wine (John 2:1-11) with a wedding feast. The saying reflects a social location of ordinary people who must mend their clothes rather than the rich who dress in fine robes (see Matt 11:8). A patch made of cloth that is not prewashed will shrink and pull away from the original garment. The "cloak" is the *himation*, the main outer garment, a rectangular cloth worn by both men and women that could be draped around the body (5:15, 27, 28, 30; 6:56; 9:3; 10:50; 11:7, 8; 13:16; 15:20, 24), in contrast to the *chitōn*, the "tunic," two pieces of cloth sewn together with openings for the head and arms, and worn closest to the skin (6:9; 14:63).

the new from the old: Since the sentence would flow evenly without this phrase it seems redundant and most likely is an addition by the evangelist to link this saying to the following one.

22. *new wine:* Wine was produced by two pressings of grapes with the juice then allowed to ferment. In new wine the fermentation is not complete. Wine was a staple of life in the ancient world (Sir 39:26; Eccl 10:19; Deut 11:14; Joel 1:10).

old leather wineskins: The fermenting wine was stored either in earthenware jugs that could hold up to ten gallons or in leather skins. Again this image shows the practice of ordinary people who were storing wine for family use.

the wine will split the skins . . . destroyed: The old skins that have been used often for fermenting would have expanded to their capacity. If new wine is put in them they will split open during fermentation, so that the loss will be complete.

new wine is for fresh wineskins: The sayings on mending the garment and on wineskins stress the opposition between the old and the new. In both sayings there is a sense of a process that must take place (shrinking, fermenting) and of a passage of time that will bring about the ultimate incompatibility of the old and the new.

INTERPRETATION

The dispute about fasting (2:18-20) and the two parabolic sayings on patching garments and on wineskins (2:21-22) form the centerpiece of the five controversies and help to interpret the surrounding material. The two previous narratives (2:1-12; 2:13-17) dealt with the forgiveness of sin, and the two that follow (2:23-28; 3:1-6) treat Sabbath regulations. Both topics were cornerstones of Jewish belief in the first century. The controversy of 2:18-22 with the removal of the groom as its own centerpiece hints at the cost of the stance that the Markan Jesus takes toward these fundamental beliefs.

The initial controversy (2:18-20) displays the familiar form of an action or saying that evokes opposition or a hostile question followed by a response, and defends the religious practice of Jesus' disciples and implicitly Jesus. The point of the story is that the "now" of Jesus' ministry in contrast to the "then" of the absence of the groom is a time for festive rejoicing, for eating and drinking, similar to a wedding banquet. The grounds for the rejoicing have unfolded in the previous narratives. People are summoned to hear the good news of the victory of God over evil, illness, and sin. Even those thought to be habitually outside the pale of God's forgiveness are welcomed to the banquet. Yet the time will come when Jesus' followers will mourn and fast, when the bridegroom is removed. This saying reflects the historical situation of the Markan community, which exists "between the times": between the past time of Jesus whose life is proclaimed to them and the future time when the Son of Man will return to gather his elect.

The two sayings on the incompatibility of the old and the new in 2:21-22 have strong claims to echo the voice of Jesus. But they have received widely different interpretations by Matthew and Luke, which suggests that Mark has also adapted them to the situation of his community. Matthew (in 9:14-17) follows Mark very closely until 9:17 when he adds to Mark 2:22, "and so both are preserved." The new and old are not so much incompatible as transformed. This reflects Matthew's view that his community preserves in a special and legitimate way the heritage of Judaism (see Matt 5:17-20). Luke (in 5:33-39) reformulates Mark's saying on the garment to "No one tears a piece *from a new garment,* and puts it on an old; if he does, he will tear the new, and the piece from the new will not match the old" (5:36). This radicalizes the incompatibility from the perspective of "the new" (Luke's Christian community). Luke adds (in 5:39) a proverb that at first glance seems to contradict the two previous sayings: "No one after drinking old wine desires the new, for he says 'the old is good.'" In the Lukan context the point seems rather to be that those who have become enamored of old practices will not be ready for the new.

The removal of the bridegroom and the following two sayings expand the controversy into a brief allegorical reflection on the relation of Jesus' new teaching with power (see 1:27) to the religious practices of his contemporaries. Jesus takes dramatic action (eating with tax collectors and sinners) and proposes vivid aphorisms to stress the presence of the "good news about God" (1:14-15) that is unfolding in his ministry. Though it is impossible to detect in exact detail Mark's redaction of individual sayings, the context of a controversy collection, and especially the allusion to Isa 53:8 on the "removal" of the bridegroom (the Servant) reflect the cost of the practice of Jesus and the stance of the Markan community toward the parent Judaism at a time when the two groups are beginning to "tear apart." The images of shrinking and fermenting suggest that this split has widened over a long period, dating back to the time of Jesus.

The tension, and often incompatibility, between the old and the new is part of every religious tradition and attends every change within that tradition. Matthew and Luke wrestled with it and adapted it to their community situation. Contemporary Christians have no less a challenge.

FOR REFERENCE AND FURTHER STUDY

Ziesler, John A. "The Removal of the Bridegroom: A Note on Mk II, 18-22 and Parallels," *NTS* 19 (1973) 190–94.

9. *Plucking Grain on the Sabbath* (2:23-28)

23. One Sabbath he happened to be walking through some fields of standing grain; and as they walked along, his disciples began plucking heads of the grain. 24. Then the Pharisees were remarking to him: "Look, why are they doing what is not permitted on the sabbath?" 25. And he answered: "Have you never read what David did, where there was need and he and his followers were hungry? 26. How he went right into the house of God when Abiathar was high priest, and he ate the loaves of bread prepared for the offering," (it is unlawful for anyone to eat these except the priests), "and he gave them to his followers." 27. Then he said to them, "The Sabbath was made for humans, and not humans for the Sabbath; 28. so that the Son of Man is lord even of the Sabbath."

NOTES

23. *One Sabbath:* The Greek dative plural form *tois sabbasin* (see 1:21) is from Hebrew *šabbat*, which refers to the day of "rest," the seventh day of the week. While the plural is used here in the singular sense, in 2:28 the singular form is used. The two occurrences of "Sabbath" provide an *inclusio* to the whole narrative in 2:23-28.

as they walked along: Literally "as they were making their way" *(hodon poiein)*. Another translation is possible: "they began to make their way through the fields." In this case the image would be that the disciples pushed the grain aside and cut through the field. In favor of our translation is that *hodon poiein* is a Latinism *(iter facere)* that can mean simply "to journey."

plucking heads of the grain: Deuteronomy 23:25 states: "If you go into your neighbor's standing grain, you may pluck the ears with your hand, but you may not put a sickle to your neighbor's standing grain." As the pericope unfolds, the point of controversy will not be taking food from the neighbor but rather that the disciples' actions implicitly constituted "work" on the Sabbath.

24. *The Pharisees:* In the five controversies there is a stylized escalation in the opponents (from some scribes in 2:6 through "scribes of the Pharisees" in 2:16 and Pharisees in 2:24 to "Pharisees and Herodians" in 3:6) and in intensity (from murmuring in 2:6 to a lethal compact to kill Jesus in 3:6).

why are they doing what is not permitted on the sabbath?: Sabbath rest is one of the most distinctive aspects of Israel's faith. Three theological perspectives ground this practice in the OT: (1) On the seventh day God completed the work of creation, and "God blessed the seventh day and hallowed it, because God rested from all the work that he had done in creation" (Gen 2:2); (2) the Sabbath is a day to remember the liberation from Egypt (Deut 5:14-15); and (3) Sabbath observance recalls the Sinai covenant as a "sign between me and you" and is itself "a perpetual covenant" (Exod 31:12-17). The most developed commandment in the Decalogue concerns the Sabbath rest (Exod 20:8-11; Deut 5:12-15). According to Exod 31:14 "whoever profanes it [the Sabbath] shall be put to death; whoever does any work on the Sabbath day shall be cut off from among the people" (see Exod 31:15; 35:2; and Num 15:32-36, where a man is stoned to death for gathering sticks on the Sabbath). Even amid the great pluralism that characterized Judaism in the first century, Sabbath observance was widely maintained. The ordinary people in Palestine as well as rigorist reform movements like the Dead Sea sect observed it strictly (CD 10:14–11:18; *Jub* 2:29-30; 50:6-13), and its observance by Jews in the Greco-Roman Diaspora evoked both admiration (Josephus, *Against Apion* 2.238; Philo, *Vit. Mos.* 2:21) and scorn (Josephus, *Against Apion* 2.20-21; Juvenal, *Satires* 14.96-105; Tacitus, *Histories* 5.5). Since the Sabbath rest had such profound religious significance and was regarded as essential to Jewish identity, and since its violation was fraught with penalties, a large corpus of legal interpretation developed among Jewish groups to determine just what constituted "work" or other violations of the Sabbath law.

what is not permitted: The "violation" here is committed by Jesus' disciples and not by Jesus, and its precise nature is obscure. Eating the standing grain was permitted (see the Note on 2:23). Among some Jewish groups their action might be equivalent to "harvesting grain," which was prohibited (Exod 34:21; *Jub* 2:29-30; 50:6-13; *m. Shab.* 7:2). They might also have violated the prohibition against eating on the Sabbath something not prepared in advance (CD 10:22). While Mark does not mention "eating," Matthew (12:1) and Luke (6:1) say that the disciples plucked and ate, which brings Jesus' biblical defense (since David and his followers presumably ate) into line with the charge.

25. *Have you never read:* The question (which is slightly ironic = surely you must have read) is an argument in favor of a rather high level of literacy in Palestine and in the Greco-Roman world.

what David did: The reference is to 1 Sam 21:1-6 (LXX 21:2-7), but with significant alterations of the OT narrative where (1) David has no companions with him; (2) there is no mention of hunger; (3) David does not enter the house of God; (4) the priest (not high priest) is Ahimelech, not Abiathar; and (5) neither David nor his companions eat the bread of presence (Gundry, *Mark* 141). Mark (or the tradition he received) freely rewrote the OT narrative to fit the controversy. The argument in this verse is from the Christian perspective of Mark's readers, and it proceeds "from the lesser to the greater." Since later, in 12:35-37 (see Ps 110:1) David will call Jesus "Lord" (12:36), Jesus can even exceed David's violation.

26. *the loaves of bread prepared for the offering:* This follows exactly the LXX's *artous tēs protheseōs*, and refers to the twelve specially baked loaves that Aaron is to set before the tabernacle on every Sabbath and that are to be eaten only by priests (see Lev 24:5-8). The phrase is variously translated as "shewbread," "bread of the presence," or "consecrated bread." Neither David nor his followers, whom he is to meet later, actually eat the bread (see 1 Sam 21:1-10).

It is unlawful . . . except the priests: This is most likely an explanatory or parenthetical comment by the evangelist rather than part of the saying of Jesus. The sentence would flow more smoothly if "he gave" followed immediately after "he ate . . . the offering." Elsewhere the evangelist explains Jewish customs to his readers (see 7:3-4).

27. *The Sabbath was made for humans, and not humans for the Sabbath:* The sentence forms a perfect chiasm: (A) Sabbath, (B) humankind, (B') humankind, (A') Sabbath. The device rhetorically stresses the primacy of the human person *(anthrōpos)* over the Sabbath, and prepares for the subsequent "Son of Man" *(ho huios tou anthrōpou)* saying. This saying is not in opposition to Jewish teaching, which did recognize serious human needs as grounds for setting aside Sabbath prescriptions. In 1 Macc 2:41 Mattathias and his friends decide to fight on the Sabbath rather than die as their kindred did (1 Macc 2:34-38). And a saying attributed to R. Simeon b. Menasyra (c. 180 C.E.) states: "The Sabbath was delivered to you, and not you to the Sabbath" (Guelich, *Mark* 124). The saying reflects Mark's view that Jesus returns to the original intent of the Law by rejecting later traditions (see 7:9-13; 10:2-9). The Sabbath commemorates God's creative and saving action for humanity, and alleviating hunger might be an example. Both Matthew (12:7) and Luke (6:5) omit this saying.

28. *so that the Son of Man is lord even of the Sabbath:* The result clause "so that" does not follow simply from the previous saying but sums up the theology of the whole pericope. The term "lord" *(kyrios)* is capitalized in some translations as if it were the christological title that is used frequently in traditions earlier than Mark (e.g., 1 Thess 1:2, 3, 6, 8; Phil 2:11; see also Acts 2:36; 4:33). However, since *kyrios* is not one of Mark's primary titles for Jesus (but see 12:36), the term here probably simply means "lord" in the sense of possessing authority over someone or something.

INTERPRETATION

With this fourth controversy the ground of the debate shifts from forgiveness of sins and table fellowship with habitual sinners to Sabbath observance. At the same time the middle three pericopes (2:13-17, 18-22, 23-28) deal with eating and drinking. In two of these (2:18-22, 23-28) Jesus defends the actions of his disciples rather than his own. There is also a linear escalation in the controversies, since Sabbath observance is central to Jewish belief and since the opposition mounts toward a final conspiracy to kill Jesus (3:6).

Though seemingly simple, the narrative in 2:23-28 contains a host of problems. In an account of the ministry of Jesus it seems improbable that Pharisees would be shadowing Jesus and his followers in Galilean wheatfields. Also, very little in Jesus' appeal to the OT in 2:25-26 corresponds to the actual OT text of 1 Sam 21:1-7. If the Pharisees had read "what David did" (v. 25) they would be as puzzled by Jesus' interpretation as are many modern readers. Also 2:27, 28 seem at first glance to be independent sayings that do not really sum up the thrust of this narrative.

The substance of this controversy concerns Sabbath observance. The action of Jesus' disciples constitutes for the Pharisees a violation of what is permitted on the Sabbath. Jesus responds by citing the example of David. The passage alluded to is from the cycle of narratives where David flees from the wrath of Saul. He goes to the shrine of Nob (called "the house of God" in Mark anachronistically, since the Jerusalem Temple was yet to be built), and tricks the priest into giving him five of the loaves of presence and the sword of Goliath. As noted, there is little correspondence in essential details, such as the explicit mention of hunger or the presence of David's companions. Mark puts on the lips of Jesus a "Christian interpretation" in which the main point of comparison is that things consecrated to God (such as the bread and the Sabbath) are not absolute values in themselves but exist for the sake of humanity (David's need and the disciples' hunger). This leads naturally to the saying about the purpose of the Sabbath.

Jesus' relation to the Sabbath is discussed in all the Gospels, though more so in Matthew than Mark. Certain clarifications are important. The Markan Jesus never questions the sacredness of the Sabbath. He participates in synagogue services on the Sabbath (1:21; 3:1; 6:2). People around him observe the Sabbath; in 1:32 the sick are brought only after sundown, and in 16:1 the women followers wait until after the Sabbath to visit the tomb. The only two Sabbath controversies in Mark appear in 2:23-28 and 3:1-6, and the issue is never the abrogation or disparagement of the biblical Sabbath but how "work" is to be interpreted (a topic of lively debate in first-century Judaism). In both cases the actions of Jesus fit in with a "restorationist" eschatology (see 10:2-9) where his ministry is the harbinger of a return to the original will of God at creation in preparation for the gathering of the elect.

The "Son of Man" saying in 2:28, even if added by Mark, constitutes the theological apex of the pericope. In the first two controversies over forgiveness (2:1-12, 13-17), Jesus' mission is epitomized by a Son of Man saying: "The Son of Man has authority on earth to forgive sin" (2:10). The final two controversies are likewise crystallized in the saying about the Son of Man's lordship over the Sabbath (2:28). Both of these sayings echo and carry forward the theme of authority *(exousia)* with which Mark's Gospel began. They also foreshadow the next set of Son of Man sayings, those between 8:22 and 10:52, where the role of the Son of Man is defined as that of the one who will suffer and give his life for others (8:31; 9:31; 10:33-34).

Though it would not be perfectly accurate to equate Jewish Sabbath observance with Christian religious obligations today, this incident can be applied in various ways to contemporary church life. Christians must constantly reassess the meaning and function of their "holy" institutions and rites in terms of both their original intent and their continuing service of human needs. Also they might attempt to recapture the rationale for the Jewish Sabbath observance. The Sabbath was a day of rest intended to memorialize the holiness of creation and liberation from slavery. The Christian "Sunday" is also a memorial of creation and of new creation as well as of the liberation achieved through the cross. In our overly commercialized society the churches may need to recover a sense of Sabbath (Sunday) "rest" if people are to experience that it was made for the sake of humans and not humans for its sake.

FOR REFERENCE AND FURTHER STUDY

Casey, P. M. "Culture and Historicity: The Plucking of the Grain (Mark 2,23-28)," *NTS* 34 (1988) 1–23.
Hultgren, Arland J. "The Formation of the Sabbath Pericope in Mark 2,23-28," *JBL* 91 (1972) 38–43.
Kister, Menahem. "Plucking on the Sabbath and Christian-Jewish Polemic," *Immanuel* 24–25 (1990) 35–51.
Morgan, C. S. "When Abiathar Was High Priest (Mark 2:26)," *JBL* 98 (1979) 409–10.
Parrott, Rod. "Conflict and Rhetoric in Mark 2:23-28," *Semeia* 64 (1993) 117–37.

10. *Healing on a Sabbath* (3:1-6)

1. Once again he [Jesus] entered the synagogue. A man who had a withered hand was there. 2. And they observed him carefully to see whether he would heal him on the Sabbath, in order that they might bring a charge against him. 3. And he said to the man, the one with the withered hand: "Stand up so everyone can see you." 4. He then said to the others: "Is it lawful to do good on the Sabbath or to do evil, to save or destroy life?" But they said nothing. 5. But in anger he looked around at all of them, and was deeply grieved at the hardness of their hearts. He then said to the man: "Stretch out your hand." He held it out, and immediately his hand was restored. 6. The Pharisees left, and immediately they began to consult over him with the Herodians, on how they might destroy him.

NOTES

1. *he entered the synagogue:* Jesus' initial act of power (1:21-28), which introduces the first major section of the gospel, was in a synagogue; the summary in 1:39

notes that he was preaching "in all the synagogues" of Galilee; and the first major section ends in a synagogue (3:1-6). While the first sojourn in the synagogue ended with amazement at "his new teaching with authority" (1:27), this visit ends with a plan to kill him (3:6), recapitulating in miniature the plot of the whole gospel.

A man who had a withered hand was there: The sentence structure in Greek, which highlights the presence of the man/human being *(anthrōpos),* shows the kind of person for whose sake the Son of Man has authority over the Sabbath. The perfect passive participle of "withered" *(exērammenen,* see 4:6) suggests a longstanding malady, perhaps from birth.

2. *observed him carefully:* The Greek verb *(paretēroun)* and its nominal forms are used for medical "observation" as well as for describing strict religious observance.

   whether he would heal him on the Sabbath: Treatment of illness is not mentioned among the thirty-nine explicit violations of the Sabbath in *m. Shab* 7:2. Apparently the physical action involved in healing would not constitute a violation, since in *m. Yoma* 8:6 Rabbi Mattiah b. Harash says that it is allowed to give medicine when a life-threatening illness may exist and "any matter of doubt as to danger to life overrides the prohibitions of the Sabbath." But there were wide variations in interpreting the Sabbath prohibitions. For example, the Essenes forbade useless talk and speaking about wealth or riches on the Sabbath (CD 10:17-19). For the rigorists who produced *Jubilees* even talking about work that one intended to do constituted a violation of the Sabbath *(Jub* 50:8).

   in order that they might bring a charge: "Charge" *(katēgorēsōsin)* is a juridical term used of a legal charge against someone (see 15:3-4) or of charging someone before God's tribunal (1 Macc 7:6; 2 Macc 10:13).

3. *he said to the man:* The beginnings of 3:3 and 4 parallel each other in order to contrast "the man" and "the others."

   Stand up . . . see you: The Greek literally reads "rise up *(egeire)* into the middle." The verb "rise up" is associated with healings in 1:31; 2:9, 11, 12; 5:41; and 10:49, and carries overtones of the restoration of health and even of life itself (resurrection). Its use here alerts the readers to the actual healing in 3:5.

4. *the others:* Lit., "them." At this point the observers are not identified as Pharisees, though this can be presumed from 3:6 ("the Pharisees left").

   Is it lawful: The rhetorical question "Is it lawful?" *(exestin)* recalls the charge against the disciples in 2:24 and the action of David in 2:26.

   to do good on the Sabbath or to do evil: This is the first of two antithetical statements, along with "to save or destroy life." It is in one sense a "trick" question since anyone present at the synagogue would answer that it is lawful to do good and unlawful to do evil. The point of the question is really, "What constitutes doing good or evil?"

   to save or to destroy life: "Saving life" on the Sabbath was allowed by the *Mishnah* (see the Note on 3:2). The phrase "to destroy" (lit. "kill," *apokteinein)* could be an allusion to the right of self-defense on the Sabbath proclaimed by the

Maccabees who were prepared to violate the Sabbath to preserve life (see 1 Macc 2:41). Since the withered hand was not a life-threatening condition, however, the cogency of Jesus' reply is debated. In the strict Jewish-Christian apocryphal *Gospel of the Hebrews* the man is identified as a stonemason who begs for healing so that his livelihood may be restored (Jerome, *Commentary on Matthew* 2, on 12:13), and so "saving life" equals the restoration of health. The rhetoric of the two verses provides an even more satisfying example. The real point is to argue that "doing good" on the Sabbath is permitted. The second antithetical question expects the answer "yes," which is why there is no response. Given the answer "yes," the argument is "from the greater to the lesser"; that is, if it is permissible to save a life on the Sabbath, then the lesser action of restoration of health is also permitted.

5. *in anger . . . deeply grieved:* The language here discloses strong emotion on Jesus' part. "Anger" *(orgē)*, used only here and in the verbal form in 1:41 (in some manuscripts), is virtually synonymous with "wrath" *(thymos;* see Isa 63:3, 6; Rom 2:8; Col 3:8). When used of humans, anger and wrath are vices (Gal 5:20; Col 3:8; Eph 4:31). The wrath of God describes God's displeasure at human evil, very often as a summons to change or reform (Deut 9:7, 8, 22; Isa 60:10; Pss 6:1; 38:1), and with reference to the disclosure of divine wrath that will characterize the eschatological day of the Lord (Zech 1:15; Matt 3:7; Luke 3:7). Both Matthew (12:12) and Luke (6:10) omit this mention of Jesus' anger and grief. Though it primarily describes the emotion of Jesus in Mark, there are christological and eschatological nuances present here. The participle "deeply grieved" *(syllypoumenos),* used only here in the NT, is the intensive form of the verb "to be sorry or grieve."

   at the hardness of their hearts: The metaphor "hard heart" suggests people who have closed themselves to God's word (Ezek 3:7; Acts 28:27; Rom 2:5); it describes the disciples in 6:52 and 8:17.

   "Stretch out your hand." He held it out . . . restored: The healing is accomplished without any explicit word of healing but simply by the command to stretch out the hand, and the verbs follow in rapid succession to enhance the power of Jesus. There is also no public acclaim or demonstration as in many miracle stories, but rather a negative reaction. In Isa 35:3 one of the hopes for the restoration of the people is that God "will strengthen the weak hands."

6. *The Pharisees left, and immediately:* The Greek adverb *euthys* ("immediately") highlights both the departure of the Pharisees and their almost concomitant conspiracy with the Herodians.

   they began to consult over him: "Consult" translates the Greek *symboulion edidoun* (lit. "give counsel"), which is very unusual, in contrast to the more familiar Latinism of 15:1, *symboulion poiēsantes* (Latin *consilium facere,* "make a consultation").

   the Herodians: This group appears in the NT only here and in Mark 12:13 (Matt 22:16 simply repeats Mark), though in 8:15 Jesus warns his disciples about the leaven of the Pharisees and the leaven of Herod. While numerous proposals have been made about their identity, the most widely accepted one is that they are supporters of Herod Antipas who ruled Galilee during the ministry of Jesus (see 6:21). Their presence in connection with the plan to kill Jesus also links the fate of Jesus and the death of John the Baptist, who is killed by Herod Antipas (see 6:14-29).

on how they might destroy him: This is the first of four such indications about Jesus' future death (see 11:18; 12:12; 14:1), culminating in the agreement in 15:1, which is couched in language similar to 3:6. There is a certain irony here, since Jesus has questioned whether it is legitimate "to destroy life" on the Sabbath (3:4), and the Pharisees and Herodians plan just such an activity on the Sabbath, and thus violate the deepest meaning of the Sabbath.

INTERPRETATION

This last of the five Galilean controversies (3:1-6) is also the most bitter and most serious. Only here does Jesus show anger toward his opponents, and only here do they plan to destroy him. The text has distinctive literary characteristics. It combines elements of a controversy (that is, an action that evokes a negative response and a counter-question of Jesus) with aspects of a miracle story (setting, description of illness, immediate and complete healing). Most surprising in a narrative that serves as a conclusion to stories where dialogue is central is that here no one speaks except Jesus. The man with the withered hand makes no request for healing; the other people in the synagogue have no reaction to the healing even though it is explicitly done in their sight (contrast 1:27-28); and the Pharisees say nothing before or after the healing. The synagogue itself has now become the site of unvoiced opposition to Jesus.

Whatever the shape of the narrative in the tradition, Mark seems to have recast it in terms of his literary and theological purposes. As mentioned above, it culminates the linear movement of the five controversies; it also lets readers know clearly that the groom will be taken away in a violent manner. It picks up the theme of the previous narrative by illustrating concretely that the Sabbath has been made for humanity and that Jesus is lord of the Sabbath, and it foreshadows the opposition to Jesus that will continue to grow from now on until that ultimate trial before the Sanhedrin and Roman authorities when the charges against Jesus will result in his death.

The five controversies that conclude the initial phase of Jesus' ministry in Galilee provide fundamental insights into the "good news of God" proclaimed by Jesus at the outset of his ministry (1:14-15). God is the one who through Jesus brings acceptance and forgiveness to people who are socially and religiously outcast. The deeper meaning of holy institutions such as the Sabbath, which honor God, can be lost sight of in the very act of careful observance of such institutions. When faced with unexpected and serious challenges to their concept of God and traditional practices, even deeply committed religious people can end up doing evil. Jesus who voices and embodies a new image of God and an alternative religious practice must be gotten out of the way. Mark's message for the church of his age contains paradigmatic value for the church of any age that must face tensions arising from rapidly changing understandings of God and of those institutions and practices vested with divine authority.

FOR REFERENCE AND FURTHER STUDY

Bennett, W. J. "The Herodians of Mark's Gospel," *NovT* 17 (1975) 9–14.

Derrett, J. Duncan M. "Christ and the Power of Choice: Mark 3:1-6," *Bib* 65 (1984) 168–88.

Meier, John P. "The Historical Jesus and the Historical Herodians," *JBL* 119 (2000) 740–46.

Smith, Stephen H. "Mark 3,1-6: Form, Redaction and Community Function," *Bib* 75 (1994) 153–74.

Stock, Augustine. "Jesus, Hypocrites, and Herodians," *BTB* 16 (1986) 3–7.

Tolbert, Mary Ann. "Is It Lawful on the Sabbath to Do Good or to Do Harm?: Mark's Ethics of Religious Practice," *Perspectives in Religious Studies* 23 (1996) 199–214.

11. *Transitional Markan Summary: Healings beside the Sea* (3:7-12)

7. Then Jesus, accompanied by his disciples, withdrew toward the sea, and a large mass of people followed, from Galilee and from Judea 8. and from Jerusalem and from Idumea and from the other side of the Jordan and from the regions around Tyre and Sidon—this large mass, since they heard about everything he did, flocked to him. 9. And he instructed his disciples to have a boat stand by because of the crowd, so that they would not crush him. 10. For he had already healed so many that all who were afflicted tried to touch him. 11. Even the unclean spirits, whenever they saw him fell at his feet, screaming in a loud voice: "You are the Son of God." 12. And he rebuked them sternly not to disclose this publicly.

NOTES

7. *Then Jesus:* The summary in 1:14-15 was the last time Mark introduced a pericope with the name of Jesus. Since the last words in direct discourse in this pericope are "Son of God" (3:11), the location of these titles implicitly states "Jesus is Son of God."

accompanied by his disciples: At this point in the narrative the term *mathētai* ("disciples") is not restricted to the four who were called first but designates a larger group of Jesus' followers (2:15, 16, 18, 23).

withdrew toward the sea: Jesus was last at the Sea of Galilee in 2:13, teaching the crowd, and the pericope preceding this one took place in a synagogue, presumably in Capernaum. The verb "withdrew" *(anechōrēsan)* has the overtone of "taking refuge" (Matt 2:12-13) or seeking seclusion (Matt 14:13). Its use here may also be due to the "plot" in 3:6. In Mark the sea is often the site for Jesus' teaching and mighty works (1:16; 2:13; 4:1; 5:21; 7:31-32).

a large mass of people: The expression *poly plēthos* is repeated chiastically in 3:8. This is an instance of Markan repetition to highlight the enclosed material (the geographical designations).

followed: There are a great number of variant readings in the manuscripts here. Many manuscripts simply omit the verb "followed." Others have the plural form and place the verb after "from Judea." The variations are principally stylistic and are caused by the verbose phrasing here.

from Galilee and from Judea: The areas mentioned are viewed from the perspective of Galilee and proceed south to east to north (the Mediterranean Sea is on the west). Judea was the place of John's preaching, and he also attracted "Jerusalemites" (1:5). Apart from Idumea, these are areas of Jesus' ministry in Mark (see 7:24, 31; 10:1).

8. *and from Idumea:* Idumea (Greek for OT Edom) is the territory from Beth-zur, south of Jerusalem on the road from Hebron to Beersheba. Herod the Great was an Idumean. Favorable reaction to Jesus from Idumeans may counter the hostile reaction of the "Herodians" in 3:6.

from the other side of the Jordan: In Greek, *peran tou Iordanou.* Perea (see 10:1) is the territory on the eastern side of the Jordan River, extending in the north to just below Pella and to the south to a line extending from the Dead Sea to the fortress (Machaerus) where John the Baptist died.

the regions around Tyre and Sidon: This is a mainly Gentile area toward the northwest, and represents the farthest extent of Jesus' ministry in Mark (see 7:24, 31). Samaria (which is never mentioned by name in Mark) and the Decapolis are noticeably absent from this list, even though Jesus will visit the latter (see 5:1-20; 7:31).

this large mass: The Greek expression *poly plēthos* is repeated from 3:7. The double mention of the crowd and their enthusiastic reception of Jesus (*poly plēthos* rather than the more familiar *ochlos*) is an ironic counter to the scorn that Greco-Roman writers heaped on ordinary people. *Hoi polloi* in Greek were the huge, uneducated mass of non-elites, and the attitude of the Roman author Horace is typical: *Odi profanum vulgus et arceo* ("I hate and avoid the common mass of people").

since they heard . . . flocked: Mark is not so much handing on literal history here as presenting a dramatic image of the magnetism of Jesus. Nor does he indicate how people heard about Jesus, leading to speculation that these regions in Mark's day were sites of Christian missionary activity (and so hearing about Jesus and coming to him).

 9. *to have a boat stand by:* See 4:1 for Jesus teaching from a boat, and 6:32 for the boat taking Jesus away from the press of the crowds. The boat features prominently during the multiple voyages of Jesus in Mark 4–8. The need for the boat and the press of the crowd magnify the power of Jesus.

10. *For he had already healed so many:* By placing the word "many" *(pollous)* first in the sentence the Greek stresses the beneficiaries of Jesus' actions. The same term will be used regarding the saving action of the Son of Man "for many" (10:45, *anti pollōn*) and the effect of "the blood of the covenant to be poured out for many *(pollōn)*" in 14:24.

all who were afflicted: The Greek *hosoi eichon mastigas* (lit. "all who received scourges") reflects the ancient view of illness as a divine affliction (see 2 Macc 7:37). Although the vocabulary is different, the text may also recall Isa 53:4-5 where the servant bears the punishments of the afflicted.

tried to touch him: This anticipates 5:27-31; 6:56; and 7:33. That the body of the Spirit-endowed person possesses power of itself is a common motif in ancient miracle stories.

11. *the unclean spirits:* The ministry of Jesus begins with victory over unclean spirits (1:24, "us"). The two major mighty works of Jesus between 1:21 and 3:6, healing and exorcism, are here summarized.

fell at his feet: The image is prostration before divine beings or high-ranking people (see Gen 17:3; Dan 3:5; Matt 2:11; 4:9; 18:26).

You are the Son of God: Mark often uses "Son of God" or a variation of it such as "beloved [or only] Son" (1:11; 9:7; 12:6), the Son (13:32), Son of God (3:11), Son of the Most High God (5:7), Son of the Blessed One (14:61), and a (or the) Son of God (15:39). This is the first use of the title after 1:1 and 11, and (like 5:7) is on the lips of unclean spirits. Apart from the centurion's confession in 15:39, this is the most forceful use of the title *"the* Son of God."

12. *he rebuked them sternly not to disclose this publicly:* See 1:25 for use of "rebuke" *(epitiman)*, and 1:34 for a similar command to a demon. As representatives of the transcendent sphere, the demons possess knowledge superior to that of humans. This is one of the most often cited "messianic secret" texts (see Introduction). For Mark's readers there is no secret, however, since they know from the very beginning that Jesus is Son of God (1:1, 11). The only question is in what sense he is, and when and how he should be proclaimed as such.

INTERPRETATION

This narrative provides a transition between the first and second subsections of the gospel. After the prologue and initial arrival of Jesus (1:1-15), Mark structures his material to portray a Jesus who is powerful in word and deed but who will suffer mortal opposition (1:16–3:6). In the next subsection (3:7–6:6) these two themes will continue, but with a subtle shift toward the division and opposition that Jesus will cause. The present section (3:7-12) summarizes major themes of the first section and prepares for the next set of narratives.

This summary looks in two directions. It begins with Jesus withdrawing with his disciples (3:7), which recalls 1:35 and anticipates 3:13; 4:10; 4:34; and 6:1 where Jesus seeks solitude with his disciples. Still the crowds flock to Jesus (3:8-9), which is a strong motif in the preceding section (1:31; 2:1; 2:13) and in the following one (3:20; 4:1; 5:21; 5:24). The summary stresses multiple healings (3:10), and healing narratives and summaries characterize both the first and second subsections (1:31, 41-44; 2:1-12; 3:1-6; 5:1-43; 6:5). Victory over demons and commands to silence (3:11) also precede and follow this summary (1:25, 34; 5:1-13, 43).

In this summary the "omniscient narrator" (that is, the storyteller possessing all that is needed for the narrative along with information not shared by the characters in the narrative) gives the readers an overview of the progress of the story. The very last direct statement (3:11), by using "Son of God," takes the reader back to 1:1 (and to 1:11) so that readers are alerted to the major christological thrust of the narrative. The crowds which come to Jesus from the areas surrounding Galilee remind the readers of the crowds that streamed out to John (1:4), but Jesus' geographical impact is much more extensive than that of John. The opening portrait of Jesus and his disciples (3:7) recalls the first public act of Jesus and the beginning of the instruction and example that Jesus gives to his disciples (1:29, 31-35; 2:13-22, 23-28). In the next section the disciples will assume more prominence, while their misunderstanding about Jesus will also increase. Mark's total narrative is not only about the identity of Jesus but also about the challenges inherent in following him.

The summary in 3:7-12, at first glance, seems awkward after the plot to kill Jesus in 3:6. It appears at first simply like a triumphalistic response to counter the rejection. Yet the motif of opposition is here too, at least implicitly. The obeisance of the demons prepares for the charge in 3:23 that Jesus is possessed and casts out demons by the power of the prince of demons. Yet readers know in advance that the demons worship Jesus; the real combat will not be between Jesus and demons, but with those "outsiders" (see 4:10-12) who misunderstand Jesus.

The summary clearly culminates in the final words of 3:11, "You are the Son of God," which take the readers back to the first words of the gospel (1:1) and foreshadow the use of this same title in the trial and crucifixion episodes (14:62; 15:39). In the title "Son of God" there is an implicit hint of opposition. Christian adoption of the title reflects in part an apologetic use of Psalm 2, the psalm of royal adoption where the central point is the divine decree: "You are my son; today I have begotten you"

(2:7; see also 2 Sam 7:14; Ps 89:26-27). The context of Psalm 2 is opposition to the king (vv. 1-3), followed by divine derision at this opposition and installation of the king (vv. 4-6). The adopted son is then assured of divine protection (vv. 7-12). In this Markan summary, then, following immediately upon the plan to kill Jesus which will unfold in tragic inevitability, the readers are informed that, as in Psalm 2, such opposition is but a prelude to the victory of God's regent. In narrative form the summary that recalls the past and prepares for the future reflects the experience of Mark's readers as they live between memory and hope.

FOR REFERENCE AND FURTHER STUDY

Burkill, T. Alec. "Mark 3:7-12 and the Alleged Dualism of the Evangelist's Miracle Material," *JBL* 87 (1968) 409–17.
Keck, Leander E. "Mark 3:7-12 and Mark's Christology," *JBL* 84 (1965) 341–58.

12. *Choosing the Twelve* (3:13-19)

13. Then he went up on the mountain, and he summoned those whom he chose personally; and they came away to him. 14. He then appointed twelve [whom he also named apostles], in order that they might be with him, and in order that he might send them on a mission to preach, 15. and to have power to cast out demons. 16. [And he constituted them as twelve]: Simon on whom he conferred the name Peter, 17. and James the son of Zebedee, along with John the brother of James, and conferred on them the name, Boanerges, which means "sons of thunder," 18. and [he called] Andrew, Philip, Bartholomew, Matthew, Thomas, James the son of Alphaeus, along with Thaddeus, Simon the Cananaean, 19. and Judas Iscariot, who was also the one who betrayed him.

NOTES

13. *he went up to the mountain:* The preceding narrative summary (3:7-12) takes place beside the sea, where Jesus is present with his disciples. The change of place signals a new event. The mountain, in addition to providing distance between Jesus and the crowds, is a traditional place for communion with God and for authoritative revelation (e.g., God's summons of Moses to Sinai in Exod 19:3-6, 16-25; and Deut 32:48–34:9; see also Mark 9:2; 13:3).

he summoned: "Summoned" translates the verb *proskaleitai* (middle voice), first used here. It is stronger than the the the simple verb "call" *(kalein)* used in the previous "call narratives" (1:20; 2:17) and has the overtone of a summons for teaching or instruction or of an invitation or call to a special task (see also 3:23; 6:7; 7:14; 8:1, 34; 10:42; 12:43; 15:44).

whom he chose personally: Literally "whom he himself wished." "Wish" is weaker in English than the Greek *ēthelen.* The rapid succession of three verbs in the third person ("he went up . . . he summoned . . . he wished") underscores the sovereignty of Jesus here. The text leaves open the possibility that those called to the mountain were a larger group out of whom the Twelve were designated.

they came away to him: This verb *(apēlthon)* was used of the reaction of those called first (1:20) and connotes not merely change of location but also of a way of life.

14. *he then appointed twelve:* The verb "appoint" is literally "make" and may reflect a Semitic usage for "appoint" or "designate" (see 1 Kgs 13:33; 2 Chr 2:18 [LXX 2:17]; 1 Sam 12:6). On the Twelve in Mark, see the Interpretation.

[whom he also named apostles]: In many translations (e.g., the Revised NAB), these words are in brackets to indicate that they may not be original in the text of Mark. The principal reasons for doubting their authenticity are these: (1) They are not in Matt 10:1-2 but are in Luke 6:13, which suggests that a later copyist added them to Mark on the basis of Luke; (2) though good manuscripts (Vaticanus, Sinaiticus) have the phrase here, from the text-critical principle *lectio difficilior potior* (the more difficult reading is preferred), many editions omit it because the "twelve apostles" became such a common expression; (3) Mark never employs the term "twelve apostles" elsewhere, and he uses the noun "apostle" only once again (6:30, though it is in a context that refers to the Twelve [see 6:7]); and (4) including the phrase complicates the sense of the sentence, since the second half of the verse reads "that he might send them out *(apostellē),*" which is tautologous after calling them "apostles," that is "those sent."

in order that they might be with him: See above under 1:16-20. The two constant elements of discipleship are "being with" or "following" Jesus and doing the things of Jesus, here being sent out to preach and cast out demons.

in order that he might send them on a mission: This is the second purpose clause explaining the reason for the choice. The verb "send on a mission" or "send out" *(apostellein)* and its nominal form "apostle" *(apostolos)* connote official representation of the sender.

to preach: Just as there is a dual purpose for the appointment of the Twelve (being with and being sent), their mission has a dual purpose. The first is to "preach" (lit. "proclaim" *[kēryssein],* or to act as heralds; see 6:12). "Proclaiming" links them to John the Baptist (1:4, 7), to Jesus (1:14, 38), to other characters in the gospel touched or healed by the power of Jesus (1:45, the leper; 5:20, the Gerasene demoniac; 7:36, the deaf and dumb man), and to the church under persecution (13:10).

15. *and to have power to cast out demons:* The mission in which the Twelve have power *(exousia)* over demons (also in 6:7, 13) again links them to Jesus whose power *(exousia)* has been manifest in the preceding section of the gospel (1:22, 27; 2:10). They fulfill the charge to preach and to exorcise in 6:12-13, but in 9:18, 28 they are unable to exorcise.

16. *[and he constituted them as twelve]:* Again editions of the Greek NT and contemporary translations question whether this phrase represents the original reading, mainly since it is easily explained as a dittography of v. 14 and is omitted by Matthew and Luke. The principal arguments for its presence are the frequent Markan practice of duplicate expressions and the need for repetition after the relatively lengthy description of the mission of the Twelve in 3:14b-15. If both of the disputed phrases in 3:14, 16 were left out, the verses would be grammatically less cumbersome and read more smoothly.

    Simon on whom he conferred the name Peter: See 1:16 on background to the name Simon. Simon is the first called in 1:16-20, and so he is the first one listed here and in all lists of the Twelve. He is the only one who truly has two names (the other names in v. 17 are either patronymics or nicknames, though Peter [= "Rocky"] may be a nickname too). In biblical thought changing the name exhibits the power of the namer; it occurs often in the context of a new stage or new mission (e.g., Abram to Abraham, Gen 17:5; Sarai to Sarah, Gen 17:15; Jacob to Israel, Gen 32:28). "Peter" derives from the Greek noun *petra* ("rock"). Mark never relates this to the Aramaic *kepha* (see Gal 2:9, 11, 14), nor does the "rock" symbolism influence his picture of Peter (see Matt 16:17-19). Rather, in Mark's Gospel, Peter has many negative qualities (see the Introduction under Discipleship).

    James the son of Zebedee . . . John the brother of James: This list departs from the story of the call of the first four disciples (1:16-20) where Andrew as Simon's brother follows Jesus before James and John do (see also 1:29). On the identity of James and John see above on 1:16-20.

    Boanerges, which means "sons of thunder": Mark's language is obscure here, since all the proposed Hebrew/Aramaic terms that could actually mean "sons of thunder" would not be transliterated in Greek as Mark does (see Guelich, *Mark* 162, for possible solutions, none of which is totally satisfying). Neither is the relevance of "sons of thunder" clear. Some relate it to the supposed fiery personalities of the two, for which there is little evidence in Mark apart from their rather mild protest in 9:38 (but see Luke 9:54).

18. *Andrew, Philip, Bartholomew, Matthew:* On Andrew see 1:16-20. Philip (= "lover of horses") was a popular Greek name (e.g., Philip of Macedon), used also by Jews (see 8:27, Caesarea Philippi [of the tetrarch Herod Philip]); he plays no role in Mark. Bartholomew (from the Aramaic *bar Tolmai* = son of Tolmai; see 2 Sam 3:3) also has no role in the Gospels, but in later Christian legends he is identified with Nathaniel (John 1:45-46). The name Matthew reflects some form of the Hebrew *Mattathiah* ("gift of God"). He is mentioned only here in Mark and is not identified with Levi the toll collector (2:14) as he is in Matt 9:9.

Thomas: The Greek name Thomas is not properly a personal name but resembles the Aramaic *te'oma'* ("the twin"). He appears in John 11:16 and in 20:24 as *ho legomenos Didymas*, the one called "the twin" (Didymas is Greek for "twin"). He becomes an important figure in post-apostolic Christianity. The Coptic *Gospel of Thomas* is ascribed to "Didymus Judas Thomas," and there exist also the apocryphal *Infancy Gospel of Thomas* and the third- (or fourth) century *Acts of Judas Thomas*, which tells of his evangelizing and martyrdom in India. There is a great devotion to him among the Syro-Malabar Christians. There is also a fifth-century *Apocalypse of Thomas*, known only through a citation in the Gelasian sacramentary.

James the son of Alphaeus, along with Thaddeus, Simon the Cananaean: This James is not "James the Less" (Mark 15:40), or James the brother of the Lord (Gal 1:19; 1 Cor 15:7); on the background to the name see 1:16-20. Thaddeus is a Greek name omitted from the Lukan list of the Twelve (Luke 6:14-16; Acts 1:13) where the name "Judas, son of James" is inserted. A variant textual reading to Matt 10:3 gives "Lebbaeus" or "Thaddeus surnamed Lebbaeus." Thaddeus has no role in the NT. "Cananaean" is most likely a Greek transliteration of the Aramaic *qan'ana'*, which means "zealous." Luke 6:15 uses the Greek form *zēlōtēs*. Since the Zealots as a political movement and revolutionary party within Judaism arose only in the days of the Jewish War (66–73 C.E.), the term most likely describes Simon's religious zeal rather than his militaristic or revolutionary bent.

19. *Judas Iscariot:* Judas appears last in every list of the Twelve. Judas is the Hellenized form of the Hebrew *Yehudâ* or Judah. Various proposals have surfaced regarding the meaning of "Iscariot" (Greek *Iskariōth*): (1) derived from the Hebrew verb *sāqar* ("act falsely") and meaning "the false one"; (2) derived from the Hebrew root *skr*, which means to "deliver" or "hand over"; in this case the phrase "the one who handed him over" could be an explanation of the Semitic original; (3) derived from a combination of *'iš* ("man") and the village of Kerioth (Josh 15:25), so that the name simply means "a man from Kerioth"; or (4) related to the "Sicarii" ("daggermen"), a group of radical Jewish assassins. Of the above proposals the second and third have the most support, while support for the fourth proposal is minimal.

who was also the one who betrayed him: Given the importance of the term *paradidonai* ("hand over" or "betray") in Mark (see the Notes to 1:14), this description of Judas may have been added by Mark. Thus the last verse in Mark's account of the choice of the Twelve echoes the fate of John the Baptist (1:14) and prepares for the fate of Jesus (8:31; 9:31; 10:33-34; 14:10-11, 18, 21, 41-42, 44; 15:1, 15) and of the disciples (13:10, 12).

INTERPRETATION

Just as Mark presents the call of disciples (1:16-20) as the initial act in the first phase of Jesus' ministry, the second phase (3:7–6:6a) begins with the appointment of the Twelve (3:13-19). This structure reinforces the view that discipleship is a theme as important to Mark as christology or the story of Jesus. The core of this second call of disciples is a list of the first twelve men named to be followers of Jesus (3:16-19), to which Mark prefaces his own theological interpretation (3:13-15).

The list of the Twelve appears here in Mark as well as in Matt 10:1-4; Luke 6:12-16; and Acts 1:13. Though there is some variation in order, every list begins with Simon [Peter] and the same four are mentioned first: Peter, Andrew, James, and John. There are minor variations among the final eight, but Judas is always last. This variation and constancy show that a group of "the Twelve" is very likely an early institution (1 Cor 15:5), probably rooted in the ministry of the historical Jesus. At the same time the lack of information about the majority of the Twelve and their relative lack of importance as individuals in the NT suggests that, as an institution in early Christianity, it may have died out in a relatively short time. The Gospel of John, though aware of the existence of the Twelve (see John 6:67, 70, 71; 20:24), contains no list of the Twelve or narrative about their choice. Though most of the Twelve are rarely mentioned in the NT, in the early Christian centuries a great number of legends developed about their apostolic lives and careers after the death of Jesus. These apocryphal Acts have been collected in Edgar Hennecke and Wilhelm Schneemelcher, eds., *New Testament Apocrypha* (Philadelphia: Westminster, 1963); and John K. Elliott, ed., *The Apocryphal New Testament* (Oxford: Clarendon Press, 1993).

The significance of the Twelve in Mark and their relation to the "disciples" *(mathētai)* is unclear. Unlike the Q source (Matt 19:28 = Luke 22:28-30), in Mark the Twelve are not designated to be the eschatological judges of a renewed Israel (over the twelve tribes). The Twelve appear in the following places in Mark: 3:14, 16; 4:10; 5:25, 42; 6:7; 8:19; 9:35; 10:32; 11:11; 14:10, 17, 20, 43. Mark has no fixed concept of "the twelve apostles," nor do the Twelve seem to have a special role among the disciples. Often they are associated with or indistinguishable from the "disciples" (a term used forty-six times). After addressing the parable of the sower to a large crowd (4:1-9), Jesus gives an esoteric instruction to "those about him with the Twelve" (4:10). In 10:32 when Jesus is on his way to Jerusalem three potentially different groups are mentioned in quick succession: the disciples, those who followed him, and the Twelve. Nor do the Twelve seem to constitute a core group within the disciples. At the transfiguration (9:2-8), the eschatological discourse (13:3-4), and Gethsemane (14:32-42) it is not the Twelve who are with Jesus but a select group of three or four (Peter, James, and John [and Andrew]). Though the narratives of the call and commissioning of the Twelve are important in the structure of Mark, their main function seems to be to symbolize the nature of discipleship (see 3:13-15) rather than to perform the actions confined to a particular group. In fact, many people in Mark's Gospel other than those called to be disciples perform the same actions as those who are called to be disciples (see Introduction on Discipleship).

It is the Markan language of 3:13-15 that gives this section its special flavor. At the mountain (a place of privileged revelation) Jesus gives his chosen disciples their commission. They are to "be with him," and they are to be people on a mission: "He appointed . . . that they might be with him, and that he might send them. . . ." Being with Jesus and being sent by him are not two distinct activities, nor is one consequent on the other. The mission of Jesus—proclaiming the gospel of God, confronting the power of evil, and healing—is to be the mission of the Twelve and implicitly of all disciples who are with him.

The traditional list of the Twelve is incorporated in a context over which falls the shadow of the cross. Jesus calls the Twelve to a mountain, and he will leave from the Mount of Olives (see 14:26) on the way to undergo his suffering and death. The call of the Twelve ends with the stark phrase about Judas "who was the one who betrayed him," foreshadowing that story of betrayal that will unfold shortly after the visit to the Mount of Olives. The narrative subtly suggests that "being with Jesus" will catch the disciples up in that same web of betrayal, suffering, and death (8:34-38; 13:9-13).

This narrative contains important themes for actualization. Like the other call narratives it presents a theology of discipleship in miniature. The true disciple is one with a sense of call; in Johannine terms, "You have not chosen me; I have chosen you" (John 15:16). This call involves "being with" and doing the things of Jesus. In Christian history there has often been a tension between "contemplation" and "action." The theology of discipleship presented here urges a combination of the two. They are two inseparable aspects of the one call. Also, as for Jesus and his first followers, action on behalf of God's kingdom will bring conflict and suffering. Finally, though somewhat muted in the narrative, the Twelve present a diverse picture. There is Simon "the rock" who emerges as unreliable in the gospel (14:66-72) and the "sons of thunder" who ambition positions of power, only to cause bickering among the others (10:35-45). Greek names like Philip and Andrew are side by side with Semitic names like Matthew and Simon, suggesting a mixture of Hellenized and more traditional Jewish families. One of the chosen ones (Judas) will ultimately reject the one who chose him, and reject the group as a whole. Both the diversity and the fragility of discipleship are part of church life throughout history and today.

FOR REFERENCE AND FURTHER STUDY

Best, Ernest. "Mark's Use of the Twelve," *ZNW* 69 (1978) 11–35.
Moloney, Francis J. "The Vocation of the Disciples in the Gospel of Mark," *Salesianum* 43 (1981) 487–516.
Rook, John T. "'Boanerges, Sons of Thunder' (Mark 3:17)," *JBL* 100 (1981) 94–95.
Villegas, Beltran. "Peter, Philip and James of Alphaeus," *NTS* 33 (1987) 292–94.

13. *The Beelzebul Controversy and the True Family of Jesus* (3:20-35)

20. Then he came home; and the crowd again gathered, so that it was impossible for them even to have a meal. 21. And when his relatives heard this, they set out to seize him, for they had been saying: "He is out of his mind." 22. But the scribes, the ones who had arrived from Jerusalem, were saying: "He is possessed by Beelzebul" and "By the prince of demons he casts out demons." 23. He then called them together and began to speak to them in parables: "How can Satan cast out Satan? 24. Whenever a kingdom is divided against itself, such a kingdom will not last. 25. Whenever a household is divided against itself, that household also will not last. 26. If Satan has risen up against himself and is divided, he will not last but is finished. 27. Again, no one can enter the house of a powerful person and carry off his possessions without first binding the powerful person, and then he will sack the house. 28. Amen I say to you: Humans will be forgiven for all their sins and blasphemies they commit. 29. But if anyone blasphemes against the Holy Spirit, that person will never receive forgiveness but is guilty of an everlasting sin"— 30. because they charged: "He has an evil spirit." 31. Then his mother and brothers arrived, but remained outside and sent people in to summon him. 32. The crowd was seated around him. Those they sent then said: "Look, your mother and brothers are outside searching for you." 33. But he gave them this answer: "Who are my mother and my brothers?" 34. He then looked around at all those who were sitting in a circle around him, and said: "Look, here are my mother and my brothers. 35. For whoever does the will of God, that person is my brother, sister, and mother."

NOTES

20. *Then he came home:* Jesus was last "at home" in 2:1-12 in a scene similar to this where the pressing crowds prevent access to him. Also in 2:1-12 the scribes make the first charge of blasphemy, and forgiveness of sin is explicitly mentioned.

21. *When his relatives heard:* "Relatives" translates the Greek *hoi par' autou* (lit. "those from him"). Though some prefer to translate this phrase as "disciples" (see 4:10, *hoi peri auton*) rather than as "relatives" or "family," the phrase is used in the Greek papyri for family members, and the Markan sandwich technique suggests that the people of 3:21 are the same as the family members of 3:31-35. The "Western" text tradition (Mss D and W) found this reading so embarrassing that they changed it to read: "When the scribes and the others heard about him, they went out to seize him, for they said, 'He is beside himself'" (Bruce M. Metzger, *A Textual Commentary on the Greek New Testament* [London and New York: United Bible Societies, 1971] 81–82).

    they set out: The verb "set out" (lit. "departed") suggests that the relatives left their homes in Nazareth (see 6:1-6) after hearing of Jesus' actions. Mark condenses the time of the journey for dramatic effect.

    to seize him: The Greek (*kratēsai*, infinitive of purpose) suggests forceful restraint or even "arrest" (6:17; 14:44). The verb is used of the hostile intent of the scribes in 12:12 and 14:1.

    for they had been saying: The subject of the Greek *elegon gar* (lit. "they were saying") is not clear. Some interpreters understand the subject to be the crowds or the people in general. But the exact verbal parallel with the charge of the scribes in 3:22 is evidence that a specific group (that is, the relatives) is also intended in v. 21. It also explains the arrival of the relatives.

    He is out of his mind: The Greek *exestē* from *ek + histēmi* (lit. "stand outside of") is used in classical Greek for being out of one's mind; see also Josephus, *Ant.* 10.114, where the people ridicule Jeremiah as if he was out of his mind (*exestēkota*). Such a charge would hardly be made up by the early church, and so this may reflect the historical view of the relatives of Jesus, none of whom had been called to the circle of the Twelve.

22. *the scribes, the ones who had arrived from Jerusalem:* The scribes, especially the Jerusalem scribes, are the most adamant opponents of Jesus in Mark (see 7:1, 5; 10:33; 11:18, 27; 14:1). Mention of "Jerusalem" here anticipates the place of Jesus' crucifixion.

    were saying: The imperfect is used of customary or continuous action.

    He is possessed by Beelzebul: Literally the text reads: "He has Beelzebul." This obscure name is never found in the Greek OT for an evil spirit, and in the NT occurs only here and in Q (Luke 11:15, 18-19; Matt 10:25; 12:24, 27). There are also variant manuscript readings: *Beelzeboul* in Vaticanus, and *Beelzebub* in the Latin and Syriac versions. Beelzebul and Beelzeboul are most likely derived from the name of the old Canaanite god meaning "Baal the Prince," or "Baal the exalted abode." Baalzebub ("Lord of the Flies") appears in 2 Kgs 1:3, 6 as a mocking distortion of the Canaanite god of Ekron. In *Test. Sol.* 3:1-6 Beelzeboul is a fallen angel who is called "prince of demons" and "ruler of the demons."

    by the prince of demons: This is an instance of Mark's fondness for duplicate expressions where the second intensifies the first (e.g., 1:32; 11:15; 13:24; 14:12). The phrase may also be a Markan explanation for Hellenistic readers of the enigmatic phrase "he has Beelzebul." The charge against Jesus is twofold:

Beelzebul infests him, and his power is subservient to the prince of demons. In this passage Mark has a density of descriptions of demons: Beelzebul, the prince of demons, Satan, and the unclean spirit. This serves to enhance the power of Jesus. By whatever name the demons are called, their power is broken by the coming of "the stronger one."

he casts out demons: This charge is most serious and tantamount to magic. A statement found in the Babylonian Talmud, *b. Sanh.* 43a, though it is debated whether it might be influenced by the Gospels, contains a reference to a certain "Yeshu" (= Jesus) who was hanged on the eve of the Passover because he practiced magic and led Israel astray (see the text and discussion in John P. Meier, *A Marginal Jew* 1:96).

23. *he then called them together . . . in parables:* This is the first occurrence of *parabolē* in Mark (subsequently in 4:2, 10, 11, 13, 30, 33, 34; 7:17; 12:1, 2; 13:28). The Greek noun derives from the verb *ballein* ("throw, place") and the preposition *para* ("alongside of"), and suggests a comparison (or placing side by side) of two different things. In C. H. Dodd's now classic definition a parable is "a metaphor or simile drawn from nature or common life, arresting the hearer by its vividness or strangeness and leaving the mind in sufficient doubt about its precise application to tease it into active thought" (*The Parables of the Kingdom* [rev. ed. New York: Scribner, 1961] 5). The Greek *parabolē* translates the Hebrew *mašal*, which embraces a wide variety of OT literary forms: proverbial sayings (1 Sam 10:12; Prov 1:1-7), riddles (Judg 14:10-18), taunt songs (Mic 2:4; Hab 2:6), allegories (Isa 5:1-7; Ezek 17:3-24), and extended parabolic narratives (Judg 9:7-15; 2 Sam 12:1-7). In apocalyptic literature it designates long discourses that reveal God's secret plans (e.g., the "Similitudes" of Enoch in *1 Enoch* 37–71). In Mark *parabolē* is used for short metaphorical sayings (3:23-27), longer narratives (4:1-9; 12:1-9), allegories (4:13-20; 13:34-37), riddles (4:10-11; 7:17), and lessons or illustrations (13:28). Though Mark 4 is often called "the parables chapter," Jesus' teaching in parables begins in 3:23. The use of "parable" in this conflict situation prepares for 4:10-12, 34 where parabolic teaching distinguishes outsiders and insiders. "Parable" also has a strong christological nuance in Mark. The Markan Jesus uses parables to speak of both himself and his mission, and he can even be called "the parable of God."

how can Satan cast out Satan?: See 1:13 above. In the OT "Satan" simply means "accuser" or "adversary" (see Job 1–2), but in the NT he becomes identified with the "prince of demons." The term, however, never loses its adversarial nuance, which is appropriate here in the "trial" to which Jesus is submitted.

24. *a kingdom is divided:* Each of the two illustrations that follow is in the grammatical form of an "eventual condition," where the second clause (apodosis) will always result from the first (protasis).

25. *a household is divided:* Though these sayings are gnomic, they would also fit events familiar to both Jesus' hearers and Mark's readers. Both the kingdom and household of Herod the Great were divided after his death in 4 B.C.E. and "came to an end." Also when Herod Antipas divorced the daughter of the

Nabatean king Aretas and married Herodias (see 6:17-19), Aretas attacked and defeated Herod Antipas' armies, which led to the eventual downfall of Herod Antipas (Josephus, *Ant.* 18.109-129; see D. C. Braund, "Herod Antipas," *ABD* 3:260). Mark's audience, whether in Syria, Palestine, or Rome, would be aware of the internal divisions that eventually brought about the defeat of the Jews in the Jewish War, and of the internal strife in Rome attending the death of Nero and its aftermath (three emperors in the year 68–69 C.E.).

26. *If Satan has risen up:* This continues the metaphor of internal division but with the addition of the verb "has risen" *(anestē)*. The condition is "factual" and presupposes the exorcising activity of Jesus, which would be a sign of the internal revolt within Satan's reign. The argument, however, is that since Satan is not "finished" there is not the internal division that would be present if Jesus were in Satan's power but acting against him.

27. *no one can enter the house of a powerful person and carry off his possessions:* The imagery shifts here from internal division to external attack, which suits the context of Jesus' attack "from the outside" on the domain of Satan. The "powerful person" *(ischyros;* lit. "the strong one") here is Satan; see 1:7 where Jesus is described as "the stronger one" *(ischyroteros).* The despoiling of the strong has a rich resonance in biblical tradition. At the Exodus the Israelites despoil the Egyptians (Exod 3:21-22; 11:2-3; 12:35-36; see Ps 105:37). In Isa 49:24-25 God is the mighty warrior who fights on Israel's side and takes away "the captives of the mighty" and "the prey of the tyrant." In Isa 53:12 the servant of YHWH "shall divide the spoil with the strong." These images bring home to Mark's readers that Jesus, like the Servant, is a liberating agent of God's deliverance from the power of evil.

    without first binding the powerful person: In the Isaiah Apocalypse (24:21-23) at the final judgment God will imprison the "host of heaven" that is opposed to him, and as part of the end-time scenario in *T. Levi* 18:12 Beliar (Satan) will be bound up by the new priest whom God will raise up. In Mark, with the coming of Jesus the power of evil has been broken, but the complete victory over evil is still in the future (see 13:24-27; compare 1 Cor 15:24-28).

28. *Amen I say to you:* This solemn formula appears only on the lips of Jesus in the Gospels, and this is the first Markan "Amen" saying (see also 8:12; 9:1, 41; 10:15; 10:29; 11:23; 13:30; 14:25, 30). The introductory "Amen" sayings recall the authoritative declaration of the prophets, "Thus says the Lord," and appear in a context of threat or promise.

    Humans will be forgiven . . . they commit: There is a double universality of forgiveness here; all humans (lit. "sons of men") will be forgiven all their sins, even if they blaspheme. Forgiveness of all sins is a hope of early Judaism (e.g., 1QS 11:11-14; *Jos As* 11:18; *2 Bar* 84:10). Even Manasseh, the most wicked of Judean kings, can pray for forgiveness to "the God of those who repent" (see *Prayer of Manasseh* 13).

29. *if anyone blasphemes against the Holy Spirit:* Blasphemy is used here not in the technical sense of invoking the divine name but in the more general sense of "abusing" or "insulting." In the Markan context the sin is attributing to

demonic power the liberating and healing activity of Jesus who begins his ministry as the one possessing God's Spirit (1:10).

that person will never receive forgiveness but is guilty of an everlasting sin: Literally "will not have forgiveness eternally, but is guilty of a sinful act into [or lasting for] eternity." "Guilty of" translates *enochos*, which has the nuance of "liable for" and "indicted for" (14:64). *Mishnah 'Abot* 3:11 lists five kinds of people who will be deprived of a share in the world to come: those who treat "holy things" as secular, those who defile the appointed times, those who humiliate neighbors in public, those who remove the sign of the covenant of Abraham, and those who expose aspects of the Torah not in accord with the Law. Here the sin is unforgivable because those who charge Jesus with demonic possession see goodness as evil, and therefore are closed to the action of God's Spirit. This makes sense for Mark's readers only in terms of the preceding narrative where Jesus, endowed with the Spirit, preaches the good news *of God* (see 1:12-15). The unforgivable sin in biblical thought is similar to "hardness of heart" (3:5).

30. *because they charged: "He has an evil spirit":* This sentence provides an *inclusio* with the charges made in 3:22 and specifies the nature of the unforgivable sin.

31. *Then his mother and brothers arrived:* The narrative of the family begun in 3:20-21 resumes here. In 3:21 the family simply hears of Jesus' action, and they think that he is out of his mind. Visually Jesus is still in the crowded house when they arrive. The mother of Jesus is mentioned only here and in 6:3, where Jesus is called the "son of Mary." On the issue of whether these were the "natural" brothers of Jesus or are so called because they were his "cousins" or "step-brothers," see the Interpretation of 6:1-6.

    and sent people in to summon him: The term for "send" *(apesteilan)* has a nuance of an official delegation that is concerned, as in 3: 21, about Jesus' sanity. Their position as "outside" prepares for the distinction between "insiders" and "outsiders" in 4:10-12.

32. *The crowd:* In these early sections of the gospel the "crowd" *(ochlos)* is favorable to Jesus. The picture of the crowd sitting in a circle (see 3:34) around Jesus visually confirms that he is one who teaches "with authority" (1:27).

    and your brothers: Some manuscripts add "and sisters" here, perhaps influenced by 3:35.

    are outside searching for you: The repetition of "outside" heightens the gap between Jesus and his relatives, as does the use of the verb *zētousin* ("seek" or "search"), which is used elsewhere of the ominous plans of Jesus' opponents (8:11; 11:18; 12:12).

33. *Who are my mother and my brothers?:* The rhetorical question simply prepares for the more solemn pronouncement in 3:35.

35. *Whoever does the will of God:* This the first in a series of "gnomic" sayings that take the form of "whoever" or "if anyone," and primarily stress the values of discipleship for those not explicitly called to follow Jesus: 9:37, whoever receives a child; in 9:38 one explicitly described as not following the disciples

casts out demons, and Jesus (9:40) says that "whoever is not against us is 'on our side'"; 10:29-31, "whoever" leaves family, etc., will receive a hundredfold; 10:43, 45 (addressed to the Twelve); and 11:23, "whoever" prays with faith will be heard. There are also gnomic sayings that express values opposed to the teachings of Jesus in 6:11; 9:42; and 10:11. In the LXX the term *thelēma tou theou* ("the will of God"), though used infrequently, suggests God's rule in creation (Sir 43:16; Ps 29:5 LXX), as well as God's directions for humans. Doing the will of God appears in the LXX in Pss 39:9 (MT 40:8); 102:21 (MT 103:21); and 142:10 (MT 143:10): "teach me to do your will, for you are my God." While the phrase appears only here in Mark, the notion is important (see the Note on *thelein* in 14:36).

is my brother, sister, and mother: The addition of "sister" here (see 3:32) is well attested in the manuscripts. Significantly absent in 3:31, 32, 35 is any mention of "father" (also in 6:3). Though some authors attribute this to the death of Joseph prior to Jesus' public ministry, the omission may have an added significance in Mark, who also envisions the Christian community as one without "fathers" (10:30).

INTERPRETATION

The tradition behind the material here is very complex, since Mark unites two independent traditions, one about the rejection of Jesus by family and relatives (3:20-21, 31-35; see also Mark 6:1-4, Matt 13:53-58; Luke 4:16-30; John 4:44), and the other about the charge that he is a sorcerer and possessed by a demon (3:22-30). Neither Matthew nor Luke reproduces the initial charge of his family (3:21), and in reporting the Beelzebul controversy they radically rewrite Mark 3:22-30. While Matthew (12:22-30) uses principally the Markan material (with the addition of the Q saying of 12:27-28 = Luke 11:19-20), Luke (11:14-23) is heavily dependent on Q. In addition, Matthew and Luke locate the Beelzebul controversy more logically after Jesus casts out a demon (Matt 12:22; Luke 11:14). They also add a Q saying in which Jesus invokes the precedent of Jewish exorcists to justify his activity (Matt 12:27 = Luke 11:19), and they have an independent tradition of the saying on blasphemy. The sayings here are rooted deeply in the Jesus tradition and exercise strong influence on the formative gospel tradition.

Mark composes this pericope to integrate the themes of christology and discipleship, and locates these originally unrelated narratives at a strategic place in his gospel, after the choosing of the Twelve, which inaugurates a new section of the gospel. The first narrative, 3:20-21 and 31-35, deals with the family of Jesus. While the natural family of Jesus thinks he is unbalanced, the true family is disclosed as those who do the will of God (3:35). Sandwiched within this narrative is the more serious charge against

Jesus made by the Jerusalem scribes: that he is possessed by Beelzebul and casts out demons by the prince of demons (3:22). The rhetoric of Jesus' response is important. Jesus begins with a rhetorical dilemma, which also functions as the proposition to be proven: "How can Satan cast out Satan?" (v. 23). The expected negative answer is then evoked by dual parabolic sayings on internal division (vv. 24-25). This initial questioning concludes in 3:26 with a further implication of the answer to the rhetorical question that if Satan suffers internal division, his reign is at an end.

The second phase of the response is the short parable about the plundering of a strong man's house (3:27), which in effect is an argument from fact since it echoes John's description of Jesus as "the stronger one" (1:7) and his own initial activity of vanquishing evil spirits (1:21-28, 32-34, 39; 3:11, 15). Jesus has plundered the house of Satan. This section then concludes with an implicit charge against his accusers that by denying the power of God at work in Jesus they are sinning against the Holy Spirit (3:28-30), where the verbal repetition of "he has an unclean spirit" (3:30) provides an *inclusio* with the charge of 3:22, "he has Beelzebul." On the narrative level the location and the *inclusio* here intensify previous themes. Jesus is truly the stronger one whose proclamation of the imminence of the kingdom inaugurates a conflict of kingdoms between God and God's adversary Satan, whose reign is collapsing.

The seriousness of the conflict is manifested by Jesus' countercharge that his accusers are committing the sin of blasphemy against the Holy Spirit. Such a statement by Jesus is heavily ironic since he has been charged by the scribes with blasphemy (2:7) and will later be condemned on this charge (14:64). By attributing the liberating and healing activity of Jesus to the world of Satan the scribes are committing the ultimate insult to God.

The "unforgivable sin" has been interpreted in various ways throughout church history. Augustine exercised a major influence by describing it as final impenitence and resistance to God's grace (Augustine, *Sermo* 71, in MPL 71.38, cols. 444–67, translated and edited by Philip Schaff, *A Select Library of the Nicene and Post-Nicene Fathers* [Grand Rapids: Eerdmans, 1956] 6:318–32). In medieval theology (e.g., Peter Lombard) it is a genus containing six species of sin: despair, presumption, impenitence, obstinacy, resisting divine truth known as such, and envy of another's spiritual welfare (see *NCE* 13:248). In the English Calvinist tradition, which has strongly influenced religious ideas in the United States, fear of this sin was an overriding concern. It consisted in resisting divine truth with malice and was a sign of final reprobation. Also in line with the Augustinian tradition, it became a weapon in theological controversy in which opponents were regarded as guilty of the unpardonable sin (see Baird Tipson, "A Dark Side of Seventeenth-Century English Protestantism: The Sin Against the Holy Spirit," *HTR* 77 [1984] 301–30). Contemporary Catholic doctrine continues the Augustinian tradition by describing it as deliberate refusal to accept God's mercy by repenting (*Catechism of the Catholic Church*, no. 1864). These views represent developments beyond the NT text and must be constantly tested against the sense intended by the biblical author.

The theme of discipleship begun in 1:16-20 is also intensified here. Jesus forms a new family that will be constituted by those whom he explicitly calls (the disciples) as well as those who are gathered around him to hear his teaching and are summoned to do the will of God. The Markan Jesus does not indicate what in the concrete constitutes doing the will of God. Despite the importance of this saying, the concept of the will of God does not appear frequently in Mark. In one crucial place, however, Mark does offer a key to what doing the will of God involves and why it makes a person into a mother, brother, or sister to Jesus. At Gethsemane (see 14:32-42), immediately prior to those events where the divisions that Jesus causes will come to a head in his final rejection by his own people and his abandonment by his disciples, Jesus prays: "Abba, Father, all things are possible to you; remove this cup from me; yet not what I will *(thelō)*, but what you will *(theleis)*" (14:36). Jesus here fulfills the conditions for disciples stated earlier in the gospel. The disciple is one who does God's will (3:35), prays to God with a faith that believes that God will bring about what is sought (11:23-24), and becomes like a child in order to enter the kingdom of God (10:15). In Gethsemane Jesus uses the familiar and familial term "Abba" in addressing God to whom all things are possible. The radical disposition of Jesus is to accept the will of God while praying that it might be otherwise.

This complex section provides a rich source for contemporary theological reflection and actualization. As noted, christology and discipleship are integrated. Jesus, who manifests God's presence by freeing people from the power of evil and by healing, is the master of an undivided household. The radically communal nature of discipleship is stressed by the incorporation into a new family that does the will of God. Therefore "doing the will of God" and becoming a member of Jesus' family is in the most radical sense being willing, like Jesus, to accept even suffering and rejection as willed by God. Peter will fail to do this in 8:32-33 when he is charged with "thinking human thoughts" and not "the thoughts of God." Solidarity with Jesus in suffering makes a person into a brother, sister, or mother to Jesus who himself is truly "son" when he can address God with faith and trust before his impending cross. Such solidarity involves membership in a new human family not determined by blood ties but by the shedding of the blood of Christ.

This passage also contains a caution against the improper use of charges about the "sin against the Holy Spirit," which can cause great anguish to people. In Mark this sin is not final impenitence or refusal to accept doctrine, but a deliberate choice to interpret the presence of divine action as evil. As C.E.B. Cranfield notes, those who make this charge against Jesus are "duly accredited theological teachers of God's people" (the scribes), whose own contact with the Spirit takes place through study of the Torah. Those who most particularly must heed the warning of this verse today are "the theological teachers and official leaders of the churches" (*The Gospel According to Saint Mark* 143).

For Reference and Further Study

Ahearne-Kroll, S. P. "'Who Are My Mother and My Brothers?' Family Relations and Family Language in the Gospel of Mark," *JR* 81 (2001) 1–25.

Barton, S. C. *Disciples and Family Ties in Mark and Matthew.* Cambridge: Cambridge University Press, 1994.

Bauckham, R. *Jude and the Relatives of Jesus in the Early Church.* Edinburgh: T & T Clark, 1990.

Best, Ernest. "Mark 3:20, 21, 31-35," *NTS* 22 (1975–76) 309–19.

Boring, M. Eugene. "The Unforgivable Sin Logion: Mark III 28-29/Matt XII 31-32/Luke XII 10," *NovT* 18 (1976) 258–79.

Crossan, John Dominic. "Mark and the Relatives of Jesus," *NovT* 15 (1973) 81–113.

Lambrecht, Jan. "The Relatives of Jesus in Mark," *NovT* 16 (1974) 241–58.

Neufeld, Dietmar. "Eating, Ecstasy, and Exorcism (Mark 3:21)," *BTB* 26 (1996) 152–62.

Robbins, Vernon K. "Beelzebul Controversy in Mark and Luke. Rhetorical and Social Analysis," *Forum* 7 (1991) 261–77.

Smith, Mahlon H. "Kinship is Relative. Mark 3:313-35 and Parallels," *Forum* 6 (1990) 80–94.

Yoonprayong, Amnuay. "Jesus and his mother according to Mk 3.20.21.31.35," *Marianum* 57 (1995) 513–643.

14. The Parable of the Sower, Sayings on the Mystery of the Kingdom of God, and the Allegory of the Seeds (4:1-20)

1. Then he began to teach them one more time by the seaside; such a huge crowd gathered around him that he climbed into a boat and sat down in it on the sea, while the whole crowd was on the land facing the sea. 2. He began then to instruct them in many ways through parables, and as he taught he would say to them: 3. "Pay attention. Look at this: a sower went out to plant seed. 4. While he was sowing, some of the seed fell along a path, and the birds flew down and ate it up. 5. Some also fell on

rocky ground, where the soil was very poor; it sprouted very quickly, since the soil was not very deep. 6. But when the sun came up, the sprouts were scorched; and since they had no root, they quickly dried up. 7. Other seeds landed among the thornbushes. But the thorns grew up, and they strangled it, and it yielded no fruit. 8. But other seeds fell on good soil. They sprouted and increased and yielded fruit. The yield was thirty, sixty, and a hundred times." 9. Then he said: "You who can hear what I said, pay attention."

10. But when he was alone, those who were with him along with the Twelve were asking him about the parables. 11. He then responded: "To you has been granted the mystery of the kingdom of God; but to those who are outside, everything occurs in parables, 12. so that they may look and see but not perceive, and that they may hear and listen but not understand, lest they convert and be forgiven." 13. He then said to them: "Don't you understand this parable? Then how will you understand all the parables? 14. The sower sows the word. 15. These are those along the path where the word is sown: Whenever they hear, Satan comes and takes away the word that is sown among them. 16. And these are the ones sown on rocky ground: Whenever they hear the word, right away they accept it joyfully. 17. But they have no inner root and are volatile; then when trouble or persecution over the word occurs, they fall away. 18. The others are those sown among thorns: They are those who listen to the word, 19. but anxiety over this world, and love of wealth, and other passions crowd in and strangle the word, and there is no fruit. 20. But those that have been sown in the good ground are those who hear the word, welcome it, and bear fruit, thirty or sixty or a hundred times what was sown."

NOTES

1. *one more time:* This verse is a virtual paraphrase of 3:7, 9, where Jesus is by the sea and directs his disciples to have a boat ready. The location by the sea recalls the call of the disciples in 1:16-20, the teaching of the crowds in 2:13, and the summary in 3:7, while anticipating another seaside assembly in 5:21.

   such a huge crowd: In this early part of the gospel Mark continually stresses the size of the crowds (2:2, 13; 3:9, 20, 32). They are in the ambivalent position of praising Jesus while limiting access to him, and of forcing him to distance himself from them (3:7, 9, 13).

   climbed into a boat . . . on the sea: The phrase causes difficulty in an already wordy sentence. Literally it says "so that Jesus sat on the sea, having entered into the boat." Some authors claim that "getting in" and "sitting" are an Aramaism for entering a boat (Taylor, *Mark* 251). Both Matthew and Luke omit the awkward "on the sea." Since sitting is a position for authoritative teaching, this phrase may foreshadow Jesus' power over the sea in 4:39-41 where he rebukes the sea and it obeys him. See the Notes on 4:35-41.

2. *in many ways:* The word *polla* can be taken as a neuter plural substantive ("many things") or adverbially as in the translation. Though most authors favor the substantive, "in many ways" refers to both the content and the method of Jesus' teaching.

3. *Pay attention. Look at this:* The Greek imperative *akouete* is similar to the beginning of the *Shema* ("Hear O Israel"), the creed recited daily by the Jewish people (Deut 6:4-5). However, Mark 4:1-34 contains little similarity to the *Shema* beyond this phrase. A more likely explanation is that the juxtaposition of hearing and seeing reflects Isa 6:6-10 and prepares for Mark 4:10-12.

   A sower went out: The Greek *exēlthen* ("go out") is used elsewhere of Jesus (1:38; 2:13; 2:17), and has led some authors to identify the sower with Jesus. Although the parable is usually called the parable of the sower, he appears only here and has minimal impact on the narrative. The real focus is the fate of the four seeds or sowings as in 4:13-20.

4. *While he was sowing:* The method of sowing is debated. Many authors follow Joachim Jeremias (*Parables* 11–12), who cites rabbinic texts to argue that in Palestine the seed is sowed first and then the whole field is plowed under. Others (K. D. White, Bernard Brandon Scott, *Hear Then the Parable*) argue that, while the field is already plowed, the method of planting the seed is "broadcast" so that some is inevitably lost. The issue is not crucial for interpretation, since the focus of the parable is the contrast between three failures and one extraordinary success.

   along a path . . . ate it up: This first sowing meets with almost instant failure. "Flew down" is a more descriptive translation of *ēlthen* than the normal "came" and captures better the realism of the parable.

5. *rocky ground:* The depiction of the fate of this seed is longer (vv. 5-6) than any other, and also repetitious. As the second half of the verse says, the rocky ground is ground with little topsoil over rocks. The term *petrōdes* is also reminiscent of the name Peter (3:16). In contrast to the first seed, there is initial growth before failure.

6. *when the sun came up:* This verse is a virtual paraphrase of the preceding one. The scorching of the sprouts at the rising of the sun is scarcely realistic since even minimal growth would have required a number of sunrises. Though generally realistic, the parables also shock by their strangeness. The sense is that the sprouts could not stand the constant heat of the sun. This prepares for the interpretation in v. 16 where the rocky ground stands for people who endure for a while but fall away at the onset of persecution.

7. *thornbushes:* Here the growth is more successful than in the previous cases. The grain has grown together with the thornbushes, but the thornbushes eventually destroy it.

   strangled it: The verb *sympignein* has the overtone of "crowd around" or "crush." The thornbushes are hardier than the grain and deprive it of food and light.

8. *they sprouted and increased and yielded fruit:* In Greek there is a switch from the singular in vv. 5-7 to the plural *alla* (lit. "other [seeds]"), and a shift from the aorist of punctiliar action to the imperfect of continuous action with two present participles ("sprouted and increased"). These subtle changes suggest both a multiplicity of sowings and a continual process of growth. The triadic pattern of sprouting, increasing, and giving fruit is in contrast to the three previous failures and suggests the ultimate "triumph" of the good seed.

thirty, sixty, and a hundred times: Again a triadic pattern appears. The extent of the harvest is a matter of contemporary debate. Jeremias argues that the "abnormal tripling" of the harvest "symbolizes the eschatological overflowing of divine fullness, surpassing all human measure" (*Parables* 150). Scott (*Hear Then the Parable* 386–88) cites evidence from Pliny (*Natural History* 18.21.95) and Varro (*On Agriculture* 1.44.2) that such harvests, though unusual, were known in antiquity. He prefers to call the harvest "superabundant." Resolution of this dispute is not crucial to interpreting the parable, since the important point is the contrast between the three failures and the bountiful yield in 4:8.

9. *You who can hear . . . pay attention:* The Greek literally says: "the one who has ears to hear, let that person hear." This verse provides an *inclusio* with the summons to hear in v. 3 and prepares for the statement on inauthentic hearing in vv. 10-12. This phrase, in the condensed form "the one who has ears, let that person hear *(ho echōn ous akousatō)* what the Spirit says," appears frequently in the book of Revelation as a summons to respond to a revelatory word (Rev 2:7, 11, 17, 29, 3:6, 13, 22; 13:9). It is rooted in the prophetic summons, most often addressed to rebellious people, to harken to God's commands (e.g., Jer 5:21; 9:20; Ezek 12:2).

10. *alone:* There is a rapid and unexplained change of scene, since Mark has nothing about the return of the boat to land or about the departure of the crowds. Yet in 4:35, after the discourse in parables, Jesus is on land, leaves the crowds, and again gets into a boat. Private instruction to Jesus' disciples appears here and in 4:34; 9:28, 35; 10:10, 32; 12:43; 13:3. While some authors see this pattern as an instance of the messianic secret (see Introduction), the private instruction does not always deal with christology. The pattern may also be influenced by the rabbinic practice of a public statement followed by a private explanation to disciples; see D. Daube, *The New Testament and Rabbinic Judaism* (London: Athlone, 1956) 141–50.

those who were with him along with the Twelve: "Those who were with him" translates *hoi peri auton.* Though similar to "his family" *(hoi par' autou)* in 3:21, the image is spatial rather than one of origin as in 3:32, 34; 9:15. This is the first mention of the Twelve after their selection (3:14) and an instance also in which they are associated with a larger group.

about the parables: The plural is strange here since only one parable has been given (4:3-9), which is not explicitly called a parable, and only one parable is explained (4:13-20). The questioners may be understood to be asking about the "many things in parables" of 4:2 and the parables of 3:23-27.

11. *has been granted the mystery:* The verb (lit. "has been given") is the perfect divine passive *(dedotai)* with the sense "God has granted." "Mystery" in the singular (contrast Matt 13:11; Luke 8:10, "mysteries" or "secrets") is used only here in the Synoptic gospels. The term is derived from the Greek *muein* ("to be silent"), and is used of the "mystery religions" (see Wis 14:15, 23, where it appears in a derogatory sense of secret rites and initiations). The sense here, however, is similar to that of Daniel 2 (vv. 18, 19, 27-29, 30, 47) where *raz* ("mystery") is used for the hidden purposes of God. The word *mystērion* appears twenty-one times in the Pauline writings, with different meanings: the revelation of the Christ event as God's previously hidden plan for human salvation (Rom 16:25-26; 1 Cor 2:7; 4:1; Eph 3:9), and a succinct statement of the content of the Christian proclamation (Col 2:2; 4:3; Eph 3:4; 6:19; 1 Tim 3:9, 16). In Rom 11:25 it appears in reference to the Jewish rejection of Jesus, the sense closest to Mark 4:11.

of the kingdom of God: In the immediate context this refers to the following parables of the kingdom (4:26-29, 30-32). Since it is also Mark's term for God's self-disclosure in the proclamation and activity of Jesus (1:15; 9:1), the mystery of the kingdom here has a strong christological focus.

to those who are outside: This echoes 3:31, 32, where the family that misunderstands Jesus is outside while the crowd is around Jesus. It also foreshadows Peter who stands outside after denying Jesus (14:68). "Outside" is not simply a spatial term but can also describe a relationship to Jesus.

everything occurs in parables: "Everything" *(ta panta)* is not specified, but refers most likely to both the teaching and the deeds of Jesus, and not simply to the parables of 4:1-34. The plural "in parables" often has the adverbial sense of "parabolically," describing the manner of speech and not simply the content (3:23; 4:2; 12:1).

12. *so that:* This verse is one of the most discussed and difficult in the New Testament. The question is whether misunderstanding and blindness were the purpose or the result of Jesus' parabolic teaching. "So that" *(hina)* is chosen deliberately to maintain the ambiguity of purpose or result. Though in classical Greek *hina* usually introduces purpose or intent, in the *Koinē* Greek of the NT period it can designate result. For other examples of *hina* in Mark that have a nuance of result, often after verbs of desiring or ordering, see 3:9; 5:18, 6:2, 8, 12; 9:9. A number of authors have proposed that *hina* here is a shortened form of *hina plērōthē* ("in order that it might be fulfilled"), followed by a quotation from the OT. Matthew (13:13) changes the *hina* to *hoti* ("because"), which makes the parabolic teaching an effect of the resistance of the hearers rather than its cause.

they may look and see but not perceive, and that they may hear and listen but not understand: This quotation of Isa 6:9-10 does not correspond exactly to the Masoretic Hebrew text (MT) or to the Septuagint. In Mark 4:12 the verbs are subjunctives, while in the Hebrew they are imperatives. The NRSV translation of the Hebrew text reads: "Go and say to this people: 'Keep listening but do not comprehend; keep looking but do not understand.'" In the LXX the verbs are in the future: "You will hear but not understand. . . ." Mark agrees with the *Targum of Isaiah* in having the verbs in the third rather than the second person, and in having the verb "be forgiven" rather than "be healed" in 4:12. Though the text of this Targum is much later than the NT, it may be based on Aramaic usage current at the time of Jesus.

lest: Equal controversy surrounds *mēpote*, which is primarily a conjunction expressing negative purpose ("lest ever"). It is also an adverb, which in post-classical Greek often means "perhaps." Jeremias *(Parables* 13–17) argues that *mēpote* is a mistranslation of the Aramaic *dil^emâ*, which can be translated "un-less." One problem with the mistranslation theory is that Mark's audience is Greek-speaking, and elsewhere he explains Aramaic phrases that appear in his gospel (5:41; 7:11, 34; 14:36; 15:34).

they convert and be forgiven: Here again the purpose of everything being in parables seems to preclude conversion. "Be forgiven" is a divine passive with the sense "God will forgive them." Those who interpret *mēpote* as "perhaps" place a period after "understand," so that this verse counters the blindness and deafness with a note of hope.

13. *Don't you understand this parable?:* The first clause can be a statement: "You don't understand," or a question: "Don't you understand?" In either case the sense is that of an implicit condition: "If you don't understand, then how can you . . ." "This parable" is multivalent. On one level it refers to the parable of the sower (4:1-9), on another level to the enigmatic saying of 4:11-12, and perhaps on still another level to the explanation of the parable in 4:13-20. The question is also strange in light of 4:10-12, where the disciples are given the mystery of the kingdom while for outsiders everything happens "in parables." A paraphrase of this verse (that might well have occurred to Mark and his first readers) might read as follows: "If you don't understand that the mystery of the kingdom is the paradox of the cross you will not understand the failure of the seeds and you will misinterpret the paradoxes of the reign of God that emerge in the following parables."

14. *The sower sows the word:* This introduction sets the tone for the whole allegory (see Interpretation); that is, the fate of the seed will stand for response to the word. In 1 Cor 3:5-9 sowing is a metaphor for preaching, and in *4 Ezra* 9:30-37 the Lord sows the Law among his people. Sowing also suggests moral activity in Hos 10:12: "sow for yourselves righteousness; reap steadfast love" (see also Job 4:8; Prov 11:18).

Whenever they hear: The verb "to hear" *(akouein)* in one of its forms appears in every description of the result of the sowing. The moods and tenses, however, convey different meanings. In vv. 15, 16 the verbs are subjunctive in a "present general" condition conveying the idea of an inevitable and constant state. Also the repetition of failed hearings illustrates the quotation of Isa 6:9-10: "that they may hear and listen, but not understand."

15. *Satan comes and takes away the word that is sowed among them:* In apocalyptic thought demons are sometimes portrayed as birds; see *1 Enoch* 90:8-13;

Apoc. Abr. 13:2-24; and Rev 18:2. In *Jubilees* 11:11-14 "Prince Mastema" (a virtual synonym for Satan) sends crows to eat the seed that is being planted. The reference in Mark to the seed taken away by Satan is not clear. Mary Ann Tolbert identifies it with the opponents of Jesus (scribes, Pharisees, and Jerusalem leaders) among whom the word of Jesus has not taken root (*Sowing the Gospel* 156), yet in 8:33 Peter is called "Satan" for not accepting Jesus' saying about his coming suffering. In favor of Tolbert's view is the use of the plural "sown among them *(eis autous)*."

16. *sown on rocky ground:* The metaphor here is mixed. The sowings on rocky ground symbolize those who accept the word joyfully but lack roots and are volatile, so that they fall away under trouble or persecution. "Fall away" (lit. "be scandalized") is not something that happens to plants. "Rocky ground" suggests a word play on the name Peter *(petrōdes),* and the fate of these seeds parallels the career of Peter in the gospel: initial enthusiasm (1:16-20) but failure under persecution or trouble (14:66-72). Also Jesus' prediction to the disciples that all will "fall away" during the Passion and that Peter will deny him (14:29-31) indicates that this sowing evokes failure in discipleship.

18. *those sown among thorns:* Philo *(Leg. All.* 3.248) interprets the thorns of Gen 3:18 as "passions" and "irrational appetites," much in the same sense as Mark does.

    who listen to the word: The verb "listen" in the periphrastic present participial form suggests people who have been listening over a longer period of time.

19. *but anxiety . . . the word:* The failure of these "listeners" is due to continuing conditions—cares of the world, love of wealth, and other desires—that strangle the word. This failed sowing also has echoes throughout Mark. For example, the rich young man who has been observing the commandments refuses Jesus' summons to follow because he has great wealth (10:17-22; see Tolbert, *Sowing the Word* 158–59). Wealth, power, and worldly concerns are obstacles to the values proposed by Jesus (see 6:14-29; 7:20-23; 10:32-45).

20. *those who hear the word, welcome it, and bear fruit:* The triad of proper responses counterbalances the triad of failures. There is also a contrast between inauthentic and authentic "hearing." As in the other three cases the initial action is simple "hearing," but here this is followed by welcoming. The verb "welcome" *(paradechontai)* contains the nuances of "receive from another," "accept as correct," and "welcome into one's home." A note of permanence is sounded in contrast to the temporary sojourn of the word in vv. 14-19.

    and bear fruit: Elsewhere in the NT bringing forth "fruit" is a metaphor for repentance, conversion, and good works (Matt 7:15-20; 21:43; John 15:2, 4, 5, 8, 16; Rom 6:22; 7:4-5; Gal 5:22-23). The use of fruit for virtues or proper moral attitudes is also frequent in the OT (e.g., Prov 11:30-31; Job 22:21 [LXX]; Sir 1:16-18; 6:18-19; 37:22-23).

    thirty, sixty, or a hundred times: The interpretation retains the surprising escalation of the parable (v. 8) so that this verse becomes an extravagant promise in contrast to the predicted rejection and failure of vv. 11-12.

INTERPRETATION

The sermon in parables in Mark 4:1-34, along with Mark 13, is one of the two major speeches of Jesus in this gospel. Aspects of the chapter suggest composition (often awkward) from different elements: the elaborate introduction of 4:1-2 with the threefold emphasis on teaching, and unclarity about the audience: in 4:1-9 Jesus speaks to the crowds, and in 4:10-12 to the disciples and others in private; in 4:13, 21, 24, 26, 30, there is no indication that Jesus has again returned to the crowd, yet 4:33 presumes this. There are different introductory formulas such as "he said to them" (4:2, 11, 13, 21, 24, 33) and simply "he said" (4:26, 30). While only one parable is given in 4:1-9, in 4:10 they ask him "about the parables." The statement in 4:10-12 that parables were given to outsiders to prevent their hearing them is in tension with 4:33 which says that Jesus used parables to adapt his teaching to his hearers. The material is diverse: a narrative parable and an application that may have been closely united (4:1-9, 13-20); an interposed saying (4:10-12) based on Isa 6:9-10, which is used in other contexts in the NT (Acts 28:26; John 12:40); four enigmatic sayings (4:21-25) that are found elsewhere in the other gospels (e.g. Matt 5:15; 10:26; 7:2); two "seed parables" (4:26-32) united by catchwords (sowing, seed); and a somewhat confusing conclusion (4:33-34). Various attempts to distinguish pre-Markan tradition from Mark's editorial additions have proved contradictory. Though Mark works with tradition here, it cannot be exactly reconstructed.

The chapter as it now stands is composed in concentric parallelism to highlight the central motifs: (A) the introduction (vv. 1-2) is parallel in length and theme to the conclusion A' (vv. 33-34); (B) the parable of the sower (4:3-9) corresponds to (B') the seed parables (4:26-32), again in length and theme; (C) the "parable theory" or reason for speaking in parables (4:10-12) is parallel to (C') the enigmatic sayings of 4:21-25; and so the center of the chapter is (D) the allegory of the seeds (4:13-20), with its stress on the difficulties in accepting the word. The structure confirms a Markan theme, present from the beginning of the gospel: The word of Jesus is a summons to conversion, but that word can meet resistance and failure.

After a scenic beginning that again stresses the magnetism and authority of Jesus, Mark 4 begins with the parable of the sower, or better "the four sowings." This unfolds with a minimum of detail but with skillful use of repetition. In what seems a haphazard manner the sower scatters seed; three of these sowings fail while the fourth yields an extraordinary harvest. This parable has often been used as a key to the ministry of the historical Jesus. C. H. Dodd stresses that since a good harvest emerged, Jesus proclaims that *now* is the time for the harvest (*Parables of the Kingdom* 145–47). Jeremias calls attention to the difference between the time of sowing and that of the harvest as well as to the discrepancy between the failures and the great harvest (*Parables* 149–51). The parable is one of assurance to the disciples that despite failure and opposition what God has begun in the ministry of Jesus will have ultimate success. J. D. Crossan joins this parable to the parable of the mustard seed, and stresses the miracle of the harvest rather than its size (*In Parables* 51). The harvest is a surprising gift that underscores the gift-like quality of the reign of God.

Close attention to the movement and images of the parable suggests another possibility. The first three sowings convey a rhythmic temporality. Each begins with the mention of a seed, proceeds to the negative situation the seed encounters—barren path, rocky soil, and choking thorns—and concludes with the failure of the seed. The parable does not hurry to its conclusion, and it achieves its dramatic effect not by simply listing the three failures in contrast to the great harvest but by depicting a progression in the growth of the seed. The first has virtually no chance of survival and is devoured by the birds before any roots are put out. The second seems to be growing—"immediately it sprang up" (v. 5)—but it withers under the heat of the sun. The third grows higher, to a stage where the buds are almost ready, but is choked off at the last minute. This rhythmic and ascending progression involves the hearers in the mystery of growth. A natural conclusion would be that the fourth seed "brought forth grain," and that the harvest was good.

The expectation of the hearers is shattered, and the rhythmic progress of nature, which lulls the hearers into acceptance, is broken in the final verse, which explodes with verbs of motion. The seeds "fell" (*epesen*) and "brought forth" (*edidou*), "growing up" (*anabainonta*) and "increasing" (*auxanomena*), and they yielded thirtyfold, sixtyfold, and a hundredfold. The contrast between a seventy-five per cent failure and such an extraordinary harvest suggests that there is no comparison between the expectation of the kingdom and its effect. The manner in which the climactic verse (4:8) explodes, after the lull of the three previous verses, conveys the advent of the kingdom in Jesus' teaching and activity (1:14-15) as something that shatters the way by which life normally operates and the patterns it involves.

The scene shifts dramatically after the parable of the sowings to a private setting of Jesus with the Twelve and others who were around him who begin to ask him about the parables. The following verses (4:10-12) are among the most obscure and debated in the whole NT, and no one explanation has carried the day. The most disturbing element is the deterministic and sectarian theology put on the lips of Jesus. Revelation is given to insiders, and outsiders are consigned in advance to misunderstanding.

Any explanation must consider the biblical understanding of God's sovereignty and the predestinarian thrust of much biblical and early Jewish thought. This appears in the "hardening" theology of the OT (Exod 4:21; 8:15, 32; 9:34), which, in effect, holds that God can be rejected or resisted by human beings only because God has so willed this in advance. It is present in the commissions to the prophets to announce divine judgment; for example, Isa 6:10: "Make the mind of this people dull and stop their ears and shut their eyes." Jeremiah is called "to pluck up and to break down, to destroy and to overthrow" (1:9) and is ordered to proclaim: "Hear this, O foolish and senseless people, who have eyes but do not see, who have ears but do not hear" (5:21). The atmosphere of these verses is also apocalyptic; i.e., hidden revelation is given to a select group, creating a strong distinction between insiders and outsiders. Determinism is a characteristic of apocalyptic. In Dan 2:28 God is one who reveals mysteries and has disclosed what will (necessarily) happen at the end of days (see *1 Enoch* 83:7; 91:5). According to the *War Scroll* from Qumran the day for the destruction of the sons of darkness has already been appointed (1QM 1:9-10), and in 1QpHab 7:13 "all the seasons of God will come about at their appointed time." In Mark 13 the course of history is determined, and the elect will be saved at the end. While shocking to modern ears, a literal reading of Mark 4:10-12 as promising revelation to an elect few, along with the predetermined rejection by outsiders, would be familiar to many of Mark's readers (see also 2 Thess 2:9-12).

The origin and function of these verses in Mark are also disputed. Many authors view 4:10-12 as a later insertion between the parable (4:3-9) and its interpretation (4:13-20). The verses are thought to originate in disputes with Jews in the early decades of emergent Christianity, especially since Isa 6:9-10 is cited in both Acts 28:23 and John 12:40 in a context of Jewish rejection of Christian claims.

Understanding Mark's meaning is complicated by an unwarranted assumption that 4:10-12 and 4:33-34 constitute a Markan "parable theory." The assumption is made that the outsiders of 4:10 and the "them" of 4:33-34 are the same. But the audience for the different parts of Mark 4:1-34 is not always clear, and is complicated by the use of two formulas: "he said," and "he said to them." In 4:1-9 Jesus clearly talks to the crowd, and in 4:10-12 to the Twelve and those around him. In 4:13 he speaks "to them" as he does in 4:21 and 26, but in 4:26, 30 (the parables of the seed growing secretly and the mustard seed) the introduction is simply "he said," while in 4:33, 34 "he said to them" reappears. Most likely the audience envisioned in 4:10-25 is the audience of 4:10, the Twelve and those around Jesus, while the audience of 4:26-32 is the crowd assembled earlier (4:1-2). While 4:33-34 represents a comment by the omniscient narrator, the narrative itself resumes in 4:35-36, where it is mentioned that Jesus leaves "the crowd" to go to the other side.

The shift of audience also corresponds to the structure proposed above, where 4:10-25 are the middle sections of the chapter (C, D, C') and deal with similar themes: failure and hiddenness. Thus 4:10-12 treats the "mystery of the kingdom" that is revealed (given) to insiders but causes blindness to outsiders. Although 4:26-32 contains the only two "kingdom" parables in this chapter, the kingdom has been proclaimed publicly (1:14-15) to a group larger than the disciples. The conclusion in 4:33-34 deals more broadly with the parabolic teaching of Jesus and reflects the pattern found elsewhere in Mark of public actions or teachings followed by private explanation (7:14-23; 9:14-28; 10:17-27; 12:41-43; 13:1-3).

The question remains: What is this Markan mystery of the kingdom given to insiders? As mentioned in the Notes, the pair "insiders and outsiders" describes a relationship to Jesus; it is not equated with the distinction between crowds and disciples. The mystery of the kingdom of God in the NT does not denote something simply incomprehensible to human reason, as in later Christian theology. Rather, it refers to the once hidden, but now revealed, salvific action of God manifest in the proclamation of a rejected and crucified Messiah (see 1 Cor 2:1-2, 7; Rom 11:25; 16:25; Eph 1:9; 3:3, 4, 9). Christian preachers, among whom we should count Mark the Evangelist, are to be "stewards of the mysteries of God" (1 Cor 4:1).

The mystery of the kingdom that causes blindness and deafness in Mark's Gospel is the paradox of God's will manifest in the cross of Jesus. As noted, "insiders" are those who do the will of God (3:31-35). In 8:31 when Jesus first predicts his future suffering he states that "it is necessary" *(dei)*, a term that suggests divine necessity or the will of God. When Peter rejects the necessity of suffering, Jesus rebukes him by saying: "You do not think the thoughts of God, but human thoughts" (8:33). Peter's failure is not due to lack of dedication or courage, but to the inability to understand the Passion as willed by God. At Gethsemane Jesus himself confronts the mystery of suffering when he prays: "Abba, Father, all things are possible to you; remove this cup from me; yet not what I will but what you will" (14:36). The will of God in Mark is that Jesus suffer and die. Jesus accepts this as God's will. Those who are truly around him and who constitute his family are those who accept God's will. Such is the mystery of God's way of reigning (4:10), which when accepted makes one an "insider" but also causes blindness and deafness in "outsiders" that, in Mark's view, precludes their conversion (4:11-12).

The interpretation of the parable of the sower in 4:13-20 is generally recognized to be not from Jesus himself, but from the early church. "The word" used absolutely in 4:14 reflects early Christian usage (e.g., Acts 4:4; 8:4; 1 Thess 1:6; Gal 6:6). Other terms that are found here but not elsewhere in the Synoptic Gospels are frequent in other NT writings, especially the Pauline letters (e.g., "sow" in the sense of preach, see 1 Cor 9:11; "root" for inward stability, see Col 2:7 and Eph 3:17; and "the lure" of riches, see Col 2:8 and 2 Pet 2:13). The situation of persecution (v. 16) represents not the context of Jesus' ministry but a more developed church setting. The tendency to turn the eschatological sayings of Jesus into ethical ones is characteristic of early church teaching. Also, though not called such, the interpretation in 4:13-20 turns the parable into an allegory, since each point is given independent significance that is to be understood by insiders.

Although Mark may have taken over this allegorical interpretation from his tradition, it has significant echoes throughout his gospel and provides one of the hermeneutical keys to his work. As Tolbert has noted, Mark 4:1-20 "provides the audience with the fundamental typology of hearing-response that organizes the entire plot of the Gospel." The sower and its interpretation "develop in imagistic or symbolic terms a theological vision of the world and Jesus' mission in it" (*Sowing the Gospel* 164–65).

The different fates of the seeds become images for different negative responses to Jesus and his teaching throughout the gospel. In 4:15 the seed along the way symbolizes situations in which Satan immediately snatches the word. This situation is hauntingly similar to what happens after Jesus proclaims "the word" (*ton logon*, used absolutely, as in 4:14) that he must suffer and die (8:31-32). In the very next phrase Peter rebukes Jesus for this saying, and Jesus immediately calls Peter "Satan." In 4:17 the fate of the seeds is that they have no root, and when tribulation or persecution comes they fall away (lit. "are scandalized"). In Mark, being scandalized is clearly the fate of those who were close to Jesus but who failed after a short time: The family and relatives of Jesus are initially amazed at his teaching and wisdom (6:2), only to be scandalized; the disciples, who Jesus prophesies will be scandalized when the shepherd is struck (14:27-28), flee when Jesus is arrested (14:50). In 4:19 the word is choked by the lure of riches and desire for other things. In the only "negative call" narrative in Mark a young man refuses to follow Jesus because he has many possessions (10:22), and Jesus speaks about the difficulty the rich have in entering the kingdom of God (10:23-25). The seed (the "word") that will bear fruit is the one that is heard and accepted (4:20). This last verse functions as an example of true discipleship for the Markan community. The summons to discipleship is in the form of a call (1:16-20; 2:13-14), and its reward will be a "hundredfold" (10:30), just as the good seed bears fruit a hundredfold (4:20). The allegory of the seeds then echoes throughout the gospel. By placing it after the revelation of the mystery of the kingdom Mark suggests that "those who were about him with the Twelve," even though they are disciples, may become "outsiders."

And yet the parable of the sower/seeds conveys a message of hope. The world is the battleground between Jesus and Satan. Jesus proclaims the good news of God's reign, which is the ultimate victory over the power of evil. The parable proclaims that, despite Satan's continuing attacks and the failure of the word due to human weakness, those who hear and accept the word into their lives will bear fruit in an extraordinary manner that surpasses human expectation.

FOR REFERENCE AND FURTHER STUDY

Beavis, Mary Ann. *Mark's Audience: The Literary and Social Setting of Mark 4.11-12.* Sheffield: JSOT Press, 1989.

Boucher, Madeleine I. *The Mysterious Parable. A Literary Study.* Washington, D.C.: Catholic Biblical Association, 1977.

Crossan, John Dominic. *In Parables. The Challenge of the Historical Jesus.* New York: Harper & Row, 1973.

Dodd, Charles Harold. *The Parables of the Kingdom.* New York: Scribner's, 1965.

Donahue, John R. *The Gospel in Parable. Metaphor, Narrative, and Theology in the Synoptic Gospels.* Minneapolis: Fortress, 1990.

Drury, John. "The Sower, the Vineyard, and the Place of Allegory in the Interpretation of Mark's Parables," *JTS* 24 (1973) 367–79.

Evans, Craig A. "On the Isaianic Background of the Sower Parable," *CBQ* 47 (1985) 464–68.

Fay, Greg. "Introduction to Incomprehension: The Literary Structure of Mark 4:1-34," *CBQ* 51 (1989) 65–81.

Heil, John Paul. "Reader-Response and the Narrative Context of the Parables about Growing Seed in Mark 4:1-34," *CBQ* 54 (1992) 271–86.

Jeremias, Joachim. *The Parables of Jesus.* New York: Scribner's, 1963.

Keegan, Terence J. "The Parable of the Sower and Mark's Jewish Leaders," *CBQ* 56 (1994) 501–18.

Knowles, Michael P. "Abram and the Birds in *Jubilees* 11: A Subtext for the Parable of the Sower?" *NTS* 41 (1995) 145–51.

Marcus, Joel. "Blanks and Gaps in the Markan Parable of the Sower," *Biblical Interpretation* 5 (1997) 247–62.

_____. "Mark 4:10-12 and Marcan Epistemology," *JBL* 103 (1984) 557–74.

Sellew, Philip. "Oral and Written Sources in Mark 4.1-34," *NTS* 36 (1990) 234–67.

Scott, Bernard Brandon. *Jesus, Symbol-Maker for the Kingdom.* Philadelphia: Fortress, 1981.

Tolbert, Mary Ann. *Sowing the Gospel. Mark's World in Literary-Historical Perspective.* Minneapolis: Fortress, 1989.

Tuckett, Christopher M. "Mark's Concerns in the Parables Chapter (Mark 4,1-34)," *Bib* 69 (1988) 1–26.

White, K. D. "The Parable of the Sower," *JTS* 15 (1964) 300–07.

15. *Four Sayings on Revelation and Two Kingdom Parables* (4:21-34)

21. He spoke again to them: "Surely a lamp is not brought in so that you might put it under a bushel basket or under a bed; no, rather that you might set it on a lampstand. 22. For, you see, there is nothing hidden except to be disclosed, nor is there any secret except that it will come to light. 23. If anyone can hear what I say, pay attention." 24. Then he said to them: "Consider what you are now hearing; the measure you use will be the measure used also on you, and even more. 25. If someone has something, that person will receive a gift; but if someone does not have anything, even what he has will be taken away." 26. And he would say: "The kingdom of God is like this. It is as if a man scatters seed upon the earth. 27. He then goes to sleep and gets up again night and day; but the seed sprouts and then begins to grow—how this occurs, he does not understand. 28. But the earth bears fruit by itself, first the stalk, then the head, and finally the full kernel of grain in the head. 29. But when the grain is ripe, without any delay he wields the sickle, since it is time for the harvest." 30. He again spoke: "How shall we find a comparison for the kingdom of God, or with what parable can we present it? 31. Consider the mustard seed! When it is sown on the ground, it is the smallest of all the seeds on earth. 32. But whenever it is sown, it grows up and becomes greater than all the bushes, and it produces great branches so that the birds of the heavens make their dwellings in its shade."

33. He was then accustomed to proclaim the word to them through such parables, to the extent that they could listen; 34. and he would not speak to them except in parables, but he explained all things to his disciples in private.

NOTES

21. *Surely a lamp is not brought in:* This construction translates the Greek interrogative particle *mēti*, which expects a negative answer. The Greek reads literally "the lamp enters" *(erchetai)*, leading some commentators to identify the lamp with Jesus (see Rev 21:23). But *erchetai* can be used in the passive sense of "be brought in." Also the Greek could be influenced by an underlying Semitic expression meaning "a lamp is brought in."

under a bushel basket: The Greek word for "bushel basket" *(modion)* is a Latinism. As in the longer parables, there is a combination of realism and unrealism here. The everyday household furnishings (lamp, basket, bed, lampstand) are realistic, but the image itself is unrealistic since the burning oil lamp might well set the basket or the bed on fire.

22. *For, you see:* This translates the explanatory *gar* in Greek and is the real point of the comparison. Light is to be revealed, not concealed.

nothing hidden . . . come to light: The saying, which is expressed in synonymous parallelism for emphasis, is not a clear explanation of v. 21, since the lamp is not really hidden. The saying stresses that concealment is temporary and that its ultimate purpose is disclosure; it thus qualifies the stress on private teaching of 4:10-12. It also fits in with the messianic secret motif and with Mark's eschatology, both of which look to the final revelation of Jesus (13:26; 14:62).

23. *If anyone can hear what I say, pay attention:* This reproduces, with the slight change from the relative to the conditional construction, the conclusion of the parable of the sower (4:9), and reintroduces the theme of "hearing" from 4:13-20. This saying also punctuates the maxims of 4:21-25, since the final two sayings move away from the theme of revelation to that of its effects on humans and human response.

24. *the measure you use . . . and even more:* Mark's "measure for measure" saying also appears in Matt 7:2 and Luke 6:38 as a conclusion to warnings against judging, in which context it makes more sense than in Mark. It is used as a variation of the Golden Rule (Matt 7:12; Luke 6:31). The saying also appears in the *Targum of Isaiah,* commenting on the difficult Hebrew text of Isa 27:8: "In the measure you will measure with, they will measure you" (Bruce Chilton, *A Galilean Rabbi and His Bible* [Wilmington, Del.: Michael Glazier, 1984] 124). While the saying may also reflect folk wisdom (e.g., "You only get as good as you give"), in Mark's context it seems to be a variation on the interpretation of the sower. The response (hearing) is the measure you use (equivalent to your response to the word), and it will be the measure to which you will be held. But in those cases where the response is favorable, even more will be added (the bountiful harvest).

25. *If someone has . . . will be taken away:* Again a probably once independent saying is placed here by Mark. Its location by Matthew and Luke at the end of the parables of the talents/pounds (Matt 25:29; Luke 19:26) seems more logical. Once more, this saying takes up a harsh idea of folk wisdom: "The rich get richer, and the poor get poorer." It appears in an apocalyptic context in *4 Ezra* 7:25 as "empty things are for the empty, full things for the full," where it is a warning that one will receive in the eschaton the "full measure" of what a person is now. Mark uses it in the context of his parables discourse (see Interpretation).

26. *And he would say:* Mark shifts here from the introductory phrase *kai elegen autois* ("he spoke to them") to the simple *kai elegen* ("he would say"), the imperfect of continuous or customary action. In the structure of the chapter adopted here the following two parables are addressed to the same audience as 4:3-9 and may have once been part of a traditional unit of "seed" parables.

The kingdom of God is like this: Though it is affirmed by virtually all NT scholars that Jesus proclaimed the kingdom of God in parables, this and the following one are the only two explicit "kingdom" parables in Mark. Both have a somewhat awkward introductory formula (vv. 26, 30).

scatters seed upon the earth: The phrasing conveys an even more random method of sowing than in 4:3.

27. *He then goes to sleep and gets up:* The sower's action is described in a rhythmic and lulling pattern linked by four uses of *kai* ("and").

   night and day: The order reflects the Jewish custom of reckoning the night as the beginning of the following day. The pattern of this verse stresses the ordinary, routine, and disengaged action of the sower, which itself would be somewhat unrealistic since common agricultural practices reflected in the parables of the sower (4:3-9) and of the weeds and the wheat in Matt 13:24-30 imply that sown fields must be overseen and tended.

   but the seed sprouts and then begins to grow: There are two verbs of growth, "sprout" *(blasta)* and "begins to grow" *(mēkynetai;* lit. "lengthens"). The repetition of verbs of growth serves, as do the verbs of rising and sleeping, to create a sense of the unhurried passage of time.

28. *bear fruit:* The use of the verb *karpophorei* echoes 4:20, where the good seed "bears fruit."

   by itself: The Greek *automatē* (an adjective employed adverbially here) is used of things that happen without visible cause. In the description of the plague of darkness in Wis 17:6 it is said that "no power of fire could give them light . . . except a dreadful self-kindled *(automatē)* fire." The adjective is used also in the LXX of Lev 25:5, 11 to describe the untilled growth during the sabbatical and jubilee years. These uses suggest that God's power stands behind the growth.

   first the stalk, then the head, and finally the full kernel: The four stages of growth (including "ripe" in v. 29) are another instance in this short parable of the repetition of words to create a sense of an unhurried and measured passage of time. They also "replace the four kinds of soil in the parable of the seeds to underscore not good hearing, but the unknown power by which the word of the kingdom achieves a happy result in the people who hear well" (Gundry, *Mark* 231).

29. *without any delay he wields the sickle:* The verb *apostellei,* which normally means "send out," is here translated "wields," since the verse is a virtual quotation of Joel 3:13: "put in the sickle, for the harvest is ripe." Since the verb is used in 3:14 and 6:7 in a missionary context and since harvest has overtones of eschatological urgency (see Joel 3:13), these nuances may well be present here.

30. *how shall we find a comparison?:* For a similar double introduction see Isa 40:18: "To whom then will you liken God, or what likeness compare him with?" This language is also characteristic of later rabbinic parables.

   with what parable: The term "parable" is used in the Jewish wider senses of "illustration" or even "riddle" (Hebrew *mashal*).

31. *the mustard seed:* The seed of the mustard plant was proverbial for its smallness; see Matt 17:20 for faith the size of a mustard seed. The mustard plant, the seeds of which are used for flavoring, grows along the Sea of Galilee to a height of two to six feet. Pliny (*Nat. Hist.* 19.170-171) describes it as a hardy plant that tends to germinate rapidly and take over a garden. The point is that the kingdom is both hardy and intrusive (see J. D. Crossan, *The Historical Jesus* [San Francisco: HarperSanFrancisco, 1991] 274).

32. *greater than all the bushes:* Given the actual size of the mustard bush, there is parabolic exaggeration and irony here.

so that the birds of the heavens make their dwellings in its shade: In the OT great trees are sometimes a symbol of national power. In Dan 4:20-21 the great tree under which "lived the beasts of the field, and in its branches dwelt the birds of the sky" is a symbol for the person and power of Nebuchadnezzar (Dan 4:19). In Ezek 17:22-23 God will take a sprig of a great cedar and plant it in order that it might produce fruit and become a noble cedar. Then "under it every kind of bird will live; in the shade of its branches winged creatures of every kind." The verbal correspondence between Mark 4:32 and Ezek 17:23, where the birds nest in the shade *(hypo tēn skian)* suggests that this is the primary OT allusion in Mark. If so, then the reign of God proclaimed by Jesus is, like the renewed Israel, the place where living creatures will find refuge. There is also a comic irony in portraying the kingdom not as a lofty cedar but as a mustard bush. For the use of this imagery in the Q version, see the Interpretation.

33. *he was accustomed:* The imperfect *(elalei)* of "speak" or "say" *(lalein)* is used of customary action.

the word: This is used absolutely here as a virtual summary of the teaching of Jesus, as in 4:14; see also 1:45; 2:1-2.

to the extent that they could listen: This statement most likely refers to the crowds, who are the audience of 4:1-9, 26-32. Some authors argue that it was originally the conclusion to the pre-Markan collection of parables.

34. *except in parables:* This is a virtual repetition of 4:33a, and illustrates the familiar Markan technique of duplicate expressions.

he explained: The noun "interpretation" *(epilysis)* and the verb "explain" *(epilyein)* are sometimes used of explanations of religious or oracular statements.

to his disciples: Though this verse is often seen as a repetition of 4:11, the focus is different. The earlier verses say nothing about explanation, but simply "to you the mystery is given." Also, the recipients of the gift are the Twelve and "those around him," while here "his disciples" receive the explanations. This verse foreshadows other instances in which Jesus interprets enigmatic teaching (and events) to his disciples. These explanations usually center on things of importance to the Markan community: proper moral conduct (7:17-21), divorce (10:10-12), and the danger of wealth (10:23-30).

INTERPRETATION

The sayings in Mark 4:21-25 derive from a collection of wisdom sayings and have parallels in Q and in the *Gospel of Thomas,* and appear in Matthew and Luke in other contexts. Luke follows Mark in repeating the saying on the lamp (4:21) in his "parable chapter" (Luke 8:16) but locates the Q version in 11:33. Matthew omits 4:21 from his parable chapter and relocates it to the Sermon on the Mount (5:15). Similarly, Luke parallels the following saying on hiddenness and revelation (4:22) in his parable chapter (8:17) and in a Q section (12:2), while Matthew omits it from the parable chapter and places it in his discourse on mission (10:26). The saying on measuring is omitted by both Matthew and Luke in their parable chapter, but they have variations of it in the Sermon on the Mount/Plain (Matt 7:2; Luke 6:38). Finally, Matthew and Luke repeat the saying on giving and receiving (4:25) at parallel places in their parable section (Matt 13:12; Luke 8:18) but repeat Q versions at the end of the parables on the talents/pounds (Matt 25:29; Luke 19:26). The presence of these sayings in such different traditions and locations argues well (by the criterion of multiple attestation) that they derive from Jesus, while the use of them by the different evangelists shows the flexibility of the developing tradition. Only Mark has made them into a unified group and located them at such a critical juncture in his parable chapter.

Even though Mark has deliberately located these somewhat enigmatic sayings here, their contextual meaning is not totally clear. The first two (vv. 21-22) are correlative to the theme of concealment/disclosure and the contrast between appearance and reality that runs through this chapter. They also counter any sectarian interpretation of the "mystery" given to the insiders of 4:10-12. The purpose of the disclosure of God's plan to the Twelve and to the disciples is ultimately that it may be revealed, that its light may be put on a lampstand. Mark's readers may well see in this a challenge to missionary activity. Living after the disclosure of the mystery of the kingdom in the death and resurrection of Jesus, they are now summoned to bring it to light, in confidence that at the final judgment (see 13:26; 14:62) all that has been hidden will be revealed.

With the formulaic call to listen in 4:23 the thrust of the sayings shifts. The final two sayings (4:24-25) maintain the atmosphere of threat and warning in the interpretation of the parable of the sower (4:13-20). Authentic listening to (and not mere "hearing") the teaching of Jesus is necessary. Human freedom ("the measure you give") can determine whether the seed will take root. Satan, rootless enthusiasm, and anxiety over worldly things can be the measure by which the seed is proved to be fruitless. But acceptance will bring with it "even more." The final saying (4:25), originally an independent bit of folk wisdom, is now related to the parable discourse. Those who, like the good soil, receive the teaching of Jesus will be even more gifted; as for those outsiders who do not really listen to the teaching of Jesus, even their present status and privileges ("what he has") will be taken away. As in much of the wisdom and prophetic biblical teaching, threat and promise alternate.

The two seed parables (4:26-29 and 4:30-32) are identified explicitly as parables of the kingdom of God by their introductory formulas. They make similar points about the nature of God's kingdom: There is a sharp contrast between small beginnings (the seeds) and great conclusions (the harvest, the great bush); something is happening in the present (the process of growth), and the process is mysterious to humans (the seed growing *automatē*, the small mustard seed turning into a large bush), which suggests divine guidance. These two seed parables may well once have formed a pre-Markan unit with the parable of the sower/seeds (4:3-9). Their message was one of hope for Jesus' discouraged followers and for the persecuted Markan community. They affirmed that despite the rejection and opposition that Jesus' "word" encountered, the "seed" sown in and through Jesus is growing and mysteriously moving toward the fullness of God's kingdom.

Taken as a whole, Mark 4:1-34 develops the major theological motifs of this gospel. A christology emerges that not only continues the portrait of Jesus as one who teaches with authority (1:27; see 4:1-2) but also proclaims that the death and resurrection of Jesus constitute the mystery of the kingdom. This is present in the material that precedes and follows this chapter. In 3:23-30 Jesus is "the stronger one" (see 1:7) who comes to despoil the kingdom of Satan (see 1:24). The kind of disbelief that attributes Jesus' power to Satan is blasphemy (3:28), the same charge that will be leveled at Jesus (14:64). In the pericope that immediately follows the parable discourse Jesus is addressed as "teacher" (4:38; see 4:1-2, 33-34), but his teaching is manifest in his control over the chaotic powers of nature (4:35-41; see Pss 65:7; 104:7; 107:23-31, where God has power over the raging sea and rescues those threatened by it).

In Mark 4 Jesus is the powerful one whose power will ultimately be made manifest even if it is now as hidden as the process of the growth of the seeds. The seed parables acquire a christological overtone and function as parables of hope for the community. Just as the seed has its own power and dynamism that is finally revealed at the harvest, so too does the mystery of the kingdom of God. The contrast between the power of Jesus, which is hidden and absent on the cross, and his glory when he returns (13:26-27; 14:62) is no less than the contrast between the smallest of all the seeds and the greatest of all the shrubs. The parables of Mark 4:1-34 are metaphors for the christology of the gospel.

Equally important in both content and context is the theme of discipleship, which in Mark is the correlate to christology. Discipleship permeates ch. 4 and is highlighted by the repeated demands for "hearing" (4:3, 9, 23, 24, 33). In biblical thought hearing *(akouein)* is intimately related to obedience *(hypakouein)*; the demands of God are expressed in the daily prayer that begins "Hear, O Israel" (Deut 6:4-9; 11:13-21; Num 15:37-41; see Mark 12:29).

In the allegory of the seeds each unsuccessful sowing begins with a "hearing" (4:15, 16, 18), and the outsiders of 4:12 "hear but do not understand." Throughout Mark failure in discipleship is equated with improper hearing. In 7:14-17 the disciples hear the "parable" about the clean and the unclean but are without understanding (7:18; see 4:12). The disciples who do not understand Jesus' teaching about the bread are described as "having ears" but not hearing (8:18). Even the opponents "hear" the teaching of Jesus but do not let his teaching take root.

On the contrary, in 4:20 there is a threefold progression in responding to the word—hearing, accepting, and bearing fruit—that becomes a paradigm for true discipleship. This structure corresponds to the progress of the good seed in 4:8: budding, increasing (growing), and bearing fruit even to a hundredfold. The calls of the disciples in Mark convey a threefold structure (1:16-20; 3:13b-19; 6:7-13). They begin with a call or summons that is heard, and that then issues in following or "being with" Jesus (3:14); this in turn is followed by preaching, teaching, and healing (3:14-15; 6:8-13). True discipleship is engagement with the life and following the way of Jesus, which will yield a bountiful harvest. Both the parables and the middle section of Mark 4:1-34 function as a warning against false discipleship: superficial hearing manifest in an initial and rootless enthusiasm, seduction by wealth, or failure in persecution. They also function to encourage the community in the face of failure and persecution (see 13:9-13). Growth is taking place; initial failure is not the whole picture. Jesus is powerful in word and work; he comes to rescue his community even when they are lacking in faith (see 4:35-41).

Eschatology (or the temporal dimension of God's kingdom) is a final theological motif of this chapter. Mark's eschatology is very much like that of Jesus: eschatology "in the process of realization" or proleptic eschatology, a combination of the "already" and the "not yet." Jesus announces that the time is fulfilled and the kingdom is imminent (1:14-15), and yet its full manifestation is in the future (8:30–9:1; 13:26; 14:62). The community lives between the resurrection and the parousia. The seed parables place the reader at a similar time, between planting and harvest. They also offer a message of hope because the future will be in extravagant contrast to the present. Such an eschatology may be opposed by some in the community who see the present as the only real time of manifestation. The Markan Jesus predicts that some will come claiming his name and authority and will perform signs and wonders (see 13:6, 21-22). Even though Mark devotes a great deal of space to miracles, especially in the first seven chapters, he subordinates them to the message of the cross, perhaps in opposition to those who invoked miracle-working powers as a sign of the presence of the kingdom. These parables that emphasize hiddenness and smallness are counters to such a perspective.

The discourse in parables offers manifold possibilities for the proclamation of the individual texts in either the context of Jesus' kingdom preaching or that of Mark's theology. A continuity exists between these contexts especially in the message of hope that the parables offer, in their stress on the contrast between appearance and reality, and in the parables as a summons to engagement with the life and teaching of Jesus. Also present is the motif of "grace." It is the power of God that gives the growth. Mark 4:1-34 offers a message of hope, but without presumption, and its warnings about false or superficial hearing can speak to a church today about the dangers of "cheap grace."

The miracle and mystery of growth provide a polyvalent cluster of images that evoke God's power and graciousness in all areas of life. In other NT books images of growth have engendered theological reflection. For John (12:23-25) the death of the seed followed by the bearing of much fruit becomes a symbol of the death and resurrection of Jesus as well as the gift of self in a life of discipleship that bears fruit and issues in life eternal. Paul adopts images of planting and growing for ministry in the community (1 Cor 3:5-10), confident that "only God gives the growth" (1 Cor 3:7). The seed that dies, only to prepare for the plant, becomes an image of the transformation hoped for in the resurrection (1 Cor 15:35-36, 42-43). The seeds that Mark planted in 4:1-34 continue to bear fruit.

FOR REFERENCE AND FURTHER STUDY

Derrett, J. Duncan M. "Ambivalence: Sowing and Reaping at Mark 4,26-29," *Estudios Bíblicos* 48 (1990) 489–510.
Funk, Robert W. "The Looking-Glass Tree Is for the Birds. Ezekiel 17:22-24; Mark 4:30-32," *Int* 27 (1973) 3–9.
McArthur, Harvey K. "The Parable of the Mustard Seed," *CBQ* 33 (1971) 198–201.
Steinhauser, Michael G. "The Sayings of Jesus in Mark 4:21-22, 24b-25," *Forum* 6 (1990) 197–217.
Weeden, Theodore J. *Mark—Traditions in Conflict.* Philadelphia: Fortress, 1971.

16. *Jesus' Power over the Wind and Waves* (4:35-41)

35. Later on that day, when evening arrived, he said to them: "Let us cross over to the other side." 36. After leaving the crowd behind, they took him along in the boat, just as he was, and other boats were with them. 37. But suddenly a fierce windstorm came up, and the waves began to break over the boat, so that all of a sudden the boat began to be swamped. 38. But he himself was in the stern of the boat, sleeping on a cushion. And they roused him and said: "Teacher! Don't you care that we are about to die?" 39. Then after getting up, he rebuked the wind and

said to the sea: "Quiet! Be still." And the wind ceased, and there was dead calm. 40. He then asked them: "Why are you so fearful? You still do not have faith, do you?" 41. And a deep sense of awe came over them, and they kept saying to one another: "Who indeed is this person when even the wind and the sea obey him?"

NOTES

35. *Later on that day, when evening arrived:* This is a parade example of Markan two-step time progressions in which the second phrase specifies the first (see 1:32, 35; 2:20; 10:30; 14:12, 15:32). The mention of evening foreshadows a similar sea miracle in 6:45-52, and it heightens the subsequent dramatic development, since a storm at sea is more frightening at night. "Evening" also signals the end of the day of parabolic teaching, much as in 1:32 at the end of the first "day" of Jesus' ministry.

    let us cross over: From this point on in the gospel Jesus is very much an itinerant who moves beyond the confines of Galilee, though Mark's geographical references are often confusing. This incident begins a series of "sea voyages" to and from the western (Jewish) side of the lake to the eastern (Gentile) side. This first voyage terminates in the east in 5:1, and Jesus returns to the west in 5:21. The next clear voyage from west to east begins in 6:45, and is marked by a sea miracle prior to arrival. The return is narrated in 6:53. After a land journey to the north that terminates east of the lake (7:31), Jesus returns to the west in 8:10. In 8:13, in language similar to 4:35, Mark narrates a voyage to the east with a journey north to Caesarea Philippi, followed by an apparent land return through Galilee (9:30).

36. *leaving the crowd behind:* The crowd has been Jesus' principal (and favorable) audience since 3:20, and the reference here links the voyage with the "solemn" assembly of the crowd in 4:1-2.

    they took him along: The verb *paralambanein* appears also in 5:40; 9:2; 10:32; 14:33. Apart from 4:36 Jesus is always the subject, and the verb has the nuance of Jesus taking a select group aside for a significant disclosure. In the two introductory verses the disciples immediately follow Jesus' command and act with initiative, in contrast to their behavior at the conclusion of the narrative.

    in the boat: The type of boat can be surmised from the archaeological discovery of the Kinneret boat in 1986 and from the mosaic of a boat found at Magdala-Taricheae. It would have been about twenty-six feet long with a width of about eight feet, and held approximately twelve to fifteen people (see John J. Rousseau and Rami Arav, *Jesus and His World* [Minneapolis: Fortress, 1995] 25–30). Mark's narrative realism is evident here.

    just as he was: This most likely refers to 4:1-2 where Jesus is seated in the boat. This reference could be taken as evidence that 4:10-25, where Jesus is outside the boat and alone with the Twelve and others, is an insertion into an earlier connected narrative.

other boats: Since the crowd has been dismissed, these boats may carry the larger group that was "around him" in 4:10. If so, this notice continues the extension of discipleship beyond the Twelve and fulfills the promise to them that they will be given the mystery of the kingdom (here the revelation of God's power in Jesus' death and resurrection).

37. *a fierce windstorm:* The phrase for "fierce windstorm" *(lailaps megalē anemou)* in Greek suggests a sudden tornado-style whirlwind descending from above.

the waves began to break over the boat: Though part of a realistic description, the "waves" *(kymata)* provide the verbal link with the OT psalms of God's power over the sea (Pss 42:7-8; 65:7-8; 89:8-9; 107:23-32).

38. *he himself was in the stern of the boat, sleeping on a cushion:* The image is of Jesus on the raised afterdeck, sleeping on a sailor's cushion (or perhaps on a bag of sand used for both ballast and comfort). "Sleeping" *(katheudōn)* recalls the farmer of 4:27 whose unconcerned sleep is a prelude to the miracle of growth and harvest. Also, an untroubled sleep is a sign of trust in the power and protection of God (Prov 3:32-34; Pss 3:5; 4:8; Job 11:18-19). The almost comic contrasts among the deep sleep of Jesus, the raging sea, and the terror of the disciples heighten the power of the word of Jesus.

they roused him: The verb *egeirousin* also echoes the action of the farmer in 4:27 who "sleeps and rises night and day." The verb *egeirein* is also used for "raising up" sick people (2:9, 11; 3:3; 5:41; 10:49) and carries an overtone of resurrection in many cases.

Teacher: Jesus is so addressed since his day of teaching (4:1-34) has been completed. The subsequent calming of the sea confirms Jesus as one whose words and deeds are powerful (see 1:21-28). Jesus is called "teacher" *(didaskale)* not only in a context of instruction (9:38; 10:17, 20, 35; 12:14, 19, 32; 13:1) but also here, and in 9:17, prior to a miracle. Jesus is also addressed as *rabbi* (a later Jewish designation for "teacher") three times, twice by Peter (9:5; 11:21) and once by Judas (14:45). In the Jewish tradition Moses was mighty in both words and deeds (Acts 7:22). The calming through word alone also fits with the title "teacher." By this image Mark's readers are given a confirmation of the teaching of Jesus.

Don't you care that we are about to die: All the verbs here are in the present, which conveys a vivid sense of urgency. "Don't you care" *(ou melei soi)* conveys a sense of disengaged objectivity on Jesus' part (see 12:14). The cry of the disciples is similar to that of the crew in Jonah 1:14: "Lord, do not let us perish." A possible point of contact between Jonah and Mark is the belief that the God of Israel has the power to save from the raging sea.

39. *Then after getting up:* The participle is *diegertheis* (with an intensive *dia*) rather than the simple *egertheis,* which conveys the image of Jesus rising to his full height on the stern of the boat in direct confrontation with the raging sea.

he rebuked: This verb *(epetimēsen)* is used often of silencing or rebuking demons or illness thought to be caused by evil spirits (1:25; 3:12; 9:25; 10:48), though it does not suggest exorcism in 8:30; 10:13, 38. The rebuke and counter-rebuke of

Peter and Jesus in 8:32-33 may have the nuance of exorcisms, since Peter is called Satan in 8:33. "Rebuke" here is appropriate in the context of Jewish belief that the sea could be the abode of demonic monsters. The syntax here (lit. "he rebuked the wind and said to the sea") should not be taken as describing two distinct actions but rather as one powerful command to the wind and the sea (which in 4:40 are conceived as a single force).

Quiet! Be still!: The first of the two imperatives, *siōpa* ("quiet"), is appropriate to the wind, while the second verb *pephimōso* is a perfect passive imperative with the nuance of "be stilled." The combination of "rebuke" and "be still" echoes closely the exorcism of 1:25. Again, the raging winds and waves are personified as evil spirits. The word of Jesus, like the word of the Lord in the OT, conquers these evil powers.

there was dead calm: The text reads literally "a great *(megalē)* calm." The great calm is in contrast to the "great" storm in 4:37 and echoes the "great" branches of 4:32.

40. *why are you so fearful?:* The adjective *deiloi* ("fearful, timid") is used only here in Mark, and conveys not simply fear but also timidity and lack of courage. Matthew (13:26) softens the rebuke by equating their timidity with being "of little faith," and Luke (8:25) asks simply, "Where is your faith?"

You still do not have faith, do you?: From the rebuke ("fearful") it is clear that faith in Mark (which is the proper response to the gospel of God; see 1:15) is not simply intellectual conviction, but also trust in God along with bold action when faced with serious threats to life and well-being (see 5:34, 36; 9:23-24; 10:52; 13:21).

41. *A deep sense of awe came over them:* The text says literally, "they feared a great fear." The cognate accusative ("fear a fear") intensifies the main verb, and the word "great" echoes the great storm and the great calm. The "fear" here is not the cowardice of v. 40 but the numinous sense of awe that accompanies a theophany or disclosure of divine power. A constant refrain in the OT Wisdom tradition is that fear of the Lord is the beginning of wisdom (Job 28:28; Pss 1:7; 111:10; Prov 1:7; 9:10; 15:33; Sir 1:11-20), and Isaiah calls the fear of the Lord "Zion's treasure" (33:6). Such a fear as grips the disciples in v. 41 is part of the ongoing pedagogy of disciples in Mark's Gospel, which leads to deeper questioning about Jesus' nature and mission.

Who indeed is this person?: A sub-motif that runs throughout Mark is the question about the identity of Jesus, often framed as "Who is this?" (see 1:27; 2:7; 4:41; 6:2, 14; 8:27; 11:27; 14:61-62; 15:2; 15:31-32). The "identity" of Jesus comes to light, properly stated, only at the foot of the cross (15:31-32, 39).

when even the the wind and the sea: The Greek *hoti* is translated here as "when" in a causal sense ("seeing that both . . ."). Though less likely, it could also function as a relative pronoun and be translated as "to whom the wind and the sea show obedience."

obey him: "Wind and sea" govern a verb in the singular, which shows they are conceived as one force. The verb "obey" *(hypakouein)* is an intensification of the verb "hear" and appears usually in response to teaching. Jesus, here the teacher mighty in word and work, receives the response of submission from the forces of nature.

INTERPRETATION

This short narrative inaugurates a series of mighty deeds of Jesus as he moves beyond the confines of Galilee across the sea (lake) to Gentile territory. It is also the first of a number of sea voyages whereby Jesus crosses the "Sea of Galilee," which is also the symbolic barrier between Jews and Gentiles. This sea crossing highlights a significant shift in the Markan narrative.

The largest concentration of miracle stories occurs between 4:35 and 8:27 (when Jesus arrives at Caesarea Philippi). These miracles include two exorcisms (5:1-20; 7:24-30), the healing and restoration to life of two women (5:21-43), two other healings (7:31-37; 8:22-26), and two miraculous feedings (6:35-44; 8:1-10). More importantly, these mighty works in Gentile territory correspond to those performed in Jewish territory (exorcisms, healings, miraculous feedings). This section is also virtually free of the opposition to Jesus that characterized the first section of the gospel. The scribes and Pharisees do not reappear until 7:1-8 (the dispute on the tradition of the elders), and the Pharisees appear alone only in 8:11-13. The narrative thus has a dual transitional function. It facilitates the movement of Jesus beyond the confines of Galilee to Gentile territory, and it moves from a long block of teaching (3:13–4:34) to a major collection of Jesus' mighty works (4:35–8:26). Theologically it is dedicated to the manifestation of Jesus as the one who brings God's power to bear on human need and suffering.

The thrust of Mark 4:35-41 is the epiphany of Jesus as the one who calms the roaring sea. It is a narrative dense with important OT intertextual references. Three main sets of motifs occur (Nineham, *Saint Mark* 146). (1) In the OT the ability to control the sea and subdue tempests was a sign of divine power (Pss 89:8-9; 106:8-9; Isa 51:9-10). (2) The image of the storm or of great waters was a metaphor for evil forces active in the world and especially for the tribulations of just people, from which only the power of God could save (Pss 18:16; 69:2, 14-15). (3) The religious person should always have trust in God, even amid the most terrible storm (Isa 43:2; Pss 46:1-3; 65:5-8, where YHWH who is the "God of salvation" in 65:5 silences "the roaring of the seas, the roaring of their waves" [*kymata*]).

Especially significant is Ps 107:23-32 (LXX 106:23-32), which Mark's narrative virtually paraphrases. According to that psalm people "went down to the sea in ships" and "saw the deeds of the Lord" (v. 23). When God raises a strong wind that lifts up waves (v. 25, *kymata*; see Mark 4:37) the mariners cry out to the Lord (v. 28; see Mark 4:38), and the Lord "made the storm be still [see Mark 4:39, "be still"], and the waves of the sea were hushed." The psalm draws on the ancient portrayal of the sea as chaotic power, often the habitation of monsters, a motif that is deeply rooted in earlier Canaanite myths of creation where a storm god defeats the sea. While in the psalm it is YHWH who both stirs up the waves and calms them in response to the prayer, in Mark Jesus sleeps at the onset of the storm but afterward calms the waves as YHWH does.

These clear resonances of the power of God in the OT give a strong christological thrust to the passage. Jesus possesses the same power over the forces of chaos that characterizes the Lord of hosts. Mark's readers would be led to see that Jesus is the agent of God's power who ultimately triumphs over the forces that threaten the community with extinction ("we are about to die"). Even the delay in the reaction of Jesus reflects those places in the OT where God seems absent during the sufferings of the elect. Later, in the eschatological discourse of Mark 13, Jesus will address just such a situation of mortal threat to believers and encourage them with the certainty of God's vindication of the elect while exhorting them to faithful vigilance in face of the absent master (13:34-37).

The narrative is also important to Mark's theology of discipleship. Those very same disciples who have been chosen in 3:7-12, who have been given the mystery of the kingdom of God (4:10-12), and who are the privileged audience of Jesus' teaching and explanation (4:34) are here chided for their timidity and lack of faith. The concern that they do not have faith is abrupt at this point in Mark. Faith has been mentioned thus far only as a proper response to the gospel (1:15), and when Jesus praises the faith of the litter bearers (2:5). Faith or lack of it, however, will appear in significant places in the following sections of Mark (5:34, 36; 6:6; 9:19, 23, 24, 42; 10:52; 11:22-24; 13:21; 15:32). Also the lack of faith on the disciples' part is distinguished from the "unfaith" *(apistia)* of the family and relatives of Jesus at Nazareth (6:6), and the "faithless generation" that Jesus must bear with (9:19).

The rebuke of the disciples here is important in the larger context of Mark. Having been given the mystery of the kingdom and having been made recipients of the private explanations of Jesus' teaching, the disciples are still on a journey to true faith. Their "failure" here, which will heighten as the narrative unfolds, simply means that their closeness to Jesus does not absolve them from the need to enter more deeply into the mystery and paradox of God's reign: that death and the power of evil will be the seeming victors, and that even Jesus, who now rescues them, will perish. Their "choral reaction" of great awe at the end is not a continuation of their earlier timidity but describes their reverence in the face of the power of God. It is truly the fear that is the foundation and beginning of wisdom.

Mark's first readers, who had experienced the upsurge of the power of chaos and evil during Nero's persecution and the civil turmoil in Rome following his death in 68 and during (or shortly before) the Jewish War of 66–73 C.E., though gifted like the disciples in the gospel with the mystery of the kingdom, may well have cried out: "Don't you care that we are about to die?!" They too (and the church of all ages) are invited to continue the journey toward a deeper and more profound faith.

17. *The Exorcism of the Gerasene Demoniac* (5:1-20)

1. Then they arrived at the other side of the lake, in the territory of the Gerasenes. 2. But as Jesus was getting out of the boat, there immediately accosted him a man from the tombs who had an unclean spirit. 3. This man made the tombs into his dwelling place, and no one was ever strong enough to restrain him, even with a chain. 4. For though they had often shackled him with manacles and chains he would rip off the manacles, and the chains would be shattered. Nobody was strong enough to subdue him. 5. He spent night and day among the tombs and on the hilltops, screeching and mangling himself with stones. 6. And after he had seen Jesus from afar he ran up and prostrated before him, 7. crying out with a shrill voice: "What do you and I have in common, Jesus, you Son of God the Most High? I want you to swear to God that you will not torture me!" 8. (For he was about to say to the man: "Depart from the man, you unclean spirit.") 9. And Jesus questioned him: "What is your name?" He then answered: "My name is Legion, for we are a multitude." 10. It begged Jesus earnestly not to send them away from the place. 11. Now there near the mountain a large herd of pigs were foraging for food. 12. Then they spoke and entreated Jesus: "Send us into the pigs, that we might infest them." 13. Jesus gave them permission, and then the unclean spirits left the man and entered the pigs. The whole herd plunged headlong down the slope of the mountain into the sea—about two thousand of them—and they drowned in the sea. 14. And those who were herding the pigs ran away and spread the report of what happened in the city and in the countryside. People came to see for themselves what happened. 15. When they approached Jesus, they saw the man who had been possessed sitting, fully clothed and talking sensibly—that is the one whom the Legion had occupied; they were awestruck. 16. Those who were there who had seen what happened to the possessed man told them the story of the pigs. 17. Then they all began to plead with Jesus to leave the area. 18. And after he had gotten into the boat the man who had been possessed begged him that he might be with him. 19. Jesus would not allow it but said to him: "Return to your home and to your relatives, and tell them everything

that the Lord has done for you, and how he had mercy on you." 20. He left immediately and began to proclaim in the Ten Cities all that Jesus had done for him. Everyone was amazed.

NOTES

1. *the other side of the lake:* The arrival at the other side *(eis to peran)* repeats 4:35 and serves as a reminder that with the help of Jesus the goal was reached after the storm.

   in the territory of the Gerasenes: Both textually and in terms of understanding the location this is one of the most disputed phrases in Mark. Matthew (8:28) reads "Gadarenes," as do some good ancient manuscripts of Mark, while Luke (8:26) reads "Gerasenes" but with the clarification "which is opposite Galilee." Some other ancient manuscripts read "Gergesenes." The real problem is correlating the suggested sites with the narrative. Gerasa, modern Jerash, was a leading city of the Decapolis, which is consistent with 5:20, but it is located roughly thirty-seven miles southeast of the sea—an extraordinary run even for demon-possessed swine. Gadara, proposed by Matthew, is five miles from the sea, but with no steep cliffs nearby. Since this story was most likely altered in transmission (see the Interpretation), one solution may simply be that the evangelist, who elsewhere lacks precise knowledge of Palestinian geography, found Gerasa in his tradition and left it. Mark locates other events in Gentile territory in relation to a significant large city (see 7:24, "the vicinity of Tyre"). Finally, much of the debate is based on a misguided understanding that Mark's realism reflects Petrine memoirs or actual events. His realism is a narrative rather than a historical realism.

2. *there immediately accosted him:* The translation, though a bit stilted, captures the Greek word order.

   a man from the tombs: The Greek reads *anthrōpos,* which could simply be "a person." The word for "tombs" *(mnēmeion)* is from the same root as the verb "remember," since tombs are memorials for loved ones. The context suggests that these were tombs cut into the mountains (5:5) rather than sarcophagi or mausoleums. According to rabbinic literature living in burial sites was one of the signs of madness, along with running about at night and tearing one's clothes (Strack-Billerbeck 1:491–92, cited in Gundry, *Mark* 258).

   who had an unclean spirit: This is Mark's more frequent term for possessed people, although only in this pericope the term *daimonizomenos* (lit. "demonized") is also used. An "unclean" spirit is especially appropriate here since the man lives in tombs and the demons are sent into pigs (both strongly unclean for Jews).

3. *This man made the tombs into his dwelling place:* The description of the demoniac in vv. 3-4 is the fullest of any in the Gospels. The triple mention of tombs (vv. 2, 3, 5) may also suggest the struggle of Jesus with the power of death (see 15:46; 16:2, 5).

no one was ever strong enough to restrain him, even with a chain: The proliferation
of negatives—literally "no one *(oudeis)*, not even *(oude)* with a chain, was ever
(ouketi) able to bind *(dēsai)* him"—as well as the indication that he had "many
times" (v. 4) broken the chains serves to heighten the power of Jesus, who is
known to be the "stronger one" (1:7) who can enter the house of the strong
one and bind him (3:27). Commentators also see an allusion here to Ps 67:7
LXX (= 68:6), which speaks of the liberation of those who have been fettered
(pepedemenous; see Mark 5:4 *pedais . . . dedesthai),* and of those who are driven
by rage and who dwell in tombs. In Rev 20:1-3 the angel from heaven comes
with chains and binds Satan for a thousand years. Though there is no direct
connection between Mark and Rev 20:1-3, the motif is similar. In Mark Satan is
still "unbound."

4. *Nobody was strong enough to subdue him:* After the exceptionally vivid description of the strength of the possessed man, the initial description of 5:3b is repeated for emphasis in chiastic fashion.

5. *on the hilltops:* The Greek for "hilltops" is literally "mountains." Though for Jews
   "the mountain" *(oros)* is a site of revelation, mountains were also places of
   refuge and danger, especially since here the tombs may be in the mountains.
   Mark here echoes much of the language of Isa 65:3-5, where Isaiah criticizes
   "the rebellious people" who imitate Gentile rituals. They sacrifice on the hills
   (65:7, 11) to gods who are demons (65:3), sleep in tombs (65:4; *mnēmasin* =
   Mark 5:5), and eat swine's flesh. Though the situations are different ("rebellious" Israelites in Isaiah and a mad Gentile in Mark), the similarity is that for
   both Isaiah and Mark spending nights in the mountain tombs is a sign of
   pagan behavior.

   screeching and mangling himself with stones: These verses convey not only the
   horror that the man evoked among those who dwelt nearby but also his self-
   destructive behavior.

6. *After he had seen Jesus from afar:* On first glance this verse is in tension with v. 2,
   where the man accosts Jesus as soon as he lands. Yet 5:2 serves more as a preview of the whole narrative by immediately introducing Jesus and the main
   character. While 5:3-5 then develops the picture of the man who accosts Jesus,
   5:6-10 narrates the meeting with Jesus and his role as an exorcist.

   he ran up and prostrated before him: Prostrating *(proskynein)* is normally a mark
   of obeisance or worship to a divine or semi-divine figure (see 15:19). The gesture conveys in action what the man will express in v. 7.

7. *crying out with a shrill voice:* The drama is heightened. In the previous verses
   the man cries out *(krazein)* night and day. Here at the first light of morning the
   man continues to cry out.

   what do you and I have in common?: This phrase, which virtually repeats 1:24, is
   the most obvious point of contact with the exorcism of the demoniac at Capernaum (1:21-28) where the demoniac cries out, asks if Jesus has come to destroy
   him, and calls him the Holy One of God. Mark clearly parallels this first exorcism on Gentile soil with the first exorcism on Jewish soil.

you Son of God the Most High: As in 1:24 and 3:11, unclean spirits know that Jesus is the Holy One or Son of God. Rather ironically, here the demoniac answers the question posed by the disciples in 4:41: The one to whom the sea and the wind give obeisance is also the one who has power over these extraordinarily violent demonic powers. Though "God, Most High," is an address known in classical and Hellenistic literature and appears in the LXX on the lips of non-Jews (Gen 14:18-20; Isa 14:14; Dan 3:26, 4:2) and therefore is appropriate for a Gentile, it is also attested in Jewish writings (see Josephus, *Ant.* 16.163, where Hyrcanus is called high priest of the Most High God; Philo, *Leg. ad Gaium* 278, 317; and 4Q233).

I want you to swear to God: Normally it is the exorcist who solemnly invokes God prior to an exorcism. Here ironically the demoniac himself acts like an exorcist. The words of the demoniac show the inner division and turmoil he suffers. He can rightly call Jesus the Son of the Most High God and can ask for salvation from the eschatological torture, but he is still occupied by powers hostile to God.

not torture me: The term for "torture" *(basanizein)* is often used in a context of eschatological judgment; see Matt 18:34; Luke 16:23, 28 (the rich man in a place of torture). In Rev 18:7, 10, 15 torment is the fate of fallen Babylon. The demoniac and/or the demons within him fear the ultimate judgment of God.

8. *(For he was about to say to the man: "Depart from the man, you unclean spirit."):* This verse causes many difficulties. Some commentators argue that here the Greek imperfect *elegen* should be translated as a pluperfect, "he had been saying," and the explanatory *gar* ("for") indicates an afterthought by the narrator. Yet prior to v. 8 there has been no command for the spirit to depart, which first comes in v. 13. This creates the anomaly that Jesus had been trying unsuccessfully to exorcise—which would be unique to this story. Another, and more helpful, explanation is that the imperfect can also connote a sense of past action that looks to the future. J. H. Moulton in *A Grammar of New Testament Greek* (Edinburgh: T & T Clark, 1963) 64–65 speaks of an "inchoative imperfect." And Friedrich Blass, Albert Debrunner, and Robert W. Funk, *A Greek Grammar of the New Testament and Other Early Christian Literature* (Chicago: University of Chicago Press, 1961) no. 323 [4]), note that the imperfect can be equivalent to *emellen* with the infinitive; that is, a person was about to do something. This translation removes the difficulty and absolves Mark of clumsy construction. Mark's explanatory comment *(gar)* explains why the demoniac pleads with Jesus to avoid eschatological damnation. By quoting 1:25 it also removes any doubt as to whether Jesus has power over the demons. What is at stake is *when* the power will be used, not whether Jesus possesses it. After questioning, Jesus then heeds the prayer by sending the demons into the swine, while the possessed man regains his sanity.

9. *What is your name?:* To know the name of the demon is to have power over the demon; the exorcist uses the name of the demon when calling on God to expel it. In *Test. Sol.* 11:5 Solomon asks a demon its name, and the demon answers: "If I tell you his name, I place not only myself in chains, but also the legion of demons under me" (see also *Test. Sol.* 5:1-13; 13:1-7). Though *Testament of*

Solomon may be influenced by Mark it reflects common exorcistic practice (G. H. Twelftree, *Jesus the Exorcist* 84–85). The question also prepares for the disclosure that the man is possessed by a multitude of demons, which enhances the power of Jesus.

my name is Legion: "Legion" is a Latin loan word in Greek (and in Aramaic) designating primarily a military unit of roughly 6000 troops. Most likely "Legion" here is simply a colloquial expression for a large number of demons, especially when conceived as a force acting in concert, as the following explanatory clause suggests ("for we are many"). Its use here has spawned a number of socio-political interpretations, as if Mark was alluding in a veiled way to the brutal "occupation" of the land by the Romans. Jesus then would be enacting a symbolic expulsion of the Romans. The problem with this socio-political explanation is that Jesus is not expelling Romans from Jewish lands, since Gerasa was a largely Greek city in the Decapolis and would not have considered the Roman military presence as oppressive as many Jews did. Paul Winter notes that after 70 C.E. the 10th Roman legion, whose emblem was a wild boar, was stationed near Gerasa (*On the Trial of Jesus* [2nd ed. Berlin and New York: Walter de Gruyter, 1974] 180–81). But the Roman legion's presence there seems too late to have influenced Mark.

10. *It begged Jesus earnestly:* The verb "beg" or "entreat" *(parakalein)* is used often of a request made by a person in need (1:40; 7:32; 8:22) or by an inferior to a superior (Matt 18:29). Its use here and in v. 12 emphasizes that Jesus is superior to the demonic powers. "It" refers to Legion making this request, especially since in v. 12 the same verb is plural.

    not to send them away: In antiquity demons tended to be "territorial" (see Luke 11:24-27).

11. *a large herd of pigs:* This reference underscores the pagan setting of the narrative and also contributes to the atmosphere of uncleanness or pollution that characterizes the story. Keeping pigs is forbidden to Jews *(m. B. Qam.* 7:7), and swineherding was, like tax collecting, one of the occupations forbidden to a Jew (see *m. Tohar.* 7:6; *m. B. Qam.* 10:2; *m. Ned.* 3:4; see also Luke 15:11-32).

12. *Then they spoke and entreated Jesus:* This sentence, itself awkward, is a repetition and specification of v. 10.

13. *Jesus gave them permission:* This banishment serves the function of the exorcism command, the *apopompē* or "sending out" (1:25; 9:25). It fulfills the expectation of 5:8.

    left the man and entered the pigs: The request of the demons is literally but rather ironically answered. They are given a "local residence," but it results in their destruction. The folklore motif of the "duped demon" may be present here.

    drowned: In the previous narrative Jesus is portrayed as one who has power over the wind and the sea; now he sends demons there. In *Test. Sol.* 5:11 the powerful demon Asmodeus begs Solomon not to send him into water. In *Test. Sol.* 11, Solomon interrogates a lion-shaped demon who has a legion of demons under him (11:3). When Solomon asks the demon by whom his power is thwarted, it responds: "By the name of the one who at one time submitted to suffer many things [at the hands of] men, whose name is Emmanouel; but now he has bound us and will come to torture us (by driving us) into the water of the cliff" (11:5; translation from *OTP* 2:973). Though this text has obvious contacts with Mark, along with *Test. Sol.* 5:11 it confirms the fear that demons have of the sea.

14. *spread the report:* The Greek is simply "they announced" *(apēggeilan)*, but with the overtone of "carrying a message." The following verses (5:14-20) are an unusually full development of the "reaction" that characterizes miracle stories. Mark has expanded the reaction in terms of his mission theology.

15. *When they approached Jesus:* After a series of verbs in the imperfect or the aorist, the verbs here return to the familiar historical present, stressing the vividness of what the townspeople see.

    fully clothed and talking sensibly: This description carefully counters his deranged state, where in place of sitting quietly he shattered chains and restlessly wandered about the mountains, mangled his (presumably bare) body, and shrieked instead of engaging in human discourse.

    the one whom the Legion had occupied: The repeated mention of the man's condition stresses again the extent of his possession and the change that came over him, since he must now be identified as having been possessed.

    they were awestruck: This translates *ephobēthesan.* Though many translations read "they were afraid," the exact same verb and form (aorist middle/passive) is used in 4:41 to describe the disciples' reaction of awe to the calming of the sea. "Afraid" can have negative psychological overtones, whereas the "fear" here is religious awe at the demonstration of the power of God.

17. *began to plead with Jesus:* The verb *parakalein* is the same one used by the demons when asking Jesus if they could stay in the territory (5:10). It stresses again the authority of Jesus.

    to leave the area: Some commentators historicize the narrative by claiming that the request is due to lack of revenue because of the death of the pigs. More likely the townspeople are both in awe at and suspicious of the power of Jesus, reactions that might have characterized pagan reactions to early Christian missionaries.

18. *begged him:* This is the fourth use of the verb *parakalein* in this relatively short pericope (see 5:10, 12, 17). It both supports the authority of Jesus and stresses that he is the one who hears human petitions.

    that he might be with him: The Greek phrase *(hina met' autou ē)* repeats exactly (with the change of the verb from the plural to the singular) the summons of the Twelve in 3:14: "he appointed Twelve to be with him." Mark's readers are to see the request of the demoniac as a petition to become a disciple of Jesus.

19. *Jesus would not allow it:* In no place (except 10:52) does Jesus take as a disciple one who seeks to follow him. Rather, he chooses those "whom he wishes" (3:13).

return to your home and to your relatives: The liberation of the man from the destructive power of evil leads to a restoration of those familial relationships that were most prized and regarded as essential in antiquity.

tell them everything: "Tell" *(apaggeilon)* is the same verb used of the initial report of the exorcism (5:14) and is part of the mission vocabulary of the early church (Acts 15:27; 26:20). Though the man has not been allowed to join Jesus' band of itinerants, he is to be a herald of the merciful deeds of God. Jesus' instruction here does not fit the "messianic secret" pattern.

that the Lord has done for you: The term "Lord" *(kyrios)* is ambiguous here. It can be used of the God of Israel (Mark 12:29, 36; 13:20), a usage the following verb would support since the acts of mercy are generally associated with God. It may also reflect the post-resurrection view of Jesus as "Lord," which is supported by the fulfillment of Jesus' order in v. 20 where the man tells everything that "Jesus" has done. But Mark never uses *kyrios* unambiguously as a title of Jesus.

20. *began to proclaim:* The same phrase describes the action of the healed leper in 1:45. In Mark "proclamation" characterizes John the Baptist (1:4, 7), Jesus (1:14, 38, 39), the disciples (3:14, 6:12), people touched by the healing and liberating power of Jesus (1:45; 5:20; 7:36), and the post-resurrection church (13:10; 14:9).

in the Ten Cities: The "Ten Cities" or "Decapolis" refers to the federation of ten Hellenistic cities east of Samaria and Galilee, across the Jordan. Pliny the Elder lists them as follows: Damascus, Philadelphia, Raphana, Scythopolis, Gadara, Hippos, Dion, Pella, Gerasa, and Canatha (*Harper's Bible Dictionary* 215). Mark's Gospel contains the earliest attested use of the term. This area was evangelized early in Christian history (Acts 9:2). There is also an early tradition that Christians fled to Pella during the first days of the Jewish War (see Mark 13:14; Eusebius, *Eccl. Hist.* 3.5.2-3). Mark's readers probably saw in the healed demoniac a prototype of the Christian missionary in these areas.

Everyone was amazed: This is the standard "choral" response to the mighty works of Jesus, especially in Mark 5 (vv. 15, 20, 42), as well as to his teaching. For a complete list of places see the Notes for 1:22.

INTERPRETATION

This long narrative has been described by Rudolf Pesch as "not only the most 'stupendous' but also the most scandalous" of the miracle stories, "which presents the unsophisticated with preposterous material to feed his [or her] credulity and at the same time invites the scorn of the sceptic." The narrative comes close to turning Jesus into a "miracle monger" who dupes the demons as well as the onlookers and bargains with demons (Pesch, "The Markan Version" 349). This judgment is especially true for those who try to uncover a historical nucleus to the story. A veritable legion of publications has emerged to explain the gallop of the demonized pigs.

This narrative is by far the most elaborate and enigmatic gospel miracle story. There are a number of internal inconsistencies such as the doublets of the meeting between Jesus and the demoniac (vv. 2 and 6) and of the life of the demoniac in the tombs with two different Greek words used for tomb (vv. 2, 3, and 5). The unfortunate man is called a person with "an unclean spirit" (vv. 2, 8) as well as one who is "demonized" (vv. 15, 16, 18). It is the only exorcism in which the explicit command to "go out" is not issued but is simply reported (v. 8). Though it has formal characteristics of an exorcism (the meeting of the demoniac and the exorcist, description of the person afflicted, request for liberation, actual exorcism, reaction), it also has "novelistic" elements such as the fate of the pigs and the developed reactions of bystanders not found in other exorcism stories. However, the final text has a clear structure: an introduction with a description of the person afflicted (vv. 1-5), the encounter with demons (vv. 6-13), the reaction of witnesses (vv. 14-17), and a conclusion about the healed man (vv. 18-20).

Pesch has addressed the problems of the narrative by postulating a four-stage development: The first stage was a narrative of Jesus as the missionary Son of God conquering demons in Gentile territory that had its original setting in the Galilean Jewish-Hellenistic (Gentile) mission; at the second stage the narrative was expanded to stress the superiority of Jesus over pagan disorder, principally by references to Isa 65:3-5 and Ps 67:7 (LXX), which made the demoniac a prototype of the Gentile world under the destructive power of evil; in stage three vv. 18-20 were added, which shifted the focus of the story from Jesus' victory over evil to the freed demoniac as a missionary; and in stage four Mark gave the story its present location and added the editorial introduction and transitional verses (vv. 5:1, 21). Though this reconstruction reflects Pesch's view of Mark as a "conservative redactor," it does highlight important elements of the narrative. Since our focus is principally on the final text of Mark we will focus on the interpretation of the story as a meaningful unit in the context of Mark's Gospel.

The location of the story is very important. Mark positions this elaborate narrative at the moment when Jesus first sets foot on pagan territory. In both structure and detail it is a virtual retelling of the first public act of Jesus in Galilee, the exorcism in Capernaum (1:21-28). Its realistic, dramatic, and elaborate features serve to illuminate the dire condition of the pagan world and the struggle involved in liberating it from evil. Both narratives, by portraying Jesus as one who liberates people from the power of evil and as a figure of power, are overtures to the subsequent narratives in their respective sections of Mark.

The narrative continues Mark's stress on Jesus as the powerful one, most recently manifest in his calming the winds and waves by a simple command. In both the calming of the sea and the exorcism of the Gerasene demoniac Jesus is the central character. In contrast to the vivid descriptions of the threat of raging sea and of the raving demoniac, Jesus appears calm, almost disengaged. In the earlier narrative he sleeps during the tempest and speaks only briefly. In the long story of the Gerasene demoniac Jesus does not speak until v. 9, when he asks the name of the demons, and he is heard only once more, in v. 19, when he commissions the liberated man to inform his relatives what the Lord has done for him. The power of Jesus is made present in a quiet, almost hidden manner, like the growing seeds of Mark 4:1-34.

The condition of the demoniac is a multi-colored tableau of the power of evil. The alternation between the plural voice of the demons and the singular voice of the demoniac captures the havoc that such possession does to personal identity. Superhuman strength is coupled with manic self-destructiveness. The possessed person is alienated from family and friends and is fated to live among the dead as unclean and as an object of fear and dread to all. In a culture like that of the first century, where the world was viewed as peopled by frightful superhuman creatures, a more vivid picture could hardly be constructed. This condition makes his liberation from evil all the more striking, and the narrative conveys this by the departure of evil into the thundering herd of swine plunging headlong into the sea, but even more by the simple picture of the man "in his right mind" and sitting with Jesus. Frantic activity has been replaced by simple presence; a mind torn by raging forces is now at peace.

As important for Mark is the missionary dimension of the narrative, which is developed here as in no other healing or exorcism story. In Mark Jesus often commands silence or concealment after a miracle (1:34, 45; 5:43; 7:36; 8:26); occasionally this is violated (1:45; 7:36). Nowhere else in the gospel does Jesus actually commission persons to spread the news of what the Lord has done for them. In hearing this command from "the Lord," Mark's readers are to see in the activity of the healed demoniac a model for their own mission to the Gentiles (see 13:10, "the gospel must be proclaimed to all nations [Gentiles]"). Since in 7:31 Jesus himself on his own "mission to the Gentiles" will travel straight through the middle of the Decapolis, the "missionary" who "begins to proclaim" what Jesus has done for him is a forerunner of the Gentile mission in the same way as John the Baptist "proclaimed" (1:4, 7) the coming of Jesus as "the stronger one." This narrative strongly echoes the beginning of the gospel and foreshadows its spread outward.

The story contains many themes for contemporary actualization. In Mark the miracles are not signs, that is, convincing demonstrations of the power of God (8:11-12). In modern terminology they can be called symbols. They function much like the parables in leading people to explore their deeper meaning. The dramatic nature of the exorcism in 5:1-20 can serve as a vivid symbol of the sense of imprisonment by violent forces that many people experience today. These forces cause isolation and alienation from friends and can be as self-destructive as the actions of the Gerasene demoniac. The narrative, however, is not simply an indictment of the power of evil. Rather, it is a story of liberation. Through the presence and power of Jesus the Son of the Most High, who can calm the raging tempest, the Gerasene demoniac experiences liberation and a return to peace and sanity. While the narrative does not warrant a simplistic "return to Jesus" as the solution to all personal and social problems, it does indicate that a power stronger than evil must intervene for real liberation to occur. It also states eloquently that liberation *from* evil is liberation *for* mission. The person who is healed and liberated returns "to his own," but with a message about the mercy of God. The churches that today proclaim and enact the Gospel of Mark must be agents of liberation from evil while moving outward to proclaim the gracious mercy of God.

FOR REFERENCE AND FURTHER STUDY

Bligh, John. "The Gerasene Demoniac and the Resurrection of Christ," *CBQ* 31 (1969) 383–90.

Dormandy, Richard. "The Expulsion of Legion. A Political Reading of Mark 5:1-20," *ExpTim* 111 (2000) 335–37.

Johnson, E. S. "Mark 5:1-20: The Other Side," *Irish Biblical Studies* 20 (1998) 50–74.

LaHurd, Carol S. "Reader Response to Ritual Elements in Mark 5:1-20," *BTB* 20 (1990) 154–60.

Pesch, Rudolf. "The Markan Version of the Healing of the Gerasene Demoniac," *Ecumenical Review* 21 (1971) 349–76.

18. *The Daughter of Jairus and the Woman with the Hemorrhage* (5:21-43)

21. And after Jesus had again crossed over the sea to the other side, a large crowd gathered around him, and he was on the seashore. 22. Then one of the leaders of the synagogue, named Jairus, arrived; and when he saw Jesus he fell at his feet. 23. He appealed earnestly to Jesus, saying: "My dear daughter is near death; please come and lay your hands on her,

so that she might be saved and have life." 24. Jesus then departed with him, but the large crowd followed him and swarmed around him. 25. There was a woman there who had been subject to bleeding for twelve years, 26. and she had suffered greatly under the care of many physicians and had used up all her resources to little avail, but rather continually became worse. 27. She had heard about Jesus, and then she came up behind him in the crowd and touched his garment. 28. For she was saying to herself: "If I can only touch even the edge of his clothes, I will be saved." 29. At that very moment the bleeding stopped, and she sensed in her body that she was healed from the affliction. 30. Simultaneously when Jesus felt in himself that power had gone out of him he turned to the crowd and said: "Who touched my clothes?" 31. The disciples then responded: "Don't you see this crowd milling about you, and you still say, 'Who touched me?'" 32. Then Jesus looked around to see the person who had done this. 33. But the woman, who had realized what he had done for her, came in fear and trembling, fell at his feet, and told him the whole truth. 34. He then said to her: "Daughter, your faith has saved you; depart in peace, and remain healed of your affliction." 35. While he was still speaking with her some friends of the synagogue leader arrived and said: "Your daughter has died; why are you bothering the teacher?" 36. When Jesus overheard what they reported, he said to the leader of the synagogue: "Don't be afraid; just have faith." 37. He then would not let anyone go with him except Peter, James, and John the brother of James. 38. When they arrived at the home of the synagogue leader he came upon a commotion, with people weeping and wailing loudly. 39. He went right in and said to them: "Why do you raise such commotion with your weeping? The child is not dead, but only asleep." 40. They laughed at him. But he threw them all out; and taking the young woman's father and mother and his disciples he entered the room where the young woman was. 41. He took the child by the hand, and said to her: *"Talitha koum,"* which is to be interpreted "Young lady, I say to you, rise up." 42. And right away the young woman stood up and began to walk, for she was twelve years old. And right away everyone was totally astonished. 43. But Jesus gave them all strict orders that no one else should know of this, and he asked that she be given something to eat.

NOTES

21. *to the other side:* The first sea voyage (see 4:35) is completed, and Jesus arrives again at the Jewish side of the lake.

    a large crowd gathered around him, and he was on the seashore: The verse virtually copies 4:1 and links this incident with the previous events on Jewish soil. In Mark the setting "along the shore" *(para tēn thalassan)* is the occasion for other important events (1:16-20, the call of the disciples; 2:13-15, the call of Levi; 4:1-34, the parable discourse; see also 3:7).

22. *one of the leaders of the synagogue:* The term *archisynagōgos* can also be translated "president of the synagogue." Acts 13:15 indicates that there could be more than one such "president." The office primarily involved oversight of the physical condition and financial well-being of the synagogue. The term is used also of such people (leaders of the assembly) in Hellenistic literature.

    named Jairus: Jairus and Bartimaeus (10:46) are the only proper names used in the miracle stories. Some have suggested that the name "Jairus" plays on Hebrew terms meaning either "he will enlighten" or "he will arouse, awaken." The problem is that Mark usually translates Semitic words (including the name "Bartimaeus"), and that the functions associated with the name Jairus would be more proper to Jesus than to the synagogue leader.

    when he saw Jesus, he fell: This parallels the beginning of the previous story where the demoniac sees Jesus and falls in worship at his feet (5:6). Here, however, the simple "falling" is a posture of petition rather than worship.

23. *He appealed earnestly to Jesus:* Appealing or beseeching *(parakalein)* is characteristic of requests for healing. "Earnestly" translates the familiar Markan adverbial use of *polla* (lit. "in many ways"). The actions and appeal of the leader again enhance the dignity of Jesus; they also show that in Mark not all Jewish leaders are opposed to Jesus.

    my dear daughter: The diminutive *thygatrion* of "daughter" (lit. "little daughter") here conveys affection and not simply age or size.

    lay your hands on her: Laying on of hands, which is sometimes used in the negative sense of harm (Gen 37:27; Lev 24:14; Neh 13:21; Luke 20:19), appears in different positive contexts: blessings (Acts 8:19), consecration (Lev 8:10), sacrificial ritual (Exod 29:10; Lev 4:15; 16:21), and healing (2 Kgs 4:34; Mark 16:18; Acts 9:12; 28:8). In *Genesis Apocryphon* 20:28-29 Abraham exorcises the plague visited upon the Egyptian king for abducting Sarai by placing his hands on him.

    be saved and have life: "Be saved" translates *sōthē,* which can also mean "be cured" or "be healed" as in many contemporary translations. "Saved" is retained because of the father's statement that she is near death, and so the request is for rescue from the power of death.

24. *large crowd:* This notice provides a virtual *inclusio* with 5:21, while the added comment that the crowd swarmed around Jesus prepares for the following intercalated incident.

25. *There was a woman there:* With this verse begins the narrative (5:25-34) of the woman who suffered from continual bleeding. For the meaning of the larger interwoven narrative see the Interpretation below. The narrative begins with an ornate sentence that uses seven consecutive participles to describe the woman's condition (vv. 25-27).

    who had been subject to bleeding: The Greek reads literally "being with a flowing of blood" *(rysei haimatos).* Though Mark gives no particulars, this phrase appears in Lev 15:19 for menstrual bleeding and in 15:25 for other unspecified forms of vaginal bleeding. In Leviticus 15 both types of bleeding cause ritual impurity. In the case of menstruation the impurity lasts for seven days and affects things the woman may touch as well as those who touch her. According to Lev 15:25, if the discharge of blood lasts "for many days . . . all the days of her discharge she shall continue in impurity." Though this pericope is generally entitled "the woman with the hemorrhage," such a title is not entirely accurate since continual hemorrhaging over twelve years would have caused death.

for twelve years: This provides another linkage with the story of Jairus' daughter, who is twelve years old (see the Interpretation).

26. *she had suffered greatly under the care of many physicians:* The double use of "greatly" *(polla)* at the hands of "many" *(pollōn)* physicians magnifies the suffering. While Sir 38:1-15 offers a very positive view of physicians and urges both prayer for healing and obedience to physicians, a negative view appears in Tob 2:10. Soranus of Ephesus (fl. ca. 98–138 C.E.), the author of the influential medical treatise *Gynecology,* lists a wide variety of treatments used to treat excessive vaginal bleeding (Soranus, *Gynecology,* tr. O. Temkin [Baltimore: Johns Hopkins University Press, 1956] 3.44). Their number and nature would suggest great uncertainty about their curative value.

and had used up all her resources: Since only those of financial means visited physicians in antiquity, and since the woman had independent resources, she must once have been a person of some status and wealth. Mark's description of her condition brings out her dire state. She is physically ill, ritually unclean, and near impoverishment. Neither religion nor social standing offers her much help.

but rather continually became worse: While Jairus' daughter is near death, this woman is quickly approaching death as well.

27. *She had heard about Jesus:* The sequence of participles continues in literally describing the woman as "having heard [news] concerning Jesus." "Hearing" echoes 3:8 where the crowds hear of Jesus and flock to him, and the "hearing" of this woman foreshadows almost verbatim the description of the Syrophoenician woman in 7:25, who also has "heard" about Jesus.

she came up behind him in the crowd: Given the size and density of the crowd, the woman violates the purity code by risking public contact with Jesus. Her action also shows initiative and courage.

and touched his garment: The languid procession of participles leads to the main verb "touched" *(hēpsato),* which conveys the shock of the narrative. Forms of the verb *haptein* appear frequently in the regulations regarding bloody discharges in Leviticus (15:19, 21, 22, 23, 27). Especially important for Mark, who has earlier designated Jesus as "the Holy One of God" (1:24), is the prescription that such a woman should not touch "any hallowed thing" (Lev 12:4). Impurity is regarded as highly contagious.

28. *For she was saying to herself:* Through the explanatory *gar* ("for"), the omniscient narrator gives readers an inside view of the woman's intentions. Such inside views function much like soliloquies in later literature.

touch even the edge of his clothes: The idea of healing through touch is very common in the Hellenistic world, since healers were thought to be figures of power. This narrative is often invoked to undergird the view that the Markan Jesus is a Hellenistic *theios anēr*, a semi-divine figure gifted with supernatural powers. Portrayals of healing through touch, however, are found in the OT accounts of healings by Elijah (1 Kgs 17:17-24) and Elisha (2 Kgs 4:25-37). Also later rabbinic traditions mention healing through touch; see Barry Blackburn, *Theios Anēr and the Markan Miracle Traditions* (Tübingen: J.C.B. Mohr [Paul Siebeck], 1991) 112–17.

I will be saved: The translation retains "saved" for *sōthēsomai* in order to preserve the notion of "rescue" from illness and possible death and to highlight the linkage with the surrounding narrative (vv. 23, 35).

29. *the bleeding stopped:* Literally the text reads "the flow of her blood dried up," which echoes Lev 12:7 where the woman will be pronounced "clean from the flow of her blood" after the purification rituals. Here there is no ritual. It is simply the power of Jesus that brings healing.

she sensed in her body: In Leviticus (especially 15:2, 3, 19, 16, 24, 26, 28) the body is frequently the source of impurity. Here the woman paradoxically recognizes that her body is healed.

from the affliction: The Greek literally reads "from the scourge" *(mastigos)* and echoes a similar use in 3:10.

30. *when Jesus felt in himself:* A typical miracle story could conclude with v. 29, but vv. 30-34 provide an extended conclusion that conveys the real meaning of the story (v. 34). Jesus' immediate self-realization about the departure of his power parallels the woman's self-realization of being healed.

that power had gone out of him: Mark portrays Jesus as a figure so charged with power that it affects people by simple touch. Since "power" *(dynamis)* is a term associated with both strength and spirit, this verse continues the motifs begun in 1:7 (about the coming of the stronger one) and 1:10 (Jesus as the "Spirit endowed" prophet; see also 6:14).

Who touched my clothes?: Such questions are often foils for the subsequent teachings or actions of Jesus (3:33; 8:27; 12:16, 23).

31. *The disciples then responded:* Though having just witnessed the mighty works of the stilling of the storm and the healing of the Gerasene demoniac, the disciples still seem unaware of the extraordinary nature of Jesus' power (4:41, "Who is this . . . ?"). This is another instance of progressive misunderstanding by the disciples (see Introduction).

33. *what he had done for her:* Since the woman already perceived in v. 29 that she was healed, this phrase suggests a deeper realization of the power of Jesus.

came in fear and trembling: This expression does not describe a psychological disposition but a reaction of human fragility in the presence of divine power (see 4:41; 5:15; and Exod 15:16; Ps 2:11; Jer 33:9; Dan 5:19; 6:26; Phil 2:12-13; Eph 6:5).

fell at his feet: With slight verbal alteration this is the same gesture as that of Jairus in 5:22—another linkage between the two narratives.

34. *He then said to her:* Jesus' response is really fourfold: calling her "daughter," a statement about her faith, a dismissal in peace, and a pronouncement that she is free of her affliction. Given the social constraints against a man and woman even talking in public (see John 4:27: "they marvelled that he was talking to a woman"), as well as against contact with a woman with menstrual bleeding, Jesus' action would be shocking.

    Daughter: This familial address is in contrast to the gestures of respect and worship given to Jesus, and recalls 3:31-35 where those who do the will of God are said to be members of Jesus' family. The woman becomes an exemplar for others.

    your faith has saved you: Faith and salvation (healing) are joined in 2:5; 5:36; 9:23; and 10:52. In these narratives saving faith describes the confidence and boldness whereby people surmount obstacles to come to Jesus.

    depart in peace: This is a standard biblical dismissal (e.g., Exod 4:18; Judg 18:6; 1 Sam 1:17; 20:42; 25:35; 2 Kgs 5:19), combining both blessing and prayer that wholeness and health (that is, peace *[shalom]*) may accompany a person. Similar in tone to Mark 5:34 is Eli's dismissal of Hannah: "Go in peace; the God of Israel grant the petition you have made to him" (1 Sam 1:17).

    remain healed of your affliction: "Remain healed" translates the imperative of the verb "be" with a nuance of a new and constant state, along with the adjective for "healthy" or "sound" *(hygiēs)*.

35. *While he was still speaking with her:* Through this connection the evangelist resumes the previous narrative begun in 5:21-24.

    Your daughter has died: This heightens the drama and provides another seemingly hopeless situation that characterizes the miracle cluster (see 4:37-38; 5:3-5, 25-26).

    why are you bothering the teacher?: This question presumes that Jairus remained present during the meeting of Jesus and the woman, and prepares for Jesus' exhortation to faith in v. 36. The title "teacher" seems initially out of place in a complex of miracle stories (4:35–5:43) with minimal teaching. However, in the ancient world wonderworkers such as Apollonius of Tyana were known also as sages. This title continues Mark's interpretation of Jesus' action as "new teaching with power" (1:28).

36. *When Jesus overheard:* Some contemporary translations render the participle *parakousas* as "ignore" (which is a possible meaning) rather than "overhear." Jesus' word of consolation to the father suggests that "overhear" is more suitable here.

    Don't be afraid; just have faith: Fear frequently appears as a motif in miracle stories (4:40; 5:33; 6:50). The fear that precedes the miracle is lack of trust and hope, not the fear (awe) that reacts to the mighty work (see 4:41).

37. *He then would not let anyone go with him:* This notation, along with the explicit command to concealment in v. 43, is often invoked in the theory of the mes-

sianic secret. But the subsequent restoration to life does not deal directly with Jesus' messiahship since there is no acclamation or reaction, nor is it totally secret since the parents and the three disciples are witnesses. Also withdrawal from the crowd is a frequent motif in miracle stories (7:33; 8:23; Acts 9:40; 1 Kgs 17:19; 2 Kgs 4:4, 33).

except Peter, James, and John the brother of James: These three are among the first disciples called (1:16-20), are mentioned first in the list of the Twelve (3:16-17), and appear with Jesus at the transfiguration (9:2) and in Gethsemane (14:33). Since this miracle is the only resuscitation in Mark, and since these three disciples will witness both his transfiguration and the depth of his abandonment at Gethsemane, they function as examples of "being with" Jesus at important revelatory moments.

38. *people weeping and wailing loudly:* Elaborate rituals of mourning are widely attested in both the Jewish and the Hellenistic worlds. In Judaism they can involve going barefoot, stripping off clothes, cutting the hair or beard, scattering ashes, fasting, loud cries of sorrow, and laments (Jer 16:6-8; Ezek 24:16-24). The NT knows of fasting (Mark 2:19), funeral dirges (Matt 11:16-17), and use of flute players (Matt 9:23). Often professional mourners were present, especially women (Jer 9:17-20; see Luke 23:27). Their presence in Mark is suggested by the presence of those who are "wailing" *(alalazontas)*. Though the early church took over Jewish mourning practices (Acts 8:2), the more elaborate pagan practices were criticized. Jesus' expulsion of the mourners and their retaliatory mockery may reflect the rejection of elaborate mourning in Mark's community (see 1 Thess 4:13).

39. *The child:* "Child" is the normal translation for *paidion,* which also has a nuance of affection (see v. 40 and John 21:5, where the risen Jesus so addresses the disciples).

is not dead, but only asleep: This statement directly contradicts the report of the messengers in v. 35 and is an example of Markan irony. Though both the OT and early Christianity used "sleep" as a euphemism for death (Dan 12:2 LXX; Ps 88:5 [87:6 LXX]; 1 Thess 5:10), in the NT death is a sleep from which one will awaken (1 Thess 4:13-18). The Markan Jesus' pronouncement is an intimation to the readers of his ultimate victory over death.

40. *They laughed at him:* Skepticism and mockery are frequent motifs in Hellenistic miracle stories (Gerd Theissen, *Miracle Stories* 56), but they are also found in the OT: Sarah and Abraham laugh when told that the aged Sarah will bear a son (Gen 17:15-17; 18:10-15), and the Shunammite woman disbelieves Elisha (2 Kgs 4:16). The mocking laughter *(kategelōn)* at Jesus echoes the mockery of the suffering just person in the OT (Job 21:3; 30:1, 9; Pss 22:7; 25:2 [24:2 LXX]), and anticipates the mockery of Jesus as the suffering just person during the Passion narrative (see 14:65; 15:16-20).

41. *He took the child by the hand:* Touching is frequent in miracle stories. However, since corpse impurity was the most severe of all impurities this touch is another instance of Jesus violating cultural codes for the greater good of humanity

(see 2:27-28; 3:4; etc.). But it is the word of Jesus, not the touch, that effects the healing.

Talitha koum: In Aramaic this phrase literally means "little lamb, arise"; the word "lamb" *(talitha)* can be a term of affection, especially for a young child (see 2 Sam 12:1-6). Foreign words *(rhēsis barbarikē)* in healing stories often function like magical incantations. Mark, however, retains and translates Aramaic terms in contexts other than miracle stories, often to underscore his point of view (3:17; 7:11, 34; 11:9; 14:36; 15:22, 34).

young lady: "Young lady" *(korasion)* is used here to highlight the distinction from the earlier description of Jairus' daughter as *paidion* ("child"). *Korasion*, the Greek diminutive of *korē* ("maiden" or "young woman"), can be used of a woman approaching marriageable age.

I say to you, rise up: The solemn formula "I say" stresses that the word of Jesus effects the raising. The term "rise" *(egeirein)* literally means "wake from sleep" (4:27, 38); it can also mean "stand up" (2:9, 11; 3:3; 10:49; 14:28), and in the passive is used of the resurrection of the dead (12:26) and of Jesus' resurrection (16:6). The verb here has a double nuance of rising from sleep and rising from (the sleep of) death.

42. *stood up:* A different verb is used here, *anestē* (lit. "rise" or "stand up"), which is also used with regard to resurrection from death in Jesus' Passion predictions (8:31; 9:31; 10:34). Formally this verse constitutes the "demonstration" of the miracle. The density of language about death and resurrection here is evidence that the Markan readers are to see this narrative as a foreshadowing of Jesus' resurrection and of their own awakening from the sleep of death.

for she was twelve years old: This is another instance of Mark's use of the explanatory *gar* ("for"), which Matthew (9:25-26) and Luke (8:54-55) omit. It hardly explains the reason that she was able to walk. Rather, it is an aside to the reader that presumably has some significance. What it means is debated. Some suggestions are the following: a detail recalled by an eyewitness (Cranfield, *St Mark* 191), a literary link with the intercalated narrative (Guelich, *Mark 1–8:26*, 303), or no theological significance at all (e.g., Gundry, *Mark* 285). Important to any interpretation are the facts that twelve is the legal age for betrothal/marriage in both Roman and Jewish law, and that the young woman is at the brink of her childbearing years (see the Interpretation).

Right away everyone was totally astonished: Though the reaction of onlookers is part of the standard pattern of the miracle stories, the phraseology here (lit. "at once they were ecstatic with a great ecstasy") conveys the extraordinary nature of this miracle.

43. *that no one else should know of this:* Explicit commands to silence follow other miracles (1:34; 7:36; 1:44; 8:26 [implicit]). Yet in other cases the command is not given (2:11; 5:20) or, when given, it is violated (1:45; 7:36). The command here, which is obeyed, is the clearest example of the "miracle secret" motif in Mark.

he asked that she be given something to eat: Like the statement "twelve years old," this seemingly unnecessary detail has puzzled interpreters, with explanations ranging from the remembrance of the "practical thoughtfulness of Jesus"

(Cranfield, *St Mark* 191) to a confirmation that the young woman really lives and is not a spirit or ghost (Gnilka, *Evangelium nach Markus* 1:218). Also in the "longer ending of Mark" (16:14) as in Luke 24:13-49 and in John 20–21, the risen Jesus appears in the context of a meal shared with his followers.

INTERPRETATION

The intercalated stories about Jesus and the woman suffering from bleeding (5:25-34) and about the raising of the daughter of Jairus (5:21-24, 35-43) are equal in narrative power and emotional effect to the just-concluded colorful and dramatic story of the Gerasene demoniac. Viewed in their larger context the four "mighty works" of 4:35–5:43 form a distinct pattern. The parables chapter resonates with a tension between hidden-ness and revelation, with a constant stress on the power of what lies below the surface (growing seeds). Yet in the four miracles of 4:35–5:43 the power of Jesus over chaotic nature, destructive demons, debilitating ill-ness, and death itself is portrayed in a more sustained and graphic man-ner than anywhere else in the gospel. This grand tableau, which visually spreads across these chapters of Mark like a medieval tapestry, ends with a visit of Jesus to his home city where his teaching is rejected (6:1-4) and his power to perform mighty works proves ineffectual (6:5). The tension between manifestation and hiddenness resumes.

Taken independently the miracles of 5:21-43 are powerful and evoca-tive narratives. The initial narrative begins with Jesus again in Jewish ter-ritory and surrounded by crowds. A synagogue leader named Jairus arrives and surprisingly falls at the feet of Jesus; this is startling since the last time Jesus appeared in a synagogue the narrative ended with a plan to kill him (3:6), even though his initial teaching and works of power oc-cured in synagogues (1:21, 23, 39). Jesus responds immediately to this man's poignant appeal that he restore health and life to his daughter who is at death's door, and he sets off with the leader and a teeming crowd. The narrative thus far unfolds like a standard miracle story with the de-scription of the critical situation and the request for healing.

This narrative is abruptly interrupted by another (5:25-34) which tells a complete story of another woman's suffering. Though the manifestation of the power of Jesus is at the center of both narratives, the intercalated narrative is really the woman's tale rather than that of Jesus. In contrast to virtually every other section of Mark that begins with an action of Jesus, it opens simply with the phrase: "There was a woman. . . ." Her plight is vividly described (vv. 25-27), and through her soliloquy in v. 28 readers are made privy to her hopes. In fact, she and the Syrophoenician woman (7:24-30) stand out from the characters in other miracle stories as "rounded" or more developed personalities rather than stereotypical characters. Both her dire state and her daring actions emerge from explicit statements and implied perspectives in the narrative.

She has been suffering from some form of vaginal bleeding for twelve years. The type of disease she suffers, according to Soranus of Ephesus, is a "grievous calamity" that left its victims weak, pale, and often unable to eat (*Gynecology* 3.40). It would also prevent their bearing children and would place the woman in a state of enduring uncleanness. Throughout the Bible a childless marriage is a great source of distress (Gen 16:1-6; 30:1-8, where Rachel says, "Give me children or I shall die"; 1 Sam 1:3-10; 2 Esdr 9:43-48). In Luke 1:18, 24-25, 57-58, Elizabeth calls her childlessness a disgrace and rejoices at the birth of her son John. Childlessness, for which the woman was almost always blamed, was a ground for divorce. The woman in Mark, since she appears alone in public and draws on her own resources to pay the physicians (v. 26), may also have been "dismissed" or divorced.

She emerges in the story, however, as a woman of daring and initiative. She acts on hearsay about Jesus and pushes her way through the dense crowd. She is sustained by a hope that she can be "saved," that is, both healed of her illness and able to resume a full life in community. Once she breaks through the physical barrier of the crowd and the religiosocial barrier of her ritual impurity and touches Jesus, her illness ceases and she senses the cure in her body. At that same moment Jesus feels a healing power depart from his body and speaks for the first time in either story. The account then switches from narration to dialogue. Jesus, who earlier in Mark possessed knowledge even of what people were thinking (2:8), asks who touched him and is virtually mocked by his disciples for asking such a question. Their misunderstanding only enhances the faith of the woman. Having experienced the power of God in her own body, the woman who a moment ago seemed fearless now approaches Jesus with the religious awe that arises from contact with divine power. Unlike the disciples who answer a question with a question, the woman speaks the simple truth, and Jesus proclaims that her faith has saved or restored her and dismisses her with a blessing and a promise of continued health—in contrast perhaps to the many times when the physicians had promised health to her.

The first narrative then resumes in 5:35-43 with the comment that Jesus had better not come to Jairus' house since the daughter had died. Having just witnessed the faith of the woman and heard Jesus' accolade of her, the synagogue leader is exhorted to equal faith. Jesus comes to the "house," a place where he brought healing power to another woman, Peter's mother-in-law (1:29-31). Having been once subjected to misunderstanding by the disciples (5:31), he is now mocked by the crowd for his ironic comment that the young girl is simply asleep. In addition to the motifs noted above, for the Markan readers those mockers may well represent outsiders (4:10-12) to whom Christian resurrection faith is folly (1 Cor 1:23) or worth only mockery (Acts 17:32). The very next words Jesus utters after those that elicit laughter is the command to the young girl to "rise up," which confirms resurrection faith. The raising of Jairus' daughter is for Mark's readers the prototype of their own hope that their God is a God not of the dead but of the living (12:27).

Though self-contained narratives, the two stories are carefully woven together. Both deal with women in life-threatening situations, and both women are called "daughter" (5:22, 34). Both women are explicitly or implicitly hoping for salvation or rescue from their situation (5:23, *sōthē*; 5:28, *sōthēsomai*). In both narratives "faith" is important; the woman's faith is praised (5:34) and Jairus is encouraged to have faith (5:36). In both narratives misunderstanding of Jesus' power (5:31, 40) is followed by its dramatic manifestation (5:34, 42).

There is another profoundly human and theological connection that is hinted at by the reference to the twelve-year illness and the young woman who is twelve years old. The young woman dies at the age of betrothal and near the time when she can bear children. In a culture where the continuation and gift of life comes primarily through women, she dies before she can bring new life into the world. The woman with a twelve-year problem of vaginal bleeding will also die without bringing forth life. In his excellent treatment of the four major impurities of Leviticus 12–15, Jacob Milgrom has argued that they all deal with varieties of the loss of life. Especially significant is that the loss of blood and semen "meant the diminution of life, and, if unchecked, destruction and death" . . . which "was a process unalterably opposed by Israel's God, the source of its life" (Jacob Milgrom, *Leviticus 1–16*. AB 3 [New York: Doubleday, 1991] 766–77). In these two narratives Jesus not only rescues the two women from death but also restores to them their life-giving capacity. Both can bring forth life from their bodies, one once racked with disease, the other deprived of life itself.

These two narratives offer many themes for contemporary actualization. Patristic authors often described the woman with the bleeding as a model of faith. Origen contrasts her as a positive example to Peter's lack of faith (see Matt 14:28-33). John Chrysostom notes that she was the first woman to approach Jesus publicly and that in the narrative Jesus uses her faith to correct the lack of faith on the part of the synagogue leader. Ephrem the Syrian sees her as an example for all Christians. These examples are from Marla J. Selvidge, *Woman, Cult, and Miracle Recital* 18–22. Contemporary scholars offer similar views. Selvidge has stressed that this woman is "an authentic model for the community" and "a teacher of the

Twelve and others" (ibid. 98–107). Hisako Kinukawa, writing from "a Japanese feminist perspective, argues that the woman "symbolizes the burden put on us women because of our femaleness" and stresses the initiative of the woman: "by being touched by her, Jesus is led to make clear that the cultic barrier established by women and men is broken down," and "by talking to her personally in public, he has broken down the social barrier of 'honor' that is restricted to men" (*Women and Jesus in Mark: A Japanese Feminist Perspective* [Maryknoll, N.Y.: Orbis, 1994] 49).

For both men and women these two narratives present important christological points as well as a "narrative theology" of faith. The Jesus who emerges from these stories is one who is compassionate in the face of human suffering and who makes the needs of these sufferers the norm for his action, to the disregard of social taboos and conventions. He talks to a woman in public and violates the stringent taboo against touching a corpse. Faith, especially as embodied by the bleeding woman, can exist in the face of seemingly hopeless situations. It involves not simply an intellectual conviction but also a bold trust that crosses barriers (symbolized both by the social constraints and the mass of people blocking access to Jesus). It can spring as in the case of Jairus from deep concern for a loved one or from desire for release from life-denying suffering. Faith is ultimately, however, the trust that contact with the power of God manifest in the teaching and actions of Jesus is victory over sickness and death.

FOR REFERENCE AND FURTHER STUDY

D'Angelo, Mary Rose. "Gender and Power in the Gospel of Mark: The Daughter of Jairus and the Woman with the Flow of Blood," in John C. Cavadini, ed., *Miracles in Jewish and Christian Antiquity: Imagining Truth* (Notre Dame: University of Notre Dame Press, 1999) 83–109.

Derrett, J. Duncan M. "Mark's Technique: The Hemorrhaging Woman and Jairus' Daughter," *Bib* 63 (1982) 474–505.

Dewey, Joanna. "Jesus' Healing of Women: Conformity and Non-Conformity to Dominant Cultural Values as Clues for Historical Reconstruction," *BTB* 24 (1995) 122–31.

Hedrick, Charles W. "Miracle Stories as Literary Compositions: The Case of Jairus' Daughter," *Perspectives in Religious Studies* 20 (1993) 217–33.

Kinukawa, Hisako. "The Story of the Hemorrhaging Woman (Mark 5:25-34) Read From a Japanese Feminist Context," *Biblical Interpretation* 2 (1994) 283–93.

Robbins, Vernon K. "The Woman Who Touched Jesus' Garment: Socio-rhetorical Analysis of the Synoptic Accounts," NTS 33 (1987) 502–15.

Selvidge, Marla J. "Mark 5:25-34 and Leviticus 15:19-20: A Reaction to Restrictive Purity Regulations," *JBL* 103 (1984) 619–23.

_____. *Woman, Cult, and Miracle Recital. A Redactional Critical Investigation on Mark 5:24-34.* Lewisburg, N.J.: Bucknell University Press, 1990.

19. *The Rejection at Nazareth* (6:1-6a)

1. Jesus then left that place and arrived in his home town; his disciples followed him. 2. When the Sabbath came he started to teach in the synagogue, and many listening to him were astonished and said: "What is the source of all this? What is this wisdom bestowed upon him? What mighty works are accomplished through his hands? 3. Isn't this one just a craftsman, Mary's son and a brother of James, Joses, Jude, and Simon? Don't his sisters still live here among us?" They were scandalized by him. 4. Jesus responded to them: "No prophet is without honor, except in his home town, among his own relatives, and in his own home." 5. Then he was unable to do any mighty deed, apart from healing a few sick people by laying hands on them. 6a. And he was shocked at their unbelief.

NOTES

1. *that place:* Mark uses this phrase to connect the story with the previous narrative of the resuscitation of Jairus' daughter.

home town: The Greek *patris* can mean "native country" or "home town." The latter is preferable in view of vv. 3-4. Though it is not explicitly mentioned here, Mark understands Nazareth as Jesus' home town (1:9) and others describe Jesus as "the Nazarene" (1:24; 10:47; 14:67; 16:6).

his disciples: Though they have no role in this narrative their presence prepares for those that follow.

2. *he started to teach:* Any Jewish layman could address a synagogue meeting if invited by the synagogue officials (see 1:21-22; also Luke 4:16-17; Acts 13:15).

in the synagogue: Jesus' public ministry in Mark begins with synagogue teaching (1:21-22), where he subsequently casts out a demon (1:23-28); he continues his work of proclamation and exorcising in synagogues (1:39), and he heals a man with a withered hand in a synagogue (3:1-6). After his rejection at the synagogue in Nazareth Jesus does not enter a synagogue again.

were astonished: This same verb (a form of *ekplēssein*) describes the reaction to Jesus' teaching at 1:22 and 11:18, in two pericopes that, like 6:1-6a, stand near the beginning of major subsections of the gospel: another instance of echoes and foreshadowings throughout the gospel (see also 7:37 and 10:26).

What is the source of all this?: This is the first of five questions that unfold rapidly and somewhat disparagingly in vv. 2-3. The first sets the tone for the following ones and can be roughly summarized as: "What is the source of this extraordinary power given to one who is no different from what we are?" Such questions are part of a cluster of "identity questions" in Mark in which people question the identity of Jesus or the origin of his power (see also 1:24, 27; 2:7; 4:41; 8:4; 11:28). On the narrative level they sustain the unfolding christology and engage the readers; for Mark's readers they also voice questions that were alive in their communities.

What is this wisdom bestowed upon him: This is the only use of "wisdom" *(sophia)* in Mark. Though the question is a natural reaction to Jesus' teaching, the subsequent one about his mighty works seems out of place where only teaching has been mentioned. The form of the question, however, recalls Mark's earlier joining of works of power with teaching (1:21-28). Wisdom is often joined with power in the OT: e.g., wisdom and power/strength as divine attributes (Dan 2:20; Isa 10:13; Jer 10:13, 16), which are given to the prophet Daniel (Dan 2:23); God's creative activity takes place through wisdom and power (Jer 10:12, 51:15); and the wise person also possesses power (Dan 2:23; 7:14; Eccl 7:19). The question of Jesus' hearers, while perhaps a subtle allusion to the charge of 3:22 (demonic possession), also expresses the narrator's view that Jesus is one gifted with God's power and wisdom (see 1 Cor 1:21).

What mighty works are accomplished through his hands?: The original Greek of this third question is syntactically difficult and has a number of textual variants. A reading favored by some translators contains *hina* ("so that"), with the preferred translation "so that mighty works are accomplished through his hands" *(New International Version).* "Mighty work" *(dynamis)* is one of the NT terms translated as "miracle." The somewhat awkward phrasing "mighty works . . . accomplished" suggests God as the primary force behind the mighty deeds with Jesus as God's designated agent. The phrase "through his hands" recalls the powerful action of God's hand in delivering the people from Egypt. See especially the "credal" statement of Deut 4:34: "Or has any god ever attempted to go and take a nation for himself from the midst of another nation, by trials, by signs, by wonders, and by war, by a mighty hand and an outstretched arm" (see also Deut 5:15; 7:19; 9:26; Exod 7:4; 32:11). In Judg 6:36 Gideon prays that "you [God] will deliver Israel by my hand." The phrase also ironically prepares for the description of Jesus as someone known for working with his hands (v. 3).

3. *Isn't this one just a craftsman?:* The series of belittling questions continues. "Craftsman" translates *tektōn* which, though most frequently rendered "carpenter," can also be anyone who works with his hands in hard material (e.g., a builder or stoneworker). Though most major manuscripts describe Jesus himself as the craftsman, there are variant readings, probably through assimilation to Matt 13:55: "Is this not *the son* of the craftsman?" Celsus, a second-century opponent of Christianity, derided it for having a laborer for its founder (see Origen, *Contra Celsum* 6.34, 36).

Mary's son: This is the only time Mary, the mother of Jesus, is mentioned by name in Mark. The appellation "Mary's son" is unusual since sons are usually named in relation to fathers (e.g., 10:35, the sons of Zebedee; Matt 16:17, Simon bar [son of] Jona). Matthew alters the description to "Is not his mother called Mary?" An early manuscript ($\mathfrak{P}^{45}$) reads "the son of the carpenter and Mary." Though some authors say that naming a person in relation to a mother is insulting, with a hint of illegitimacy, other men at the time of Jesus were identified by their mothers: e.g., John the son of Dorcas (Josephus, *War* 4.145; see Acts 9:36), and Joseph the son of Iatrine (= "midwife"; Josephus, *Life* 185 (see Tal Ilan, "Man Born of Woman . . ." [Job 14:1]: The Phenomenon of Men

Bearing Metronymes at the Time of Jesus," *NovT* 34 [1992] 23–45). Also Mark uses the converse by identifying the women at the cross in terms of their sons rather than their husbands: "Mary the mother of James the Less and of Joses" (15:40).

brother of James, Joses, Jude, and Simon: Of the four brothers named here only two (James and Jude) appear elsewhere in the NT, though some authors argue that Jesus' mother is the same as Mary the "mother of Joses" at the cross (15:40, 47). Since the family of Jesus had patriarchal names (Jacob, Joseph, Judah, Simeon—in their OT forms), some have suggested that they reflect either a "pious" Jewish family (Gundry, *Mark* 296) or one with resurgent religious feeling and pride in their ancestral heritage (Meier, *Marginal Jew* 1:207).

Don't his sisters still live here among us?: The sisters of Jesus are not named. The mention of Jesus' trade and of his brothers and sisters serves to stress his ordinariness, which provides the source of the scandal. On the issue of whether these brothers and sisters of Jesus were "real brothers and sisters" see the Interpretation.

they were scandalized by him: The verb "scandalized" *(eskandalizonto),* etymologically from *skandalon* ("a stone that trips a person"), means that the family and friends of Jesus could not move beyond their own prejudgments to accept the actions and teaching of Jesus (see 3:20-21, 31-35). They become like the outsiders in 4:10-12 for whom the teaching of Jesus was a riddle.

4. *No prophet is without honor except in his home town:* Jesus applies to himself an aphorism that seems to have circulated independently, with minor variations. The simplest form is Luke 4:24: "No prophet is accepted in his home town." John 4:44 reads: "A prophet does not have honor in his own home country." A more developed version reads: "A prophet is not acceptable in his home town; a doctor does not heal those who know him" (*Gos. Thom.* 31; *P. Oxy.* 31:1-2). Parallels to the aphorism are found in Hellenistic literature: e.g., "it is the opinion of all the philosophers that life is difficult in their native land" (Dio Chrysostom, *Discourses* 47.6), and "until now my own country ignores me" (Philostratus, *Life of Apollonius of Tyana*, Letter 44). None of the proposed parallels, however, uses the word "prophet." So it seems that Mark presents it as an echo of the OT motif of the rejected prophet (2 Chr 24:19; 36:16; Neh 9:26, 30; Jer 35:15; Ezek 2:5; Hos 9:7; Dan 9:6, 10), which Luke expands into a major theme of his gospel (see especially Luke 4:16-30). Also in Isa 53:3 (LXX) the "Suffering Servant" is without honor *(atimos)* among all people. The figures of the rejected prophet and of the Servant influence Mark's picture of Jesus.

among his own relatives: Mark may have added "among his own relatives" as an echo of the misunderstanding by the family in 3:20-21, 31-35. The "dishonor" suffered by Jesus moves from the larger circle of his home town to his relatives and then to his actual family ("home"). In a village culture such as that of first-century Nazareth, to stand out or apart from one's family was an occasion for shame or dishonor for the whole family.

5. *he was unable to do any mighty deed:* The reason for this inability appears in 6:6a, the unbelief of his friends and family. This means that Jesus does not come as

a magician or miracle worker who dazzles his audience with works of power that compel belief (see 15:32: "come down from the cross that we may see and believe"). It does mean that where there is no openness to the power of God (6:2) or where that power becomes a stumbling block to preconceptions the "mighty work" as an invitation to deeper faith and discipleship cannot take place.

apart from healing a few sick people: Bultmann sees a contradiction between vv. 5a and 5b and views it as evidence that the whole incident here is artificially composed (*History of the Synoptic Tradition* 30). Matthew rewrites the whole of Mark 6:5 to say simply that "he did not do many mighty works there" (13:58), thus removing any hint that Jesus' power was limited. Mark's exception implies that the object of the disbelief by the townspeople was the complete prophetic mission of Jesus (his wisdom and mighty works). Jesus still retains the power to do mighty works in the face of disbelief. What he cannot do is compel acceptance. There may also be a very subtle allusion to Isa 53:3-5 here. Though God's Servant is without honor and rejected by all people in v. 3, in v. 4 he is said to bear the infirmities of the people who are healed through his suffering (53:5).

6a. *he was shocked at their unbelief:* "Shock" *(ethaumazen)* is a normal (positive) reaction by crowds to the power of Jesus. It is used only here of Jesus and represents a paradoxical counterreaction to unbelief. Matthew omits this reaction of Jesus in line with his other editorial changes of passages in Mark that might seem to diminish the power or dignity of Jesus. Though "unbelief" *(apistia)* is used only here and in 9:24 ("help my unbelief"), it reflects the stark alternatives in Mark between belief and unbelief and between understanding and lack of understanding. It also functions here much like blasphemy against the Holy Spirit in 3:29, that is, as a misuse of human freedom that closes the person to the action of God. Matthew softens Mark's stark alternatives by describing the followers of Jesus as people of "little faith" (6:30; 8:26; 14:31; 16:8).

INTERPRETATION

The narrative of Jesus' rejection in his home town is reported by the three Synoptic Gospels, but in different places and with different emphases. Matthew (13:53-58) recounts it at the very end of the parables chapter to stress the divisions the teaching of Jesus effects, while Luke enlarges the incident and places it at the outset of the ministry of Jesus (4:16-30) as a scenic introduction to his major theme of Jesus as the rejected prophet. John highlights rejection by Jesus' "own people" in the Prologue (1:11) and quotes the aphorism on prophetic rejection in 4:44; in John 6:42 people also speak of his human parentage (see Mark 6:3) as a counter to his claim that he is the bread come down from heaven. This incident is a parade example of a narrative that is deeply rooted in the historical ministry of Jesus while being freely adapted to the theologies of the individual gospels.

In Mark this rejection brings to an end a subsection of the gospel that begins in 3:13 with the choice and naming of the Twelve (3:13-19). In the preceding subsection the teaching and activity of Jesus have unfolded in greater detail (Mark 4:1-34, the teaching in parables and 4:35–5:43, dramatic words and acts of power). The rejection at Nazareth (6:1-6a) begins with an allusion to this activity, since it is both the wisdom of Jesus and his mighty works that puzzle his relatives and the people of his home town. The incident also follows Jesus' first foray beyond his native territory (5:1-20), which anticipates a more extensive journey and foreshadows the rejection of Jesus by people in Gentile territory (7:24–8:21). The rejection, here by family and friends, also echoes the earlier rejection by religious authorities that concludes the first subsection of the gospel (3:6). Similarly, the presence of the disciples, who have no role in the visit to Jesus' home town, prepares for the mission of the Twelve in 6:6b-13. This mission reflects the pattern that all the major divisions and subdivisions of Mark begin with discipleship stories (1:16-20; 3:13-19). The mission of the Twelve also will highlight the fact that while the natural family of Jesus seems bewildered at his wisdom and mighty works, the Twelve engage in teaching and activity modeled closely on that of Jesus (6:13, preaching of repentance, exorcising, healing) and so constitute his new family (3:31-35).

The emphasis of the narrative in 6:1-6a is clearly on the rejection of Jesus the prophet embodied in the five questions in vv. 2-3 and in Jesus' aphoristic response in v. 4. This has led some authors to argue that the whole narrative is simply an expansion of the aphorism. Bultmann, for one, calls it a typical scene constructed from a saying, the biographical apophthegm of 6:4 (*History of the Synoptic Tradition* 30). Still, its presence in all four gospels in different settings as well as its nature as an incident that would scarcely have been created by the early church confer a ring of authenticity on the rejection—especially since James, one of these relatives of Jesus, emerged as a leader in the early church (see Gal 1:19; 2:9, 12; Acts 12:17; 15:13; 21:18; 1 Cor 15:7). Whatever the nature of the historical incident, the narrative has been enhanced by allusion to the OT motif of the rejected prophet (see Notes).

The most debated historical issue surrounding this section (and 3:20-21, 31-35) is whether the brothers and sisters of Jesus were biological brothers and sisters and the other children of Mary and Joseph. Throughout church history three major solutions have evolved: (1) These were the natural children of Joseph and Mary; this opinion was held in the ancient church by Hegesippus (2nd c.), Tertullian (160–220 C.E.), and Helvidius (4th c.), and is held today by many non-Catholic scholars and recently by the Catholic scholars Rudolf Pesch (*Marksuevangelium* 1:322–24) and John P. Meier (*A Marginal Jew* 1:327–32); (2) the "Epiphanian" solution is that they were the children of Joseph by an earlier marriage; and (3) the view of Jerome is that they were "cousins" of Jesus, perhaps the sons of Mary's sister. One or other of these latter views has been held by most Roman Catholics and by many non-Catholics too (see Richard Bauckham, "The Brothers and Sisters of Jesus: An Epiphanian Response," *CBQ* 56 [1994] 686–700).

None of these views would necessarily compromise the doctrine of the virginal conception of Jesus, since even if the brothers and sisters were natural children of Joseph and Mary they could have been born after Jesus (see Matt 1:25). Since the sources pertinent to the discussion of this question range widely through the NT, a commentary on Mark cannot address the issue adequately, nor is resolution of this issue important to understanding Mark. In Mark the natural family of Jesus, whether they are blood brothers and sisters, stepbrothers and stepsisters, or cousins, is suspicious of Jesus as being mad, regards him as a source of shame to the family, rejects him at Nazareth, and is supplanted by the new family gathered in response to Jesus' teaching and presence (3:31-35; 10:29-31).

This passage also touches on issues that are developed in later theology. We have noted that Matthew softens the surprise of Jesus at the unbelief of the townspeople in function of his "higher christology." Developing theology would struggle with the strange conjunction here of the stark humanity of Jesus with a sense that he is beyond human explanation. This will unfold in subsequent centuries in the great paradox of Christian faith: Jesus as *verus deus, verus homo* ("true God and true human").

Equally generative of later theological development is the contrast between the overwhelming power of Jesus (wisdom and mighty works) and his inability to work miracles because of the unbelief of the townspeople. The power of God that works through Jesus seems limited by human resistance. Though discussion of the problem of the sovereignty of divine grace and human freedom takes place more in dialogue with Pauline literature, the Markan narrative is a foundational text for such reflection. As one commentator notes: "just as his power is our salvation, so our unbelief is his powerlessness" (Erich Grässer, "Jesus in Nazareth," in Erich Grässer et al., *Jesus in Nazareth*. BZNW 40 [Berlin and New York: Walter de Gruyter, 1972] 35).

The narrative contains several themes for actualization. It offers a counter to any movement toward a docetic or spiritualized Jesus. The human Jesus is vividly portrayed here. He is simply "Mary's son," whose display of power and teaching seems to contradict the familiar view that his relatives had of him. He worked with his hands like the vast majority of people of his day. The scandal of the ordinariness of Jesus' origin was used against Christians in the early centuries as are scandals of the all-too-humanness of the church today.

Most obviously and "proverbially," the theme of the prophet's rejection is important. Prophetic figures are rarely respected or honored by those closest to them. Prophets are deeply rooted in a tradition but they often must take stands against what they see as the destructive development of their tradition. Also prophets are called to speak God's word for those who have no one to speak for them and to take the side of the marginal as did the prophets of ancient Israel, and as did Jesus when he turned from his own and healed the sick who, in Mark, are never far from him. Such conduct can be both surprising and alienating. Those who feel called to a prophetic mission should not be surprised or shocked at rejection. From 3:6 onward when the plan to kill Jesus emerges through his alienation from his neighbors here (6:1-6a) and later from his disciples (8:14-21), the shadow of the cross falls over the story of Jesus the prophet of God.

For Reference and Further Study

Batey, Richard A. "Is Not This the Carpenter?" *NTS* 30 (1984) 249–58.
Bauckham, Richard. "The Brothers and Sisters of Jesus: An Epiphanian Response," *CBQ* 56 (1994) 686–700.
Crossan, John Dominic. "Mark and the Relatives of Jesus," *NovT* 15 (1973) 81–113.
Grässer, Erich. "Jesus in Nazareth (Mark VI.1-6a): Notes on the Redaction and Theology of St. Mark," *NTS* 16 (1969–70) 1–23.
Ilan, Tal. "'Man Born of Woman . . .' (Job 14:1). The Phenomenon of Men Bearing Metronymes at the Time of Jesus," *NovT* 34 (1992) 23–45.
McArthur, Harvey K. "Son of Mary," *NovT* 15 (1973) 38–58.
Meier, John P. "The Brothers and Sisters of Jesus in Ecumenical Perspective," *CBQ* 54 (1992) 1–28.

20. *The Mission Charge to the Twelve* (6:6b-13)

6b. He then left for a teaching tour of the surrounding villages. 7. Having summoned the Twelve, he then began to send them on a mission two by two, and conferred on them power over the unclean spirits. 8. He directed them to take nothing for the journey except a staff—no bread, no beggar's bag, no money in their belts. 9. But they were to wear sandals, and not to put on two tunics. 10. He also told them: "Wherever you go into a home, remain there until you leave that place. 11. If any place does not welcome you or listen to you, leave immediately and shake the dust from your feet as evidence against them." 12. They departed and proclaimed a message of repentance. 13. They cast out many demons, anointed many sick people with oil, and cured them.

NOTES

6b. *left for a teaching tour:* The comment links this report to 6:1 where Jesus began his sojourn by teaching and also provides a transition from the rejection by his family and hometown people to a preaching tour of the surrounding area. Mark constantly stresses Jesus as a teacher, especially in transitional and summary statements (see especially 1:21; 2:13; 4:1; 6:2, 34; 9:31; 10:1). Much of Jesus' teaching takes place while he is "on the move."

7. *having summoned:* The use of "summon" *(proskalein)* recalls the initial choice of the Twelve (3:13, "he summoned those he wanted"). The verb connotes an authoritative summons (15:44). Jesus also "summons" disciples *(mathētai,* 8:1; 10:42; 12:43) and crowds (7:14; 8:34).

   the Twelve: Thus far in Mark the Twelve have been chosen in 3:14-15 and given the mystery of the kingdom in 4:10-12. The commissioning in 6:7-11 enlarges their role. Subsequently they will accompany Jesus on the journey to Jerusalem while misunderstanding the nature of his power (9:35; 10:42), will celebrate a final meal with him (14:12-21), and will flee at his arrest (14:43-46, 50). Mark does not give to the Twelve the eschatological significance as judges of the twelve tribes of Israel that is found in Matt 19:28.

   send them on a mission: The same verb *(apostellein)* is used here as well as in 3:13-14. But at the initial call it described the purpose of Jesus, "in order that he might send them on a mission," while here this purpose is fulfilled. The verb conveys a sense of delegated and representative authority, so that the mission of the Twelve is both from Jesus and through the power of Jesus.

   two by two: Because of the use of the juridical term *martyrion* ("evidence" or "witness") in v. 11, the paired missionary activity may reflect the law that two witnesses are needed when charging a person (Deut 19:15; Num 35:30; 2 Cor 13:1). Another possibility is that it reflects the concrete missionary practice of the early church (1 Cor 9:2-6).

   power over unclean spirits: Just as the initial ministry of Jesus began with the confrontation with evil spirits, so too will the ministry of the Twelve. The power *(exousia)* that characterized the initial ministry of Jesus (1:22, 27, 2:10) was given to the Twelve at their initial call (3:15) and is again conferred and exercised for the first time (6:12-13).

8. *He directed them:* The following instructions present very specific directives about lifestyle not found in the initial commissioning and seemingly unrelated to the initial commission of v. 7 and its fulfillment in vv. 12-13.

   for the journey: Literally "for the way" *(hodos).* Since *hodos* in Mark also connotes the "way of discipleship" the instructions are not simply traveling directives but are also symbolic of the demands of discipleship.

except a staff: On the practical level the staff is used for support and protection. The staff in the OT is also symbolic of power and authority (frequently in Exodus and Numbers for the staff of Moses or Aaron; e.g., Exod 4:20; 7:9-20; 8:16-17; 14:16; see also Mic 7:14; Ps 23:4). The parallels in Matt 10:10 and Luke 9:3 expressly forbid the staff. In 2 Kgs 4:29-37 Gehazi the servant of Elisha is told to take Elisha's staff and lay it on the face of the son of the Shunammite woman as a prelude to the actual healing by Elisha (see Mark 6:13). On the parallels between the travel gear of the Twelve and the wandering Cynics, see the Interpretation.

no bread, no beggar's bag, no money in their belt: The instructions demand trust in both God and neighbor and presuppose the practice of hospitality and support that is characteristic of early Christian missions (Acts 16:15, 40; 18:1-3; Phil 4:14-15). The beggar's bag *(pēra)*, also translated as "sack" (for food, etc.), was carried by traveling philosophers and wonderworkers. The prohibition of the sack and of money may reflect a desire to distinguish Jesus' disciples from venal traveling philosophical and religious missionaries.

9. *they were to wear sandals:* Again, in contrast to Matt 10:10 and Luke 10:4, Mark allows sandals. Mark's missionaries resemble the Israelites preparing to eat the Passover meal prior to their departure from Egypt, with "your sandals on your feet, and your staff in your hand" (Exod 12:11). If there is an exodus motif here it is very subtle, perhaps as a prelude to the Markan feeding in the wilderness (6:32-44), the testing of the people (as the disciples are tested and fail; see 8:14-21), and a revelation on a mountain top (9:2-8).

and not to put on two tunics: The "tunic" *(chitōn)* is the garment normally worn close to the skin. Josephus *(Ant.* 17.136) mentions a slave who wore two tunics, and so the term can also be extended to include outer garments (see Mark 14:63). The prohibition against a change of clothes underscores the eschatological urgency of the mission.

10. *Whenever you go into a home, remain there:* The home that welcomes them is to be a base for the missionaries, and they are not to move around.

until you leave that place: While the home is the missionary base, the "place" is the larger venue presupposed for the mission. The instructions here again may reflect a network of early Christian homes that welcomed missionaries, even as they were rejected in their preaching (see Acts 17:1-9; 18:1-11).

11. *shake the dust from your feet:* In Acts 13:51 this is a symbolic judgment against those who reject the missionaries; in Jewish sources it is an act of deprecation used by Jews when returning from pagan (unclean) lands *(m. Toh.* 4:5).

as evidence against them: The act is explained as "evidence" or "witness" *(eis martyrion autois)* either "against" or "for" them as a sign of judgment or a call to repentance. Mark uses the same phrase in 1:44 for the leper's appearance before the priests. In 13:9 the appearance of Christians before assemblies, rulers, and kings because of the name of Jesus will also be *eis martyrion autois.*

12. *proclaimed a message of repentance:* The initial proclamation of the Twelve reproduces in part that of Jesus in Mark 1:14-15.

13. *cast out many demons:* Exorcisms and confrontation with the power of demons follow their proclamation as they did that of Jesus in 1:21-28.

anointed many sick people with oil: Oil is used for medical purposes in Luke 10:34. Here instead of the simple phrase "cured" or "healed," a ritual of anointing is mentioned, most likely introduced as a reflection of early Christian practice (see Jas 5:14-15).

and cured them: The principal activities of Jesus—proclamation, exorcism, and healing—characterize the mission of the disciples.

INTERPRETATION

After the rejection in his home town, Jesus in 6:6b-13 sends the Twelve on a mission that virtually reproduces his own activity up to this point. The narrative is interrupted by the vivid story of the murder of John the Baptist (6:14-29) and resumed when "the apostles" report on the mission (6:30-32). The intercalated narrative about John not only creates the impression of passing time but also informs the reader of the suffering and opposition that await those associated with Jesus—as the Twelve are in their mission.

The mission charge has a complex development. While Mark and Matthew have only one mission of the Twelve (Mark 6:6b-13; Matt 10:1-15; Luke 9:1-6), Luke has a second mission of the Seventy(-two) in 10:1-16 that is derived from Q. Since most scholars claim that Luke better represents the original order of Q it appears that many of the Q sayings are integrated by Matthew in his version of the Markan mission charge (10:1-15) and in other contexts (9:37-38; 11:24). The major differences shared by Matthew and Luke against Mark are the direction not to take a staff (Matt 10:10; Luke 9:3; cf. Mark 6:8) and the prohibition of sandals (Matt 10:10; Luke 10:4; cf. Mark 6:9). The major differences between Mark and Q concern features that are absent in Mark such as the saying on the harvest (Luke 10:2; Matt 9:37-38), the sending "as lambs among wolves" (Luke 10:3; Matt 10:16), the instruction to give the greeting of peace (Luke 10:5; Matt 10:12-13), the sayings on laborers worthy of their hire (Luke 10:7; Matt 10:10b), the explicit proclamation of the kingdom (Luke 10:9; Matt 10:7), the saying on Sodom (Luke 10:12; Matt 10:15), and the woes against Chorazin and Bethsaida (Luke 10:13-15; Matt 11:21-23). The Q mission charge is both more elaborate and more prophetic (in the sense of threats of future judgment) than that of Mark. Though there is no *direct* evidence that Mark knew Q (as a fixed collection), he seems to have known individual sayings found in Q.

The mission charge in Mark and Q has been the principal textual foundation for the recently proposed portrait of Jesus as a wandering Cynic.

Though this topic is more pertinent to historical Jesus research, at least one major proponent (Burton Mack) argues that the Markan Jesus is also a Cynic. Such claims are highly problematic.

Cynicism, so called most likely from the Greek *kyōn* ("dog") in the sense of a "dogged" person or one who "barked at" people, is rooted in the Socratic tradition. Its principal "founding figures" were Diogenes of Sinope (404–323 B.C.E.) and Crates of Thebes (fl. ca. 330 B.C.E.). It was less an organized philosophy than a critical perspective on the pretensions of others. It was characterized by an itinerant lifestyle, aphoristic teaching, and anti-establishment and anti-social behavior. The "traveling gear" of the Cynic closely resembles the directives in the mission charge in Q. Pseudo-Diogenes writes: "When I'd chosen in favor of this Cynic way, Antisthenes took off the shirt and the cloak I was wearing, put a doubled threadbare cloak on me instead, slung a satchel on my shoulder with some bread and other scraps of food, and put in a cup and a bowl. On the outside of the satchel he hung an oil flask, and a scraper, and then, finally, he gave me a staff, too" (Ps.-Diogenes 30.3, cited from Francis G. Downing, *Christ and the Cynics: Jesus and Other Radical Preachers in the First Century Tradition* [Sheffield: Sheffield Academic Press, 1988] 47). According to Diogenes, Antisthenes "was the first to double his cloak, and use just that, and carry a staff and a satchel" (Diogenes, *Lives of Eminent Philosophers* 6.13, in Downing, *Christ and the Cynics* 47).

Even given the relatively meagre evidence for the Cynic lifestyle and still less for their activity in Galilee, there are some significant differences from Jesus and his disciples. Cynics are told to be anti-social. Lucian of Samasota (2nd century C.E.) describes one of their practices: "Seek out the most crowded places, and when you're there, keep to yourself, quite unsociable, exchanging greetings with no one, neither friend nor stranger" (Lucian, *Philosophies for Sale* 10, in Downing, *Christ and the Cynics* 48). Both Mark (6:10) and Q (Luke 10:5-8; Matt 10:11-12) prescribe just the opposite.

If Mark reacts in any way to the Cynic tradition it is rather to distinguish Jesus and his disciples from that tradition and implicitly to reject it as a lifestyle for Christian missionaries. Jesus' disciples are to wear sandals and not carry the begging bag that was characteristic of the Cynics. They are to stay with settled communities and are to move on only when their stay is unfruitful. Further indication that the Markan Jesus is not the Cynic Jesus is the Markan Jesus' fidelity to the Torah. Rather than rejecting traditional values, Jesus promotes true observance of the Sabbath, encourages marriage, accepts and even welcomes children, and is constantly in the presence of crowds and disciples. He is far from the solitary and individualistic rejection of human contact attributed to the Cynics. The Cynic Jesus is a problematic reconstruction of the historical figure and a nonexistent model for the Markan Jesus.

The mission charge in Mark is less detailed and dramatic than the one in Q as reconstructed from Matthew and Luke. Mark recounts it "with a certain vagueness and lightness of touch" (Cranfield, *St Mark* 203). Its narrative purpose is to continue the pattern of having a discipleship story at the beginning each major section. It also sets the tone for this section in which the Twelve feature prominently while at the same time they grow in their misunderstanding of Jesus so that ultimately even they are said to have "hard hearts" (8:14-21). The narrative also serves to link the ministries of Jesus, of his historical disciples, and of the Markan community. Each comes out or is sent out to preach (*kēryssein:* 1:14; 3:14; 6:12; 13:10). Each will meet failure and rejection in the mission.

The enduring theological significance of this passage is its role as a call to the church never to forget its origin in a community of missionaries: the Twelve are also among the first recipients of a resurrection appearance in 1 Cor 15:3-7, a tradition that has been described as "community founding" and mission inaugurating. The church's self-identity is as a community that is sent; it is to "travel light" and to proclaim the word in freedom and fearlessness. Like Jesus it is to confront the power of evil and serve as an agent of God's healing power. As many churches today are engaged in a continuing quest for identity in a complex world, this rather simple narrative should always be a conversation partner.

FOR REFERENCE AND FURTHER STUDY

Caird, G. B. "Uncomfortable Words: II. Shake Off the Dust from Your Feet," *ExpTim* 81 (1969) 40–43.
Draper, Jonathan A. "Wandering radicalism or purposeful activity? Jesus and the sending of messengers in Mark 6:6-56," *Neotestamentica* 29 (1995) 183–202.
Mack, Burton L. *The Lost Gospel. The Book of Q & Christian Origins.* San Francisco: HarperCollins, 1993.

21. *The Identity of Jesus and the Execution of John the Baptist* (6:14-29)

14. Then Herod the king heard about him [Jesus], for his reputation had become well known. Some people were saying: "John the Baptist has been raised from the dead, and this is why miraculous powers are working in him." 15. Others would say: "He is Elijah." And others surmised: "He is a prophet like one of the prophets." 16. But Herod heard this [speculation] and said: "John, the one I beheaded, has been raised up."

17. For it was Herod himself who had given the order that John was to be arrested and confined in a prison at the instigation of Herodias, the wife of his brother Philip, whom he had himself married. 18. For John used to say to Herod: "It is illegal for you to be married to your brother's wife." 19. But Herodias held a grudge against John and wanted to destroy him but could not find a way. 20. (You see, Herod was afraid of John. He also realized that John was a just and holy man, and even protected him. When he heard him speak he was very perplexed, yet he enjoyed listening to him.) 21. Her opportunity arrived one day, when Herod on his birthday hosted a banquet for his high officials, his military commanders, and the elites of Galilee. 22. Then Herodias' daughter entered the banquet hall and performed a dance, which delighted Herod and the dinner guests. Herod then said to the young woman: "Ask me for whatever you want, and I will give it to you." 23. He even made an oath to her: "Ask me for whatever you want, and I will give it to you—even if it is half of my kingdom." 24. She left and asked her mother: "What should I request?" She answered: "The head of John the Baptist." 25. Right away she hurried back and made this request to the king: "My wish is that you give to me right now the head of John the Baptist on a platter." 26. The king was very dejected but was unwilling to refuse her, because of the oaths and the presence of the dinner guests. 27. Still he immediately dispatched an executioner to bring him John's head. He went out and beheaded John in the prison, 28. and brought his head on a platter and gave it to the young woman, who then gave it to her mother. 29. When John's disciples heard about this, they came and took his body and laid it in a tomb.

NOTES

14. *Herod:* The "Herod" described here is Herod Antipas, born in 20 B.C.E., the son of Herod the Great and Malthace (a Samaritan). After the death of Herod the Great he became tetrarch (the ruler of a specified territory) of Galilee and Perea from 4 B.C.E. to 39 C.E. In Luke 13:31-32 Jesus calls him "that fox." Also in Luke 23:6-16 (see Acts 4:27), Herod Antipas concurs in the execution of Jesus. He ruled like a typical Hellenistic client king and was known for his extensive building projects, especially the cities of Sepphoris and Tiberias, cities there is no report of Jesus ever entering, even though Sepphoris was only four miles from Nazareth.

the king: Herod was technically not a king, and Matthew (14:9) and Luke (9:7) correctly call him a "tetrarch." The description is also ironic, since it was Herod's desire to be a king that led to his downfall (Josephus, *Ant.* 18.240-56).

for his reputation had become well known: The Greek reads simply "his name," but here "name" is used in the sense of the publicity given the name. The statement here is in ironic contrast to the reception that Jesus receives in "his home town" (6:1-3) and verifies his statement that prophets are not accepted in their own home or by their relatives (6:4). Mark also continues the motif of the spread of Jesus' fame throughout Galilee (1:28; 3:7). The whole section in 6:14-29 contains many uses of the "explanatory *gar*": that is, *gar* ("for") is used to explain or comment on other verses (6:14, 17, 18, 20). This may indicate that Mark was adapting an early legend that was unfamiliar to his readers.

John the Baptist has been raised from the dead: This is a strange opinion to attribute to Jewish people. Though groups such as the Pharisees hoped for the general resurrection, expectation of individuals returning to life before the eschaton is virtually unknown at this time. The perfect tense *egēgertai* ("has been raised") implies that John has been raised and is still alive, which the next phrase confirms.

miraculous powers: The reports of Jesus' miracles that have characterized the narrative to this point have reached even Herod, though he shares the confusion between John and Jesus voiced by the people at large. "Miraculous powers" translates *dynameis* (lit. "mighty works"; see also 6:5; 9:39), which is Mark's preferred term for miracles. He uses "signs" not for the works of Jesus (see 8:11-13) but for the works of false prophets (13:22).

are working in him: According to popular thought preternatural powers resided in a miracle worker just as "evil powers" occupied a demoniac.

15. *Others would say: "He is Elijah":* Elijah, whose historical ministry was set in the 9th century B.C.E., evokes a host of associations for Jewish readers. He is the prophet *par excellence* of conflict with oppressive royal power (1 Kgs 17–19, 21; 2 Kgs 1–2). He (along with Enoch in Gen 5:22-24) had not died but ascended in a whirlwind and a fiery chariot to heaven (2 Kgs 2:11-12). He will return to prepare for the day of the Lord (Mal 4:5 = 3:23-24 in Hebrew), and in the NT he becomes the precursor of the Messiah. Elijah is first mentioned here, but features prominently in the subsequent narratives where Mark will identify John as Elijah (8:28; 9:4, 5, 11, 12, 13; 15:35). The Elijah traditions in the NT are complex. At times Elijah is the precursor of John the Baptist, the fiery reformer who announces the day of the Lord; at other times John is identified with Elijah as the precursor of the Messiah (Jesus). In post-biblical Jewish tradition he becomes a protector of the poor; a place is always set for him at the Passover Seder table, and he is patron of the newborn (Jerome T. Walsh, "Elijah," *ABD* 2:463–66).

a prophet like one of the prophets: Popular opinion views Jesus as a prophet in ironic contrast to his neighbors and relatives who do not honor him as a prophet (6:1-6a). The proposed identifications of Jesus become less specific, moving from John to Elijah to a general prophetic figure. Since the Hebrew prophets were not primarily miracle workers this latter opinion may refer to a general hope for the return of a prophet like Moses (Deut 18:15, 18; see Acts 7:37). Moses and Elijah will appear with Jesus in 9:4. The Qumran community hoped for the coming of "the prophet and the Messiahs of Aaron and Israel" (1QS 9:11), and there were different prophetic figures who arose in the first century: e.g., the Samaritan prophet (Josephus, *Ant.* 18.85-89), Theudas (Acts 5:36; Josephus, *Ant.* 20.97-98), and the unnamed Egyptian prophet (Josephus,

War 2.261-63 = *Ant.* 20.169-71; Acts 21:38). The Markan Jesus speaks of the future coming of false prophets who will perform signs and wonders (13:22).

16. *John, the one I beheaded:* The temporal flow of the narrative is interesting. Herod's question about the identity of Jesus presupposes the earlier death of John, so the account of John's death serves as a "flashback." Here, more strongly than in the subsequent narrative, the responsibility for the death of John is solely Herod's.

   has been raised: This second reference to the "raising" of John (see 6:14) is another instance of the Markan technique of intercalation or bracketing of significant material (the proposed identifications of Jesus) by similar phrases.

17. *For it was Herod himself who had given the order . . . confined in a prison:* The "flashback" begins with the explanatory *gar.* Mark's account here differs considerably from that of Josephus (*Ant.* 18.116-119). In Mark, John is imprisoned and executed presumably in Galilee (6:21), while according to Josephus (*Ant.* 18.119) John is imprisoned and executed in Machaerus, a fortress on the northeast corner of the Dead Sea.

   at the instigation of Herodias, the wife of his brother Philip, whom he himself had married: Compared to Josephus (*Ant.* 18.109-119) and what is known from other ancient sources, Mark's report is significantly inaccurate. Herod Antipas' first marriage was to the (unnamed) daughter of Aretas IV, the Nabatean king. Herod Antipas later married Herodias after dismissing Aretas' daughter, who escaped to her father. This precipitated the conflict between Aretas and Herod Antipas that led to his ultimate downfall and exile to Gaul in 39 C.E. Herodias had originally been married to another Herod, a half-brother of Antipas (a son of Herod the Great and Mariamne II). Herodias and this Herod had a daughter named Salome, who married another half-brother of Herod Antipas named Philip (yet another son of Herod the Great by his wife Cleopatra of Jerusalem). Mark is thus incorrect in calling Herodias the (former) wife of Philip; where Mark and Josephus agree is that the girl (unnamed in Mark, Salome in Josephus) is the daughter of Herodias. Though scholars often conflate Mark and Josephus (*Ant.* 18.109) to create a "Herod Philip," no such person is independently attested. Given the confusing relation of the descendants of Herod by his ten wives (many of whose sons and grandsons are called "Herod"), Mark's confusion (along with that of many generations of readers) is understandable.

18. *It is illegal for you to be married to your brother's wife:* Such a marriage would be in violation of Lev 18:16 and 20:21: "If a man takes his brother's wife, it is impurity; he has uncovered his brother's nakedness; they shall be childless." Josephus (*Ant.* 18.116-119) attributes John's execution to Herod's fear of John's preaching and of his popularity among the people, which Herod feared might lead to rebellion. Since, according to Josephus, John summoned people to virtuous living and to his baptism ("righteousness toward one another and piety toward God"), there is no absolute contradiction between Josephus and Mark (see also 1:4). Absent from Mark is Josephus' emphasis on Herod's explicit political motive.

19. *held a grudge against John:* The Greek *eneichen* literally means "had it in for" John. Herodias is starkly introduced simply as one who had long wished to kill John; this is underscored by the sequence of verbs in the imperfect: "held a grudge . . . wanted . . . could not find a way." Herodias is here pictured as like Jezebel (1 Kgs 19:1-3) who plots the death of Elijah.

20. *You see, Herod was afraid of John:* This whole verse is an editorial comment introduced by the explanatory *gar* ("you see"). Herod's fear seems in contrast to his matter-of-fact statement in v. 16: "John, the one I beheaded."

    a just and holy man: There is agreement in this description of John by Mark and Josephus (*Ant.* 18.117-118), who calls John a good man preaching *dikaiosynē* ("righteousness") and *eusebeia* ("piety," i.e., proper relationship with God). These two qualities are the sum of virtue for Hellenistic Jews.

    protected . . . perplexed . . . enjoyed listening: The three verbs here are parallel and opposite to the three verbs describing Herodias in 6:19. Again the contrast between a strong and vengeful woman and a vacillating king shows the influence of the conflict between Jezebel and Elijah (especially 1 Kgs 18:1-46; 21:1-29). Herod here exemplifies the fate of the seed ("word") in the allegory of the seeds (4:13-20), where the seed that falls on rocky ground represents those who receive the word with joy but have no root in themselves (4:16-17).

21. *her opportunity arrived:* After the parenthetical comment the narrative resumes with the focus again on Herodias.

    on his birthday hosted a banquet: The somewhat gratuitous mention of Herod's birthday may be ironic. In classical Greek the term for "birthday" *(genesia)* is used frequently for a memorial of the birthday of a deceased person, while *genethlia hēmera* is used for the actual birthday. Since in Hellenistic Greek *genesia* is used for both, the overtones of the term tell Mark's readers that Herod's "birthday" will always be commemorated as the day on which John died.

    his high officials, his military commanders, and the elites of Galilee: This list is an accurate description of the upper classes in a Hellenistic city. The "high officials" are literally people of power *(megistanes)*, who are aligned with the military *(chiliarchoi)* and those of high status ("elites" or *prōtoi*). In Mark 10:43 Jesus will contrast the attitudes expected of his disciples to those of "rulers" and "great ones" who lord it over their subjects. The list of banquet guests heightens the contrast between worldly power and John the prophet.

22. *Then Herodias' daughter entered the banquet hall and performed a dance:* Some important manuscripts (Sinaiticus, Vaticanus, and Codex Bezae) contain the masculine singular genitive *autou,* so that the text would read "When his daughter Herodias entered . . . and performed a dance." Other admittedly inferior manuscripts read *autēs* so that she is Herodias' daughter, which is supported by the logic of the story (see 6:24). Most contemporary translations (the NRSV excepted) render the phrase as "Herodias' daughter." Though commonly identified as "Salome," the daughter is never named here or anywhere in the NT. The daughter is later (in 6:22, 28) called a *korasion* ("young woman"), the same term used in Mark 5:42 for a twelve-year-old girl. The daughter here could be as young as twelve, and so the narrative could con-

ceivably depict a child's performance rather than the sensuous and seductive dance of later art and literature—and imagined by many commentators on the text. One commentator has called it a "prostitute's dance," for which there is no textual evidence.

which delighted: The verb *ēresen* (from *areskein*) means simply "please" or "accommodate," and does not suggest sexual overtones (see 1 Macc 6:60; 8:21, where "the speech [or proposal] pleased" them).

Ask me for whatever you want, and I will give it to you: The setting (a banquet and a dance) and the language here reflect the words of King Ahasuerus to Esther in Esth 5:6 and 7:2. There is great irony here since Herod was a client king of Rome and had no power to subdivide his kingdom.

23. *He even made an oath to her:* Though "royal oaths" are characteristic of Hellenistic rulers, the taking of oaths was a serious religious issue in Judaism and early Christianity, and oaths were not to be treated lightly (see Matt 5:34-36; Jas 5:12; and the Mishnaic treatise *Nedarim*). Herod seems to become more alienated from his Jewish roots as the narrative progresses.

24. *she left:* In contrast to 6:14-16 with its slow-moving list of opinions about John and Herod's musings, from v. 22 ("she entered") the pace of the narrative is very rapid, with frequent entrances and departures that draw the readers quickly into the tragic inevitability of John's fate.

the head of John the Baptist: Herodias' grudge against John and her desire to kill him (6:19) can now be played out.

25. *Right away:* The Greek text is dense with terms denoting speed and urgency: "right away," "she hurried back" (lit. "she entered with haste" or "with eagerness"), and "give to me right now" *(exautēs).*

26. *The king was very dejected:* "Very dejected," *perilypos* in Greek, conveys very strong emotion and is used elsewhere in Mark only of Jesus in Gethsemane: "My soul is very sorrowful even unto death" (14:34). Herod's inability to do what is right is like the attitude of the rich young man who leaves Jesus "sorrowful" *(lypomenos),* and his emotion here recalls by contrast his earlier joy at listening to John (6:20). He is again an illustration of seed that falls on rocky ground (4:16-17; see above on 6:20).

because of the oaths and the presence of the dinner guests: Though Herodias stands behind John's death, the ultimate blame falls on Herod who becomes an example of those "who are supposed to rule over Gentiles" (10:42). Pilate caves in to similar pressure in ordering Jesus' execution in Mark 15:14-15.

27. *executioner:* The Greek term *spekoulator* is a loan word from Latin and originally meant "spy" or "scout." The narrative portrays the executioner as a virtual participant at the feast since Herod "immediately" dispatches him and the executioner leaves. His presence adds a macabre note to the celebration.

beheaded: Mark uses an unusual Greek term here, *apekephalisen.* Josephus uses the more normal *pelikizein (Ant.* 14.39; 14.140; 15.36; *War* 1.185; 2.241; see Rev 20:4). He recounts that Antony beheaded Antigonus so that such a dishonor would diminish Antigonus' fame among the Jews *(Ant.* 15.9-10). In *War* 2.241

beheading is parallel to crucifixion. It was a type of execution designed to de-
fame the person so treated.

in the prison: According to Josephus (*Ant.* 18.119) John was imprisoned in
Machaerus; see above under v. 17. Mark's account presumes a prison very
near the banquet hall and apparently in Galilee (unless we are to assume that
Herod brought all these people down to Machaerus).

28. *brought his head on a platter:* The term *pinax* (lit. "flat board") refers here to a
serving dish customarily used at feasts. There is brutal irony here in picturing
John's head as one of the "courses" at a royal banquet. The narrative now concludes very rapidly: The executioner "brought" in the head and gave it to the
young woman, and she gave it to her mother. There is no indication that
Herod saw the head, and no further description of the reaction of Herodias.

29. *When John's disciples heard about this:* John's disciples are mentioned elsewhere
only in 2:18 where their fasting practice is contrasted to that of Jesus' disciples.
According to the gospel traditions John worked principally in Judea (Mark
1:2-6; Matt 3:1-12; Luke 3:1-18; John 1:19-42; 3:22-24), and Jesus begins his
ministry in Galilee only after the arrest of John. Jesus evokes the memory of
John in disputes with Jerusalem authorities (11:30-33), so that John's disciples
would presumably be still working in Judea.

they came and took his body and laid it in a tomb: Since proper burial was a sign of
honor and of divine favor John is honored in death. His fate and his burial
foreshadow the proper burial to be given to Jesus (15:45-47), only not by those
explicitly called his disciples but by Joseph of Arimathea with the faithful
women as observers. The Greek terms used here for "corpse" *(ptōma)* and for
"tomb" *(mnēmeion)* recur in 15:45-46. The latter term literally means "a token
of remembrance." John and Jesus will be remembered together whenever the
gospel is proclaimed.

INTERPRETATION

Sandwiched between the sending and the return of the Twelve (6:6b-
13 and 6:30-32), the death of John the Baptist (6:14-29) is a complex narrative that begins with Herod's curiosity over Jesus (6:14-16) and then leads
into a retrospective account of the death of John (6:17-29). It is retrospective since John's arrest was narrated before Jesus' initial proclamation
(1:14). It is also the longest narrative in the gospel about anyone except
Jesus and is replete with textual and historical difficulties that argue for a
narrative (like that of the story of the Gerasene demoniac, 5:1-20) that developed over a long period. It has been called a "legend" or a "novelistic
tale," and is one of those gospel narratives that has been most portrayed
in Christian art and in other artistic forms (film, opera, etc.).

The introduction (6:14-16) betrays many characteristics of the evangelist's style and was most likely composed by Mark in order to link the

fates of John and Jesus closely together. The opinions voiced about John also foreshadow the opinions about Jesus expressed before Peter's "messianic confession" (8:27-30). Herod Antipas' guess that John had been "raised up" (6:16) also foreshadows belief in the resurrection of Jesus.

The retrospective account of John the Baptist's death in 6:17-29 first provides background information (6:17-20) and then tells a chilling tale of court intrigue and human weakness (6:21-29). According to the background information what got John into trouble was his prophetic denunciation of Herod's irregular marriage to Herodias (for the details, see the Notes). John accuses Herod of violating the OT commandment against marrying one's brother's wife (see Lev 18:16; 20:21). The party most aggrieved by John's denunciation is Herodias, while Herod himself is portrayed as fascinated by John and as enjoying his company.

The account of John's death in 6:21-29 ranks as one of the great stories in world literature. The cast of characters includes the scorned woman (Herodias), the charming and seductive young dancer (Herodias' daughter), the powerful and elite members of Galilean society, the righteous prophet (John), the weak-willed king (Herod Antipas), and the ruthlessly efficient executioner.

When Herodias' daughter's dance pleases her husband and the guests at his birthday party, the scorned woman seizes upon her husband's foolish public statement ("Ask me for whatever you want") and uses the occasion to have the righteous prophet killed in a particularly grisly manner ("the head of John the Baptist on a platter"). The request is granted with horrendous efficiency: "He went out and beheaded John in the prison and brought his head on a platter and gave it to the young woman, who then gave to her mother" (6:27-28). Just as the story began with foreshadowings of Jesus' resurrection, so it ends in 6:29 with the burial of John by his disciples, which is narrated in such a way as to anticipate some elements in the burial of Jesus. As John went, so Jesus will go.

While Mark 6:14-29 is good literature, is it accurate history? The only other independent ancient description of John's death comes from Josephus in *Ant.* 18.116-119. According to him Herod Antipas was alarmed at John's popularity and feared a rebellion if he were not stopped: "Herod decided therefore that it would be much better to strike first and be rid of him before his work led to an uprising" (18.118). So, according to Josephus, Herod had John brought in chains to the fortress Machaerus, and there he was put to death. Herod emerges as a political pragmatist who nevertheless ultimately paid for his deeds with the destruction of his army by "divine vengeance" on account of his mistreatment of John (18.116, 119).

It is difficult (though probably not impossible) to harmonize the accounts of John's death by Mark and Josephus. Herod could have invited his Galilean friends down to Machaerus. Herod could have been both fascinated with and threatened by John. Herod could have seen the birthday party and the girl's request as a dramatic and memorable way of getting rid of John and of impressing his guests at the same time. But it is more enlightening to focus on the differences in perspective, especially on Mark's concern with morality as opposed to Josephus' concern with politics.

Mark 6:14-29 breathes the air of the OT court tales. Herod's boast that he will give the girl whatever she asks "even if it is half of my kingdom" (6:23) links this story to the book of Esther (see 5:6 and 7:2). The scene at Herod's banquet that gets out of control evokes memories of Belshazzar's feast in Daniel 5 and the deposing of Queen Vashti in Esther 1. And the plots of the wicked queen against the righteous prophet are reminiscent of Jezebel's efforts to rid herself and her husband Ahab of the prophet Elijah in 1 Kings.

From Mark's moral perspective there is a sharp contrast among the major figures in the story. On the one hand John remains the faithful prophet who stands up for the Torah, accuses Herod of an illegal marriage, and dies for his bold witness. On the other hand there is the wicked schemer Herodias and the weak-willed Herod Antipas. While fascinated by John and even respecting him as "a just and holy man" (6:20), Herod makes a foolish promise (see the story of Jephthah's foolish vow in Judg 11:29-40) and has John executed because he wants to save face in the presence of his powerful friends. His honor is more important than the prophet's life. Thus Herod shows himself to be an example of those rulers who "lord it over" their subjects (see 10:42) and provides a foreshadowing of the weak-willed behavior of Pontius Pilate in judging the case of Jesus (15:1-15).

Mark's account of John's death prepares for his story of Jesus' death. By sandwiching 6:14-29 between the accounts of Jesus sending out the Twelve in 6:6b-13 and their return in 6:30-32 Mark also reminds his readers that prophetic figures like John and Jesus can expect suffering and even death at the hands of those rulers who "lord it over" others and put their honor and reputation above truth and righteousness. This story would be a sobering reminder to a church under pressure from the Roman imperial authorities.

FOR REFERENCE AND FURTHER STUDY

Aus, Roger. *Water into Wine and the Beheading of John the Baptist: Early Jewish-Christian Interpretation of Esther 1 in John 2:1-11 and Mark 6:17-29.* Atlanta: Scholars, 1988.

Bach, Alice. "Calling the Shots: Directing Salome's Dance of Death," *Semeia* 74 (1996) 103–26.

Glancy, Jennifer A. "Unveiling Masculinity. The Construction of Gender in Mark 6:17-29," *Biblical Interpretation* 2 (1994) 34–50.

Hoehner, Harold W. *Herod Antipas. A Contemporary of Jesus Christ.* Cambridge: Cambridge University Press, 1972.

Horsley, Richard A. "Like One of the Prophets of Old: Two Types of Popular Prophets at the Time of Jesus," *CBQ* 47 (1985) 435–63.

Matera, Frank J. "The Incomprehension of the Disciples and Peter's Confession (Mark 6,14–8,30)," *Bib* 70 (1989) 153–72.

Meier, John P. "John the Baptist in Josephus: Philology and Exegesis," *JBL* 111 (1992) 225–37.

Tyson, Joseph B. "Jesus and Herod Antipas," *JBL* 79 (1960) 239–46.

22. *The Feeding of the 5000 by the Sea of Galilee* (6:30-44)

30. Then the apostles gathered around Jesus and reported to him everything that they had done and had taught. 31. He responded: "Come away by yourselves to a desolate place, and rest for a while." (For people were coming and going in large numbers, and they could not even find enough time to eat.) 32. So they went away by themselves in a boat to a desolate place. 33. But they were seen departing, and the crowds recognized them and ran on foot from all the cities, arriving there before they did. 34. But when he [Jesus] came ashore he saw the large mass of people and had compassion on them because they were like a flock without a shepherd. He then began to teach them many things. 35. When it became late in the day his disciples came up to him and said: "This is a desolate place, and it is already late in the day; 36. send the crowd away so they can go to the surrounding fields and villages and buy themselves something to eat." 37. But he spoke up and answered them: "Give them something to eat yourselves." But they countered: "Do you expect us to leave and buy bread worth two hundred denarii and then distribute it to them?" 38. But he asked them: "How many loaves of bread do you have? Go and find out." After checking they said: "Five, and two fish." 39. He instructed every one to recline as if for a banquet on the green grass. 40. And they sat down in clusters of a hundred and fifty. 41. Then he took the five loaves and the two fish, and looking up to heaven, he said a blessing and broke the loaves and gave them to the disciples to distribute to the crowds, and they also divided the two fish among them all. 42. Everyone ate and was satisfied. 43. Then they collected twelve wicker baskets filled

with what was left of the loaves and the fish. 44. The number of those who had eaten the loaves was five thousand men.

NOTES

30. *The apostles gathered around Jesus:* Apart from the disputed reading of 3:14 this is the only time the "disciples" are called "apostles." The description fits the context since they had been "sent out" by Jesus in 6:7.

    everything that they had done and had taught: This recapitulates their mission from 6:12-13 where they, like Jesus, proclaim the need for conversion and perform exorcisms and healings. This verse repeats the essence of discipleship for Mark: being with Jesus and doing the things of Jesus: teaching and works of power (see 1:16-20; 3:7-12).

31. *to a desolate place:* We have used "desolate" rather than "deserted place" (*erēmos topos,* see v. 35), since "deserted" suggests that few people are present. The desolate place or desert wilderness (*erēmos*) evokes the locales of John's original call to repentance (1:3-5) and of Jesus' temptation (1:12-13), as well as the place to which Jesus retreats to pray (1:35, 45).

    rest for a while: The verb for "rest" (*anapausasthe*) may allude to the Greek text of Ps 23:2 (22:2 LXX) where the shepherd cares for the psalmist by restful waters (lit. "water of rest [*anapauseōs*]"). Other possible allusions to this psalm are the green grass (Ps 23:2 [22:2]; Mark 6:39) and the provision of a meal by the shepherd (Ps 23:5 [22:5]; Mark 6:41-42). "Rest" is also used for the land promised to the people after the wilderness wandering (Exod 33:1-14; Deut 12:9-10; Josh 1:13; Jer 31:2). In Matt 11:28-29 Jesus promises rest to all who are weary, and in Heb 4:9-11 eschatological rest from toils and persecution is promised to God's people.

    coming and going in large numbers: The presence of large crowds (*polloi*), which prevents the disciples from eating, echoes 3:20 and continues the frequent motif in the early part of Mark that the crowds virtually hem Jesus in (2:4, 13; 3:9, 32; 4:1, 36; 5:21, 24, 30-32). This reinforces the magnetism of Jesus' presence while ironically anticipating the opposition of the crowd during the Passion (14:43; 15:8, 11, 15).

    find enough time to eat: "Find enough time" translates the Greek verb *eukairoun* and has the nuance of finding both the opportunity and the leisure. Explicit mention of "eating" prepares for the subsequent narrative when, ironically, the disciples will not eat but will serve the hungry.

32. *they went away by themselves:* "By themselves" (*kat' idian*) is used elsewhere of special instruction (4:34; 9:28; 13:3) or revelation (9:2) given by Jesus to the disciples. Yet here the privacy is short-lived, and no private instruction is given.

    desolate place: As in v. 31, *erēmos topos* evokes the journey of the people of Israel in the wilderness (LXX *erēmos*) and the miraculous feedings there (Exod 16:1-35; Num 11:1-10; Pss 78:24; 105:40). This "sea voyage," the third in Mark (see 4:35–5:1; 5:21-22), is along the west side of the lake. Though Mark does not mention a specific locale, Luke 9:10 places it near Bethsaida and John 6:23 near Tiberias.

33. *the crowds recognized them:* This is another instance where the desire of Jesus for privacy or secrecy is thwarted (see 1:44-45; 5:20; 7:24, 36).

    ran on foot from all the cities: Though some authors suggest that the sea voyage of v. 32 is to the east side of the lake, the land journey of the crowds makes this improbable. Mark uses "cities" *(poleis)* in a loose sense of inhabited places in contrast to deserted or less populated areas (1:33, 38 *[kōmopoleis]*; 6:56), but most properly of Jerusalem (11:19).

34. *had compassion on them:* "Compassion" (see also 1:41; 8:2; 9:22) translates the Greek *esplanchnisthē*, the verbal form of the noun *splanchnon/a*, used for the inner parts of the body ("guts") and for the seat of the emotions as well as for the heart. The term is a virtual synonym for *oiktrimoi* (Hebrew *raḥûm* and *raḥămîm*, "merciful love"), which in the OT is a quality of God (Isa 54:7-8, "with everlasting love I will have compassion on you"; Pss 86:15; 111:4; 112:4; 145:8). "Compassion" is the bridge from sympathy to action (see Luke 10:33; 15:20).

    because they were like a flock without a shepherd: This evokes the OT image of Israel as in need of protection and guidance (Num 27:17; 1 Kgs 22:17; 2 Chr 18:16). Also God is the shepherd of Israel (Zech 11:17) as is the king, God's vice-regent (Ezek 34:15, 23). In Isa 40:11 God will "feed his flock like a shepherd," which may influence the feeding motif of the narrative.

    he then began to teach them many things: "Began to teach" is a characteristic Markan phrase that often introduces especially significant material (4:1; 6:2; 8:31). Teaching and feeding are not in opposition, since eating and drinking often symbolize receiving wisdom (Sir 15:3; 24:19-21; Prov 9:5). John 6:35-50 contains the fullest NT exposition of this motif. Mark also juxtaposes miracles with teaching to support his picture of Jesus as a teacher with authority and power (1:22, 27).

35. *his disciples:* After "apostles" in v. 30, the usual term "disciples" reappears. Some commentators argue that this is the beginning of the original narrative that Mark here reworks.

    desolate place, and it is already late in the day: This provides an *inclusio* with vv. 31-32, and the concise description of the place and the time ("late in the day") prepares for the crisis of feeding. The time is also the normal time for the evening meal and fits in with the temporal sequence of v. 47 (evening) and v. 48 (the fourth watch of the night; that is, between three and six in the morning).

36. *send the crowd away:* The stark use of the imperative *apolyson* ("you send away!") gives a peremptory character to the disciples' request that contrasts with the description of Jesus as deeply moved by the people. This verse begins a staged dialogue between Jesus and the disciples in which their literal misunderstanding will enhance the miracle.

37. *Give them something to eat:* Taken literally the command is strange. In vv. 30-35 the disciples are so pressed that they do not have time to eat, and then they retreat by boat to a desolate place, scarcely carrying food for 5000 people. The

command by Jesus provides the dramatic tension, which is then resolved by Jesus' action.

yourselves: The emphatic use of *hymeis* ("you yourselves") by Jesus stresses that the disciples should be active in feeding the people in contrast to their own desire simply to send the people away for food. Mark draws a very subtle contrast between Jesus as the one who cares and has compassion for the people and the insensitivity of the disciples.

buy bread worth two hundred denarii: The denarius was the normal wage for a day laborer (Matt 20:2). The figure is thus not insignificant, and stresses the size of the crowd and the seeming impossibility of providing food for them.

38. *how many loaves of bread:* Literally "how many breads *(artous)* do you have?" The term "bread" is used seventeen times between 6:8 and 8:19 and provides a submotif to the whole section, highlighted by two serious misunderstandings about bread by the disciples (6:52; 8:17-19).

Five, and two fish: Bread and fish (most likely preserved fish; see *opsarion* in John 6:9). For the numbers in the various multiplication accounts see the Note on 8:5.

39. *as if for a banquet:* The Greek here reads *symposia symposia* where the duplication conveys a distributive sense (i.e., all reclining in banquet style). The use of "recline" and "symposium" would evoke for Mark's Greco-Roman readers the image of the formal dinner party, which was often the setting for significant teaching (e.g., Plato's *Symposium*). See 6:34: "he began to teach them many things."

on the green grass: John (6:4) locates this feeding near Passover, which would be in the spring when the grass is green after the winter rain.

40. *in clusters:* Literally "garden plots" *(prasiai)* by garden plots," or group by group. Cranfield (*St Mark* 218) calls attention to an example in rabbinic literature where students studying the Torah are arranged like "garden-beds." Though later than Mark, this image could continue the motif of wisdom teaching that runs through this section.

of a hundred and fifty: There are mixed images here since the previous verse suggests a small symposium, which would never include a hundred people. In Exod 18:25 Moses arranges the Israelites in companies of thousands, hundreds, fifties, and tens, but there for the sake of delegation of authority (Exod 18:10-24). More pertinently, the Qumran community adopted these groupings for enhancing their community identity as the true Israel (1QS 2:21-22; CD 13:1; 1QM 4:1–5:17) and specifically for the messianic banquet (1QSa 2:11-22; see Guelich, *Mark* 341). The intermixture of motifs and images may be due to different interpretations of the feeding as the tradition developed.

41. *Then he took:* Five actions by Jesus are described: "taking," "looking up to heaven," "saying a blessing," "breaking," and "giving" the loaves to the disciples to distribute.

looking up to heaven, he said a blessing: Looking to heaven is the gesture of prayer, and the blessing would presumably be the standard Jewish blessing of bread before a meal: "Blessed are you, O Lord our God, who brings forth bread from the earth." In biblical thought blessing does not make an object holy. Rather, it is a form of the praise of God, which acknowledges the object as already created holy by God and praises God for setting it aside for human use.

and broke the loaves and gave them to the disciples: The Jewish head of the family would break the bread, eat a piece, and then give the bread to others.

distribute: The Greek *paratithēmi* (lit. "set before") is used often in the context of offering food as a sign of welcome or hospitality (Gen 18:8; 24:33; 2 Sam 12:20; Luke 11:6; Acts 16:34). In contrast to the desire of the disciples to get rid of the people (v. 36), Jesus makes the disciples welcome them as guests in a household.

the two fish: Fish appear also in each Markan feeding account, but they are simply mentioned here in contrast to 8:7 where Jesus says a blessing over the fish.

42. *Everyone ate and was satisfied:* "Satisfied" *(echortasthēsan)* suggests an extravagance of food that allowed the people to eat as much as they wanted. This is confirmed by the following verse. There could be a subtle allusion here to the manna that was always enough for every one of the Israelites in the desert (Exod 16:13-21; see also Deut 8:10 where being satisfied is an aspect of life in the promised land). This brief sentence is the only indication of the actual miracle; in contrast to other less dramatic miracles, there is no reaction of wonder or amazement by the crowd here.

43. *twelve wicker baskets:* The Greek for "basket" *(kophinos)* is a loan word from Latin *(cophinus)*. The satirist Juvenal says that these baskets were especially characteristic of the poorer classes of Jews in Rome *(Satires* 3.14; 6.542). In the Bible "twelve" is a dominant reference to the twelve sons of Jacob, and therefore the twelve tribes of Israel, in contrast to the seven (or seventy) nations of the world. The first feeding here symbolizes Jesus' sharing of bread (teaching) and sustenance with the Jewish people (see Interpretation).

44. *The number of those who had eaten the loaves was five thousand men:* Biblical numbers lend themselves to constant speculation. No certainty exists here other than that this number is larger than those to be fed in 8:9. One possibility is that the ratio of those fed by Jesus, one thousand per loaf, far exceeds the number of those fed by Elisha, one hundred with twenty loaves (see 2 Kgs 4:42-44). The use of "men" *(andres),* found only here in Mark, is somewhat strange since the crowds that follow Jesus are composed of men, women, and children (made explicit in Matt 14:21). Its usage here may reflect the biblical way of counting families by the heads of households and also the grouping of males at Qumran for the eschatological meal.

INTERPRETATION

The narrative of a miraculous feeding is the only miracle of Jesus attested in all four Gospels (the feeding of the 5000 appears in Mark 6:32-44;

Matt 14:13-21; Luke 9:10b-17; and John 6:1-15) and the only one that is recounted in two variant forms (the feeding of the 4000 appears in Mark 8:1-10 and Matt 15:32-39). Though some authors consider the introduction (Mark 6:30-31) a separate pericope dealing with the return of the disciples, these verses both retrospectively provide an inclusio with the sending out of the disciples (6:6b-13) and offer a smooth transition to the feeding narrative, highlighted by the mention of the "desolate" place (6:31, 32, 35) and the concern with eating (6:31, 36, 37).

Innumerable theories have been offered to explain the relation of the different versions of the feeding to each other and to a postulated primitive narrative. Though our approach centers on the Markan meaning, the complicated tradition history of the accounts means that as often-told stories they provide a rich texture of allusions and motifs that are not always internally consistent.

These narratives are dense with OT intertextual allusions. The feedings occur "in the wilderness" or desolate places and are "gift miracles" similar to the water from the rock (Exod 17:1-7) and the miraculous feeding of the Israelites through manna (a form of bread) in the wilderness (Exod 16:1-36; Num 11:4-9). In the Wisdom tradition feeding is associated with teaching, and bread with knowledge (see below). The closest OT parallel to this story is the miraculous feeding of one hundred men with twenty barley loaves by Elisha (2 Kgs 4:42-44). Verbal and thematic parallels are noteworthy. In both narratives the protagonist (Jesus, Elisha) gives a seemingly impossible order involving a small amount of food and a large number to be fed (Mark 6:37; 2 Kgs 4:42); in both cases those receiving the order protest (Mark 6:37; 2 Kgs 4:43); in both cases Jesus and the prophet are insistent that food is to be given (Mark 6:39, 41; 2 Kgs 4:43); and in both cases there is food left over after a large number of people have eaten (Mark 6:43; 2 Kgs 4:44).

After the return of the apostles the narrative follows the general structure of a miracle story with a setting that describes a situation of need (6:35), an implicit or explicit request (6:35-36), the mighty work itself (6:41-42), and some demonstration of the action (6:43-44). A number of interesting elements pose the question of the relation between the two Markan feedings (6:30-44; 8:1-10). The narratives are very similar in setting, content, and structure, but show significant differences. The first account is considerably longer. Differences are present in the number fed (5000 versus 4000), in the amount of food originally available (fives loaves and two fish versus seven loaves and a few fish), and in the discourse between Jesus and the disciples, which is harsher in the first narrative than in the second (compare 6:36-37 with 8:3-4). Somewhat surprising in 8:1-10 is that the disciples give no indication of knowing that Jesus will perform a mighty work, even after their participating in the feeding of 6:30-44.

Various proposals have emerged (and will continue to emerge) to relate the narratives: (1) there was a single early narrative that took different forms in the tradition and that Mark edited differently in each instance; (2) 8:1-10 is an early pre-Markan narrative that Mark used in his composition of 6:30-44; and (3) there were two different pre-Markan versions of the story and both were edited by Mark. A growing majority of interpreters holds that there was an early narrative that the individual evangelists reworked and adapted to their theological perspectives.

This first feeding narrative occurs in a pattern that will be repeated later in the gospel. Mark narrates a miraculous feeding (6:30-44; 8:1-8), which is followed by a "sea journey" (6:45-52; 8:9-10), a dispute with Pharisees (7:1-13; 8:11-13), and further instructions to the disciples (7:14-23; 8:14-21), and concludes with a narrative about the gift of hearing or sight (7:31-37; 8:22-26; see the references to seeing and hearing in 4:12 and 8:18). While more elaborate proposals have emerged (see Paul Achtemeier, "Miracle Catenae"), Mark's penchant for duplicate narratives and expressions suggests a deliberate parallelism, where actions that Jesus performs mainly in Jewish territory are paralleled among the Gentiles.

More important than discovering the traditions behind Mark is recognizing the manner in which Mark uses this narrative, whatever the extent of his editing may have been. The feeding of the 5000 is dramatically juxtaposed to the macabre banquet of Herod in 6:14-29. Herod's banquet is a birthday celebration for the select upper classes and held presumably in a palace; the banquet offered by Jesus is for ordinary people and held on the green grass for those who come on foot from various towns. Herod's banquet begins with Herodias' grudge against John, and Jesus' banquet starts with his compassion on the hungry crowds. Herod gives orders that John should be executed, whereas Jesus gives orders that the crowd should be fed. The two banquet scenes become narrative embodiments of the contrast between the followers of Jesus and the powerful ones, a contrast that will conclude the journey to Jerusalem (10:35-45).

The feeding of the 5000 also provides a contrast to the rejection of Jesus in 6:1-6a. There Jesus says that a prophet does not receive honor among his own, but in 6:30-44 Jesus performs a mighty work that far surpasses the actions of the prophet Elisha. At Nazareth a small group of relatives and townsfolk questions where Jesus received his wisdom, but in 6:30-44 he teaches and gives bread to a crowd far surpassing the population of Nazareth. At Nazareth where Jesus is rejected he can perform no mighty work; in the wilderness with the crowds streaming after him he performs the most public miracle in the whole gospel.

The narrative continues to fill out the evolving picture of Jesus. The introduction (6:30-34) highlights the contrast between Jesus' desire for solitude and his concern for the large mass of people who come from "all the cities." Since the crowds prevent Jesus and his disciples from enjoying the solitude they sought (6:31), Jesus' initial reaction of compassion is somewhat surprising. This is another instance of Mark's readiness to portray the strong emotions of Jesus. Here, in contrast to the later narrative, Jesus' compassion is not motivated by the crowd's hunger but by the observation that they are a flock without a shepherd. His initial response is not to feed them with food but to teach them many things (to give them spiritual food, or wisdom). Undergirding this narrative is the metaphorical use of feeding for teaching, and the metaphorical use of eating bread for learning wisdom (see Prov 9:5; Sir 15:3; 24:19). In later Jewish thought the manna given by Moses in the wilderness symbolizes the Torah. Also the first "mighty work" of Jesus in Mark is described as a new teaching with authority (1:21-28). Mark's readers are called on to realize that the teaching of Jesus that is handed down in the gospel narrative is as important for life and sustenance as bread in the wilderness was for the Exodus generation.

The story moves at a slow pace with the relatively lengthy exchange between Jesus and the disciples (vv. 35-38). Their initial suggestion to send the crowd away to buy their own food is countered by the seemingly impossible command of Jesus to "give them something to eat yourselves," which the disciples, quite reasonably, understand as a command to purchase food. Mark heightens the narrative tension further in v. 38 when Jesus then asks the disciples about their own supply of food and instructs the crowd to sit in orderly groups on the ground. This elaborate preparation holds the readers and hearers in high suspense and provides a contrast to the relatively simple way in which the actual "multiplication" occurs. Even if the narrative evokes images of the messianic banquet (see the Notes), it is as a hidden Messiah that Jesus eats with his people.

The actions of Jesus are described in language that foreshadows his final meal with the disciples on the eve of his own death. All the feeding accounts and the Last Supper narratives (Mark 14:22-25; Matt 26:26-29; Luke 22:15-20; 1 Cor 11:23-25), despite significant differences in detail and postulated different developments (see Meier, *A Marginal Jew* 2:950–67), describe Jesus as first uttering either a blessing or a prayer of thanksgiving, then "taking" bread, "breaking" it, and (except Paul) "giving" it to disciples or crowds to eat. While the absence of wine or any blessing of wine and the similarity of the actions ("take," "bless," and "break") to the normal Jewish blessing before meals lead some authors to deny any "eucharistic" overtones to the feeding narratives, the similarities outweigh the differences. This is supported also by John's omission of the institution narrative at the Last Supper, while in John 6 retaining and heightening the feeding narrative to signify the eating and drinking of the body and blood of Jesus (even though wine is not mentioned in John's narrative). From the post-resurrection perspective of Mark's readers the symbolism of Jesus sharing his word and food with a great crowd would animate their celebration of the Lord's Supper and sustain their hope of the final banquet when all people will be gathered together (Isa 25:6; *2 Bar* 29:1-8).

This narrative provides many options for actualization. One way not to actualize the passage is to say that the people were so moved by the preaching of Jesus that they divided their food with others. This "nice thought" interpretation goes back to the nineteenth-century rationalistic attack on miracles but has now achieved a strong foothold in mainline Christian preaching. Rather, the narrative offers a picture of Jesus as compassionate toward the leaderless people and concerned about their physical hunger. A church that invokes the name of Jesus must be concerned about the spiritual and physical hungers of people today. The location in a desolate place evokes God's care of the Jewish people during the wilderness wanderings. Since Vatican II has chosen "pilgrim people" as one of the central metaphors for the church, this aspect of the narrative can readily be actualized. Those Christian groups that see a eucharistic reference here might reflect that the narrative combines Jesus' teaching with his provision of food. Vatican II recaptures this double dimension of the narrative when it speaks of the Eucharist in terms of the table of "both the word of God and the body of Christ" (*Dei Verbum* 21). This formulation counters an overemphasis on the automatic effect of eucharistic presence, which itself is mediated by faith in the word of Jesus.

FOR REFERENCE AND FURTHER STUDY

Achtemeier, Paul J. "The Origin and Function of the Pre-Marcan Miracle Catenae," *JBL* 91 (1972) 198–221.
Bassler, Jouette M. "The Parable of the Loaves," *JR* 66 (1986) 157–72.
Boobyer, George H. "The Eucharistic Interpretation of the Miracles of the Loaves in St. Mark's Gospel," *JTS* 3 (1952) 161–71.
_____. "The Miracles of the Loaves and the Gentiles in St. Mark's Gospel," *SJT* 6 (1953) 77–87.
Fowler, Robert M. *Loaves and Fishes. The Function of the Feeding Stories in the Gospel of Mark.* Chico: Scholars, 1981.
Grassi, Joseph A. *Loaves and Fishes: The Gospel Feeding Narratives.* Collegeville: The Liturgical Press, 1991.
Oyen, Geert van. *The Interpretation of the Feeding Miracles in the Gospel of Mark.* Turnhout: Brepols, 1999.

23. *Jesus Walks on the Water and Astounds the Disciples* (6:45-52)

45. Then right away Jesus made his disciples get into the boat and go before him to the other side, in the direction of Bethsaida, while he himself sent the crowd away. 46. Then after sending them on their way he went up to the mountain to pray. 47. By the time evening came the boat was in the middle of the sea, while he was by himself on the land. 48. But he noticed that they were being tossed around while trying to row, for the wind was in their face, and at about the fourth watch of the night he came to them walking on the surface of the sea, and was about to pass by them. 49. But when they saw him walking on the sea they thought it was a ghost and they cried out. 50. For they all had seen him and were terrified. But at once he began to speak with them, and said: "Be courageous; I am; do not be afraid." 51. Then he got into the boat with them and the wind died down. But they were utterly bewildered, 52. for they had not understood the meaning of the loaves, but rather their heart was hardened.

NOTES

45. *made his disciples:* The Greek *anagkazein* has the overtone of "forced." There is no indication of why the voyage is so urgent.

   go before him toward the other side, in the direction of Bethsaida: The geographical references here are confusing. Throughout this section of Mark, Jesus has been on the west side of the lake (6:1, 32). Bethsaida is at the northeast corner of the lake (Sea of Galilee) where the River Jordan comes into the lake, and yet in 6:53 the voyage seems to terminate at Gennesaret, which is on the west side of the lake. Some authors postulate that Mark awkwardly juxtaposes originally independent stories (feeding of 5000 and walking on water). We have translated *pros Bēthsaidan* as "in the direction of Bethsaida," leaving open the possibility that Mark understands that the adverse winds forced a return to the west.

46. *he went up to the mountain to pray:* In OT thought a mountain often has a sacral quality (Gen 22:14; Exod 3:1; Deut 11:29; Josh 8:30) and is a privileged place of contact with God: Mount Sinai (Exod 19:3, 16, 24), and Mount Zion (Pss 68:16; 84:5). This motif is repeated in the NT: the Mount of Transfiguration in Mark 9:2-8 and parallels and the Mount of Olives in Mark 14:32-42 and parallels.

   to pray: Jesus is alone and at prayer in 1:35, here in 6:46, and during the Gethsemane episode in 14:32-42. In the first two instances prayer serves as a refuge for Jesus from the crowds. In the first two cases no words from the prayers are quoted, so that Jesus' prayer in Mark is primarily being in God's presence (see also 9:2).

47. *evening came:* See 4:35, also an evening voyage on the sea. "Evening" means usually "dusk" (1:35, evening, at sundown; 4:35; 11:19; 13:35; 14:17; 15:42) and

is in tension with the following time reference ("the fourth watch"), which may suggest the merging of different traditions.

48. *he noticed:* Since Jesus is apparently still on the mountain or at least on land (v. 47), his "sight" manifests his preternatural power and prepares for the following action.

about the fourth watch of the night: Since Mark follows the Roman custom of dividing the night into four watches (see 13:35), the time would be between 3:00 and 6:00 in the morning, which is the time when God's help is especially needed (Isa 17:14).

walking on the surface of the sea: The "sea miracles" of Mark all draw on OT motifs of the power of God over the forces of chaos symbolized by the sea, but each with a particular nuance. A close parallel is provided by Job's praise of God's power: "who alone stretched out the heavens, and trampled the waves of the sea" (Job 9:8; cf. 26:28; 38:16; see also Ps 77:19; *Odes of Solomon* 39:10). Here Jesus exercises serene power in contrast to his rebuke of the threatening waves in 4:38.

he was about to pass by them: "Was about to" translates the disputed *ēthelen*, which can also mean "he wanted to." Our translation is determined by the meaning of "pass by them." The infinitive *parelthein* "is practically a 'technical term' for the appearance of a divine being, in the sense of his drawing near and showing himself before human eyes" (Heil, *Jesus Walking* 70), and evokes God's ephiphany to Moses (Exod 33:19-23; 34:6) and Elijah (1 Kgs 19:11). Those who favor "wanted to" interpret this verse as an instance of Jesus' desire for self-concealment in Mark. But this idea is contradicted by the self-revelatory formula of v. 50. Mark stresses rather the epiphany of Jesus, which heightens the subsequent misunderstanding of the disciples.

49. *they thought it was a ghost:* The Greek term *phantasma* ("ghost") has the nuance of an illusion. The scene is portrayed as a concise but powerful drama where the utter darkness, the power of the waves, the appearance of a spectre, and the cries and fear of the disciples stand in contrast to the calming words and actions of Jesus.

50. *he began to speak with them:* As in OT theophanies, the words communicate the presence of the divine.

I am: Many translations render this phrase "it is I," which can obscure the echo of the powerful OT divine revelational formula "I am" used in the context of God's saving presence (Exod 3:14; Isa 41:4; 43:10-11). In Mark it will also be used by false claimants to the name of Jesus (13:6) and by Jesus himself in response to the question of the high priest (14:62).

do not be afraid: The revelational formula is bracketed by two commands: "be courageous," and "do not be afraid," which signal both the presence of the divine and an imminent commission from God as in the infancy (Luke 1:13, 30; Matt 1:20) and resurrection narratives (Mark 16:6; Matt 28:5, 10; Luke 24:5). "Fear not" is also a frequent command by Jesus prior to a saving miracle (e.g., Mark 4:40; 5:36; Luke 8:50).

51. *the wind died down:* This not only serves as the confirmation of the power of Jesus but also evokes the power of God over the forces of destruction and chaos (Ps 89:10-11) and the rescue of seafarers (Ps 107:29; Jonah 1:14). Here in contrast to 4:35-41 Jesus gives no command to the sea; his simple presence in the boat calms the waves, which suggests that the main Markan focus here is on the epiphany rather than on the wondrous action.

     they were utterly bewildered: Of itself this does not connote failure or disbelief on the disciples' part, but it is a standard reaction in the face of Jesus' power (1:27; 2:12; 5:42). The following verse, however, shows that Mark puts a more negative cast on their amazement.

52. *For they had not understood the meaning of the loaves:* The Greek literally reads "for they had not understood about the loaves *(epi tois artois)*." Some translations supply "the incident of," which unduly limits the deliberate ambiguity of Mark in his use of *epi*. See the Interpretation. Mark 6:52-53 has been at the center of the controversy over whether a fragment of Mark has been found among the Dead Sea Scrolls. In 1972 José O'Callaghan proposed that a very small Greek fragment from Cave 7 at Qumran (7Q5) was a fragment of Mark 6:52-53, a position that has been revived and defended by Carsten P. Thiede (*The Earliest Gospel Manuscript? The Qumran Papyrus 7Q5 and its Significance for New Testament Studies* [Exeter: Paternoster, 1992). The problem is that this fragment contains only ten Greek letters that can be read clearly. Even if they are in a sequence that would correspond to Mark 6:52-53, some emendation is required. Most papyrologists and specialists in the Dead Sea Scrolls regard the hypothesis as highly dubious (see Robert H. Gundry, "No *NU* in Line 2 of 7Q5: A Final Disidentification of 7Q5 with Mark 6:52-53," *JBL* 118 [1999] 698–707). Moreover, it would be very strange if a fragment of the section of Mark that precedes Jesus' mitigation of OT purity laws (7:1-23) would have been preserved by a community that so stressed ritual purity as the Qumran people did. See Stefan Enste, *Kein Markustext in Qumran.*

     their heart was hardened: "Heart" is singular in Greek and so suggests a collective response. The perfect passive "hardened" *(pepōrōmenē)* could be a theological passive suggesting that God hardened their hearts. Hardness of heart connotes imperviousness to God's revelation; e.g., the hardening of the heart of Pharaoh throughout the plague narratives (Exod 7:13, 14, 22; 8:15, 19, 32; 9:7, 12, 34, 35; 10:1, 20, 27; 11:10; 14:8). In the NT under the influence of Isa 6:9-10 the motif is often used apologetically to describe the rejection of Jesus (John 12:40; Acts 28:26-27; 2 Cor 3:14-15; Eph 4:18). Because of the biblical view of God's sovereignty such hardening is attributed to God's design, while acknowledging human responsibility, which in later theology becomes the problem of predestination and human freedom.

INTERPRETATION

This passage concludes the first cycle of narratives that comprises a feeding followed by a sea miracle, here in Jewish territory and for Jewish people. It is also the second of three sea miracles in Mark (4:35-41; 6:45-52; 8:14-21), where Jesus comes to the rescue of beleaguered disciples only to have them fail to understand who he is (4:40; 6:52; 8:17-19); the latter two passages contain the harshest criticism of the disciples in the gospel: that their hearts are hardened.

Formally the episode constitutes a "sea rescue epiphany" and is dense in intertextual resonances of the OT. The sea is both the source of life (Gen 1:10, 20; Ps 23:2) and the domain and symbol of destructive power (Pss 18:16; 69:1-2; 74:13; 104:26; 106:11; Isa 57:20; Jer 47:2). God's power is often expressed in the control of waters (Gen 1:2, 6-9; 8:1-3; 9:11; Job 26:5, 8; Ps 33:7), and God's saving power is manifest in the liminal events of bringing the people through the waters of the Red Sea (Exod 14:21-28; 15:8-10; Isa 43:16; 51:10; 63:12) and of the Jordan (Josh 3:13-16; 4:18-23). Divine rescue from the power of water is also a frequent theme in the Psalms (18:16; 69:1-2; 77:16-17; 78:13-16).

On the narrative level this story continues and extends the theme of misunderstanding by the disciples and foreshadows the second great misunderstanding in 8:14-21. As in the second narrative, it comes after two great manifestations of Jesus' power: the feeding of multitudes and the display of his power over raging waters. While in the present narrative the narrator comments that the disciples' hearts were hardened, in 8:17 Jesus himself confronts them with this charge, which shows the escalating nature of their misunderstanding.

As noted in the introductory comments on Mark's theology, the ambivalent picture of the disciples is one of the great puzzles of Markan studies. The recent insights of Whitney T. Shiner are helpful in understanding this puzzle. He notes that the misunderstanding does not yield to understanding, but exists simultaneously with clear revelation by Jesus. The disciples become the foil for a narrative presentation of the enigmatic sayings of 4:10-12; that is, that the mystery of the kingdom of God is a gift that divides the world into insiders and outsiders. Mark is not interested in the moral or ethical aspect of the disciples' failure but in their narrative theological function. The reader is told why they fail: because in some mysterious way God willed their failure and hardened their hearts. The discordance between the readers' understanding and the disciples' perception furthers the dramatic flow of Mark.

In both cases the disciples' hardening and misunderstanding center around the meaning of "bread." Again multiple interpretations surface: from the disciples' simple misunderstanding of the nature of Jesus' power to multiply food, through a view that this power presents an incorrect christology of Jesus as the powerful and available presence of God, to opinions that link the misunderstanding to the nature of the Christian Eucharist. The Markan Jesus would then be thought to teach the Markan community that Jews and Gentiles are to be united at the eucharistic banquet, since the early Christian Eucharist was associated with a meal (1 Cor 11:17-26) and since disputes over Jewish dietary laws were so widespread (Acts 10:9-23; 15:1-21; Gal 2:11-15; Rom 14:1-23). The eucharistic interpretation is supported by the two feedings in two different territories and by Mark's placing of this narrative before the discourse about clean and unclean food in 7:1-23.

FOR REFERENCE AND FURTHER STUDY

Derrett, J. Duncan M. "Why and How Jesus Walked on the Sea," *NovT* 23 (1981) 330–48.

Enste, Stefan, *Kein Markustext in Qumran: Eine Unterschung der These: Qumran-Fragment 7Q5 = Mk 6,52–53*. Göttingen: Vandenhoeck & Ruprecht, 1999.

Heil, John Paul. *Jesus Walking on the Sea. Meaning and Gospel Functions of Matt. 14,22-33; Mark 6,45-52 and John 6,15b-21*. Rome: Biblical Institute Press, 1981.

Madden, Patrick J. *Jesus' Walking on the Sea. An Investigation of the Origin of the Narrative Account*. Berlin and New York: Walter de Gruyter, 1997.

Quesnell, Quentin. *The Mind of Mark. Interpretation and Method through the Exegesis of Mark 6,52*. Rome: Biblical Institute Press, 1969.

Shiner, Whitney T. *Follow Me! Disciples in Markan Rhetoric*. Atlanta: Scholars, 1995.

Smith, Stephen H. "Bethsaida via Gennesaret: The Enigma of the Sea-Crossing in Mark 6,45-53," *Bib* 77 (1996) 349–74.

24. *A Markan Summary of the Healing Power of Jesus* (6:53-56)

53. Then after completing the crossing, they came to land at Gennesaret and anchored there. 54. And when they got out of the boat, people recognized him right away, 55. scattered throughout the whole region, and started carrying on their straw mats all the sick to wherever they heard he was. 56. And wherever he entered the villages, cities, or hamlets, they placed their sick in the town marketplaces and begged him that they might at least touch the fringe of his garment. And all those who touched it were restored to health.

NOTES

53. *After completing the crossing:* See 6:45 on the geographical problem here, since the voyage does not terminate on the other side of the lake as the verb *diaperasantes* implies (see 5:21).

Gennesaret: Used only here in Mark, this term refers not to a city but to the fertile and thickly populated plain between Tiberias and Capernaum.

54. *recognized him right away:* Immediate and widespread recognition is a strong Markan motif, and here it contrasts the nameless people who recognize Jesus with the disciples who shortly before confused Jesus with a ghost (6:49). The sequence of Greek participles modifying verbs in the imperfect tense intensifies the action and underscores the enthusiasm of the crowds.

55. *throughout the whole region:* "Whole" (*holos*) is used frequently by Mark to intensify the extent of Jesus' magnetism (see 1:28, 33, 39, "the whole of Galilee").
    on their straw mats: The same term was used in the story of the paralytic (2:1-12); the *krabattos* was the multipurpose bed and stretcher of the poor.
    wherever they heard he was: The "hearing" underscores the motif of the proclamation of the power of Jesus, since those who first recognized Jesus become the heralds of his presence.

56. *Wherever he entered villages, cities, or hamlets:* The double use of *hopou* ("wherever") at the end of v. 55 and at the beginning of v. 56 underscores the universalizing aspect of the power of Jesus. The collocation of the three geographical terms covers the main settled centers of Galilean life. Galilee at the time of Jesus was heavily populated and, despite some attempts to picture Jesus as a rural itinerant preacher, Mark stresses his impacting those places where people gather.
    marketplaces: The Greek term *agora* is used for the town center, which is the major site of political, commercial, and religious activity. Mark uses this word in the following incident when he speaks of the place that occasions impurity for the Pharisees (7:4), and later as a locale for religious ostentation by the scribes (12:38). Somewhat ironically, the *agora* is the place were Jesus heals the sick.
    begged: The verb *parakalein* echoes the requests of the leper (1:40), the Gerasene demoniac (5:10, 12, 17, 18), and the synagogue leader (5:23); it appears in prominent miracles in Mark. It literally means "call to the side of," and its nominal form becomes the "Paraclete" in John 14–16 with overtones of "advocate" or "defender." The sick are, in effect, asking Jesus to be on their side, which echoes the description of Jesus as the compassionate shepherd (6:34).
    the fringe of his garment: See 5:28. In antiquity an aura of power was believed to surround the "holy man" or healer. The fringe (*kraspedon*) is also used for the tassels that Jewish males were to have hanging from the four corners of their garments (Num 15:38-39; Deut 22:12).
    were restored to health: Literally "were saved" (*esōzonto*), with the double sense of being freed from suffering and restored to wholeness (and the overtone of "salvation").

INTERPRETATION

This passage is the second of the two longer Markan transitional summaries of the mighty deeds of Jesus (see 3:7-12); for short summaries see 1:28; 39, 45; 2:13; 4:33; 6:6b; a complete list is in Taylor, *Mark* 85. They present an expansive picture of the works of Jesus and provide transitions to new sections. Concrete terms like "straw mats," "beg," and "touching the garment" remind the reader of earlier miracles, while this passage also prepares for those mighty works that will take place in Gentile territory (7:24–8:10). Missing here are any references to exorcisms (cf. 3:7-12), perhaps because there is only one exorcism in the rest of the gospel (9:14-29).

Coming shortly after the missionary journey of the disciples (6:7-13, 30-31), Mark 6:53-56 also looks to the missionary practice of the early church. The passage is replete with actions and movements: a boat is moored; people run; they bring the sick to any place where Jesus is. This anticipates the travels of those who proclaim the gospel (6:12-13). They, too, are to travel to villages, cities, and hamlets so that the word they proclaim may be heard. They are also to be agents of God's healing and saving power to those who call *(parakalein)* on them as "advocates." The *agora* is now the center of the healing power of God, and not simply the locus of political and economic power.

25. *The Dispute over Clean and Unclean* (7:1-23)

1. Then the Pharisees and some of the scribes who had arrived from Jerusalem gathered around him. 2. They noticed that some of his disciples were eating loaves of bread with unclean, that is, unwashed, hands. 3. (For the Pharisees, and in fact all the Jews, never have a meal without washing their hands up to the wrist, as a way of observing the tradition of the elders; 4. nor do they have a meal when returning from a marketplace unless they first wash themselves. There are also many other traditions that they observe, such as washing drinking cups and measuring bowls and bronze kettles [and beds].) 5. Then the Pharisees and the scribes asked him [Jesus]: "Why then do your disciples not follow the tradition of the elders but eat bread with unclean hands?" 6. He responded: "Isaiah prophesied correctly about you hypocrites, when it is written: 'This people honors me with their lips but their heart is far from me. 7. Their worship of me is empty, when they teach human precepts as doctrines.' 8. By abandoning the command of God, you hold on to human tradition."

9. He spoke to them again: "Is it correct that you set aside the command of God in order to uphold your tradition? 10. For Moses said: 'Honor your father and your mother, and anyone who curses father or mother shall die.' 11. Yet you say: 'If a person should say to father or mother: "Anything you deserve from me is *korban*"' (that is, dedicated to God), 12. then you would not allow him to do anything further for father or mother. 13. In this way you nullify the word of God in favor of that

tradition of yours which you hand down; and you do many other things just like this." 14. He then summoned the crowd again and spoke to them: "All of you listen carefully and understand: 15. Nothing outside a person can enter and make a person unclean; rather the things that come out make that person unclean." 17. But when he left the crowd and came into the house his disciples questioned him about this riddle, 18. and he responded to them: "Are you still so obtuse? Don't you realize that whatever enters a person from outside has no power to make that person unclean; 19. and the reason is that it does not really enter a person's heart, but goes into the stomach and then passes out into the toilet." (In this manner he declared all foods to be clean.) 20. For he said: "It is that which comes out of a person that can make a person unclean. 21. For it is from within, from human hearts that pour forth evil designs, sexual immoralities, thefts, murders, 22. adulteries, forms of greed, malicious acts, deceit, promiscuity, the evil eye, blasphemy, arrogance, and folly. 23. All these evils pour out from within and make a person unclean."

NOTES

1. *the Pharisees:* The Pharisees have appeared earlier in controversy with Jesus at 2:16, 24; and 3:6. The Greek text could be translated so as to say that both the Pharisees and the scribes were from Jerusalem. Scholars debate the extent of Pharisaic activity in Galilee during the ministry of Jesus.

   and some of the scribes . . . from Jerusalem: Throughout the gospel the scribes are stronger opponents of Jesus than the Pharisees are; in 3:22 the scribes from Jerusalem appear without Pharisees and accuse Jesus of being possessed by Beelzebul. Their presence again here shows the seriousness of the dispute, and throughout the gospel "Jerusalem" foreshadows the place of the Passion and death of Jesus.

2. *some of his disciples:* The actions of the disciples rather than those of Jesus himself evoke opposition also in the disputes over religious obligations in 2:18, 24. "Some" may signify that other disciples of Jesus were thought to have obeyed the food laws. Both the charge and the different practices of the disciples of Jesus (see Gal 2:11-14) may reflect an early church setting for this dispute.

   eating loaves of bread: The plural "loaves" *(artous)* links this dispute with the previous sequence of "bread narratives" (6:8, 37, 38, 41, 44, 52).

   unclean: The Greek word for "unclean" is simply "common" *(koinos)*, a term that links the different parts of this narrative (7:1, 5, 15, 18, 20, 23). In classical Greek the term is opposed to "private" *(idios)*, but it appears in 1 Macc 1:47, 62 in reference to unclean animals (swine) and unclean food (see also Acts 10:14, 28; 11:8; Rev 21:27). The meaning "unclean" arises from a distinction between what is available for "common" or general use and what has been particularly set apart or dedicated to God (Greek *hagios* from *hagiazein*, "set apart" or "consecrate"; Hebrew *qāddeš*).

that is, unwashed hands: This phrase represents the first explanatory comment by the evangelist in a passage that is dense with similar explanations (see vv. 3-4, 11, 19). The custom of handwashing before ordinary meals is not attested in the OT. Leviticus 15:11 speaks of a ritual of handwashing, but only after contact with unclean objects. Ritual washings in the context of prayer are attested in Jdt 12:7, *Letter of Aristeas* 305, and *Sybilline Oracles* 3.591-93. At the wedding in Cana (John 2:6) there is mention of "six stone water jars for Jewish rites of purification," which would suggest a custom observed by the guests. The *Mishnah* (ca. 200 C.E.) contains a tractate on rules of impurity associated with the "Hands" *(Yadayim)*, with directions for handwashing (*m. Yad.* 1:1–2:4; *m. Hag.* 2:5-6), including long comments on washing before touching bread (*m. Yad.* 2:4). Since the *Mishnah* codified oral traditions, the Gospel of Mark is evidence that such a custom existed among some Jewish groups in the first century C.E.

3. *For the Pharisees, and in fact all the Jews:* The previous sentence breaks off at the end of v. 2 and is not resumed until v. 5. Here the evangelist interjects a long parenthesis that explains to non-Jewish readers the origin of the charge against Jesus' disciples. The reference to "all the Jews" manifests a Markan penchant for universalizing scenes, though it is Mark's sole use of "the Jews" as a group (in contrast to the Gospel of John). Many authors, most recently Booth (see below), argue that the ritual washings listed in vv. 3-4 were practiced only by priests or by certain groups of Pharisees.

up to the wrist: The Greek text literally reads "unless they wash their hands with the fist *(pygmē)*," a "puzzling little word" (Gnilka, *Das Evangelium nach Markus* 1:281), that has spawned a number of manuscript variations and continual interpretations. A few manuscripts simply omit the term while other good ancient manuscripts read *pykna* ("often" or "thoroughly"), which provides the basis for the *NRSV* and *NAB* translations. Proposed interpretations of *pygmē* include "with the fist," that is, rubbing water into one hand with a closed fist; a unit of measure, found in secular Greek, with the meaning of washing hands to the elbow; or with a handful of water, that is, with a cupped fist. Our translation follows Matthew Black (*An Aramaic Approach to the Gospels and Acts* [Oxford: Clarendon Press, 1967] 9), and also is in accord with some of the provisions found in the *Mishnah* (especially *m. Yad.* 2:3, which speaks of hands rendered clean "up to the wrist").

the tradition of the elders: "Tradition" *(paradosis)* is authoritative teaching that is handed on orally from teacher to teacher or from school to school. Josephus (*Ant.* 13.297) says that the Pharisees handed on to the people certain regulations from the teaching of the fathers that were not found in the laws of Moses, and that they were rejected by the Sadducees for this reason (see also *Ant.* 18.12). The phrase "tradition of the elders" appears in *Ant.* 10.51, and a similar expression is found in Philo, *Spec. Leg.* 4.150. The Mishnaic tractate *ʾAbot* (1:1-18) begins with a long chain of tradition stretching from Moses to Simeon ben Gamaliel (after 135 C.E.). Early Christians adopted the terminology for authoritative teaching about Jesus Christ (see 1 Cor 11:2, 23; 15:3).

4. *when returning from a marketplace:* The verb "returning" or "coming" is not present in the Greek but is supplied to capture the sense of the verse. One could also render "marketplace" *(agora)* more generically as "public gathering."

   unless they first wash themselves: Certain manuscripts contain the unusual verb *rantisōntai* ("sprinkle," Heb 9:19, 21), in place of *baptisōntai* ("wash themselves"). Some authors understand either verb in the active rather than the middle sense and supply a direct object such as "food" or items bought in the marketplace. There is, however, little evidence that food washing was customary, while personal washing before meals was practiced, especially at the communal meals of Pharisaic associations (*ḥăberîm*, see Luke 7:44).

   many other traditions: Mark supplies his readers with a general description of Pharisaic ritual practices, followed by specific examples. The repeated emphasis on tradition highlights the substance of the dispute.

   drinking cups and measuring bowls and bronze kettles: The *Mishnah* (*m. Kelim*, especially 8:2–11:3) contains careful instructions for washing cooking utensils. "Measuring bowl" translates *xestos*, itself a loanword from the Latin *sextarius*, a unit of measurement transferred to a cup or bowl (e.g., "pint"). Similar practices are attested also in Q (Luke 11:39; Matt 23:25-26).

   [and beds]: Some ancient manuscripts add *kai klinōn* ("and beds"), perhaps under the influence of Lev 15:25-30. Yet in Leviticus the issue is the cleansing of beds after menstrual impurity, which would be a surprising addition in Mark to a discussion of eating impurities. Others suggest that the term *klinē* ("bed") be translated as dining couch, but there is little evidence for such a custom.

5. *not follow the tradition of the elders:* After the long parenthesis the narrative resumes by putting in dialogue form the objection made by the Pharisees and scribes in v. 2. The explanation in vv. 3-4 also raises the intensity of the narrative by stressing the importance of tradition to the questioners.

   but eat bread with unclean hands: Many authors argue that this verse combines two originally separated debates, one about violating tradition and the other about ritual purity when eating. Whatever the origin of the statements, which can never be determined exactly, Mark combines them in such a way that the binding power of tradition becomes the focus of the whole narrative.

6. *Isaiah prophesied correctly:* Mark here cites Isa 29:13. But the quotation, while agreeing more closely with the LXX against the Hebrew text, also has variations from the LXX. Though Mark cites and alludes to Isaiah frequently (e.g., Mark 1:3; 2:7; 3:21; 9:12; 10:34, 45; 11:17; 12:32, 40; 13:8, 13, 31; 14:49, 61; 15:27), the verb "prophesy" appears only here. Mark places himself in the stream of prophetic criticism of misplaced emphasis on religious observance to the detriment of works of justice and charity such as care for one's parents (7:10-13; see Amos 5:21-24; Isa 1:10-20; 58:1-14; Jer 6:16-21; 22:1-23).

   about you hypocrites: Both the noun *hypokritēs* and the verbal root *hypokrinein* are images from the world of Greek drama. The verb means "to play a part" or "to make believe," and the noun comes to mean "pretender" or "dissembler." The term can describe objective discrepancy without the overtone of deliberate subjective pretense that accompanies the English "hypocrite" (Gnilka, *Evangelium* 1:282).

honors me with their lips: Mark is close to the LXX here in abbreviating the Hebrew text (*NRSV* translation): "Because these people draw near with their mouths and honor me with their lips."

7. *their worship of me is empty:* Here Mark follows the LXX, while the Hebrew text has no such phrase.

when they teach human precepts as doctrines: This is the greatest alteration from both the Hebrew and LXX. The Hebrew ends with "their worship of me is a human commandment learned by rote," and the LXX reads "[by] teaching commandments *(entalmata)* of men and doctrines *(didaskalias)*." Mark's alteration subtly sharpens the "empty worship" by omitting the "and" from the LXX, thus having Isaiah charge the people with making human precepts into doctrines rather than simply teaching human precepts and doctrines.

8. *By abandoning the command of God:* The participle "abandoning" *(aphentes)* modifies the verb "hold on to," which emphasizes the causal connection between observance of human doctrines and neglect of the divine command. "Command" *(entolē)* is used by Mark only here (vv. 8, 9) and in 10:5, 19; 12:28, 31. In every case the citation is from the Pentateuch, and each citation contains a central belief of Israel. In 7:10a (Exod 20:12; Deut 5:16) and in 10:19 (Exod 20:12-17; Deut 5:16-21) the Decalogue is cited; in 7:10b (Exod 21:17; Lev 20:9) the Holiness Code, which is virtually dictated by God to Moses (Exod 20:22), is cited; in 10:4 (Deut 24:1, 3) Moses is explicitly mentioned; and in 12:29 (Deut 6:4-5) the *Shema* is called the prime *entolē* to which is joined the command to love neighbor (Lev 19:18). Mark contrasts the solemnity of an *entolē* with human traditions and foreshadows the primary "commandment" to love God and neighbor (12:28-31). At stake in the dispute is what really constitutes fidelity to God's revelation versus human tradition. Such citations on the lips of Jesus show that the dispute between Jesus and those who challenge him is not about the authority of the Torah, but precisely over applications and interpretations of the Law by specific Jewish groups.

9. *Is it correct:* Most translations render the Greek word *kalōs* ("beautiful, good, morally correct") in an ironic sense: e.g., "You have a fine way of rejecting the command of God . . . !" *(NRSV)* or "How well you have set aside the command of God . . . !" The translation proposed here interprets the sentence as a question. Evidence is provided by Matthew, who introduces the quotation of the command to honor parents with a question: "Why do you transgress the command of God . . . ?" (Matt 15:3 = Mark 7:9). The Markan verse is a virtual restatement of v. 8, which has led some interpreters to see a separate source here. Given Mark's penchant for repetition, such an assumption is not necessary. Also, rhetorically the question of v. 9 introduces a more serious charge than that of Isa 29:13. In vv. 10-13 the issue is the opponents' infidelity to the Torah.

10. *Moses said:* The quotations that follow agree almost verbatim with the LXX text of Exod 20:12 and 21:17 (see Deut 5:16). Matthew (15:4) reads "God" in place of "Moses," thereby increasing the seriousness of the dispute.

11. *Anything you deserve from me is korban:* The term *korban* is left untranslated, since Mark himself presents it in this way along with an interpretation. It is a Hebrew noun translated in Lev 2:1, 4, 12, 14, as "gift." Josephus (*Ant.* 4.73) has a sentence similar to Mark's. After describing the Nazirite vow he writes: "Again those who describe themselves as 'Korban' to God—meaning what the Greeks would call 'a gift.'" In *Against Apion* 1.167 he describes an oath taken by the Jews as *korban* and again explains it as a gift. The term has been found on a first-century ossuary that reads: "All that a man may find to his profit in this ossuary is an offering *(korban)* to God from him who is within" (see Joseph A. Fitzmyer, "Aramaic Qorban inscription from Jebel Hallet et-Turi and Mark 7:11, Matt 15:5 : [reply to J. T. Milik]," *JBL* 78 [1959] 60–65).

12. *then you would not allow him to do anything further for father or mother:* The practice alluded to seems to have involved dedicating a certain (probably large) gift to the Temple prior to the death of one's parents. Since this gift may have been accompanied by a solemn oath, its use or profit was no longer permitted to the donor (or to his parents). The Torah contains solemn prescriptions on the observance of vows (Num 30:1-2; Deut 23:21-23), and so there is a conflict here of two solemn obligations: honoring parents and observing vows.

13. *you nullify:* "Nullify" *(akyrountes)* or "make void" is a legal term (Josephus, *Ant.* 18.304; 20.183) used only here, in the Matthean parallel (15:6), and in Gal 3:17 where the Law does not "annul" a covenant ratified by God.

    the word of God: Though Mark describes Jesus as speaking "the word" (2:2; 4:33), the "word of God" appears only here in Mark (see Matt 15:6) and is never used of Jesus' word. Luke, however, uses it more frequently and often in reference to the word of Jesus (3:2; 5:1; 8:11, 21; 11:20). In early Christian literature it becomes a virtual synonym for the Christian message about Jesus (e.g., Acts 6:2, 7; 8:14; 11:1; 12:24; 13:7; 13:46; 17:3; 18:11; 1 Thess 2:13; Rom 9:6; Col 1:25; 2 Tim 2:9; Heb 13:7). Here the Markan Jesus equates the revelation of Scripture (the Torah) with the word of God.

    and you do many other things just like this: This is a polemical phrase that reflects Mark's desire to distance the teaching of Jesus from the Pharisees' purity rules and thus prepares for the following discussion.

14. *He then summoned the crowd again:* Thus far in the narrative Jesus has been talking only to the Pharisees and the Jerusalem scribes. With the change of audience not only is a new phase in the dispute inaugurated, but the content (external versus internal defilement) is radically different since the first dispute dealt with *how* a person should eat (with washed or unwashed hands) while here the implicit discussion is *what* a person may eat or not eat. This was an issue of great concern in the early church (see Acts 10:9-16; 15:1-21; Gal 2:11-14; 1 Cor 8–10; Rom 14:1–15:13).

    listen carefully and understand: Similar calls for attentiveness and discernment occur in 4:3, 9, 23-24; 9:7. This solemn summons, along with the designation of the following saying as a *parabolē* (7:17) and the private instruction given to disciples (7:18-23), create echoes of Mark 4:1-34.

15. *Nothing outside a person can enter and make a person unclean:* The stark beginning of the sentence with the word "nothing" underscores the radical nature of the aphorism.

   rather the things that come out make that person unclean: The contrast and the *mashal* (proverb with the overtone of "riddle") prepare for the subsequent interpretation. Like many of the proverbial sayings of Jesus, this would strike his hearers as paradoxical or strange. For a culture concerned about food laws just the opposite of Jesus' saying would seem to be true: What goes in causes defilement. For many commentators this saying in v. 15 is the core of the whole narrative, and there is a vigorous debate over whether it represents an authentic saying of Jesus or is a creation of the early community to explain and defend its neglect of Jewish food laws.

[16.] *Anyone who has ears ought to hear:* Some ancient manuscripts (e.g., Codex Alexandrinus and Codex Bezae) contain this verse, but since the best manuscripts omit it, and since it may be a scribal addition influenced by 4:9, 23, virtually all modern editions and translations omit it.

17. *when he left the crowd:* This is an instance of the familiar Markan pattern of private explanation to the disciples following public teaching (4:10-12; 4:34; 7:17-23; 10:10-12; 10:23-31). The explanations address concerns of Mark's audience.

   about this riddle: The Greek *parabolē* has the nuance of both proverbial saying and riddle. Here the latter nuance is strong since for the disciples the saying would seem strange.

18. *Are you still so obtuse?:* The last time the disciples appeared (6:52), they also lacked understanding—about the loaves. Now they continue to be obtuse. This criticism of the disciples' lack of understanding echoes 4:13, 40, and anticipates the similar language of the harsh rebuke in 8:17.

   whatever enters a person from outside has no power to make that person unclean: This is another instance of the familiar Markan technique of bracketing important material (the obtuseness of the disciples) by virtually identical phrases or sentences. This clause duplicates v. 15, but "nothing" is altered to (literally) "whatever (*pan* = everything) . . . has no power." Some authors argue that v. 18 reflects Semitic syntax (see Ps 143:2 [142:2 LXX]; Rom 3:20; Gal 2:16). Such syntax is not unknown in Greek, and the positive phraseology describing the beginning of the digestive process prepares better for the explanation of vv. 19-20 than the negative phrasing of v. 15 does.

19. *it does not really enter a person's heart:* This part of the saying has an ironic character, since no one believed that food could enter a heart. The heart in biblical thought is very much the center of a person's life, the seat of human activity and emotion, and the battleground between good and evil. People give praise and thanksgiving to God from their hearts (Isa 30:29; Pss 9:1; 13:5; 16:9; 19:8; 28:7), yet from the heart flow evil inclinations and rebellion (Gen 6:5;

8:21; Pss 55:21; 66:18; 78:18). "Heart" here also links this part of the chapter with the quotation from Isa 29:13 in v. 6.

goes into the stomach: "Stomach" *(koilia)* is used most often in the OT positively for "womb" (e.g., Num 5:21-22, 27; Isa 44:2, 24; 46:3; 49:1, 5), a usage followed in the NT (Luke 1:15, 41, 42, 44; 2:21; 11:27), but also for the place of digestion (1 Tim 5:23; Rev 10:9-10), and often with negative overtones (Phil 3:19; 1 Cor 6:13). Paul describes those who impose strict dietary regulations on others as those who "do not serve our Lord Jesus Christ, but their own stomach" (Rom 16:18).

passes out into the toilet: The vivid imagery of the digestive process embellishes the contrast between inner and outer purity and also prepares for the list of repugnant vices and attitudes that is to follow.

(In this manner he declared all foods to be clean.): This translates literally the simple participial phrase "cleansing all foods," which is most likely a later explanatory comment to the readers. It can modify the subject of the verb "he said" either in v. 18 or in v. 20. If the latter, the declaration refers primarily to vv. 21-23; if the former, it refers to the whole complex of thought between vv. 18-23. The ambiguity may be intended by the evangelist.

20. *that which comes out of a person:* The second half of the saying of v. 15 is here repeated but now after the illustration, and prepares for the following list.

21. *from within, from human hearts:* This is the third use of "heart" in the pericope and illustrates clearly that the heart can be far from God (v. 6).

    evil designs: This general description introduces a traditional list of twelve vices, the first six of which are in the plural and the last six in the singular. Mark uses "designs" *(dialogismoi)* with a negative overtone (see 2:6, 8; 8:17). Such lists of vices and of virtues are very frequent among the Hellenistic moralists, and though not frequent in the OT they are found often in later Jewish literature (e.g., Wis 14:25-26; *3 Bar* 4:17; *1 Enoch* 91:6-7; *Jub* 23:14; *4 Macc* 1:2-4) and at Qumran (1QS 4:9-11). In the Gospels they appear only here and in the Matthean parallel (15:18-19), but they are frequent in the Pauline letters (Rom 1:29-31; Gal 5:19-20; 1 Cor 6:9-10; 1 Tim 1:9-10; 2 Tim 3:2-4). The introductory "evil designs" and the "evil eye" (envy) are the only Markan vices not found also in the Pauline lists. The lists serve different functions: moral instruction, exhortation, apologetic, and polemic. Mark uses the list of vices here primarily to illustrate things that "come out of" a person.

    sexual immoralities, thefts, murders, adulteries, forms of greed, malicious acts: Mark's list differs from both Jewish and Hellenistic lists in stressing sins against other individuals rather than sins against God or one's nation (Gundry, *Mark* 366). Theft, murder, and adultery reflect the content of the second half of the Decalogue (Exod 20:13-15; Deut 5:17-19).

22. *the evil eye:* This term should be understood not in the popular sense of casting a spell upon someone but in its applied sense of "envy" (see Matt 20:15).

    blasphemy: The term is used here in the "secular" sense of slander (see 2 Tim 3:2).

folly: The list concludes with "folly" *(aphrosynē)*, which has the same generic ring as does "evil designs." It also recalls the widespread OT criticism of folly (Pss 14:1; 49:10; 53:1; Sir 11:19-20).

23. *All these evils pour out from within:* This verse is a summary and virtual repetition of v. 20 and stresses the main point of vv. 15-23: that true defilement is rooted in inner distortion rather than in external observance.

INTERPRETATION

This passage stands at the midpoint of a larger section of Mark in which, after being rejected by his own (6:1-6a), Jesus embarks on a mission to Jews and Gentiles (6:7–8:21). Jesus has performed mighty works in Jewish territory, most immediately the feeding of 5000 people (6:30-44), followed by a sea crossing (6:45-52) where somewhat surprisingly the disciples are said not to have understood about the loaves (6:52; see 6:37). After a typical Markan summary stressing the magnetic power of Jesus (6:53-56), a dispute arises with Pharisees and scribes from Jerusalem precisely over how "loaves" (7:2) are to be eaten. The dispute soon escalates into a larger dispute over food laws and over the relation of external and internal purity. The resolution of this dispute, in which Jesus declares all food to be clean, prepares for the journey of Jesus to Tyre, Sidon, and the Decapolis. A Gentile woman (7:24-30) and a man (7:31-37) experience his healing power; he then feeds 4000 people in Gentile territory (8:1-10) and has another dispute with Pharisees (8:11-13). This is followed by another sea voyage during which disciples again have a misunderstanding about bread (8:14-21). A transitional healing miracle (8:22-26) brings this major section of the gospel to a close and provides a bridge to the great central section of the gospel (8:27–10:52). The controversy of Mark 7:1-23 echoes the previous ministry of Jesus in Jewish territory and foreshadows the mission to the Gentiles.

This narrative follows and simultaneously expands the general pattern of earlier controversies: an action by Jesus and disciples (7:2), an objection to this action (7:5), a riposte by Jesus (7:6-13, 15-23), and a saying that is the real point of the dialogue (7:13, 15). Though appearing to be a coherent narrative centering around the theme of cleanness or ritual purity, the passage is filled with difficulties. The initial question about eating with unwashed hands, after a lengthy explanation by the evangelist (7:3-4), is restated as a debate about tradition. The first response from Jesus, citing the prophet Isaiah (7:6-8), addresses the issue of God's command versus human tradition. The connection with rituals of eating is virtually forgotten except for the possible ironic connection of "honoring with lips" (7:6) to rituals of eating. The next section of the narrative continues the polemic against human traditions that can distort God's command by citing the custom of the *korban* (7:9-13). Only then do the following verses turn to issues of clean and unclean in the form of a dual proclamation, one to the crowds (what happened to the Pharisees and the scribes?), followed by a private explanation to the disciples about what is clean and unclean.

The narrative combines three distinct disputes: the question of how one is to maintain purity when eating (7:1-8), a criticism of the misuse of the laws and commands of God by overemphasizing human traditions (7:9-13), and further instructions to a different audience (the crowd and the disciples) on what causes ritual impurity (7:14-23). The narrative is more dense with explanatory comments than any other section of Mark (see Notes), and is quite repetitious, especially in the second half. This is clearly a narrative that has gone through a complex development, though the exact stages may not be recoverable.

The dispute has been a battleground not only over issues of Markan theology but also over the relation of the historical Jesus to Jewish purity laws. Though our primary focus is on the theology of Mark and not on reconstructing the ministry of Jesus from Mark, because of the importance of this pericope to Jesus research some comments are necessary. The major point of dispute is 7:15: "Nothing outside a person can enter and make a person unclean; rather, the things that come out make that person unclean." Does this saying represent the attitudes and teaching of the historical Jesus, even if the wording is not a stenographic report?

Until recently there was a rather strong consensus, even among "radical" NT scholars like Bultmann, that Mark 7:15 represented an authentic saying of Jesus. A variation on this is Matt 15:11: "It is not what goes into the mouth that causes a person to be unclean, but what comes out of the mouth causes uncleanness" (which corresponds almost verbatim to *Gos. Thom.* 14). If authentic, the saying supposedly represents Jesus' radical attitude toward Jewish ritual practices and his abrogation of them for his disciples. Other parts of the pericope such as the metaphor from digestion (vv. 19-20), the declaration that all foods are clean (v. 19b), and the list of vices are thought variously to represent different stages in the development of the narrative. Many problems, however, attend the claim of authenticity, the most cogent being that if Jesus articulated such a clear vision of the inability of food to affect one's religious standing before God, why is it that precisely this issue caused such major disputes throughout the early church (Acts 10:9-16; 15:1-21; 1 Cor 8–10; Rom 14:1–15:13), most notably among those who were closest to the historical Jesus—Peter and the Jerusalem community under the leadership of James, the brother of the Lord (Mark 6:3; Gal 2:11-14)? The argument against authenticity asks whether such a radical saying of Jesus would not have been known and invoked in disputes that threatened to split the early communities.

Recent studies of the Jewish context of Jesus' ministry, along with a more precise reading of the text of Mark 7:1-23, have called into question the picture of Jesus as opposing Jewish legalism and as abrogating ritual concerns and substituting moral purity (vv. 17-23). Very few areas of NT studies are as controversial as the question of Jesus' relation to the Jewish purity laws. Two of the scholars most learned in this area, Jacob Neusner and E. P. Sanders, have often expressed diametrically opposite views. However, some generalizations are widely accepted. The concept of a single or normative Judaism has waned in recent years. Neusner speaks of the "Judaisms" of the first century. Examples would be the "Judaism" of Qumran, which was adamantly opposed to the "Judaism" of the Temple priesthood and the Pharisees. Diaspora Judaism represented by someone like Philo of Alexandria who was learned in the Platonic tradition, wrote in Greek, and offered allegorical interpretations of the OT ritual laws (while simultaneously urging their observance) coexisted with Judaisms that looked forward to an apocalyptic cataclysm.

The issue is complicated also by difficulties in defining exactly the teaching of the Pharisees at the time of Jesus. While it is historically accurate to view the Judaism of the *Mishnah* (which itself developed into "rabbinic Judaism") as in continuity with Pharisaic Judaism, they are not identical. The Pharisees were groups of lay people dedicated to the dual Torah, that is, to the written Torah and the oral tradition, both of which were regarded as deriving from God's revelation to Moses on Sinai. They were also dedicated to the sanctification of everyday life in a manner that touched all aspects of experience.

In regard to the dispute in 7:1-23 there is evidence from Qumran, other parts of the NT, and the *Mishnah* that eating was surrounded by many rituals of purification. The *Mishnah* contains whole treatises on such issues. Though handwashing is mentioned in 7:3-4, it is not clear that the prescriptions found here are accurate descriptions of first-century practice. Nevertheless, when the statements of Mark are taken in conjunction with later Jewish traditions there is good evidence that some Pharisees observed rituals of sanctification that included handwashing, and that they may have criticized Jesus' disciples for their nonobservance. The basic point is that Jesus' response as presented in Mark 7:1-23 should not be seen as his rejection of all Jewish ritual laws (or of the Law in general), nor does he disagree with all Jewish groups or even with all Pharisees.

A close reading of 7:1-23 shows that, at least apart from the later addition of 7:19b ("In this manner he declared all foods to be clean") by the final editor, Jesus upholds the authority of the Torah by citing the Decalogue. Jesus does not so much abrogate ritual laws as criticize their potential misuse. Neither does he contrast moral integrity with ritual observance. In the Torah itself (Leviticus 1–18), after the long list of laws governing things that cause impurity, Leviticus 19 (especially vv. 11-18) mandates justice and charity in social dealings and rejects the kinds of destructive social actions mentioned in Mark 7:21-23. Even though the "vice list" may be a later addition to an original dispute, the Jesus who voices this list is firmly within the tradition of Judaism. Cleanness of heart in the Jewish tradition is not opposed to the sanctification of everyday life through rituals of consecration and purification. It is simultaneously supported by them and fosters them.

The part of the narrative that moves beyond the view of virtually every first-century Jew is the statement in which Jesus pronounces "all foods to be clean" (7:19b). Such a view would also have been strange to most of the early Christian communities. The Notes have indicated those places where eating unclean food or observing other food laws threatened to divide the community. As late as his letter to the Romans (ca. 58 C.E.), Paul addressed this problem. Those whom Paul calls "weak" in the community observe particular food laws (14:2, 21). Paul urges "the strong" (among whom in theory he counts himself) to accept them, and voices sentiments that are similar to Mark 7:19b: "I know and am persuaded in the Lord that nothing is unclean *(koinon)* in itself" (Rom 14:14); and "everything is clean" *(panta kathara,* 14:20). Not even Paul, however, mandates that the "weak" give up their observance of food laws. Rather, he urges that they be accepted by the strong, and that the weak abandon attacks on the strong. If Paul's statement that he is "persuaded in the Lord" refers to a saying similar to Mark 7:15 this would be virtually the only evidence that such a saying was known by or influenced early Christian behavior. More likely both this saying and 7:19b are evidence that the final edition of Mark's Gospel took place in a Greek-speaking environment that had begun to move more radically away from Jewish practice than the historical Jesus or many of the traditions incorporated into the gospel had anticipated.

The harshest criticism of Pharisaic practice comes from Jesus' attack on the practice of *korban.* Yet, though the institution of *korban* (that is, the use of dedicatory formulas to restrict access to property) is known, there is little evidence for the precise custom criticized by Jesus. Also, when the oral tradition was codified the *Mishnah* recognized that a vow taken against a biblical precept can be absolved, especially those vows that worked to the detriment of parents *(m. Ned.* 9:1; 11:11). While the Pharisees were organized in table fellowship groups *(ḥăberîm),* it is not known whether such a custom characterized all Pharisees or only certain groups.

As noted above, this narrative holds a central place in the literary structure of Mark as an overture to the further mission to the Gentiles. It also addresses questions most likely still alive in the Markan community. The relation to Jewish laws concerning food was highly disputed in the early church. Raymond E. Brown (in *CBQ* 45 [1983] 74–79) has indicated that four distinct postures toward Jewish law and ritual emerged in the early church: (1) Jewish Christians and their Gentile converts who insisted on observance of all prescriptions of Mosaic Law, including circumcision of males (see Acts 11:2; Gal 2:3); (2) Jewish Christians and their Gentile converts who did not insist on male circumcision but did require converted Gentiles to keep some Jewish observances (which could be called moderately conservative Jewish Gentile Christianity; see Acts 15; Matthew); (3) Jewish Christians and their Gentile converts who did not insist on male circumcision and did not require observance of Jewish kosher laws (Paul's advice in Romans 14–15); and (4) Jewish Christians and their Gentile converts who did not insist on male circumcision or other Jewish ritual laws, and who *saw no abiding significance in Jewish cults and feasts* (Mark 7; John; Hebrews).

According to this analysis Mark 7 derives from the final stages of the composition of the gospel, which took place shortly after the destruction of the Jerusalem Temple (or when that destruction seemed inevitable). During this period Judaism itself was regrouping under the leadership of the Pharisees, and all Jews were involved in a process of self-definition and revision. Early Christian groups under the impact of the destruction of the Temple and in reaction to Jewish self-definition often defined themselves *over against* Jewish groups. Mark 7:1-23 should be seen in the context of a Christian community invoking the words of Jesus, some perhaps historical and others attributed to Jesus in the tradition, in order to define their attitude toward Jewish law and custom and in function of their missionary outreach to Gentiles.

Certain cautions and opportunities for contemporary actualization emerge from this narrative. The cautions arise around a tendency to characterize first-century "Judaism" as legalistic and external in contrast to the more spiritual and compassionate moral code presented by Jesus. The controversy in Mark 7 unfolds within first-century Judaism. The Markan Jesus contrasts his interpretation of the Law and the Prophets to interpretations by specific Jewish groups—a widespread process within the different "Judaisms" of the first century. Also, the spiritualization of the food laws manifest in vv. 17-23, which is presented to the disciples in the house, may well represent a later Christian development handed on in meetings of the "house churches." But this is not simply a "hellenization" of Jesus' message, since such stress on interior morality was also strong in Judaism itself, especially in the Diaspora Judaism represented by someone like Philo.

Nonetheless, the narrative does offer an opportunity for contemporary Christians to reflect on how and why strong religious commitment and devotion to tradition can result in a certain moral rigidity, and it sounds the warning that certain laws and customs must be continually re-assessed in light of revelation, just as the Markan Jesus invokes the Torah against "human tradition." The Second Vatican Council called Scripture the "soul of theology" and in its "Decree on the Training of Priests" (*Optatam totius* 16) said that special attention needs to be given to the development of moral theology, and that its scientific exposition should be more thoroughly nourished by scriptural teachings. In the intervening years since the Council there have been many attempts to ground moral theology in Scripture. At the same time there is currently a strong counter-tendency to "build a fence around the law" with a renewed stress on codified moral directives, which seems to owe more to traditional teachings than to the biblical vision. There must be a constant interplay between Scripture and tradition lest Christians today end up "nullifying the word of God" (7:13).

For Reference and Further Study

Booth, Roger P. *Jesus and the Laws of Purity: Tradition History and Legal History in Mark 7*. JSNTSS 13. Sheffield: JSOT Press, 1986.

Brown, Raymond E. "Not Jewish Christianity and Gentile Christianity but Types of Jewish/Gentile Christianity," *CBQ* 45 (1983) 74–79.

Cuvillier, Elian. "Tradition et rédaction en Marc 7:1-23," *NovT* 34 (1992) 169–92.

Focant, Camille. "Le rapport à la loi dans l'évangile de Marc," *RTL* 27 (1996) 281–308.

Lambrecht, Jan. "Jesus and the Law: An Investigation of Mark 7:1-23," *ETL* 53 (1977) 24–52.

Malina, Bruce J. "A Conflict Approach to Mark 7," *Forum* 4/3 (1988) 3–30.

McEleney, Neil J. "Authenticating Criteria and Mk 7:1-23," *CBQ* 34 (1972) 431–60.

Neusner, Jacob. *Judaism: The Evidence of the Mishnah*. 2nd. ed. Atlanta: Scholars, 1988.

Neyrey, Jerome H. "A Symbolic Approach to Mark 7," *Forum* 4/3 (1988) 63–91.

Pilch, John J. "A Structural Functional Analysis of Mark 7," *Forum* 4/3 (1988) 31–62.

Räisänen, Heikki. "Jesus and the Food Laws: Reflections on Mark 7.15," *JSNT* 16 (1982) 79–100.

Salyer, Gregory. "Rhetoric, Purity, and Play: Aspects of Mark 7:1-23," *Semeia* 64 (1993) 139–69.

Sanders, E. P. *Jewish Law from Jesus to the Mishnah. Five Studies*. London: SCM, 1990.

Svartvik, Jesper. *Mark and Mission. Mk 7:1-23 in its Narrative and Historical Contexts*. Stockholm: Almqvist & Wiksell, 2000.

26. *The Syrophoenician Woman* (7:24-30)

24. He then rose up, left that place, and set out on a journey to the region around Tyre. He went into a house and did not want anyone to know he was there, but it was impossible to avoid being discovered. 25. Right away upon hearing about him, a woman whose little daughter was possessed by an evil spirit came and threw herself down at his feet. 26. (But this woman was a Greek, a Syrophoenician by birth.) And she begged him to expel the demon from her daughter. 27. But he said to her: "Let the children first eat all they want; for it is not right to take food from the children and throw it to the little dogs." 28. But the woman retorted and said to him: "Sir, even the little dogs under the table make a meal of the crumbs that the children give them." 29. And he said to her: "Because of what you said, go home; the demon has already left your daughter." 30. When she arrived home, she found her little child lying on a bed, but the demon was gone.

NOTES

24. *He then rose up:* Mark uses this somewhat solemn phrase (lit. "rising up," *anastas*) when Jesus embarks on significant new activity; see 1:35 and 10:1 (which repeats 7:24 almost verbatim). Here Jesus begins his journey northward, leaving Galilee to travel to Gentile territory. In 10:1 Jesus begins his final journey to Jerusalem where he will die and be raised up (see the use of the same verb, *anastēnai,* in the predictions of Jesus' raising up in 8:31; 9:9, 31; 10:34).

the region around Tyre: This phrase refers to those lands bordering Galilee that were under the jurisdiction of Tyre. Possibly under the influence of Matt 15:21 and Mark 7:31 some important manuscripts here add "and Sidon," which is twenty-two miles north of Tyre. Tyre itself was an ancient Phoenician city with a large mixed population. Herod the Great visited Tyre periodically and built halls, porticoes, temples, and marketplaces for the city (Josephus, *War* 2.459). But Josephus says that the inhabitants of Tyre were bitter enemies of the Jews (*Against Apion* 1.13), and at the outbreak of the Jewish War in 66 C.E. the Tyrians killed and imprisoned many Jews (Josephus, *War* 2.478). The significance of the place name is that Jesus enters territory that is not only Gentile but also potentially hostile.

he went into a house: The house in Mark is often the site of healing, teaching, preaching, or controversy (see 1:29; 2:1, 15; 3:20, 32-33; 5:38; 7:17; 9:33). Since Mark's community gathered as a "house church" (13:34-37; see Rom 16:5), Mark's readers may have seen these actions of Jesus as proleptic of their community life.

did not want anyone to know he was there: Frequently in Mark, Jesus seeks privacy or anonymity only to be discovered or proclaimed. By this technique Mark heightens the power and numinous presence of Jesus (see 1:43-45; 3:11-12; 7:36; 8:30). See also "Messianic Secret" in the Introduction.

it was impossible to avoid being discovered: The report about Jesus' fame, even in Gentile territory, echoes the earlier gathering of the people from "Tyre and Sidon" in 3:8, thus heightening the fame of Jesus among the Gentiles.

25. *Right away upon hearing about him, a woman whose little daughter was possessed by an evil spirit:* The Greek text with its repetition of the possessive *(autēs)* after the relative pronoun *(hēs)*—literally "whose daughter of her had a spirit"—reflects Semitic grammar and may be evidence for the age of the tradition. Also the Greek of this verse is very terse, with two participles ("hearing" and "coming") in rapid succession, which suggests the hurried and eager action of the woman. "Evil spirit" translates *pneuma akatharton* (literally "unclean spirit"; see 1:23, 26; 3:11, 30, 5:8; 6:7; 9:25), since "unclean" or "impure" in English can suggest sexual immorality while "impurity" in biblical thought is what is in contrast to the realm of the "holy" or the "pure." Those destructive spirits opposed to God are therefore paradigmatically "unclean." In the following verse Mark calls this spirit simply a "demon," a term he uses frequently with the verb "expel" (1:34, 39; 3:15, 22; 6:13; 9:38).

26. *(But this woman was a Greek, a Syrophoenician by birth.):* This description reflects Mark's frequent use of duplicate expressions where one term is specified by the following term (e.g., 1:32, 35; 4:35; 14:12; 15:42). A "Greek" (used only here in Mark) does not mean someone who is ethnically Greek but can be used as a generic term for a non-Jew. It also suggests someone who had assimilated Greek culture and language. Mark further describes her as "Syrophoenician," perhaps to distinguish her from a "Libophoenician," which was used for Phoenicians from North Africa (as were the Carthaginians). The somewhat elaborate nomenclature introduced by the repetition of *gynē* ("woman"; see 7:25a), with the adversative particle *de* in place of Mark's frequent *kai* parataxis, may highlight the social status of this woman (literally she was a Greek "lady") as well as her memory in the Christian tradition. In later church tradition she becomes known as Justa and her daughter as Berenice (Pseudo-Clementine *Homilies* 2.19; 3.73).

27. *Let the children:* The response of Jesus is uniquely harsh, since no other suppliant in the gospel is treated in this manner. The "bread" saying seems unconnected with the request—which itself is not specified but is presumably a request for healing/exorcism. Though the specific term "children" *(tekna)* is not used frequently in the LXX for Israel (but see Isa 63:8-9), the idea of the people of Israel as God's children is frequent (Deut 32:20, 43; Ps 82:6 ["you are gods, children of the Most High]; Isa 1:1; 17:9; 63:8; Hos 11:1).

    first: "First" anticipates a "second" feeding and may reflect the Pauline view of the progress of the gospel "to the Jew first, and also to the Greek" (Rom 1:16). There may also be an allusion to the two feeding miracles in 6:30-44 (for Jews) and 8:1-10 (for Gentiles).

    eat all they want: "Eat all they want" is literally "be satisfied." The verbal pattern of "bread," "eat," and "be satisfied" appears in both feeding narratives (6:42; 8:2); its use here both echoes the first narrative and foreshadows the subsequent one.

it is not right: "Right" *(kalos)* has the overtone of morally good, proper, or contributing to salvation (BAGD, s.v.) rather than simple propriety.

food from children: The metaphorical use of eating here links this pericope with the larger context of the two feeding narratives and discussions of bread *(artos).* As the response of the woman will confirm, the "feeding/eating" here serves as a metaphor for the larger arena of acceptance and a claim to God's benefits.

and throw it to little dogs: The reply of Jesus seems brutally harsh, since to call someone a dog was an insult (1 Sam 17:43; Isa 56:10-11). Dogs were regarded as unclean animals and almost always have a negative connotation (1 Sam 24:14; 2 Kgs 8:13; Prov 26:11; see Matt 7:6, "do not give what is holy to dogs"). Lazarus' degradation is highlighted by his desire to eat the scraps left for dogs and by the dogs licking his wounds (Luke 16:19-22), and opponents and heretics are called "dogs" (2 Pet 2:22; Phil 3:2; Rev 22:15; Ignatius, *Eph* 7:1). Though the diminutive *kynarion* (lit. "little dog") is often used for house dogs in contrast to the street scavengers, the verb "throw" suggests casting food outside for the dogs to eat.

28. *But the woman retorted and said to him:* The double verb "retorted" *(apekrithē)* and "said" *(legei)* reflects a "high" rhetorical style, and is found elsewhere only on the lips of Pontius Pilate (15:9).

    Sir: The vocative *kyrie* (lit. "lord") may be deliberately ambiguous, since it can be simply a reverential mode of address or a reference to a divine figure (though *Kyrios* is not a major christological title in Mark).

    even the little dogs under the table: The woman responds to Jesus' insulting metaphor with a counter-metaphor, comparing herself (and implicitly the Greeks) with the house pets who in Greek culture were often present at meals. The "dog talk" in this pericope is symbolic of a deeper cultural gap between Jews and Greeks.

    make a meal of the crumbs that the children give them: The woman's response adapts Jesus' metaphor to her own situation. In contrast to Jesus' statement of "rightness" the woman evokes the custom of children feeding the dogs. Her metaphor counters the exclusive right of the children to food by the image of children who share their food, even with the little dogs. Just as Jesus' initial response is uniquely harsh, the response of the woman is the sole place where Jesus is "bested" in verbal repartee.

29. *And he said to her: "Because of what you said, go home:* "Because of what you said" translates the Greek "because of your word *(logos)."* Often in miracle stories the healing is in response to the faith of petitioners (2:5; 5:34; 10:52; see 9:22, "all things are possible to the one who believes"). Here the healing occurs only after the woman bests Jesus in verbal repartee. Matthew seems to "correct" Mark at this point by substituting "Woman, great is your faith" (15:28) for Mark's "because of what you said."

    the demon has already left your daughter: Unlike other "exorcisms," there is no physical confrontation between the exorcist and the demon, nor is there any explicit word of command. The healing from a distance and the use of the perfect tense of the verb "has already left" *(exelēlythen)*, which describes completed action in the past, heighten the power of Jesus. Healing at a distance is a documented motif in ancient miracle stories. The Talmud contains a story of the healing of Rabban Gamaliel's son by Hanina ben Dosa (*b. Berakoth* 34b), and Philostratus tells of such a healing by Apollonius of Tyana (*Life of Apollonius* 3.38 [LCL]). Mark's community may read this as a hope for the power of the gospel in the Gentile world.

30. *lying on the bed:* In an earlier story (2:1-12) the paralytic is brought on his *krabbatos* (a mat or bed for the poor). "Bed" *(klinē)*, which is used in Greek for both a dining couch and a bed, while echoing 2 Kgs 4:32, may also suggest a higher social level for the woman and her daughter.

the demon was gone: This serves as the "confirmation of the miracle," one of the standard motifs of a miracle story. The perfect participle used here *(exelēlythos)*, by echoing the perfect indicative in the previous verse, again heightens the effective power of the word of Jesus.

INTERPRETATION

After a relatively long debate with Pharisees over Jewish food laws the Markan Jesus rises up and leaves for non-Jewish territory. Mark's readers would interpret the pronouncement that all foods are clean (see 7:19b) as a warrant for acceptance of Gentiles (see Rom 14:14). The following incidents in Mark (7:24–8:21) take place in Gentile territory and culminate in a miraculous communal meal with Gentiles (8:1-10) that elicits further discussion and misunderstanding (8:11-21). When the gospel is read on two levels as a remembrance of Jesus and as directives to the Markan community these narratives can be seen as grounding the practice of the church in the example of Jesus while at the same time reflecting the continuing difficulties caused by this practice.

The restoration to health of the daughter of the Syrophoenician woman has formal characteristics of both a miracle story (exorcism) and a controversy. A person in need confronts Jesus with a request followed by a description of the disease or need (7:24). But the story breaks off and continues with a debate between Jesus and the woman over the appropriateness of his providing help for Gentiles. Having been bested in the debate, Jesus pronounces the daughter already freed of the demon, and the miracle is confirmed when the woman returns home and finds the young woman lying (quietly) in bed.

The narrative contains certain anomalies. It is virtually the only miracle in which Jesus is completely alone. Even in other incidents where Jesus withdraws from the crowds, the disciples are present. Here and in the following narrative (7:31-37) the disciples are absent, so much so that Mark notes that Jesus must summon the disciples in 8:1. There is no mention of faith, which characterizes so many of the miracle stories (see the Notes), and the harshness with which Jesus answers the initial request of the woman is unparalleled. Not even the bizarre Gerasene demoniac receives such a seeming rebuke as does this woman.

Matthew (15:21-28) seems uneasy with the ambiguities of the Markan story. In his account the disciples are present and contribute to the dramatic action by trying to keep the woman away from Jesus. Matthew explains Jesus' somewhat harsh initial response to the woman (15:23) through the saying of Jesus: "I was sent only to the lost sheep of the house of Israel" (see Matt 10:6, 23). And finally Matthew has Jesus praise the faith of the woman; only then does the healing take place.

Intertextually the story has echoes of the Elijah and Elisha narrative cycles. The initial story of the Elijah cycle takes place in Zarephath (1 Kgs 17:8-24), a city that "belongs to Sidon" (1 Kgs 17:8; see Mark 7:24). Elijah is commanded to "rise up" (1 Kgs 17:9; LXX *anastēthi*); see Mark 7:24, where Jesus "rose up." Then he alone meets the widow of Zarephath, and a miraculous feeding takes place. Later the woman's son falls ill and dies; after the death of her son the woman verbally confronts the prophet: "Why have you come against me, O man of God?" Though the healing of the son is narrated in more detail than in the case of the Syrophoenician woman's daughter, the words of the prophet take the form of a simple pronouncement: "See, your son lives" (17:23); compare Mark 7:29: "the demon has already left your daughter."

Echoes of a similar story in the Elisha cycle, the restoration to life of the son of the Shunammite woman in 2 Kgs 4:18-37, also appear in Mark 7:24-30. The locale (Shunem) is in the north. After some years this woman's son dies, and she seeks out Elisha. After an initial dialogue the woman grasps the feet of the prophet (4:27; see Mark 7:25). The woman manifests the same initiative and persistent concern as the Syrophoenician woman (4:28-31). Elisha finds the child lying on a bed (4:32, *klinē;* see Mark 7:30), and the prophetic word announcing the healing is also a simple pronouncement: "Take your son" (4:36). The Elisha story is followed soon after by a narrative of a miraculous feeding (see Mark 8:1-10). These echoes of the Elijah and Elisha narratives support the motif of the prophet who goes to a person outside Israel (the widow of Zarephath and the Shunammite; see Luke 4:25-27).

The story also has affinities with the only miracle story in Q, the healing of the centurion's servant (Matt 8:5-13; Luke 7:1-10). In Mark and in the Q story the petitioner is a non-Jew (Mark 7:25; Matt 8:5, 10; Luke 7:2, 4, 9); in both cases there is a rather long dialogue between Jesus and the petitioner (Mark 7:27-28; Matt 8:8-10; Luke 7:6-9). Also the petitioner in each case acts in an unexpected manner. Readers would not expect a woman to confront Jesus and even get the better of him in an argument, nor would they expect a centurion to address Jesus as "Lord" and profess his unworthiness (Matt 8:8; Luke 7:6). In both Mark and Q there is an instantaneous healing from a distance (Mark 7:29; Matt 8:13; Luke 7:10). Both of these narratives also perform a similar function: They ground the outreach of the church to the "nations" (Mark 11:17; 13:10) in the ministry of Jesus.

The narrative in Mark 7:24-30 is itself intriguing in its realism and parabolic character. Though, as throughout the gospel, Jesus is the principal and most developed character, the woman is "rounded" in the sense of exhibiting more surprising and realistic traits than virtually any other character. Immediately upon hearing of Jesus she acts quickly and decisively for the sake of her daughter. As in the parables, the realism is somewhat shattered in the reply of the woman. Despite her seeming posture of humble suppliant ("threw herself down at his feet"), she responds with equal alacrity to Jesus' insult about not giving the children's food to dogs. Is the reader intended to visualize her still at the feet of Jesus? Another surprising twist comes when Jesus "capitulates" (7:29, "because of what you said"), and thus seems less solemn and more human than in other parts of the gospel.

The narrative portrays an array of "boundary crossings." Jesus leaves the traditional land of Israel to go to the regions of Tyre (and Sidon), lands that first-century readers knew as bitter enemies of the Jews. The woman crosses the boundaries separating Jews and Gentiles, and males and females. As a "Greek lady" (see Notes) she crosses the social barrier between itinerant preacher and landed property owner. The woman also crosses the boundary between stereotypical male dominance and female submissiveness. Jesus' harsh reply would be expected in a first-century androcentric culture; what would be shocking are the courageous reply of the woman and Jesus' ultimate capitulation.

In its immediate context the narrative provides a dramatic vignette of what is involved after Jesus warns against the power of tradition to make void the word of God and calls into question purely external observance of food laws. Such laws often served as "boundary markers" between Jews and Gentiles. Rather strangely, after seeming to view as irrelevant what "goes into a person" (7:16), in his response to the woman Jesus distinguishes the "children" (Jews) from the "little dogs" (Gentiles) precisely by what goes into them, that is, by what they eat: table food or crumbs. The woman, who in this culture is a double outsider (a woman alone with a man, and a non-Jewish woman at that; see John 4:9, 27), paradoxically teaches Jesus the implications of his earlier teaching and of his journey into Gentile territory. The liberation from evil that was promised to the "children" is now to be made available for non-Jews. Since table fellowship with Gentiles was one of the most divisive areas in early Christianity (see Gal 2:11-14), the woman articulates the Gentile perspective. The benefits of God's reign proclaimed and enacted thus far by Jesus and given first to the Jews (Rom 1:16) are to be made available to "the little dogs."

The wider context of the narrative is also significant. Throughout this whole subsection (6:6b–8:21) motifs of food and eating resonate—from the murderous banquet of Herod, through the feeding of 5000 Jewish people and the discussion of clean and unclean food, to the feeding of 4000 people in Gentile territory, with the startling conclusion in 8:21 that the disciples really did not understand the feedings. The story of Jesus and the Syrophoenician woman provides a hermeneutical key to the whole section. Those boundaries that separated Jews and Gentiles in early Christianity and that so often involved disputes over eating are to be broken down. Even the disciples of Jesus do not seem to understand this (8:21). But the Gentile woman does, and so she provides for subsequent generations a model of the "outsider"—the woman who challenges readers against setting limits to those who would be called sons and daughters of God.

FOR REFERENCE AND FURTHER STUDY

Baudoz, Jean-François. *Les miettes de la table. Étude synoptique et socio-religieuse de Mt. 15,21-28 et Mc. 7,24-30.* EB n.s. 27. Paris: Gabalda, 1995.
Dewey, Joanna. "Jesus' Healings of Women: Conformity and Non-Conformity to Dominant Cultural Values and Clues for Historical Reconstruction," *BTB* 24 (1994) 122–31.
Dufton, Francis. "The Syrophoenician Woman and Her Dogs," *ExpTim* 100 (1989) 417.
Perkinson, Jim. "A Canaanitic Word in the Logos of Christ; or The Difference the Syro-Phoenician Woman Makes to Jesus," *Semeia* 75 (1996) 61–85.
Pokorny, Petr. "From a Puppy to the Child: Some Problems of Contemporary Biblical Exegesis Demonstrated from Mark 7.24-30/Matt 15.21-28," *NTS* 41 (1995) 321–37.
Rhoads, David. "Jesus and the Syrophoenician Woman in Mark. A Narrative-Critical Study," *JAAR* 62 (1994) 343–75.
Sugirtharajah, Rasia S. "The Syrophoenician Woman," *ExpTim* 98 (1986) 13–15.

27. Jesus Restores Hearing and Speech to a Suffering Man (7:31-37)

31. And once again he set out from the region around Tyre and traveled by way of Sidon toward the Sea of Galilee through the region of the Decapolis. 32. And the people brought to him a person who was deaf and could barely speak, and they begged him to lay his hand upon him. 33. But he took him aside privately away from the crowd; then he put his

fingers in his ears, and then he spat and touched the man's tongue. 34. Then gazing heavenward, he sighed deeply and said to him: "Ephphatha!"; that is, "Be opened." 35. At that moment his ears were opened, and his tongue was loosened, and he spoke correctly. 36. And he [Jesus] ordered them not to tell anyone. But the more he ordered them, the more extravagantly they proclaimed it. 37. Then everyone was totally awestruck and said: "He has done all things well; he even has made the deaf to hear and given a voice to the voiceless."

NOTES

31. *And once again he set out:* The combination of *kai* (and") with *exelthōn* ("set out") was used earlier in Mark to signal significant transitions in Jesus' activity (1:45; 6:34).

    from the region around Tyre and traveled by way of Sidon: On Tyre see the Note on 7:24. Sidon is about twenty-two miles north of Tyre. In post-exilic Jewish literature "Tyre and Sidon" become virtual shorthand for the southern Phoenician territory (Joel 3:4; Zech 9:2; 2 Esdr 1:11; see Acts 12:20). "By way of" translates the Greek *dia* (lit. "through"), which is used with the genitive to speak of journeys bypassing one place on the way to another. The movements of Jesus here are not "logical," since if he is on his way to the Decapolis, a further journey north would be unnecessary. Mark wants to have Jesus move north, then east, and finally south to compass the whole of the southern Phoenician (Gentile) territory prior to his journey to Jerusalem in 8:22–10:52.

    through the region of the Decapolis: Literally "along the middle *(ana meson)*" of the district. Mark describes Jesus as remaining near the east side of the lake (8:10). The Decapolis was first mentioned as the locale of the healed demoniac who proclaimed "all that Jesus had done" (5:20), thus foreshadowing his present mighty work. On the Decapolis see the Notes under 5:20. A pattern Mark creates is that Jesus is first known in those Gentile areas he enters and then he performs mighty works there. This is similar to the Johannine pattern where people proclaim Jesus but faith comes from direct contact (see John 4:28-30, 39-42).

32. *the people brought:* The shift to the historical present here (lit. "bring") makes the narrative more vivid. Mark wants the reader to know that the fame of Jesus announced earlier (5:20) is such that ordinary people (and not simply disciples) have hope in the power of Jesus (they "beg" him).

    a person who was deaf and could barely speak: The Greek "deaf" (*kōphos*) means completely unable to hear, while *mogilalos* (lit. "speaking with difficulty"), which is recognized as tragic in the Bible (Ps 38:13), depicts accurately the suffering of those born deaf even today. Although some translations (e.g., Syriac) interpret the term as referring to a total inability to speak, 7:35 suggests some power of speech. The malady also recalls the hopes for the returning exiles in Isa 35:5-6: "the eyes of the blind shall be opened, and the ears of the deaf unstopped" (see also Isa 42:19). The language also echoes God's words to Moses in Exod 4:11: "Who gives speech to mortals? Who makes them mute or deaf, seeing or blind? Is it not I, the Lord?" This allusion adds a christological dimension to the narrative: Jesus, like the Lord, has power over hearing and speech.

and they begged him to lay his hand upon him: The Greek for "beg" *(parakalein)* has many nuances. Literally it means "call alongside of," with the sense of soliciting an advocate (see the "Paraclete" in John) and comes to mean "entreat, beg, implore." The request for healing is part of the formal structure of a miracle, and the verb *parakalein* is used similarly in 1:40, 5:23; and 8:22. Healing by touching is another common motif in Markan miracle stories (1:31, 41; 5:23; 5:41; 8:22; 9:27).

33. *took him aside privately away from the crowd:* This is another Markan duplicate (or really triplicate) expression: "took him aside" *(apolambanein)*, "privately" *(kat' idian)*, and "from the crowd." In every other instance *kat' idian* is used to describe Jesus' seclusion with his disciples (4:34; 6:31-32; 9:2, 28; 13:3). Though this action is adduced as evidence for the theory of the Messianic Secret, only here and in 8:22-26 does Jesus take someone aside for healing.

he put his fingers in his ears: The readers (but no one else) realize that the healing here is accompanied by six actions: taking aside, putting hands in the ear, spitting, touching the tongue, a deep groan (7:34), and a command of healing.

then he spat: In both the Greco-Roman and the Jewish worlds (and in many places today), "spittle" or saliva was regarded as having a therapeutic function (see John 9:6; Pliny, *Natural History* 28.4.7; Tacitus, *Histories,* 4.81; Suetonius, *Vespasian* 7 [variation of same story]; and *b. Shab.* 108b. Tacitus recounts the "miracles" of Vespasian at Alexandria where a blind man begs him to anoint his eyes with spittle; see 4.82).

and touched the man's tongue: The reader is to envision Jesus' spitting in his hands and then "anointing" the man's tongue. On the "magical" aspects of Jesus' actions, see the Interpretation.

34. *gazing heavenward, he sighed deeply:* Looking heavenward is often a sign of prayer (see Ps 123:1; Luke 18:13; John 17:1; Acts 7:55). For sighing, Martin Dibelius (*From Tradition to Gospel* 84–86) cites the Leiden Magical Papyrus where sighing is part of the technique of miracle workers. Yet this is the only place where Jesus sighs deeply or groans *(estanaxen)* prior to a miracle. A cognate verb *(anastenazein)* is used in 8:12, but there it refers to Jesus' displeasure over the request for a sign.

Ephphatha: A few authors claim that this is the Greek vocalization of a Hebrew *niph'al* imperative, but most see it as the vocalization of the Aramaic *'eppatah,* the imperative of *pĕtah* ("open"). Though the use of foreign words *(rhēsis barbarikē)* as an incantation is a frequent motif in magical papyri and in exorcisms, such words often take the form of unintelligible "abracadabras." Whatever the function of the Aramaic term in the pre-Markan tradition, Mark makes it intelligible through his translation ("Be opened"), so that it serves as a word of power that frees the man from his infirmity rather than as a mysterious magical incantation (see Exod 4:11 and above under v. 32).

35. *his ears were opened:* Mark writes literally that the man's "hearing(s)" *(akoai)* was opened up, in contrast to *ōta,* which would designate simply his "ears."

    He spoke correctly: This confirms the meaning of *mogilalos* (v. 32) as "speak with difficulty," since the healing brings intelligible speech. This verse conforms to the standard pattern of visible demonstration at the end of miracle stories.

36. *But he [Jesus] ordered them:* Although Jesus performs the miracle in private (7:33), all the pronouns are in the plural. Many commentators solve this tension between the private healing and the commands to the public, along with the crowd's reaction in 7:37, by postulating a mixture of tradition in 7:32-35 and Markan editorial addition in 7:36-37 as part of the Messianic Secret motif. However, it can be argued more simply that the "private" healing is simply one-to-one apart from the crowd (not in a house as in the previous narrative). The reader is to imagine that then the correct speech of the man was heard at a distance, and so the crowd was admonished to remain silent.

    not to tell anyone: Explicit or implicit commands to silence after a miracle are found here and in 1:34; 1:44-45; 5:43; and 8:26. As in 1:44-45, the command is violated, and the fame of Jesus spreads all the more.

    they proclaimed it: "Proclaiming" *(kēryssein)* has a religious overtone and is associated with the message Jesus brings about God as well as the message the post-resurrection church brings about Jesus. In Mark the following figures "proclaim": John the Baptist (1:4, 7), Jesus (1:14-15, 38-39), people who have experienced Jesus' mighty works (1:45–5:20; 7:36), the disciples (3:14; 6:12), the community under persecution (13:10), and the post-resurrection community (14:9).

37. *Then everyone was totally awestruck:* The Greek text rings with vivid superlatives. The main verb *exeplēssonto* is an intensive form of the root verb *plēssein* and means to be "struck out of one's senses," while "totally" translates the adverb *hyperperissōs,* which intensifies the already extravagant adverb *perissōs* ("beyond measure"). The original audience of the miracle now becomes an excited chorus that heralds the power of Jesus.

    He has done all things well: The language here *(kalōs panta pepoiēken)* echoes the LXX of Gen 1:31: "and God saw everything that he had done *(epoiēsen),* for behold it was exceedingly good *(kala lian)."* Jesus' action restores the fallen creation and anticipates the messianic age.

    the deaf to hear and given a voice to the voiceless: This is another (see 7:32) allusion to Isa 35:5-6 where the restoration of hearing is part of the new day of salvation. In the light of v. 36 Mark's readers may take this as a symbol of the power of God at work among the Gentiles; they hear the saving word ("be opened") and proclaim it.

INTERPRETATION

Mark continues the journey of Jesus through Gentile territory with a vivid narrative of the healing of a deaf mute—which strangely is not found in either Matthew or Luke. At this point in his gospel Matthew in 15:29-31 enlarges Mark's narrative into a vivid picture of Jesus seated on a mountain (cf. Matt 5:1) and healing "the lame, the maimed, the blind, and the dumb," with the result that the great crowds (Matt 15:30) glorify the God of Israel (15:31). Matthew captures the universal dimension of Mark's concrete narrative. In Mark, along with the story of the Syrophoenician woman, this narrative conveys the *bona messianica*, the benefits hoped for in the messianic age when death and sickness will be overcome. They serve as a prelude to the feeding of the 4000 (Mark 8:1-10), the gift of food in Gentile territory parallel to the more extensive feeding of the 5000 at 6:30-44.

Intertextually the malady also recalls the hopes of the returning exiles in Isa 35:5-6 that "the eyes of the blind shall be opened, and the ears of the deaf unstopped" (see also Isa 42:19). The language also echoes Exod 4:11 (see the Notes).

The story is a prime example of the vivid quality of Mark's narrative style. The ailment of the man is described in detail, as are Jesus' initial contacts with him: He takes him aside, puts his fingers in his ears, spits, and touches his tongue. Prior to the healing command Jesus "sighs." Then he speaks in a "foreign" tongue, and the healing occurs. The reaction to the miracle is strongly dramatized. Such details make this narrative similar to magical cures current in the Hellenistic world. Groaning and use of a foreign tongue may reflect techniques found in the magical papyri. The actions seem to be a form of sympathetic magic; placing the fingers in the ears mimics their opening, and spitting and "anointing" the tongue imitate expelling an obstacle to speech. These similarities may explain the omission of the story by Matthew and Luke. More positively, such gestures are appropriate in a Gentile setting in which Jesus appears as both similar to pagan healers and superior to them (since ultimately the healing is due to a command of Jesus).

Jesus' command to silence in 7:36 is not, however, part of the magical tradition. This narrative contains in miniature the tension surrounding the so-called "Messianic Secret" in Mark. The more Jesus commands silence, the more extravagantly the people speak out (lit. "proclaim"), and those who hear of it are totally awestruck. This pattern supports the view that the "secret" texts deal not with whether Jesus is a powerful Son of God but rather with what kind of Son he is and when and how he can be proclaimed as such. Only at the gospel's climax, under the shadow of the cross, will a Gentile centurion utter the ultimate confession of Jesus as God's Son (15:39).

This narrative also serves to contrast the reaction of others (even Gentiles) who respond positively to Jesus and the growing misunderstanding of him on the part of the disciples. In a prior incident (6:45-52), when faced with an equally strong manifestation of Jesus' power, the disciples are fearful and confused, and they do not understand what they hear about the bread (6:52), and in 7:18 Jesus again criticizes their lack of understanding. Their perception will continue to decline in subsequent narratives, especially in 8:18 where they are judged as neither hearing nor seeing properly.

Here the Markan Jesus continues his mission of announcing and enacting the good news begun in 1:14-15. Readers now know that this message and the power that Jesus manifests will be heard and experienced by others than those who were originally called to be his disciples and will even extend beyond the confines of Jewish territory. Jesus is here a model for the Markan church—for a church in mission beyond the bounds of its own culture, which joins the proclamation of the gospel to the ministry of confronting human suffering.

FOR REFERENCE AND FURTHER STUDY

Collins, Raymond F. "Jesus' Ministry to the Deaf and Dumb," *Melita Theologica* 35 (1984) 12–36.

Horton, Fred L., Jr. "Nochmals *ephphatha* in Mk 7:34," *ZNW* 77 (1986) 101–08.

Morag, Shelmo. "*Ephphatha* (Mark vii. 34): Certainly Hebrew, not Aramaic?" *JSS* 17 (1972) 198–202.

Rabinowitz, Isaac. "*Ephphatha* (Mark 7:34): Certainly Hebrew, not Aramaic," *JSS* 16 (1971) 151–56.

28. *The Second Feeding Narrative: The 4000* (8:1-10)

1. In those days, when a large crowd had again assembled, since they did not have anything to eat, he called his disciples to his side and said to them: 2. "I have compassion on the crowd because they have already stayed with me for three days and they have nothing to eat. 3. But if I send them home while they are so hungry, they will collapse on their journey, for some of them have traveled a long distance." 4. Then his disciples replied to him: "How is it possible for anyone here in such a remote place to feed these people with bread?" 5. He then asked them: "How many loaves of bread do you have?" They replied: "Seven." 6. He then directed the crowd to sit down on the ground, and he took the seven loaves; and after giving thanks, he broke them and gave them to his disciples to distribute, and they set them before the people. 7. They also had some small fish. And after uttering a blessing over them, he told them to distribute these also. 8. They began eating and were satisfied; then they

[the disciples] picked up seven baskets full of the fragments that were left over. 9. There were four thousand people there, and then Jesus sent them away. 10. Right away he got into the boat with his disciples and arrived at the region of Dalmanutha.

NOTES

1. *In those days:* This constitutes a more solemn introduction to a section than the frequent "and" (*kai* parataxis), and is used elsewhere to underscore the significance of a particular event (see 1:9, the initial arrival of Jesus to be baptized by John; 2:20, the day when the bridegroom will be taken away; 4:35, the first "sea miracle"; 13:17, 24, 32, the days of the final tribulation; 14:25, "that day" when Jesus will drink the new wine).

    large crowd: A similar designation (see 6:34) appears in the first feeding narrative (6:32-44). The two narratives are explicitly linked by the term "again."

    since they did not have anything to eat: In contrast to the first narrative, where Jesus in 6:34 has compassion on them because they are leaderless (sheep without a shepherd) and where the disciples call attention to the hunger of the people, here Jesus is the first to notice their hunger and it moves him to compassion. The lack of something to eat is repeated almost verbatim at the end of v. 2. Physical hunger is a more dominant motif here than in the first feeding.

2. *I have compassion:* The same verb is used by the narrator in 6:34 ("he had compassion"), though here on the lips of Jesus it carries greater force.

    they have already stayed with me: Again in contrast to 6:32-44 where the crowds pursue Jesus and arrive at the lakeshore before him, the crowds have presumably been with Jesus on his journey through the Decapolis, which is underscored by the long homeward journey they face in 8:3.

    already . . . three days: "Three days" appears elsewhere in Mark only in the Passion predictions of 8:31; 9:31; 10:33-34, and in the references to the building of the temple not made with hands (14:58; 15:29). While here the term may simply underscore the hunger consequent upon the length of the journey, other nuances are possible. A "three day" journey is frequent in the OT, often in anticipation of a significant event (Gen 30:36; Exod 3:18; 5:3; 8:27; Num 10:33; Josh 1:11). A three-day fast, or period of hunger, precedes important events (1 Sam 30:12; Esth 4:16).

3. *a long distance:* Literally the Greek reads: "they have come from afar (*apo makrothen).*" In Josh 9:6 (LXX) and Isa 60:4 (LXX) this phrase designates "Gentiles," a usage followed by the early church (Acts 2:39; 22:21; Eph 2:11-12). Given the local context of these narratives in Gentile territory, Mark's readers may think of the ingathering of the Gentiles into their community.

4. *his disciples replied:* Though Jesus has not asked the disciples to feed the crowd as in 6:37, they perceive his intention. Since they have already witnessed the feeding of the 5000, the disciples' question serves to underline their growing obtuseness, which will culminate in 8:18-19.

5. *Seven:* The numbers in the feeding narratives provide endless fascination. In the first Synoptic feeding narrative (Mark 6:38; Matt 14:17; Luke 8:13; John 6:9) there are five loaves and two fish, while here and in Matt 15:34 there are seven loaves along with a few fish in both cases. Though "seven" is one of the most popular numbers in the Bible and the Ancient Near East, specific nuances have been attributed to Mark's use of it here: "Seven" may suggest Gentiles as in the seven commandments of the Noachic covenant (Gen 9:4-7), the seven Hellenists chosen in Acts (6:3), the seven churches of Revelation 2–3, or the seven pagan nations of Canaan (Acts 13:19; Deut 7:1).

6. *to sit down:* In contrast to 6:39-40, the OT allusions are omitted as well as the possible allusions to the messianic banquet (see the Notes for 6:39-40).

   he took . . . giving thanks . . . broke . . . gave: The actions of Jesus here parallel 6:41 but with significant variations. Mark 8:6 omits looking up to heaven (6:41) and employs the Greek *eucharistēsas* ("after giving thanks") rather than *eulogēsas* ("he said a blessing"). The language used for the actions of Jesus here (e.g., *eucharistēsas*) is closer to the Pauline tradition (1 Cor 11:23-24). This may reflect the formula of thanksgiving used in Gentile churches and so would be appropriate in the Markan setting.

7. *after uttering a blessing:* The second blessing of fish is not found in the earlier narrative, and also here the more Jewish form *eulogēsas* appears. This may suggest the idea of an editorial rewriting to bring the two accounts closer together.

8. *were satisfied:* This characterizes both accounts (see 6:42) but is heightened here because of the earlier comment in v. 3 that the people were so hungry they would collapse on their return journey.

   seven baskets: Seven is harmonized with the number of loaves and carries similar nuances. The Greek term here for "basket" *(spyris)* suggests a smaller and somewhat more elegant basket than the "wicker basket" *(kophinos)* of 6:43, which Roman authors saw as characteristic of Jewish groups in Rome.

9. *four thousand:* Again there is great speculation about the number and its contrast with the 5000 of the earlier account. "Four" has been associated with the four corners of the universe or the four points of the compass, suggesting the ingathering of the Gentiles. It could also be a simple stylistic variation.

10. *he got into the boat with his disciples:* Jesus and his disciples embarking in a boat is a frequent narrative transitional device (3:9; 5:21; 6:32; 8:13) and is often the occasion for significant revelation (4:1-9; 4:35-41; 6:45-52; 8:13-21).

    the region of Dalmanutha: There are two variant readings here. Though major manuscripts read "region" *(merē)*, Matt 15:39 and some manuscripts of Mark 8:10 read "mountains" *(oria)*. "Dalmanutha" presents a more puzzling problem. It appears only here in the NT, and its location and meaning are uncertain. Matthew reads "the mountains of Magadan," with manuscript variations of "Magdala." Matthew and the manuscript tradition suggest that it was located at the northwest corner of the Sea of Galilee. A recent suggestion derives Dalmanutha from an Aramaic term for "wall," and it may have been one of the enclosed cities of that region (James F. Strange, "Dalmanutha," *ABD* 2.5). Since the Matthean variant "Magdala" is derived from the Aramaic word for "tower" it is possible that the same "walled city" was called by different names.

INTERPRETATION

Here Mark recounts a second multiplication of loaves and fishes similar to the first (6:30-44). Both accounts are gift miracles in which Jesus meets the needs of people who have no access to food. In both, the disciples question the seeming impossibility of Jesus' command to feed the crowds, and the allusions to the OT are basically the same, though in more condensed form here (e.g., the location in a "desolate place" is mentioned only once, 8:4; cf. 6:31, 32, 35). The actions surrounding the distribution of food (taking, giving thanks, breaking, and distributing) are virtually the same.

The narrative occurs in a pattern similar to the first feeding in which a miraculous feeding (6:30-44; 8:1-9) is followed by a "sea journey" (6:45-52; 8:10), a dispute with Pharisees (7:1-13; 8:11-13), and further instructions to disciples (7:14-23; 8:14-21), and concludes with a narrative about the gift of hearing or sight (7:31-37; 8:22-26; see the references to seeing and hearing in 4:12 and 8:18). One major difference in the pattern is that the second feeding comes after two miracles done in Gentile territory (7:24-30, 31-37) in which Jesus is described as the one "who does all things well" (7:37), rather than after the questioning about Jesus' identity and the death of John (6:14-29). It is part of Jesus' mission to the Gentiles in Mark and stresses an abundance of food for both Jews and Gentiles.

In the account itself a major difference is the omission of any reference to the teaching of Jesus or to his compassion for the crowd as leaderless sheep without a shepherd. In the second feeding it is the hunger of the people that evokes the compassionate response of Jesus. This is heightened by his comment to the disciples that the crowd has remained with him three days after having traveled a long distance and his fear that people will literally collapse on their journey. The second feeding provides a more vivid picture of Jesus as one who observes human suffering and meets human needs. While Jesus is portrayed more vividly in this narrative, the disciples are far less a narrative presence here. In 6:30-44 it is the disciples who initially call attention to the hunger of the people after Jesus' lengthy teaching. When this evokes Jesus' command to feed them, the disciples counter with a protest about the impossibility of buying bread for so many people, and this is followed by rather elaborate instructions for eating. In 8:3-5 the dialogue of Jesus with the disciples is more muted, and their misunderstanding is less dramatic. In both narratives the disciples appear as those who distribute the food and gather the fragments.

This narrative thus concludes the mission of Jesus to the Gentiles, since even in Mark's somewhat confused geography Jesus will soon begin his journey southward from the Jewish city of Bethsaida (8:22) to Jerusalem. Readers will soon learn that Jerusalem is to be the place of Jesus' death and resurrection. Since table fellowship between Jews and Gentiles was a source of much controversy in the nascent church, Mark offers his community a picture of a Jewish Jesus and Jewish disciples who are concerned for the sustenance of both Jews and Gentiles, evocative perhaps of Paul's understanding of the power of the gospel "to the Jew first and also to the Greek" (Rom 1:16).

Actualization of the narrative would follow many of the same guidelines suggested for the feeding of the 5000, with the added nuance that Christians should be concerned to meet the hungers of all people. The eucharistic allusion, which was strong in the first feeding account, is also present here. This suggests that the Eucharist should be the memory and food of Jesus that break down barriers between different groups.

FOR REFERENCE AND FURTHER STUDY

Seethaler, Angelika. "Die Brotvermehrung—ein Kirchenspiegel?" *BZ* 34 (1990) 108–12.
See also the list of books and articles on Mark 6:30-44.

29. *Pharisees and Scribes Seek a Sign* (8:11-13)

11. Then the Pharisees came forward and began to argue with him by seeking from him a sign from heaven, in order to test him. 12. Then he sighed from the depths of his spirit and said: "Why does this generation seek a sign? Amen I say to you, no sign shall be given to this generation." 13. Then he dismissed them, again got into the boat, and went off toward the other side.

NOTES

11. *The Pharisees:* The Pharisees appear as opponents of Jesus in 2:16 (scribes of the Pharisees); 2:24; 3:6 (with the Herodians); 7:1; 10:2; and 12:13 (with Herodians)—usually in disputes over legal issues. Thus their introduction here is somewhat out of character. They are absent from the Passion narrative and play no role in the death of Jesus.

began to argue: Mark often uses "begin" *(archesthai)* as a simple modal verb with little nuance of a break in time. "Argue" *(syzētein)* often connotes a dispute within a group (1:27; 9:10, 14, 16; 12:28); its root, "seek" *(zētein)* provides a word play with "seeking" in v. 12, the first of a number of hostile instances of "seeking" (8:12, 18; 12:12; 14:1, 11, 55).

a sign from heaven: In both classical and Hellenistic Greek *sēmeion* ("sign") refers to a mark by which something is known. Here it means "authenticating sign" and does not carry the nuance of "symbol" as in English or in the Johannine usage. In Mark and the other Synoptics it is never used for the miracles of Jesus (which in Mark are primarily called *dynameis*, "works of power"). In Mark it is associated with claims and actions of false prophets (13:22). The sign "from heaven" can be either some cosmic event heralding the end of the age (13:22-26) or a reverential way of speaking about God (that is, a sign from God or a divine sign). The second interpretation seems more likely in light of the theological passive in Jesus' response, "no sign shall be given," that is, by God. See the Interpretation about reasons for seeking signs.

in order to test him: The sentence in Greek consists of a series of participles without conjunctions that has the effect of joining more closely the "seeking" and the hostile testing (see 10:2; 12:15). It also evokes the motif of testing of the righteous one (see Wis 2:17-21) to see if that person is truly "God's child" (2:18). The "testing" of Jesus as the righteous sufferer not only by his opponents but also by God (1:13; 14:32-42) is a major motif of Mark's christology.

12. *he sighed from the depths of his spirit:* The Greek for "sigh" *(anastenazein)* is used only here in the NT, and not only suggests anguish at the challenge but also prepares readers for the solemn form of response that will follow. "Spirit" *(pneuma)* suggests Jesus' inner disposition (2:8) and is also associated with power. Rather ironically, when denying this sign Jesus appears as even more powerful than he does in the feeding narratives.

this generation: Though "generation" *(genea)* means descent from a common ancestor, it comes to mean all those born or living at the same time (BAGD). The nuance here is negative (see Gen 7:1; Ps 95:10)—a theme that is made explicit in 8:38 ("this evil and adulterous generation") and in 9:19 ("unbelieving generation"). In light of 13:30 ("this generation will not pass away until all these things are accomplished") it may also reflect the common eschatological belief that evil will reign in the period before the end time.

Amen I say to you: This is a particularly solemn form of speech that echoes Jesus' response to an earlier and more serious challenge when he is charged with casting out demons by the power of Beelzebul (3:28). It appears frequently in Mark in a context of both threat (3:28; 8:12; 9:1; 13:30; 14:18, 30) and promise (9:41; 10:15, 29; 11:22; 12:43; 14:9, 25). During the Passion narrative, when the "Amen" sayings of Jesus are fulfilled (14:18, 30), the reader will realize the reliability of the other "Amen" sayings.

no sign shall be given: The Greek here ("if a sign will be given to this generation") does not make literal sense. After the solemn affirmation, however, the Greek construction appears to be an elliptical form of a Hebrew oath formula (e.g., "if I do such a thing, may I die"). A modern variation of the formula would be "I'll be damned if such and such happens." This is the only NT use of the formula and is in stark contrast to Jesus' attack on oaths in Matt 5:33-37, which may explain Matthew's omission of this oath in 16:1-4.

13. *Then he dismissed them:* In most translations Jesus simply "leaves" *(apheis)* them. The verb can also mean "dismiss" or "send away." "Dismiss" captures better the authority of Jesus, who has silenced his adversaries since they never re-appear or actually speak in the narrative.

the other side: We learn from 8:22 that this final sea voyage in Mark ends at Bethsaida. This verse, like 8:10, serves as a transition from one audience (the Pharisees) to another (the disciples).

INTERPRETATION

Some editions/translations introduce the request for a sign by Mark 8:9b-10, the dismissal of the crowd and the sea voyage to Dalmanutha, since Mark often begins pericopes with the arrival of Jesus at a new place. More accurately, those verses are bridges or transitional verses for a narrative that itself is transitional from the actual feeding to the discussion of its deeper significance (8:14-21).

The narrative is in the form of a riposte or challenge to the authority of Jesus. In contrast to the crowds that thronged around him in the previous narrative, here Jesus and the Pharisees are isolated with very little supporting cast. The visual starkness of the scene underscores the sharp verbal response of Jesus.

The Pharisees are demanding a sign from God that will apparently confirm the authority and power of Jesus. In the OT prophetic messages and activity were often confirmed by divine signs (2 Kgs 20:8-9; Isa 7:11-14; 55:13; Ezek 12:11; 24:27), and prophets were expected to demonstrate signs of their authenticity (see Deut 18:20-22). John 6:14 reflects a similar tradition when, in commenting after the feeding of the 5000, it says: "when the people saw the sign which he had done, they said: 'This is indeed the prophet who is to come into the world.'" As Richard A. Horsley has suggested, during the time of Jesus there were "oracular" prophets (e.g., 1 Cor 12:28; 13:2; 14:1-5) and "action" or "sign" prophets. Mark warns against false prophets in 13:22, and Matthew (7:22) knows of both kinds while also warning about the danger they cause. Josephus cautions against "impostors and demagogues" who "under the guise of divine inspiration" provoked revolutionary acts by promising people signs of divine action (*War* 2.259; *Ant.* 20.168; cf. Acts 5:36-37). In defending himself against the "super-apostles" Paul can say: "the signs of a true apostle were performed among you in all patience, with signs and wonders and mighty works" (2 Cor 12:12). The question of authenticating signs for prophets was urgent in the first century.

The intertextual development of the "sign challenge" provides a window into the growth and change of early traditions. Mark's critical presentation of sign-seeking is similar to Paul's criticism: "Jews ask for signs and Greeks seek wisdom" (1 Cor 1:22). Comparison of Mark 8:11-13 with Matt 12:38-42; 16:1-4; and Luke 11:16, 29-32 suggests that there were two early versions of a "sign challenge," one in Mark in which no sign is given, and another in Q where only the sign of Jonah is given. Matthew (when following Mark) develops the Markan narrative into a discourse about reading the signs of the times and expands the denial of the sign ("no sign will be given") by adding "except the sign of Jonah" without specifying in what sense Jonah was a sign (Matt 16:1-4). When adapting the Q version of the pericope Luke also says that no sign will be given except the sign of Jonah, but he then makes it refer to the preaching of Jonah to the people of Nineveh, who repented, in contrast with those who resisted the teaching of Jesus (Luke 11:29-32). Matthew edits Q to make the sign of Jonah refer not simply to the preaching of Jesus but to Jonah's three days in the belly of the whale, a type of the three days the Son of Man will spend in the heart of the earth. Matthew thus extends the rejection of Jesus' preaching to the rejection of the post-resurrection proclamation of the church. The Gospel of John has a complex tradition. In John 4:48 Jesus says critically to the official at Capernaum: "Unless you see signs and wonders, you will not believe." Yet in the first half of the gospel (John 1–12) Jesus performs many signs that conceal greater truths and are intended to lead people to deeper faith, even though the most profound faith is in the person of Jesus rather than in signs (20:29-31). Mark's version of the dispute, with its pointed and powerful response from Jesus, argues for his dependence on an early tradition.

Mark does not deny that the mighty works of Jesus are manifestations of God's power, but he insists that these works are experienced by people with faith (2:5; 5:34; 10:52); miracles do not produce faith. The demand to Jesus to produce another sign and his denial of the sign at the end of a sequence of mighty works (Mark 7:24–8:10) foreshadows the mocking challenge to Jesus to come down from the cross "that we may see and believe" (15:32). Mark's Gospel, which begins with a radical call to faith (1:15), ends with that same radical demand.

FOR REFERENCE AND FURTHER STUDY

Buchanan, George W. "Some Vow and Oath Formulas in the New Testament." *HTR* 58 (1965) 319-36.

Edwards, Richard A. *The Sign of Jonah in the Theology of the Evangelists and Q.* London: S.C.M., 1971.

Gibson, Jeffrey B. "Another Look at Why Jesus 'Sighs Deeply': *anastenazo* in Mark 8:12a," *JTS* 47 (1996) 131–40.

_____. "Jesus' Refusal to Produce a 'Sign' (Mk 8.11-13)," *JSNT* 38 (1990) 37–66.

Horsley, Richard A., and John S. Hanson. *Bandits, Prophets, and Messiahs. Popular Movements at the Time of Jesus.* San Francisco: Harper & Row, 1985.

Swetnam, James. "No Sign of Jonah," *Bib* 66 (1985) 126–30.

30. *A Further Misunderstanding by the Disciples and the Conclusion of the Bread Section* (8:14-21)

14. Now they [the disciples] forgot to take loaves of bread, except for a single loaf that they had with them in the boat. 15. Then he [Jesus] spoke up and began to warn them strongly: "Look out; be wary of the leaven of the Pharisees and the leaven of Herod." 16. Meanwhile they supposed among themselves that it was because they had no bread. 17. And he was aware of this and said to them: "Why do you suppose that it is because you have no bread? Do you not yet understand or grasp what has happened? Is the heart of all of you still hardened? 18. Do you have eyes and not really see, and ears and not really hear? And don't you remember? 19. When I broke the five loaves for the five thousand, how many baskets full of fragments did you take up?" They answered: "Twelve." 20. "And when the seven for the four thousand, how many containers full of fragments did you pick up?" Then they said: "Seven." 21. Then he said to them: "And still do you not grasp what has happened?"

NOTES

14. *forgot to take loaves of bread:* This introductory phrase seems artificial and serves almost as a stage prop to prepare for the central topic of the narrative, the disciples' misunderstanding of the bread miracles.

    single loaf: The allusion to the "single loaf" is unclear. Given the subsequent criticism of the disciples, it may recall the command of Jesus to the disciples not to take even a single loaf on their missionary journeys (6:8). Many commentators find it to be a veiled allusion to the presence of Jesus, especially since the word "bread" *(artos)* is not used after this narrative until 14:22, when Jesus pronounces that the bread is his body.

15. *be wary of the leaven of the Pharisees:* Since Luke 12:1 hands on a version of this saying in a complex of Q material some authors argue that a version of this

warning appeared in both Mark and Q. Leaven or yeast is a hidden and small element that, though essential to fermentation in baking, is also sometimes a symbol of corruption because it can cause bread to become stale or moldy. "Leaven" is then used symbolically for a morally corrupting element (see 1 Cor 5:6-8; Gal 5:9; also in Greco-Roman authors such as Plutarch, *Quaestiones Romanae* 109, and Persius, *Satires* 1.24). The reference to the Pharisees recalls the dispute over signs in 8:11-13. Though Matthew (16:12) describes the leaven of the Pharisees as their teaching, Mark leaves the reference open-ended. While the Pharisees are often opponents of Jesus in Mark, their primary objections are to his actions (2:16, 18, 24; 3:1-6; 7:1-5). Because of the proximity of 8:11-13, the "leaven of the Pharisees" is most likely their desire for an authenticating sign from Jesus.

the leaven of Herod: This is also altered by Matthew (16:6) to "the leaven of the Sadducees," since Herod never "teaches." In Mark the "corrupting influence" of Herod may be an echo of 3:6 where Pharisees and Herodians plot to kill Jesus, or a reference to Herod's misunderstanding of Jesus in 6:14-16. The two "misunderstandings" set the stage for the misunderstanding by the disciples.

16. *they supposed among themselves:* As frequently in Mark, the reader is made privy to private thoughts (2:6-8; 5:28; 6:26; 9:34; 10:41).

    because they had no bread: The misunderstanding by the disciples is similar here to the technique of ironic misunderstanding found in John where a fairly crass interpretation leads to a deeper spiritual truth (e.g., John 3:3-4; 4:10-12; 7:35, 41-42; 11:50).

17. *Do you not yet understand or grasp what has happened?:* Literally "do you not know or understand?" Both "know" *(noeite)* and "understand" *(syniete)* have nuances that are different from the English "intellectualistic" use of the terms. The terms mean rather to accept something or get hold of it. In the OT knowledge and understanding are often a gift of God and are located in the heart (Isa 6:9-10), and their objects are often the works of God (Ps 28:5; Job 36:24-29; see Hans Conzelmann, "συνίημι, κτλ.," *TDNT* 7:888–96). Jesus' rebuke echoes the charge against the outsiders in 4:10-12 (quoting Isa 6:9-10), and links this pericope closely with the first misunderstanding about the bread (6:52), which also occurs in a boat. The addition of "not yet" *(oupō)* adds a certain poignancy to Jesus' words, with the sense of not understanding "even after seeing all that I have done?"

    Is the heart of all of you still hardened?: In contrast to most translations we have followed the Greek in retaining the singular "heart," which underscores the unified misunderstanding on the disciples' part. "Hardened heart" is a frequent OT usage for willful resistance to signs of God's presence, especially by Pharaoh (e.g., Exod 10:1, 20, 27; 11:10; 14:8) and by Israel (e.g., Ezek 3:7; 11:19). This is the harshest criticism of the disciples in the gospel.

18. *eyes and not really see, and ears and not really hear:* This is a direct quotation from Jer 5:21 (cf., Ezek 3:7; 12:2) and is similar to Mark's use of Isa 6:9-10 in 4:10-12. There is also biting irony here, since this rebuke comes at the end of that long section of the gospel characterized by Jesus' public and visible works of

power. These works evoke resounding praise and acclamation, which the disciples could hardly fail to see and hear.

And don't you remember?: This question serves to introduce the recollection of the two feedings, where the answer of the disciples implies that they do remember. Yet seeing, hearing, and remembering are not enough to surmount the disciples' misunderstanding. This indicates that the misunderstanding is on a far deeper level than the question of bread.

19. *baskets full of fragments:* The word "full" here and in v. 20 stresses the superabundant results of the miracle and in turn heightens the obtuseness of the disciples.

20. *seven for the four thousand:* In each retrospective reference to the feedings the distinctive terminology of each feeding is used, which shows Mark's clear intention to both unite and highlight their significance.

21. *And still do you not grasp what has happened?:* This question virtually repeats 8:17 and is another instance of Mark's "sandwiching technique." Though most translations interpret the sentence as a question, it could also be taken as an exclamation of Jesus' disappointment. Due to its location at the end of the first major section of the gospel, the question ranges beyond the misunderstanding over the bread and confronts readers with the question whether a true grasp of Jesus can exist simply on the basis of his powerful teaching and powerful deeds (1:21-28). They must still confront the mystery of the cross.

INTERPRETATION

This pericope, which is variously named by commentators as "Warning Against the Leaven of the Pharisees and of Herod" (Guelich), "The Blindness of the Disciples" (Nineham), and "The Mystery of the Loaves" (Taylor), is one of the most enigmatic in Mark's Gospel. Its Greek style is cramped and allusive, and the flow of the narrative is obscure. There are a number of textual variations, and Matthew (16:5-12) alters the passage by omitting the enigmatic phrase about one loaf and the reference to the hardened heart of the disciples. He also alters the text by explicitly describing the leaven as the "teaching" of the Pharisees and of the Sadducees (substituting the latter for Mark's "the leaven of Herod").

It begins with the somewhat strange statement that the disciples forgot to bring bread (lit. "breads" or "loaves") and had only one loaf. Jesus then issues a double warning against the leaven of the Pharisees and of Herod that seems unrelated to the forgetfulness of the disciples. Yet Jesus never returns to the Pharisees and Herod. His warning is followed by a familiar pattern of misunderstanding by the disciples, of which Jesus is simultaneously aware. He then reproaches the disciples in the harshest criticism of them yet in the gospel by citing Jeremiah's critique of Judah for not recognizing the wondrous acts of God (Jer 5:21: "Hear this, O foolish and senseless people, who have eyes but do not see, who have ears but do not hear"), which is similar to the use of Isa 6:9-10 in his criticism of outsiders earlier in the gospel (4:10-12). This is followed by his subsequent rhetorical question: "Is the heart of all of you still hardened?," which recalls the earlier rebuke over their misunderstanding of the first miracle of the bread (6:52).

Interpretations of this narrative divide over just what is alluded to by the disciples' "bread obtuseness." Many commentators argue for a christological interpretation; that is, neither the Pharisees nor the disciples have a true understanding of Jesus and continue to doubt his power (Morna D. Hooker, *Gospel* 192; Robert H. Gundry, *Mark* 407–10; Dennis E. Nineham, *Saint Mark* 213–14). Others see here a hidden debate over the Eucharist in the Markan community and suggest that some fail to see that Jesus himself is the one bread that will bring Jews and Gentiles together, or that the community faced a crisis situation like that in 1 Cor 5:1-13 in celebrating the Eucharist without having confronted the presence of "old leaven" (i.e., a corrupting influence) in its midst (Quentin Quesnell, *Mind of Mark*). A variation of this is the suggestion that there are people in Mark's community for whom the Eucharist is a celebration of the power and presence of God rather than a memorial of Jesus' suffering and death (Paul Achtemeier, *Mark*).

While this enigmatic narrative may continue to conceal its meaning, a number of considerations suggest a combination of a christological and a eucharistic meaning. The term "bread" appears sixteen times between 6:8 and 8:19, and only once in the remainder of the gospel when Jesus is himself the bread (14:22). Structurally this narrative is of great importance. The earlier rebuke that climaxed a sea voyage (6:45-52) concludes a sub-section of the gospel beginning at 6:7 where the high point of Jesus' activity is the feeding of 5000 in Jewish territory. The present narrative concludes a section where Jesus, also in the context of a sea voyage, has fed the 4000 in non-Jewish territory. It also concludes the motif of "bread" that has been interwoven through the previous three chapters. The explicit mention of the two feedings by Jesus in 8:19-20 shows that Mark views this narrative as a culmination to the first major section of the whole gospel (1:1–8:21). Here the disciples are challenged to see Jesus as the one bread who unites both Jews and Gentiles.

In its criticism of the disciples this narrative not only looks backward to the blindness of the disciples but also prepares for the transitional narrative of the gift of sight in 8:22-26. The healing of the blind man in 8:22-26 serves as a "bookend" or bracketing pericope for the great middle section of the gospel (8:27–10:45), which then concludes with another giving-of-sight story (10:46-52). In the following major division of the gospel (8:22–10:52) misunderstanding by the disciples is one of the constitutive elements of the plot. The dialogue between Jesus and his disciples in 8:14-21 and their obtuseness clearly recall important elements in the whole first part of the gospel and foreshadow imminent deeper divisions not over bread but over the meaning of the life and death of Jesus. In following the spiritual journey of the disciples, Mark's readers are invited to enter for themselves more deeply into the challenge that Jesus' words will pose for them in the following section.

FOR REFERENCE AND FURTHER STUDY

Beck, Norman A. "Reclaiming a Biblical Text: The Mark 8:14-21 Discussion About Bread in the Boat," *CBQ* 43 (1981) 49–56.
Countryman, L. William. "How Many Baskets Full? Mark 8:14-21 and the Value of Miracles in Mark," *CBQ* 47 (1985) 643–55.
Gibson, Jeffrey B. "The Rebuke of the Disciples in Mark 8:14-21," *JSNT* 27 (1986) 31–47.
Manek, Jindrich. "Mark viii,14-21," *NovT* 7 (1964–65) 10–14.
Mitton, Charles L. "Leaven," *ExpTim* 84 (1972–73) 339–43.

31. *The Gradual Healing of a Blind Man* (8:22-26)

22. Then they [Jesus and his disciples] came to Bethsaida. And they brought a blind man to him and begged him to touch him. 23. Then he [Jesus] took hold of the blind man's hand and led him outside the village. And he spat on his eyes, laid his hands on him, and asked him: "Do you see anything?" 24. And he began to see again and said: "I see humans as I see trees—but moving about." 25. Then once again he [Jesus] laid his hands on his eyes. And he came to see again clearly, and his sight was restored, and he was seeing everything distinctly. 26. Then he [Jesus] sent him home with the word: "Do not even enter the village."

NOTES

22. *they [Jesus and his disciples] came:* In the Greek text all the verbs are in the historical present ("come . . . bring . . . beg"), one of Mark's favorite constructions designed to make a story more vivid. The name of Jesus is never mentioned in the passage, with the result that it is hard sometimes to know who is doing what to whom. To clarify matters at key points we have inserted the name of Jesus in square brackets.

to Bethsaida: a town on the northeast corner of the Sea of Galilee. The small fishing village (the name means "house of fishermen") was raised to the honor of a city by the tetrarch Philip and renamed Bethsaida Julias in honor of the emperor Augustus' daughter. The feeding of the 5000 takes place in the area (see Mark 6:45). For recent archaeological excavations at et-Tell and its identification as NT Bethsaida, see Fred Strickert, *Bethsaida: Home of the Apostles* (Collegeville: The Liturgical Press, 1998).

they brought . . . begged: The subject switches from Jesus and his disciples to an impersonal "they," who presumably are friends of the blind man. As in 2:3-5, their faith shown in bringing the blind man to Jesus is rewarded by his healing.

a blind man: This is the first healing of a blind person in Mark (see also 10:46-52) and the first use of the word *typhlos* ("blind") in this gospel. By contrast, Matthew uses *typhlos* frequently, especially in the context of summaries of Jesus' activities and multiple healings.

to touch him: For the powerful healing touch of Jesus see Mark 1:41 and 7:33. The assumption is that divine power resides in Jesus and that contact with him can bring about physical healing (see 5:28; 6:56).

23. *took hold of the blind man's hand:* The healing is more complicated and gradual than the friends probably expected, and it takes place apart from them and whatever crowd may have gathered in the village (*kōmē* as opposed to *polis*), thus preparing for Jesus' command in 8:26.

    spat on his eyes, laid his hands on him: The healing ritual is reminiscent of that in Mark 7:33 where Jesus spits and touches the tongue of the man who was deaf and spoke with difficulty. See also the story of the man born blind in John 9:6-7. For accounts about Vespasian healing a blind man by applying his own saliva to the man's eyes see Tacitus, *Histories* 4.81, and Suetonius, *Vespasian* 7. For a reference to Abraham laying hands on Pharaoh to drive out his evil spirit see the Qumran *Genesis Apocryphon* (1QapGen) 21:29.

    Do you see anything?: Literally "if you see anything." This unusual construction can be explained either as elliptical ("I ask if you see anything") or as a reflex of a Hebrew construction in which the Greek word *ei* ("if") serves as the equivalent of the Hebrew interrogative marker *h-*.

24. *to see again:* The Greek verb *anablepein* implies that the man had lost his sight and now comes to see again (in contrast to John 9:1, 20, where the man was born blind). But his recovery of sight is not yet complete.

    I see humans as I see trees—but moving about: Literally "I see humans that like trees I see them walking." The point is that the man does not yet see things sharply and distinctly, and so he can barely tell the difference between humans and trees. The fact that he does know the difference between humans and trees confirms that he once had sight. His problem is that he now can only tell humans from trees by the fact that humans walk and trees do not.

25. *once again he [Jesus] laid his hands on his eyes:* From 8:23 it was not clear where Jesus laid his hands the first time. In 7:33 Jesus puts his fingers in the ears of

the deaf man and touches his tongue. That Jesus must perform the healing ritual "once again" indicates that it was not entirely successful the first time.

he came to see again clearly, and his sight was restored, and he was seeing everything distinctly: The completeness of the cure is emphasized by three different and quite striking verbs. That "he came to see again" *(dieblepsen)* can be taken to mean that he began (inceptive) to see clearly again or that he succeeded (effective) in seeing clearly again. That "his sight was restored" *(apekatestē)* confirms that the story is about the recovery of sight and suggests that God was the agent of his healing (the divine passive construction). That "he was seeing everything *(eneblepen)* distinctly" calls attention to the intensity of his seeing *(emblepein* means "look at, fix one's gaze upon") and to his own ongoing ability to see (imperfect, "was seeing"). The final adverb *tēlaugōs,* found only here in the NT, means "far shining" and then "clearly, plainly, distinctly" and underscores the cure's completeness.

26. *he [Jesus] sent him home:* Whereas Jesus sent the Gerasene demoniac home with instructions to proclaim openly what the Lord had done for him (5:19), here he sends the formerly blind man home as a way of avoiding publicity, presumably as part of the "secrecy" motif.

Do not even enter the village: In this reading there is no reason given why the man should not enter the village/city of Bethsaida. The other readings in the manuscripts reflect attempts to supply the reason: "Do not tell anyone in the village"; "Do not even enter the village, and do not even tell anyone in the village"; and "Go to your home and do not tell anyone." The reading adopted here appears in good manuscripts, is "more difficult" because it gives no reason, and thus explains the genesis of the other readings (because they supply a reason).

INTERPRETATION

The account of the gradual healing of the blind man in Mark 8:22-26 is both unusual and pivotal in Mark's narrative. It is unusual because Jesus the healer is not immediately and completely successful. This may explain why both Matthew (but see Matt 9:27-31) and Luke omit the episode. It is pivotal because it provides a bridge between Jesus' activities in Galilee (1:14–8:21) and his journey to Jerusalem (8:27–10:52) and sets the theme and tone of the journey narrative: the need to come to understand the teaching and healing activity of Jesus in light of the mystery of the cross.

The narrative is a healing story with some dialogue. A blind man is brought to Jesus (8:22); those who bring him implicitly display faith in Jesus' power to heal him. The first stage in the healing (8:23-24) involves a complex (almost "magical") ritual and takes place outside of Bethsaida. The result is a partial restoration of the man's sight at least so that he can distinguish humans from trees insofar as the former walk about. The second stage (8:25) brings about a full restoration of the man's sight. The episode ends (8:26) not with the amazement of the crowd or a proclamation by the man who was healed, but rather with Jesus sending him home and commanding him not to enter the village.

There are many verbal similarities between Mark 7:31-37 and 8:22-26. Both accounts include the ritualistic actions of spitting and touching but also coincide in the words used to introduce the scenes (7:32-33a and 8:22-23a) and the concluding commands to silence (explicit in 7:36 and implicit in 8:26). They are linked further by their common reference to Isa 35:5-6a, which is explicit in 7:37b ("the ears of the deaf [shall be] unstopped . . . the tongue of the speechless sing for joy") and implicit in 8:22-26 ("the eyes of the blind shall be opened").

Even more important to the structure of Mark's Gospel are the links with the Bartimaeus story in 10:46-52. These two miraculous giving-of-sight stories bracket the journey narrative (8:27–10:45) and by their position acquire important symbolic significance. Throughout the journey narrative we will come to see more clearly the mystery of the cross—Jesus' death and resurrection—in the life of Jesus and in the lives of those who follow him. There are, of course, differences between the two accounts. Whereas the man of Mark 8:22-26 is healed gradually and told not to go to his village, Bartimaeus makes a confession of faith in Jesus as the (healing) Son of David, is cured instantly and completely, and follows Jesus on "the way" toward Jerusalem.

By placing 8:22-26 at the beginning of the journey narrative Mark has imbued the story of the gradual giving of sight to a blind man with symbolic or spiritual value. It will take time for Mark's readers to absorb the idea of Jesus as the suffering Messiah. Indeed, the disciples who are the immediate audience for Jesus' teaching on the way do not "get it" until after Jesus' death and resurrection.

Jesus' final command that the newly re-sighted man should not even enter the village (8:26) also moves forward the "secrecy" motif (see 1:44; 5:43; 7:36). In the course of the journey narrative Mark's readers will come gradually to see what kind of a Messiah Jesus really is and that he cannot be understood or appreciated apart from the mystery of the cross.

Rather than being distracted or put off by the "magical" healing rituals, Jesus' initial lack of success as a healer, and his command not to enter the village, teachers and preachers need to focus on the theological significance that Mark has given to the story by placing it at the beginning of the journey in which the true character of Jesus' messiahship will be revealed. Moreover, most of us can identify with the experience of faith as a gradual process in which sometimes things look blurry and at other times we come to see clearly.

FOR REFERENCE AND FURTHER STUDY

Baudoz, Jean-François. "Mc 7,31-37 et Mc 8.22-26. Géographie et théologie," *RB* 102 (1995) 560–69.

Collange, Jean-François. "La déroute de l'aveugle (Mc 8,22-26). Ecriture et pratique chrétienne," *Revue d'Historie et de Philosophie Religieuses* 66 (1986) 21–28.

Howard, J. Keir. "Men as Trees, Walking: Mark 8.22-26," *SJT* 37 (1984) 163–70.

Johnson, E. S. "Mark 8:22-26: The Blind Man from Bethsaida," *NTS* 25 (1978–79) 370–83.

Marcus, Joel. "A Note on Markan Optics," *NTS* 45 (1999) 250–56.

Miller, J. I. "Was Tischendorf really wrong? Mark 8:26b Revisited," *NovT* 28 (1986) 97–103.

Sugirtharajah, Rasia S. "Men, Trees and Walking: A Conjectural Solution to Mk 8:24," *ExpTim* 103 (1992) 172–74.

32. *Peter's Confession, the First Passion Prediction, Peter's Misunderstanding, and the Demands of Discipleship* (8:27-38)

27. Then Jesus and his disciples went toward the villages of Caesarea Philippi. And on the way he questioned his disciples and said to them: "Who are people saying that I am?" 28. They said in reply: "[Some say] John the Baptist, and others Elijah, and still others one of the prophets." 29. And he questioned them further: "But you—who do you say that I am?" Peter answered him: "You are the Messiah." 30. But he forbade them to tell anyone about him. 31. And he began to teach them that it is necessary that the Son of Man suffer many things and be rejected by the elders and chief priests and scribes, and be put to death, and after three days rise again. 32. And he was saying this quite openly. But Peter took him aside and began to rebuke him. 33. But he [Jesus] turned, looked at his disciples, and rebuked Peter, saying: "Get behind me, Satan, for your mind is not on the things of God but on the things of humans." 34. And he summoned the crowd along with his disciples, and he said to them: "If anyone wishes to follow after me, let that person deny himself and take up his cross and follow me. 35. For whoever wishes to save his soul will lose it. But whoever will lose his soul on account of me and of the gospel will save it. 36. For what does it profit a person to gain the whole world and suffer the loss of his soul? 37. For what may a person give as a recompense for his soul? 38. For whoever is ashamed of me and of my teachings in this adulterous and sinful generation, the Son of Man will be ashamed of him when he comes in the glory of his Father along with the holy angels."

NOTES

27. *Jesus and his disciples:* Since Mark 8:22-26 contained no explicit mention of Jesus or his disciples (hence the need for square brackets in our translation), the evangelist has to reintroduce the characters who will be most prominent in the journey narrative (8:27–10:45).

the villages of Caesarea Philippi: The term "villages" refers to the small settlements (like "suburbs") surrounding the larger city. Located on the southern slope of Mount Hermon and near one of the sources of the river Jordan, this area represents the northern tip of the land of Israel. The emperor Augustus had given the city (which was then named Panion after the Greek god Pan) to Herod the Great. Herod's son Philip rebuilt the city and named it after the emperor and himself (thus Caesarea Philippi, not to be confused with Caesarea Maritima on the Mediterranean coast).

on the way: The journey taken by Jesus and his disciples will go from Caesarea Philippi (8:27) to Jerusalem (11:1). On the way there will be a stop at the Mount of Transfiguration (9:2), a passing through Galilee (9:30) and a stop at Capernaum (9:33), arrival in the region of Judea and beyond the Jordan (10:1), a resolute focus on going up to Jerusalem (10:32), and arrival in Jericho (10:46). More important than the geographical itinerary, however, is the spiritual itinerary in which Mark's readers are led to face the mystery of the cross and its implications for the way of discipleship.

he questioned . . . and said: One might expect the disciples to question the teacher. The key verb in 8:27-30 is "say" *(legein)*, and most of the statements are introduced by a double verb of saying: "he asked . . . saying" (8:27b), "they said . . . saying" (8:28a), and "Peter answered and said" (8:29b).

28. *John the Baptist . . . Elijah . . . one of the prophets:* The same list of popular identifications of Jesus appeared in the introduction to the account of the death of John the Baptist under Herod Antipas (Mark 6:14-15). Since Jesus received John's baptism (Mark 1:9) and at some point was attached to John's movement and shared at least some of John's expectations about the coming kingdom of God, it is not surprising that Jesus should be identified as John returned to life. The traditions about Elijah's mysterious departure (2 Kgs 2:1-12) and his role as precursor of "the great and terrible day of the Lord" (Mal 4:5) probably led to speculation about Jesus, as the prophet of God's kingdom, being Elijah (but see Mark 9:11-13). Certainly it was natural that Jesus, who claimed to speak for God about the coming kingdom of God, should be regarded as a prophet. There may even have been a hint about Jesus as the prophet like Moses mentioned in Deut 18:15. While there is some truth in each of these three identifications, there is much more to Jesus' identity than any one of them conveys.

29. *Peter answered:* As is often the case in Mark's Gospel (see 8:32; 9:5; 10:28; 11:21), Peter serves as the spokesman for Jesus' disciples. He was among the first disciples called (1:16-20) and his name appeared first in the list of the Twelve (3:16).

You are the Messiah: Both *māšîaḥ* in Hebrew and *christos* in Greek mean "the anointed one." In the OT priests, prophets, and kings were anointed in rites that seem also to convey the idea of their divine election. In Jesus' time Messiah/Christ/Anointed was by no means a univocal term, and so one can correctly speak about Judaisms and their messiahs. However, one prominent form of messianism in the Second Temple period is represented by the hope for a future Davidic king who would restore justice and the good fortunes of God's people (see *Psalms of Solomon* 17). Such a messiah would naturally be a threat to the Roman rulers and their Jewish collaborators in the land of Israel. In light of what Jesus did (especially his acts of "power") and said (his claims about sonship, his pivotal role in God's plan, and his sayings about the Temple), it is likely that some people did identify Jesus as such a messiah—at least this is what Mark suggests (see 1:1).

30. *He forbade them to tell anyone about him:* From the historical perspective it would have been dangerous for the disciples to proclaim that Jesus is the Messiah, since it would infuriate the Roman and Jewish officials. In fact, such popular speculation may have contributed to the events leading to Jesus' death (see Mark 14:61). From the Markan narrative and theological perspective, however, the disciples (and Mark's readers) need clarification about what kind of messiah Jesus really is (not the kind described in *Psalms of Solomon* 17) and what the implications of Jesus' messiahship are for his disciples (surely not to be rulers over an earthly kingdom). During the journey narrative at least part of the messianic secret will be unfolded: that Jesus is a suffering Messiah.

31. *he began to teach them:* Mark uses the auxiliary verb *archesthai* ("begin") twenty-six times in his gospel and twice here in successive verses *(ērxato).* Having accepted Peter's confession that he is the Messiah, Jesus now begins to explain the true nature of his messiahship and what it might mean for his followers.

    it is necessary: The impersonal verb *dei* ("it is necessary"), used here for the first time, carries an overtone of apocalyptic determinism and will become increasingly prominent as the gospel proceeds (see 9:11; 13:7, 10, 14; 14:31). It injects the idea of divine agency as God's plan unfolds in Jesus' Passion and in the end-time events (three occurrences in ch. 13). It also foreshadows Jesus' prayer in Gethsemane when he recognizes and accepts his imminent death as God's will (see 14:36). These events will take place according to the will of God.

    the Son of Man: Last used in 2:28, this title for Jesus will also become prominent in what follows (see 8:38; 9:9, 12, 31; 10:33, 45; 13:26; 14:21, 41, 62). It appears in each of three Passion predictions (8:31; 9:31; 10:33-34). In the OT (Ezekiel and Daniel) there is no explicit connection between the Son of Man and suffering.

    be rejected by the elders and chief priests and scribes: In the Markan Passion narrative these three groups constitute the leaders of the Jewish opposition to Jesus. The Pharisees, so prominent in the controversy stories during Jesus' public ministry, will disappear in the Passion narrative. The "elders" represent the Jewish leaders, perhaps members of the Sanhedrin and other influential figures. The "chief priests" include primarily Annas and Caiaphas and the upper levels of the Temple personnel. The "scribes" are the "intellectuals," not only skilled in reading and writing but also trained in traditional wisdom and the Torah (the law for Jews); for a description of the ideal scribe see Sir 39:1-11 (see also Christine Schams, *Jewish Scribes in the Second-Temple Period* [Sheffield: Sheffield Academic Press, 1998]).

be put to death: The same verb *apokteinein* appears in the other two Passion predictions (see 9:31; 10:34).

after three days rise again: The more usual NT terminology for the resurrection of Jesus is "on the third day" (see Hos 6:2) and "be raised" (divine passive). The Markan Passion predictions, however, are consistent in using "after three days" (apparently counting parts of Good Friday and Easter Sunday as full days) and the verb *anastēnai* ("rise") rather than *egeirein* ("raise"). While it is customary to describe Mark 8:31; 9:31; and 10:33-34 as Passion predictions, they each reach their climax by referring to Jesus' resurrection.

32. *he was saying this quite openly:* The imperfect *elalei* suggests repeated action on Jesus' part (see 2:2; 4:33). The adverb *parrēsia* derives from the noun for "courage, boldness, frankness," and here it means "openly, plainly." Nevertheless, the disciples fail to grasp Jesus' meaning.

Peter took him aside . . . to rebuke him: The precise reason for Peter's action is not specified, but the context suggests that Peter could not make the connection between the Messiah (8:29) or the Son of Man (8:31) and suffering. Compare Matt 16:16-22, where Peter extends and heightens his confession of Jesus' identity ("the Messiah, the Son of the living God," 16:16b), is blessed as the recipient of a divine revelation and appointed to be the "rock" on which the church is to be built (16:17-19), and makes a direct statement about Jesus' death ("God forbid, Lord! This shall never happen to you," 16:22).

33. *turned, looked at his disciples, and rebuked Peter:* Whereas Peter intends his rebuke of Jesus to be private, Jesus makes his rebuke of Peter with the disciples as his audience, thus making it a teaching opportunity. The two rebukes are linked by the verb *epitiman*—a term used earlier in the context of an exorcism (1:25) and the stilling of the storm (4:39).

Get behind me, Satan: The language is reminiscent of Matt 4:10. But, of course, Mark's temptation account is considerably shorter (1:12-13) and does not include this phrase. The Hebrew verb *śāṭan* means "test" or "tempt," which expresses well the role of the Satan figure in Job 1–2 and Zech 3:1-2. In NT times the figure of Satan becomes the principle of evil in the cosmic struggle that shapes human history until the eschaton (see Mark 1:12-13). By rejecting the plan of God that involves a suffering messiah/Son of Man, Peter puts himself on the wrong side of the struggle.

not on the things of God but on the things of humans: For similar constructions involving the verb *phronein* see Rom 8:5 ("the things of the flesh . . . the things of the spirit") and Col 3:2 ("things that are above . . . things that are on earth"). Jesus' charge against Peter reminds Mark's readers that the story of Jesus has a cosmic-eschatological significance, a theme introduced already in the prologue (1:1-13).

34. *The crowd along with his disciples:* The instructions about discipleship that fol-low are directed not only to those who are already disciples but also to anyone who might wish to learn about and become part of Jesus' movement.

   to follow after me: The verb *akolouthein* ("follow") has been Mark's favorite term for becoming a disciple of Jesus since the call of the first disciples (see 1:18; 2:14-15).

   deny himself and take up his cross and follow me: Translators who seek to use in-clusive language (as we generally do) face a problem in 8:34-38. To use plural forms instead of Mark's Greek singulars can blunt the element of personal challenge. While Mark probably envisioned both male and female disciples (see especially 15:40-41), he used masculine singular forms (as was customary in Greek) throughout 8:34-38. The basic meaning of *aparneisthai* ("deny one-self") is to act in a selfless way and to give up one's place as the center of things. The reference to the cross *(stauros)* immediately evokes in us (and surely in Mark's first readers too) thoughts about Jesus' own crucifixion, and underlines the basic dynamic of the whole journey narrative: Prospective dis-ciples must be willing to share the "way" of Jesus the suffering Messiah/Son of Man. While the cross saying does evoke the post-Easter situation, it is not impossible that the historical Jesus used such language. Crucifixion was a public punishment visited upon rebels and slaves, and the one being crucified was forced to carry the horizontal cross-beam to the place of execution (see 15:21, where Simon of Cyrene is compelled to help Jesus in doing so). The third condition ("and follow me") repeats the key word of the protasis. Whereas the first occurrence of "follow" refers to becoming a disciple, the second occurrence conveys the importance of persevering in following Jesus.

35. *save his soul . . . lose his soul:* The Greek word *psychē* also causes problems for translators. The traditional rendering as "soul" carries more philosophical (especially Platonic) connotations than the Semitic anthropology (Hebrew *nepeš*) can bear, though the Jewish apocalypses 4 *Ezra* and 2 *Baruch* (both writ-ten in the late first century C.E.) often use the word "soul" in what approaches the "Greek" sense. But to translate *psychē* as "life" (as many modern transla-tions do) probably says less than Mark wished to say. What is at stake is the inner core of the person, what constitutes the self, perhaps in the Markan con-text in the situation of potential martyrdom. The language of "saving" and "losing" suggests that there is also an eschatological or "afterlife" dimension to the saying (see 9:1), and that more than earthly happiness or peace of heart in the present is at issue.

   on account of me and of the gospel: Some manuscripts omit "of me." Both Matt 16:25 and Luke 9:24, however, contain "of me," though neither has "and of the gospel." For other Markan uses of *euaggelion* as the good news about Jesus' death and resurrection see 1:14, 15; 10:29; 13:10; and 14:9 (see also 16:15).

36. *profit . . . gain . . . loss:* The commercial vocabulary heightens the contrast with the spiritual dimension conveyed by *psychē* and confirms that *psychē* means more than "life" understood as physical survival in this world.

37. *recompense:* The word *antallagma* ("something given in exchange," see Sir 26:14) continues the commercial imagery and its contrast with *psychē* as the most precious aspect of the person (that is, something that money cannot buy).

38. *ashamed of me and of my teachings:* See "on account of me and of the gospel" in 8:35. Some manuscripts omit *logous* ("teachings") and simply read "me and mine."

    this adulterous and sinful generation: Compare Matt 12:39: "an evil and adulterous generation seeks a sign." Influenced by various OT phrases (Isa 1:4; Hos 2:4; etc.), this expression (found only here in the NT) criticizes the religious and moral behavior of Jesus' contemporaries (with "adultery" perhaps as a symbol for idolatry and apostasy as in Hosea and elsewhere in the OT).

    the Son of Man: Whereas in 8:31 the title appears in the context of Jesus' Passion and resurrection, here the context is the eschatological judgment. While it is possible that at some point in the pre-Markan tradition "Son of Man" referred to a glorious figure different from Jesus (as in Dan 7:13-14 and *1 Enoch* 37–71), for Mark the eschatological Son of Man is Jesus. This identification is confirmed by Matt 10:33: "Whoever denies me before humans, I will deny him before my heavenly Father."

    when he comes in the glory of his Father along with the holy angels: This "snapshot" of Jesus' parousia prepares for Mark 13:26 ("the Son of Man coming on the clouds with great power and glory") and 14:62 ("the Son of Man seated at the right hand of the Power and coming with the clouds of heaven"). Its presence at the end of Jesus' instructions gives the whole teaching on discipleship in 8:34-38 an eschatological framework (see Dan 7:13-14) and confirms that *psychē* must mean more than "life."

INTERPRETATION

Jesus' question to Peter in Mark 8:29 ("Who do you say that I am?") is the central theme of the entire gospel. From 1:21-28 onward Mark has emphasized Jesus' authority as a wonder-worker and a teacher. At the same time Mark has highlighted a series of misunderstandings and rejections of Jesus by the Pharisees and Herodians (3:6), Jesus' family (3:21) and neighbors in Nazareth (6:1-6), and his own disciples (8:14-21). The purpose of the Markan journey narrative in 8:27–10:45 is to clarify who Jesus is (christology) and what it means to follow him (discipleship). The key to understanding Jesus properly will turn out to be the mystery of the cross: Jesus the healer and teacher is the suffering Messiah/Son of Man. To follow him means to be willing to share in his Passion and death as well as his resurrection. The journey narrative is introduced (8:22-26) and concluded (10:46-52) by episodes in which Jesus bestows the gift of sight on two blind men. By following the journey narrative Mark's readers also come to see Jesus and his "way" more clearly.

The journey begins in 8:27-30 with Peter's confession of Jesus as the Messiah. This serves as the starting point for the rest of the material in the journey narrative, which is designed to explain what kind of Messiah Jesus is and what implications this identity has for his followers. In 8:31-38 we meet a pattern that will be repeated in 9:30-37 and 10:32-45: a prediction of Jesus' Passion, death, and resurrection (8:31); a misunderstanding by his disciples (8:32-33); and instructions on true discipleship (8:34-38). This pattern in turn provides the framework for the other discourses and narratives along the way.

Peter's confession of Jesus as the Messiah in 8:29 is the first use of *christos* since Mark 1:1. While prominent in the OT and some early Jewish writings (see the notes on 8:29), the term "Messiah" could be and was applied to many figures. Its obvious connection with King David in particular and Israelite kingship in general made it a dangerous title in first-century Palestine, since its use could inflame Jewish nationalism and lead to brutal repression from the Roman officials; see Richard A. Horsley, *Jesus and the Spiral of Violence* (San Francisco: Harper & Row, 1987). Its use with reference to Jesus played a large part in his execution as "King of the Jews" under Pontius Pilate (see 15:2, 12, 18, 26, 32). According to 15:32 the chief priests and scribes mocked Jesus in these terms: "Let the Christ, the King of Israel, come down from the cross. . . ."

Written roughly twenty to thirty years after Jesus' death, Paul's letters freely use *Christos* almost as a surname for Jesus ("Jesus Christ") and take its meaning for granted. It is even part of the very early pre-Pauline credal formula in 1 Cor 15:3-5: "Christ died for our sins. . . ." Paul appears to have had no problem in referring to Jesus as *Christos*.

Mark, however, does seem to have had a problem: How could Jesus the Jewish Messiah/Christ have died such a shameful death on a Roman cross? So the evangelist needed to interpret and redefine the title "Messiah" to take in the reality of the cross. In addition to the opening verse (1:1) and Peter's confession (8:29), Mark uses the word *Christos* in the following contexts: being given a cup of water in "the name of Christ" (9:41); the debate about "Christ the Son of David" (12:35); the warning against "false Christs" (13:21-22); the high priest's query whether Jesus is "the Christ, the Son of the Blessed" (14:61); and the taunt from the high priests and scribes about "Christ the King of Israel" coming down from the cross (15:32). There is also an effort to subordinate the title "Messiah" to "Lord" (12:35-37), while the Roman centurion at the cross affirms that Jesus is "Son of God" (15:39) rather than the Messiah/Christ.

The first of the three Passion predictions appears in 8:31. In content and language it is linked with the other Passion predictions in 9:31 and

10:33-34 ("Son of Man . . . kill . . . after three days . . . rise again"). An obvious question raised by these Passion predictions is whether the historical Jesus spoke in such detail about the fate awaiting him in Jerusalem. In fact, it is hard to escape the impression that the language of these texts has been influenced to some extent by the events described in Mark 14–16. Nevertheless, given the political situation in Palestine in Jesus' time it is also likely that Jesus recognized that his teachings and actions, as well as the popular enthusiasm that they were generating, might well get him into trouble with the Roman and Jewish authorities.

In the context of Mark's literary and theological plan, however, the even more important question is: Why did Jesus' disciples so totally fail to grasp what Jesus was telling them beforehand? According to Mark 8:31; 9:31; and 10:33-34, Jesus presented his disciples with a clear program for what would happen when they reached Jerusalem. But immediately after each prediction Jesus is misunderstood—by Peter (8:32-33), the whole group (9:32-34), and James and John (10:35-37). At this point in the gospel (see 8:14-21) the disciples have become negative examples for Mark's readers. By their misunderstandings and subsequent acts of treachery in the Passion narrative they serve as models of behavior to be avoided.

Peter's failure to accept the mystery of the cross is corrected and balanced by positive teachings about following Jesus in 8:34-38: the challenge to follow Jesus even to the cross (8:34), losing and gaining one's soul/life (8:35), the extraordinary value of one's *psychē* (8:36-37), and not being ashamed of the Son of Man (8:38). Although these sayings may once have existed separately, Mark (or a predecessor) brought them together on the basis of their content (discipleship) and keywords ("wish . . . for . . . soul . . . gain and lose . . . be ashamed"). In form the instruction is typical of Jewish Wisdom books (Proverbs, Sirach, etc.). The inclusion of the final saying about the Son of Man and the last judgment (8:38) has the effect of giving the collection a christological and eschatological dimension. The content of these sayings would have been especially challenging and comforting to a Christian community facing persecution, as seems to have been the case with Mark's first readers.

Mark 8:27-38 is a rich resource for those who seek to make Mark's Gospel come alive in the lives of Christians today. It sets before us the basic question of Mark's Gospel and indeed of the entire NT: Who do you say that I am? It confronts us with the mystery of the cross and challenges us to integrate the reality of Jesus' suffering (and our own) into our understanding of Jesus and discipleship. And it spells out the demands, value, and rewards of faithful following of Jesus. In a sense Mark 8:33, with its contrast between God's thoughts and human thoughts, is the nub of the gospel. Mark presents his first readers and today's reader with an exercise in "right thinking" about suffering.

For Reference and Further Study

Aichele, George. "Jesus' Frankness," *Semeia* 69–70 (1995) 261–80.

Bayer, Hans F. *Jesus' Predictions of Vindication and Resurrection.* Tübingen: J.C.B. Mohr [Paul Siebeck], 1986.

Beardslee, William A. "Saving One's Life by Losing It," *JAAR* 47 (1979) 57–72.

Bennett, W. J. "The Son of Man must . . .," *NovT* 17 (1975) 113–29.

Claudel, Gerard. *La confession de Pierre, trajectoire d'une péricope évangelique.* Paris: Gabalda, 1988.

Malina, Bruce J. "'Let Him Deny Himself' (Mark 8:34 & Par): A Social Psychological Model of Self-Denial," *BTB* 24 (1994) 106–19.

Osborne, B. A. E. "Peter: Stumbling Block and Satan," *NovT* 15 (1973) 187–90.

Rebell, Walter. "'Sein Leben verlieren' (Mark 8.35 parr.) als Strukturmoment vor- und nachösterlichen Glaubens," *NTS* 35 (1989) 202–18.

Rhoads, David. "Losing Life for Others: Mark's Standards of Judgment," *Int* 47 (1993) 358–69.

33. *The Transfiguration* (9:1-13)

1. And he said to them: "Amen I say to you: There are some people standing here who will not experience death until they see the kingdom of God come with power." 2. And after six days Jesus took with him Peter and James and John. And he brought them up a high mountain where they were alone by themselves. And he was transformed before them. 3. And his garments became gleaming, extraordinarily white, such as no bleacher on earth could whiten them. 4. And Elijah with Moses appeared to them, and they were conversing with Jesus. 5. And Peter spoke up and said: "It is good that we are here. Let us make three booths—one for you, one for Moses, and one for Elijah." 6. For he did not know what to say, since they were awestruck. 7. And there was a cloud overshadowing them, and a voice came from the cloud: "This is my beloved Son. Listen to him." 8. And suddenly when they looked around, they no longer saw anyone with them except only Jesus. 9. As they were coming down from the mountain, he ordered them that they should not tell anyone what they saw until the Son of Man had risen from the dead. 10. And they kept this matter to themselves, while discussing what it means to rise from the dead. 11. And they asked him: "Why do the scribes say that Elijah must come first?" 12. Then he said to them: "Elijah does indeed come first and restores everything. And how does it stand written about the Son of Man—that he should suffer much and be treated with contempt? 13. But I tell you that Elijah has already come and they did to him whatever they wished, as it has been written about him."

NOTES

1. *And he said to them:* Mark often uses this expression to make connections (see 2:27; 4:11, 21, 24; 6:10; 7:9; 8:21), especially when, as here, the connection is not immediately obvious. The verse serves as a bridge between 8:34-38 and 9:2-8.

   Amen I say to you: Whereas "Amen" often concludes prayers or statements, the use of "Amen" to introduce a statement is unusual and is often regarded as a speech-characteristic of the historical Jesus. Used already in 3:28 and 8:12, it becomes increasingly frequent in the second half of Mark's Gospel (see 9:41; 10:15, 29; 11:23; 12:43; 13:30; 14:9, 18, 25, 30).

   some people standing here: The Greek perfect participle *hestēkotōn* seems to carry a present sense here. In this context it refers most obviously to Peter, James, and John (9:2), though it could refer to the larger group of 8:34.

   experience death: The verb *geuesthai* ("taste") is used metaphorically with regard to death also in John 8:52 and Heb 2:9.

   the kingdom of God come: For the kingdom of God as the central theme of Jesus' preaching see Mark 1:15. The major interpretive problem here is posed by the perfect participle *elēlythuian*. Should it be taken as present in sense ("come") as seems to be the case with *hestēkotōn* ("standing") earlier in the verse? Then the kingdom is still future (though imminent). Or should it be taken as a true perfect ("has come")? Then the kingdom has already come (realized eschatology), and the task of "some standing here" is to recognize its presence. The former explanation better suits Mark's eschatology as expressed in 1:15.

   with power: The term *dynamis* is used by Mark with reference to Jesus' miracles (6:2, 5, 14; 9:39), to God (12:24; 14:62), and to the heavenly "powers" and to the coming of the Son of Man (13:25-26). Its appearance here *(en dynamei)* contributes to the eschatological mood of the episode that follows.

2. *after six days:* This precise time reference is puzzling. To what does it refer? It is explained in several ways: as part of a pre-Markan source that the evangelist carelessly took over, as an allusion to the theophany that Moses experienced after six days on Mount Sinai according to Exod 24:15-17, as pointing back to Peter's confession in 8:29, or as pointing forward to Jesus' "Passion week" in Jerusalem.

   Peter and James and John: Among the first disciples called (1:16-20), these three form an inner circle here as well as in 5:37 and 14:33.

   he brought them up: Mark does not say why Jesus brought them there. Luke's explanation ("to pray," Luke 9:28) is part of his editorial theme that Jesus prays at all the decisive moments in his life.

   a high mountain alone by themselves: The usual identifications include Mounts Hermon, Carmel, and Tabor (the traditional site since the fourth century). More important than the precise geographical location is the motif that mountains (Moriah, Sinai, Jerusalem, etc., as well as Olympus and many other non-Jewish sites) are places of communication with divine beings and of divine revelation. The emphatic adverbial clause "alone by themselves" *(kat' idian monous)* highlights the mysterious character of the episode.

he was transformed: The episode is known as the transfiguration on the strength of the Latin translation *transfiguratus est,* which was taken over into early English Bible versions. The Greek verb *metamorphōthē* implies a change in "form" *(morphē).* While the concept of metamorphosis was well known in the Greco-Roman world (see Ovid's *Metamorphoses*), in the context of early Christian theology a better approach may be through the christological hymn preserved in Phil 2:6-11: "who being in the form *(morphē)* of God . . . emptied himself . . . being born in the likeness of humans." In the transformation/transfiguration event the inner circle among Jesus' disciples receives a glimpse of Jesus' divine *morphē.*

3. *his garments became gleaming:* The dazzlingly white garments presumably show forth the glory of the one who wears them (see Rev 3:4; 7:9). Some commentators point out the absence of a reference to the face of Jesus in 9:3 (compare Matt 17:2 and Luke 9:29). The verb *stilbein* ("gleam, glitter, glisten") appears only here in the NT.

   extraordinarily white: The piling up of terms contributes to the brilliance of the scene. The comparison that follows concerns one who cleans or whitens woolen cloth ("bleacher, fuller"). The idea is that not even the best bleacher could produce something as dazzlingly white as the garments of the transformed Jesus were.

4. *Elijah with Moses:* The two figures are generally taken as emblematic of the Prophets (Elijah) and the Law (Moses). They are both prophetic figures who suffered because of their fidelity to God. Their presence at the transfiguration of Jesus points to Jesus' role in fulfilling God's promises made in the OT. It also contributes to the eschatological dimension of the scene (see Rev 11:3-13). According to 2 Kgs 2:11 Elijah "ascended in a whirlwind into heaven," and according to Mal 4:5 (see also 3:1) he is to return before the day of the Lord. The mystery surrounding the burial of Moses (see Deut 34:6) generated Jewish traditions about his assumption and his eschatological significance (see *Assumption of Moses*). Many commentators worry about the peculiar order "Elijah with Moses" (compare "Moses and Elijah" in Matt 17:3 and Luke 9:30 as well as in Mark 9:5). According to John Paul Heil ("A Note on 'Elijah with Moses' in Mark 9,4," *Bib* 80 [1999] 115), in Mark's Gospel the party mentioned second and introduced by "with" *(syn)* is the more notable figure, and so all the Synoptic evangelists are saying the same thing.

   appeared: The aorist passive of *oran (ōpthē)* occurs only here in Mark. Compare its recurrent use (four times) in Paul's list of the appearances of the risen Christ in 1 Cor 15:4-8.

5. *Peter spoke up and said:* The double reference to speaking highlights Peter's role as spokesman for Jesus' disciples on the journey (see 8:29, 32; 10:28; 11:21).

   Rabbi: The Hebrew word *rabbi* taken over into Greek literally means "my great one" or "my lord." By Mark's time (70 C.E.) it was probably not yet a technical term for the Jewish teacher, but shortly afterwards it was becoming one, as Matt 23:8 ("you are not to be called Rabbi") shows and as Luke 9:33 suggests. (Luke substitutes *epistata* ["teacher"] for "Rabbi" in this scene.) In fact, Matthew avoids anyone applying "Rabbi" to Jesus except in the case of Judas' betrayal (see Matt 26:49). All this suggests that Mark's uses of *rabbi* (see also 11:21 and 14:45) and *rabbouni* (10:51) should be taken as expressions of politeness or majesty rather than as identifying Jesus as a Rabbi in the later sense of that term.

It is good that we are here: Why it is good is not specified. Perhaps we are to assume that it was because the experience was such a pleasure, or because it gave the disciples a chance to serve Jesus and his visitors. Or perhaps we are just to take it (as Mark seems to do in 9:6a) as an awkward and foolish comment on Peter's part.

three booths: The primary reference is probably to the booths or tabernacles used in the ancient Israelite fall agricultural festival (see Lev 23:39-43), but whether there is an even more direct reference to that feast is unclear. Peter's point seems to be this: Just as Jews camped out in the fields during the fall harvest festival rather than going back and forth to their homes, so Peter thinks that he can prolong the experience of Jesus' transfiguration by building shelters (see the "eternal tents" in Luke 16:9) for the three principal figures: Jesus, Moses, and Elijah.

6. *he did not know what to say:* The comment underlines Peter's failure to understand fully what was going on before his eyes. See 2 Pet 1:16-18, where "Peter" looks back on the transfiguration and describes himself and the other disciples as "eyewitnesses of his [Jesus'] majesty."

they were awestruck: The adjective *ekphoboi* applies to Peter, James, and John. Their "fear" is primarily awe and respect at the mighty acts of God in Jesus (see 4:41; 5:15, 33; 6:50; 16:8), not sheer terror at fear of injury or death. The description foreshadows Mark 16:8 where the women are awestruck in the face of the empty tomb and the proclamation of Jesus' resurrection.

7. *a cloud overshadowing them:* In an area such as the Holy Land where much of life depends on the regular cycle of rains from October to April, the cloud was a symbol of life and hope. Since God was assumed to be the author of life and the ground of hope it is not surprising that the cloud became also a symbol of the divine presence. In Exod 40:34-38 a cloud covers the tent of meeting, which is filled with the glory of the Lord. At the dedication of Solomon's Temple in Jerusalem "a cloud filled the house of the Lord" (1 Kgs 8:10-11). Evoking a familiar epithet for the Canaanite god Baal, Ps 68:4 calls Yhwh the one "who rides upon the clouds."

a voice came from the cloud: The cloud symbolism and the reference to Jesus as "my beloved Son" indicate that the speaker is God.

This is my beloved Son: The scene is reminiscent of Jesus' baptism in Mark 1:9-11, but here there is third-person language ("This is . . . ") rather than second-person address ("You are . . . "), thus giving the impression that the three disciples heard the voice. Moreover, here there is no "with you I am pleased" clause as in Mark 1:11 (but see Matt 17:5). Also the heavenly voice here identifies Jesus as "my beloved Son" while in 1:11 he is literally "my Son, the beloved." These differences aside, Mark 1:11 and 9:7 are obviously related because they identify Jesus as the Son of God at the beginning of his Galilean ministry (1:11) and the beginning of the journey narrative (9:7), and both point forward to the centurion's identification of Jesus at his death on the cross: "Truly this man was the Son of God" (15:39).

Listen to him: The voice approves Jesus as the representative and revealer of God, thus lending divine authority to his difficult teachings about christology and discipleship during the journey narrative. The disciples are urged to hear and obey him.

8. *suddenly:* Mark effectively conveys the abruptness of the story's ending not only by the unusual adverb *exapina* ("suddenly") but also by the double negative (*ouketi oudena,* which is literally "no longer no one"), the adversative *alla* ("except"), and the final phrase *monon meth' heautōn* ("only . . . with them").

9. *As they were coming down from the mountain:* The reference to the mountain has the effect of linking the episode in 9:9-13 with the transfiguration (see 9:2). The link in turn allows Mark to explore the relationships among the coming kingdom of God (9:1), the glory of Jesus (9:2-8), and the suffering of the Son of Man (9:9-13).

   that they should not tell anyone: This command to silence is unusual because it is given to three disciples only (Peter, James, and John) and has a time limit (Jesus' resurrection; see 8:31).

   until the Son of Man had risen from the dead: The translation "until" smoothes out the complicated Greek expression *ei mē hotan* ("if not [= except] when"). Here, as in the three Passion-resurrection predictions (8:31; 9:31; 10:33-34), the title "Son of Man" dominates. The verb *anastę* (aorist subjunctive) is translated as a perfect, even though the action is future. This verse, along with 8:29b-30, is a key text in William Wrede's interpretation of the Messianic Secret.

10. *they kept this matter to themselves:* It is not clear whether *logos* refers to the transfiguration event ("this matter") or to Jesus' command to silence in 9:9 ("this word"). Nor is it clear whether "to themselves" belongs with what precedes ("kept to themselves") or to what follows ("while discussing among themselves").

    what it means to rise from the dead: Since at least in some Jewish circles (especially the Pharisees) resurrection was a prominent belief (see 12:18-27), the disciples surely would not have been hearing about it for the first time. It is more likely that their puzzlement involved how it might happen that Jesus as an individual person and before the end-time and final judgment could be raised from the dead, since resurrection was generally understood to be a collective and eschatological event. Some manuscripts solved the problem by reading "what it means 'when he has risen from the dead.'"

11. *the scribes say that Elijah must come first:* While there is something of a change of topic (Elijah) here from 9:9-10, the new topic picks up on a major figure (Elijah) in 9:2-8 and relates him to the suffering Son of Man (9:9-10). Here the scribes are referred to in their capacity as experts in the interpretation of Scripture. The idea that Elijah must come first is based on Mal 4:5 (3:23 in Greek): "I will

send you the prophet Elijah before the great and terrible day of the Lord comes." The disciples want to know how the Son of Man can rise from the dead (9:9) when Elijah has not yet come. Their eschatological scenario has Elijah coming back first and then the general resurrection of the dead on the day of the Lord.

12. *Elijah does indeed come first and restores everything:* Rather than rejecting the disciples' eschatological scenario, Jesus accepts and interprets it. The notion that Elijah "restores everything" conveyed by *apokathistanei* (puts all things in order and returns them to their original condition to prepare for the divine visitation) may be based on Mal 4:6 (3:24 in Greek): "He will turn the hearts of parents to their children and the hearts of children to their parents."

about the Son of Man—that he should suffer much and be treated with contempt: No OT text refers directly to the suffering of the Son of Man or of the Messiah. But here as elsewhere in the NT, the OT Scriptures as a whole are taken as pointing toward the suffering of Jesus (see 1 Cor 15:3-5). The second part of 9:12 has the effect of reminding the disciples (and Mark's readers) that Jesus' suffering is a more important precedent to the fullness of God's kingdom than Elijah's coming is.

13. *Elijah has already come:* As in 9:12a, Jesus accepts the disciples' eschatological scenario and implies without a direct statement that John the Baptist was equal to Elijah—an identification already suggested by the prophetic lifestyle he adopted (see Mark 1:6 and 2 Kgs 1:8).

they did to him whatever they wished: The fate of John described in 6:14-29 foreshadows that of Jesus the Son of Man. The idea that John's fate was foretold in Scripture may rest on the analogy between Elijah's opposition to Jezebel (1 Kgs 19:1-3) and John's opposition to Herodias (Mark 6:17-19).

INTERPRETATION

The Markan episode traditionally known as the transfiguration actually consists of three elements: the saying about the imminent coming of God's kingdom (9:1), the narrative about the transformation or transfiguration of Jesus (9:2-8), and the discussion between Jesus and his disciples about Jesus as the suffering Son of Man and John the Baptist as an Elijah figure (9:9-13). While different in literary form and content, in their present place in Mark's Gospel they confront Jesus' disciples and Mark's readers with the mystery of the kingdom of God and the place of Jesus' suffering, death, and resurrection within it. Mark may well have been the one who was responsible for putting the three units together. Their combination evokes themes that are central to his gospel.

The saying about the imminent coming of God's kingdom (9:1) promises that some contemporaries of Jesus would see "the kingdom of God come with power" before they die. This saying, along with Mark 13:30 (see

Matt 24:34; Luke 21:32) and Matt 10:23, provides the strongest evidence that Jesus regarded the kingdom of God as future and imminent (that is, to come soon). These sayings are balanced off by Luke 11:20 (see Matt 12:28); Matt 11:12 (see Luke 16:16); and Luke 17:21, which imply that God's kingdom is already present or at least inaugurated in Jesus' ministry. When the two sets of sayings are put together, the result is the "already/ not yet" dynamic that is typical of NT eschatology.

The kingdom saying in Mark 9:1 is taken by most commentators as part of the preceding unit with 8:34-38. In fact it serves as a bridge from the final (eschatological) saying on discipleship in 8:38 to the story of the transfiguration in 9:2-8. By placing it just before the transfiguration Mark has given an interpretation to both the saying and the narrative. On the one hand Mark's readers are led to suppose that those "standing here" are Peter, James, and John, and that the transfiguration itself represents *a* (if not *the*) coming of God's kingdom in power. On the other hand the readers are provided with a clue toward understanding Jesus' transfiguration as a preview or anticipation of the fullness of the kingdom of God and of the risen Jesus' place within it.

The narrative about the transformation or transfiguration of Jesus (9:2-8) describes the setting and the brilliant figure of Jesus (9:2-3), the appearance of Moses and Elijah as well as Peter's suggestion (9:4-6), the cloud and the voice coming from it (9:7), and the abrupt ending of the event (9:8). The major interpretive question regarding Mark 9:2-8 is, What is its literary genre? The three most prominent explanations are these: historical report, resurrection appearance, and apocalyptic vision. While no one of these interpretations is entirely convincing, each contains some important truth.

Those who regard the transfiguration as a historical report cover a wide spectrum of opinions. They range from those who want to take every element as literal fact to those who say that some irrecoverable experience of the "brilliance" of Jesus on the part of his disciples led to the imaginative representation that now stands in the NT. The story certainly has many "supernatural" features that are beyond the capacity of the historian: the symbolism of the high mountain, the transfiguration itself, the appearance of Moses and Elijah, and the heavenly voice. That it reflects the disciples' experience of Jesus' brilliance is entirely likely. But the precise details of that experience are hard to determine.

Some interpreters suggest that the transfiguration story was originally an account of an appearance of the risen Christ that has been read back into the career of the earthly Jesus. It fits well with the NT descriptions of other appearances of the risen Christ (e.g., Acts 9:3; 22:6; 26:13). The hypothesis is initially attractive (because it gives a context to the changed appearance of Jesus and to the disciples' amazement) and not implausible, though a better case can be made for Matt 16:17-19 (or even Luke 5:1-11) as originally a post-Easter story. But some key elements found in the NT appearance stories, especially the theme of mission, are missing. At any rate, the transfiguration is at least a preview of the glory of the risen Jesus and so is an anticipation of the resurrection.

Still others regard the transfiguration as an apocalyptic vision such as one finds in Daniel and other Jewish apocalypses (*1 Enoch, 4 Ezra, 2 Baruch,* etc.). Indeed, Matt 17:9 explicitly describes the experience as a "vision" *(horama).* This suggestion helps to explain the supernatural elements as well as the eschatological context of the story. But there is no first-person narrative ("I saw") or an angelic interpreter and a detailed interpretation of the vision. However, it is fair to say that the transfiguration does provide a preview of Jesus as a major character in the coming of God's kingdom in its fullness.

No one of these literary genres—historical report, resurrection appearance, apocalyptic vision—fully explains the transfiguration of Jesus, but each of them does explain something. A more helpful approach to the text is to say that it is a "christophany," that is, a manifestation or revelation of who Jesus Christ really is. The term is a variation of the word "theophany," a scene in which God reveals God's own self to humans (see, for example, the encounter between God and Moses in Exodus 3). In the transfiguration Jesus Christ is revealed as a glorious figure, someone on a level with (and even superior to) Moses and Elijah, and is called "Son of God" by a heavenly voice. In the Markan context of the journey narrative the transfiguration gives a glimpse of Jesus' true identity and the glorious goal to which his journey will lead. Meanwhile the disciples are understandably puzzled and react with a mixture of awe and foolishness.

If one can speak of an OT model for the transfiguration story the best candidates are the descriptions of Moses on Mount Sinai in Exodus 24 and 34. There are many common features: the high mountain (Mark 9:2 and Exod 24:12, 15-18; 34:3), the presence of a special group (Mark 9:2 and Exod 24:1-2, 16), radiance from the central figure (Mark 9:6 and Exod 34:29-30, 35), fear among the onlookers (Mark 9:6 and Exod 34:29-30), the cloud (Mark 9:7 and Exod 24:15-18; 34:5), and the voice from the cloud (Mark 9:7 and Exod 24:16). The common features are so numerous that it is hard to escape the impression that the transfiguration story presents Jesus as not only the Son of God but also a Moses figure.

The discussion between Jesus and his disciples (9:9-13) relates Jesus' identity to the mystery of the cross and to Elijah/John the Baptist. When Jesus echoes the Passion prediction of 8:31 in 9:9 the disciples wonder how the Son of Man (whose glory they have experienced) could be put to death so as to rise from the dead. They also wonder about the sequence of eschatological events. For them resurrection is an end-time event, and

Elijah must come before this can happen. This was only one of the several eschatological scenarios current among Jews in Jesus' time, but it was a common one (see 4 *Ezra* and 2 *Baruch*). But rather than rejecting their scenario, Jesus uses it to link John the Baptist to the prophet Elijah—a link already suggested by the inclusion of Mal 3:1 in the OT quotation in 1:2-3, by John's Elijah-like prophetic lifestyle (1:6), and by his fearlessness in speaking out against rulers in Israel (6:14-29). However, some people were apparently identifying Jesus with Elijah (see 6:15; 8:28), and only in 9:11-13 does it become completely clear that it is John rather than Jesus who is the Elijah figure. At Jesus' death on the cross some of the by-standers imagine that he is calling on Elijah (see 15:35-36). Nevertheless, while establishing that John the Baptist is Elijah in the eschatological scenario, Mark 9:11-13 serves to link John and Jesus, especially with re-gard to their sufferings, to the full coming of God's kingdom.

While each of the three sections in 9:1-13 can be taken separately, it is pastorally useful to follow Mark's insights in letting them interpret one another. What emerges from the combination is a deeper appreciation of Jesus' death and resurrection as pivotal events in the coming of God's kingdom in its fullness, the overwhelming brilliance of the person of the "real" Jesus, and the persistent presence of the mystery of the cross. The call to "listen to him" (9:7) highlights the proper response to Jesus and his place in the paschal mystery. It may point backward in particular to the teaching on the cost of discipleship in 8:34-38. The lectionary practice of reading the transfiguration story on the second Sunday of Lent captures the Markan dynamic nicely.

FOR REFERENCE AND FURTHER STUDY

Agua-Perez, Augustin del. "The Narrative of the Transfiguration as a Derashic Scienification of a Faith Confession," *NTS* 39 (1993) 340–54.

Allison, Dale C. "Elijah Must Come First," *JBL* 103 (1984) 256–58.

Faierstein, Morris M. "Why Do the Scribes Say that Elijah Comes First?" *JBL* 100 (1981) 75–86.

Fitzmyer, Joseph A. "More About Elijah Coming First," *JBL* 104 (1985) 295–96.

Heil, John Paul. *The Transfiguration of Jesus: Narrative Meaning and Function of Mark 9:2-8, Matt 17:1-8 and Luke 9:28-36.* Rome: Biblical Institute Press, 2000.

Marcus, Joel. "Mark 9,11-13: 'As It Has Been Written,'" *ZNW* 80 (1989) 42–63.

Murphy-O'Connor, Jerome. "What Really Happened at the Transfiguration?" *Bible Review* 3/3 (1987) 8–21.

Nardoni, Enrique. "A Redactional Interpretation of Mark 9:1," *CBQ* 43 (1981) 365–84.

Pellegrini, Silvia. *Elija—Wegbereiter des Gottessohnes. Eine textsemiotische Unter-suchung im Markusevangelium.* Freiburg: Herder, 2000.

Perrin, Norman. "The Composition of Mark ix,1," *NovT* 11 (1969) 67–70.

Robinson, John A. T. "Elijah, John and Jesus: An Essay in Detection," *NTS* 4 (1958) 263–81.

Stein, Robert H. "Is the Transfiguration (Mark 9:2-8) a Misplaced Resurrection Account?" *JBL* 95 (1976) 76–96.

Taylor, Justin. "The Coming of Elijah, Mt. 17,10-13 and Mk 9,11-13: The Development of the Texts," *RB* 98 (1991) 107–19.

Viviano, Benedict T. "Rabbouni and Mark 9:5," *RB* 97 (1990) 207–18.

34. *Healing a Possessed Boy* (9:14-29)

14. And when they came to the disciples, they saw a large crowd around them and scribes discussing with them. 15. And immediately the whole crowd, when they saw him, were utterly amazed. And they ran up and greeted him. 16. And he asked them: "What are you discussing with them?" 17. And a man from the crowd answered him: "Teacher, I brought you my son who has a mute spirit. 18. And whenever it takes hold of him it dashes him down, and he foams at the mouth and grinds his teeth and becomes rigid. And I asked your disciples to cast it out, and they were not able to do so." 19. But he answered them: "O unbelieving generation! How long will I be with you? How long will I put up with you? Bring him to me." 20. And they brought him to him. And when the spirit saw him it immediately threw him into convulsions. And he fell on the ground, and he was rolling about and foaming at the mouth. 21. And he [Jesus] asked his father: "How long is it since this has happened to him?" He said: "From childhood on. 22. And it often throws him down into fire and into water so as to destroy him. But if you can, have compassion on us and help us." 23. But Jesus said to him: "'If you can!' All things are possible to one who believes." 24. Immediately the father of the boy shouted out and said: "I believe. Help my unbelief." 25. When Jesus saw that a crowd came running together he rebuked the unclean spirit and said to him: "You mute and deaf spirit, I command you. Go out from him, and never enter him again." 26. And after shouting and convulsing him greatly it went out. And he became like a dead man so that many said that he was dead. 27. But Jesus took hold of his hand and lifted him up, and he arose. 28. And when he entered the house his disciples were asking him in private: "Why could we not cast it out?" 29. And he said to them: "This kind cannot go out by any means except by prayer."

NOTES

14. *when they came to the disciples, they saw:* Some manuscripts have singular verbs ("he came . . . he saw"), perhaps to make a smoother transition from 9:9-13

where Jesus is the center of attention. The disciples include at least the other members of the Twelve and perhaps an even larger group.

a large crowd: There is some tension between the references to the large crowd at the beginning of the story (see also 9:17) and to the crowd that "came running together" as if they were gathering for the first time in 9:25.

scribes discussing with them: The scene seems to envision the scribes engaged in debate with Jesus' disciples ("them"). It is hard to decide whether *synzētein* should be rendered in a neutral way ("discussing") or polemically ("arguing"); for other Markan uses of this verb see 1:27; 8:11; 9:10, 16; 12:28. The scribes play no further role in the story.

15. *were utterly amazed . . . ran up and greeted him:* The excitement of the crowd at Jesus' arrival is conveyed by the verb *ekthambein*, which appears elsewhere in Mark with reference to Jesus' strong emotions in Gethsemane (14:33) and to the women's confusion at finding Jesus' tomb empty on Easter morning (16:5, 6). The crowd's actions in running up to Jesus and greeting him foreshadow the actions of the rich man in 10:17.

16. *them . . . them:* In each case the precise identity of "them" is not clear. It could be that Jesus is asking the disciples what they were discussing with the scribes (see 9:14). But since in 9:17 a man from the crowd answers, it could also be that Jesus asks the crowd.

17. *Teacher, I brought to you my son:* Thus far in Mark, Jesus has been called "teacher" only twice (4:38; 5:35). As the narrative proceeds this title will become increasingly frequent (see 9:38; 10:20, 35; 12:14, 19, 32; 13:1; 14:14). The fact that the man brought his son to Jesus implies his faith in Jesus' power to heal his son. But of course Jesus was away on the high mountain during the transfiguration.

a mute spirit: The translation of *alalon* (lit. "speechless") as "dumb" is both offensive and inaccurate. The Greek expression *pneuma alalon* conveys the idea that the boy's condition is due to demonic possession, and so he can be healed only by the expulsion of the demon or evil spirit *(pneuma)*. The spirit that possesses the boy renders him incapable of speaking and is speechless itself *(alalon)*. Compare the earlier exorcisms where the demons speak and correctly identify Jesus as "the Holy One of God" (1:24) and as "the Son of the Most High God" (5:7).

18. *whenever it takes hold of him:* The description of the boy's attacks is vivid: "dashes him down . . . he foams . . . grinds his teeth . . . becomes rigid." The assumption is that the *pneuma alalon* initiates the attack and the other symptoms follow. The final symptom ("becomes rigid") is based on the verb *xērainetai* ("become dry or withered"). For Matthew's diagnosis of the boy's condition as epilepsy see his term in Matt 17:15, *selēniazetai* (lit. "moonstruck"), which reflects the widespread belief that epilepsy was related to the phases of the moon *(selēnē)*.

your disciples . . . were not able: Since Jesus was absent, the man turned to Jesus' disciples in the hope that they could do what Jesus could do. This was a legitimate assumption in light of Mark 6:7 (where Jesus gives the Twelve authority over unclean spirits) and 6:13 (where the disciples succeed in casting out many demons).

19. *O unbelieving generation!:* Jesus' exasperation at the unbelieving/faithless *(apistos)* people of his own day (see 8:38) echoes Deut 32:5: "a perverse and crooked generation." That OT text in turn influenced some manuscripts of Mark to expand 9:19a to "O unbelieving and perverted generation!"

How long: The repetition of *heōs pote* ("until when") expresses the feelings of a teacher who has been persistently misunderstood (see 4:40). There is probably also a hint of Jesus' own sense of his approaching death here. For Jesus' amazement at the unbelief displayed by his neighbors and then by his disciples see 6:6a and 8:14-21. His frustration here is echoed in 8:12: "Why does this generation seek a sign? Amen I say to you, No sign will be given to this generation."

Bring him to me: Jesus apparently overcomes his personal exasperation and agrees to drive out the demon and so to bring healing to the boy and peace of heart to the father.

20. *the spirit saw him . . . and he fell:* The masculine aorist participle *idōn* ("seeing") does not fit well grammatically with the neuter noun *pneuma,* but from the perspective of sense they belong together. The structure of the verse, with its change of subjects, highlights the role of the evil spirit in bringing on the boy's physical symptoms. For an earlier description of the symptoms see 9:18.

21. *How long is it since . . . ?:* The word *hōs* here carries the sense of "from what point" or "since when." The boy has endured this condition most of his life.

22. *it often throws him down:* From the viewpoint of the narrative the evil spirit throws the boy into convulsions with the goal of destroying him by burning him or drowning him. The miracle is not simply a physical healing; it is first and foremost an exorcism.

if you can: What begins as a formula of politeness becomes the central motif of the story: the power of faith. The man presumably brought the child to Jesus out of a mixture of desperation and hope (see 9:17).

have compassion on us and help us: For previous uses of the highly emotional verb *splanchnizesthai* ("be moved with pity, have compassion") see 1:41; 6:34; and 8:2. In each of those cases Jesus is the one who is moved with pity and shows compassion toward another. The verb *boēthein* ("help, come to the aid of another") appears in Mark only here and in 9:24. The plural "us" includes at least the father and his son, and perhaps the whole family and their friends.

23. *If you can!:* The statement conveys more impatience on Jesus' part (see 9:19). The Greek text places the neuter definite article *to* before "if you can," which has the effect of emphasizing that part of the father's request in 9:22 so as then to hold it up to criticism.

All things are possible to one who believes: The saying is somewhat ambiguous and not entirely apropos. With it Jesus appears to criticize both his disciples and the father. For a similar affirmation see 10:27: "All things are possible with

God." See also Jesus' challenge to Jairus in 5:36: "Do not fear, only believe." The faith Jesus expects is basically trust in his Father, but this faith probably also involves trust in the gospel (1:15) and in him as the herald of the gospel. These verses on faith and prayer foreshadow the instruction in 11:22-25.

24. *"I believe. Help my unbelief":* The father's cry is one of the most memorable and beloved statements in the NT because it captures the mixed character of faith within the experience of most people. The fact that the father brought the boy to Jesus shows some faith on his part already. But his hesitancy expressed in the use of "if you can" shows a less than perfect faith in Jesus and his healing power. The only previous use of *apistia* ("unbelief") described the reception Jesus got from the people of Nazareth (see 6:6a). Jesus is asking the father to move to an even more perfect level of faith.

25. *a crowd came running together:* Mention of a large crowd was made already in 9:14, 15, and 19. This verse gives the impression that only now is a crowd forming and that there is some chance of a riot. For earlier references to disorderly crowds see 1:45; 2:2; 3:9-10, 20; 4:1; 5:24; and 6:31.

    rebuked the unclean spirit: Although the verb *epitiman* generally appears in contexts where something or someone needs correction (see 3:12; 8:30, 32, 33; 10:13, 48), it also occurs in the exorcism at the synagogue in Capernaum (1:25) and in the stilling of the storm (4:39). Here the spirit who attacks the boy is identified as "unclean" for the first time. The uncleanness here is not so much ritual or even moral; the idea is that the spirit is on the side of "the evil one" (see 3:22-30).

    You mute and deaf spirit, I command you: The spirit *(pneuma)* has already been identified as "mute" or "speechless" *(alalon)* in 9:17. The adjective *kōphos* can mean both "mute" and "deaf," and so here "deaf" seems more likely. The term *epitassein* ("command") also appears in the exorcism at the synagogue in Capernaum (1:27; see also 6:27, 39). The emphasis on "I" highlights Jesus' personal authority as an exorcist.

    Go out from him, and never enter him again: The double command not only expels the demon but also makes sure that he never returns. For the motif of the demon who does return see Matt 12:43-45 and Luke 11:24-26. Compare Jesus' earlier commands to demons in 1:25 ("Be silent, and come out of him!") and 5:8 ("Come out of the man, you unclean spirit").

26. *after shouting and convulsing him greatly:* For a similar description as part of an exorcism see 1:27: "The unclean spirit convulsed him and cried out with a loud voice and came out of him."

    he became like a dead man: See 9:18 where the father says that the final stage in the boy's attacks leaves him in a rigid state. Unlike 1:27 where the reaction of the bystanders is amazement at the exorcism, here they imagine that the boy is dead. Compare the case of Jairus' daughter in 6:35-43.

27. *Jesus took hold of his hand and lifted him up:* These gestures accompanied the healing of Peter's mother-in-law in 1:31 and the restoration of Jairus' daughter in 5:41. The language of lifting up *(egeirein)* evokes the idea of resurrection—

a motif confirmed by the addition of another "resurrection" verb, *anistēmi* ("arose"), immediately afterward. The story breaks off abruptly without a triumphal ending, and the scene shifts to a house where Jesus and his disciples engage in private conversation about the disciples' failure to expel the demon.

28. *his disciples were asking him in private:* For other cases where Jesus explains difficult matters to the disciples in private see 4:10; 7:17; and 10:10. Here the disciples are puzzled by their own failure to perform the exorcism—something that Jesus did so easily and that Jesus had empowered them to do (see 6:7).

29. *This kind cannot go out:* The reference to the demon as "this kind" suggests that it possessed extraordinary force. The translation "go out" captures the active sense of the Greek verb *exelthein,* though the meaning is passive ("be cast out").
    except by prayer: This qualification fits with the emphasis on faith in the narrative. It suggests that the disciples, too, needed greater faith to cast out the demon. The phrase "and fasting," though it is found in many good manuscripts (see also the "shadow" verse in many manuscripts of Matt 17:21), is generally regarded as a later addition reflecting the growing prominence of fasting in early Christian circles .

INTERPRETATION

In the context of the Markan journey narrative this lone miracle story —the healing of the possessed boy—in 9:14-29 reminds us that even with the glory of Jesus made manifest in his transfiguration the power of evil continues to exist, and that the disciples' faith remains inadequate. The story is properly called an exorcism and not simply a healing story. The assumption is that an evil spirit is causing the boy's physical symptoms. The passage continues the theme introduced in the temptation narrative (1:12-13) that the ministry of Jesus is part of a cosmic and eschatological struggle between good and evil. Just as Jesus' Galilean ministry began with a revelation of him as the Son of God (1:9-11) and a struggle with an evil spirit (1:12-13), so here in the journey narrative the revelation of Jesus as the Son of God (9:1-13) is followed by a struggle with an evil spirit (9:14-29).

The long narrative begins with an account of the disciples' failure to bring healing to the possessed boy (9:14-19). This first part introduces not only the characters (Jesus, the disciples, the crowd, the father and son, the demon) but also the theme of faith ("O unbelieving generation," 9:19). Then in 9:20-27 there is a detailed report about the healing of the boy, which revolves around the theme of the father's faith ("I believe. Help my unbelief," 9:23). Finally in 9:28-29 Jesus and the disciples discuss in private the reason for the disciples' failure to heal the boy. This sets the stage for Jesus to pronounce that this kind of demon can be driven out only by prayer. Thus Mark 9:14-29 combines the literary forms of a healing story, an exorcism, and a pronouncement.

The narrative as a whole is distinctive for its details and its length. It shares many elements with the exorcism in the synagogue at Capernaum (1:23-27) and is almost as long as the story of the Gerasene demoniac (5:1-20). There is a good deal of repetition in the descriptions of the boy's sufferings (see 9:17-18, 20, 22, 26)—so much that some scholars (notably Rudolf Bultmann) have argued that two originally distinct exorcism accounts have been joined together. It appears that Matthew and Luke both found Mark's narrative too long, and so they shortened it by omitting many of the graphic details and thus highlighting the theme of faith (see Matt 17:14-21 and Luke 9:37-43a).

Matthew in 17:15 summarizes the detailed Markan descriptions by diagnosing the boy's condition as epilepsy. See the note on Mark 9:18 for Matthew's term *selēniazetai* and the perception of a connection between epilepsy and the phases of the moon. In some circles in antiquity epilepsy was called the "sacred disease" because its sudden onset and extreme effects on the person were regarded as displays of divine power. Mark, however, is not particularly interested in the medical diagnosis, nor does he view the boy's condition as sacred. Rather, Mark presents it as a case of demonic possession, as the result of an evil spirit taking over the boy, inflicting terrible sufferings on him and trying to kill him.

One major theological theme is faith. The man brings the boy to Jesus out of a hope that Jesus might heal him (9:17). The disciples, acting on their own, fail to heal the boy (9:18). When this is brought to Jesus' attention by the father, Jesus laments over the unbelief of this generation and expresses his frustration with them (9:19). When asked by the father to do something for the boy "if you can," Jesus affirms that "all things are possible for one who believes" (9:23). In response the father issues his great proclamation: "I believe. Help my unbelief" (9:25). When the disciples ask about their failure Jesus points to the importance of prayer as an act of faith (9:29). From beginning to end, the story is about faith.

Another great theological theme is the power of Jesus as healer and lifegiver. Mark's interpretation of the boy's condition as demonic possession places the episode in the context of Jesus' ongoing battle against the forces of evil. The fact that only Jesus—and not the disciples—could heal the boy highlights his power as the healer par excellence. And Jesus' actions in ministering to the boy after the demon had been expelled ("Jesus took hold of his hand and lifted him up, and he arose," 9:27) point forward toward Jesus' own resurrection.

For many people today the description of the boy's physical symptoms as the result of demonic possession presents personal and theological problems. Those who are sick can suppose that they are possessed by a demon or (more commonly) are being punished for their sins. These is-sues are not easy for teachers and preachers to address with reference to this biblical text; for a treatment of these matters see Daniel J. Harrington, *Why Do We Suffer? A Scriptural Approach to the Human Condition* (Franklin, Wis.: Sheed & Ward, 2000). Such questions can easily distract from the more positive and central themes in the passage: the nature and impor-tance of faith and the power of Jesus as a healer and as the ground of our hope in the resurrection.

FOR REFERENCE AND FURTHER STUDY

Achtemeier, Paul J. "Miracles and the Historical Jesus: A Study of Mark 9:14-29," *CBQ* 37 (1975) 471–91.
Pilch, John J. *Healing in the New Testament. Insights from Medical and Mediterranean Anthropology.* Minneapolis: Fortress, 2000.
Sterling, Gregory E. "Jesus as Exorcist: An Analysis of Matthew 17:14-20; Mark 9:14-29; Luke 9:37-43a," *CBQ* 55 (1993) 467–93.
Wohlers, Michael. *Heilige Krankheit. Epilepsis in antiker Medizin, Astrologie und Religion.* Marburg: N. G. Elwert, 1999.

35. *A Second Passion Prediction and More Instructions for Disciples* (9:30-50)

30. And they left there and passed through Galilee, and he did not want anyone to know it. 31. And he continued teaching his disciples and say-ing to them: "The Son of Man will be handed over into the hands of men, and they will kill him. And when he is killed, he will rise after three days." 32. But they failed to understand the statement, and they were afraid to ask him. 33. And they entered Capernaum. And when he was in the house he asked them: "What were you discussing along the way?" 34. But they kept silent. For along the way they had been discussing among themselves who is the greatest. 35. And he sat down and called the Twelve and said to them: "If anyone wishes to be first, he shall be last of all and servant of all." 36. And he took a child, stood him in their midst, embraced him, and said to them: 37. "Whoever receives one such child in my name receives me. And whoever receives me receives not me but the one who sent me." 38. John said to him: "Teacher, we saw some-one casting out demons in your name, and we forbade him because he does not follow us." 39. But Jesus said: "Do not forbid him. For no one who will do a mighty work in my name can soon after speak evil of me. 40. For whoever is not against us is for us. 41. For whoever gives you a

cup of water because you have the name of Christ, Amen I say to you, such a one will not lose his reward. 42. Whoever scandalizes one of these little ones who believe in me, it would be better if a donkey's millstone were put around his neck and he were thrown into the sea. 43. And if your hand scandalizes you, cut it off. It is better that you enter into life disabled than having two hands to go away into Gehenna, into unquenchable fire. 45. And if your hand scandalizes you, cut it off. It is better to enter into life maimed than having two feet to be cast into Gehenna. 47. And if your eye scandalizes you, throw it away. It is better to enter into the kingdom of God with one eye than having two eyes to be cast into Gehenna, 48. where their worm does not die and the fire is not quenched. 49. For everyone will be salted with fire. 50. Salt is good. But if the salt becomes insipid, how will you season it? Have salt among yourselves, and live in peace with one another."

NOTES

30. *they left there:* This marks the end of Jesus' public ministry in Galilee, since the teachings between the second Passion prediction in 9:31 and 10:1 (which takes Jesus and the disciples to Judea and beyond the Jordan) are directed toward the disciples.

   he did not want anyone to know it: The geographical notices in 9:30 and 10:1 suggest that the reason why Jesus did not want anyone to know about his presence in Galilee was so that he might devote his time and energy to instructing his circle of disciples for one last time in their home area. However, as what follows shows (see 9:32), Jesus had little success in getting them to understand the mystery of the cross.

31. *He continued teaching . . . and saying:* The use of the imperfect tense in both cases indicates repeated action on Jesus' part.

   The Son of Man will be handed over into the hands of men: As in the other Passion predictions (8:31 and 10:33-34), Jesus refers to himself as the Son of Man, thus linking these sayings to uses of the title in reference to his humanity (see 2:27-28) and to the coming of the glorious Son of Man figure on the day of the Lord (see 13:26). The keyword in this shortest of the three Passion predictions is *paradidotai* ("be handed over"). It appears in the present tense, though the meaning is future. The passive voice leaves open the identity of the agent. On the historical level, of course, the agent is Judas, who is described in 3:19 as "the one who handed him over." On the theological level, however, the verb *paradidotai* evokes the idea of the divine plan unfolding (see Isa 53:6, 12). From 9:31 onward the verb becomes increasingly prominent (see 10:33; 13:9, 11, 12; 14:10, 11, 18, 21, 41, 42, 44; 15:1, 10, 15) with reference to the suffering of Jesus and of his disciples. Its recurrence promotes the concept that God is the real agent behind the Passion and that everything proceeds according to God's will. See 1:14 where the use of *paradidonai* serves to place the arrest of John the Baptist in this same context.

they will kill him: The second Passion prediction provides less specific information about the circumstances surrounding Jesus' death than 8:31 and 10:33-34 do. This fact leads some scholars to regard it as the most original form of Jesus' Passion prediction. The version in Luke 9:44 ("the Son of Man is to be delivered into the hands of men") is even shorter. In none of the Passion predictions is there an explicit mention of crucifixion as the precise mode of Jesus' death.

he will rise after three days: Mark again uses the somewhat peculiar active formula (for the NT) found also in 8:31 and 10:34. The more common divine passive formula appears in Matt 17:23 ("on the third day he will be raised"), with its more exact time calculation and divine passive construction.

32. *they failed to understand:* After the first Passion prediction and the instructions accompanying it (8:27–9:29), it is hard for readers to grasp why the disciples continue to be so dense (they do not even want to know). Whereas in the first case Peter at least had the courage to object to Jesus' Passion prediction (8:32), here the disciples do not even raise a question. Mark is suggesting that instead of profiting from Jesus' teachings they are regressing, and thus they function as increasingly negative examples in contrast to the positive example displayed by Jesus.

33. *entered Capernaum . . . in the house:* Capernaum had served as a base for Jesus and his first disciples in the early stages of his public ministry (see 1:21; 2:1). Perhaps we are to imagine that the house belongs to Peter (see 1:29-31), though some scholars suppose that it belonged to Jesus (see 2:1, 15).

What were you discussing along the way?: While *dialogizesthai* can have a private and neutral sense ("consider, ponder, reason"), Mark generally gives it a public and negative sense such as "argue" (see 2:6, 8; 8:16, 17; 11:31). Its occurrences here and in 9:34 probably help to explain the embarrassment that the disciples display by their silence in 9:34. The repetition of "along the way" in 9:33 and 9:34 keeps up the journey motif and places Jesus' teachings in the framework of "the way" of discipleship.

34. *they kept silent:* The verb *siōpan* appears in several different contexts in Mark (see 3:4; 4:39; 10:48; 14:61). The closest parallel occurs in 3:4, where the people in the synagogue at Capernaum are reduced to an embarrassed silence by Jesus' teaching about doing good on the Sabbath. The disciples here seem to realize the contradiction between Jesus' teachings and the topic of their conversation.

who is the greatest: The comparative form of the adjective *meizōn* ("greater") has a superlative meaning ("greatest") in this context. It is probably wise to resist reading this text through its parallel in Matt 18:1: "Who is greatest in the kingdom of heaven?" Neither in Mark 9:34 nor in Luke 9:46 is there a specific reference to the kingdom of God. So here we are to assume that the disciples were arguing about places of prominence within their own group in the present. In a hierarchical society where status and honor were very important values the topic would have been both natural and worth discussing.

35. *he sat down:* For sitting as a posture for Jesus as a teacher see Mark 4:1 as well as Matt 5:1; 13:1; Luke 5:3; and John 8:2.

and called the Twelve: Why the Twelve should be singled out here is puzzling, since they seem to have been the ones who were having the discussion in 9:33-34. But as members of Jesus' inner circle they especially need this advice.

If anyone wishes to be first, he shall be the last of all and servant of all: The saying flows nicely from the scene that has been set up and so is an example of a pronouncement story or *chreia.* With this teaching Jesus challenges and subverts the assumptions of his culture about rank and status. The content of the teaching appears at somewhat greater length in 10:43-44 (see also Matt 23:11 and Luke 9:48; 22:26-27).

36. *he took a child:* Some commentators note that in Aramaic the word *ṭalyaʾ* can mean both "servant" and "child," and so they discern a catchword link with "servant" *(diakonos)* in 9:35. The child *(paidion)* could be either male or female (as the case of Jairus' daughter in 5:39 shows). Jesus' symbolic gesture takes the conversation in a different direction from 9:33-35—from the servant to those being served. In first-century Palestinian society a child would symbolize not so much innocence or unspoiledness as lack of social status and legal rights. A child was a "non-person" totally dependent on others for nurture and protection, and of course one could not expect to gain anything either socially or materially from kindness to a child. By placing the child in the midst of his circle of disciples Jesus is clearly using this symbolic action as a way of instructing his disciples. By embracing the child Jesus displays his acceptance of the child (who is a social nonentity) as worthy of respect and care.

37. *Whoever receives one such child in my name receives me:* The key phrase is "in my [Jesus'] name"; it is picked up as a catchword in the next episode (see 9:38, "in your name"). In the perspective of Jesus even the most apparently insignificant people are important because they too (and especially) carry the name of Jesus and belong to him. See the great Last Judgment scene in Matt 25:31-46 for a dramatic development of this teaching.

whoever receives me receives not me but the one who sent me: The presupposition of this saying is the practice of rulers or communities (including synagogues and churches) who sent out emissaries and expected that the emissaries (or "apostles," which means "those who are sent") would be treated with the respect and dignity appropriate to the one doing the sending. This custom is at the root of the early Christian institution of apostleship. In this case there is a kind of chain of sending or mission (as frequently in John's Gospel) from God ("the one who sent me") through Jesus to his emissaries (who can include even social nonentities like a child).

38. *John said to him:* This is the only case in Mark in which John the son of Zebedee acts entirely on his own. For other Markan references to this John see 1:19, 29; 3:17; 5:37; 9:2; 10:35, 41; 13:3; and 14:33.

in your name: For the "name" of Jesus as linking the various parts of the discourse see 9:37. The "strange exorcist" was apparently using the name of Jesus as a kind of magical instrument (see 1:24; 5:7) and having positive results.

we forbade him: The verb *kōlyein* has a wide range of meanings ("hinder, prevent, forbid"). The issue for translators and interpreters is the means the disciples took: was it verbal ("forbid") or physical ("hinder, prevent")? Besides its uses in 9:38-39 *kōlyein* appears elsewhere only in 10:14 with reference to the disciples preventing children from approaching Jesus.

because he does not follow us: The "strange exorcist" was not part of the circle of Jesus' disciples. It is curious that John should criticize him for not following "us" rather than Jesus (cf. "follow with us" in Luke 9:49-50). Perhaps we are to imagine John as referring back to the mission of the Twelve (6:7-13). More likely this was a subtle way of underscoring John's failure to understand that Jesus is the real source of the disciples' power. Two other readings are found in the manuscript tradition of Mark 9:38b: "who does not follow us, and we forbade him," and "who does not follow us, and we forbade him because he does not follow us." Both attempt to make the text a little smoother and so are most likely secondary readings.

39. *Do not forbid him:* For an OT parallel (if not a direct influence) see the story of Eldad and Medad in Num 11:26-29. Despite their not being "among those registered," Eldad and Medad prophesied in the camp of the Israelites. When Joshua urges Moses to stop them, Moses takes a tolerant attitude: "Are you jealous for my sake? Would that all the Lord's people were prophets, and that the Lord would put his spirit on them" (Num 11:29). See also Acts 19:13-16 where Jewish exorcists try unsuccessfully to use "the name of the Lord Jesus" over people possessed by demons.

For no one . . . can soon after speak evil of me: This first explanation is not in Luke 9:50, and Matthew omits the entire episode. Mark's text bases Jesus' tolerance on the assumption that someone who experiences Jesus' power will naturally speak well of him. In the early church such a saying could have been used to combat factionalism or exclusivism, though its use in such circumstances need not explain the creation of the statement.

40. *For whoever is not against us is for us:* The second explanation ("For . . . ") is a generalization and development of the first. It appears also in Luke 9:50. For a different perspective see Matt 12:30//Luke 11:23: "Whoever is not with me is against me."

41. *a cup of water:* In later contexts (10:38-39; 14:23, 36; 15:36) the word *potērion* ("cup") carries the idea of the cup of suffering. That is not the case here. Matthew uses this saying in his missionary discourse (see Matt 10:42) and specifies the recipients as "these little ones."

because you have the name of Christ: Literally the text reads "in name because you are of Christ." The word "name" *(onoma)* links this saying to 9:37-39. The use of the title "Christ" is unusual in the context of Jesus' own discourse and may suggest a post-resurrection perspective. Whereas 9:37 concerns receiving others (especially social "nobodies") in the name of Christ, this saying concerns strangers who do an act of kindness to disciples in the name of Christ.

Amen I say to you: For other Markan uses of the solemn introductory formula with "Amen" see 3:28; 8:12; 9:1; 12:15, 29; 11:23; 12:43; 13:30; 14:9, 18, 25, 30.

reward: The nature of the reward and its timing (present or future/eschatological) are not specified.

42. *Whoever scandalizes:* A *skandalon* is an obstacle or stumbling block that trips up someone on the way. Here and in 9:43, 45, 47 the verb derived from it *(skandali-zein)* is used metaphorically to refer to enticing someone to sin and thus putting an obstacle in the way of that person on the path of discipleship. We have used the English verb "scandalize" to reflect the presence of the Greek root, but since "scandalize" has a somewhat archaic sound to people today, the translation "put stumbling blocks in the way of" might convey the sense better.

one of these little ones who believe in me: The "little ones" are simple believers in Jesus. The phrase "in me" is absent from some important manuscripts, but it is implied even where it is absent; see also Matt 18:6.

a donkey's millstone: The expression *mylos onikos* refers to the upper stone on a large mill *(mylos)* that would have been powered by a donkey *(onos)* and used for grinding wheat. The donkey's millstone would have had the effect of an anchor or a heavy weight (like "cement overshoes"), and its use would make certain that the guilty person would die by drowning. The obvious exaggeration helps to bring out the seriousness involved in leading simple believers in Jesus into sin.

43. *if your hand scandalizes you:* The three sayings in vv. 43, 45, and 47 follow the same basic pattern: If one part of your body (hand, foot, or eye) proves to be an obstacle to your entering the kingdom of God, cut it off and so avoid being cast into Gehenna. These sayings are associated with v. 42 by the keyword "scandalize." But whereas v. 42 concerns one who scandalizes simple believers in Jesus, these three sayings treat parts of the body by which one may be led into sin. Given the widespread use of the body as a political/communal metaphor in antiquity, it is possible that these three sayings should be read as referring to problems encountered within the Christian community (the "body of Christ") and the use of excommunication to deal with troublemakers (see 1 Cor 5:1-5).

enter into life disabled: The expression "enter into life" in vv. 43 and 45 is replaced by "enter into the kingdom of God" in v. 47, thus suggesting an equivalency or at least a parallelism. The term translated as "disabled" *(kyllos)* refers to a limb that is abnormal or incapable of being used, and by extension to the person who has such a limb. It is paralleled by "maimed" in v. 45 and by "one-eyed" in v. 47.

go away into Gehenna, into unquenchable fire: The verb "go away" is paralleled by the (divine) passive "be cast" in vv. 45 and 47. The word "Gehenna" referred first of all to the "Valley of Hinnom" situated west and south of Jerusalem and running into the village of Silwan. During the Judean monarchy it became the site of a "high place" (the notorious "Topheth") where forbidden religious practices including human sacrifices by fire (see 2 Chr 28:3; 33:6; Jer 7:31; 32:35) took place. Jeremiah's oracle of judgment against it (see Jer 7:31) set the stage for Gehenna to be taken as a term for what we call "hell" or "hell-fire" (see *1 Enoch* 27:2; *4 Ezra* 7:36; Matt 5:22, 29-30; 23:33; Luke 12:5), the place of punishment to which sinners go. The appositional clause "into unquenchable fire" is apparently based on Isa 66:24, which is quoted at the end of this unit in Mark 9:48.

44. The quotation of Isa 66:24 found in all the best textual witnesses in Mark 9:48 and alluded to at the end of 9:43 is inserted in some inferior manuscripts also after each of the first two "scandal" sayings in this unit (vv. 44 and 46). This explains why in most modern translations the verse numbers for vv. 44 and 46 are omitted (since the numbering was based on the so-called *Textus receptus,* which is now recognized as not based on the best manuscripts).

45. *maimed:* The term translated as "maimed" *(chōlos)* can also mean "lame" or "crippled." This is its only occurrence in Mark.

    to be cast into Gehenna: Here and in v. 47 the passive verb *blēthenai* implies divine agency. Some manuscripts add "of fire" to "Gehenna."

46. See the notes on v. 44 for the nonoccurrence of Isa 66:24 in the best manuscripts, and on v. 48 for the origin and meaning of the text.

47. *throw it away:* The first two sayings have "cast it off." The variation here ("throw it away") fits better with the eye as the offending part of the body, and introduces a rhetorical variation that emphasizes the third member in the set of three sayings.

    to enter into the kingdom of God: The second major variation from the rhetorical pattern suggests an equivalence between "life" and "the kingdom of God." For entering the kingdom of God see Mark 10:15, 23-25. The variation serves to qualify the kind of life Jesus has been talking about as eternal life with God and not simply earthly happiness. It also prepares for the radical teaching about how hard it is to enter the kingdom of God in Mark 10:1-31.

48. *where the worm does not die and the fire is not quenched:* The verse is based (with some modification) on the Septuagint of Isa 66:24, the last verse in that OT book. In Isa 66:14-24 the saying appears in the eschatological context of the in-gathering of all Israel and of all the nations, and of the appearance of "the new heavens and the new earth." Isaiah 66:24 functions as a final threat against those in Israel who have rebelled against God and warns such persons that they will suffer eternal punishment (rather than annihilation). For "fire and worms" as instruments of eschatological punishment see Jdt 16:17. The quotation of Isa 66:24 is absent from the parallel passage in Matt 18:8-9, but its presence in Mark 9:48 with the reference to "fire and salt" provides the keyword link to the "fire and salt" saying in 9:49 and leads to the inclusion of two more "salt" sayings in 9:50.

49. *For everyone will be salted with fire:* The first of the three "salt" sayings appears to be based on the purifying capacity of salt. Its images of salt and fire most likely imply a period of testing and purification before the coming of God's kingdom in its fullness (see Matt 6:13). Other manuscripts introduce the role of salt in sacrifices from Lev 2:13b: "with all your offerings you shall offer salt." There are two other versions of Mark 9:49 in the manuscripts: "For every sacrifice will be salted with fire"; and "For everyone will be salted with fire,

and every sacrifice will be salted with salt." The third version combines the first two readings. The second version probably originated from a scribe's marginal note drawing attention to a possible link to Lev 2:13b (see Bruce M. Metzger, *A Textual Commentary on the Greek New Testament* [3rd ed. London and New York: United Bible Societies, 1971] 102–103). The first (and most likely original) reading may have some relation to the Q version of John the Baptist's saying preserved in Matt 3:11//Luke 3:16: "He will baptize you with the Holy Spirit (or more likely, wind) and fire."

50. *if the salt becomes insipid, how will you season it?:* Commentators regularly point out that while technically salt does not lose its taste completely it can become so contaminated or diluted that its taste is hard to recognize (see Job 6:6; Matt 5:13; Luke 14:34-35). The second "salt" saying, however, is not about chemistry. It builds on the uses of salt as a seasoning and as a preservative. There may be a reference here to the role of Jesus' disciples as "salt of the earth" (Matt 5:13) and agents of spiritual wisdom (see Col 4:6, which also contains the verb *artyein*).

Have salt among yourselves, and live in peace with one another: The third "salt" saying alludes to the use of salt in making covenants and offering sacrifices: "You shall not omit from your grain offerings the salt of the covenant with your God" (Lev 2:13a; see also Num 18:19; 2 Chr 13:5). It urges that Jesus' disciples cultivate hospitality and peace (see 1 Thess 5:13).

INTERPRETATION

The basic pattern of Passion prediction, misunderstanding on the part of the disciples, and instructions about discipleship introduced in Mark 8:31-38 is repeated in 9:30-50. After a reminder about the journey motif in 9:30, Jesus delivers the shortest of the three Passion predictions in 9:31. When the disciples fail to understand in 9:32, Jesus delivers teachings about greatness in his movement (9:33-37), outsiders who act in the name of Jesus (9:38-41), giving scandal (9:42) and being a scandal to oneself (9:43-48), and various aspects of "salt" (9:49-50). This section ends the second great Passion prediction unit with a reference to discipleship as involving service and sacrifice (see also 8:34-38 and 10:35-45).

In this part of the journey Jesus turns his attention to the circle of his disciples, and he presents them with the most direct and concise version of the fate that awaits him in Jerusalem (9:31). The disciples not only fail to understand the Passion prediction but even fear to pursue the topic (9:32). Then they show the depth of their misunderstanding by arguing about who is the greatest among them (9:34) and by trying to restrict the power of Jesus to their own narrow circle (9:38).

The disciples' misunderstanding provides the occasion for Jesus to define true greatness in his movement as the humble service of others (9:35), to urge the disciples to find Jesus and his Father in the most apparently insignificant people (9:37), and to remind the disciples that they cannot confine Jesus' power to their own group (9:39-40). Thus the disciples' misunderstanding serves as an opportunity for Mark's readers to understand better who Jesus is and what it means to follow him.

The second half of the passage—from Mark 9:37 onward—shows the strong influence of "catchword" or "keyword" composition, which is very likely a sign of pre-Markan oral transmission. The saying about receiving a child "in my name" (9:37) leads into the episode about casting out demons "in your name" (9:38-40) and the saying about those who give a cup of water "because you have the name of Christ" (9:41). The saying about scandalizing others (9:42) introduces three sayings about parts of the body being occasions for scandal (9:43-48). The reference to fire in 9:48 (from Isa 66:24) leads into the salt and fire saying in 9:49, which is accompanied by two more salt sayings in 9:50.

This block of teaching is structured by means of a series of keywords: name, scandal, fire, and salt. The logic here is external and formal; it does not proceed solely by argument or the force of ideas. The use of keywords suggests a process of memorization prior to the composition of Mark's Gospel. The passage is evidence for both oral tradition and Mark's incorporation of pre-existing material in his gospel.

The episode of the "strange exorcist" in 9:38-41 is remarkable for the attitude of tolerance it counsels toward those who are outside the circle of Jesus: "whoever is not against us is for us" (9:40). It is ironic that this advice appears shortly after the account of the disciples' failure to cast out a demon in 9:14-29. Read in the context of a gospel written for a small Christian community facing persecution, this instruction would have encouraged a positive attitude toward the adherents of other religions while reinforcing belief in the absolute centrality of the "name of Christ" in the economy of salvation. It would also serve as critique of Christian exclusiveness.

In treating the "scandal" sayings in 9:42-48 we have followed the widely accepted line of their interpretation as general sayings about discipleship. There is, however, an approach represented by Will Deming (*NTS* 36 [1990] 130–41) and Raymond F. Collins in *Sexual Ethics and the New Testament* (62–72) that links on the basis of a text in the Babylonian Talmud (*b. Niddah* 13b) each of the four scandal sayings with specific sexual sins: scandalizing "little ones" as child abuse (v. 42), scandal through one's hand as masturbation (v. 43), scandal through one's foot as adultery (v. 45), and scandal through one's eye as lustful glances (v. 47; see Matt 5:28-29). Collins does admit, however, that by the time Mark's Gospel was composed the sexual connotations were lost and "Jesus's stumbling sayings became general sayings on discipleship" (p. 70).

There is rich material for preachers and teachers in Mark 9:30-50. The passage reminds prospective followers of Jesus that facing the mystery of the cross is essential, that greatness in the community of Jesus involves the service of others and trying to recognize his presence in persons without power or status, that Jesus' power transcends the circle of his disciples, that scandal toward others and toward oneself is to be avoided as much as is possible, and that Jesus' disciples must live up to their vocation to be "salt" of the earth.

The passage also contributes to our appreciation of Mark's Jesus. Not only does Jesus heroically embrace the mystery of the cross (9:31) but he also exemplifies his own ideal of greatness as the service of others (9:35). He promotes an identification between himself and his Father ("the one who sent me") with the least important in his society (9:37; see Matt 25:31-46). He shows a remarkable tolerance and greatness of spirit in allowing the "strange exorcist" to act in his name (9:38-40). He promises a reward to those who show kindness toward his followers (9:41) and challenges his own disciples to even greater perfection by avoiding whatever is contrary to entering life in God's kingdom (9:42-48). The disciples' misunderstanding leads to the readers' greater understanding of both discipleship and christology.

The "good news" of this passage is that those who do Jesus' work without formally being his followers are "for him," and that those who give even a cup of water to those who "belong to Christ" will be rewarded. Jesus' words here are a challenge to read the signs of the times and to discern those who are confronting the power of evil and so are "for us."

FOR REFERENCE AND FURTHER STUDY

Achtemeier, Paul J. "An Exposition of Mark 9:37-50," *Int* 30 (1976) 178–82.
Collins, Raymond F. *Sexual Ethics and the New Testament: Behavior and Belief.* New York: Crossroad, 2000, 62–72.
Deming, Will. "Mark 9.42-10.12, Matthew 5.27-32, and *B. Nid.* 13b: A First-Century Discussion of Male Sexuality," *NTS* 36 (1990) 130–41.
Derrett, J. Duncan M. "*Mylos onikos* (Mk 9:42 par.)," *ZNW* 76 (1985) 284.
Fleddermann, Harry. "The Discipleship Discourse (Mark 9:33-50)," *CBQ* 43 (1981) 57–75.
Koester, Helmut. "Mark 9: 43-48 and Quintilian 8.3.75," *HTR* 71 (1978) 151–53.
Lattke, Michael. "Salz der Freundschaft in Mk 9:50c," *ZNW* 75 (1984) 44–59.
Milikowsky, Chaim. "Which Gehenna? Retribution and Eschatology in the Synoptic Gospels and in Early Jewish Texts," *NTS* 34 (1988) 238–49.
Wahlde, Urban C. von "Mark 9, 33-50: Discipleship, the Authority that Serves," *BZ* 29 (1985) 49–67.

36. *Marriage and Divorce* (10:1-12)

1. And he left there and came into the regions of Judea [and] beyond the
Jordan. And again crowds gathered around him; and as was his custom,
he was again teaching them. 2. And Pharisees approached him and asked
him if it is lawful for a man to divorce his wife. For they were testing him.
3. He answered and said to them: "What did Moses command you?"
4. They said: "Moses allowed a man to write a certificate of divorce and
divorce her." 5. Jesus said to them: "Because of your hardness of heart he
wrote this command for you. 6. But from the beginning of creation, 'Male
and female he made them. 7. Because of this a man will leave his father
and mother, and he will be joined to his wife, 8. and the two will be one
flesh.' So they are no longer two but one flesh. 9. What God has joined
together, let no man separate." 10. And in the house once more the disciples were asking him about this. 11. And he said to them: "Whoever
divorces his wife and marries another commits adultery against her. 12.
And if she divorces her husband and marries another, she commits adultery."

NOTES

1. *came into the regions of Judea [and] beyond the Jordan:* The verbs "came . . . gathered" are examples of Mark's frequent use of the historical present construction in which present tense verbs are clearly past in meaning. The present
tense makes the story more vivid, and the device is often used by storytellers
in all ages ("So he says to me . . . and I say to him"). The problem regarding
the geography of Jesus' journey is reflected in three major variants in the
manuscripts: (1) "the regions of Judea and beyond the Jordan"; (2) "the regions of Judea beyond the Jordan"; and (3) "the regions of Judea through beyond the Jordan." The first reading is generally accepted by textual critics and
commentators, though one might expect a different order: "beyond the Jordan
and into the regions of Judea." In other words, one might assume that Jesus
was avoiding Samaria and coming into Judea by crossing into Perea east of
the Jordan and recrossing the Jordan back into Judea.

   again crowds . . . he was again teaching: Whereas in Galilee Jesus had been focusing his teachings on his disciples (9:30-50), now in Judea he begins to teach
publicly again. This point is emphasized by the repetition of the adverb *palin*
("again"), by the reference to his "custom," and by use of the imperfect *edidasken* ("he was teaching"). The plural *ochloi* ("crowds") is unique in Mark,
whereas the singular *ochlos* appears thirty-six times.

2. *Pharisees approached him:* Many manuscripts of Mark do not have this phrase,
and its presence in some may be due to a harmonization with Matt 19:3. However, Jesus is now in Judea where he will frequently enter into debate with
various Jewish groups (see 11:27–12:44), and the issue of the grounds for divorce was a controversial topic among Pharisaic sages.

if it is lawful for a man to divorce his wife . . . they were testing him: The verb *apoly-ein* when used in the context of marriage is generally translated "divorce." However, that rendering may not fully capture what happened to the woman when the husband decided to dismiss or send her away from his household. At least according to their reading of Deut 24:1-4 the Pharisees knew very well that it was lawful for a man to divorce his wife. One gets the impression that the opponents knew beforehand that Jesus' position on this matter was in conflict with common opinion and with Deut 24:1-4, and their question to Jesus was designed to show to the wider public his lack of orthodoxy. In that sense they were "testing" him.

3. *What did Moses command you?:* In fact Moses gives no "command" about divorce. Rather, in Deut 24:1-4 (the only passage in the Torah that deals with divorce) the possibility of divorce is taken for granted. What is at issue there is the case of a man who divorces his wife and wants to remarry her after she has been married to some other man and divorced by him. According to Deut 24:4 the first husband is not allowed to take her again as his wife. In the Torah and elsewhere in the Bible (even in the case of Joseph and Mary in Matt 1:19) it is assumed that divorce is the husband's prerogative.

4. *Moses allowed:* By using the word "command" in v. 3 Jesus has put his opponents on the defensive and forced them to use the more correct term "allowed." Their admission that Moses allowed divorce leaves the question of "commanding" open and prepares for Jesus' contention that Moses did so because of the people's hardness of heart.

   a certificate of divorce: According to Deut 24:1, 3, the husband wrote out a document declaring that he had divorced his wife and sent her away. An example of such a writ of divorce has been found among the Dead Sea scrolls from *Murabbaʿat* (Mur 19 ar): "I divorce and repudiate of my own free will, I Joseph son of Naqsan, . . . you my wife, Miriam . . . so that you are free on your part to go and become a wife of any Jewish man that you please." Possession of this certificate provided the woman with the legal proof that the marriage had ended and made it possible for her to marry someone else. In this sense the certificate offered the woman legal protection against the claims of her former husband and the possibility of starting a new life.

5. *your hardness of heart:* The term *sklērokardia* appears in the NT only here (and the parallel in Matt 19:8) and in the second-century ending of Mark's Gospel: "he [Jesus] upbraided them [the disciples] for their unbelief and hardness of heart" (Mark 16:14). Nevertheless, hardness of heart is a major biblical theme. Since in biblical anthropology the heart is the source of understanding and judgment as well as the emotions, hardness of heart involves closing off one's mind and emotions from the truth. In the early chapters of Exodus Pharaoh is portrayed as an example of hardness of heart. In Ps 95:7 the people of Israel are urged not to follow the bad example of their ancestors as they wandered in the wilderness: "Harden not your hearts as at Meribah, as in the days of Massah in the desert." In Mark 3:5 Jesus' opponents in the synagogue are accused of hardness of heart and in 4:10-12 the general public's failure to understand the

parables is explained in terms of the prophecy about hardness *(pōrōsis)* of heart in Isaiah 6:9-10. In Mark 6:52 the failure of Jesus' own disciples to understand him and his deeds is attributed to their "hardened" *(pepōrōmenē)* heart. In the context of the debate about marriage and divorce in Mark 10:1-12 Jesus interprets Deut 24:1-4 as a temporary concession by God to the spiritual weakness of the people.

6. *from the beginning of creation:* The following quotations from Gen 1:27 (and 5:2) and 2:24 are taken as expressing God's original will for humankind before the "fall" in Genesis 3. The idea is that these texts override or "trump" Moses' concession to hardness of heart in Deut 24:1-4. The basis for this idea is the concept of the "new creation" inaugurated in Jesus' ministry. Now God's original plan for men and women set forth in Genesis 1 and 2 can be actualized. That "from the beginning of creation" is simply a way of referring to the first chapters in the book of Genesis ("Creation") seems unlikely.

   Male and female he made them: The quotation of Gen 1:27 (see also 5:2) is identical in wording to the Septuagint. The text describes God's creation of humankind on the sixth day according to the Priestly Creation account (Gen 1:1–2:3). The fact that God created humankind as "male and female" provides the presupposition for Jesus' positive teaching about married people constituting "one flesh."

7–8. *Because of this . . . one flesh:* The quotation of Gen 2:24 is identical in wording to the Septuagint. The central clause ("and he will be joined to his wife") is missing in many manuscripts. Its absence can be explained as an error by a scribe whose eye skipped from *kai* ("and") to *kai* ("and") at the beginning of v. 8, or its presence in many other manuscripts can be explained as a correction by a scribe who wanted to give the full text of Gen 2:24. The passage describes the climax of the second (Yahwist-Elohist = JE) creation account (Gen 2:4-25) according to which Adam was created first and then the woman Eve was formed from his rib. In the context of the argument in Mark 10:6-9 marriage between a man and woman represents a kind of reunification.

8. *no longer two but one flesh:* The phrase summarizes the point made by the combination of Gen 1:27 and 2:24 and expresses the positive ideal of marriage put forward by Jesus.

9. *What God has joined together:* The verb *synezeuxen* ("joined together") consists of the preposition/prefix *syn* ("with") and the root *zeug-*, which can describe two animals united by a "yoke" *(zeugos)*. By extension it refers to a pair, or in this case a married couple. According to the logic of Mark 10:6-9 the original will of God in creating man and woman was that they should constitute "one flesh" in an indissoluble union.

   let no man separate: Since according to Deut 24:1-4 only the husband could initiate divorce proceedings the "man" here must be the husband (but see 10:12) rather than a third party such as a judge. Thus the Markan Jesus does away with the institution of divorce by prohibiting the husband from initiating the procedure.

10. *in the house:* Where the house is and who owns it are not clear, especially since Jesus and his disciples are now in Judean territory. For Jesus giving the disciples private instructions about his teaching see also 4:10-12; 7:17-23; and 10:23-31.

11. *Whoever divorces his wife and marries another commits adultery against her:* This concise statement of Jesus' teaching about divorce and remarriage is close to the versions in 1 Cor 7:10 ("the husband should not divorce his wife") and Q ("everyone who divorces his wife and marries another commits adultery," Luke 16:18//Matt 5:32). The final phrase "against her" in Mark 10:11 introduces the idea that a wife too can be the victim of a husband's adultery. In the patriarchal society of Jesus' day where the wife was regarded as the husband's property, adultery was primarily an offense against the husband. The expression "against her" injects a certain note of equality between husband and wife. Whether "against her" refers to the first or second wife is not clear.

12. *And if she divorces her husband and marries another, she commits adultery:* This sentence is generally regarded as an addition to Jesus' teaching that was made to address situations related to Roman legal practice whereby a woman could initiate divorce proceedings. It also follows from the note of equality introduced at the end of v. 11 ("against her"). For an even earlier version of this adaptation to Roman law (Corinth was a Roman colony), see 1 Cor 7:10: "the wife should not separate from her husband." The exceptive clauses in Matt 5:32 and 19:9 ("except on the ground of unchastity") are generally understood as adaptations of Jesus' teaching on divorce to Jewish law and custom.

INTERPRETATION

In the context of the journey narrative Mark 10:1-12 presents Jesus' radical teachings on marriage and divorce. The positive ideal set forth is that husband and wife become "one flesh," and the fulfillment of this ideal means no divorce.

The main part of the passage takes the form of a controversy story in which Pharisees (with hostile intent) seek to bring Jesus into conflict with what they regarded as the clear teaching of Holy Scripture. After setting the scene in the early phase of Jesus' Judean ministry (10:1), Mark has the Pharisees pose their question to Jesus: "Is it lawful for a man to divorce his wife?" (10:2). When Jesus asks them what Moses said on this matter they refer to Deut 24:1-4 in 10:3-4. Thus Jesus unveils their hostility, since it becomes obvious that they already knew the "biblical answer" to the question. The implication is that they only wanted to bring out Jesus' "unorthodox" views on the matter. The rest of the controversy (10:5-9) presents Jesus' distinctive views on marriage and divorce. Having dismissed the text from Deuteronomy as a concession to human weakness (10:5), Jesus appeals in 10:6-8 to two texts from Genesis (1:27 and 2:24) as expressing

God's original plan for men and women ("no longer two but one flesh"). From this divine ideal Jesus draws the conclusion in 10:9 that divorce is contrary to that ideal: "What God has joined together, let no man separate." The public controversy is followed by Jesus' private instruction (10:10-12) in which he reiterates his condemnation of divorce and applies it to both men and women.

Jesus' radical teachings on marriage and divorce in Mark 10:1-12 must be understood in the context of first-century Palestine and the Greco-Roman world. The world of Jesus was very much a patriarchal society. Many marriages were arranged, and the arrangements were made between the bride's father and the groom (and his father). Marriage was regarded first of all as a legal arrangement between the groom and the bride's father. Once the couple were engaged they might get to know one another under supervision and would marry after a year or so (see Matt 1:18-19). The marriage ceremony involved the signing of the proper legal documents and the bringing of the bride into the groom's household (or that of his father) as Matt 25:1-13 depicts.

In the context of first-century Palestinian Judaism, Jesus' teachings on marriage and divorce were radical. While polygamy had become increasingly rare except for elites such as the Herods, divorce was not uncommon. On the basis of the case treated in Deut 24:1-4 a husband could divorce his wife if he found "something objectionable" (*ʿerwat dābār*) in her. The procedure involved the husband giving the wife a certificate of divorce (testimony that he had really divorced her and that she was now free to marry someone else) and sending her away. The certificate, of course, did provide the divorced woman with protection against the husband's future legal claims and made her legally free to marry someone else.

Despite the protestation of the prophet Malachi ("I hate divorce," Mal 2:16) most Jews in Jesus' time took divorce for granted. The great teachers debated the grounds for divorce and in particular the meaning of *ʿerwat dābār*. According to the Mishnah (*m. Gittin* 9:10) the school of Shammai gave it a strict interpretation as sexual misconduct on the woman's part (*debār ʿerwah*), whereas the school of Hillel said "Even if she spoiled a dish for him," and Rabbi Aqiba said "Even if he found another more beautiful than she is."

Some texts from the Dead Sea scrolls have both enriched and complicated the discussion. The *Damascus Document* 4:19–5:2 cites Gen 1:27 ("male and female he created them") in the context of a discussion about marriage, though there the issue seems to be polygamy. *4QInstruction* 416 2 iv 1 cites Gen 2:24 ("a man will leave his father . . . the two will be one flesh") but as part of an instruction about the husband's authority over his wife. The *Temple Scroll* 57:15-19 stipulates that the king must take a wife with royal Jewish lineage and that "she alone shall be with him as long as she lives." Scholars are divided over whether the text refers to polygamy or divorce, and over whether what is stipulated for the ideal king applies to anyone else.

The legal documents from *Murabba'at* in the vicinity of the Dead Sea include marriage contracts and certificates of divorce from the early second century C.E. They help us to see the legal formulas ("I release and divorce my wife today") and regulations (about the return of dowries, etc.) involved in Jewish marriages and divorces at the time. Josephus confirms that only the husband could divorce the wife and says that "a divorced woman may not marry again on her own initiative unless her former husband consents" (*Ant.* 15.259), though Josephus himself provides examples in which the wife at least pushed the husband into divorcing her.

Against this background Jesus' positive ideal of marriage as becoming "one flesh" and therefore that there can be "no divorce" stands out. That the historical Jesus taught this is confirmed by applying the criteria of dissimilarity, multiple attestation, and coherence. In a society in which divorce was widely accepted and the controversial issue was the grounds for divorce Jesus' teaching about no divorce went against custom and the cultural grain. As we will see below, the early church too had some problems with Jesus' prohibition of divorce. Moreover, the "no divorce" teaching appears in several independent sources: 1 Cor 7:10-11, Q (Luke 16:18//Matt 5:32), and Mark 10:1-12 (see Matt 19:1-12), and the radical character of this teaching is consistent with Jesus' many other radical teachings (e.g., Mark 9:33-50 and 10:17-31). By his "no divorce" teaching Jesus did not so much abolish the OT law (since he interpreted Deut 24:1-4 as a concession to the people's hardness of heart) as he went to the root of the OT commandment (as he does throughout Matt 5:20-48) and thus made sure that it was not infringed.

That early Christians had some problems with Jesus' "no divorce" teaching is indicated by Paul's advice to new Christians who found themselves in mixed marriages (1 Cor 7:12-16) and by the so-called exceptive clauses in Matt 5:32 and 19:9 ("except for *porneia*"). Whether *porneia* refers to sexual misconduct on the wife's part or marriage within degrees of kinship forbidden by Leviticus 18 (see Acts 15:20, 29), there is some exception being introduced. And Mark 10:12 extends Jesus' teaching on divorce and remarriage to conform to Roman legal procedures whereby a woman could initiate divorce proceedings. In the early church there was both acceptance of Jesus' "one flesh"/"no divorce" teaching and attempts to deal with problems that arose when it was applied.

The tension both in Judaism and in the early church raises the question of the actualization of Jesus' "one flesh"/"no divorce" teaching throughout history and today. It is important to recognize that in the debate about divorce in Jesus' day patriarchal family life and structures were taken for granted, that there is no manifest concern for what we today call psychological (in)compatibility, and that marriage is not yet being understood in sacramental terms. Also it is hard to know exactly how Jesus intended his teaching on these matters, and how we should take it. Is it an ideal to strive for, a challenge to be faced, an extreme example, or divine law? And which part of the NT evidence is more important—Jesus' absolute prohibition of divorce or the exceptions introduced by Paul and Matthew? And how is Jesus' teaching best actualized? Within the Christian churches there is a wide spectrum of approaches to marriage and divorce. Divorce and remarriage remains a complex and difficult pastoral issue. All the churches need to face it courageously if they wish to move forward the cause of church unity.

Recognition of the complexities involved in the NT evidence about marriage and divorce should not be allowed to obscure the positive character of Jesus' teaching about husband and wife constituting "one flesh." This teaching must be placed in the context of Jesus' proclamation of God's kingdom and the radical demands it may make on people. On the one hand Jesus has a vision of a restored creation in which unity and mutuality in marriage mirror God's original plan. On the other hand Jesus summons men and women to a discipleship that recognizes the radical demands of God by precluding divorce just as in some cases it may preclude marriage (see Matt 19:10-12). At the same time the church that follows Jesus' prophetic mandate must also incorporate in its life his pastoral sensitivity toward those in irregular relationships (see John 4:7-42; 7:53–8:11).

Jesus' teaching on marriage was as radical in the first century as it is in the twenty-first century. Those who teach and preach on Mark 10:1-12 should take care to convey the positive and constructive approach to marriage that it presents.

For Reference and Further Study

Brewer, David I. "Nomological Exegesis in Qumran 'Divorce' Texts." *RQ* 18 (1998) 561–79.

Collins, Raymond F. *Divorce in the New Testament*. Collegeville: The Liturgical Press, 1992.

_____. *Sexual Ethics and the New Testament: Behavior and Belief*. New York: Crossroad, 2000, 22–41.

Donahue, John R. "Divorce: New Testament Perspectives," *Month* 14 (1981) 113–20.

Fitzmyer, Joseph A. "The Matthean Divorce Texts and Some New Palestinian Evidence," *TS* 37 (1976) 197–226.

Green, Barbara. "Jesus' Teaching on Divorce in the Gospel of Mark." *JSNT* 38 (1990) 67–75.

Ilan, Tal. *Jewish Women in Greco-Roman Palestine.* Peabody, Mass.: Hendrickson, 1996.

Kaye, Bruce N. "'One Flesh' and Marriage," *Colloquium* 22 (1990) 46–57.

Keener, Craig S. " . . . *and marries another": Divorce and Remarriage in the Teaching of the New Testament.* Peabody, Mass.: Hendrickson, 1991.

Vawter, Bruce. "Divorce and the New Testament," *CBQ* 39 (1977) 528–42.

37. *Jesus Blesses Children* (10:13-16)

13. And they were bringing children to him in order that he might touch them. But his disciples rebuked them. 14. When Jesus saw this he grew angry and said to them: "Let the children come to me; do not prevent them. For of such is the kingdom of God. 15. Amen I say to you, whoever does not receive the kingdom of God like a child may not enter it." 16. And he took them in his arms and blessed them, laying hands upon them.

NOTES

13. *they were bringing children:* The subject of the verb is left indefinite ("people were bringing"). The *paidia* ("children") could be of any age from infancy to twelve years old. According to Luke 18:15 they were infants *(brephē).*

    that he might touch them: That is, "lay hands on them." According to v. 16 those who brought the children to Jesus were seeking his blessing. In the context of NT times there were two dimensions to receiving a blessing: physical contact with a holy person and a transfer of spiritual power, and having a holy person call down the blessing of God the Holy One on another person. As v. 16 shows, the two aspects are not mutually exclusive.

    his disciples rebuked them: The disciples' action here continues the negative presentation of them in this whole section where they are constantly concerned about positions of power and influence (in contrast to the "non-status" of children). Why exactly the disciples rebuked them is not clear. Was it because they seemed to be wasting Jesus' valuable time? Or were they creating a commotion? The closest parallel comes in the Bartimaeus story where the bystanders rebuke Bartimaeus for calling out to Jesus (10:48). But as here, Jesus there ignores them and ministers to Bartimaeus.

14. *he grew angry:* For earlier displays of exasperation or emotion on Jesus' part see Mark 1:43; 3:5; 8:12; 8:17-21; and 9:19. As the rest of this narrative indicates, the reason for Jesus' anger *(aganaktein)* was the disciples' failure to understand the gift of the kingdom of God and those who receive it.

Let the children come to me: In later Christian writings this text became the NT basis for the baptism of infants, but there is no reason to read this idea back into Mark (though it may have resonated with some in the Markan community). Here the saying functions as the occasion for Jesus to teach about the kingdom of God with reference to the example of children.

do not prevent them: For the problem of translating the verb *kōlyein* see the Notes on Mark 9:38-39.

of such is the kingdom of God: The Greek construction—the possessive *tōn toioutōn* and the verb "be" *(estin)*—is best taken as the equivalent of "to such belongs." What is at issue is the receptiveness of children in receiving everything as a gift. The kingdom of God is not a proprietary right; rather, it is a gift from God.

15. *Amen I say to you:* For other Markan uses of this solemn and otherwise unusual introductory formula see 3:28; 8:12; 9:1, 41; 10:29; 11:23; 12:43; 13:30; and 14:9, 18, 25, 30.

    receive the kingdom of God like a child: Children are naturally dependent on others for food, clothing, and other necessities. They receive all these things as gifts. How much more must all of us receive the kingdom of God as the greatest gift of all (see Luke 18:17).

    may not enter it: For the idea of entering the kingdom of God see also Mark 9:47 and 10:23-25. The string of "entering" sayings in this part of the gospel adds an important dimension to the Markan presentation of the kingdom of God. Only those who accept the kingdom of God as a gift can expect to enter it.

16. *he took them in his arms:* The verb *enagkalizesthai* appears elsewhere in Mark only at 9:36 where the service of the least important persons in society is described with reference to a child. The embrace or "hug" indicates Jesus' loving acceptance of the child as a model of receptiveness vis-à-vis the kingdom of God.

    blessed them, laying his hands upon them: Jesus calls down God's power on the children and at the same time transfers his power to them. This final verse explains why the people brought the children to Jesus in the first place or at least how the Markan Jesus understood their intent.

INTERPRETATION

It is fitting that a passage about children (10:13-16) should follow one about marriage (10:1-12), since women and children were especially vulnerable in this society. But this passage primarily concerns the kingdom of God and what kinds of people can be part of it. Only those who receive God's kingdom as a gift from God and make no claim upon it on the basis of their own status or power will enter God's kingdom.

After the scene is set and the main characters introduced (10:13a), there is an angry confrontation between Jesus and his disciples (10:13b-14a).

This allows Jesus to impart important teachings about God's kingdom (10:14b-15) and to carry out his symbolic embrace and blessing of the children (10:16).

In an earlier episode (9:36-37) Jesus used the example of a child as a way of teaching about the service of others, especially those who seemed to be social nobodies. There the emphasis was on the child's lack of social status and legal rights. Here children are presented as symbolizing powerlessness, dependence, and receptiveness.

The scene described in 10:13-16 stands out for its beauty and simplicity. It is one of the very few passages about children in the NT and in writings from the Greco-Roman world (where there was no interest in the romantic notion of children as innocent or unspoiled creatures). Here the focus is on the dependence of children and the fact that they necessarily receive everything as a gift.

In Jesus' view the greatest thing is the kingdom of God. By its nature the kingdom of God is transcendent (and so not a human product or achievement) and eschatological (its fullness is future). No human can bring it about or put a claim on it. It is God's kingdom. Only those who recognize it as such can enter this kingdom. For everyone, the kingdom of God is pure gift on God's part, and it must be received as such. Thus the passage presents a twofold message. On the one hand it shows Jesus' positive concern for children. He takes children seriously as human persons, calls attention to the wisdom they display in regarding everything as a gift, and seals his genuine affection for them with an embrace and a blessing. On the other hand the passage makes an important contribution toward our understanding of Jesus' teaching about the kingdom of God. Since the kingdom is transcendent and eschatological it must be received as a gift. The logic of God's kingdom is the logic of divine grace. A recognition of this fact can guard against careless theological discourse about our building up or bringing in the kingdom of God.

FOR REFERENCE AND FURTHER STUDY

Bailey, James L. "Experiencing the Kingdom as a Little Child: A Rereading of Mark 10:13-16," *Word & World* 15 (1995) 58–67.

Beisser, Friedrich. "Markus 10,13-16 (parr) — doch ein Text für die Kindertaufe," *Kerygma und Dogma* 41 (1995) 244–51.

Jeremias, Joachim. *Infant Baptism in the First Four Centuries*. Philadelphia: Westminster, 1962.

Légasse, Simon. *Jésus et l'enfant*. Paris: Gabalda, 1969.

Robbins, Vernon K. "Pronouncement Stories and Jesus' Blessing of Children: A Rhetorical Approach," *Semeia* 29 (1983) 43–74.

38. Riches and Poverty (10:17-31)

17. As he was setting out on the way a certain man ran up, knelt before him, and asked him: "Good teacher, what must I do in order to inherit eternal life?" 18. Jesus said to him: "Why do you call me good? No one is good except God alone. 19. You know the commandments: You shall not murder; you shall not commit adultery; you shall not steal; you shall not bear false witness; you shall not defraud; honor your father and mother." 20. He said to him: "Teacher, all these I have observed from my youth." 21. Jesus looked at him, loved him, and said: "One thing is lacking to you. Go, sell whatever you have, and give to the poor, and you will have treasure in heaven; and come, follow me." 22. But his face fell at this saying, and he went away sad, for he had many possessions. 23. And Jesus looked around and said to his disciples: "How difficult it is for those who have riches to enter the kingdom of God." 24. But his disciples were amazed at his words. Jesus addressed them again, and said to them: "Children, how difficult it is to enter the kingdom of God. 25. It is easier for a camel to pass through the eye of a needle than for a rich person to enter the kingdom of God." 26. They were astounded even more and were saying to one another: "Then who can be saved?" 27. Jesus looked at them and said: "With humans it is impossible, but not with God. For all things are possible with God." 28. Peter began to say to him: "Behold, we left everything behind and have followed you." 29. Jesus said: "Amen I say to you, there is no one who left house or brothers or sisters or mother or father or children or land for my sake and for the gospel's sake 30. who will not receive now in this age a hundredfold houses and brothers and sisters and mothers and children and land, with persecutions, and in the age to come eternal life. 31. Many who are first will be last, and the last first."

NOTES

17. *As he was setting out on the way:* The geographical notice keeps alive the journey motif (see 8:27; 9:2, 9, 14, 30, 33; 10:1). As he often does, Mark introduces a new episode without giving Jesus' name, though it is obviously about Jesus.

a certain man . . . knelt before him: Only in Mark 10:22 do we learn that he was rich. According to Matt 19:22 he was a young man *(neaniskos)*, and according to Luke 18:18 he was a "ruler" *(archōn)*. His action in kneeling before Jesus indicates his respect and reverence for Jesus. The only other Markan use of the verb "kneel" *(gonypetein)* is in 1:40, where a leper approaches Jesus and begs for healing.

Good teacher, what must I do in order to inherit eternal life?: The address "good teacher," while unusual in Jewish circles, carries no obvious negativity (despite Jesus' response in the next verse). The man wants to know Jesus' views on what are the necessary requirements for entering the kingdom of God (see 10:23)—for which "eternal life" seems to be a synonym (see Dan 12:2). The preceding passage (10:13-16) insisted that entering the kingdom is a gift from God.

18. *Why do you call me good?:* Why Jesus takes offense at being called "good teacher" is puzzling. One gets the impression that Jesus regards the address as insincere flattery issuing from a hostile intention (see 10:2; 12:14). But he quickly (see v. 21) changes his mind. Matthew smoothes out the interchange by having the man ask, "Teacher, what good deed must I do . . .?" and having Jesus answer, "Why do you ask me about what is good?" (Matt 19:17).

No one is good except God alone: While the adjective "good" obviously applies to God in the Jewish tradition, it also applies to many other things (see Gen 1:4, 10, 12, 18, etc.). For some this statement raises theological questions. Is Jesus admitting his inadequacies vis-à-vis God? Or is this an implicit claim to his divinity? Does *agathos* here mean something more than "good"—such as "gracious" in the sense that the kingdom (as in 10:13-16) is a gift from God alone?

19. *You know the commandments:* The commandments listed here come from the second part of the Decalogue, which concerns relationships with other human beings. Their order—murder, adultery, stealing, false witness, honoring parents—highlights murder and adultery. But why emphasize murder in the case of a sincere seeker of God's kingdom?

you shall not defraud: The commandment may reflect Exod 20:17 (see also Exod 21:10 and Deut 24:14). Its omission in some manuscripts of Mark and in Matt 19:18 and Luke 18:20 from the list of the Ten Commandments is good evidence that it was indeed part of Mark's text.

20. *Teacher:* The questioner has dropped "good" from his address to Jesus (see vv. 17-18).

all these I have observed: In terms of the conversation thus far it would appear that observing the Ten Commandments was enough for someone to inherit eternal life. To what else is the man being called?

from my youth: The man's claim suggests that he is no longer young, despite Matt 19:22.

21. *Jesus looked at him, loved him:* The mood of the encounter has shifted from its tense beginning in vv. 17-18. Jesus apparently now admires the sincerity and integrity of someone who has carefully observed the Ten Commandments all his life.

One thing is lacking to you: Jesus wishes to extend to the man an invitation to join his movement and become a disciple ("come, follow me"). Matthew interprets this invitation in terms of perfection: "If you would be perfect . . ." (Matt 19:21).

sell whatever you have, and give to the poor: As the example of Job shows, a pious man was expected to prosper and then to serve as a benefactor for those in need (see Job 1:1-5; 29:1-25). Being a benefactor in turn won gratitude from the beneficiaries and a good reputation in society at large. Jesus is asking the man to divest himself of all his goods once and for all and so deprive himself of the role of benefactor.

you will have treasure in heaven: For this theme see Matt 6:19-21. See also 4 Ezra 7:77 where Ezra is told: "For you have a treasure of works laid up with the Most High; but it will not be shown to you until the last times." Jesus challenges the man to admit that there are even greater blessings than being rich in this life and playing the benefactor.

22. *his face fell:* The verb *stygnazein*, which appears only here in Mark, means "be or become gloomy or dark," and by extension "be shocked or appalled."

    he went away sad: The man finds himself unable to respond positively to Jesus' invitation to become a disciple. This invitation entailed an itinerant lifestyle unencumbered by many possessions (see Matt 8:19-22; Luke 9:57-62).

    for he had many possessions: Only at the end of the narrative do we learn that the man was rich. He had to choose between holding on to his many possessions and joining in Jesus' movement. His desire to retain his possessions made it impossible for him to accompany Jesus as he moved about the land of Israel.

23. *Jesus looked around and said to his disciples:* As in 10:10-12 (and 4:10-12 and 7:17-23), Jesus supplements his public teaching with private instruction for his own disciples.

    How difficult it is for those who have riches to enter the kingdom of God: The adverb *dyskolōs* and the adjective *dyskolos* appear in Mark only in 10:23-24. The term *chrēmata* ("riches") is even stronger than *ktēmata* ("possessions") in 10:22. For entering the kingdom of God see the note on 10:15. The obstacle posed by riches seems to be that the thought and energy given to accumulating and preserving one's riches can distract from making God's kingdom the focus of attention.

24. *his disciples were amazed:* For other Markan uses of *thambeisthai* see 1:27 and 10:32. The disciples' amazement apparently stems from the common assumption that riches are a sign of God's favor and blessing (see Deut 28:1-14).

    Children, how difficult it is to enter the kingdom of God: The address to the disciples as "children" *(tekna)* appears only here in Mark; but see 2:5 for an affectionate use of the singular form of address *teknon.* Whereas v. 23 expressed the difficulty for the rich to enter the kingdom of God, v. 24 is a general statement about how hard it is for anyone to enter the kingdom. Some manuscripts understandably qualify the general statement by inserting such phrases as "for those who trust in riches," "for a rich man," and "for those who have possessions." The Western text moves the general statement in v. 24 to after v. 25. While this order is more logical, it is probably not more original.

25. *for a camel to pass through the eye of a needle:* The hyperbole (obvious exaggeration) illustrates just how difficult it is for a rich person to enter God's kingdom. The substitution of *kamilon* ("rope") for *kamēlon* ("camel") in a few manuscripts represents an effort to blunt the hyperbole. The idea that there was an "Eye of the Needle Gate" or "Camel's Gate" in Jerusalem has no historical foundation and again serves only to blunt the hyperbole.

26. *They were astounded even more:* Their further amazement stems from Jesus' general statement in v. 24 and his saying about the camel in v. 25. If the rich

who have leisure to observe God's commandments and the resources to give alms find it difficult to be saved, how much more difficult it must be for everyone else!

Then who can be saved?: Jesus has led the disciples to ask the most basic theological question about entering God's kingdom and inheriting eternal life. They are being forced to acknowledge the "gift" character of salvation and God's initiative in it.

27. *With humans it is impossible, but not with God:* The appearance of this saying and its positive version ("all things are possible with God") moves Jesus' teaching about entering the kingdom of God from a focus on what humans must do (see vv. 19 and 21) to a recognition of God as the one who initiates the process of salvation and invites people to enter the kingdom (as in 10:13-16). There are echoes of Gen 18:14 ("Is anything impossible for God?"; see also Job 10:13; 42:2; Zech 8:6).

28. *Peter began to say:* Peter plays his customary role as spokesman for the disciples (see 8:29, 32; 9:5; 11:21). The use of *archesthai* as a transition marker is a characteristic feature of Mark's vocabulary and syntax (26 times). One could translate its occurrence here simply as "Then Peter said." Matthew and Luke omit most of these constructions.

    we left everything behind and have followed you: For the first disciples (including Peter) leaving behind their families, homes, and businesses see Mark 1:16-20. While "left . . . behind" is in the aorist tense, the second verb appears in the perfect ("have followed") in some manuscripts and in the aorist ("followed") in others. The second verb refers to their having become disciples of Jesus, and so this episode provides a contrast with the episode of the man in 10:17-22 who rejected Jesus' invitation to become his disciple.

29. *Amen I say to you:* This solemn introduction to a saying by Jesus becomes increasingly frequent in the second half of the gospel; see the note on Mark 9:1.

    house . . . land: The list begins with "house" *(oikia)* and ends with "land(s)" or "fields" *(agrous)*. Those who constitute the household are mentioned in between.

    for my sake and for the gospel's sake: The phrase places Jesus and the gospel ("good news") on the same level. For other uses of *euangelion* ("gospel") in Mark see 1:1, 14, 15; 8:35; 13:10; 14:9; [16:15]. The early Christian summaries of faith identify Jesus and the gospel (see Rom 1:3-4; 1 Cor 15:1, 3-5), but whether the historical Jesus used this language about himself is often questioned.

30. *who will not receive:* Literally vv. 29-30 read "there is no one . . . but will receive."

    a hundredfold: Most manuscripts of Luke 18:30 and some manuscripts of Matt 19:29 have "manifold."

    now in this age . . . in the age to come: The terms reflect the classic Jewish apocalyptic distinction between the present time ("this age/world") and the future fullness of God's kingdom ("the age/world to come"). The list of benefits describes the inaugurated or anticipated aspects of the kingdom of God to be experienced already in the Christian community. Thus the picture of "this age" is more positive than that of Jewish apocalypticism in which the present age/world was often viewed as overwhelmingly evil.

houses . . . land: The list is the same as that in Mark 10:29, except for the omission of "and father" in 10:30. Although the omission may simply be due to a scribal error, one can argue that in the new family of Jesus constituted by those who seek to do God's will (Mark 3:31-35) there is no need or place for any father apart from God (note the same omission in 3:34-35; see also Matt 23:9).

with persecutions: This phrase, which interrupts the smooth and positive flow, is generally attributed to Mark. If so, it is a precious clue to the historical situation of persecution in which he wrote. Regardless of the origin of the phrase, it is a brilliant reminder of the mystery of the cross in the midst of a list of the positive benefits of discipleship.

31. *Many who are first will be last, and the last first:* This saying appears in the Synoptic parallels (Matt 19:30; Luke 13:30 = Q) as well as in Matt 20:16. It gives the impression of having once circulated as an independent saying and of being only loosely attached to its present contexts. The point is the reversal of values that will accompany the full coming of God's kingdom.

INTERPRETATION

Mark 10:17-31 is the longest sustained treatment of any ethical issue in the gospel and reflects Jesus' ethic of radical discipleship. The passage consists of three sections that deal with different aspects of the theme of riches and poverty. The first episode (10:17-22) is a narrative about a good-hearted and pious man who nonetheless feels compelled to refuse Jesus' invitation for him to become a disciple because "he had many possessions." He cannot face up to Jesus' challenge to sell his possessions, give the proceeds to the poor, and follow Jesus. The second episode (10:23-27) is a private instruction for the disciples in which Jesus reminds them how hard it is for the rich to enter the kingdom of God. The third episode (10:28-31) contains Jesus' promise to his disciples that in return for putting aside their worldly goods and following Jesus they will be rewarded more than amply ("a hundredfold") not only with eternal life in the fullness of God's kingdom but also in the present time.

While the three episodes are loosely joined together and may have been originally separate, they do express three important approaches to the theme of riches and poverty in the NT: riches as an obstacle to discipleship, God's preferential option for the poor, and the rewards (present and eschatological) for voluntary poverty undertaken for the sake of God's kingdom. These attitudes may well be rooted in the ministry and teaching of Jesus. They also give us an insight into early Christian approaches to these issues.

The first episode (10:17-22) portrays riches as an obstacle to discipleship. In the context of Mark's Gospel discipleship means adopting the itinerant lifestyle of Jesus and his first followers. The particulars of this lifestyle are sketched in Jesus' missionary discourse directed to the Twelve in Mark 6:7-13. Being with Jesus and sharing in his mission of teaching and healing demand the adoption of the simplest possible way of life ("one staff, no bread, no bag, no money") and subordinating one's personal comfort to the mission. The kind of poverty envisioned in Mark's Gospel is apostolic or mission-oriented rather than ascetic in the sense that self-denial becomes an end in itself. The man's rejection of Jesus' invitation arises from his unwillingness to adopt the simple and itinerant lifestyle suited to Jesus' ministry and the conditions of first-century Palestine. His possessions were an obstacle to his participating in Jesus' mission. The positive message of the episode is that those who follow Jesus should voluntarily cultivate a simple lifestyle in the service of the apostolic mission and not allow concern for earthly possessions to prevent them from carrying out their mission.

The second episode (10:23-27) obliquely touches the "privileged" spiritual position of the materially or economically poor by reflecting on how hard it is for the rich to enter God's kingdom. The logic of this theme is stated most clearly in Luke's collection of beatitudes and woes: "Blessed are you poor. . . . Woe to you who are rich" (Luke 6:20, 24). It is celebrated in Mary's Magnificat: "He has filled the hungry with good things, and the rich he has sent away empty" (Luke 1:53). The idea of God's preferential option for the poor is developed indirectly in Mark 10:23-27, especially by Jesus' statements about how being rich and having many possessions can prevent one from entering God's kingdom. The unspoken assumption is that the rich can become so preoccupied with material goods that these become too important and so distract one from recognizing that God's kingdom is a divine gift often best appreciated by those who are economically poor.

The third episode (10:28-31) promises rewards to those who take up poverty in the service of Jesus' mission of proclaiming the kingdom of God. Their rewards are both future or eschatological ("in the age to come eternal life") and present or ecclesiological ("in this age a hundredfold houses and brothers and sisters . . ."). This theme is also well expressed by Luke in the parable of the rich man and Lazarus (Luke 16:19-31—the future aspect) and again in Mary's Magnificat (Luke 1:46-55, especially in 1:52—the present aspect). Mark does not give much attention to the theme of sharing material goods; this is, of course, a major theme in Luke-Acts (see Luke 16:19-31 and Acts 2:43-47 and 4:32–5:11).

While leaving family and possessions is deeply rooted in the Jesus tradition (e.g., the Q sayings in Luke 9:57-62; 12:49-53; 14:25-26), Mark alone adds the promise of a new family and new possessions. The family that has been left behind will be replaced by a new family. The hundredfold that the Markan reader knows from Mark 4:7, 20 is the fruit of hearing and doing the word of God in a new family based not on natural kinship but on the power of God. This perspective appears throughout the NT where familial language is used of the Christian community. Early Christians addressed each other as "brother" and "sister." Paul calls Onesimus his "child" (see Phlm 10), compares his own work among the Thessalonians to that of a nurse caring for children and of a father encouraging his children (1 Thess 2:7-12), and calls the mother of Rufus his "mother" (Rom 16:13). The practice of hospitality and welcome toward traveling missionaries allowed early Christians ultimately to "possess" many houses (see Mark 10:29). The omission of "fathers" in Mark's list of rewards is evidence for many scholars that Mark's house churches also challenged the dominant patriarchal model of family life.

The kind of poverty promoted by Mark and other NT writers is not simply monastic community of goods or a primitive form of communism as envisioned in the Qumran *Rule of the Community.* Rather, it is first and foremost poverty undertaken voluntarily in the service of proclaiming and witnessing to the kingdom of God. It is intended to contribute to an appreciation of the centrality of God's kingdom by minimizing the distractions involved in becoming and staying rich, and it promises rewards not only in the world to come but also in the present. Mark's addition of "with persecutions" in 10:30, however, is a sobering reminder of the reality of the world in which Mark's community lived and worked (as do many Christians today).

While developed in and tied to the conditions of the itinerant mission of Jesus and his first followers in first-century Palestine and the Roman empire, the basic principles of the Markan teaching on poverty and riches —possessions as a possible obstacle to discipleship, the difficulty the rich may experience in entering God's kingdom, and the present and future rewards for those who follow Jesus in simplicity and poverty—continue to provide a challenge to all who dare to call themselves Christians and especially those who do so in the "rich nations" of the world today.

FOR REFERENCE AND FURTHER STUDY

Best, Ernest. "Uncomfortable Words: VII. The Camel and the Needle's Eye (Mark 10:25)," *ExpTim* 82 (1970–71) 83–89.

Guinan, Michael D., ed. *Gospel Poverty.* Chicago: Franciscan Herald, 1977.

Gundry, Robert H. "Mark 10:29: Order in the List," *CBQ* 59 (1997) 465–75.

Légasse, Simon. *L'appel du riche (Marc 10,17-31 et paralleles).* Paris: Gabalda, 1966.

May, David M. "Leaving and Receiving: A Social-Scientific Exegesis of Mark 10:29-31," *Perspectives in Religious Studies* 17 (1990) 141–51, 154.

MacHardy, W. D. "Mark 10:19: A Reference to the Old Testament?" *ExpTim* 107 (1996) 143.

O'Neill, J. C. "'Good Master' and the 'Good' Sayings in the Teaching of Jesus," *Irish Biblical Studies* 15 (1993) 167–78.

Schmidt, Thomas E. "Mark 10.29-30; Matthew 19.29: 'Leave Houses . . . and Region?'" *NTS* 38 (1992) 617–20.

Soares-Prabhu, George M. "Anti-Greed and Anti-Pride. Mark 10:17-27 & 10:35-35 in the Light of Tribal Values," *Jeevadhara* 24 (1994) 130–50.

39. *A Third Passion Prediction and More Instructions for Disciples* (10:32-45)

32. They were on the road, going up to Jerusalem, and Jesus was preceding them; and they were amazed, but those following him were afraid. And taking aside the Twelve again, he began to tell them what was to happen to him: 33. "Behold we are going up to Jerusalem; and the Son of Man will be handed over to the chief priests and the scribes, and they will condemn him to death, and they will hand him over to the Gentiles; 34. and they will mock him and spit upon him and scourge him and kill him; and after three days he will rise." 35. And James and John, the sons of Zebedee, approached him and said to him: "Teacher, we wish that you do for us whatever we ask you." 36. He said to them: "What do you wish that I should do for you?" 37. They said to him: "Grant to us that we should sit one at your right hand and one at your left in your glory." 38. Jesus said to them: "You do not know what you are asking. Can you drink the cup that I drink or be baptized with the baptism with which I am baptized?" 39. They said to him: "We can." But Jesus said to them: "The cup that I drink you will drink, and the baptism with which I am to be baptized you will be baptized with. 40. But to sit at my right hand or left is not for me to give, but it is for those for whom it has been prepared." 41. And when the ten heard this, they became furious at James and John. 42. And Jesus called them to himself and said to them: "You know that those who are supposed to rule over the Gentiles lord it over them and their great ones wield authority over them. 43. But it is not to be so among you. But whoever may wish to become great among you shall be your servant, 44. and whoever may wish to be first among you shall be slave of all. 45. For the Son of Man did not come to be served but to serve and to give his life as a ransom for many."

NOTES

32. *they were on the road, going up to Jerusalem:* The introduction to the third Passion prediction in 10:33-34 is quite elaborate and somewhat confusing. The opening phrases bring the "journey" motif back into the reader's consciousness (see 10:1, 17). Jerusalem is the place where the three Passion predictions will be fulfilled. In Mark's narrative this will be Jesus' only visit to Jerusalem.

Jesus was preceding them: The use of the participle *proagōn* ("preceding, walking ahead") highlights Jesus' preeminence among the wayfarers and his willing acceptance of the fate that awaits him in Jerusalem. For Jesus as the *archēgos* ("forerunner, leader, pioneer, scout") see Acts 3:15; 5:31; and Heb 2:10; 12:2.

they were amazed, but those following him were afraid: The second group seems to be made up of disciples *(akolouthountes)*. Were the members of the first group bystanders, local people, or members of a larger group of Jesus' disciples (beyond the Twelve)? And why were they so amazed?

taking aside the Twelve again: The first two Passion predictions were also directed to the Twelve (see 8:27-33; 9:31-32). In all three cases the disciples fail to understand, and they demonstrate their lack of understanding by their inappropriate responses.

he began to tell them: This is another example of one of Mark's favorite constructions; see the note on Mark 10:28.

what was to happen to him: The third Passion prediction is much more detailed than the first two. It matches the Markan Passion narrative so closely that most interpreters suspect that it has been composed by Mark (or at least filled out by him) in light of the Passion narrative.

33. *going up to Jerusalem:* Since Jerusalem is set in the mountains one necessarily goes up to it no matter what direction one comes from. Psalms 120–134 were used by pilgrims as they made their way up to the Holy City and so are known as "the Songs of Ascents."

the Son of Man will be handed over to the chief priests and the scribes: As in the first two Passion predictions (8:31; 9:31), Jesus refers to himself as "the Son of Man." According to 8:31 he will "be rejected by the elders and chief priests and scribes." See Mark 14:53 for the fulfillment of this prophecy.

they will condemn him to death: See Mark 14:64 ("all condemned him as deserving death") for the fulfillment of this prophecy.

they will hand him over to the Gentiles: See Mark 15:1: "they bound Jesus and led him away and handed him over to Pilate." The third Passion prediction places the ultimate responsibility for Jesus' death on Pilate and the Romans.

34. *they will mock him . . . and kill him:* For the mockery see Mark 15:20 (and also 14:65); for the spitting see 15:19; for the scourging see 15:15; and for the execution see 15:24, 37.

after three days he will rise: As in the other Passion predictions there is no explicit mention of crucifixion. Also as in the other Markan Passion predictions the phrases "after three days" (rather than "on the third day") and "he will rise" (rather than "he will be raised") are used.

35. *James and John:* For the call of Zebedee's sons to follow Jesus see Mark 1:19-20. Throughout the gospel they along with Peter form an inner circle among the Twelve (see 5:37; 9:2; 14:33; also 1:29). This is the only incident in which they act on their own. Is Peter's absence significant? In fact Matthew seems to have found their request so offensive that he blames it on "the mother of the sons of Zebedee" (Matt 20:20-21).

    we wish that you do for us whatever we ask you: Their request is the equivalent of asking Jesus for a "blank check." Their self-centeredness shows how they, like Peter in 8:32-33 and the other disciples in 9:33-34, failed to grasp the meaning of Jesus' Passion prediction. Whereas the disciples in 9:33-34 were apparently arguing about places of preeminence in the group formed by Jesus during his earthly ministry, James and John are seeking places of special prominence at the parousia (second coming) of Jesus and the full coming of the kingdom of God.

36. *What do you wish that I should do for you?:* Jesus' response is best taken as a polite question (see 10:51). Another rendering takes it as a statement: "Whatever you wish, I will do for you." But since Jesus ends up refusing their request (see v. 40), taking it as a question seems more appropriate.

37. *that we should sit:* It is hard to know whether James and John are evoking the image of the messianic banquet (see Luke 14:15-24; Matt 22:1-10) or that of the heavenly throne room (see Revelation 4–5).

    one at your right hand and one at your left: Mark seems to use the two Greek words for "left" (*aristeros* in v. 37 and *euōnymos* in v. 40) indiscriminately. See 15:27 where Jesus is crucified with two bandits *(lēstai)* "one at the right" and the other at his left *(euōnymos).*

    in your glory: For other Markan references to the glorious parousia of Jesus see 8:38; 13:26; and 14:62. The disciples' willingness to ignore the content of Jesus' very detailed Passion prediction reveals the depth of their misunderstanding of him.

38. *Can you drink the cup that I drink:* Here the image of the cup is best understood in terms of the OT theme of the cup of suffering or the cup of wrath (see Jer 25:15-29; Ps 75:8; Isa 51:17, 22). For the cup of suffering that Jesus will drink see Mark 14:24 and (especially) 14:36. While there is probably no primary reference to the Eucharist intended, the image does bring out the idea that sharing in the Lord's Supper (see 14:24) means sharing in Jesus' suffering and death.

    or be baptized with the baptism with which I am baptized: The Greek verbs *baptein* and *baptizein* have as their root meaning "dip, immerse." They can convey the idea of death by drowning. While again it is unlikely that a primary reference to baptism is intended, the image does serve to remind Mark's readers that they were baptized into the death of Christ (see Rom 6:3-4). The baptism that Jesus will undergo is his Passion and death. Being "in Christ" involves a participation in his death.

39. *We can:* The disciples' confident but foolish response illustrates the depth of their misunderstanding and prepares ironically for the cowardice they will display when Jesus is arrested (see 14:50).

you will drink . . . you will be baptized with: One of the mysteries of the Passion narratives is why Jesus' disciples were not immediately rounded up, arrested, and put to death. According to early Christian tradition (see Acts 12:2 for the case of James) most of the Twelve eventually suffered death by martyrdom (but see John 21:21-23). Jesus' saying in v. 39 does not necessarily prophesy that James and John will undergo martyrdom, but it does prophesy that they will suffer on account of their identification with Jesus, and in that sense they share his cup and his baptism.

40. *to sit at my right hand or left is not for me to give:* The assumption is that only God (the Father) can make these assignments. This saying is often linked to Mark 13:32: "But of that day or that hour no one knows, not even the angels in heaven, nor the Son, but only the Father." Both Mark 10:40 and 13:32 suggest that some functions or powers are left to God the Father.

    but it is for those for whom it has been prepared: Some early translations took the Greek as *allois* ("for others") rather than as *all' hois* ("but . . . for whom"). It is not clear for whom these places were reserved. On the basis of Matt 8:11//Luke 13:28 one might suppose that it was for the patriarchs Abraham, Isaac, and Jacob. At the end of the verse some manuscripts add "by my Father," very likely under the influence of Matt 20:23.

41. *when the ten heard this:* There was no indication of the presence of the rest of the Twelve in 10:35-40. Their introduction here provides a narrative connection between the presumptuous request by James and John in 10:35-40 and Jesus' teaching about true leadership as the service of others in 10:42-45.

    they became furious: In Greek this is another example of one of Mark's favorite constructions ("began" plus an infinitive). For the verb *aganaktein* ("be angry, indignant") applied to Jesus see the note on Mark 10:14.

42. *those who are supposed to rule over the Gentiles lord it over them:* In Jesus' instruction to the Twelve he begins by appealing to what they would already have known from their experience in first-century Palestine under Roman rule. The terms "rule" *(archein)* and "lord it over" *(katakyrieuousin)* help to characterize this experience as one of being subject to unlimited and overwhelming imperial power. The participle *dokountes* ("who are supposed") introduces a note of irony and prepares for Jesus' vision of the kingdom of God and of servant leadership.

    their great ones wield authority over them: The idea of worldly leadership as the exercise of raw power is further developed by the noun *megaloi* ("great ones") and the verb *katexousiazousin* ("wield authority"). The root of the verb is the same as that of the noun *exousia* ("authority"). From the beginning of Mark's Gospel a major theme has been the *exousia* of Jesus (see 1:22, 27; 2:10) and his transmission of it to his disciples (see 3:15; 6:7). The teachings that follow will illustrate how Jesus and his followers are to manifest their *exousia* by serving others.

43. *But it is not to be so among you:* The use of the present tense *(estin)* for the verb "be" carries the sense of a command ("it shall not be so"). Some manuscripts change it to a future tense *(estai)*, perhaps by assimilation to vv. 43b and 44.

43b–44. *Whoever may wish . . . slave of all:* The two sentences provide an excellent example of synonymous parallelism. Their structure is basically the same, with some minor variations for emphasis. While in the NT epistles *diakonos* is often used to refer to a church official ("deacon"), here it carries the more basic sense of "servant." Jesus' ideal of a servant-leader as *diakonos* also appears in Mark 9:35. The verb *diakonein* is used in the context of serving others in Mark 1:13; 1:31; 10:45; 14:47. The phrase "slave of all" is deliberately paradoxical. A slave *(doulos)* usually belongs to one owner and does the bidding of that one owner. By recommending that his followers become the "slave of all" Jesus underlines his ideal of universal service toward others.

45. *the Son of Man did not come to be served but to serve:* The title "Son of Man" appears in all three Passion predictions (8:31; 9:31; 10:33-34). This verse not only summarizes the three but also provides a theological interpretation of them in terms of Jesus as the servant *(diakonos)*. Jesus is the best example of his own ideal of servant leadership ("not to be served but to serve").

to give his life: Here *psychē* carries the general Semitic sense of "life" rather than "soul"; see the notes on Mark 8:35-37 for the problem of translating *psychē*. For "giving one's life" as a way of referring to martyrdom see 1 Macc 2:50 ("give your lives for the covenant of our ancestors") and 6:44 ("so he gave his life to save his people and to win for himself an everlasting name").

as a ransom: The term *lytron* ("ransom") refers to the price for releasing a captive or for a slave to buy his or her freedom. For a theological use of the term see 4 Macc 17:21 where the martyrdom of the mother and her seven sons (see 2 Maccabees 7) is interpreted as an atoning sacrifice and a ransom: "the tyrant was punished, and the homeland purified—they having become, as it were, a ransom for the sin of our nation." The related Greek word *apolytrōsis* appears frequently in the NT epistles (see Rom 3:24; 8:23; 1 Cor 1:30; Eph 1:7, 14; 4:30; Heb 9:15; 11:35) as one way of describing the effects of Jesus' death and resurrection.

for many: The Greek phrase *anti pollōn* echoes the Suffering Servant passage in Isa 53:12: "he bore the sin of many, and made intercession for the transgressors." The preposition *anti* conveys the idea of "in return for" in the sense of expiatory sacrifice. The term *pollōn* literally means "many" but can also carry the sense of "all" (e.g., "many have been created but few will be saved" in *4 Ezra* 8:3). See Jesus' words over the cup according to Mark 14:24: "This is my blood of the covenant, which is poured out for many *(hyper pollōn)*."

INTERPRETATION

Mark's journey narrative thus far has twice featured the pattern of Passion prediction (8:31; 9:31), misunderstanding on the part of Jesus' disciples (8:32-33; 9:32), and teachings about discipleship and christology (8:34–9:29; 9:33–10:31). The teachings cover many topics and take various forms, to the point that it is possible to lose sight of the journey framework.

Hence Mark has to keep reminding his readers about the journey. The third instance of the pattern (10:32-45), though it consists of three units, is more focused and compact. It is a fitting conclusion to the journey narrative.

The first unit (10:32-34) is a very detailed Passion prediction, so detailed that it is hard to escape the impression that its wording reflects the episodes described later in the Markan Passion narrative. The second unit (10:35-40) is a dialogue between the two sons of Zebedee and Jesus in which James and John manifest their failure to comprehend the mystery of the cross. The third unit (10:41-45) is an instruction in which Jesus proposes to the disciples his ideal of servant leadership as the humble service of others and interprets his own suffering and death as a "ransom for many"—an expiatory or atoning sacrifice.

Jesus first presented his ideal of servant leadership in Mark 9:35 in the context of the disciples' discussion about who is the greatest (9:33-37). There the issue seems to have been greatness among Jesus' followers during his earthly ministry. In 10:35-45 this ideal is presented at greater length in the context of the request by the sons of Zebedee to have prominent places in the coming kingdom of God and Jesus' glorious parousia.

The Dead Sea scrolls provide some important background for this Markan text. The Jewish community (probably Essenes) that apparently stood behind the several rulebooks found at Qumran was highly structured. Members with a Jewish priestly lineage stood at the head. This community also looked forward to God's imminent intervention on their behalf in which those who in their estimation had remained faithful to the God of Israel would be vindicated on earth and would be invited to a glorious and eternal existence with the angels in the heavenly court. According to the "Messianic Rule" (1QSa) their meals and community meetings were structured so as to reflect how things would be at the messianic banquet in the kingdom of God. The priest (and priest-messiah) comes first, and then the messiah of Israel, the heads of thousands, and the heads of the congregation's clans in a descending order of status (see 1QSa 2:11-22). There is a kind of mutual relationship envisioned here between the community meal and the future messianic banquet, in which rank and honor are very important factors.

While the Qumran text is better taken as a parallel than as a direct source it does help us to see what was at stake in Jesus' disciples' debate about rank in the Jesus movement and about honor in the coming kingdom of God. In a society that prized status and honor Jesus' disciples want to know where they stand (see 9:33-37) and what place they could expect in the kingdom (10:35-40). But the responses that they get from Jesus in 9:33-37 and 10:41-45 serve to reveal how badly they misunderstand Jesus.

According to Jesus true greatness involves the service of others. His ideal of servant leadership should prevail among his disciples during his earthly ministry. The same ideal exposes the foolishness of speculations about preeminence in the coming kingdom.

The OT background of Jesus' concept of servant leadership is best found in the Servant Songs in Second Isaiah (42:1-9; 49:1-7; 50:4-9; 52:13–53:12). The Fourth Servant Song (52:13–53:12) contains the most extensive description of the Servant's sufferings and a theological interpretation of them as a sacrifice and an expiation for Israel's sins. There is a longstanding debate about the identity of the Servant in the context of Israel's history during the sixth-century-B.C.E. exile in Babylon. Was he an individual such as the king of Judah, the high priest, or a leader of a prophetic school? Or was the Servant a collective entity such as Israel itself, the exile community in Babylon, or some group within the exile community? Whatever the historical answer to this fascinating question may be, the important point for us is that early Christians identified the Servant as Jesus and viewed him as the key to understanding the Servant Songs (see especially the episode of Philip and the Ethiopian eunuch in Acts 8:26-40).

The allusion to Isa 53:12 in Mark 10:45 ("a ransom for many") takes Jesus' instructions about leadership and service out of the realm of Wisdom teaching and into the realm of christology. The allusion probably evoked other phrases from Isaiah 53: "a man of suffering . . . he has borne our infirmities . . . he was wounded for our sins . . . the Lord has laid on him the iniquity of us all . . . like a lamb that is led to the slaughter . . . he was cut off from the land of the living . . . you make his life an offering for sin . . . he bore the sin of many and made intercesssion for the transgressors." Rather than being a foreign body attached to the end of Mark 10:41-45, the "ransom" saying provides the key to the whole passage and to Mark's Gospel as a whole. Moreover, the "ransom" saying links Mark's Gospel to Paul's focus on the soteriological effects of Jesus' death and resurrection (see *apolytrōsis* and its many synonyms).

The three units in Mark 10:32-45 work together and interpret one another. The Passion prediction in 10:33-34 and the "ransom" saying in 10:45 provide the framework both for the illustration of the disciples' failure to understand the kingdom of God proclaimed by Jesus (10:35-40) and for Jesus' own presentation of his ideal of leadership as the service of others (10:41-44). Taken together, these texts provide a profound conclusion to the teaching in the Markan journey narrative about christology and discipleship.

As in 10:28-31 where Jesus presents his followers with a countervision to the ethos of the time, he now gives them a lesson on the exercise of power. Gentile rulers lord it over their subjects, and their "great ones" make their authority felt (in contemporary terms "throw their weight around"). Gentile (that is, Roman) power was exercised primarily through force, intimidation, and a network of patronage that tried to insure absolute loyalty to the emperor. But the way in which power is maintained in that the world of rulers and the ruled is anathema to true followers of Jesus. His teaching about the servant leadership he exemplified is opposed to any fascination with power and precedence in church life. The church of every age must be wary of imitating those oppressive structures of power and prestige that characterize the rulers of this world, and must imitate the kind of servant leadership embodied in Jesus, who gave his life that others might be free.

FOR REFERENCE AND FURTHER STUDY

Collins, Adela Yarbro. "The Signification of Mark 10:45 among Gentile Christians," *HTR* 90 (1997) 371–82.

Dawson, Anne. *Freedom as Liberating Power. A socio-political reading of the exousia texts in the Gospel of Mark.* Fribourg: Universitätsverlag, 2000.

Lindars, Barnabas. "Salvation Proclaimed. VII. Mark 10,45: A Ransom for Many," *ExpTim* 93 (1981–82) 292–95.

McKinnis, Ray. "An Analysis of Mark X 32-34," *NovT* 18 (1976) 81–100.

Moulder, W. J. "The Old Testament Background and the Interpretation of Mark 10:45," *NTS* 24 (1977–78) 120–27.

Seeley, David. "Rulership and Service in Mark 10:41-45," *NovT* 35 (1993) 234–50.

Selvidge, Marla J. "'And Those Who Followed Feared' (Mark 10:32)," *CBQ* 45 (1983) 396–400.

Watts, Rikki E. "Jesus and the Suffering Servant," in William H. Bellinger, Jr. and William R. Farmer, eds., *Jesus and the Suffering Servant. Isaiah 53 and Christian Origins.* Harrisburg, Penn.: Trinity Press International, 1998, 125–52.

40. *The Healing of Blind Bartimaeus* (10:46-52)

46. And they came to Jericho. And as he was leaving Jericho along with his disciples and a large crowd, Bartimaeus, the son of Timaeus, a blind beggar, was sitting by the road. 47. When he heard that it was Jesus of Nazareth he began to shout out and say: "Son of David, have mercy on me!" 48. And many were rebuking him to be silent. But he shouted out all the more: "Son of David, have mercy on me!" 49. And Jesus stopped and said: "Call him." And they called the blind man and said to him: "Take courage! Arise! He is calling you." 50. He threw off his outer gar-

ment, sprang up, and came to Jesus. 51. And Jesus said to him: "What do you wish that I should do ?" The blind man said to him: "My master, that I may see again!" 52. And Jesus said to him: "Go. Your faith has saved you." And immediately he regained his sight and followed him on the way.

NOTES

46. *They came to Jericho:* The narrative begins with a verb in the historical present (lit. "they come"). The journey started in Caesarea Philippi (see 8:27), but apart from the confusing notice in 10:1 there have been few particulars about the route until the mention of Jericho. Located fifteen miles northeast of Jerusalem, five miles west of the Jordan River, and six miles north of the Dead Sea, Jericho is a kind of oasis in the midst of some rough terrain. The city had something of a revival under Herod the Great, who built a winter palace in the area.

as he was leaving Jericho: According to Luke 18:35 the Bartimaeus incident took place as Jesus was approaching Jericho. Luke then situates the Zacchaeus incident (Luke 19:1-10) after Jesus entered the city and as he was passing through it. Matthew follows Mark in placing the episode outside of Jericho but smoothes out the awkward sequence and tells it as the healing of two blind men (see Matt 20:29-34).

a large crowd: These may have been inhabitants of Jericho, or other pilgrims on the way to Jerusalem for Passover, or a combination of the two.

Bartimaeus, the son of Timaeus: Except for Jairus (see 5:22), this is the only personal name given by Mark apart from those of Jesus and his disciples along with John the Baptist and Herod (Antipas) until the Passion narrative begins. The Aramaic word for "son" is *bar,* and so "the son of Timaeus" is a translation or explanation of the name. The name "Timaeus" is harder to explain; a connection with the figure in the Platonic dialogue seems unlikely, yet it is difficult to find a Semitic name that might have generated the name Timaeus. The proper name is omitted by Luke (18:35) and Matthew (9:27).

a blind beggar, was sitting by the road: For an earlier healing of a blind man see Mark 8:22-26. The word for "beggar" *(prosaitēs)* is found only in John 9:8 elsewhere in the NT, though beggars were probably a common phenomenon in ancient Palestine. While here *hodos* ("road, way") is simply a geographical indication, in 10:52 the same word functions theologically as a reference to the "way" of discipleship.

47. *Jesus of Nazareth . . . Son of David:* The adjective *Nazarēnos* appears also in Mark 1:24; 14:67; and 16:6. For references to Jesus as Son of David see 12:35-37, though there the point is that Jesus is more than the Son of David. The Son of David par excellence was Solomon, and in NT times Solomon was frequently portrayed as a magician and healer (see Dennis C. Duling, "Solomon, Exorcism, and the Son of David," *HTR* 68 [1975] 235–52).

have mercy on me: Bartimaeus' cry for compassionate help is evidence of his faith in Jesus' power to heal and in Jesus' role as the agent of God's mercy (see Luke 6:36). Bartimaeus the "beggar" asks not for money but for healing.

48. *many were rebuking him:* For earlier uses of "rebuke" *(epitiman)* see 1:25; 3:12; 4:39; 8:30, 32, 33; 9:25; and 10:13. The fact that Bartimaeus is not dissuaded but shouts out all the more confirms the depth of his faith in Jesus.

49. *Jesus stopped and said: Call him." And they called the blind man:* Jesus shows his authority by having those who were trying to silence Bartimaeus in v. 48 (perhaps his own disciples as in 10:13) now serve as his messengers.

    Take courage! Arise!: The verb *tharsein* appeared in Mark 6:50 when Jesus encouraged the disciples as he walked on the waters. The verb *egeirein* (see 1:31; 2:9, 11, 12; etc.) often has a hint of resurrection about it.

50. *He threw off his outer garment, sprang up, and came to Jesus:* These vivid details are omitted in Matt 20:32-33 and Luke 18:40-41, presumably as "unnecessary." Although Matthew and Luke succeed in highlighting the theological dynamics of the narrative they lose something of the vividness that makes Mark's story of Bartimaeus memorable and attractive. Some interpreters find a symbolic significance in Bartimaeus' actions as putting off his old and evil way of life. But for a blind man to be a beggar in first-century Palestine was not particularly disgraceful.

51. *What do you wish that I should do?:* See the same (somewhat peculiar) construction in Mark 10:36.

    My master: The Greek word *Rabbouni* is a heightened or emphatic form of "Rabbi." It derives from the Hebrew *rabboni,* a combination of *rabbon* ("master") and the first-person singular suffix. In the NT the title is used with regard to Jesus only here and in John 20:16 (when Mary Magdalene recognizes that what she thought was the gardener was the risen Jesus). It is doubtful that either Rabbi or Rabbouni had become a technical term for a Jewish teacher in Jesus' time; see the note on Mark 9:5.

    that I may see again: The verb *anablepein* often appears in the context of regaining sight that had been lost. The following verse suggests that Bartimaeus' newly found sight was both physical and spiritual.

52. *Go. Your faith has saved you:* There is no healing word or touch here (compare 8:22-26). There is simply Jesus' declaration that Bartimaeus' faith has "saved" him—a verb *(sōzein)* that can refer to both physical and spiritual healing (even "salvation"). See the same declaration by Jesus in the story of the woman with the flow of blood in Mark 5:34.

    immediately he regained his sight: The healing is instantaneous and complete, in contrast to the gradual healing in Mark 8:22-26.

    followed him on the way: The combination of the words "follow" and "way" suggests that Bartimaeus became a follower of Jesus and went up to Jerusalem with him (though he is never heard from again).

INTERPRETATION

The healing of blind Bartimaeus is on the surface a miracle story, but it is also, and more profoundly, a dialogue about faith. After setting the scene in 10:46 Mark narrates Bartimaeus' repeated cry in vv. 47-48: "Son of David, have mercy on me!" When Jesus summons him in v. 49, Bartimaeus rushes to Jesus in v. 50. Jesus elicits his request ("that I may see again") in v. 51, and in v. 52 declares him healed from his blindness ("your faith has saved you"), and Bartimaeus follows Jesus on the way up to Jerusalem.

The blind Bartimaeus displays prophetic insight. His choice of the epithet "Son of David" evokes Jesus' royal lineage as well as contemporary Jewish traditions about Solomon as a magician and healer. The beggar Bartimaeus here asks for more than money ("that I may see again"), and he gets even more than he asks for ("your faith has saved you"). Bartimaeus emerges as an exemplar of faith in Jesus and seems to accept Jesus' invitation to become his disciple.

As the conclusion of Mark's journey narrative the Bartimaeus episode in 10:46-52 is linked to the earlier healing of a blind man in 8:22-26 (which constitutes the beginning of the journey). Besides bearing witness to Jesus' power as a healer, the two accounts by their very position in Mark's outline have obvious symbolic significance.

Both texts are stories about blind men who receive the gift of sight from Jesus, and both feature a large amount of dialogue. In 8:22-26 there are ritualistic or even magical elements (use of spittle, laying on of hands), whereas in 10:46-52 there are no healing actions or words, and what stands out is the faith of Bartimaeus ("your faith has saved you"). In 8:22-26 the healing is complicated and gradual, whereas in 10:46-52 it is immediate and complete. In 8:22-26 the man is sent home and told not to enter the village, while in 10:46-52 Bartimaeus follows Jesus on the way.

The Markan journey narrative has been primarily concerned with coming to see who Jesus is and what it means to follow him. At the outset Mark 8:22-26 reminds the reader how difficult it can be to see these things clearly, while at the end Mark 10:46-52 illustrates a clear-sighted faith in Jesus the Son of David as the agent of God's healing power and the enthusiastic and wholehearted response that he evokes from people of faith. More important than the restoration of Bartimaeus' physical sight is his spiritual insight into the person of Jesus.

The Bartimaeus story also serves as a bridge to the next phases in Mark's story of Jesus' public ministry: his teaching in deed and word in Jerusalem (chs. 11–12); his apocalyptic discourse (ch. 13); and his Passion, death, and resurrection (chs. 14–16). In Markan geography Jerusalem is the place where Jesus is rejected and put to death.

The way of Jesus turns out to be the way of the cross: the way of rejection by his Jewish contemporaries, the way of betrayal by his own disciples, and the way of suffering and death at the hands of the Jewish and Roman authorities. Along the journey described in 8:22–10:52 Jesus has taught his disciples who he is, what awaits him (see 8:31; 9:31; 10:33-34), and what it means to follow him. Bartimaeus has received the gift of sight and sets out on the way of Jesus: the way that leads to Jerusalem.

For Reference and Further Study

Achtemeier, Paul J. "'And He Followed Him': Miracles and Discipleship in Mark 10:46-52," *Semeia* 11 (1978) 115–45.

Beavis, Mary Ann. "From the Margin to the Way: A Feminist Reading of the Story of Bartimaeus," *Journal of Feminist Studies in Religion* 14 (1998) 19–39.

Culpepper, R. Alan. "Mark 10:50: Why Mention the Garment?" *JBL* 101 (1982) 131–32.

Duling, Dennis C. "Solomon, Exorcism and the Son of David," *HTR* 68 (1975) 237–52.

Eckstein, Hans-Joachim. "Markus 10,46-52 als Schüsseltext des Markusevangeliums," *ZNW* 87 (1996) 33–50.

Guijarro-Oporto, Santiago. "Healing Stories and Medical Anthropology: A Reading of Mark 10:46-52," *BTB* 30 (2000) 102–12.

Johnson, Earl S. "Mark 10:46-52: Blind Bartimaeus," *CBQ* 40 (1978) 191–204.

Olekamma, Innocent Uhuegbu. *The Healing of Blind Bartimaeus (Mk 10,46-52) in the Markan Context. Two Ways of Asking.* Frankfurt: Peter Lang, 1999.

Robbins, Vernon K. "The Healing of Blind Bartimaeus (10,46-52) in Marcan Theology," *JBL* 92 (1973) 224-43.

Steinhauser, Michael G. "The Form of the Bartimaeus Narrative (Mark 10,46-52)," *NTS* 32 (1986) 583–95.

41. *Jesus' Entry into Jerusalem* (11:1-11)

1. And when they came near to Jerusalem, to Bethphage and Bethany, at the Mount of Olives, he sent two of his disciples. 2. And he said to them: "Go to the village opposite us; and immediately as you enter it, you will find a colt tethered, on which no one has yet sat. Untie it and bring it. 3. And if anyone says to you, 'Why are you doing this?,' you say, 'Its master has need of it, and he will send it back here again immediately.'" 4. And they went off and found the colt tethered at the door out in the street, and they untied it. 5. And some of those standing there were say-

ing to them: "What are you doing, untying the colt?" 6. But they told them just as Jesus said, and they let them go. 7. And they brought the colt to Jesus, and they put their garments on it, and he sat on it. 8. And many spread their garments on the road, and others spread leafy branches that they cut from the fields. 9. And those who were going ahead and those who were following were shouting out: "Hosanna. Blessed is the one who comes in the name of the Lord. 10. Blessed is the kingdom of our father David that is coming. Hosanna in the highest." 11. And he came into Jerusalem, into the Temple, and he looked around at everything. As the hour was already late, he went out to Bethany with the Twelve.

NOTES

1. *they came near to Jerusalem:* The initial verb and many of the other verbs in this narrative are in the historical present tense in Greek, one of Mark's favorite literary devices.

   to Bethphage and Bethany, at the Mount of Olives: Bethphage ("house of unripe figs") was a village on the Mount of Olives; its exact location is uncertain. Bethany is a village about two miles east of Jerusalem; its name today is El-Azariah, which reflects a traditional connection with the tomb of Lazarus (see John 11:1-44). During "Holy Week" Bethany apparently serves as Jesus' home base (see Mark 11:11-12; 14:3-9). The Mount of Olives is a large hillside to the east of Jerusalem. It was so named because it is a comparatively good place for growing olive trees. According to Zech 14:4 the Mount of Olives is the place where the Lord (YHWH) will reveal himself in the decisive battle against the nations: "On that day his feet shall stand on the Mount of Olives . . . one half of the mount shall withdraw northward and the other half southward."

2. *Go to the village opposite us:* Since Bethany is serving as Jesus' home base the village is most likely Bethphage (which seems to have been located between Bethany and Jerusalem from the east).

   you will find: Do Jesus' instructions reflect a prior arrangement or a gift of prophecy? The narrative can be read in either way. The idea of a prior arrangement satisfies most of the evidence (but see v. 3c).

   a colt tethered, on which no one has yet sat: The OT background of Jesus' symbolic action is the description of the divine warrior in Zech 9:9: "Lo, your king comes to you; triumphant and victorious is he, humble and riding on a donkey, on a colt, the foal of a donkey." The Greek word *pōlos* can refer to the young offspring of various animals including donkeys and horses. Matthew (in 21:2, 7) envisions the presence of two animals—the donkey and her colt—on the basis of an excessively literal reading of Zech 9:9. The fact that no one has yet ridden on the animal apparently contributes to the "purity" of Jesus' prophetic action.

3. *Its master has need of it:* The Greek word *kyrios* makes the interpretation difficult. It could simply (and most likely) refer to the owner of the animal with

whom Jesus has made the arrangement, but it could also refer to God ("the Lord") or to Jesus himself (though *Kyrios* is not a prominent christological title in Mark, despite 12:35-37). However, most translators and interpreters identify Jesus as the subject. As noted in v. 2, the story can be read in two different ways: as reflecting either a prior arrangement or Jesus' prophetic gift.

he will send it back here again immediately: The subject of the verb is most likely the owner, but why then the promise that the owner will send it back, and why the very precise phrasing ("here again immediately") with its suggestion of some anxiety?

4. *at the door out in the street:* The two disciples find things precisely as Jesus told them, and they do exactly as he told them. The word *amphodos* ("street") refers to a road with houses on both sides, or to a "city quarter," or to a "crossroads." The idea is that the animal is out in public sight and the bystanders can see the two disciples untying it.

5. *some of those standing there:* For similar expressions see Mark 9:1 and 15:35. In questioning the two disciples the bystanders do exactly as Jesus had foretold in v. 3.

6. *they told them just as Jesus said:* Or "just what Jesus instructed." The explanation that Jesus had suggested to the two disciples in v. 3 is successful and has the desired effect. Some commentators, however, wonder why the bystanders so easily accept the disciples' explanation.

7. *they put their garments on it, and he sat on it:* Here "they" presumably includes at least the two disciples who brought the animal to Jesus. Their actions serve to create a kind of "throne" for Jesus and contribute to his messianic fulfillment of Zech 9:9 ("your king comes to you . . . on a donkey").

8. *many spread their garments on the road:* Here the "many" presumably includes a wider group than Jesus' disciples. For the royal/messianic significance of this action, see 2 Kgs 9:13: "they all took their cloaks and spread them for him on the bare steps; and they blew the trumpet and proclaimed 'Jehu is king.'"

others spread leafy branches that they cut from the fields: According to John 12:13 these were branches of palm trees, but palm branches would be better suited for the feasts of Tabernacles (see Lev 23:39-43) and Hanukkah (see 1 Macc 13:51; 2 Macc 10:7) than for Passover. The word *stibas* ("a bed of straw, leaves, etc.") occurs only here in the NT.

9. *those who were going ahead and those who were following:* This most likely means the whole crowd; that a division into (choral?) groups is intended is unlikely. How large the crowd was and what impact Jesus' action had on Jerusalem as a whole is hard to judge. We need not imagine that the whole city is taking notice.

Hosanna: This is the Greek transliteration of the Hebrew *hôšaʿ-naʾ* ("save, please") as in Ps 118:25 ("save us, we beseech you, O Lord!"). While in the OT "Hosanna" is a petition or cry for divine help, in Mark 11:9-10 it seems to function as an expression of joy or homage.

Blessed is the one who comes in the name of the Lord: Taking up from "Hosanna" in Ps 118:25, this sentence is a direct quotation of Ps 118:26. It may originally have been a greeting spoken by Jewish priests to welcome people as they entered the Temple area. Since Jesus does enter the Temple area in v. 11, it is appropriate that Ps 118:26 should be applied to him here.

10. *Blessed is the kingdom of our father David that is coming:* This is not a biblical quotation, though it can be taken as a commentary or interpretation of Ps 118:26 in v. 9. The most extensive presentation of a Davidic messiah in NT times appears in *Psalms of Solomon* 17: "See, Lord, and raise up for them their king, the son of David, to rule over your servant Israel in the time known to you, O Lord" (v. 21). But compare Mark 12:35-37, which suggests that as "Lord" *(kyrios)* Jesus is superior to David. Whether or not Jesus might have intended to encourage this kind of Davidic messianism, such a prophetic demonstration surely would have alarmed the Roman officials and their Jewish collaborators.

    Hosanna in the highest: A paraphrase (based on Job 16:19 and Ps 148:1; see also Luke 2:14) would be "grant salvation, you (God) who dwell in the highest heavens."

11. *he came into Jerusalem:* In Mark's narrative this is Jesus' first and only visit to Jerusalem. Luke 2:41-52 recounts his visit there as a boy, and John assumes several visits. From a historical perspective John may well be correct.

    into the Temple: We are to imagine Jesus entering the Temple area, which was very large and consisted of several courts. Only the high priest could enter the Holy of Holies on the Day of Atonement.

    and he looked around at everything: Some commentators take this as proof that Jesus had not visited Jerusalem before, since it makes Jesus look like a tourist. The phrase prepares for Jesus' second symbolic action in "cleansing" the Temple courtyards (see Mark 11:15-17).

    the hour was already late: So ends the first day in Mark's Passion Week schema (see 11:12, 19-20).

    he went out to Bethany with the Twelve: The crowd has disappeared and the popular excitement has died down. Jesus returns to his temporary home base some two miles east of Jerusalem. The Twelve were last mentioned in 10:32.

INTERPRETATION

Mark's account of Jesus' entry into Jerusalem is best understood as a symbolic action or prophetic demonstration, analogous to the public actions used so effectively by OT prophets and in the twentieth century by Mahatma Gandhi and Martin Luther King, Jr. A large part of the narrative (vv. 1-7) is devoted to describing the preparations for the event. The event itself (vv. 8-10) consists of Jesus' "triumphal" entry into the city. The story concludes (v. 11) with Jesus' visit to the Temple area and with the return of Jesus and the Twelve to Bethany.

The OT prophets made abundant and effective use of symbolic actions as means of teaching about God's ways and judgments (see Isa 20:1-6; Jer 13:1-11; 28:1-17; 32:1-15; Ezek 2:1–3:3; Hos 1:2–2:1). These actions often take the form of bizarre behavior but serve to convey God's will for the people; as enacted parables they are designed to make people think and ask questions.

That Jesus' entry into Jerusalem was intended as a symbolic action or prophetic demonstration is indicated by the elaborate preparations made in vv. 1-7. The question whether Jesus' instructions reflect a prior arrangement or his prophetic foreknowledge is secondary to the messianic overtones developed with the help of allusions to Zech 9:9 ("your king comes . . . riding on a donkey") and 14:4 ("on that day his feet stand on the Mount of Olives"). Moreover, the crowd's interpretation of Ps 118:26 in terms of "the kingdom of our father David that is coming" confirms the nature of the event as a prophetic demonstration of Jesus' messiahship and his pivotal role in ushering in the kingdom of God.

In the context of Mark's outline Jesus' entry into Jerusalem in 11:1-11 constitutes the beginning of "Holy Week" and serves as the context for unfolding the events that lead to Jesus' death as the suffering Messiah and his resurrection. Right from the start of Holy Week we know that Jesus is the Messiah and what his significance is for the coming of God's kingdom. But we need to learn exactly what kind of messiah Jesus really is.

Mark 11:1-11 also introduces the motif of Jesus' mounting opposition to the Temple—a theme that appears in the following episodes (11:12-25), in the controversies of ch. 12, and most dramatically in the apocalyptic discourse in ch. 13. For the role of Jesus' critical attitude toward the Temple in bringing about his death see Mark 14:58 and 15:29.

On the historical level it is likely that Jesus inaugurated his final ministry in Jerusalem with such a symbolic demonstration. We will never know how many people witnessed it and what effect it had on the general population, and whether the demonstration took the precise shape that Mark attributes to it is also debatable. But it does appear that the two prophetic actions undertaken by Jesus early in Holy Week—the "triumphal" entry (11:1-11), and the "cleansing" of the Temple (11:15-17)—help to explain what got Jesus killed.

Josephus in his *Antiquities* 17.269-285 describes a series of messianic pretenders (Judas, Simon, Athronges) who arose in Israel in the early first century C.E. He summarizes the situation in this way: "Anyone might make himself king as the head of a band of rebels." Another outbreak of such figures occurred in the mid-first century C.E. (see *Ant.* 20.160-72). For the purpose of illuminating Mark 11:1-11 the case of the Egyptian prophet (*Ant.* 20.169-72) is most helpful. Having declared himself a prophet, this man "advised the masses of the common people to go out with him to the mountain called the Mount of Olives. . . . For he asserted that he wished to demonstrate from there that at his command Jerusalem's walls would fall down, through which he promised to provide them an entrance into the city."

The usual Roman response to such outbreaks was swift and massive punishment. The Jewish leaders, especially those responsible for the Temple and the smooth running of society, generally collaborated with the Romans in these cases. It was in the best interests of both groups not to allow such rebellious movements to gain further popular support.

The kind of Davidic messianic expectation expressed by the crowd in v. 10 ("Blessed is the kingdom of our father David that is coming") rested on the biblical idealization of David as the founder of the Israelite monarchy (see 1 and 2 Samuel). The fullest presentation of Davidic messianism in NT times appears in *Psalms of Solomon* 17 ("their king shall be the Lord Messiah," v. 32). That psalm looks for a Son of David who will serve God's people as their military and political leader as well as the judge of the nations. That Jesus was addressed twice as "Son of David" by Bartimaeus in the previous episode (10:47, 48) helps to explain why such hopes for Israel's future may have clustered around Jesus as he entered the city his ancestor David had made the capital of his kingdom a thousand years before.

Yet, according to Mark, Jesus is in the final analysis a very different kind of messiah. He enters the city "humble and riding on a donkey" (Zech 9:9). The kingdom he proclaims and enacts is not that of his ancestor King David but rather that of his heavenly Father. And the decisive event in his activity in Jerusalem will not be some kind of military victory but rather his death on the cross and his resurrection (which represents victory over death).

The narrative about Jesus' entry into Jerusalem in Mark 11:1-11 establishes Jesus' identity as the Messiah and the Son of David. As the Holy Week narrative proceeds, however, the popular expectations about Jesus as Messiah and Son of David will be found wanting. Mark's readers will be confronted with the startling paradox of Jesus as the suffering Messiah.

FOR REFERENCE AND FURTHER STUDY

Derrett, J. Duncan M. "Law in the New Testament: The Palm Sunday Colt," *NovT* 13 (1971) 231–58.

Duff, Paul B. "The March of the Divine Warrior and the Advent of the Graeco-Roman King. Mark's Account of Jesus' Entry into Jerusalem," *JBL* 111 (1992) 55–71.

Fitzmyer, Joseph A. "Aramaic Evidence Affecting the Interpretation of Hosanna in the New Testament," in idem, *The Dead Sea Scrolls and Christian Origins.* Grand Rapids: Eerdmans, 2000, 119–29.

Kinman, Brent R. "Jesus' 'Triumphal Entry' in the Light of Pilate's Assize," *NTS* 40 (1994) 442–48.

Smith, Stephen H. "The Literary Structure of Mark 11:1–12:40," *NovT* 31 (1989) 104–24.

Tatum, W. Barnes. "Jesus' So-Called Triumphal Entry. On Making an Ass of the Romans," *Forum* 1 (1998) 129–43.

42. *The Fig Tree and the Temple* (11:12-25)

12. On the next day as they left Bethany, he was hungry. 13. And when he saw from a distance a fig tree having leaves, he went to see if by chance he might find something on it. But when he came up to it he found nothing but leaves. For it was not the season for figs. 14. And he answered and said to it: "May no one ever again eat fruit from you." And his disciples were listening. 15. And they came to Jerusalem. And on entering the Temple he began to drive out the sellers and the buyers in the Temple, and he overturned the tables of the money changers and the seats of those selling pigeons. 16. And he did not allow anyone to carry a vessel through the Temple. 17. And he taught and said to them: "Is it not written, 'My house shall be called a house of prayer for all the nations?' But you have made it a cave for bandits." 18. And the chief priests and scribes heard, and they were seeking how they might destroy him. For they feared him, since all the crowd was spellbound by his teaching. 19. And when it was evening, they went out from the city. 20. And as they passed by in the morning they saw that the fig tree had withered up from its roots. 21. And Peter remembered and said to him: "Rabbi, look! The fig tree that you cursed has withered up." 22. And Jesus answered and said to them: "Have faith in God. 23. Amen I say to you, whoever may say to this mountain, 'Be taken up and cast into the sea' and does not doubt in his heart but believes that what he says will come about, it will be done for him. 24. Therefore I say to you, all the things that you ask in prayer, believe that you have received, and it will be done for you. 25. And whenever you stand praying, forgive if you have anything against someone, in order that your Father who is in heaven may forgive you your trespasses."

NOTES

12. *On the next day:* In the early days of Holy Week (see 11:1, 12, 20-21; 14:3, 17) Jesus and his disciples move between Bethany and Jerusalem, about a two-mile distance.

he was hungry: This is the only mention in Mark of Jesus being hungry. For an earlier incident in Galilee involving food taken by the disciples of Jesus see 2:23-28.

13. *a fig tree having leaves:* A fig tree in Palestine could be expected to have leaves by Passover (April). In Mic 7:1 the image of the fig tree is used in the context of God's hunger and Israel's infidelity: "I have become like one who . . . finds no cluster to eat; there is no first-ripe fig for which I hunger." In Hos 9:10 Israel's ancestors are compared to "grapes in the wilderness . . . the first fruit on the fig tree in its first season." The prophet Hosea goes on to describe the results of Israel's wickedness in terms of a withered tree without fruit: "Ephraim is stricken, their root is dried up, they shall bear no fruit."

For it was not the season for figs: The season for ripe figs in Palestine begins in June. The parenthetical explanation is generally attributed to Mark. The effect, however, is to highlight what seems to be irrational behavior on the part of Jesus. As a native of the land of Israel Jesus presumably should have known better than to expect ripe figs at Passover. This in turn suggests a theological-allegorical dimension to the episode.

14. *May no one ever again eat fruit from you:* The verb *phagoi* ("eat") is in the optative mood, and according to 11:21 it is to be understood as a curse ("the fig tree that you cursed"). As 11:20 suggests, Jesus' curse of the fig tree had more of an effect than simple fruitlessness, since it was withered up from its roots.

his disciples were listening: This note prepares for the resumption of the fig tree episode with Peter's response in vv. 20-21 and Jesus' teaching on prayer in vv. 22-25.

15. *they came . . . he began to drive out:* The narrative begins with two of Mark's favorite constructions: the historical present (lit. "they come"), and *archesthai* ("begin") plus the infinitive. John places the "cleansing" of the Temple at the beginning of Jesus' public activity (see John 2:13-22). Of course, John's Gospel features several visits to Jerusalem by Jesus over a three-year span. Mark (followed by Matthew and Luke) narrates only one visit to Jerusalem, which leads immediately to Jesus' arrest and execution.

on entering the Temple: See the note on 11:11. The area of the large Temple complex Jesus enters is presumably the Court of the Gentiles, where commercial activity was both permissible and necessary if sacrifices were to be offered.

the sellers and the buyers: Most of the commerce undertaken in the Temple complex was related to the sacrificial cult. This general phrase is specified by way of content in what follows.

the tables of the money changers: The Greek term *kollybistēs* ("money changers") derives from *kollybos*, which was a small Greek coin that came to stand for the rate of exchange. The money changers provided Jewish or Tyrian coins in exchange for Greek or Roman money. These coins could then be used for buying materials for sacrifices (animals, grain, wine, oil, etc.) and for paying Temple taxes and dues (see Exod 30:11-16).

the seats of those selling pigeons: Pigeons or turtledoves were used in sacrifices offered for women (see Lev 12:6-8; Luke 2:22-24), lepers (Lev 14:22), and others (Lev 15:14, 29). The birds served as sacrifices for those who could not afford more expensive animals.

16. *to carry a vessel through the Temple:* What is in view is the whole Temple complex, not merely the places of sacrifice or the Holy of Holies. The word "vessel" *(skeuos)* could refer to the money bags of the sellers and buyers or of those who used the Temple as a bank, or more generally it may describe what was needed to carry on the business of the Temple cult. According to the *Mishnah* "one should not enter the Temple Mount with his walking stick, his overshoes, his money bag, or with dust on his feet. And one should not use the Temple Mount for a shortcut" (*m. Berakot* 9:5). Jesus, like the rabbis, seeks to preserve the sacred character of the Temple complex.

17. *'My house shall be called a house of prayer for all the nations':* The OT text is from Isa 56:7 (LXX), part of the opening exhortation in Third Isaiah (chs. 56–66). It appears in a prophetic discourse that is critical of the poor level of Torah observance in the newly built Second Temple (late sixth century B.C.E.). The "house" is the Jerusalem Temple. The phrase "all the nations" recalls the vision of Isa 2:2-4 (see also Isaiah 66) according to which Jerusalem and its Temple will be the place of worship and instruction for all the nations of the world: "Many peoples shall come and say, 'Come, let us go up to the mountain of the Lord, to the house of the God of Jacob, that he may teach us his ways and that we may walk in his paths'" (Isa 2:3). It is this vision of a purified and renewed Temple that will welcome non-Jews that Jesus evokes in the Temple incident. For Mark's readers (many of whom were Gentile Christians) the expression "for all the nations" would have been especially significant.

a cave for bandits: The phrase usually translated as "den of thieves" comes from Jer 7:11: "Has this house, which is called by my name, become a den of robbers in your sight?" The use of Isa 56:7 and Jeremiah 7:11 as a commentary on Jesus' actions in Mark 11:15-16 indicates that at least part of Jesus' problem with the Jerusalem Temple was its commercialism and the dishonest practices associated with it. The term *lēstēs* ("bandit") will appear in the Passion narrative in the contexts of Jesus' arrest ("as against a bandit," 14:48) and his crucifixion ("they crucified two bandits," 15:27). The target of this accusation ("you have made it . . .") seems to be the chief priests and scribes (11:18).

18. *the chief priests and scribes . . . were seeking how they might destroy him:* The phrase "how they might destroy him" is identical to the first notice of a plot against Jesus (see 3:6). But whereas in 3:6 the plotters are the Pharisees and Herodians, here they are the chief priests and scribes who along with the elders will be the prime movers on the Jewish side in having Jesus arrested and put to death (see 11:27, 31; 12:1; and 14:1, which has the same verb for "seeking" *[ezētoun]*). In fact there are no mentions of the Pharisees in Mark's Passion narrative.

all the crowd was spellbound by his teaching: This sentence probably refers back to the popular enthusiasm at Jesus' entry in 11:1-11. In Mark 11:32 and 12:12 the chief priests and elders of the people are said to fear losing the respect of the crowd *(ochlos)*. In the Passion narrative, however, the leaders gain control over the crowd and manipulate it to call for Jesus' death (see 15:8, 11, 15).

19. *when it was evening:* This ends the second day in Mark's "Holy Week." Since according to 11:20 they come upon the withered fig tree the next morning, Jesus and his disciples presumably went back to Bethany (see 11:11-12). Some manuscripts read "he went out"; but see 11:20 for the plural form.

20. *they passed by in the morning:* See the note on 11:12 for Mark's "Holy Week" framework and for Jesus' movements between Bethany and Jerusalem.

    the fig tree had withered up from its roots: According to 11:14 Jesus had said only that no one would ever again eat from the fig tree. His curse thus has an even greater effect (see Hos 9:10, 16 and the note on Mark 11:13).

21. *Peter remembered:* Peter again acts as the spokesman for the disciples (see 8:29, 32; 9:5; 10:28). His address to Jesus as "Rabbi" is unusual in Mark; see 9:5 (Peter) and 14:45 (Judas). His comment interprets Jesus' saying in 11:14 as a curse and confirms that the fig tree has indeed withered up.

22. *Jesus answered and said:* What follows in Mark 11:22-25 is a brief catechesis on faith and prayer (see 9:28-29) consisting of a topic sentence (v. 22b) and three sayings (vv. 23, 24, 25) that may originally have been independent. In the Markan context the discourse points to God as the source of power for Jesus and for all believers.

    Have faith in God: The sentence could also be taken as a question: "Do you have faith in God?" Some manuscripts preface the clause by "if." But it is best taken as an imperative. The word "believe" *(pisteuein)* appears in vv. 23 and 24 and functions as one of the keywords (along with "prayer") in the unit. The expression *pistis theou* ("the faith of God") does not appear elsewhere in the NT. In this context the genitive *theou* must be an objective genitive; that is, God is the object of faith (see Mark 5:34; 9:23-24; 10:52).

23. *Amen I say to you:* For other uses of this solemn introduction see 3:28; 8:12; 9:1, 41; 10:15, 29; 12:43; 13:30; 14:9, 18, 25, 30.

    whoever may say to this mountain: Many of the verbs ("say . . . does not doubt . . . but believes") are in the subjunctive mood, thus emphasizing the conditional character of the saying (all depends on faith). Attempts to tie the saying to a particular mountain (the Mount of Olives or the Temple Mount) or sea (the Sea of Galilee) are fruitless and miss the point of the hyperbole. For other versions of the saying see Matt 17:20; Luke 17:6 (a tree instead of a mountain); and 1 Cor 13:2 ("faith so as to move mountains").

    believes that what he says will come about: The verb *pisteuein* ("believe") links the saying to v. 22 ("have faith in God") and to v. 24 ("believe"). The point is that through faith people can do what is humanly impossible.

    it will be done for him: This is a divine passive construction; the assumption is that God will bring it about.

24. *Therefore I say to you:* The second saying also receives a solemn introduction.

all the things you ask in prayer: The Greek text has two verbs ("you pray for and ask"). The verb "pray" *(proseuchesthai)* serves as a link to v. 25 ("whenever you stand in prayer").

believe that you have received: For "believe" see vv. 22 and 23. The verb "receive" is in the aorist tense rather than in the future, suggesting that faithful prayer is so sure to achieve its results that it is as good as already answered.

and it will be done for you: As in 11:23, this is divine passive. For other Synoptic Gospel teachings about the role of faith in prayer and about confidence (indeed, certainty) that God will answer prayers of petition see Matt 7:7-11 and Luke 11:9-13. The teaching that faith in God guarantees success in prayer is so unusual in Judaism and early Christianity and so well attested in the Gospels that it is generally traced back to the historical Jesus.

25. *whenever you stand praying:* The participle "praying" links this saying to v. 24, though it does treat a different topic: the need for reconciliation before prayer. Among Jews the usual posture for prayer was standing (see Luke 18:9-14), though there are references to kneeling for prayer (see 1 Kgs 8:54; Dan 6:10).

forgive if you have anything against someone: A similar situation is evoked in Matt 5:23-24, though there the setting is offering a gift at the altar (presumably at the Jerusalem Temple). But the point is the same: Forgive and be reconciled with your human enemies before seeking forgiveness from and reconciliation with God.

your Father who is in heaven: This title for God, not found elsewhere in Mark, suggests some familiarity with the Jewish-Christian version of the Lord's Prayer in Matt 6:9-13. For other echoes of the Lord's Prayer see Mark 14:36.

may forgive you your trespasses: The word "trespasses" *(paraptōmata),* not found elsewhere in Mark, is another link to the Lord's Prayer and especially to the coda in Matt 6:14-15 where *paraptōmata* appears twice. Both Matt 6:12 and 6:14-15 (as well as Luke 11:4) insist on the close relationship between divine forgiveness and our willingness to forgive one another.

[26.] Some manuscripts, most likely under the influence of Matt 6:15, have the following sentence: "But if you do not forgive, neither will your Father who is in heaven forgive you your trespasses." The better manuscripts of Mark omit it. Since the traditional numbering system was based on manuscripts that did contain the verse, it is now a null or empty number in most editions and translations.

INTERPRETATION

Mark's familiar technique of beginning one story, interrupting it with a second story, and returning to the first story (e.g., 1:21-28; 2:1-12; 5:21-43) helps to explain the movement of 11:12-25. The cursing of the fig tree (11:12-14) leads into the "cleansing" of the Temple (11:15-19). Then the narrative returns to the (now withered) fig tree (11:20-21), accompanied by a loosely associated instruction on prayer (11:22-25). The two narratives—the fig tree and the Temple action—clearly have symbolic value. Indeed, like 11:1-11 they are prophetic actions that follow in the tradition of the enacted parables of the OT prophets (especially Jeremiah, Ezekiel, and Hosea). The problem is trying to discern what exactly they symbolize.

The cursing of the fig tree (11:12-14, 20-21) is curious in several respects. Jesus' behavior seems irrational, since as a native of Palestine he should not have expected to find ripe figs at Passover time. The result of his curse is the destruction of the fig tree (as with the pigs in 5:1-20), and this is the only miracle or act of power that Jesus performs during his ministry in Jerusalem.

Mark presents Jesus' withering of the fig tree as an event, indeed as an act of divine power or miracle on Jesus' word alone—an impression confirmed by the addition of vv. 22-25. Many commentators, however, suggest that the "event" may well have developed out of the parable of the barren fig tree preserved in Luke 13:6-9. In the parable a man plants a fig tree in his vineyard and it fails to bear any fruit for three years. When he is about to have it cut down his vinedresser intercedes and suggests that it be given intensive care for one more year, when a decision can be made whether to cut it down.

Whether Mark 11:11-12, 20-21 reflects a historical event or the historicizing development of a parable is a matter of longstanding debate among scholars, but all agree that the episode has some symbolic value—as does the cleansing of the Temple in 11:15-17. In it Jesus curses a fig tree for its failure to bear fruit (even though out of season), and the result is that the fig tree is withered up and effectively destroyed. But what does the withered fig tree symbolize? At this point scholars tend to speak with great confidence but with little agreement. The fig tree has been said to symbolize the Jewish crowds, the Jewish religious leaders, the Temple, the sacrificial worship enacted in the Temple, Israel as God's people, Judaism as a religious system, or even the Markan community.

Perhaps the best explanation is that the withered fig tree represents the failure by many in Israel to accept Jesus as God's messenger and Jesus' message of the kingdom of God. This interpretation looks back to Jesus' seed parables of the kingdom of God in Mark 4:1-34, especially the parable of the sower (4:3-20) and its themes of the mixed reception of Jesus' preaching.

The "cleansing" of the Temple (11:15-19) is generally regarded as reflecting a prophetic demonstration undertaken by Jesus (though a few view it as a creation by the early church). Indeed, the entry into Jerusalem (11:1-11) and the Temple action (11:15-19) go a long way toward explaining why the Jewish and Roman leaders acted so quickly to arrest and execute Jesus. Passover as a Jewish pilgrimage feast drew large crowds to

Jerusalem. The great Passover theme of liberation from slavery could easily ignite a political and nationalistic uprising among the Jewish pilgrims. The two public symbolic actions undertaken by Jesus just before Passover amounted to a claim of his messianic identity (11:1-11) and a critique of the Jerusalem Temple (11:15-19). In the "trial" before the Sanhedrin in Mark 14:55-65 the two charges raised against Jesus are that he threatened to destroy the Temple and replace it (14:58; see also 15:29-30), and that he claimed to be "the Christ, the Son of the Blessed" (14:61; see also 15:31-32).

While the Temple action does help to explain on both the historical and literary levels why Jesus was arrested and executed, Jesus' own intentions in performing this symbolic action (and even Mark's reading of it) remain obscure and open to many interpretations. The least that can be said is that Jesus' Temple action was a protest against the excessive commercialization and secularization of the Temple complex (see 11:17 and *m. Ber.* 9:5). The assumption is that, even though the sellers and buyers were performing necessary services for those wishing to offer sacrifices, perhaps they should have done so outside the Temple complex itself and so better preserved the sacred character of the Temple precincts.

Many scholars, however, are not satisfied with such a modest interpretation, and some object to the episode's traditional title as "the cleansing of the Temple," since they think that far more was at stake. The most common interpretations are that Jesus' Temple action was a political-revolutionary action, an attack on the holiness of the Temple, an attack on the Jewish sacrificial system, a symbol of the imminent building of God's eschatological temple to replace the Second Temple, or a demonstration of Jesus' sovereignty over the Jerusalem Temple. The assessment by Etienne Trocmé in *L'Évangile selon Saint Marc* (290) is typical of the sweeping conclusions drawn from this episode: "It is the end of the Temple that Mark proclaims, thus distancing himself from the conciliatory solution of the church of Jerusalem. In the eyes of our evangelist, Jesus' intervention in the sanctuary has deprived it of all legitimacy, even as a simple place of prayer" (translation by Daniel J. Harrington). But as with the fig tree episode, a more modest and less ambitious interpretation may be preferable.

Another puzzle in this passage is the function of the catechesis on faith and prayer in 11:22-25. Since Mark seems to have viewed the withering of the fig tree as an act of divine power on Jesus' part (see 11:20-21), the most plausible explanation for his attaching the instruction seems to have been his desire to emphasize that God is the source of Jesus' power and that through faith and prayer believers can share in that divine power.

Despite its many interpretive problems, Mark 11:12-25 serves to clarify Jesus' identity and mission as he embarked on his ministry in Jerusalem. The fig tree episode foreshadows the mixed and indeed predominantly hostile reception Jesus will receive in Jerusalem. The Temple action establishes the inadequacy of the Jerusalem Temple as the only place to worship the God of Israel and helps to explain the course of events that issued in Jesus' death on the cross, and the instruction on faith and prayer points to God's power and God's ability to bring about apparently impossible results—such as redemption through Jesus' death on the cross (see 10:45).

FOR REFERENCE AND FURTHER STUDY

Betz, Hans Dieter. "Jesus and the Purity of the Temple (Mark 11:15-18): A Comparative Religion Approach," *JBL* 116 (1997) 455–72.

Böttrich, Christfried. "Jesus und der Feigenbaum. Mk 11:12-14,20-25 in der Diskussion," *NovT* 39 (1997) 328–59.

Casey, Maurice. "Culture and Historicity: The Cleansing of the Temple," *CBQ* 59 (1997) 306–32.

Cotter, Wendy J. "For It Was Not the Season for Figs," *CBQ* 48 (1986) 62–66.

Dowd, Sharyn Echols. *Prayer, Power and the Problem of Suffering: Mark 11:22-25 in the Context of Markan Theology.* Atlanta: Scholars, 1988.

Evans, Craig A. "Jesus' Action in the Temple: Cleansing or Portent of Destruction?" *CBQ* 51 (1989) 237–70.

_____. "Jesus and the 'Cave of Robbers': Toward a Jewish Context for the Temple Action," *Bulletin of Biblical Research* 3 ((1993) 93–110.

Hedrick, Charles W. "On Moving Mountains. Mark 12:22b-23/Matt 21:21 and Parallels," *Forum* 6 (1990) 219–37.

Murphy-O'Connor, Jerome. "Jesus and the Money Changers (Mark 11:15-17; John 2:13-17)," *RB* 107 (2000) 42–55.

Neusner, Jacob. "Money-Changers in the Temple: The Mishnah's Explanation," *NTS* 35 (1989) 287–90.

Oakman, Douglas E. "Cursing Fig Trees and Robbers' Dens: Pronouncement Stories Within Social-Systemic Perspective. Mark 11:12-25 and Parallels," *Semeia* 64 (1993) 253–72.

Sanders, E. P. *Jesus and Judaism.* Philadelphia: Fortress, 1985.

Seeley, David. "Jesus' Temple Act," *CBQ* 55 (1993) 263–83.

Telford, William R. *The Barren Temple and the Withered Tree: A Redaction-Critical Analysis of the Cursing of the Fig-Tree Pericope in Mark's Gospel and Its Relation to the Cleansing of the Temple Tradition.* Sheffield: JSOT Press, 1980.

43. *The Authority of Jesus* (11:27-33)

27. And they came again to Jerusalem. And while he was walking in the Temple the chief priests and scribes and elders approached him. 28. And they said to him: "By what authority do you do these things? Or who

gave you this authority that you may do them?" 29. But Jesus said to them: "I will ask you something. Answer me, and I will tell you by what authority I do these things. 30. The baptism of John—was it from heaven, or from human beings? Answer me." 31. And they were discussing among themselves, saying: "If we say 'from heaven,' he will say, 'Why then did you not believe him?' 32. But if we say 'from human beings'"— for they feared the crowd. For all held that John was really a prophet. 33. And they answered Jesus and said: "We do not know." And Jesus said to them: "Neither will I tell you by what authority I do these things."

Notes

27. *they came again to Jerusalem:* The verbs here and elsewhere in the passage are in the historical present. According to Mark's chronological framework the events of the third day in "Holy Week" began with 11:20 and continue in Jerusalem through the controversies with various groups (11:27–12:44) and the apocalyptic discourse at the Temple Mount (13:1-37).

    the chief priests and scribes and elders: These three groups were mentioned in the first Passion prediction (see 8:31) and they appear again in the Passion narrative (see 14:43, 53; 15:1) as the prime movers on the Jewish side against Jesus. As the Jewish leaders most responsible for keeping order in Jerusalem and in the Temple area they would be especially concerned about the possible effects of Jesus' entry into the city (11:1-11) and his Temple action (11:15-19) in fomenting civil unrest or a riot (see *thorybos* in 14:2).

28. *By what authority do you do these things?: Exousia* is better rendered as "authority" than as "power." The question of Jesus' *exousia* was raised at the very beginning of his public ministry (see 1:22, 27; 2:10), with the implication that his authority is from God and transcends the authority of other Jewish teachers and leaders as well as that of Roman officials (even the emperor). For Jesus sharing his authority with his disciples see 3:15 and 6:7. In the Markan narrative context "these things" refers most obviously to his entry to the city and Temple action, though it could include more generally all his teaching and healing activities.

    Or who gave you . . . . : The second question is almost the same as the first, though it does help to underline the early Christian claim that God (answering the question "who . . . ?") is the real source of Jesus' authority.

29. *I will ask you something:* The use of the counter-question (answering a question by asking another question) is a standard device in rabbinic debates. For Jesus' frequent use of this technique in the earlier Markan series of controversies see 2:9-10; 2:19; 2:25-26; 3:4.

30. *from heaven or from human beings?:* For Mark's account of John's baptism and the response it received from the people see Mark 1:2-8. Like the other evangelists and Josephus (see the Interpretation below), Mark emphasizes the great enthusiasm that John's baptism generated: "And there went out to him

all the country of Judea and all the people of Jerusalem" (1:5). In this context "from heaven" is another way of saying "from God." For the connection between God and John's baptism see Mark's account of Jesus' baptism by John in 1:9-11.

31–32. *If we say 'from heaven'. . . . :* Jesus' question has the effect of putting his opponents in a dilemma. If they say that John's baptism was from God they have to explain why they refused to believe John. If they say that it was only a human creation they run the risk of losing popular support (see 11:18) from the many people who regarded John as a prophet. Underlying their dilemma is the even more basic question: Which is more important—the kingdom of God proclaimed by John and Jesus or the Jerusalem Temple (whose guardians were the chief priests, scribes, and elders)? Although Mark does not use the term "prophet" to describe John directly, the description of his prophetic lifestyle (see 1:6) evokes the figure of Elijah (see 2 Kgs 1:8) and thus places John in the category of prophet.

33. *we do not know:* In reducing Jesus' opponents to silence by means of the counterquestion and its dilemma the narrative demonstrates Jesus' superior wit and suggests that just as John's baptism was surely from God, so Jesus' authority to do "these things" also comes from God. Thus Jesus evades a direct confrontation with his powerful opponents (while winning the debate) and still indicates that God is the real source of his authority.

INTERPRETATION

Just as a block of five controversy stories were part of Jesus' early ministry in Galilee (2:1–3:6), so another block of five controversy stories plus a parable is part of Jesus' early ministry in Jerusalem (11:27–12:37). The first unit in the second block concerns the source of Jesus' authority (11:27-33). In the Temple area the chief priest, scribes, and elders ask Jesus a question: "By what authority do you do these things?" (11:27-28). Rather than answering their question directly Jesus asks them about the authority behind John's baptism (11:29-30). When the opponents recognize that Jesus has put them in a dilemma, they refuse to answer him (11:31-33a). So Jesus refuses to answer them (11:33b).

From the way in which the story is told it is clear that Jesus wins the debate. Whereas the opponents set out to trap Jesus into claiming in public a divine authority for himself, they find themselves trapped by Jesus' question into having to take a public position about the baptism of John. The opponents, of course, are the representatives and guardians of Jerusalem Temple piety. John the Baptist was a popular prophet in the area around the Jordan River. He proclaimed the coming kingdom of God and the need to prepare for the divine judgment that will accompany it. These were two different ways of being a religious Jew in the first century:

Temple-centered or kingdom-centered. Jesus was associated with John and his style of kingdom-centered piety.

That John was a popular figure is clear from Josephus' account of his ministry in the time of Herod Antipas: "When others too joined the crowds about him [John the Baptist], because they were aroused to the highest degree by his sermons, Herod became alarmed. Eloquence that had so great an effect on humankind might lead to some form of sedition, for it looked as if they would be guided by John in everything that they did" (*Ant.* 18.118). As in the case of Jesus' Jerusalem opponents, so Herod Antipas was afraid that popular enthusiasm for John might issue in civil unrest.

This episode contains Mark's last mention of John the Baptist. Throughout the gospel thus far the careers of John and Jesus have been intertwined. The prologue (1:1-13) portrays John as the forerunner of Jesus, the one who baptized Jesus, and the one whose arrest preceded Jesus' own public ministry. In the controversy about fasting in 2:18-22 the contrast in religious practices between John's disciples and Jesus' disciples leads to affirmations about Jesus as the bridegroom and about his ministry as a special time. The account of John's execution under Herod Antipas (6:14-29) foreshadows Jesus' own Passion and death. According to 8:27-30 some people identified Jesus as John the Baptist restored to life (see also 6:14). In 9:12-13 Jesus suggests that John the Baptist was the Elijah figure prophesied by Malachi as the forerunner of God's kingdom (see Mal 4:5-6).

John and Jesus are intertwined again in the first Jerusalem controversy (11:27-33). For both John and Jesus the source of their authority is God, and what they do is done by them as God's agents. Just as the controversies early in Jesus' Galilean ministry establish that his *exousia* is from God (see 1:22, 27; 2:10), so early in his Jerusalem ministry it becomes clear that Jesus' *exousia* is from God. The beauty of Mark 11:27-33 is that the story makes this point indirectly while demonstrating the cleverness of Jesus in debate with his most powerful opponents in Jerusalem. Their frustration with Jesus and their fear that popular enthusiasm for him (as for John) might issue in an uprising will become factors in the events that lead to Jesus' death on the cross (see 14:1-2).

FOR REFERENCE AND FURTHER STUDY

Dawson, Anne. *Freedom as Liberating Power. A socio-political reading of the exousia texts in the Gospel of Mark.* Fribourg: Universitätsverlag, 2000.

Shae, Gam Seng. "The Question on the Authority of Jesus," *NovT* 16 (1974) 1–29.

Webb, Robert L. *John the Baptizer and Prophet. A Socio-Historical Study.* Sheffield: JSOT Press, 1991.

Wink, Walter. *John the Baptist in the Gospel Tradition.* Cambridge: Cambridge University Press, 1969.

44. *The Parable of the Vineyard* (12:1-12)

1. And he began to speak to them in parables: "A man planted a vineyard and set a hedge around it and dug a pit and built a tower and let it out to tenant farmers and went away on a journey. 2. And when the proper time came he sent to the tenant farmers a servant to collect from the tenant farmers some of the fruits of the vineyard. 3. And they seized him and beat him and sent him away empty. 4. And again he sent to them another servant. And that one they beat about the head and treated disrespect- fully. 5. And he sent another (and that one they killed) and many others —some of them they beat, but others they killed. 6. He still had one son, the beloved. He sent him last of all to them, saying: "They will respect my son." 7. But those tenant farmers said to themselves: "This is the heir. Come, let us kill him, and the inheritance will be ours." 8. And they seized and killed him, and threw him outside the vineyard. 9. What [then] will the owner of the vineyard do? He will come and have the tenant farmers put to death, and will give the vineyard to others. 10. Have you not read this scripture: 'The stone that the builders rejected—this has be- come the cornerstone. 11. This was the Lord's doing, and it is marvelous in our eyes'?" 12. And they were seeking to arrest him but feared the crowd, for they knew that he told the parable against them. And they left him and went away.

NOTES

1. *he began to speak to them in parables:* The passage begins with the common Markan construction "he began" plus the infinitive (see also 4:1). The audi- ence ("to them") is most likely the same as the audience for 11:27-33 ("the chief priests and scribes and elders"). This is confirmed in 12:12. Since both 12:1a and 12:12 appear to be Markan redactional elements, the framework in which the evangelist has placed the parable suggests that the tenant farmers are to be identified with the leaders of the Jewish people. There is only one parable, and so it seems that "in parables" refers to the mode of Jesus' teach- ing (see 4:1-34) rather than its quantity.

A man planted a vineyard: The opening of the parable evokes the song of the vineyard in Isa 5:1-7 as a symbol for Israel ("the vineyard of the Lord of hosts is the house of Israel," Isa 5:7). The language reflects the Greek (LXX) version of Isaiah. The hedge was intended to keep animals out of the vineyard; the pit was for pressing the grapes into wine; the tower served as both a lookout post and a place of shelter.

let it out to tenant farmers: The owner's actions in letting the vineyard out and going on a journey are not part of Isa 5:1-7. The word *geōrgos* literally means "one who works the soil" or "farmer." Since the parable concerns a vineyard it is common to translate *geōrgoi* as "vinedressers." The translation "tenant farm- ers" reflects better the economic arrangement (common in ancient Palestine and all over the Greco-Roman world) whereby absentee landowners let out their land to local farmers in return for a large share of the profits. From the start it appears that the parable evokes the following identifications: the vineyard = Israel, the owner = God, and the tenant farmers = Israel's leaders.

went away on a journey: Some object that such behavior does not fit with the identification of the owner as the God of Israel. But Mark 12:1-12 is a parable, not systematic theology, and the owner's absence does fit with the entrusting of the historical leadership of God's people to the kings, priests, and other leaders within Israel.

2. *when the proper time came:* The phrase may reflect the legislation of Lev 19:23-25 according to which it was forbidden to eat fruit from a tree for the first three years from its planting, the fruit of the fourth year was set apart for a sacrifice to God, and only in the fifth year might the fruit be freely eaten.

   a servant: The word here and in 12:4 is *doulos* ("slave" or "servant"). The servants who are sent by the owner and mistreated by the tenant farmers are most obviously the biblical prophets, especially in their role of confronting the religious and political leaders of Israel. The mission of the servants is to obtain the owner's share of the profits from the tenant farmers. The word "fruits" is a common biblical idiom (see Matt 7:16-20) for "results" on both the material and moral/spiritual levels.

3. *beat him and sent him away empty:* Not only do the tenant farmers refuse to give an accounting to the owner's servant but they also show disrespect for the one who sent him by beating up his emissary.

4. *another servant . . . they beat about the head and treated disrespectfully:* The two verbs here may convey a single idea that might be expressed as follows: "they dishonored him by striking him on the head" (see Mark 14:65 and Matt 5:39). Some find a progression in the bad treatment given to the servants in vv. 3-5: "beat . . . beat about the head . . . killed."

5. *he sent another . . . and many others:* Following the rules of good storytelling, the parable breaks off the series of servants at three and at the same time alludes to the mistreatment of many others who were sent by God to call Israel's leaders to an accounting. These servants need not be defined exclusively as the biblical prophets. They can include biblical figures such as Moses and David as well as more recent figures like John the Baptist.

6. *one son, the beloved:* The one beloved son stands in contrast to the many "servants" or "slaves" mentioned in 12:3-5. In the background may be the story of Abraham and Isaac in Genesis 22: "Take your son, your only son Isaac, whom you love" (Gen 22:2). The two other occurrences of the adjective *agapētos* ("beloved") in Mark involve the identification of Jesus as God's beloved Son: the heavenly voices ("my beloved son") at the baptism (1:11) and at the transfiguration (9:7). At least at the Markan level of the parable's history the beloved son is Jesus.

   They will respect my son: While in the active voice the Greek verb *entrepein* means "to make someone ashamed," in the middle and passive voices it carries the sense of "have regard for, respect." The owner mistakenly assumes that the tenant farmers will treat his son well out of respect not only for the status of the son but also out of regard for the one who sent him.

7. *This is the heir . . . and the inheritance will be ours:* The only son would have been the heir to the owner's property, including the vineyard. Why the tenant farmers imagined that, with the son dead, the property would be theirs is puzzling. Perhaps they thought that in the confusion they could seize the vineyard or that it might revert to them as just recompense for the labor that they had put into it.

Come, let us kill him: The sentence is the same as the LXX version of Gen 37:20. It expresses what Joseph's brothers plan to do to him before they decide to sell him into slavery. There may be a hint of Joseph/Jesus typology here, especially with regard to the theme of the two as innocent sufferers. A more promising motif is the jealousy or envy that motivated Joseph's brothers as a type of what motivated the tenant farmers (who in the parable represent Jesus' opponents; see 12:1a, 12; 15:10).

8. *they seized and killed him:* For the verb "seize" see 12:3, and for "killed" see 12:5. The tenant farmers treat the beloved son in the same way they treated the owner's slaves.

threw him outside the vineyard: At the most basic level this means that the tenant farmers refused to give the beloved son a decent burial (see 15:42-47)—an indignity even beyond what they did to the servants. A possible parallel is provided by Heb 13:12-13: "Jesus also suffered outside the city gate . . . Let us then go to him outside the camp . . ." Both Mark 12:8 and Heb 13:12-13 may reflect the fact that Jesus was crucified outside the walls of Jerusalem.

9. *What [then] will the owner of the vineyard do?:* In the context of the parable the Greek word *kyrios* is properly rendered as "owner," but given the identification between the vineyard and Israel suggested by the quotation of Isa 5:1-2 in Mark 12:1, in the final analysis the *kyrios* is the God of Israel.

He will come and have the tenant farmers put to death: For OT examples of the motif of God turning Israel over to the nations see Amos 5:16-18; Isa 5:18-26; 47:6; Jer 2:29-37; 5:14-17. The OT prophets (Isaiah, Jeremiah, Ezekiel) uttered many threats against the Jewish leaders in Jerusalem. It is tempting to take this sentence as reflecting the events of 70 C.E.—the destruction of Jerusalem and its Temple. But is the prophecy before or after the fact?

will give the vineyard to others: Note that the vineyard (= Israel) is not destroyed (compare Isa 5:5-6). It is the tenant farmers (= the Jerusalem leadership) who are punished. Who the "others" are is not clear. It is tempting to take them to be Gentile Christians, though this is unlikely since most of the leaders of the church in Mark's day were still ethnic Jews.

10. *Have you not read this scripture:* Mark's usual way of introducing a biblical quotation is with *gegraptai* ("it was written"); see 1:2; 7:6; 11:17; and 14:27. In Mark 10:24 and 14:49 the plural noun *graphai* refers to the "scriptures." Since 15:28 is generally regarded as a scribal addition, this is Mark's only use of *graphē* in the singular as a word for "scripture."

the stone that the builders rejected . . . : Mark 12:10-11 is a quotation of the LXX text of Ps 118:22-23. Though not directly related to the preceding parable, it makes a similar point: In rejecting Jesus as God's Son and God's stone the Jerusalem leaders made a terrible mistake. Perhaps the similarity between the Hebrew words for "son" *(ben)* and "stone" *(?eben)* was the reason why the parable in 12:1-9 and the biblical quotation in 12:10-11 were joined together. For other uses of Ps 118:22-23 in the NT see Matt 21:42; Luke 20:17; Acts 4:11; 1 Pet 2:7 (see also Rom 9:33; 1 Pet 2:6, 8). The prominence of Ps 118:22-23 in the NT may have been due to its inclusion in an early Christian anthology of OT quotations (a testimony book).

this has become the cornerstone: There is a longstanding debate about the meaning of *kephalē gōnias* ("lit. "the head of the corner"). Does it refer to the cornerstone in the foundation of a building or to the capstone placed at the top of the building as a sign of its completion? In either case the stone once rejected by the builders has become essential to the building's survival.

11. *This was the Lord's doing:* Literally "this was by the Lord." Ps 118:22-23 may have originally referred to a surprising victory or to a king's sudden rise to power. In the context of Mark's narrative it points forward to Jesus' Passion and death (his rejection by the "expert" builders) and to his resurrection (his vindication by God and the recognition of his central place in God's plan for his people). The surprising work of God in Jesus (especially in the mystery of the cross) should elicit wonder and admiration from humans.

12. *they were seeking to arrest him but feared the crowd:* See 11:18 and 11:27, which already suggest that the primary audience for the parable ("to them," in 12:1) was the Jerusalem leadership—the chief priests, scribes, and elders.

he told the parable against them: Mark's redactional note confirms that he regarded the parable as a criticism of the Jerusalem leadership, not of all Israel. In other words, the problem is with the tenant farmers and the builders, not with the vineyard and the building.

they left him and went away: Nevertheless, the leaders do not cease in their efforts at trapping Jesus and turning the crowd against him (see 12:13; 14:1-2, 10-11, 43, 53-65; 15:1-15). In 15:10 they are accused of having turned Jesus over to Pilate out of "envy" *(phthonos).*

INTERPRETATION

The parable of the vineyard (12:1b-9) is accompanied by an OT fulfillment quotation (12:10-11), and both are set in a narrative framework (12:1a, 12) that points blame at the Jewish leaders in Jerusalem for rejecting Jesus the Son and the stone. The parable itself consists of the situation (12:1b), the owner's sending his servants and their mistreatment by the tenant farmers (12:2-5), the owner's sending his son and his mistreatment by the tenant farmers (12:6-8), and the owner's punishment of the tenant farmers (12:9). The quotation of Ps 118:22-23 in 12:10-11 is related thematically to the parable since in both cases the "experts" (tenant farmers, builders) fail to recognize the ultimate importance of the one(s) they reject and mistreat. The Markan editorial framework (12:1a, 12) serves to emphasize that the parable and the biblical text both criticize the leaders in Jerusalem, not Israel collectively as a people.

While the nucleus of the parable might go back to Jesus there are some factors that suggest composition or extensive editing in early Christian circles or at least an elaborate process of transmission from Jesus to Mark's Gospel. First, the biblical quotations and allusions—Isa 5:1-2 in Mark 12:1, Gen 37:20 in 12:7, and Ps 118:22-23—all reflect the wording of the Greek Septuagint. Second, while Mark 12:1-9 is not technically an allegory (since not every element is given an interpretation), it is more allegorical—the owner = God, the vineyard = Israel, the tenant farmers = Israel's leaders, the servants = the prophets, the beloved son = Jesus—than most of the parables in the Synoptic Gospels. Third, the high claim made by Jesus about himself in 12:6 ("one son, the beloved") in a public setting stands in tension with the reserve that generally surrounds Jesus' identity. Some interpreters suggest that Jesus may have originally told the parable about John the Baptist as the "one son, the beloved," but there can be little doubt that Mark interpreted it as a story told by Jesus about himself (see the Note on 12:6 and its links to Mark 1:11 and 9:7). Finally, if one reads 12:9 as referring to the destruction of Jerusalem in 70 C.E. and to the church's Gentile mission (we do not), then even a post-70 date would be likely.

It is possible that the "stone" quotation of Ps 118:22-23 was taken from a collection of OT quotations developed to support specific beliefs. Among the Dead Sea scrolls there are examples of anthologies of OT texts on the messiah (4Q175), the future consolations of Israel (4Q176), and the last days (4Q177). For a full presentation of the evidence see Martin C. Albl, *"And Scripture Cannot Be Broken." The Form and Function of the Early Christian Testimonia Collections* (Leiden: Brill, 1999). Albl points to five prominent *testimonia* traditions that can be glimpsed in the NT: messianic prooftexts, Ps 110:1, Isa 6:9-10 and the "hardening" tradition, Zech 12:10 and the "two advents," and the "stone" *testimonia* (as in Mark 12:10-11).

However complex the origin of its components may be, Mark 12:1-12 in its present form is a rich theological text. It has been described as Mark's Gospel in miniature or even the whole Bible in miniature. It roots Jesus in the context of Israel's history by its use of OT texts: the song of the vineyard (Isa 5:1-7), the history of the prophets and their rejection, the jealousy and envy shown by Joseph's brothers (Gen 37:20 = Mark 12:7), and the "stone" text (Ps 118:22-23). It places Jesus at the decisive moment in God's dealing with his people and identifies Jesus as the fully accredited and beloved agent (son) of God (12:6-8). And it raises the theme of God's judgment against those leaders in Israel who reject the Son of God

(12:9), and holds out the promise of a marvelous vindication (resurrection) on behalf of Jesus as God's "stone" that the builders rejected.

The surprising feature about this parable/allegory is the action of the owner who continues to send emissaries in the face of brutal rejection. The question of 12:9 ("What will the owner do?") thus engages the readers in the larger question about how they think about God. Rather than simply attacking unbelieving Israel for rejecting him, Jesus presents a God who is longing for a response. The prophetic books often refer to the long-suffering God who reaches out for a human response (see Hos 2:2, 14-20; Jer 3:11-14; Ezek 16:59-63). In this parable Jesus brings to the fore such a searching God. In contrast, the dialogue of the tenants shows that they are a people who have eyes but do not see and who are hard of heart (Isa 6:9; Mark 4:11-12; 8:18).

This text is sometimes read as if it teaches the replacement of Israel as God's people by the church, but as has been mentioned already, the target of the passage's criticism is not Israel as God's people but rather its political and religious leaders in the time of Jesus. These leaders are portrayed as the tenant farmers who mistreat God's emissaries (the prophets and God's Son Jesus) and as the "builders" who reject the "stone" that becomes the most important part (whether as the cornerstone or the capstone) in the whole building (Jesus' place in the history of salvation). The "others" to whom the vineyard (Israel) is given are better understood as Jesus and his (Jewish) disciples than as the Romans or as Gentile Christians. A careful reading of this parable can be a safeguard against its misuse as teaching Christian theological supersessionism whereby the church replaces Israel as the people of God.

For Reference and Further Study

Brooke, George J. "4Q500 1 and the Use of Scripture in the Parable of the Vineyard," *Dead Sea Discoveries* 2 (1995) 268–94.

Cahill, Michael. "Not a Cornerstone! Translating Ps 118,22 in Jewish and Christian Scriptures," *RB* 106 (1999) 345–57.

Evans, Craig A. "Jesus' Parable of the Tenant Farmers in Light of Lease Agreements in Antiquity," *JSP* 14 (1996) 65–83.

_____. "On the Vineyard Parables of Isaiah 5 and Mark 12," *BZ* 28 (1984) 82–86.

Milavec, Aaron. "The Identity of 'the Son' and 'the Others': Mark's Parable of the Wicked Husbandmen Reconsidered," *BTB* 20 (1990) 30–37.

_____. "Mark's Parable of the Wicked Husbandmen as Reaffirming God's Predeliction for Israel," *JES* 26 (1989) 289–312.

Schottroff, Willy. "Das Gleichnis von den bösen Weingärtnern (Mk 12,1-9 parr.). Ein Beitrag zur Geschichte der Bodenpacht in Palästina," *ZDPV* 112 (1996) 18–48.

Snodgrass, Klyne. *The Parable of the Wicked Tenants: An Inquiry into Parable Interpretation.* WUNT 27. Tübingen: J.C.B. Mohr [Paul Siebeck], 1983.

_____. "Recent Research on the Parable of the Wicked Tenants: An Assessment,"
Bulletin of Biblical Research 8 (1998) 187–215.

Weren, Wilhelmus J. C. "The Use of Isaiah 5,1-7 in the Parable of the Tenants
(Mark 12:1-12; Matthew 21,33-46)," *Bib* 79 (1998) 1–26.

45. *Taxes to Caesar* (12:13-17)

13. And they sent to him some of the Pharisees and Herodians to trap
him in speech. 14. And they came and said to him: "Teacher, we know
that you are true and do not care about anyone's opinion. For you are not
a respecter of persons, but in truth you teach the way of God. Is it lawful
to give the census tax to Caesar, or not? May we give it or not give it?"
15. But he recognized their hypocrisy and said to them: "Why do you put
me to the test? Bring to me a denarius so that I may look at it." 16. And
they brought one. And he said to them: "Whose image is this, and whose
inscription?" They said to him: "Caesar's." 17. Jesus said to them: "The
things of Caesar give back to Caesar, and the things of God to God." And
they were amazed at him.

NOTES

13. *they sent to him:* The first verb and several others in the passage are in the historical present—a help toward vividness in storytelling. From the flow of the
narrative it appears that the subject pronoun ("they") refers to the chief
priests, scribes, and elders (see 11:27; 12:1, 12). Having failed to get the better
of Jesus in debate (11:27-33) and having recognized that they were the targets
of his parable about the tenant farmers (12:1-12), they enlist the aid of various
Jewish groups (see 12:13, 18, 28) to get Jesus' controversial views out into the
open and so to get him in trouble with the Romans and/or with the "crowd."

    the Pharisees and Herodians: These two groups were previously paired in Mark
    3:6 as entering into a plot against Jesus. Their collaboration is the first indica-
    tion of the seriousness of the opposition Jesus will face throughout Mark's
    narrative (see also 6:1-6; 8:14-21). The Herodians were supporters of the Hero-
    dian dynasty in general and of Herod Antipas in particular. Their presence in
    Jerusalem might seem strange, since the Romans had deposed Herod Archae-
    laus in 6 C.E. and replaced the Herod family in Jerusalem and Judea with a
    series of Roman governors or prefects (the most famous being Pontius Pilate
    from 26 to 36 C.E.). But the "Herodians" could be in Jerusalem for the Passover
    pilgrimage (as Herod Antipas was, according to Luke 23:6-12). Since the

Herodian dynasty owed its existence to its support of and by the Roman empire the Herodians presumably would support paying taxes to Caesar. The Pharisees' involvement in political affairs varied widely over the years, depending on who had political power and how much influence they had over them. In Jesus' time the Pharisees' political involvements in Judea do not seem to have been strong. In the Markan narrative, however, they appear to function as the representatives of the view that opposes paying taxes to Caesar. While more nationalistic groups and movements might better represent this position, it might also be hard to imagine such groups engaging alongside the Herodians (and the chief priests) in debate with Jesus in Jerusalem at Passover time.

to trap him in speech: The verb *agreuein* ("to catch" as in hunting or fishing) occurs only here in the NT. The opponents hope to catch Jesus by means of his own words. This notice warns the reader that the flattering introduction to the question in 12:14 is insincere and is intended to "set up" Jesus for a fall.

14. *you are true and do not care about anyone's opinion:* The adjective "true" (*alēthēs*) could also be rendered "frank" or "sincere." The second part is literally "it is not a care to you about anyone" (or "anything"). These flattering expressions are designed both to ingratiate the questioners with Jesus and to put him "on the spot" so that he would have to give a truthful and straightforward response (and get himself into trouble). Perhaps in the background here is Jesus' ability to outwit the leaders in 11:27-33 by not giving them a direct answer.

you are not a respecter of persons: Literally "you do not look into the face of persons." This common OT idiom (see Lev 19:15; Deut 10:17; Mal 2:9; etc.) has its NT equivalent in the Greek word *prosōpolempsia* in the sense of showing "partiality" (see Rom 2:11; Eph 6:9; Col 3:25; Jas 2:1).

in truth you teach the way of God: The opponents have already addressed Jesus as "teacher" (*didaskale*) and applied the adjective "true" to him. "The way of God" refers to the kind of life that is in accord with God's will and leads to life with God. The opponents' attempt at flattery in 12:14 follows a chiastic outline: (A) "true"; (B) not caring about anyone's opinion; (B') not a respecter of persons; (A') "in truth."

Is it lawful to give the census tax to Caesar, or not?: The word *exestin* ("be right, lawful, permissible") has already appeared several times in Mark (2:24, 26; 3:4; 6:18; 10:2), and in every case with reference to the OT Law. Here *exestin* is rendered as "lawful" both for consistency and also because the debate can be traced back to the first commandment (see Exod 20:2-6; Deut 5:6-10). The Greek word for "tax" or "poll tax" is *kēnsos*, which is a loanword taken over from the Latin *census*. This tax was imposed on Jews by the Romans and was regarded as a sign of their subjugation to the Roman emperor ("Caesar") and his local representatives.

May we give it or not give it?: To pay the census tax was to acknowledge the Roman emperor's sovereignty and to accept Jewish subjugation. To refuse to pay it was to reject that sovereignty and subjugation, and so to run the risk of being accused of rebellion. The questioners think that they have caught Jesus in a trap. If he says yes he loses favor with the many Jews who resent Roman occupation. If he says no he is exposed as a rebel against Rome.

15. *But he recognized their hypocrisy:* Jesus sees through the opponents' attempt at flattery in 12:14 and the trap they have set for him. This is the only occurrence of *hypokrisis* in Mark (see 7:6 for the noun *hypokritēs*). The word has roots in theatrical presentations and carries the sense of outward show and pretense. Jesus correctly diagnoses their question as a test ("Why do you put me to the test?"); for earlier uses of *peirazein* ("test") with respect to Jesus see 1:13 (by Satan) as well as 8:11 and 10:2 (by the Pharisees).

    Bring to me a denarius: A denarius was a Roman coin made of silver. According to Matt 20:2 it was the daily wage paid to a workman in first-century Palestine. For other occurrences of the word in Mark see 6:37 and 14:5. Jesus' request implies that he did not have such a coin on his person, and so one had to be brought to him.

16. *Whose image is this, and whose inscription?:* In Jesus' time the image on the Roman denarius would have been that of the emperor Tiberius (who reigned between 14 and 37 C.E.). The inscription would have included various imperial titles, some of which could imply claims of his divinity or that of his predecessor *(Tiberius Caesar Divi Augusti Filius Augustus).* For the OT roots of the Jewish tradition against artistic depictions of gods see Exod 20:4-6 and Deut 5:8-10.

    They said to him: "Caesar's": As in 11:27-33, Jesus has answered his opponents' question with his own question and has forced them to entangle themselves in a dilemma. The coin bearing Caesar's image and Caesar's name clearly belongs to Caesar.

17. *The things of Caesar give back to Caesar:* "The things of Caesar" include his coinage as well as the whole imperial apparatus. Since the opponents are using Caesar's coins they have accepted the sovereignty of Caesar and their people's subjugation to him. Having involved themselves in the imperial system, they have incurred the obligation of paying the census tax to Caesar. The verb *apodidonai* carries the sense of fulfilling an obligation ("give back, render"), an obligation incurred by accepting the Roman imperial system.

    the things of God to God: With this comment about the "things of God" (see 8:33) Jesus takes the debate to another level. He challenges his opponents to be as observant about their duties to God as they are about their duties toward the Roman emperor and his representatives—or even more so.

    they were amazed at him: This is the only Markan use of *exthaumazein;* for uses of *thaumazein* ("wonder") see Mark 5:20; 6:6; and 15:5, 44. For why they were amazed see the Interpretation.

INTERPRETATION

The second in the series of five controversy stories demonstrates Jesus' cleverness in eluding the trap set by his opponents and leads up to his pronouncement about the "things of Caesar" and the "things of God." Here the opponents are Pharisees and Herodians, brought together at the instigation of the chief priests, scribes, and elders ("they sent," 12:13). After an introduction full of flattery they put the question to Jesus about whether it is lawful to pay the census tax to Caesar (12:14). Recognizing their hypocrisy, Jesus asks that a Roman coin (denarius) be brought to him, and he puts to them a counter-question about whose image and inscription are on the coin (12:15-16). Finally in 12:17 he issues his own statement: "The things of Caesar give back to Caesar, and the things of God to God." The opponents retreat in amazement and are reduced to silence.

Why are they amazed? At the level of debate technique Jesus again (see 11:27-33) outwits his opponents. He sees through their flattery and hypocrisy. He recognizes that they are testing him in an effort to trap him into offending the Roman officials and/or the common people in Palestine, and so he refuses to answer their question directly. Rather, he makes them answer their own question. Finally he issues a general statement that is open to several interpretations.

The most obvious interpretation is that Jesus recommends that the census tax be paid to the Romans. But his recommendation is based on the fact that Judea and Galilee are part of the Roman empire and are using the empire's coinage. In other words, the opponents by their participation in the Roman system have already answered their own question affirmatively. Since they use Caesar's coins they should pay Caesar's taxes: "The things of Caesar give back to Caesar . . ."

The addition of "and the things of God to God," however, makes Jesus' response more ambiguous. The addition can be taken as merely a pious afterthought or homiletic application: Be as serious (and more so) in fulfilling your obligations to God as you are in fulfilling your obligations to the Roman government and their local representatives. But it can also be read as suggesting that one's obligations to God override one's obligations to Caesar. This kind of thinking inspired various Jewish revolutionary movements during the first century and became especially prominent in the Jewish War of 66–73 C.E. Read in this way, Jesus' pronouncement could be taken as siding with those who refused to pay the emperor's tax.

Still another possible function of adding "and the things of God to God" was to turn the discussion into a theological debate about who really rules. Is it the Roman emperor or the God of Israel? In the background of this debate seems to be the OT commandment prohibiting the worship of other gods (see Exod 20:2-3; Deut 5:6-7) and the manufacture of images of them (Exod 20:4-6; Deut 5:8-11). In some parts of the Roman empire (especially outside of Rome itself) there seems to have been support for worshiping the emperor as a god. This is at least part of the background of the crisis treated in the book of Revelation. So it is possible to read Jesus' pronouncement in Mark 12:17 as his theological statement about the relative claims of Yhwh and the Roman emperor regarding divine sovereignty.

The ambiguity involved in Jesus' statement in Mark 12:17 helps to explain other NT texts about attitudes toward the Roman empire. In Rom 13:1-7 Paul urges cooperation with Roman officials as the instruments of God and diligence in paying taxes to the Roman authorities. Whether Paul felt compelled to say such things because of the difficult situation of the Roman Christians in the mid-fifties of the first century or because he expected the Roman empire to be replaced soon by the kingdom of God (see Rom 13:11-12), at least his words in 13:1-7 recommend that Christians be "good citizens" of the Roman empire. The same positive attitude is recommended in 1 Pet 2:13-14: "For the Lord's sake accept the authority of every human institution, whether of the emperor as supreme, or of governors, as sent by him to punish those who do wrong and to praise those who do right."

A very different attitude toward the Roman empire can be discerned in the book of Revelation. It appears that a local official in western Asia Minor (present-day Turkey) was promoting the cult of the emperor Domitian (81–96 C.E.) and of the goddess Roma, and demanding that Christians participate (see Rev 13:1-18). For early Christians this demand produced a crisis of conscience. John the Seer takes the position that Christians may not participate, and in Revelation 17 he presents a lurid description of the emperor as a beast and the goddess Roma as a prostitute. The basic question of Revelation is: Who really is "my Lord and my God"?

For the Markan community in Rome this passage could provide positive proof (as did Rom 13:1-7 and 1 Pet 2:13-17) to their non-Christian rulers and neighbors that Jesus recommended cooperation with the Roman empire and its officials—despite the fact that Jesus had been executed under the Roman official Pontius Pilate. At the same time, however, it may also have raised for these Christians the theological questions that are involved in the phrase "and the things of God to God."

"And they were amazed at him." There were many reasons why Jesus' opponents were amazed at him in this debate. The richness and ambiguity of the text as well as the diversity in NT approaches to the Roman empire caution against taking this passage as providing *the* early Christian approach to issues of "church and state."

In subsequent centuries and even today this text has been used to affirm the autonomy of civil power and the separation of the religious and secular spheres. Yet Mark clearly subsumed the things of Caesar under the things of God, especially by locating this passage in the context of controversies that culminate in the "great commandment" to love God with one's whole heart, soul, mind, and strength, and to love the neighbor as oneself (12:28-34). While Christianity does not mandate any particular social structure, no power of "Caesar" takes precedence over love of God and neighbor.

The reaction of Jesus' opponents ("they were amazed") offers a good starting point for those who teach and preach this text and try to open up its literary and theological profundity.

For Reference and Further Study

Cassidy, Richard J. *Christians and Roman Rule in the New Testament*. New York: Crossroad, 2001.

Donahue, John. R. "A Neglected Factor in the Theology of Mark," *JBL* 101 (1982) 563–94.

Finney, Paul C. "The Rabbi and the Coin Portrait (Mark 12:15b, 16): Rigorism Manqué," *JBL* 112 (1993) 629–44.

Giblin, Charles Homer. "The 'Things of God' in the Question Concerning Tribute to Caesar (Lk 20:25; Mk 12:17; Mt 22:21)," *CBQ* 33 (1971) 510–27.

Herzog, William R. "Dissembling, a Weapon of the Weak: The Case of Christ and Caesar in Mark 12:13-17 and Romans 13:1-7," *Perspectives in Religious Studies* 21 (1994) 339–60.

Pilgrim, Walter E. *Uneasy Neighbors: Church and State in the New Testament*. Minneapolis: Fortress, 1999.

Reiser, Marius. "Numismatik und Neues Testament," *Bib* 81 (2000) 457–88.

46. *The Debate about Resurrection* (12:18-27)

18. And Sadducees, who say that there is no resurrection, came to him and asked him a question, saying: 19. "Teacher, Moses wrote for us that if someone's brother may die and leave behind a wife and not leave a child, his brother may take the wife and raise up offspring for his brother. 20. There were seven brothers. And the first took a wife. And when he died he did not leave any offspring. 21. And the second one took her, and she died, not leaving offspring. And the third likewise. 22. And the seven did not leave offspring. And last of all the woman also died. 23. In the resurrection when they rise, whose wife will she be? For the seven had her as wife." 24. Jesus said to them: "Is not this why you are wrong— because you do not know the Scriptures or the power of God? 25. For when they rise from the dead they neither marry nor are married; but they are like angels in heaven. 26. About the dead that are raised, have you not read in the book of Moses—about the bush—how God said to him: 'I am the God of Abraham and the God of Isaac and the God of Jacob?' 27. He is God not of the dead but of the living. You are quite wrong."

NOTES

18. *Sadducees:* Jesus' questioners belonged to a movement or party that took its name from the priest Zadok in the time of David and Solomon (see 2 Sam 8:17; 15:24; 1 Kgs 1:8), or perhaps from the Hebrew word for "righteous ones" (*ṣăddîqîm*)—or both. While there may have been some connection between them and the Essenes in the second century B.C.E., by the first century C.E. they were quite different movements. According to Josephus (*Ant.* 18.16-17) they were "men of the highest standing" but with limited popular influence.

who say that there is no resurrection: Josephus writes: "The Sadducees hold that the soul perishes along with the body. They own no observance of any sort apart from the laws" (*Ant.* 18.16). According to Acts 23:8 "the Sadducees say that there is no resurrection, nor angel, nor spirit." Both in doctrine and in popular appeal the Sadducees were very different from the Pharisees. In rabbinic literature they appear as foils to the Pharisees (whose views are generally accepted by the rabbis).

asked him a question: The Sadducees apparently know beforehand that Jesus sided with the Pharisees on the matter of resurrection. According to Josephus the Sadducees were fond of entering into debate with distinguished Jewish teachers: "they reckon it a virtue to dispute with the teachers of the path of wisdom that they pursue" (*Ant.* 18.16). Mark 12:18-27 assumes and illustrates the two most distinctive positions of the Sadducees according to Josephus: There is no resurrection, and there is no revelation apart from the Torah. For various views about immortality and resurrection in NT times see the Interpretation. The Sadducees' question to Jesus is hostile in intent and seeks to reduce to absurdity the case for life after death.

19. *teacher:* For other addresses to Jesus as "teacher" (*didaskale*) see Mark 4:38; 9:17, 38; 10:17, 20, 35; 12:14, 32; and 13:1.

Moses wrote for us: What follows in Mark 12:19 is a paraphrase and summary of Deut 25:5-6. Since this text is part of the Torah, the Sadducees are putting it forward as promoting their view that there is no resurrection. The biblical case concerns the institution of levirate marriage (from the Latin *levir*, "brother-in-law"). According to Deut 25:5-6 a man has the right and duty to take his deceased brother's widow as his own wife and to raise up offspring from her "so that his name may not be blotted out of Israel." There were probably also considerations about keeping land and other property within the husband's family. According to Deut 25:7-10 the living brother could refuse to take up this obligation and the widow could go through a procedure (*ḥalîṣâ*) that released him from this duty (but only after some public embarrassment) and freed her to marry someone else. The institution of levirate marriage provides the background for the stories of Judah and Tamar in Genesis 38 and of Ruth and Boaz in the book of Ruth.

20–22. *There were seven brothers:* The point of the extreme example is to reduce belief in resurrection to absurdity. The case assumes that life after death is very much like life before death, where the norm is marriage between husband and wife. There may be some connection with the story of Sarah in the book of Tobit: "For she had been married to seven husbands, and the wicked Asmodeus had killed each of them . . ." (Tob 3:8).

23. *In the resurrection when they rise:* The term "resurrection" refers to rising from death to life; it is more than resuscitation or reanimation. The earliest OT texts that affirm this belief are Isa 26:19 ("Your dead shall live, their corpses shall rise") and Dan 12:2-3 ("Many of those who sleep in the dust of the earth shall awake, some to everlasting life . . . Those who are wise shall shine like the brightness of the sky . . ."). The phrase "when they rise" is not present in many good manuscripts of Mark and in the Synoptic parallels (see Matt 22:28; Luke 20:33), but it does fit Mark's pleonastic style, and it is easy to see why scribes and other evangelists might omit it.

    whose wife will she be: As in the controversies with the chief priests, scribes, and elders (11:27-33) and with the Pharisees and Herodians (12:13-17), the Sadducees imagine that they have trapped Jesus—in this case into contradicting the Torah. The logic of their example is that since in the resurrection the same woman cannot be the wife of seven different men, therefore there can be no resurrection of the dead.

24. *Is not this why you are wrong:* The form of the question demands an affirmative answer. The passive form of *planan* ("you are led astray, or deceived" = "you are wrong") appears again at the end of Jesus' response in 12:27. For the active form see 13:5, 6.

    the Scriptures or the power of God: The topics are taken up in reverse order. The Scriptures are treated in 12:26-27 and the power of God (to raise the dead and to give eternal life) is treated in 12:25.

25. *they neither marry nor are married:* In the context of the Jewish world of the first century (see the discussion on Mark 10:1-12) the active and passive plural forms of the verb *gamizein* ("marry") refer to men and women respectively. The case that the Sadducees have concocted in 12:20-23 is based on the assumption that human relationships before death continue in life after death. But those who believe in eternal life (such as Jesus and the Pharisees) envision a different kind of existence. They believe that God has the power to bring about a new way of being in communion with God.

    they are like angels in heaven: In the Dead Sea scrolls (especially *Hodayot* or *Thanksgiving Hymns*) the idea of eternal life as angelic existence is prominent. The hope of the righteous is to participate with the angels in the splendor of the heavenly court and the heavenly liturgy. In the book of Revelation John is invited to come up to the heavenly throne room for a glimpse of what eternal life with God is like (see chs. 4–5). In 1 Cor 15:35-50 Paul denies that resurrected life is simply the exact continuation of earthly life and goes on to describe the condition of those who are raised from the dead as having a "spiritual body" (*sōma pneumatikon*).

26. *About the dead that are raised:* Note that the discussion concerns life after death for the righteous; nothing is said here about punishments for the wicked after their death.

the book of Moses—about the bush: In this case the book of Moses is Exodus and the passage "about the bush" is ch. 3, the episode of the burning bush. The quotation that follows is taken from Exod 3:6, 15, 16.

I am the God of Abraham and the God of Isaac and the God of Jacob: This statement occurs three times in Exodus 3: when Moses turns to look at the burning bush (3:6), when Moses asks "I am who I am" for further identification (3:15), and when God instructs Moses on what he is to tell the assembly of elders (3:16). The effect of these passages in the OT context (see also Exod 4:5) is to link the God of the patriarchs in Genesis to the God who reveals himself to Moses in Exodus.

27. *He is God not of the dead but of the living:* Here in the NT context the statement of divine identity makes a different point—one that is designed to prove from the Torah (Exod 3:6, 15, 16; 4:5) that belief in the resurrection of the dead is found even in the Sadducees' Scriptures. The idea is that if God identifies himself as the God of the patriarchs (Abraham, Isaac, and Jacob) long after their death, then those same patriarchs must somehow still be alive and enjoying angelic existence with God in heaven (see 12:25). Note that the basis for eternal life is communion with God. In the Jewish and NT contexts resurrected life is a gift from God and not something that is simply part of human nature (the immortal soul) or owed to all humans.

You are quite wrong: See the same verb *planasthe* (omitted in Matt 22:33 and Luke 20:38) at the beginning of Jesus' response in 12:24.

INTERPRETATION

The third controversy story in Jerusalem features the Sadducees as Jesus' opponents and concerns belief in the resurrection of the dead. After noting that the Sadducees say there is no resurrection (12:18) the passage sets up the debate by having the Sadducees cite the OT law about levirate marriage from Deut 25:5-6 (12:19) and lay out an extreme case in which seven brothers in turn marry the same woman (12:20-23). The case is supposed to prove a conflict between part of the Torah (Deut 25:5-6) and belief in the resurrection of the dead. In his response (12:24-27) Jesus argues that the Sadducees fail to understand both the power of God to bring life out of death and the nature of resurrected life (12:25). He goes on to contend that there are statements in the Torah itself (Exod 3:6, 15, 16; 4:5) that imply resurrection, since they assume that the long-deceased patriarchs Abraham, Isaac, and Jacob were still alive when God revealed himself to Moses.

This passage purports to present Jesus' position on an issue that divided the Sadducees and the Pharisees. According to Josephus (*Ant.* 18.12-17) the Pharisees believed that "souls have power to survive death and that there are rewards and punishments under the earth for those who have led lives of virtue and vice," whereas "the Sadducees hold that the soul perishes along with the body." Here Jesus sides with the Pharisees.

A strong belief in life after death was something of a novelty in the Judaism of Jesus' day. While prominent in the Psalms, life in Sheol was always a shadowy and ill-defined kind of existence. Wisdom teachers like Ben Sira encouraged their students to strive for the immortality of a good reputation ("a good name"), while most people sought immortality through their children. In the book of Daniel (written around 165 B.C.E.), however, the hope for eternal life was linked to the hope for the vindication of the righteous in Israel who were suffering during the persecution under the Seleucid King Antiochus IV Epiphanes: "Many of those who sleep in the dust of the earth shall awake, some to everlasting life . . ." (Dan 12:2). In the book of Wisdom (composed in Alexandria in the first century B.C.E.) Jewish hope for an afterlife takes the form of immortality of the soul: "The souls of the righteous are in the hand of God" (Wis 3:1). It is possible that Greek beliefs about the immortality of the soul influenced Jewish expectations (even those of the Pharisees).

The resurrection of the body represents a form of life after death that is more in keeping with the traditional Jewish concept of the human person as at once body and soul (and/or spirit). This doctrine holds that after physical death the whole person is restored to life. The best example occurs in 2 Maccabees 7 where the seven brothers and their mother refuse to disavow their Jewish faith and suffer great tortures in the hope that they will be fully vindicated and restored in the resurrection of the dead. Thus the third brother offers his tongue and hands to the torturers because "I hope to get them back again" (7:11). This holistic understanding of life after death underlies many of the accounts about encounters with the risen Jesus in the Gospels.

Jesus' debate about resurrection in Mark 12:18-27 is unusual on many counts. Whereas many of Jesus' debates in Mark and the other Synoptic Gospels are with Pharisees, only here in Mark does he debate with Sadducees. And he takes the side of the Pharisees. Moreover, the biblical texts to which Jesus appeals to ground his belief in resurrection (Exod 3:6, 15, 16; 4:5) seem weak at least to modern readers, however persuasive they may have been to first-century Jews. The passage contains no allusion to Jesus' own resurrection; indeed, its argumentation has been aptly described as pre- or non-Christian. Other NT texts that promote belief in resurrection—the most prominent being 1 Corinthians 15—ground that belief in the resurrection of Jesus: "If Christ has not been raised, your faith is futile . . . But in fact Christ has been raised from the dead, the first fruits of those who have died" (1 Cor 15:17, 20). These considerations have led John P. Meier to argue that Mark 12:18-27 may represent very closely the teaching of the earthly Jesus on the resurrection of the dead.

In the context of Mark's narrative Jesus' debate with the Sadducees about resurrection concerns the proper interpretation of Scripture. The basis of the Sadducees' argument is that belief in resurrection contradicts the law about levirate marriage in Deut 25:5-6. The basis of Jesus' response is that the Sadducees fail to understand the power of God (to restore the dead to life) and their own Scriptures. Jesus' position here fits well with his sayings about entering the kingdom of God or hell in Mark 9:43-48 and with his reference to his entering God's kingdom after his own death in 14:25 ("until that day when I drink it new in the kingdom of God"). And, of course, the three "Passion" predictions (8:31; 9:31; 10:33-34) all refer to the resurrection of Jesus. For the Markan community Jesus' teaching about life after death and rewards for heroic behavior would have brought consolation and hope, just as the book of Daniel must have done for Jews in Palestine in the second century B.C.E. The theology presented here would also have provided Mark's community with an apologia against Gentile rejection of resurrection on the basis of a crassly materialistic understanding of the Christian proclamation (see Acts 17:31-34).

The theological significance of this gospel passage lies in its emphasis on God as the basis for belief in life after death. Rather than tracing hope for an afterlife to human nature (the immortal soul), the text bases the doctrine of resurrection on the power of God and on communion with God ("I am the God of Abraham . . ."). Resurrection is a gift from God. It is a vindication of the righteous who remain faithful to God in times of testing and suffering. And Jesus becomes the first and best example of his own teaching.

FOR REFERENCE AND FURTHER STUDY

Cavallin, Hans C. C. *Life after Death: Paul's Argument for the Resurrection of the Dead in I Cor. 15.* Lund: Gleerup, 1974.

Cohn-Sherbok, Daniel M. "Jesus' Defence of the Resurrection of the Dead," *JSNT* 11 (1981) 64–73.

Collins, John J. *Apocalypticism in the Dead Sea Scrolls.* London: Routledge, 1997.

Downing, Francis G. "The Resurrection of the Dead: Jesus and Philo," *JSNT* 15 (1982) 42–50.

Main, Emmanuelle. "Les Sadducéens et la résurrection des morts: comparaison entre Mc 12, 18-27 et Luc 20, 27-38," *RB* 103 (1996) 411–32.

Meier, John P. "The Debate on the Resurrection of the Dead: An Incident from the Ministry of the Historical Jesus?" *JSNT* 77 (2000) 3–24.

Nickelsburg, George W. E. *Resurrection, Immortality, and Eternal Life in Intertestamental Judaism.* Cambridge, Mass.: Harvard University Press, 1972.

47. *The Great Commandment(s)* (12:28-34)

28. And one of the scribes, hearing them debating and seeing that he answered them well, approached and asked them: "Which commandment is first of all?" 29. Jesus answered: "The first is this: 'Hear, O Israel, the Lord our God, the Lord is one. 30. And you shall love the Lord your God with all your heart and with all your soul and with all your mind and with all your strength.' 31. The second is this: 'You shall love your neighbor as yourself.' There is no other commandment greater than these." 32. And the scribe said to him: "Well said, Teacher. You have truly said that He is one, and there is no other but He. 33. And to love Him with all the heart and with all the understanding and with all the strength, and to love the neighbor as oneself is much more than all holocausts and sacrifices." 34. When Jesus saw that he answered wisely, he said to him: "You are not far from the kingdom of God." And no one anymore dared to ask him a question.

NOTES

28. *one of the scribes:* In the previous two controversies Jesus' questioners were Pharisees and Herodians (12:13) and Sadducees (12:18). For scribes as allies of the chief priests and elders see 11:27. But this scribe is positively disposed toward Jesus (12:29), agrees with him (12:32-33), and is praised by him (12:34).

    hearing . . . seeing . . . approached: The piling up of participles is characteristic of Mark's style.

    Which commandment is first of all?: The rabbis would later count 613 commandments in the Torah—248 of them positive in form and 365 negative in form. They also debated about the distinction between "heavy" and "light" commandments (see Matt 5:19). The "first" or most important commandment was a common topic in Jewish circles and it is reasonable to assume that a teacher like Jesus would be asked for his response as a matter of course.

29. *The first is this:* In fact Jesus quotes two OT commandments (see 12:31a, 33), suggesting that no one commandment suffices as an answer to the scribe's question. Yet in the final analysis (see 12:31b) the two love commandments constitute the one great commandment.

    Hear, O Israel, the Lord our God, the Lord is one: This quotation from Deut 6:4 serves as the introduction or preamble to the love commandment in 6:5. The Hebrew imperative singular "hear" provides the title *(Shema)* for the block of three OT quotations (Deut 6:4-9; 11:13-21; Num 15:37-41) that were (and are) recited three times a day by pious Jews. In NT times the verse was understood to mean that the God of Israel is the one and only God. Recognition of the God of Israel as the one and only God provides the reason why one should love this God with all one's being.

30. *you shall love the Lord your God:* The first commandment is a quotation of Deut 6:5 and part of the Jewish daily prayer. Thus Jesus' answer is thoroughly

within the Jewish tradition and takes the form of the biblical passage that was most familiar to Jews of his time. In the NT there are surprisingly few references to our love for God (see Luke 11:42; Rom 8:28; 1 Cor 2:9; 8:3; 16:22; Eph 6:24; 1 John 4:20-21). It is more common to speak of believing, knowing, and obeying God.

with all your heart . . . soul . . . mind . . . strength: The reason for piling up all these parts of the person is to insist that the whole person is to love God. The term "mind" *(dianoia)* is not part of the Hebrew text; its appearance here and elsewhere (see Matt 22:37) may reflect greater concern among Jews with the things of the "mind" in Hellenistic times. The point is that God deserves our total love, with nothing being held back or excepted.

31. *The second is this:* For the "first" commandment see 12:28 and 29.

    You shall love your neighbor as yourself: The second commandment is a quotation of Lev 19:18b. It assumes that people naturally love themselves enough to care for themselves, protect themselves, and look after their own interests. The challenge is to show the same kind of love to others. The OT context of Lev 19:17-18 suggests a fairly narrow definition of "neighbor" as one's kin or part of one's people. Jesus' parable of the Good Samaritan in Luke 10:29-37 serves to broaden the definition of "neighbor" beyond family and ethnic relationships.

    There is no other commandment greater than these: While distinguished as "first" and "second," Deut 6:5 and Lev 19:18b—linked by the word "love"—constitute one commandment that transcends all others in importance.

32. *the scribe said to him:* The episode in 12:32-34 in which the scribe agrees with Jesus and is praised by him is not part of the parallel Synoptic passages (see Matt 22:35-40 and Luke 10:25-28).

    He is one, and there is no other but He: The scribe's paraphrase of Deut 6:4 (see Mark 12:29) underscores the belief that the God of Israel is the one and only God and so is deserving of total love from humans. It also provides the theological foundation for the double love commandment in the following verse and shows that the scribe has understood Jesus perfectly.

33. *to love Him . . . to love the neighbor as oneself:* The scribe repeats (without hostility or irony) almost exactly Jesus' quotations of Deut 6:5 and Lev 19:18b in Mark 12:30-31. His list of the components of the person omits the "soul" and uses *synesis* ("understanding") rather than *dianoia* ("mind"). The variations are minor and show again that what is at stake is total love for God.

    is much more than all holocausts and sacrifices: The two love commandments are taken as one ("is much more"). The scribe goes beyond (or draws a conclusion from) Jesus' statement in 12:30-31 by proclaiming the superiority of love of God and of neighbor over the many laws in the Torah about sacrifices. For similar sentiments in the OT see 1 Sam 15:22; Hos 6:6; Prov 21:3. This position fits well with the episodes in Mark 11 that highlight the superiority of Jesus and his preaching of God's kingdom over the Jerusalem Temple.

34. *he answered wisely:* The adverb *nounechōs* ("intelligently, thoughtfully") appears only here in the NT. Since Jesus could hardly praise the scribe for merely repeating what Jesus had just said (which was a quotation of two familiar OT texts), this is most likely a comment about the scribe's final statement concerning the superiority of love over sacrifices.

You are not far from the kingdom of God: Here there is something of an echo of Jesus' approbation of the rich man in Mark 10:21. The scribe is not far from the kingdom of God in several senses. He has grasped Jesus' teaching about the supreme importance of God's kingdom and receiving it as a gift from God (see Mark 10:13-16). If he lives by the love commandment he will be able to "enter" into the life of God's kingdom (see 9:43-48). And he has been conversing with Jesus in whose life and teaching God's kingdom is present in a special way (see 1:15).

no one anymore dared to ask him a question: In Matt 22:46 this notice is deferred until the end of the fifth and final Jerusalem controversy.

INTERPRETATION

The debate about the great commandment(s) is not so much a controversy or conflict story as it is a conversation between teacher and student, and so it is often called a scholastic dialogue. In 12:28 a scribe approaches Jesus with a standard question of the day: "Which commandment is first of all?" In 12:29-31 Jesus answers by quoting the OT commandments about love of God (Deut 6:4-5) and love of neighbor (Lev 19:18b). In 12:32-33 the scribe shows his agreement with Jesus by paraphrasing Jesus' answer and adding that the love commandment is more important than holocausts and sacrifices. Finally in 12:34 Jesus declares that this scribe is not far from God's kingdom.

A rabbinic anecdote about Shammai and Hillel, two Jewish teachers roughly contemporary with Jesus, illustrates the context of the question put to Jesus in Mark 12:28-34. According to the Babylonian Talmud (*b. Shabbat* 31a) a Gentile approached Shammai and said to him: "Make me a proselyte on the condition that you teach me the whole Torah while I stand on one foot." Shammai chased him away with the stick that was in his hand. But when the Gentile approached Hillel and asked him the same question, Hillel gave him this answer: "What is hateful to you, do not do to your neighbor; that is the whole Torah, while the rest is commentary; go and learn it." Hillel's answer (which is sometimes called the "Silver Rule"), of course, is a version of the "Golden Rule" that is attributed to Jesus in Matt 7:12 and Luke 6:31 (see also Tob 4:15).

Jesus' own summary of the Torah is thoroughly traditional. It consists of two OT commandments (Deut 6:4-5 and Lev 19:18b), the first of which was recited by pious Jews three times a day in the *Shema*. Like Hillel's

Silver Rule, it provided a vantage point from which all the commandments could be understood and practiced. If there is a novelty in Jesus' teaching, it consists in putting the two love commandments together and making them into one commandment. In a Palestinian Jewish context it is unlikely that Jesus' double love commandment would have been intended or understood as abrogating the rest of the Torah. Rather, its function would have been to simplify and facilitate the observance of all the commandments in the Torah. By emphasizing inner dispositions (love of God and neighbor) and by going to the root of all the commandments, Jesus provides a help and guide to doing God's will as it was revealed in the Torah.

The Markan community probably read this text with a different focus. For new Christians living in a polytheistic environment where sacrifices were offered to all kinds of gods, it was important to absorb the belief that the Father of Jesus Christ is the one and only God ("He is the one, and there is no other but He") and that love of this God and love of neighbor are "much more than all holocausts and sacrifices." Since Jewish monotheism was admired by many Gentiles, Mark's community could have invoked this teaching of Jesus in their mission to the "nations." They may also have taken the task of fulfilling the double love commandment as the equivalent of fulfilling the whole Law—perhaps along the lines suggested by Paul in his letter to the Romans: "the one who loves another has fulfilled the Law . . . love is the fulfilling of the Law" (Rom 13:8, 10).

What is unique about Mark's version of the debate about the love commandment(s) are the friendly attitude displayed by the scribe and Jesus' affirmation of him as "not far from the kingdom of God." In Matt 22:34-40 the question comes from a Pharisee who is a "lawyer" (an expert in the Jewish law) in what is introduced as a "test." In Luke 10:25-28 a "lawyer" sets out to "test" Jesus by asking: "What must I do to inherit eternal life?" Then Jesus educes from the questioner the double love commandment, approves his answer, and tells him: "Do this and you will live."

The other evangelists also put a different "spin" at the end of the episode. Matthew takes the double love commandment as part of his theme that Jesus came not to abolish the Law and the Prophets but to fulfill them (see Matt 5:17), and so he adds the comment in Matt 22:40 that "on these commandments hang all the Law and the Prophets." Luke takes the occasion to expand the understanding of "neighbor" in Lev 19:18b by appending the parable of the Good Samaritan (Luke 10:29-37). In answer to the lawyer's question ("And who is my neighbor?"), Jesus asks him (and us) to identify first with the man who was beaten and left for dead. In those circumstances my "neighbor" would be anyone who might help me—even a Samaritan. Finally Jesus turns the parable into an example story by saying: "Go and do likewise."

Jesus' teaching on the love commandment(s) in Mark 12:28-34 sets a high theological and ethical standard. It is based on the biblical conviction that the Father of Jesus "is one, and there is no other but He." By his command to love God, Jesus summarizes the foundational ethics of the Torah and provides a basis by which Christians can appreciate the heritage of the Jewish Scriptures. The command is also a response to the love that God has shown us: "We love [God] because he first loved us" (1 John 4:19). And this love has been revealed especially in Jesus: "God's love was revealed among us in this way: God sent his only Son into the world so that we might live through him" (1 John 4:9). Jesus also insists that love of God and love of neighbor go together and ultimately form one commandment. But by also keeping them conceptually distinct ("the first . . . the second") he resists attempts to substitute one for the other and so to ignore either love of God or love of neighbor (see 1 John 4:20-21).

FOR REFERENCE AND FURTHER STUDY

Donahue, John R. "A Neglected Factor in the Theology of Mark," *JBL* 101 (1982) 563–94.

Fuller, Reginald H., ed. *Essays on the Love Commandment.* Philadelphia: Fortress, 1978.

Furnish, Victor P. *The Love Command in the New Testament.* Nashville: Abingdon, 1972.

Perkins, Pheme. *Love Commands in the New Testament.* New York: Paulist, 1982.

48. *The Messiah and the Son of David* (12:35-37)

35. As Jesus was teaching in the Temple he said: "How do the scribes say that the Messiah is the Son of David? 36. David himself in the Holy Spirit said: 'The Lord said to my lord: Sit at my right hand, until I put your enemies beneath your feet.' 37. David himself calls him 'lord.' And so how is he his son?" And a great crowd was listening to him with delight.

NOTES

35. *Jesus was teaching in the Temple:* The final Jerusalem "controversy" takes place in the Temple complex (but not in the Holy of Holies or the places of sacrifice). For earlier references to Jesus' activities in this setting see Mark 11:11, 15, 16, 27. This place will also serve as the setting for Jesus' eschatological discourse

(see 13:1, 3). Compare Matt 22:41 where the Pharisees are identified as Jesus' debating partners and engage Jesus in a true controversy.

the Messiah is the Son of David: In the OT the term "messiah" ("anointed one") is applied to priests, prophets, and kings. Jesus' question about the Son of David here narrows the range down to kings. During the period of the monarchy (from David to the Babylonian exile) the kings of Judah traced their lineage back to King David; see Isa 11:1, 10 ("a shoot from the stump of Jesse . . . the root of Jesse") and Jer 23:5 ("I will raise up for David a righteous branch"). After the return from exile there was a persistent (but not universal) hope among Jews for a king who would restore God's people to the "glory days" of David and would manifest skills even greater than those of David as a warrior, political leader, and judge. See *Psalms of Solomon* 17 for the fullest statement of such hopes in the first century B.C.E.

36. *David himself in the Holy Spirit:* In his introduction to the quotation of Ps 110:1 Jesus shares two assumptions with his Jewish contemporaries: David composed the Psalms, and he did so under divine inspiration. In the argument that follows in Mark 12:36b-37a these two assumptions are essential to the point being made.

   The Lord said to my lord: The wording of the Greek version of Ps 110(109):1 is also essential to the argument. The Hebrew text has "an oracle of YHWH to my lord": in other words, "a saying from the God of Israel to my lord the king." The psalm was very likely part of the coronation ritual for the kings of Judah in First Temple times and promised that YHWH would stand behind and guide the king during his reign. In the Greek Bible tradition the divine name "YHWH" is customarily rendered as "Lord" (*kyrios*), as is the title accorded to the king (*kyrios* = Hebrew *'adonaî*). So in the Greek version "the Lord" (God) speaks to "my lord" (the king). But if David wrote the psalm, who then is "my lord" with respect to David?

   Sit at my right hand . . . beneath your feet: The quotation is the same as the LXX except for the final phrase: "a footstool of your feet" (LXX) versus "beneath your feet" (Mark 12:36). In the context of ancient Israel's kingship the divine invitation to "sit at my right hand" designated the close relationship between God and the king as well as the exalted status that the king now holds as a member of the heavenly court. This part of Ps 110:1 was widely used in early Christian circles to provide a biblical precedent for Jesus' resurrection, ascension, and exaltation (for quotations see Acts 2:34-35; 1 Cor 15:25; Heb 1:13; for allusions see Mark 14:62 parr.; [16:19]; Rom 8:34; Eph 1:20; Col 3:1; Heb 1:3; 8:1; 10:12). In the NT context the second part of the promise ("until I put your enemies beneath your feet") serves to emphasize God's action in vanquishing the powers of Sin and Death through Jesus' death and resurrection—the central theme of Paul's letter to the Romans.

37. *David himself calls him 'lord':* The logic of the passage is that since David wrote Ps 110:1 and refers to "my lord" he must be talking about someone other than and superior to himself.

so how is he his son?: Unless it was true, it would be peculiar to refer to one's own son as greater than oneself ("my lord"). In the Markan context the idea is that neither "Son of David" nor "Messiah" adequately expresses the real identity of Jesus. He is more than David's son and more than the messiah of Jewish expectations. In fact, Jesus deserves to share the title *kyrios* with God. It should be noted, however, that Mark does not make much use of *kyrios* as a christological title for Jesus.

the great crowd was listening to him with delight: For other references to the "crowd" *(ochlos)* during Jesus' Jerusalem ministry thus far see Mark 11:18, 32; 12:12. The crowd's positive reaction to Jesus confirms the fears of the chief priests, scribes, and elders. Compare Matt 22:46 where the response of the crowd is silence (taken from Mark 12:34).

INTERPRETATION

The episode about the Messiah and the Son of David in Mark 12:35-37 is not so much a controversy or conflict story (as it becomes in Matt 22:41-45) as it is an argument based on biblical interpretation. Here there are no opponents and Jesus asks his own question (12:35). The matter at issue is: "How do the scribes say that the Messiah is the Son of David?" The biblical text under discussion is Ps 110:1: "The Lord said to my lord: Sit at my right hand . . ." (12:36). In 12:37a Jesus seizes on the double use of "lord" understood as God speaking to the newly anointed, notes that the text calls the latter "my lord," and concludes that the Messiah must be more than the Son of David since David calls him "my lord." The crowd takes delight in Jesus' display of biblical reasoning (12:37b).

The argument in 12:35-37 assumes that David under the inspiration of the Holy Spirit composed Psalm 110, and that the Messiah is a Son of David and so a royal figure. It probably also assumes that Jesus himself is a descendant of David (see Matt 1:1-17; Luke 3:23-38). The argument is based on the Greek text but still stands with the Hebrew text (*ʾadonî* = "my lord"). The point is that the Messiah must be more than David and more than a Son of David since David refers to him as "my lord."

Israel's hopes for a Messiah like David were rooted not only in Ps 110:1 but also in texts like 2 Sam 7:12-13 ("I will raise up your offspring . . . and I will establish his kingdom") and Isa 11:1 ("a shoot shall come out of the stump of Jesse"). With the return from exile there arose the idea of both a royal/political messiah and a priestly messiah (see Ezekiel 40–48; Zechariah 1–8; Qumran texts). But there was no single kind of messianic expectation. Indeed, some varieties of Judaism had no place for a messiah figure.

The fullest description of a Davidic messiah appears in the first-century B.C.E. *Psalms of Solomon* 17. This text asks God to "raise up for them their king, the Son of David, to rule over your servant Israel in the time known to you, O God" (17:21). The hope is that the Messiah will "purge Jerusalem from Gentiles . . . and smash the arrogance of sinners" (17:22-23), and that he will "gather a holy people . . . and judge peoples and nations" (17:26, 28). Then "their king shall be the Lord Messiah" (17:32).

In the context of Jewish expectations about the Messiah in Jesus' time, Ps 110:1 lent itself to a messianic interpretation. Originally part of the coronation rite in First Temple times, the psalm was taken in Second Temple times to prophesy a figure who would establish righteousness in the world and restore Israel to glory (see 4 *Ezra*/2 *Esdras* 11–13). Whereas in the NT epistles Ps 110:1 generally serves to establish Jesus' resurrection and ascension (see the note on 12:36), here (and in the parallels in Matt 22:41-45 and Luke 20:41-44) it is used to establish that Jesus, though he is rightfully called the Messiah and the Son of David, has a dignity that is even greater than what those titles imply. He is "Lord" *(kyrios)*—a title that at least in Jewish circles placed him on a level with the "Lord" who is God.

In the Roman empire *kyrios* was also used as a title for the emperor. And so for early Christians to proclaim Jesus as "Lord" could be taken to suggest that the emperor is not. In fact, a major concern in the book of Revelation is exactly this: Who is "my Lord and my God?" Is it the Roman emperor or Jesus? Whether the early Christians liked it or not, their practice of proclaiming Jesus as "Lord" had political overtones and consequences.

In his narrative context Mark sought to remind his readers that Jesus of Nazareth—whom they regarded as the fulfillment of Jewish messianic expectations and as Lord—is the one who suffers betrayal and abandonment, and meets a death reserved for rebels and slaves (crucifixion). Taken by itself, Mark 12:35-37 is a proclamation of the lordship of Jesus. Taken in the context of Jesus' ministry in Jerusalem, the passage serves as a reminder of the true identity of the one who will soon enter into his Passion and death. The mystery of the cross is part of Jesus' identity as Messiah and Lord.

FOR REFERENCE AND FURTHER STUDY

Gourgues, Michel. *A la droite de Dieu. Résurrection de Jésus et actualisation du Psaume 110,1 dans le Nouveau Testament*. Paris: Gabalda, 1978.

Hay, David M. *Glory at the Right Hand. Psalm 110 in Early Christianity*. SBLMS 18. Nashville: Abingdon, 1973.

Loader, William R. G. "Christ at the Right Hand—Ps. CX. 1 in the New Testament," *NTS* 21 (1974–75) 81–108.

49. *The Scribes and the Widow* (12:38-44)

38. And in his teaching he said: "Beware of the scribes who like walking around in long robes and greetings in the market places, 39. and the first seats in the synagogues and the first couches at dinners, 40. who devour the households of widows and make long prayers for show. These will receive much more condemnation." 41. As he sat opposite the treasury he was watching how the crowd put money into the treasury. And many rich people were putting in large sums. 42. And a certain poor widow came and put in two small copper coins that were worth a penny. 43. And he summoned his disciples and said to them: "Amen I say to you, this widow put in more than all those contributing to the treasury. 44. For all those contributed from their abundance. But she from her poverty put in everything she had—her whole life savings."

NOTES

38. *Beware of the scribes:* In NT times scribes were not only proficient in reading and writing contracts and other administrative documents but also knowledgeable in Jewish law and so suited to take an active role in Jewish society. Since the Torah was the basic law for the Jewish people, the scribes combined in themselves the roles of lawyer and theologian. During Mark's account of Jesus' ministry in Jerusalem thus far the scribes have been linked to the chief priests and elders as opponents of Jesus (see 11:18, 27). This same group will hatch the plot to kill Jesus in 14:1. While in 12:35-37 Jesus contested the scribes' reading of Ps 110:1, shortly before he had praised the wisdom of a scribe and declared him to be not far from the kingdom of God (see 12:28-34).

    who like walking around in long robes and greetings in market places: The scribes criticized here are accused of ostentatiousness, of making a display of themselves so as to attract the attention of the general public by means of their dressing in long flowing robes (*stolai*) and by their "glad handing" in places (*agorai*) where large crowds might convene.

39. *the first seats in the synagogues and the first couches at dinners:* The first seats (*prōtokathedriai*) in the synagogues (places where Jews gathered for Scripture readings and prayer as well as for cultural events) may even have faced the congregation. Those who occupied them would surely be seen. The first couches (*prōtoklisiai*) at banquets were places of honor (see Luke 14:7-11), and those who reclined on them would be noticed and get a reputation as important persons.

40. *who devour . . . and make long prayers:* The grammatical construction changes from the genitive plural participle of 12:38 (*thelontōn* "who like") to a pair of nominative plural participles (*katesthiontes . . . proseuchomenoi*). Moreover, the charges escalate from self-promotion in 12:38-39 to dishonesty and hypocrisy in 12:40.

the households of widows: Lawyers with a reputation for importance and for piety might more easily have themselves appointed as trustees over the estates of widows and so gain a share in their estates. The "household" *(oikia)* refers to the whole estate, not simply the house. The reference to widows prepares for the contrast that follows in 12:41-44. Jesus accuses these scribes of deliberately campaigning to gain public notice in order to enhance their reputation and put themselves in a better position to make a profit on the most defenseless members of Jewish society.

long prayers for show: See the critique of hypocrisy in prayer in Matt 6:5-6 and the teaching about the value of short prayers in Matt 6:7-15 (especially 6:7-8).

much more condemnation: Because these scribes pray primarily as part of their campaign of self-promotion their reward consists in being seen by others (see Matt 6:5). Because their prayers are insincere (since they are really directed at humans rather than to God) God will judge them very severely.

41. *he sat opposite the treasury:* In the ancient world temples, including the Jerusalem Temple (see 2 Maccabees 3), also functioned as banks or treasuries, and so were often targets for robbers and foreign kings in search of money. The assumption in Mark 12:41-44, however, is that Jewish people were contributing money for upkeep of the Jerusalem Temple. Whether the Greek word *gazophylakion* is to be taken generically as "treasury" or more concretely as the collection-box or receptacle is a matter of dispute among scholars. According to the *Mishnah* (*m. Sheqalim* 6:5) there were thirteen trumpet-shaped chests in the sanctuary, each one labeled for its different purpose (yearly taxes, bird offerings, etc.).

how the crowd put money into the treasury: The concrete interpretation of the *gazophylakion* is more consonant with the public nature of the event suggested by Mark's narrative. The coins made of "copper" *(chalkos)* would reverberate when tossed into the trumpet-shaped receptacles and thus draw attention to both the gift and the giver.

many rich people were putting in large sums: For the rich man's obligation and desire to be a benefactor and dispenser of favors see the self-portrait of Job in Job 29. Given the public character of the contributions and the noise made by the trumpet-shaped receptacles, there is a link suggested between the self-promotion of the scribes and the actions of the rich in donating to the Temple treasury.

42. *a certain poor widow:* A woman whose husband had died had no inheritance rights in ancient Israel. While a levirate marriage could be arranged (see Deut 25:5-10; Mark 12:18-27) and a priest's daughter could return to her father's household (see Lev 22:13), most widows had to rely on their children or on charity. And so, many OT texts (e.g., Deut 14:29; Jer 49:11; Pss 68:5; 146:9) present God as the ultimate defender of widows (and orphans). The OT prophets frequently criticize the exploitation of widows (e.g., Isa 1:17, 23; Jer 7:6; Ezek 22:7; Zech 7:10). The appearance of the poor widow in Mark 12:42 was anticipated in 12:40 by the charge made against those scribes "who devour the households of widows."

two small copper coins that are worth a penny: The Greek word *lepta* (here translated "small copper coins") designated the smallest monetary denomination in circulation. The Greek *kodrantēs* (here translated "penny") is a Latin loanword *(quadrans),* for a coin equal to a quarter of an *as* (a Roman monetary denomination). The presence of Latin loanwords in Mark, especially in explanatory phrases such as this one, is at least consistent with the view that the gospel was composed in Rome.

43. *he summoned . . . Amen I say to you:* The notice that Jesus called his disciples to himself and the use of the solemn introductory formula ("Amen I say to you") prepare for and contribute to the importance of Jesus' pronouncement on the situation in 12:43b-44.

    this poor widow put in more: How Jesus knew this has been a matter of dispute among scholars. While it may be due to Jesus' "supernatural" knowledge, it is sufficient for the verisimilitude of the narrative that Jesus made a judgment based on the woman's appearance and on the sound made by her two small copper coins reverberating in the trumpet-shaped receptacles. See the discussion on the similar problem in Mark 11:1-7.

44. *from their abundance . . . from her poverty:* It is a general truth that very rich people can easily afford to be generous givers since they suffer no real harm in doing so. But the poor person who gives despite his or her "deficiency" or "want" *(hysterēsis)* is ultimately the more generous giver.

    everything she had—her whole life savings: Is the widow being too generous? Should she really give her own meagre life savings to support the Jerusalem Temple? For the debate about whether Jesus approves of her action see the Interpretation.

INTERPRETATION

While Jesus' critique of the scribes' efforts at self-promotion (12:38-40) and his apparent praise of the generous widow (12:41-44) can be taken separately, they are better understood as a diptych that contrasts two kinds of "religious" persons. The scribes are criticized first for drawing public attention to themselves (12:38-39) and then for using their piety as a cloak for making a profit on vulnerable members of society (12:40). The poor widow in 12:41-44 is praised for her generosity shown in contributing what she had to the Temple treasury. Because she contributes "out of her poverty" she is actually more generous than all the rich people who contribute large sums out of their surplus. By placing the story of the widow between Jesus' condemnation of the scribes (12:38-40) and his announcement of the Temple's destruction in 13:1-2 Mark seems to hold up the widow as an example of the true piety and generosity that exists among God's people. At least this is the traditional and most obvious interpretation of the figure of the widow. (But see below.)

The ideal scribe is beautifully sketched by Ben Sira (who seems to have run a school for prospective scribes) in Sir 38:24–39:11. Beyond the basic skills of reading and writing, prospective scribes were expected to study "the law of the Most High" and the wisdom of the ancients, to travel so as to broaden their experiences, to pray regularly and to ask God for wisdom, and in all these ways to achieve the immortality that comes from having a good "name."

Ben Sira's positive ideal of the scribe is affirmed in the NT by what is often called Matthew's self-portrait: "Every scribe who has been trained for the kingdom of heaven is like the master of a household who brings out of his treasure what is new and what is old" (Matt 13:52). Other Synoptic passages, however, are critical of scribes, or "lawyers" as they are sometimes called. In Luke 11:45-52 (which reflects Q) the "lawyers" are the objects of three "woes" from Jesus on the grounds that they make life difficult for ordinary people, that they build tombs for the very kinds of persons they would kill, and that they take away "the key of knowledge." Matthew in ch. 23 greatly expands the critique found in Q, and lumps together the scribes and Pharisees as the objects of Jesus' criticisms. In teaching and preaching on Mark 12:38-40 one should note that these criticisms are not applied to all scribes without exception (see 12:28-34), and be aware that this passage as well as Luke 11 and Matthew 23 all carry the potential to encourage anti-Semitism when applied to all Jews at all times.

It is clear that the poor widow stands in contrast to the evil scribes. Whereas the scribes are ostentatious and devious she is little noticed, sincere, and generous. Whereas the scribes put all their efforts into promoting themselves and thus expanding their opportunities for financial gain, the poor widow contributed "everything that she had—her whole life savings" to the upkeep of the Jerusalem Temple.

The widow is surely generous. But is she generous to a fault? Does Jesus really approve her action? Thus far in Mark 11–12 the Jerusalem Temple and its officials have been treated from a critical perspective (see especially 11:15-19), and in 13:2 Jesus will prophesy the destruction of the Jerusalem Temple—an event that was to occur in 70 C.E. under the Romans. Thus the context of Mark 12:41-44 raises the question whether the generosity of the poor widow should be taken as an occasion for praise (the usual approach) or for lament (an approach suggested by Addison G. Wright and others). When interpreted as cause for lament the widow's action would illustrate the perils of institutional religion whereby the Temple establishment manipulated this generous woman into parting with what little she possessed. At the very least, attention to the Markan context leaves open whether the widow is presented as a model to be imitated for her sincerity and generosity or as someone to be pitied as a victim of religious exploitation.

FOR REFERENCE AND FURTHER STUDY

Derrett, J. Duncan M. "'Eating Up the Houses of Widows': Jesus' Comment on Lawyers," *NovT* 14 (1972) 1–9.

DiCicco, Mario M. "What Can One Give in Exchange for One's Life? A Narrative-Critical Study of the Widow and Her Offering, Mark 12:41-44," *Currents in Theology and Mission* 25 (1998) 441–49.

Fleddermann, Harry T. "A Warning about the Scribes (Mark 12:37b-40)," *CBQ* 44 (1982) 52–67.

Malbon, Elizabeth Struthers. "The Poor Widow in Mark and Her Poor Rich Readers," *CBQ* 53 (1991) 589–604.

Schams, Christine. *Jewish Scribes in the Second-Temple Period*. Sheffield: Sheffield Academic Press, 1998.

Sugirtharajah, Rasiah S. "The Widow's Mites Revalued," *ExpTim* 103 (1991) 42–43.

Wright, Addison G. "The Widow's Mites: Praise or Lament?—A Matter of Context," *CBQ* 44 (1982) 256–65.

50. *Jesus' Eschatological Discourse* (13:1-37)

1. As he came out of the Temple one of his disciples said to him: "Teacher, look! What wonderful stones and what wonderful buildings!" 2. And Jesus said to him: "Do you see these great buildings? There will not be left here one stone upon another stone that will not be pulled down." 3. And as he was sitting on the Mount of Olives opposite the Temple, Peter and James and John and Andrew asked him in private: 4. "Tell us, when will these things happen, and what is the sign when all these things are to be accomplished?"

5. Jesus began to speak to them: "Beware lest anyone leads you astray. 6. Many will come in my name, saying: 'I am he,' and they will deceive many. 7. When you hear about wars and reports of wars, do not be alarmed. It is necessary that these happen, but this is not yet the end. 8. For nation will rise against nation and kingdom against kingdom; there will be earthquakes in various places; there will be famines. These are the beginning of the birthpangs. 9. But look out for yourselves. They will hand you over to councils, and in synagogues you will be beaten, and you will stand before governors and kings on my account to testify to them. 10. And it is necessary that the gospel first be preached to all the nations. 11. And when they lead you away, handing you over, do not worry beforehand about what you are to say. But whatever may be given to you in that hour, say this. For you are not the ones speaking but the Holy Spirit. 12. And brother will hand over brother to death, and father, child; and children will rise up against parents and kill them. 13. And

you will be hated by all on account of my name. But whoever endures to the end—this one will be saved.

14. "But when you see the abomination of desolation standing where he should not (let the reader understand), then let those who are in Judea flee into the mountains. 15. Let one who is on the roof not come down or enter to take anything from his house, 16. and let one who is in the field not turn back to take his outer garment. 17. Woe to those who are pregnant and nursing in those days. 18. Pray that this not happen during winter. 19. For those days shall be a tribulation such as has not been from the beginning of the creation that God created until now and never will be. 20. And unless the Lord shortened the days no human being would be saved. But on account of the elect whom he elected he shortened the days. 21. And then if anyone says to you, 'Look, here is the Messiah! Look, there!'—do not believe him. 22. For false messiahs and false prophets will arise and perform signs and wonders so as to lead astray the elect, if possible. 23. But you, take heed. I have told you everything beforehand.

24. "But in those days after that tribulation the sun will be darkened, and the moon will not give its light, 25. and the stars will be falling from heaven, and the powers in the heavens will be shaken. 26. And then they will see the Son of Man coming in clouds with much power and glory. 27. And then he will send his angels and gather his elect from the four winds, from the end of the earth to the end of heaven.

28. "From the fig tree learn the lesson. As soon as its branch becomes tender and produces leaves you know that summer is near. 29. So also you, when you see these things take place, you know that he is (or: they are) near—at the gates. 30. Amen I say to you that this generation will not pass away until all these things take place. 31. Heaven and earth will pass away, but my words will not pass away. 32. But about that day or hour no one knows, neither the angels in heaven nor the Son, but only the Father. 33. Take heed! Be alert! For you do not know when that time is. 34. It is like a man who goes away, leaves his household, and puts his servants in charge, giving to each his work; and he orders the gatekeeper to be on watch. 35. Watch therefore! For you do not know when the master of the household is coming—whether late or midnight or cock crow or early— 36. lest he come suddenly and find you all sleeping. 37. What I say to you, I say to all: Watch!'"

NOTES

1. *As he came out of the Temple:* The geographical notice links the apocalyptic discourse in ch. 13 to the symbolic actions and debates described in chs. 11–12. From the narrative perspective it also allows a broader view of the Jerusalem Temple—which in turn pales into insignificance in comparison with the cosmic events described in the discourse from 13:5 onward.

what wonderful stones and what wonderful buildings!: The Jerusalem Temple complex, especially since the rebuilding project under Herod the Great, featured monumental buildings and walls made out of huge stones. In the Markan narrative this is the first and only visit to Jerusalem. The disciples react as might be expected of "hayseeds" from Galilee on their first visit to the "big city" and to the central shrine of the Jewish people. Jesus takes a more detached view in 13:2.

2. *There will not be left here one stone upon another stone that will not be pulled down:* For prophecies about the destruction of Jerusalem and the First Temple see Mic 3:12 and Jer 26:18: "Zion shall be plowed as a field; Jerusalem shall become a heap of ruins, and the mountain of the house a wooded height." Recent excavations near the Temple Mount in Jerusalem have revealed how the Roman armies in 70 C.E. used fire to undermine the foundations of the walls and then tumbled the huge stones down into a heap of rubble. In this sense Jesus' prophecy was fulfilled. However, the "fulfillment" neither proves nor disproves the proposal that Mark 13:2 represents a prophecy after the fact (*vaticinium ex eventu*). Jesus, standing in the prophetic tradition, may very well have prophesied the destruction of the Second Temple, or the wording of the prophecy attributed to him in Mark 13:2 may reflect the course of events at Jerusalem in 70 C.E. For other references to Jesus' prophecy about the destruction of the Second Temple see Mark 14:57-58; 15:29; Matt 26:61; John 2:19; Acts 6:14. Note that in Mark 13:2 there is no mention of rebuilding the Temple.

3. *as he was sitting on the Mount of Olives:* By sitting Jesus adopts the posture of the teacher (see 4:1). The Mount of Olives is parallel to the eastern side of the city of Jerusalem and offers a good view of the Temple complex and of the whole city of Jerusalem. According to Zech 14:4 it was to be the site of YHWH's final victory over Israel's enemies. According to Josephus, an Egyptian prophet urged a crowd to go with him to the Mount of Olives where he promised that "at his command Jerusalem's walls would fall down" (*Ant.* 20.169-72).

   Peter and James and John and Andrew: These four men were the first disciples called by Jesus according to 1:16-20. The first three named here, as a kind of inner circle among the Twelve, witnessed the restoration of Jairus' daughter to life and the transfiguration of Jesus (5:37; 9:2; see also their presence in Gethsemane in 14:33). This probably explains why Andrew is the last named here.

4. *when will these things happen:* From what has been said so far, "these things" and "all these things" in 13:4 most naturally refer to the destruction of the Jerusalem Temple (see 13:2). But in what follows there is no clear reference to the fate of the Temple. Matthew recognized this problem and so has the disciples say: "Tell us, when will this be, and what will be the sign of your coming and of the end of the age" (Matt 24:3).

5. *Jesus began to say to them:* Jesus' speech begins with the common Markan construction "he began" (*ērxato*) plus the infinitive (used twenty-six times; see 1:45; 2:23; 4:1; etc.).

   Beware lest anyone leads you astray: For other uses of the imperative *blepete* ("beware, look out") in Mark 13 see vv. 9, 23, and 33. The tenor of Jesus' eschatological discourse according to Mark 13 is to cool down end-time excitement and to urge cautious discernment in the face of dramatic cosmic events.

6. *Many will come in my name, saying: 'I am he':* The figures referred to here may well be messianic claimants (see Acts 5:36-37; Josephus, *Ant.* 17.261-85; 20.167-72). See 13:21-22 for prophecies about false messiahs. However, the phrase "in my name" implies that these figures claim to teach in the name of Jesus or even to be the risen Jesus returned from the right hand of God (see 14:62). The expression *egō eimi* ("I am he") may push their claims even higher, since this is an OT revelation formula applied to YHWH (see Exod 3:14; Deut 32:39; Isa 41:4; 43:10) and used by Jesus while he is walking on the waters in Mark 6:50 and extensively in John's Gospel where Jesus acts as both the revealer and the revelation of God.

   they will deceive many: The cautious attitude recommended here regarding such figures underscores the general warning in 13:5.

7. *When you hear about wars and reports of wars:* For the construction "when" *(hotan)* plus the second person plural subjunctive see also 13:11 and 14. For wars as signs preceding the revelation of the Messiah/Son of God see *4 Ezra* 13:31: "They shall plan to make war against one another, city against city, place against place, people against people, and kingdom against kingdom."

   It is necessary that these things happen: A major theme in Mark 13 is that everything is taking place according to the divine plan, and so for righteous and faithful believers there is nothing to fear. For Mark's other uses of *dei* ("it is necessary") in the apocalyptic discourse see 13:10 and 14; for his uses of *dei* in the context of Jesus' suffering and death see 8:31; 9:11; and 14:31.

   but this is not yet the end: In this context (see also 13:13) *to telos* ("the end") refers to the coming of the Son of Man and the gathering of the "elect" into eternal life with God (see 13:24-27).

8. *nation will rise against nation:* See the quotation of *4 Ezra* 13:31 in the note on the preceding verse. Threats of wars, earthquakes, and famines are common in OT prophetic books. For example, Isaiah forecasts wars among nations (Isa 19:2), earthquakes (13:13), and famines (14:30). In Jewish and early Christian apocalypses these threats appear (as in Mark 13) as part of the divine plan leading to the full revelation of the kingdom of God.

   the beginning of the birthpangs: These drastic happenings—wars, earthquakes, and famines—are compared to the labor pains *(ōdines)* that a woman endures in giving birth to a child. For the coming ("footprints") of the Messiah as a time of moral and physical decay (and so a period of severe testing for righteous people), see *m. Sotah* 9:15: "With the footprints of the Messiah: presumption increases, and dearth increases. The vine gives its fruit and wine at great cost. . . ." By insisting that these events are only the "beginning" the Markan Jesus continues his effort to cool down end-time excitement and to place these events in the unfolding of God's plan leading to "the end."

9. *But look out for yourselves:* The present plural imperative *blepete* ("look out") appears also in Mark 13:5, 23, and 33, thus punctuating the eschatological

discourse with warnings to be on guard and to be cautious about jumping to the conclusion that whatever is happening now is "the end."

councils . . . synagogues . . . before governors and kings: The first two bodies—councils and synagogues—could exercise authority over Jews (and Jewish Christians). The *synedria* here refer to local councils of Jewish leaders (see Matt 5:22; 10:17; Acts 22:5), not to the Sanhedrin at Jerusalem that according to Mark 14:53-65 was responsible for conducting the trial of Jesus. That local synagogues had the power to make judgments and to inflict punishments on Jewish Christians is indicated by Paul's statement in 2 Cor 11:24-25a: "Five times I have received from the Jews the forty lashes minus one. Three times I was beaten with rods." The mention of "governors" would include such Roman officials as Pontius Pilate as well as Felix and Festus (see Acts 23:24; 24:27), while "kings" might include Herod Antipas and Agrippa I along with various Gentile client kings and even the Roman emperors. The point is that Jesus' disciples can expect to stand trial before both Jewish and Gentile judges.

on my account to testify to them: The two concluding phrases emphasize that the disciples will undergo trials on account of their fidelity to Jesus (see also 13:13). The expression *eis martyrion autois* is best taken as referring to the testimony that Jesus' disciples will have to give before their judges (as 13:11 indicates). For different uses of the same phrase see 1:44 ("as a testimony for them") and 6:11 ("as evidence against them").

10. *And it is necessary that the gospel first be preached to all the nations:* For other uses of *dei* ("it is necessary") in this discourse see 13:7 and 14. Here, as in 13:7, it bears the sense of the unfolding of God's plan. The word *euangelion* ("gospel") is one of Mark's favorite terms (see 1:1, 14, 15; 8:35; 10:29; and 14:9 [and 16:15]). For the combination of *kēryssein* ("preach") and *euangelion* see 1:14 and 14:9. That Mark himself has inserted this sentence is suggested by the characteristically Markan vocabulary, the fact that the verse interrupts the smooth flow of thought from 13:9 to 13:11, and the unlikelihood that Jesus spoke so clearly about the Gentile mission (since there was so much dispute about it in the early church according to Acts and Paul's letters). The result of the Markan insertion is to extend greatly the timetable of the divine plan until the gospel has been preached to all the nations of the world. For Paul's reflections on these topics see Romans 9–11 (especially 11:25-26a: "until the full number of Gentiles come in").

11. *when they lead you away, handing you over:* The verse is best taken as a continuation of 13:9. Its description of being arrested and led away to trial probably spoke to the experiences of Christians in Mark's own community (though not exclusively to them).

do not worry beforehand about what you are to say: According to Paul in addressing the Corinthian Christians, "not many of you were wise by human standards, not many were powerful, not many were of noble birth" (1 Cor 1:26). Even allowing for some rhetorical exaggeration on Paul's part it is fair to say that most early Christians would have been terrified at the prospect of having to defend themselves in a public trial.

you are not the ones speaking but the Holy Spirit: The saying seeks to allay their anxiety by reminding them that the Holy Spirit (see Mark 1:8, 10, 12; 3:29; 12:36) will provide a proper defense. For the Holy Spirit as the "Paraclete" or defense attorney see John 14:16, 26; 15:26; 16:7; and 1 John 2:1.

12. *And brother will hand over brother . . . :* The verb "hand over" *(paradidonai)* appeared previously in 13:9 and 11. The verse as a whole is based on Mic 7:6: "for the son treats the father with contempt, the daughter rises up against her mother, the daughter-in-law against her mother-in-law; your enemies are members of your own household." A slightly different adaptation of Mic 7:6 was part of Q (see Matt 11:35-36; Luke 12:52-53). The motif of divisions in families and among friends became part of Jewish apocalyptic scenarios (see *Jub* 23:19; *4 Ezra* 5:9; 6:24; *2 Bar* 70:3), and Mic 7:6 is quoted as part of passage on "the footprints of the Messiah" in *m. Sotah* 9:15, right after "children will shame elders, and elders will stand up before children." This kind of biblical and apocalyptic language may well have resonated with the experiences of members of the Markan community during times of persecution.

13. *you will be hated by all on account of my name:* For a vivid description of hatred toward the righteous on the part of the wicked see Wis 2:12a: "Let us lie in wait for the righteous man because he is inconvenient to us and opposes our actions." For background information that may be especially pertinent to the Markan community see Tacitus' description of "the notoriously depraved Christians" and their "deadly superstition" *(Annales* 15.44). Whereas in Mark 9:37-41 there is mention of acting in the name of Jesus, here the idea is suffering on account of loyalty to the name of Jesus (see Matt 5:11-12; Luke 6:22-23).

whoever endures to the end: Patience *(hypomonē)* is an important virtue in Jewish and early Christian apocalypses. One must remain faithful until God's plan is fully unfolded ("to the end *[telos]*": see 13:7) and the righteous are vindicated and the wicked punished.

this one will be saved: The use of the verb *sōzein* here clearly goes beyond the ordinary meanings of "rescue" and "heal" and breaks into the realm of "salvation" understood in the spiritual and eschatological sense.

14. *But when you see:* For the construction "when" *(hotan)* plus a second person plural subjunctive verb see 13:7, 11, and 29.

the abomination of desolation: The Greek phrase *to bdelygma tēs erēmōseōs* is a rendering of the Hebrew expression *šiqqûṣ mĕšômem* (or *sômem*) in Dan 11:31 and 12:11 (see also 9:27), which means "the abomination that makes desolate." In Daniel it refers to the pagan altar erected by the Seleucid King Antiochus IV Epiphanes in 167 B.C.E. upon the altar of holocausts in the Jerusalem Temple. It is a Jewish parody on the name of the deity "Baal Shamen" ("the Lord of the Heavens") who was to be worshiped there. According to the Jewish parody Baal Shamen is really an "abomination" (with *šiqqûṣ* substituted for Baal) that brings about desolation (*sômem* or *mĕšômem* being substituted for the Hebrew word for "heavens," *šamayîm*). In the Markan context the phrase refers to some dramatic sacrilege that is to take place.

standing where he should not: The masculine singular accusative participle *hestēkota* ("standing") does not agree grammatically with the neuter singular noun *bdelygma*, which complicates efforts at identifying how Mark intends it to be taken. The participle's reference to a person ("standing") may suggest the emperor Caligula's (unsuccessful) attempt to have a statue of himself set up in the Jerusalem Temple in 40 C.E. (see Josephus, *Ant.* 18.261; Philo, *Legat.* 188, 207–08). In this interpretation what Caligula tried to do was a reprise of what Antiochus IV Epiphanes did. Otherwise, there may be a reference to the mysterious figure of the Antichrist described in 2 Thess 2:4: "He opposes and exalts himself above every so-called god or object of worship, so that he takes his seat in the temple of God, declaring himself to be God." Or perhaps it is an allusion to the imminent or already completed destruction of Jerusalem and its Temple in 70 C.E. under the Roman general (and later emperor) Titus.

(let the reader understand): This parenthetical comment is generally taken as a direction to Mark's readers to understand "the abomination of desolation" as an analogy or precedent and to apply it to their own situation in the first century C.E. But it could be a note for the person who read Mark's Gospel in a public church service to call attention to the grammatical peculiarity of the preceding phrase "standing where he [sic] should not"; see Ernest Best, "The Gospel of Mark: Who was the Reader?" *Irish Biblical Studies* 11 (1989) 124–32.

let those who are in Judea flee into the mountains: The area around Jerusalem is mountainous, and the advice here is especially appropriate as a response in the face of an invading army ("head for the hills"). The Markan community, while in different geographical circumstances, could easily make the application to its own situation ("let the reader understand").

15–16. *one who is on the roof . . . one who is in the field:* Again the examples fit well in a Palestinian setting. The flat roofs of houses were used for sleeping and other activities, especially when the sun was down. Someone working in a field would probably take off the outer garment or coat *(himation).* In both cases what is going to happen will be so sudden and so dramatic that those affected by it will not have time to gather their belongings from inside the house or to fetch their outer garments. As in 13:14b, the idea is to get out of the way and move as quickly as possible.

17. *pregnant and nursing:* Since quick movement is essential in the situation, the dramatic moment will be hard on pregnant women and nursing mothers who might find such a response especially difficult.

18. *not . . . during winter:* Winters in Palestine are often cold and rainy (the rainy season lasts from October to April), and the wadis or river beds can become impassable. Moreover, there would be little or no food for people trying to live off the land since no produce would be available in the fields.

19. *For those days shall be a tribulation:* The statement echoes Dan 12:1b: "There shall be a time of anguish, such as has never occurred since nations first came into existence." In Daniel 12 the "tribulation" *(thlipsis)* is the climax of a long overview of history from the Persian kings to Antiochus IV Epiphanes. The re-

sult of this "great tribulation" will be the resurrection and vindication of the righteous faithful in Israel.

from the beginning of creation . . . and never will be: Mark expands Dan 12:1b and highlights the importance of the great tribulation by tracing it back to creation and looking toward the future, and by his characteristic device of repetition: "from the beginning of the creation that God created until now and never will be."

20. *unless the Lord shortened the days:* The assumption is that God has worked out a schedule or timetable for the end-time events (see Dan 12:7, 11, 12). The motif of God cutting short the days appears in *1 Enoch* 80:2 as well as *2 Bar* 20:2 ("I now took away Zion to visit the world in its own time more speedily") and *1 Enoch* 83:1 ("For the Most High will surely hasten his times"). Another assumption is that the events accompanying the coming of God's kingdom will be a period of testing or trial ("the beginning of the birthpangs" according to 13:8). Thus God's cutting short those days is an act of divine mercy on behalf of the elect. Again repetition strengthens the point: "The Lord shortened the days . . . he shortened the days."

the elect whom he elected: This is another example of Markan repetition ("elect . . . elected"). In this context the "elect" would be members of the Christian community. Their "election" is the result of God's favor or grace, not their own merits (see "among those whom he favors" in Luke 2:14c and its Qumran parallels).

21. *if anyone says to you . . . do not believe him:* The advice is part of Mark's program to dampen end-time excitement (see also 13:5-8, 10, 13).

'Look, here is the Messiah! Look, there!': For the Q version of a related saying see Luke 17:23 (and Matt 24:26): "They will say to you, 'Look there!' or 'Look here!' Do not go; do not set off in pursuit." Whereas the warning in 13:5-6 was directed against those who will come in the name of Jesus and say "I am he," here the warning is aimed clearly at messianic pretenders. Some Jewish apocalyptic scenarios included a messiah figure, and one way to inflame end-time excitement was to proclaim someone to be the Messiah—as Rabbi Aqiba did with regard to Simeon Bar Kokhba in the Second Jewish Revolt in 132–135 C.E.

22. *false messiahs and false prophets:* For Josephus' judgment on the harm done to the Jewish people by false messiahs see *Ant.* 17.285: "Anyone might make himself king as the head of a band of rebels whom he fell in with, and then would press on to the destruction of the community, causing trouble to few Romans and then only to a small degree but bringing the greatest slaughter upon their own people." For OT criteria for discerning false prophets see Deut 18:20 ("any prophet who speaks in the name of other gods") and 18:22 ("if a prophet speaks in the name of the Lord but this thing does not take place or prove true"); see also Deut 13:1-5. While the term *pseudochristoi* appears only here (and in the parallel Matt 24:24) in the NT, many NT texts show a strong concern with *pseudoprophētai* (see Matt 7:15; 24:11; Luke 6:26; Acts 13:6; 2 Pet 2:1; 1 John 4:1; Rev 16:13; 19:20; 20:10).

will . . . perform signs and wonders: Most manuscripts contain the verb *dōsousin* ("will give"), and this reading is textually preferable to *poiēsousin* ("will perform, do"), but for the purpose of English translation only it seems better in this case to follow the "easier" reading. The combination of "signs and wonders" is a stock OT expression (see Deut 4:34; 6:22; 7:19; 13:2; 28:46; 29:2; 34:11; Jer 32:20, 21). The Greek equivalent *sēmeia kai terata* appears frequently elsewhere in the NT (see John 4:48; Acts 2:19, 22, 43; etc.; Rom 15:19; 2 Cor 12:12; 2 Thess 2:9; Heb 2:4).

so as to lead astray the elect: For the "elect" see Mark 13:20 and 27. The figure identified as "the man of lawlessness" (see the note on 13:14) in 2 Thess 2:9-10 may be in mind here also: "The coming of the lawless one is apparent in the working of Satan, who uses all power, signs, lying wonders, and every kind of wicked deception for those who are perishing because they refused to love the truth and so be saved."

23. *take heed:* For other uses of *blepete* in Mark 13 see vv. 5, 9, and 33.

   I have told you everything beforehand: From the narrative perspective "you" refers back to the four disciples who constitute Jesus' audience (see 13:3-5). By telling them (and all Mark's readers) beforehand, the Markan Jesus again restrains end-time excitement (see the Note on 13:21) and reinforces the value of patient endurance (see 13:13).

24. *in those days after that tribulation:* See the references to "those days" in 13:17 and 19 and the two mentions of "days" in 13:20. For the "tribulation" *(thlipsis)* see 13:19. Whereas the portents coming before the tribulation pertain to earthly events (wars, earthquakes, famines), those coming after it are cosmic (sun, moon, stars, etc.).

24–25. *the sun will be darkened . . . the powers in the heavens will be shaken:* The wording used for the cosmic portents is based on various OT texts, especially Isa 13:10: "For the stars of the heavens and their constellations will not give their light; the sun will be dark at its rising, and the moon will not shed its light." For other pertinent OT texts see Isa 34:4; Joel 2:10, 31; 3:15; Amos 8:9; Hag 2:6, 21. But in Mark 13 these cosmic portents are meant to signal the coming of the Son of Man, which is not their context in the OT. The "powers *(dynameis)* in the heavens" may refer to the heavenly bodies in general (sun, moon, stars) or to the "elemental spirits" *(stoicheia tou kosmou)* that were thought to rule over them (see Gal 4:3; Col 2:8, 20; 2 Pet 3:10, 12).

26. *the Son of Man coming in clouds:* The expression evokes Dan 7:13: "I saw one like a human being [literally 'a son of man'] coming with the clouds of heaven." That this figure is described as being "like" a human being suggests that it is something else—most likely an angel, probably Michael (see Dan 12:1). In the Markan context, however, the Son of Man is Jesus (see Mark 2:10, 28; 8:31, 38; 9:9; 9:31; 10:33, 45; 14:21, 41). Psalm 68:4 celebrates YHWH as the one "who rides upon the clouds"—a title taken over from the Canaanite storm god Baal who was known as the "cloud rider." For the cloud as the symbol of YHWH's presence see 1 Kgs 8:10-11. This complex of images recurs in the Jewish trial scene when Jesus affirms that he is "the Messiah, the son of the

Blessed" and that "you will see the Son of Man seated at the right hand of
Power [= God] and coming with the clouds of heaven" (14:62).

27. *he will send his angels:* In this judgment scenario the Son of Man takes the leading role (see Matt 25:31-46) and the angels serve to gather those who are to be
judged (see Matt 13:49-50).

    gather his elect from the four winds: For other references to the "elect" see Mark
    13:20, 22. The "four winds" are the four points of the compass (north, south,
    east, and west). For the scattering of God's people see Zech 2:6: "I have spread
    you abroad like the four winds of heaven." For God gathering the people from
    their dispersion see Deut 30:4: "Even if you are exiled to the ends of the world
    [Heb. 'heaven'], from there the Lord your God will gather you, and from there
    he will bring you back" (see also Isa 11:11, 16; 27:12; Ezek 39:27). Here the Son
    of Man does what God does in the OT.

    from the end of the earth to the end of heaven: The phrase combines elements from
    Deut 13:7 (the end of the earth) and 30:4 (the end of heaven), and thus em-
    braces all creation.

28. *From the fig tree learn the lesson:* For information about the fig tree's growth
cycle see the Note on 11:13. Many trees in the land of Israel are evergreens. The
fig tree, however, goes through an annual cycle of growing leaves and bearing
fruit, and so is a good signal for discerning the seasons of the year. The word
translated "lesson" is *parabolē* (see Mark 4:1-34). The root meaning of "parable" is placing one thing beside another *(paraballō)*. In this case the natural
growth cycle of the fig tree is set beside "these things happening" in 13:29. See
the parable in 13:33-37 that complements and balances off this initial parable.

    As soon as its branch becomes tender and produces leaves: This process takes place
    in April, around Passover (see 11:13). It is a sure sign that winter is over and
    summer is near.

29. *when you see these things take place:* In the narrative context "you" still refers to
the four disciples named in 13:3-5 (but see 13:37). That the parable is supposed
to enlighten them is emphasized by the address, "So also you." What are
"these things?" The most obvious answer in this context is the series of events
leading up to the coming of the Son of Man and the vindication of the elect
described in 13:26-27.

    you know that he is (or: they are) near—at the gates: The verb *ginōskete* is the same
    as in 13:28, and both are probably best taken as indicatives ("you know")
    rather than as imperatives. Just as you know from the leaves on the fig tree
    that summer is near, so you know from "these things" what will happen next.
    But what is that? There is no subject of the verb *estin* ("is"), and the implied
    subject could be singular ("he" or "it") or plural ("they" as a neuter). In this
    context "he" as a reference to the Son of Man seems to be the most obvious
    subject. The expression "near at the gates" means "imminent" or "close at
    hand." It has no biblical background beyond evoking the image of an army
    about to attack a city. The mention of "gates" does, however, provide a link to
    the "gatekeeper" in 13:34.

30. *this generation will not pass away until all these things take place:* The saying is linked backward to 13:29 by "these things" and forward to 13:31 by "pass away." It receives the solemn introduction, "Amen I say to you." The most obvious meaning of *genea* is "generation"—that is, the contemporaries of Jesus (or Mark) who would be expected to have died in the next twenty to thirty years (see 8:38–9:1). This suggests that the expectation was that "all these things" would occur fairly soon, at least by the end of what we call the first century C.E. Efforts to interpret *genea* as referring to the Jewish people ("race") are not convincing. As in 13:29 "all these things" is problematic. The most obvious meaning is the coming of the Son of Man and the vindication of the elect (see 13:26-27). The expression may also have been taken to refer to Jesus' death and resurrection as the decisive event in salvation history and/or to the destruction of Jerusalem and its Temple in 70 C.E. If indeed "all these things" does refer to the return of Jesus as the glorious Son of Man, his non-appearance does not seem to have created much consternation for the evangelists (who insisted on constant vigilance). The specificity (and imminence) of the timing stated here ("this generation") is balanced by the claim in 13:32 that no one knows the day or the hour.

31. *Heaven and earth will pass away, but my words will not pass away:* The saying is based on Isa 51:6 ("the heavens will vanish like smoke, the earth will wear out like a garment") and 40:8 ("the word of our God will stand forever"). It is linked to the preceding verse by the verb "pass away" and serves to underscore the authority of Jesus as a teacher. But to what does "my words" refer? The most obvious answer is that it refers to what Jesus has been teaching in his apocalyptic discourse (though it could embrace the whole of his teaching). This saying constitutes the center of a carefully constructed unit: A—parable (13:28-29), B—time saying (13:30), C—saying about Jesus' authority (13:31), B'—time saying (13:32), A'—parable (13:33-37).

32. *about that day or hour:* This saying balances off (but does not necessarily contradict) the "this generation" saying in 13:30. Here the issue is the exact time (presumably within "this generation") when "these things" will take place.

    no one knows, neither the angels in heaven nor the Son, but only the Father: That God should know the precise time for "these things" is understandable, since they take place according to God's plan. But that the Son (who is placed on the same level as the angels) should not know this too strikes most Christian readers as surprising. There has been some preparation for this statement in Jesus' admission to the sons of Zebedee that it is not within his power to decide who will sit at his right or left hand in the kingdom of God (see 10:40). These sayings are not the kind of material that early Christians would have created on their own, and so they may well represent the authentic voice of Jesus and provide an important perspective on the meaning of the Incarnation (see Phil 2:6-11). However, they have also provided ammunition throughout the centuries for those who question Jesus' divinity and equality with the Father in the Trinity.

33. *Take heed! Be alert!:* For earlier uses of *blepete* in Mark 13 see vv. 5, 9, and 23. The two imperative plurals are calls to pay attention as the discourse nears its end

and prepare for the two occurrences of the imperative plural *grēgoreite* ("watch") in vv. 35 and 37. Many manuscripts read "be alert and pray," probably under the influence of Mark 14:38 ("watch and pray"). For other links to the Gethsemane episode see the Notes on 13:36 and 37.

you do not know when that time is: Since no one knows the exact time (see 13:32), the proper response is to be on guard always, that is, to act as if the last judgment was to occur at any moment and to live so that one will be judged positively. This is a strong motive in NT ethical teaching.

34. *like a man who goes away:* This parable balances off the the parable of the fig tree in 13:28-29 where the focus was on the end-time signs. It begins like the parables of the talents (Matt 25:14-15) and the pounds (Luke 19:12-13) but makes a different point: Always be on guard (rather than "use your 'talents' productively"). Because the owner has assigned a task to each servant (or slave, *doulos*) and put the gatekeeper in charge, on his return he can easily judge who has acted appropriately (that is, according to his orders).

orders the gatekeeper to be on watch: The mention of the "gatekeeper" *(thyrōros)* provides a verbal link with 13:29 ("at the gates *[thyrai]*"). The sentence also introduces the verb *grēgorein* ("be on watch"), which appears in the imperative plural construction in 13:35 and 37 and is the keyword of the subunit constituted by 13:33-37.

35. *you do not know when the master of the household is coming:* One would normally expect the owner to arrive during daylight, since travel after dark was difficult and dangerous, but one cannot be certain about that. Therefore one should act as if he was coming at any moment. In the context of Mark 13 there seems to be an identification between the Son of Man (13:26-27) and the owner of the house. In the broader Markan context there may also be a reference to the full coming of God's kingdom, of which the Son of Man's coming is an element (see the parables of the kingdom in 4:26-29 and 30-32). When the master of the household comes there will be an accounting and a judgment regarding the work done by the servants (the last judgment).

whether late . . . or early: The Romans divided the night into four periods or watches. But see Troy W. Martin, "Watch during the Watches (Mark 13:35)," *JBL* 120 (2001) 685–701. There have already been references to "the first watch" in 6:48 and to "late" *(opse)* in 11:11, 19. For "cock crow" see 14:30, 72. The master could come at any time during the night (or day), and so the servants should always have everything in order.

36. *lest he come suddenly and find you all sleeping:* While the gatekeeper has been given oversight, every servant has been assigned a task and will be judged accordingly when the master returns. The mention of the servants "sleeping" *(katheudontas)* prepares for the picture of the disciples sleeping in the Gethsemane episode (see 14:37, 40, 41).

37. *What I say to you, I say to all:* While in the narrative context the discourse has been directed to the four disciples—Peter, James, John, and Andrew—mentioned in 13:3-5, this final directive indicates that it is significant for all Mark's readers.

Watch!: The keyword *(grēgorein)* in the subunit (13:34, 35, 37) is also a keyword in the Gethsemane pericope (see 14:34, 37, 38). It is an appropriate summary of the ethical stance that emerges from the Markan eschatological discourse.

INTERPRETATION

Mark 13 is often referred to as the "Little Apocalypse" (as opposed to the book of Revelation or "Great Apocalypse"), and as the "Synoptic Apocalypse" (because versions of it appear also in Matthew 24–25 and Luke 21). The word "apocalypse" means "revelation," and as a literary form an apocalypse purports to reveal the mysteries of the future and/or of the heavenly realm. Some apocalypses like Mark 13 describe the course of history as well as a climactic cosmic transformation. Since their content often concerns the "last things" (death, resurrection, judgment, rewards and punishments, the afterlife), apocalypses are said to deal with "eschatology" (the study of the "last things"). The most extensive Jewish apocalypses are Daniel, *1 Enoch, 4 Ezra (2 Esdras* 3–14), and *2 Baruch.* Other Jewish writings from Jesus' time (including some of the Dead Sea scrolls), though not formally apocalypses, contain many eschatological or apocalyptic elements.

In the Markan apocalypse Jesus acts as the revealer of the future and of the heavenly realm. The setting for his revelation (13:1-4) is the Mount of Olives opposite the Jerusalem Temple complex and already associated with "the day of the Lord" (see Zech 14:4). There Jesus answers the question put to him by four of his disciples about when "these things" will take place. The conversation quickly shifts from Jesus' prediction about the Temple's destruction to the course of future events and the great cosmic transformation that will accompany the coming of God's kingdom in its fullness.

In the first part of the discourse (13:5-13) Jesus describes impersonators of him ("I am he") as well as wars, earthquakes, and famines as only "the beginning of the birthpangs" (vv. 5-8), and goes on to warn that Jesus' followers can expect persecutions and family divisions (vv. 9-13). In the second part (13:14-23) Jesus deals with the "great tribulation" that is triggered by the "abomination of desolation" (vv. 14-20) and warns against being led astray by the appearance of false messiahs and false prophets (vv. 21-23). In the third part (13:24-27) Jesus describes the cosmic portents that will lead up to the triumphant manifestation of the glorious Son of Man and the vindication of the "elect." The final unit (13:28-37) is an exhortation consisting of parables and sayings, with mixed messages but urging total confidence in the plan of God and constant vigilance as this plan unfolds and reaches its climax.

The great critical question regarding Mark 13 concerns the origin of the material in it. How much comes from the OT and Jewish apocalyptic sources, from Jesus, from the early church, and from Mark? Some elements are clearly biblical quotations and allusions (see the Notes on 13:14, 19, 24-25, 26, 30). Other elements very likely echo the voice of Jesus (see the Notes on 13:2, 32) and the experience of early Christians and especially Mark's community (see the Notes on 13:6, 9, 11-13, 21-22). Still other elements reflect Mark's distinctive vocabulary and style (see the Notes on 13:10, 19, 20, 28-37).

One popular scholarly theory contends that Mark 13 is based on a Palestinian Jewish apocalyptic scenario that was developed in response to the emperor Caligula's plan to have a statue of himself erected in the Jerusalem Temple around 40 C.E. (see the Notes on 13:14). According to this theory Mark (and perhaps some early Christian writer before him) expanded the Jewish apocalypse with sayings of Jesus and other traditions. Many learned attempts, however, at unscrambling the various elements have revealed the difficulty of the undertaking and the wisdom of reading the text as it now stands in Mark's Gospel and as a literary unit.

Apocalyptic is sometimes called the "literature of the dispossessed." It usually arises among (at least relatively) oppressed or alienated people who have little chance of fighting back against the powerful and of gaining political, military, and economic power. The book of Daniel originated in such a Jewish group around 165 B.C.E. The Seleucid King Antiochus IV Epiphanes, with the apparent support of some local Jewish leaders in Jerusalem (see 1 Macc 1:11-15), sought to transform the Temple into a shrine dedicated to the "Lord of Heaven" (Baal Shamin) and to replace the Torah as the law of the Jewish people. Some pious persons in Jerusalem viewed these actions as calamitous, since Antiochus was depriving Jews of their ancestral Temple, Law, and land. The group in which the book of Daniel originated looked to the God of Israel as their only source of hope. Their book presents an interpretation of world history in which the four great empires (Babylon, Media, Persia, and Greece) finally yield their power to the God of Israel and "the saints of the Most High." Their belief was based on the conviction that the God of Israel would fulfill the promises made to his people, and eventually vindicate the righteous and punish the wicked.

The book of Revelation is the only full-scale NT apocalypse (though there are many apocalyptic passages elsewhere in the NT). Written late in the reign of the emperor Domitian (around 95 C.E.), it addressed Christian communities in western Asia Minor who were either suffering persecution or facing the threat of it. The main problem seems to have been caused by a local official who was insisting that Christians should participate in civil religious rites in which the Roman emperor and the goddess Roma (a personification of the empire) were to be worshiped as gods. John the seer regarded these demands as a threat to the essential doctrines of Christian faith, and so through the book of Revelation he counseled non-participation and nonviolent resistance. It was customary in some circles to call emperor Domitian "my lord and my god." But for Christians those titles were appropriate to the risen Jesus alone (see John 20:28). So the book of Revelation explores the question: Who really is my Lord and my God? It answers that the risen Jesus, the slain Lamb, is really the "King of kings and Lord of lords" (19:16). It advises Christians to remain faithful under persecution, out of the conviction that there will be a dramatic transformation in which the risen Jesus will be revealed as the real King and Lord to all creation and the righteous faithful will be finally and fully vindicated.

Attention to the two biblical apocalypses helps to illumine many features of Mark 13. The "Little Apocalypse" addresses Christians who have suffered and can expect to suffer more for their faith (see 13:9-13). The short-term answer to their question about why they suffer is that it is because of their fidelity to Jesus and his message of God's kingdom. The long-term answer is that their suffering is part of God's unfolding plan—the climax of which is to be the revelation of the glorious Son of Man (Jesus) and the vindication of God's elect (those Christians who have remained faithful). This is a Christian version of the problem of suffering and theodicy. This approach affirms the omnipotence and justice of God but defers their full manifestation to the future revelation of God's kingdom. It regards the present sufferings of the innocent as a test or discipline to be endured with patience in the hope for ultimate vindication by God.

In some respects Mark 13 can appear as a foreign body in this gospel. Elsewhere in Mark, Jesus does not make much use of the exotic images and formulas found in Jewish apocalyptic writings. Nevertheless, many of Jesus' most important teachings according to Mark have their roots in Jewish apocalypticism—to the extent that Ernst Käsemann once called Jewish apocalyptic "the mother of Christian theology."

Mark's introductory summary of Jesus' preaching in 1:15 ("the time is fulfilled, and the kingdom of God has come near") evokes the idea of the eternal kingdom to be established by God (see Dan 2:44) that the "holy ones of the Most High" will receive and possess forever (Dan 7:18). In his parables of God's kingdom (Mark 4:1-34) Jesus emphasizes its future dimension by images of the abundant harvest (see 4:8, 20, 29) and the fully grown mustard tree (4:32), while also giving attention to its present or inaugurated dimension. Jesus' many healings and exorcisms in Mark are best understood as anticipations of and pointers to the full manifestation of God's kingdom. His wise teachings have as their goal to help sincere people "enter the kingdom of God" (see 9:43-48). His radical teachings about marriage and riches (see 10:1-31) are based in part on the belief that the kingdom of God is the most important entity and that its full coming will mean a return to God's original plan for creation (see 10:6-8). Resurrection is part of the complex of end-time events that will mark the full coming of God's kingdom (see Dan 12:1-3).

Mark 13 makes an important contribution to the gospel's christology, especially with its image of the "Son of Man coming in clouds" (13:26). Throughout the gospel "Son of Man" is a prominent title for Jesus. It sometimes appears as a reference to Jesus himself or in his role as a representative human being (see 2:10, 28; 14:21, 41). It occurs in all three Passion predictions (8:31; 9:31; 10:33-34) and related texts (9:9, 12; 10:45). But "Son of Man" also refers to a pivotal figure in the events associated with the full coming of God's kingdom. In Mark 8:38 we are told that the Son of Man "when he comes in the glory of his Father with the holy angels" will be ashamed of those who have been ashamed of him and his teachings. Mark 13:26 places the manifestation of the glorious Son of Man as the climax in the series of events that constitute the unfolding of God's plan for creation, and in the trial scene Mark 14:62 identifies Jesus as the glorious figure of Dan 7:13. Thus Mark 13:26 is a pivotal text in a very important theme of Mark's christology.

What are we to make of the apocalyptic imagery in Mark 13? It is easy enough to point out the OT roots and Jewish parallels to individual phrases and motifs (as has been done in our Notes). It is more difficult to say what these phrases and motifs meant for Mark and might mean for people today. The basic problem is that the kingdom of God is a divine, future, and transcendent entity. It is God's kingdom to bring, and we can only pray for its coming ("Thy kingdom come") and look forward to it in hope. Though it has been inaugurated in Jesus' life and ministry, its fullness remains future. And it is transcendent in that as a divine and future entity it goes beyond the limits of human thought and speech. In talking about the fullness of God's kingdom, then, one is forced to use imaginative language.

We will never know how literally Mark intended the apocalyptic imagery in ch. 13 to be taken. That Mark believed that the coming of God's kingdom would involve a time of testing for God's people, a cosmic transformation, the revelation of the risen Jesus as a glorious figure, and the vindication of the righteous seems clear enough. But what exactly he meant by the "abomination of desolation" or how precisely he expected the details in his scenario to be fulfilled we will not know until "these things" take place (or do not take place).

In fact, much of Mark's editorial work in ch. 13 went into persuading his readers against being carried away by apocalyptic enthusiasm. He punctuates the discourse with the warning *blepete* ("beware, take heed";

see 13:5, 9, 23, 33). In two sections (13:5-6 and 21-22) he warns against charlatans who will come in Jesus' name and against false messiahs and false prophets. By inserting 13:10 ("it is necessary that the gospel first be preached to all the nations") Mark extends greatly the timetable of eschatological events. One of the basic reasons for the presence of the apocalyptic discourse in the gospel seems to have been to prevent excessive speculation on these matters: "I have told you everything beforehand" (13:23).

Mark's editorial intent becomes even clearer in the concluding exhortation in 13:28-37. This passage has a concentric structure (see the Note on 13:31) and is constructed with the help of several keywords ("these things," "gate," "pass away," "watch"). By his use of the parables and sayings Mark manages both to keep alive eschatological expectation and to instill an attitude of constant vigilance since "that day or hour" remains unknown.

Christian teachers and preachers are often terrified by Mark 13 and other NT apocalyptic passages. This is so because the concepts and images seem very foreign and because throughout the centuries these texts have been misused by "false messiahs and false prophets" to manipulate people and even to convince them to perform destructive acts. Nevertheless, as this Interpretation has tried to show, Mark 13 plays an important role in Christian theology and life and should be taken seriously.

The first step toward breaking down prejudice against apocalyptic is to appreciate its literary conventions, especially its reuse of OT images and myths in the new context of the future unfolding of God's plan. The next step is to appreciate the historical circumstances in which the Jewish and Christian apocalypses were composed as the "literature of the dispossessed." The third step is to try to grasp the abiding theological significance that an apocalyptic text such as Mark 13 might have.

Mark 13 uses the conventions of apocalyptic to address Christians who have undergone suffering for the name of Jesus and can expect even more. These people constituted a tiny minority in the Roman empire and necessarily placed their hope of vindication in God. In the apocalyptic vision they found a reason for Jesus' suffering and their own ("it is necessary") as well as a promise that their suffering would soon end in glory (as they believed Jesus' suffering did). The language of Jewish apocalyptic—the kingdom of God, Messiah and Son of Man, resurrection, the last judgment—provided many of their most important theological ideas. The conviction that the world would be transformed and that they would reign with the risen Jesus in glory gave them a horizon of hope against which they could interpret their present sufferings, and the insistence on constant vigilance helped them to find significance and ethical direction in their actions in the present.

For Reference and Further Study

Collins, Adela Yarbro. "The Apocalyptic Rhetoric of Mark 13 in Historical Context," *Biblical Research* 41 (1996) 5–36.
Dyer, Keith D. *The Prophecy on the Mount. Mark 13 and the Gathering of the New Community.* Bern: Peter Lang, 1998.
Evans, Craig A. "Predictions of the Destruction of the Herodian Temple in the Pseudepigrapha, Qumran Scrolls, and Related Texts," *JSP* 10 (1992) 89–147.
Gaston, Lloyd. *No Stone on Another. Studies in the Significance of the Fall of Jerusalem in the Synoptic Gospels.* Leiden: Brill, 1970.
Geddert, Timothy J. *Watchwords: Mark 13 in Markan Eschatology.* Sheffield: JSOT Press, 1989.
Hartman, Lars. *Prophecy Interpreted. The Formation of Some Jewish Apocalyptic Texts and of the Eschatological Discourse in Mark 13 par.* Lund: Gleerup, 1966.
Lambrecht, Jan. *Die Redaktion des Markus-Apokalypse. Literarische Analyse und Strukturuntersuchung.* Rome: Pontifical Biblical Institute, 1967.
Pesch, Rudolf. *Naherwartungen. Tradition und Redaktion in Mk 13.* Düsseldorf: Patmos, 1968.
Taylor, N. H. "Palestinian Christianity and the Caligula Crisis. Part I. Social and Historical Reconstruction," *JSNT* 61 (1996) 101–24; "Part II. The Markan Eschatological Discourse," *JSNT* 62 (1996) 13–41.

51. *Contrasting Beginnings of Jesus' Last Days* (14:1-11)

1. Now Passover and the Feast of Unleavened Bread were to begin the next day. And the chief priests and the scribes were exploring ways that they might secretly capture him and put him to death. 2. For they were saying: "Not in the midst of the crowded festival, or some riot may break out among the people."

3. Then he (Jesus) was in Bethany at the house of Simon the leper, and during dinner a woman came in carrying an alabaster jar of very expensive ointment, genuine nard; and shattering the alabaster jar, she poured it over his head. 4. But some who were there muttered indignantly to themselves: "Why is there a total loss of this ointment? 5. For this ointment could have been sold for almost a year's wages, and the money given to the poor." And they loudly berated her. 6. But Jesus responded: "Leave her alone; why do you so trouble her? She has treated me with honor. 7. For you will have the poor everywhere in your midst; and whenever you wish, you have the power to do good for them; but you will not always have me. 8. But she has done what she could; in advance, she has anointed my body for burial. 9. Amen, Amen, I tell you wherever the gospel is proclaimed throughout the whole world, especially what

she has done will be spoken of in memory of her." 10. Then Judas Iscariot, who was one of the Twelve, went off to the chief priests in order to hand him [Jesus] over. 11. When they heard of his plan they were happy and promised to give him money. And he kept looking for the best way to hand him over.

NOTES

1. *Passover and the Feast of Unleavened Bread:* Passover (Greek plural *ta pascha*) translates the Hebrew *pesaḥ* (most likely from the verb "pass over") and commemorates when the Lord passed through Egypt to strike down the firstborn of the Egyptians and passed over "the houses of the Israelites in Egypt" (Exod 12:1-28). By the rhetorical figure of synecdoche (understanding a part for the whole) the term is used for the commemoration of the deliverance from Egypt, for the feast, and for the sacrificial lamb (Mark 14:12). Passover is the most solemn of Jewish feasts, a pilgrimage feast and also a family festival (either a single family or others joined together) where a choice lamb is to be sacrificed and eaten as a memorial of God's deliverance of Israel from Egypt. It is joined to the festival of unleavened bread *(azyma)*, or better the period when only unleavened bread can be eaten, and is also a commemoration of the liberation from Egypt. The joint feast is to begin on the fourteenth day of the first month (Nisan), includes the sacrifice of the lambs and the Passover meal, and extends over eight days. The ritual for Passover comes to be called the *seder* ("order" or "arrangement"), which is used by contemporary Jews and Christians as a synonym for the feast.

   were to begin the next day: The Greek literally says "was after two days." By Jewish time reckoning, which measured days from sunset to sunset, the day of preparation for the feast would be the 14th of Nisan when the Passover lamb was slaughtered; the meal was eaten at evening on the 15th (Mark 14:12). Mark's time reference is then to the 13th of Nisan. If the crucifixion was on the eve of a Sabbath (15:42, Friday), then by our calendar Mark 14:1 would refer to the day extending from Tuesday sunset to Wednesday sunset. John, who stresses that Jesus is the Paschal lamb, has a different chronology according to which Jesus is crucified on the day of preparation for the Passover (19:31). For attempts to reconcile the Synoptic and Johannine chronology see Raymond E. Brown, *The Death of the Messiah* (New York: Doubleday, 1994) 1350-78.

   the chief priests: In 8:31 and 10:33 the chief priests are the principal agents of Jesus' death, and (along with the scribes) feature prominently in the Passion narrative (where the Pharisees do not appear). During the reign of the Hasmonean kings Israel was a theocracy and a Temple state where Jewish priest-kings ruled in God's name. Since the Jewish priesthood was hereditary there were a large number of priests and many grades or orders of the priesthood (see Luke 1:5), with some being quite poor and living at subsistence level. At the top of the religious hierarchy stood the high priest, who in Jesus' time was Caiaphas. His tenure (18–36 C.E.) coincided with both the ministry of Jesus and the prefecture of Pontius Pilate. The term "chief priests" most likely describes a "Jerusalem priestly aristocracy with positions of privileged power over the temple and its treasury" (Brown, *Death of the Messiah* 1426).

scribes: The "scribes" were experts trained in the Law (which was the Law of Moses or the Torah). In Mark there seem to be two kinds of scribes: those who are associated with the Pharisees and who oppose Jesus in Galilee (2:6-7, 16; 7:1, 5; 9:14), and those associated with the Jerusalem leaders who desire Jesus' death (14:1, 53; 15:1, 31). The scribes, along with the chief priests and "elders" (*presbyteroi:* see 14:43, 53; 15:1), who reflect the OT institution of wise counselors, seem to have constituted the governing aristocracy in Jerusalem. Since Rome governed its empire under Roman leaders (prefects or governors) through local elites and assemblies *(gerousiai),* these groups may have exercised a similar function in Jerusalem.

exploring ways: Literally "seeking" *(zētein).* This culminates three earlier references in Mark to plans to put Jesus to death (3:6; 11:18; 12:12) and is an instance of the Passion narrative influencing the composition of the whole gospel.

secretly: The Greek noun *dolos* has overtones of stealth or subterfuge. It modifies the participle "capturing." The reason for their concern appears in the following verse: fear of a riot breaking out.

capture him and put him to death: "Capture" *(kratēsantes)* is preferable to the usual "arrest," which suggests modern legal procedures leading up to an "arrest." Mark portrays an *ad hoc* mob action; see 14:43 where a "crowd," and not an official group, comes with swords and wooden clubs.

2. *For they were saying:* The particle *gar* ("for") gives the reason for their stealth. In this phrase we hear the voice of the "omniscient narrator" who gives the readers information unknown to the characters in the story.

Not in the midst of the crowded festival: Most translations read "on the feast day" *(heortē),* which creates a chronological problem since in Mark's chronology they do arrest Jesus after the Passover meal and hence on the feast. Since the population of Jerusalem quadrupled during Passover, and since it was so volatile a time that the Roman prefect moved from Caesarea Maritima to Jerusalem, civil disturbance was greatly feared, especially after Jesus entered Jerusalem hailed by large crowds (11:1-11) and was so popular among the people that the Jerusalem leaders were afraid to capture him publicly (12:12).

3. *Bethany:* Mark here intercalates the narrative of the woman's deed (14:3-9) between the plot to kill Jesus (14:1-2) and the account of Judas' betrayal (14:10-11; see the Interpretation). Bethany (Hebrew "house of the poor," or "house of Ananiyah"), the site of modern El-Azariah, is located at the foot of the eastern slope of the Mount of Olives, about two miles from Jerusalem toward Jericho. It serves as the home base for Jesus during his final days in Jerusalem (Mark 11:1, 11-12). In John it is the home of Mary, Martha, and Lazarus (11:1-44); Luke seems to locate the ascension in the vicinity of Bethany (see Luke 24:50-51 and Acts 1:6-11).

Simon the Leper: An incident similar to this occurs in Matt 26:6-13 (closely following Mark 14:3-9); Luke 7:36-50; and John 12:1-8 (see the Interpretation). Luke locates the story early in Jesus' Galilean ministry in the house of Simon "the Pharisee," and John places it in the house of Mary and Martha. The basic action of anointing (but not the identity of the woman) is constant in all versions.

the leper: The host is so called only in Mark, and this is a somewhat strange note, given the social constraints on lepers (see Mark 1:40-45). In the pre-Markan tradition it was most likely assumed that this "Simon" had been healed of his leprosy and/or that the house belonged to him; the Qumran *Temple Scroll* 46:17-18 indicates that lepers lived east of Jerusalem. Mark may have added this designation to recall the earlier meeting of Jesus and the leper in Galilee (1:40-45), which continues the motif that Jesus dines and associates not with the powerful of this world (compare Mark 6:14-29) but with marginal people.

during dinner: The literal expression "reclining at table," which suggests a more formal dinner late in the afternoon, is used in secular Greek for a "symposium" or a dinner where teachers instruct disciples (see Plato, *Symposium*).

a woman: Only in John is this woman named Mary (not Magdalene but Martha's sister). Unlike Luke 7:39 there is no indication in Mark/Matthew that she is "a sinner." Somewhat ironically, though her deed will be remembered wherever the gospel is proclaimed (14:9), she never speaks and she remains anonymous.

alabaster jar: In Greek literally "without handles," these jars made of a white translucent material could be luxury items.

very expensive ointment, genuine nard: The description of the ointment as "expensive" and "genuine" highlights the generosity and exuberance of the woman. Nard is a very costly perfume derived from a plant native to India. English "spikenard" is derived from the thorns on the Latin form of the plant *(spica nardi)*. In Song of Songs 1:12 nard (here also a personification of the bride, 4:13) gives off a fragrance for the king's banquet.

genuine: The unusual Greek word *(pistikos)* is found only here and in John 12:2. Some derive it from *pistos* ("faithful" or "genuine"), while others think it comes from a Greek form of the Latin *spicatum* or from the pistachio tree *(pistakia)*. "Genuine" seems more likely, and stresses again the quality of the woman's gift.

shattering: Only Mark mentions the "shattering," which adds a note of energy and enthusiasm to the woman's actions. This verb *syntribein* appears elsewhere in Mark at 5:4 to describe the violent shattering of chains by the Gerasene demoniac. Also flasks used to anoint corpses were often broken and left in the coffin (Robert H. Gundry, *Mark* 812).

poured it over his head: Similar to verbs of "filling," *katachein* governs the genitive case and suggests a large amount of ointment flowing on Jesus' head. Luke and John narrate the anointing of Jesus' feet rather than his head. In Jewish history the heads of priests (Exod 29:4-7) and of kings (2 Kgs 9:3-6) were anointed, and Luke views it as a sign of respect for guests (7:46). Yet Jesus will say in 14:8 that the anointing here is preparation for his burial, and it is set at a meal bracketed by actions of Jesus' enemies, which may reflect Ps 23:5 (see Interpretation).

4. *some who were there muttered indignantly to themselves:* Though Matthew (26:8) has Jesus' disciples complain about the waste, and John attributes the complaint to Judas, Mark has no explicit mention of the disciples' presence at the dinner. Mark used the verb *aganaktein* ("complain, grouse") earlier to describe the disciples' displeasure with the request of James and John (10:41), and muttered complaints about Jesus' actions appear early in his ministry (1:27; 2:6-8), which provides another link to the beginning of Jesus' Galilean ministry.

total loss: Literally "why this destruction?" *(apōleia)*, from the verb *apollymi* ("perish, destroy utterly"). This again emphasizes the extravagance of the woman's action. It also provides a link to the story of the woman in Mark 12:44 who gives her "whole life" as an offering to the Temple.

5. *almost a year's wages:* Literally "three hundred denarii." Again Mark stresses the extravagant generosity of the woman, since a denarius was the average daily wage for a laborer (see Matt 20:2).

and the money given to the poor: At important Jewish festivals such as Passover there was a special concern for almsgiving.

they loudly berated her: The verb *(embrimasthai)*, used of the snorting of a horse, suggests strong physical expressions of anger (see Mark 1:43).

6. *But Jesus responded:* Mark's use of the adversative *de* ("but") highlights Jesus' counter to the complaining dinner guests.

why do you so trouble her?: The Greek literally says, "Why do you place burdens on her?" It suggests an unjust charge that will be countered by Jesus' interpretation of her action.

treated me with honor: In secular Greek *kalos* (with its sense of beautiful and honorable) is often paired with *agathos* to describe an ideal of gracious humanity, so that the woman's action is stronger than contemporary translations such as "done a good deed."

7. *For you will have the poor everywhere in your midst:* In its more familiar translation, "the poor you will always have with you," this is one of the most misinterpreted verses in the NT. In context it evokes the "poor law" from Deut 15:1-11, which contains a series of prescriptions about remission of debts and care for the poor, so that "there will be no one in need (Hebrew *'ebyôn*, "poor") among you."

you have the power to do good for them: Jesus does not proclaim the inevitability of poverty with a consequent lack of concern for the situation of the poor; as the next part of the verse affirms, their presence is a stimulus to care and almsgiving. Also at Passover time it was customary to make donations for the poor.

but you will not always have me: This constitutes another "Passion prediction" (see 8:31; 9:31; 10:33-34) and orients the whole incident to the unfolding Passion, while echoing the earlier prediction of Jesus that the bridegroom will be taken away (2:20).

8. *But she has done what she could:* The Greek is elliptical, and reads literally "what she had, she did," where "have" is used in the sense of "be able" and reflects the description of the generous widow in 12:44. The contrast is between the possibility for good action by the complaining guests and the actual deed of the woman.

   in advance, she has anointed my body for burial: Though "anointing" is a symbol with multiple meanings (hospitality, royal or priestly anointing, a sign of joy, and healing), Jesus' words here point directly to the anointing of a corpse. In effect, at the very beginning of the Passion Jesus is already a "dead man walking." Along with echoing 12:44, the woman's action foreshadows the devotion of the women at Jesus' tomb (16:1-2).

9. *Amen, Amen, I tell you:* "Amen" generally appears in the Hebrew Bible at the conclusion of commands, blessings, curses, doxologies, and prayers; it confirms what has been said before (Bruce Chilton, "Amen," *ABD* 1.184). In Mark it occurs (at the beginning of Jesus' sayings) to confirm eschatological threats (3:20; 8:21; 9:1, 13:30), promises (9:41; 10:15, 29; 11:22; 14:25), implicit blessings (12:42), and prophetic predictions (14:18, 30). Here the promise motif is highlighted.

   wherever the gospel is proclaimed: The combination of "gospel" and "proclaimed" appears elsewhere in Mark only at 1:14 and 13:10. Thus it characterizes the three phases of Jesus' ministry: the time of his arrival (1:14), the time of his Passion (14:9), and the time of his absence when the community will proclaim the gospel (13:10). The gospel is both the good news *about* and *from* Jesus.

   throughout the whole world: Mark anticipates the universal spread of the gospel throughout the world *(kosmos),* understood here primarily as the humanly inhabited world rather than the cosmos (cf. Col 1:6; 2:8; Eph 1:4). Many authors view this verse as an addition by Mark to stress the world-wide mission of the church (see 13:10). Others have suggested that this saying and John 12:2 reflect the tradition in *Midrash Rabbah on Ecclesiastes* (7:1): "The fragrance of a good perfume spreads from the bedroom to the dining room; so does a good name spread from one end of the world to the other" (Raymond E. Brown, *John I–XII.* AB 29A [Garden City, N.Y.: Doubleday, 1966] 453). The late date of the *Midrash,* of course, makes direct literary influence questionable.

   what she has done will be spoken: In Mark the gospel is communicated through preaching and teaching, even in the face of suffering and persecution (see 4:1-20; 13:10-11).

   in memory of her: The Greek *eis mnēmosynon* (used only here and in Matt 26:13) can mean "as a memorial to her" in the sense that her deed will always be part of the proclamation of the gospel. The term may also carry an eschatological nuance that God will remember the woman and will acknowledge her deed at the final judgment (*1 Enoch* 98:3; 103:1-4; see Matt 25:31-46, where nameless people minister to Jesus in the person of the least). In contrast to Luke (23:19) and Paul (1 Cor 11:24), Mark has no statement about action "in remembrance *(anamnēsin)* of me" at the Lord's Supper.

10. *Judas Iscariot:* Mark first mentions Judas in the choice of the Twelve (3:13-19); the Gospels always list him last, with the description, "the one who handed him over" (Matt 10:4; Luke 6:16). On the derivation of "Iscariot" see the Note on 3:19.

went off to the chief priests in order to hand him over: The departure of Judas immediately contrasts with the action of the woman. In contrast to John, who places Judas at the Last Supper, Mark does not recount Judas' return until the arrest in 14:43. The use of the verb "hand over" *(paradidonai)* links the fates of John (1:14), of Jesus (8:31; 9:31; 10:32-33; 14:10-11, 18, 21, 41-42, 44; 15:1, 15), and of the disciples after the departure of Jesus (13:10, 12).

11. *they were happy:* This provides a bridge to 14:1 where the officials are seeking *(zētein)* a way to arrest Jesus without causing a riot. On the historical issues involved, see the Interpretation.

give him money: Mark's account is very sober; he does not mention Judas' desire for money (Matt 26:15), or his being possessed by Satan (John 13:27), or say that his motivation was the desire for personal gain (Acts 1:18). The developing tradition intensifies Judas' evil character.

kept looking for the best way: "Kept looking" translates the imperfect *ezētei* and culminates previous indications of plans to harm Jesus (3:6; 11:18; 12:12; and especially 14:1).

the best way: This is also a bridge to 14:1 since their aim seems to involve stealth—which Luke (22:6) makes explicit by noting that they wanted to arrest him away from the crowd.

INTERPRETATION

The Passion narrative begins with the familiar Markan sandwiching technique: A—the plan of officials to arrest Jesus (14:1-2); B—the story of a woman anointing Jesus (14:3-9); and A'—the agreement of Judas to hand Jesus over (14:10-11). This provides a dual and contrasting beginning to Jesus' last days, where an act of devotion anticipating Jesus' death is literally surrounded by plans to bring about his death.

The two stories are replete with OT motifs that run throughout the Passion narrative. Especially influential is the motif of the suffering just person who is unjustly persecuted and surrounded by enemies, found in the Psalms (22; 31; 35; 38; 69; 71), the Prophets (Jer 11:18-19; Isa 52:13–53:12), and the Wisdom literature (especially Wis 2:12-20, "let us lie in wait for the righteous man," v. 12; and 3:1-9). See also Ps 23:5 ("You set a table before me as my enemies watch. You anoint my head with oil; my cup overflows)," which offers an interesting parallel to Mark. Jesus is at table; his enemies watch; and his *head* (only in Mark) is anointed not by God but by a woman whose action is to be remembered whenever the gospel of God is proclaimed (Mark 1:14).

The plans against Jesus throughout the narrative (3:6; 11:18; 12:12) culminate in these stories of opposition, while the prophetic service of the woman echoes the passages about the healing of Peter's mother-in-law (1:29-31) and the action of the widow (12:44), and anticipates the story about the women at the burial and at the empty tomb (15:40-41, 47; 16:1-8). Each phase of Jesus' ministry—his initial preaching in Galilee, his Jerusalem sojourn, and now his Passion, death, and resurrection—is heralded by a woman performing a "prophetic anointing." The sandwich thus creates a contrast between those who truly follow Jesus and those who are opposed to him. This is vividly illustrated by the contrast between openness and secrecy. The officials hope to capture Jesus secretly, and Judas goes off in private to seek them out, while the woman's action is to be proclaimed openly as part of the gospel throughout the world.

The narrative of the woman's action is one of the few to appear in all four gospels (Mark 14:3-9; Matt 26:6-13; Luke 7:36-50; John 12:1-8). While there is overlap in the details, there are major differences, so that the interrelationship of the narratives and the shape of the earliest tradition are disputed. In all the accounts a woman at a meal anoints Jesus' body and objections are raised. Luke is least like the others since he places the episode during the Galilean ministry in the house of Simon the Pharisee, and the focus of the story is repentance expressed in loving action. While Mark, Matthew, and John all place it at the start of the Passion narrative, only Mark and Matthew mention the anointing of the head and note that it anticipates the anointing for burial. Since this narrative was so widely yet differently used, it very likely reflects some incident in Jesus' life (by the criterion of multiple attestation), though its origin and growth are widely debated.

The narrative of the anointing has a dual focus. One focus is christological: on the anticipation of Jesus' death. Though Mark clearly states that the anointing is for burial, the anointing of *his head* also evokes royal, and hence messianic, overtones since the heads of kings and priests were anointed (the Dead Sea scrolls attest to an expectation of a priestly and a royal messiah/anointed one; see CD 19:10; 20:1; 1QSa 2:12). The narrative with which the Passion begins thus continues and qualifies the "messianic" entry of Jesus into Jerusalem where he is hailed as Son of David (11:9-10). But here Jesus is anointed as the Messiah who rules only through suffering and death.

The other focus is on the action of the woman and her interaction with the guests at the dinner. As in all the versions, the action of the woman seen in its cultural context is shocking: her entering what would have been an all-male gathering, touching Jesus, and the exuberant outpouring of precious ointment. The invocation of using the money for the poor provides a foil for Jesus' answer that while the poor can be served at every

Passover he will depart from them at this Passover, and that this woman perceives this and so anoints him as the suffering Messiah.

There is also a sad irony to this passage. Though the woman is heralded as one whose deed would be remembered wherever the gospel is proclaimed, most Christians are more familiar with the action of Judas than with the prophetic devotion displayed by the woman. Her action in its Markan form appears only in the Palm Sunday reading of the Passion (Cycle B) but can be omitted; when the Matthean Passion is read (Cycle A), the lectionary begins with Matt 26:14, the betrayal of Judas, omitting the story even from the long form of the Passion narrative.

This passage offers many themes for actualization and reflection: the diptych of devotion and betrayal, the paradox of a messiah anointed for burial, the lavish prophetic action of the woman, the perennial persecution of just people, and the need to correct the possible misunderstanding of "you will have the poor everywhere in your midst." While some of these themes are familiar, it is incumbent on the church today to see that Jesus' words—that this woman's actions are forever joined to the proclamation of the gospel—remain a part of church life and proclamation.

FOR REFERENCE AND FURTHER STUDY

Barton, Stephen C. "Mark as Narrative. The Story of the Anointing Woman (Mk 14:3-9)," *ExpTim* 102 (1991) 230–34.

Broadhead, Edwin K. *Prophet, Son, Messiah. Narrative Form and Function in Mark 14–16.* Sheffield: JSOT Press, 1994.

Collins, Adela Yarbro "The Composition of the Passion Narrative in Mark," *Sewanee Theological Review* 36 (1992) 57–77.

_____. "The Genre of the Passion Narrative," *Studia Theologica* 47 (1993) 3–28.

Heil, John Paul. "Mark 14,1-52: Narrative Structure and Reader-Response," *Bib* 71 (1990) 305–32.

Kelber, Werner H., ed. *The Passion in Mark: Studies on Mark 14–16.* Philadelphia: Fortress, 1976.

Senior, Donald. *The Passion of Jesus in the Gospel of Mark.* Wilmington, Del.: Michael Glazier, 1984.

52. *Jesus' Final Meal with His Disciples* (14:12-25)

12. Then on the first day of the Feast of Unleavened Bread when they were sacrificing the Passover lambs, his disciples asked him: "Where do you want us to go and prepare so you can eat the Passover meal?" 13. And

he dispatched two of his disciples with the following instructions: "Go up to the city, and a person carrying a jug of water will meet you; follow him. 14. And wherever he goes into a house, say to the owner of the house: 'The teacher says, Where is my guest room, where I am to eat the Passover meal with my disciples?' 15. Then he himself will show you a large upper room well furnished and ready; and there you shall prepare for us." 16. And the disciples left, came to the city, and found it just as he had told them; and they prepared for the Passover.

17. And when it was evening he arrived with the Twelve; 18. and while they were reclining and eating the meal Jesus said to them: "Amen I say to you that one of you will hand me over, one who is eating with me." 19. They began to be very sad, and to say to him one by one: "It is not I, is it?" 20. But he replied: "One of the Twelve, the one who is dipping bread with me in the dish, 21. for the Son of Man goes forward as it has been written of him, but destruction awaits that person by whom the Son of Man is handed over; it would be better for that one if he had never been born."

22. And during the meal he took bread, blessed, broke it into pieces, and then gave it to them and said: "Take, this is my body." 23. And he took a cup, gave thanks, and gave it to them; and all drank from it. 24. Then he said to them: "This is my blood of the covenant, which is being poured out for many. 25. Amen, I say to you, I will never again drink of the fruit of the vine until that day when I will drink it new in the kingdom of God."

NOTES

12. *On the first day of the Feast of Unleavened Bread:* The chronology is confusing here, since the paschal lamb was normally eaten on the first day of the feast. Yet Mark describes the "first day" as the day of preparation when the lambs were slaughtered, corresponding to Wednesday, while the meal would be celebrated that evening (15 Nisan; see Mark 14:17).

were sacrificing the Passover lambs: The imperfect *ethuon* ("were sacrificing") carries the nuance of customary action and should be understood as "when they customarily sacrificed." The word "lambs" is supplied from the context and is not mentioned explicitly in Greek (see Exod 12:1-20; Lev 23:5-8; Num 28:16-25). Though the early legislation of Exod 12:6 states that the lambs are to be kept until 14 Nisan and slaughtered "between the evenings" (that is, in the twilight of 14 Nisan), due to the large number of pilgrims in Jerusalem at Passover the sacrifices began late in the afternoon.

his disciples: Throughout Mark's Gospel "disciple" designates the Twelve and a larger group. Mark 14:12-16 uses the term "disciples," but in 14:17 Jesus arrives for the feast with "the Twelve." The different terms may reflect the use of two separate sources. Mark may also have in mind a larger group than the Twelve at the supper.

so you can eat the Passover meal: Though seemingly directed to Jesus alone ("you"), the sense is "celebrate the Passover together," since Jesus assumes the role of the head of the family.

13. *he dispatched two of his disciples:* In 14:13-16 Mark virtually repeats 11:1-6 (the instructions on finding the colt), but here the prophetic activity of Jesus is enhanced. The following verses stress that Jesus' words will be fulfilled "to the letter" (v. 16), which continues the motif of Jesus as a prophet whose words will come to pass (see 1 Sam 10:1-13; 1 Kgs 17:8-16).

carrying a jug of water: This is somewhat strange, since normally men carried water in leather bottles while women carried water in jars and jugs.

14. *whenever he goes into a house:* In contrast to the possible rejection of the disciples foreseen in 6:11, here they are welcomed hospitably.

The teacher: Jesus is so addressed throughout Mark, often in contexts of performing mighty deeds (4:38; 5:35; 9:17), as well as by disciples (9:38; 10:35; 13:1), would-be followers (10:17, 20), and adversaries (12:14, 19, 32). The use of the definite article suggests that "the teacher" was known to the householder, as does the description of the room as "my guest room."

my guest room: The Greek *katalyma* suggests a temporary resting or stopping place and is also used by Luke for the "inn" where Joseph and Mary found no room for the birth of Jesus (Luke 2:7). During Passover Jerusalem residents were expected to make space available for pilgrims to celebrate the meal.

a large upper room, well furnished and ready: In crowded Jerusalem the eating quarters of the family were often on the upper story above the din of the street or of a shop below. The designation "large" (*mega:* literally "great") suggests that more than the Twelve and Jesus were present, while "well furnished" (Greek *estrōmenon:* literally "spread over, carpeted") describes a festive room with covered couches for the guests to recline on (see 14:18). The term also echoes the garments spread out *(estrōsan)* before Jesus when he first entered Jerusalem (11:8).

16. *just as he had told them:* The narrative concentrates on the instructions of Jesus, while their fulfillment is narrated concisely, again confirming his authority.

17. *when it was evening:* The Passover supper was usually begun between the officially determined sunset and the descent of darkness.

the Twelve: From this point on Mark speaks of "the Twelve" primarily in a negative sense (14:20, 42). The term "disciple *(mathētēs)* reappears only in 14:32 and 16:7.

reclining and eating: Though Exod 12:11 says that the meal should be eaten with staff in hand and ready for a quick departure, by the first century Jewish groups had adopted the Greco-Roman custom of reclining (on one elbow) while eating. Since slaves did not recline while eating, the new custom may reflect the theme of liberation from Egyptian slavery (see Gundry, *Mark* 827).

One of you will hand me over: In a solemn pronouncement (see 14:9) Jesus announces his imminent betrayal. The expression "one of you" stresses that the betrayal will come from Jesus' chosen Twelve. Though the readers have known this since 3:19, where Judas was described as the one "who betrayed him," the disciples now know of the betrayal for the first time; in 14:10 Judas' action is also made known to the readers but hidden from the disciples.

one who is eating with me: This is a reference to Ps 41:10: "Even the friend who had my trust, who shared my table, has scorned me." The psalm is a thanksgiving after suffering and expresses hope in God despite suffering and opposition. See also the lament in Ps 55:10-11 over betrayal by one who walked with the psalmist. Since eating together was a sign of special intimacy in the ancient world, the tragedy of Judas' action is heightened.

19. *to be very sad:* The Greek verb *lypeisthai* has overtones of distress and anxiety, here not so much over the impending fate of Jesus as over the fact that one of the Twelve is to be the betrayer.

    one by one: In this short phrase Mark offers a condensed but poignant picture of the uncertain disciples.

    It is not I, is it?: The Greek particle *mē* introduces a question that expects a negative answer. The question reflects Mark's picture of the flaws of the Twelve throughout the gospel; they are never really sure of their own commitment.

20. *One of the Twelve:* Through the familiar technique of double statement, where the second intensifies the first, Mark stresses the gravity of the betrayal in the context of that very meal that celebrates freedom from slavery and the unity of the community, and specifies clearly that it is one of the Twelve who were called earlier "to be with him" (3:14).

    the one who is dipping bread with me in the dish: This is a virtual repetition of v. 17 and is a metaphorical way of expressing deep union. It reflects the words of the sufferer in Ps 41:4-10, where the enemies "wonder in malice when I will die," and "even my bosom friend in whom I trusted, who ate of my bread, has lifted his heal against me" (Ps 41:9); see also Ps 55:12-15.

21. *the Son of Man:* This is one of the four "Son of Man" sayings in the Passion narrative, three of which stress his suffering (14:21 [two], 41) and one his return in power (14:62).

    goes forward as it is written of him: The divine necessity of suffering is stressed as in the Passion predictions (8:31; 9:31; 10:33-34). Though the Greek for "go forward" *(hypagein)* is used by John (7:35; 8:14; 16:5) to describe Jesus' return to the Father, this motif is not explicit in Mark. While Jesus' sufferings are described as grounded in what "is written," no text in the Jewish Scriptures explicitly mentions a suffering Son of Man. Nevertheless, throughout the Passion narrative Mark interprets Jesus' suffering in light of OT texts, and so reflects the early Christian view that the death and resurrection of Jesus were "according to the Scriptures" (1 Cor 15:3-5).

    destruction awaits: This translates "woe" *(ouai),* which is somewhat archaic in English. Though rooted in laments over death, Jesus' use of "woe" is resonant of the frequent prophetic judgment oracles and continues the motif of Jesus as the suffering prophet (see Hos 7:12-14; Amos 5:17-19; 6:3-5; especially Mic 2:1-2; Isa 5:7-23; 28:1-2).

by whom the Son of Man is handed over: Since the suffering and death of Jesus are always presented as in accord with God's will, this verse presents the classic theological dilemma of God's sovereign will versus human freedom, a topic that is not addressed directly in the gospel (see also Mark 4:10-12).

it would be better . . . he had never been born: This harsh statement is either in tension with or an illustration of Jesus' earlier statement that every sin can be forgiven except the sin against the Holy Spirit (3:28-29). In *1 Enoch* 38:2 the seer says that for those who deny the Lord of Spirits "it had been good for them if they had not been born." Mark reflects a similar apocalyptic determinism.

22. *during the meal:* After the prophecy of betrayal Mark returns to the setting of the meal (see 14:18). Though Mark sets this meal in a Passover context the principal element of the Passover meal, eating the lamb, is never mentioned (see Interpretation).

took bread: Jesus' actions recall his earlier actions at the feedings of the 5000 (6:41) and of the 4000 (8:6) with the addition of "having given thanks" *(eulogēsas;* see *eucharistēsas,* 14:23). Though Mark writes *artos,* the bread presumably would be the "unleavened bread" *(azymos)* eaten throughout the extended Passover festival.

blessed: Mark here uses the participle *eulogēsas* (lit. "blessing") for the words over the bread. "Blessing" is an act of thanksgiving and praise of God and reflects the Jewish custom of blessing food at the beginning and end of meals (Josephus, *War* 2.131).

broke it into pieces, and then gave it to them: These actions reflect the normal custom of the *paterfamilias* distributing food to the family members during a festive Jewish meal.

Take, this is my body: Through liturgical practice we tend to think of two distinct meanings for the bread and the cup, but "my body" and "my blood of the new covenant" are two ways of expressing the total self-gift of Jesus "for the sake of the many." Since in this kind of construction Aramaic has no specific form of the verb "to be," the original words would simply be "This my body," though the Greek states it more clearly with "is" *(estin).* Jesus' words have spawned a host of different interpretations with important implications for ecumenical dialogue. Some scholars say Jesus was simply pointing to the bread while others say that the sentence could mean "This is I myself" or "This means or represents my body." Theological statements of "real presence" or "transubstantiation" are developments from this text (and other NT texts), but the Markan emphasis is on the action of Jesus in his self-giving that is about to take place on the cross.

23. *And he took the cup, gave thanks, and gave it to them:* Apart from the omission of "he broke," the action here reproduces that associated with the bread. Though "wine" is not explicitly mentioned, by metonymy the cup represents what it contains (here, wine). In the Passover ritual (as reconstructed by Joachim Jeremias) four cups of wine punctuate the meal, and this cup would be that taken after eating the lamb. The repetition of "gave it to them" stresses the self-giving

action of Jesus, and readers might hear an echo of the cognate verb "hand or give over" *(paradidonai)*, which is used of Jesus' death (see 14:21).

all drank from it: Just as Jesus breaks the one loaf and all share in it, they all drink from one cup, which underscores the participation of the disciples in the events symbolized by Jesus' actions. Paul states this explicitly in 1 Cor 10:16-17.

24. *This is my blood of the covenant:* Through these words the Markan Jesus interprets his actions at the supper. Although some manuscripts add "new" before "covenant," the oldest ones such as Vaticanus and Sinaiticus omit it. The addition of "new" is due most likely to the influence of Luke 22:20 and 1 Cor 11:25. Blood is a powerful symbol with many meanings, primarily associated with life. Though the terms "covenant" and "blood" are not joined frequently in the OT, the term "blood of the covenant" appears when Moses ratifies the Sinai covenant by sprinkling the people with blood (see Exod 24:1-8; also Heb 9:19-21; 10:28-30). The shedding of Jesus' blood is taken as the ratification of the covenant.

covenant: Covenant *(diathēkē)*, used only here in Mark, is one of the primary religious institutions of Israel. The people are constituted as such by the Sinai covenant in Exodus 19–24 (known as the Book of the Covenant), which was foreshadowed by covenants of promise made with Abraham. In the OT two major kinds of covenant appear: one modeled on the ancient Near Eastern suzerainty treaties, which begin with a historical prologue and involve mutual rights and obligations and are ratified by sacrifice (e.g., the Sinai covenant); and the other described as "patron" covenants (George Mendenhall, "Covenant," *IDB* 1.714–23) or "the divine charter" (Gen 9:8-15; Genesis 15; 2 Samuel 7), whereby God binds himself to the future of a people (through Abraham or David), and which, when broken, can be renewed (Jer 31:31-34).

which is being poured out for many: The neuter nominative participle "poured out" *(to ekchynnomenon)* specifies that it is Jesus' life that is being poured out ("my blood"); the same verb is used for the shedding of blood in Isa 59:7 and Ps 13:3.

for many: The Greek *hyper pollōn* reflects pre-Markan formulas in which the death of Jesus is always "for" others (e.g., 1 Cor 11:24; Rom 5:8; 8:32; Gal 1:4; 2:20). It also echoes Mark 10:45, where the Son of Man came to give his life as a *lytron anti pollōn* ("a ransom for many"). "Many" in English is often equivalent to "not all," but in Aramaic and Hebrew usage "many" can be understood here and in 10:45 in an inclusive sense (Jeremias, *Eucharistic Words* 179). The Markan Jesus understands his imminent death as bringing about a covenant community that will benefit all humans.

25. *Amen, I say to you:* This solemn introduction, used at the beginning of the dinner to introduce the prophecy of betrayal (14:18), both concludes the supper and introduces a new motif. Since the prophecy both of betrayal and of abandonment by the disciples will be fulfilled in the gospel itself, readers are also assured that the prophecy of drinking the new wine in the kingdom will be fulfilled.

I will never again drink of the fruit of the vine: In Jewish thought fasting from food and drink had many meanings: repentance (Joel 2:11-13), mourning (2 Sam 12:22-24), preparation for contact with the holy (2 Chr 20:20-22), petitionary prayer (Isa 58:2-4; Ezra 8:22-24), and preparation for the day of the Lord (Joel 2:12-14). The phrase "fruit of the vine" is a Semitic expression for wine. Since the ministry of Jesus is the time of celebration at the presence of the bridegroom, and since fasting will begin only when the bridegroom is taken away (2:19-21), Jesus' vow of fasting at the Supper is a prophetic symbol of his imminent death (see Jeremias, *Eucharistic Words* 212: "At the Last Supper therefore Jesus neither ate of the Passover lamb nor drank of the wine; probably he fasted completely").

until that day when I drink it new in the kingdom of God: Jesus, who fasted at this meal, looks forward to a time of feasting. The death of Jesus is not, however, the end, since he looks toward a new presence in the kingdom of God. Other Jewish groups celebrated meals in anticipation of the eschatological banquet (IQSa 2:11-22), which is often referred to as the "messianic banquet," though in some texts a messiah is absent (see Isa 25:6; *1 Enoch* 62:14; *2 Bar* 29:1-8; Matt 8:11-12; 22:1-10; Luke 13:28-19; Rev 2:7; 19:9).

kingdom of God: This saying forms a great arch to Jesus' initial proclamation of the nearness of God's kingdom in 1:14-15 and anticipates the coming kingdom. It also foreshadows the ironic proclamation of the crucified Jesus as king (15:2, 9, 12, 18, 26) and the presence at his burial of Joseph of Arimathea as one who was waiting "for the kingdom of God" (15:43-46).

INTERPRETATION

The account of Jesus' final meal with his disciples is divided into three sections: the preparations for the meal (14:12-16), the initial phase of the meal with the prediction of Judas' betrayal (14:17-21), and the institution of the Lord's Supper (14:22-25). The Markan composition here creates a series of "sandwiches." Judas' betrayal (14:10-11), which provides the frame for the initial story of the woman's action, also provides a frame for the preparations for the Passover (14:12-16), which is followed by Jesus' prediction of betrayal (14:17-21). This again serves to frame the institution narrative, which is followed by the prediction of Peter's betrayal (14:27-31). By initiating the Passover meal with the prediction that he will be handed over and concluding it with the prediction of the failure of the disciples Mark rounds off the pattern begun in 8:31 and repeated in 9:31 and 10:33-34, that Jesus will be handed over while the disciples will fail to comprehend his suffering. The Passover meal not only assures the reader that the words of Jesus are to be believed, but also creates a tapestry of betrayal and failure interwoven with acts of loving service, culminating in Jesus' statement that his blood will be poured out for many (14:24).

Historical reconstruction of this section of Mark is immensely complex and not the task of this commentary. Clear evidence for a tradition of the Lord's Supper some twenty years prior to Mark is found in 1 Cor 11:23-26. The tradition does not exist in identical form in the several places where it is attested: Matt 26:26-29, which closely follows Mark 14:22-25; Luke 22:15-20, which has considerable differences and significant manuscript variations; and *Didache* 9:1–10:15. Joseph Fitzmyer reflects a majority of scholars in postulating two early forms of the Last Supper narrative: a Jerusalem tradition represented in Mark/Matthew and an Antiochene tradition found in Luke/Paul (Joseph A. Fitzmyer, *The Gospel According to Luke X–XXIV.* AB 28A [Garden City, N.Y.: Doubleday, 1985] 1393).

Likewise disputed are when the meal was held and what kind of meal was eaten. The Synoptic tradition and Paul place the meal on the eve of Passover (that is, the evening before the death of Jesus) and so present it as an actual Passover meal. But John places it on the day of preparation when the Paschal lambs were slain (John 13, but without an institution narrative). This involves the question whether John and the Synoptics were following different calendars as well as possible variations among Jews of Jesus' time regarding the celebration of Passover (see Fitzmyer, *Gospel According to Luke,* and also Kodell, Marshall, Chilton in the bibliography for this section).

The picture of a Passover meal emerges from explicit statements in the Synoptics (Mark 14:12; Matt 26:17; Luke 22:7-8). In his magisterial work *The Eucharistic Words of Jesus,* Joachim Jeremias offered a careful reconstruction of the sequence of events in the Jewish Passover meal and argued strongly that the NT evidence reflects Jewish Passover practice. But subsequent research has questioned whether the evidence Jeremias draws from later Jewish documents *(Mishnah* and *Talmud),* written well after the destruction of the Second Temple, can be used to describe first-century practice, since the destruction of the Temple caused major changes in the celebration. Likewise, there is no consensus on how Passover was celebrated by the large number of Jews living outside of Palestine, especially since it was a pilgrimage feast to be celebrated in Jerusalem. Again a variety of other Jewish meal patterns have been proposed as the basis of the NT accounts: Jewish festival meals with multiple wine courses; ḥabûrâ or fellowship meals with companions, similar to those of the Pharisees; and tôdâ or meals of thanksgiving. Though Mark's account is vital in any historical reconstruction, Mark does not always exhibit a detailed knowledge of Jewish customs and elsewhere feels the need to explain Jewish practices to his community (see 7:3-4). Hence Mark may not be an entirely reliable guide to the historical reconstruction of the Last Supper.

This section of Mark is heavily influenced by OT motifs, reflecting the early tradition that Christ "died for our sins according to the Scriptures"

(1 Cor 15:3) in addition to the more general Passover motifs. Jesus continues to be presented as "the suffering just one" of the Psalms (see especially Psalms 41 and 55). Particularly influential throughout the developing Passion tradition is Zechariah 9–14, which stresses the suffering of the royal Messiah. Jesus enters Jerusalem amid shouts, like the king of Zech 9:9, humble and riding on an ass. The somewhat unusual phrase "blood of the covenant" reflects Zech 9:11: "As for you also, because of the blood of my covenant with you, I will set your captives free from the waterless pit"; and in Zech 11:4 the "shepherd of the flock" (see Mark 6:34) is doomed to slaughter. Jesus' prediction of the striking of the shepherd and the scattering of the sheep are an adaptation of Zech 13:7, and the apocalyptic judgment scene of Zechariah 14 takes place on the Mount of Olives. The latter chapters of Zechariah have been called the "Zechariah Passion" (Barnabas Lindars, *New Testament Apologetic* [Philadelphia: Westminster, 1961] 117). See also the use of Zech 12:10 in John 19:37: "They will look on the one whom they have pierced."

Since the purpose of this commentary is to call attention to the distinctively Markan emphases, our focus here is on Mark's presentation of the supper. Mark clearly sees the supper as a Passover meal, though there is no explicit reference to the eating of lamb. Mark's stress on the contrast between Jesus and his failed followers, achieved by the various "sandwiches," was noted above. In the institution narrative itself Mark stresses the words, actions, and interpretation of the bread and wine. The bread and wine become bearers of the very presence of Jesus, which inaugurates a new covenant to be fully realized in the kingdom of God.

Just as the covenant at Sinai was ratified by the sprinkling of blood, Jesus' new covenant will be so ratified (Exod 24:5-8). Since blood symbolizes "life," the sprinkling is a participation of all the people in the life of the victim offered. Covenants in the Jewish tradition are the culmination of a process of engagement between the partners and are usually preceded by a historical prologue that recounts the benefits given by the principal agent of the covenant. The good news of Jesus the Messiah (1:1) that Mark has narrated to this point recounts God's saving deeds in Jesus, which are then ratified by the covenant sacrifice.

In line with Mark's eschatology throughout the gospel, this covenant possesses an "already" and a "not yet" quality. Jesus gives his very self (body and blood) as a covenant sacrifice, but the fulfillment of his union with the disciples will take place only in the kingdom of God. This is the final kingdom saying of Jesus, and it completes the eschatological vision of the kingdom as something that has arrived in the ministry of Jesus and grows secretly but whose full flowering is in the future. This eschatological dimension is underscored by the departure for the Mount of Olives where Jesus, according to Mark 13, had prophesied the destruction of the Temple, his return as Son of Man, and the gathering of the elect.

Actualizing Jesus' Last Supper according to Mark presents numerous challenges and opportunities. The eucharistic celebration of the church combines many perspectives: recollection of the Exodus deliverance, continuation of Jesus' presence through a meal, the sacramental reenactment of his Passion and death, the foretaste of the heavenly banquet, the presentation of Jesus as a model of loving service (the footwashing in John), and an anticipation of the heavenly banquet. Mark's somewhat sober narrative stresses above all the sacrificial death of Jesus "for many" and so is a caution against overstressing the communal meal as the leading motif of the Eucharist. We recall not only a meal, but the final meal of one who was to be executed as a criminal for our sake.

The liturgical rites normally correspond to no one NT account but draw elements from all of them. Since the Eucharist is so central in much Christian piety there is a tendency to meld together the different accounts. There is also a danger of exaggerated focus on the words of institution and the real presence. Vatican II provided an excellent guideline for proper interpretation by speaking of the "twofold table of the Lord's Word and of the Supper." In Markan terms this means that it is the Jesus of the gospel, God's chosen prophet and suffering servant, who gives his life for many. It also means that reception of the Eucharist cannot be separated from responding to the challenge of discipleship that permeates the gospel, though the failure of the chosen Twelve serves as a warning that meeting this challenge is never complete. As a covenant "in my blood" the Eucharist is a promise that Jesus will be with the believer in the present and in the future banquet of the kingdom. The ancient hymn of the church captures the Markan meaning well: "*O sacrum convivium in quo Christus sumitur, memoria passionis ejus recolitur, et nobis datur pignus aeternae gloriae*" ("O sacred banquet in which Christ is received, the memory of his Passion is brought to life, and to us is granted a pledge of eternal glory").

FOR REFERENCE AND FURTHER STUDY

Casey, Maurice. "The Date of the Passover Sacrifices and Mark 14:12," *Tyndale Bulletin* 48 (1997) 245–47.
_____. "The Original Aramaic Form of Jesus' Interpretation of the Cup," *JTS* 41 (1990) 1–12.
Chilton, Bruce D. *Jesus' Prayer and Jesus' Eucharist. His Personal Practice of Spirituality.* Valley Forge, Penn.: Trinity Press International, 1997.
Feeley-Harnik, Gillian. The Lord's Table. *Eucharist and Passover in Early Christianity.* Philadelphia: University of Pennsylvania Press, 1981.

Jeremias, Joachim. *The Eucharistic Words of Jesus.* New York: Scribner's, 1966.

Kodell, Jerome. *The Eucharist in the New Testament.* Wilmington, Del.: Michael Glazier, 1988.

Marshall, I. Howard. *Last Supper and Lord's Supper.* Grand Rapids: Eerdmans, 1981.

Ossom-Batsa, George. *The Institution of the Eucharist in the Gospel of Mark.* Bern-Frankfurt: Lang, 2001.

Smith, Barry D. "The More Original Form of the Words of Institution," ZNW 83 (1992) 166–86.

53. *Prediction of Peter's Denial* (14:26-31)

26. And after singing hymns they went out to the Mount of Olives. 27. Then Jesus said to them: "You all will fall away, because it is written: 'I will strike the shepherd, and the sheep will be scattered.' 28. But after I am raised up I will go before you into Galilee." 29. But then Peter said to him: "Even if everyone falls away, it will not be I." 30. Then Jesus said to him: "Amen I say to you that you, today on this very night before the cock crows twice, will deny me three times." 31. But he was responding vehemently: "Even if it is necessary for me to die along with you, I will never deny you." Then the others said the same thing.

NOTES

26. *And after singing hymns:* Though most translations render *hymnēsantes* as "having sung a hymn," the plural is probably more accurate. According to later Jewish tradition the Passover concluded with singing of the *Hallel* psalms, 114/15 to 118, which are hymns of praise and thanksgiving to God, especially for the Exodus.

    they went out: The Greek verb *exēlthon*, from *exerchesthai*, is the same one used in the LXX of David's flight from Jerusalem (2 Sam 15:16; see below).

    the Mount of Olives: This is a small ridge, known for extensive olive groves, about three miles long, running north to south across from the Kidron Valley, east of Jerusalem (Warren J. Heard, Jr., "Olives, Mount of," *ABD* 5:13). Mark locates it "opposite the Temple," where Jesus had earlier predicted the Temple's destruction (13:2-4). According to the vision of the day of the Lord in Zechariah 14 the feet of Lord will stand in judgment on this mountain. Here Mark also echoes 2 Sam 15:30 where David, having been betrayed by a trusted friend, flees Jerusalem and ascends the Mount of Olives where he weeps and prays to God.

27. *You all will fall away:* The Greek verb *skandalisthēsesthe* is often translated "be scandalized," which connotes in English "shock" or "cause offense." The Greek verb, from the noun *skandalon* ("trap, snare, something which makes

you fall"), is stronger. Mark uses the term earlier in 4:17 to describe the seed that falls away in time of persecution, thus foreshadowing this prediction (see also 6:2; 9:42, 45).

it is written: This is a standard Markan formula for the fulfillment of the OT, either followed by a specific quotation (1:2; 7:6; 11:17) or with a general reference (9:12; 14:21).

'I will strike the shepherd, and the sheep will be scattered': Though a citation of Zech 13:7, the Markan version corresponds exactly neither to the LXX nor to the Masoretic Text. These read: "Arise, O sword, against my shepherd [LXX, shepherds] and against the man who stands next to me,' says the Lord of Hosts. 'Strike the shepherd, and the sheep are scattered [LXX: and draw out the sheep]; I will turn my hand against the little ones.'" The context in Zechariah 13 is not a prophecy of dispersal but rather a negative judgment on the unfaithful shepherd and the faithless sheep (see Ezekiel 34). Mark also changes the imperative "strike" *(pataxate)* to the first person future, "I will strike," with God most likely understood as the agent of striking. This reflects the Markan theology that Jesus' suffering is willed by God, which becomes explicit in the Gethsemane narrative (see also 8:31 and the prophetic fulfillment texts). Mark has earlier compared Jesus to the compassionate shepherd (6:34), and the scattering of the sheep foreshadows the flight of the disciples in 14:50.

28. *But after I am raised up:* This provides the dramatic contrast to the pessimistic prediction in 14:27 and continues the theme of death followed by resurrection begun in 8:31. The passive articular infinitive *to egerthēnai* stresses that, just as the suffering of Jesus was divinely willed (8:31; 14:36), God is also the agent of his resurrection.

I will go before you: The use of *proagein* here echoes the context of the third Passion prediction where Jesus "goes before" the disciples on the way to Jerusalem (10:32). After his resurrection Jesus will resume his role of leadership of the community.

into Galilee: Galilee in Mark is both a geographical and symbolic place. There Jesus begins his ministry of proclaiming the good news of the kingdom, calls his first disciples, and does the bulk of his mighty works and teaching about the kingdom, while Jerusalem proves to be the place of his rejection and of his suffering and death. The promise of a post-resurrectional meeting in Galilee is the promise of a new mission (see 16:7).

29. *But then Peter said to him:* As on other occasions Peter assumes the role of speaker for the larger group, though usually with a misunderstanding that then evokes subsequent correction from Jesus (8:29; 9:5; 10:28; 11:21). Mark's use of the adversative *de* ("but") and *ephē* ("said") rather than the characteristic *legei* accentuates Peter's protest.

Even if everyone falls away, it will not be I: Peter's initial words "even if" grammatically presuppose a condition that will be fulfilled, but ironically will not be. On "fall away" see above, v. 27. The grammatical dissonance here underscores the surprise of the denial. The translation "not be I" captures the Greek word order, which puts Peter's *ouk egō* (lit. "not I") at the end of the sentence.

30. *Amen I say to you that you:* On "Amen" see the Note on 14:9. The double use of the personal pronoun *soi* ("to you") and *su* ("you") ironically corresponds to Peter's strong use of "I" *(egō)* and his desire to isolate himself from others who will deny Jesus. He is now singled out as the leader of those who deny Jesus.

today on this very night before the cock crows twice: Duplicate or, in this case, triplicate designations of time are characteristic of Mark. They also stress here the immediacy with which Jesus' prediction is fulfilled.

before the cock crows twice: Mark does not use the technical term for a cock's crow *(kokkyzein)*, but prefers *phōnēsai*, which can be used of either a human voice or an animal sound. Thus he subtly contrasts Peter's earlier "sound" *(ephē)* that he would never deny with the "sound" heralding his denial. The other gospels omit the reference to the cock crowing twice *(dis)*, which foreshadows what happens in 14:68, 72. Some feel that its presence arises from the similarity of its sound to *tris*, "three times." Also in Greco-Roman writing a second cock crow is associated with the dawn or sunrise (see Brown, *Death of the Messiah* 137), which again foreshadows the time sequence of 14:72 and 15:1.

you will deny me: Though Jesus had predicted that all would "fall away" and Peter had protested that he would not "fall away" (which could suggest weakness), Jesus' prediction is couched in the stronger language of "deny" *(aparneisthai)*, which has overtones of "repudiate." Apart from referring to Peter's denial, the term appears only in Mark 8:34 where disciples are summoned to "deny themselves," which follows the first major misunderstanding by Peter where Jesus calls him "Satan." Ironically here, rather than denying himself Peter will deny Jesus. The term becomes part of the vocabulary of Christian apostasy when some fail in the face of persecution (see Mark 4:17; *BAGD* 108).

three times: This foreshadows the three denials of 14:68, 70, 71 and contrasts with the three times Jesus comes to his disciples in Gethsemane (14:37-41). For Mark's readers it might also reflect Roman judicial procedures mentioned by Pliny, where Christians were asked three times whether they were Christians (*Epistles* 10.96.2-3). Though the literary evidence is from a period later than Mark these procedures seem to have been used prior to Pliny (ca. 110 C.E.); see G.W.H. Lampe, "St. Peter's Denial and the Treatment of the *Lapsi*," in David Neiman and Margaret Schatkin, eds., *The Heritage of the Early Church*. Orientalia Christiana Analecta 195 (Rome: Pontifical Oriental Institute, 1973) 114–33.

31. *But he was responding vehemently:* Mark's use of the adversative *de* ("but") suggests a strong counter to Jesus' statement, and the imperfect "was responding" *(elalei)* has the overtone of "begin" or "launch into" and "continue on." The adverb "vehemently" *(ekperissōs)* is found nowhere else in the NT or the LXX or in classical Greek. It derives from the verb *perisseuein*, which means "more than was enough," and has overtones of excess. Matthew, who presents a more reverential treatment of Peter, omits the adverb in 26:35.

Even if it is necessary for me to die along with you: Peter's response repeats and intensifies his earlier protest, moving from not "falling away" to a readiness to suffer the same fate as Jesus, just as his later denials will increase in vehemence (see 14:66-72). The use of *dei* ("is necessary") adds to the almost pathetic irony of the scene, since Peter originally rejected Jesus' prediction that it would be necessary for him to suffer and die (8:31). The verb "die with" *(synapothanein)* is found only here in the NT (Matt 26:35 changes it to the normal *apothanein*). It is also rare in classical Greek, where it has overtones of "clinging to another even in death." Suffering with Jesus became an ideal in early Christianity (see 2 Cor 7:3; 2 Tim 2:11).

I will never deny you: "Will never" *(ou mē;* see Mark 9:1) expresses an emphatic negative in a somewhat solemn, oath-like form. Again the language is stronger than Peter's protest in 14:29 that he will not be among those who fall away.

Then the others said the same thing: The disciples quickly ratify Peter's decision, which continues the pathetic irony, since they will sleep rather than watch with Jesus in the next pericope (14:32-42), and will flee at his arrest (14:50).

INTERPRETATION

Mark structures the stages of his Passion narrative not only temporally but also by geographical location. In this transitional passage Jesus leaves the upper room and travels to the Mount of Olives prior to his arrival in Gethsemane and his subsequent arrest and death in Jerusalem. The substance of the passage deals with the prediction of the striking of the shepherd and the scattering of the sheep, followed by the prediction of Peter's denial and Peter's protest of fidelity. The structure of the narrative is similar to that of 8:31-33, where Jesus' prediction of his suffering is followed by Peter's resistance to the prediction and a further confirmatory statement by Jesus.

This brief passage is rich in intertextual echoes of the OT. After singing hymns that may be related to the joyful memory of the Exodus, Jesus' journey to the Mount of Olives reflects the flight of David from Jerusalem after betrayal by a trusted friend, where he will pray to God (2 Samuel 15; see the Notes). Likewise the explicit citation of Zech 13:7 (with important changes; see the Notes) reflects the widespread use of Zechariah 9–14 by the early church to underscore that the death of Jesus was "according to the Scriptures" (see Brown, *Death of the Messiah* 1451 for use of Zechariah in the Passion narrative). This section continues the pervasive motif of the suffering person who will be abandoned by followers at a time of trial (Job 19:13-22; Pss 41:8-10; 55:12-14; Zech 13:5-7).

The narrative takes its focus from the quotation of Zech 13:7 that the shepherd will be struck and the sheep will scatter. This provides another Passion prediction by Jesus, which like the earlier ones looks forward to resurrection but differs by announcing the coming failure of Jesus' followers rather than the hostile actions of others (8:31; 9:31; 10:33-34). Reminiscent of Peter's earlier misunderstanding in 8:32-33, the narrative focuses on Peter, who again counters Jesus' teaching with a protest of his own fidelity, only to receive the ominous prediction that he will deny Jesus three times.

The prediction of Peter's denial (Mark 14:30; Matt 26:34; Luke 22:34; John 13:38) and his actual denial (Mark 14:66-72; Matt 26:69-75; Luke 22:56-62; John 18:25-27) are among those few incidents that appear in all four Gospels. As the kind of narrative that would embarrass the early community, it very likely has solid grounding in the actual events surrounding Jesus' death. It is especially stark in light of the negative picture of Peter from Mark 8:31 on and the promise of a post-resurrection appearance to the disciples (14:27) rather than an actual appearance. As the tradition develops in the other gospels the negative picture is softened. Luke describes the disciples not as those who will flee but as those "who remained with me in my trials" (22:28), and has Jesus pray for Peter and predict his conversion and subsequent leadership of the community (22:31-32). John provides an elaborate rehabilitation of Peter through his triple expression of love in John 21:15-19. This trajectory is paradoxical evidence of the antiquity and reliability of the Markan portrait.

Though historically rooted, Jesus' prediction of denial by Peter underscores the OT motif of the just person being betrayed by a companion, as mentioned above. It may also have conveyed a powerful message to Mark's Roman readers who had experienced apostasy and interfamilial betrayal during persecution (see also Mark 13:9-13). In describing the persecution of Christians under Nero, the Roman historian Tacitus (writing around 115 C.E.) states that many Christians were arrested on the basis of evidence furnished by other Christians (*Ann.* 15.44). A community that then faced the task of reconciliation with those who failed under persecution would take consolation from Mark's picture of Peter, who failed his Lord and yet was known by the Roman church as one of the "righteous pillars" of its early days (*1 Clem.* 5:2).

This section continues two major christological themes of the Passion narrative: the suffering just person with overtones of the Servant of Isa 52:13–53:12, and the prophet whose words can be trusted. What Jesus predicts here will come to pass. He will be struck; the sheep will scatter; Peter will deny him three times; but he will be raised up and go before his disciples to Galilee to again gather his flock. The message is then ultimately one of assurance and hope. Though Jesus will be mocked as a false prophet in 14:65, the gospel readers know he can be trusted.

Presentation of this narrative today should be joined with the actual denial in 14:66-72. But the narrative moves beyond the denial by its promises of resurrection and of the subsequent meeting with the failed disciples. With literary artistry Mark assures the readers of this by telling a story in which Jesus' predictions are fulfilled, so that the word of Jesus can engender trust. The failure of the disciples is not the last word. Rather, God's power can triumph not only over death but also over human betrayal and failure. In both art and proclamation the church traditionally honors Peter and Paul as its first great apostles. We should not forget that one failed Jesus when tested and the other was a persecutor of Jesus and the church (1 Cor 15:9; Acts 8:1; 9:4-5).

FOR REFERENCE AND FURTHER STUDY

Brown, Raymond E. *The Death of the Messiah. From Gethsemane to the Grave.* 2 vols. New York: Doubleday, 1994.
Cook, Stephen L. "The Metamorphosis of a Shepherd: The Tradition History of Zechariah 11:17 + 13:7-9," *CBQ* 55 (1993) 453–66.
Glasson, Thomas F. "Davidic Links with the Betrayal of Jesus," *ExpTim* 85 (1973–74) 118–19.
Wilcox, Max. "The Denial Sequence in Mark XIV.26-31, 66-72," *NTS* 17 (1971) 426–36.

54. *Jesus in Gethsemane* (14:32-42)

32. And they came to a plot of land whose name was Gethsemane, and he said to his disciples: "Sit here while I pray." 33. And he took along Peter and James and John with him, and he began to be distressed and troubled. 34. And he said to them: "My soul is sorrowful unto death. Remain here and keep on watching." 35. And going forward a little, he was falling on the ground and praying that if it is possible the hour might pass away from him. 36. And he said: "Abba, Father, all things are possible for you. Take away this cup from me. But not what I wish but what you wish." 37. And he came and found them sleeping, and said to Peter: "Simon, are you sleeping? Were you not strong enough to watch one hour? 38. Keep watching and praying lest you enter into testing. The spirit is willing but the flesh is weak." 39. And again he went away and prayed, saying the same words. 40. And again he came and found them sleeping, for their eyes were very heavy. And they did not know what they should answer him. 41. And he came a third time and said to them: "Do you go on sleeping and taking your rest? He is being paid off. The hour has come. Look, the Son of Man is being handed over into the hands of sinners. 42. Get up. Let us go. Look, the one who hands me over has come near."

NOTES

32. *And they came to a plot of land whose name was Gethsemane:* The movement that is key to the passage is helped along by the frequent uses of "and" *(kai)* as a connector and of the historical present tense (lit. "they come . . . he says"). The name "Gethsemane" means "oil press" *(gat šemani)* in Hebrew and Aramaic. It refers to a plot of land on the Mount of Olives with olive trees and an olive oil press. For earlier references to the Mount of Olives see Mark 11:1; 13:3; and 14:26. See also its role in the day of the Lord according to Zech 14:4.

    and he said to his disciples: "Sit here while I pray": Third person plural language ("they") yields to third person singular language ("he"). This is the last use of *mathētēs* ("disciple") until 16:7 ("go, tell the disciples"). Jesus' purpose in coming to Gethsemane is to pray; see 1:35 and 6:46 for other references to Jesus at prayer in places of solitude.

33. *he took along Peter and James and John with him:* For other Markan uses of *paralambanein* ("take along") see 4:36; 5:40; 7:4; 9:2; 10:32. The reference in 9:2 is most important (but see also 5:37, 40), since it too involves Peter, James, and John at the transfiguration (which has some links to the Gethsemane episode). The three disciples who form a core group among the Twelve serve as witnesses here (as at the restoration of Jairus' daughter to life and at the transfiguration).

    he began to be distressed and troubled: The beginning of Jesus' upset at his impending fate is described with the help of Mark's familiar "he began" *(ērxato)* construction plus two infinitives that express deep feelings: *ekthambeisthai* ("be distraught," see 9:25 and 16:5-6; for *thambeisthai* see 1:27; 10:24, 32), and *adēmonein* ("be troubled"). The precise cause of Jesus' disturbance is not specified (see Ps 55:5-6).

34. *he said to them:* Here "them" must refer to Peter, James, and John, whom Jesus has separated from the rest of the disciples. As the story proceeds he will further separate himself from these core disciples.

    My soul is sorrowful: Jesus' words reflect Pss 42:5, 11; 43:5: "My soul is cast down within me." Jesus the innocent sufferer makes his own the language of the OT lament psalms (see also Pss 31:10-11; 55:5). See the Interpretation.

    unto death: The phrase suggests that Jesus' sorrow is so intense that it threatens his life. See Sir 37:2: "Is it not a sorrow like that for death itself when a dear friend turns into an enemy?"

    Remain here and keep on watching: The aorist imperative *meinate* ("remain") is synonymous with *kathisate* ("sit") in 14:32. The present imperative *grēgoreite* suggests continued action ("keep on watching"). The prominence of the verb *grēgorein* in the parable of the man going on a journey at the end of the eschatological discourse (13:34, 35, 37) and in the Gethsemane episode (14:34, 37, 38) suggests that here too it has an eschatological context with reference to the time of testing that Jesus' Passion represents.

35. *And going forward a little:* Jesus seems to be separating himself from Peter, James, and John. He will return to them three times (see 14:37, 40, 41).

falling on the ground and praying: While separating from the disciples and falling to the ground are appropriate preparations for prayer, in the case of Jesus they also capture the distress he is experiencing (see 14:33). The imperfect tenses "was falling . . . praying" express continuing action on Jesus' part.

if it is possible the hour might pass away from him: This is an indirect statement of what is stated directly in 14:36. See 14:33-34 where the same device of indirect statement ("he began to be distressed and troubled") and direct statement ("My soul is sorrowful . . .") was used. The phrase "if possible" does not cast doubt on the power of God so much as it asks that God somehow change the divine plan regarding Jesus' suffering and death. Asking God to change his mind is a common theme in biblical prayers. The "hour" *(hōra)* most obviously refers to the moment of Jesus' Passion and death, but very likely also carries an apocalyptic overtone in the light of Mark 13:32 ("about that . . . hour no one knows"). In fact, early Christians like Mark regarded Jesus' death and resurrection as the decisive moment toward the full coming of God's kingdom. Brown in *The Death of the Messiah* (168) makes the point well: "Mark is representing a moment that is both historical and eschatological. The suffering and crucifixion of Jesus are a physical trial for him but also part of a cosmic struggle."

36. *Abba, Father:* The address in the direct statement of Jesus' prayer combines the Aramaic *(Abba)* and Greek *(ho patēr)* forms of the word "Father." The use of "Abba" in early Christian prayer is witnessed in Rom 8:15 and Gal 4:6 and is generally regarded as reflecting Jesus' own way of addressing God. It may also underlie the address "Father" in the Lukan version of the Lord's Prayer (see Luke 11:2).

all things are possible for you: The phrase restates positively what was said more tentatively in 14:35 ("if it is possible") and counters any misunderstanding about Jesus' faith in God's power. It also echoes Jesus' own statement in Mark 10:27: "All things are possible with God."

Take away this cup from me: The "cup" *(potērion)* metaphor is synonymous with "the hour" in 14:35, and so it very likely has both historical (Jesus' suffering) and eschatological (the coming of God's kingdom) aspects. In the OT the "cup" image is often used by the prophets to describe the suffering that God will bring on the enemies of God's people or on the wicked (see Isa 51:17; Jer 25:15-16; 51:7; Ezek 23:33; Ps 75:8). Jesus' prayer about the "cup" in 14:36 should be interpreted in light of his challenge to James and John to "drink the cup that I drink" (10:38-39) and his words over the cup at the Last Supper ("my blood of the covenant poured out for many," 14:24). In all three cases there is a reference to the suffering of Jesus in the metaphor of the cup.

But not what I wish but what you wish: The repetition of "but" *(alla)* is emphatic, if also peculiar. The double use of the verb *thelein* ("I wish . . . you wish") adds to the power of Jesus' statement. It also served as the basis for the doctrine that Jesus had both a human and a divine will (against the heresy of Monotheletism = Jesus had only one will). Brown in *The Death of the Messiah* (177–78) expresses Jesus' problem with the following question: "Could not the Father bring about the kingdom in some other way that did not involve the horrendous suffering and crucifixion of the Son delivered into the hands of sinners?" The final words of Jesus' prayer echo a petition in Matthew's version of the Lord's Prayer (Matt 6:10: "Thy will be done . . .") and here express his perfect acceptance of the cross as God's will.

37. *he came and found them sleeping:* The two verbs *erchetai* and *heuriskei* are both in the historical present tense. Whether "them" includes all the disciples who originally accompanied Jesus (see 14:32) or only Peter, James, and John (see 14:33) is not clear.

Simon, are you sleeping?: Having just mentioned the name of Peter in the introduction to the quotation, Mark has Jesus address him here as "Simon." See Mark 3:16: "Simon (to whom he gave the name Peter)." Peter, who shortly before had boasted that he would never fall away (14:29) and that he was willing to die rather than deny Jesus (14:31), is now made into the symbol of the disciples' weakness and failure to stay with Jesus as he enters into his Passion.

Were you not strong enough to watch one hour?: The verb *ischyein* ("be able, strong enough") is related to the adjective *ischyros,* and so provides a link to John the Baptist's description of Jesus as "the stronger one" *(ischyroteros)* in 1:7 and Jesus' designation of Satan as "the strong one" in 3:27. The verb *grēgorein* ("watch") links the Gethsemane pericope to the parable of the man going on a journey in 13:34-37 (see the Note on 14:34). By his unexpected return Jesus enacts that parable and gives the "hour" an eschatological overtone here too.

38. *Keep watching and praying:* The present imperatives suggest continuing action. For the themes of watching and praying in combination see Pss 42:8; 63:6; 77:2.

lest you enter into testing: The "testing" *(peirasmos)* is not only the historical testing Jesus is undergoing but also the eschatological testing or trial referred to in Mark 13:19-20 as the "great tribulation." Jesus has already entered into that testing. Since the disciples are so unprepared for it, Jesus urges them to pray that they not enter it now. There is an echo of the petition in the Matthean version (6:13) of the Lord's Prayer here: "Lead us not into temptation *(peirasmos)."*

the spirit is willing but the flesh is weak: While Jesus' comment sounds like a proverb, it fits the situation in Gethsemane very well. The opposition is between the "spirit" as what is noble and godly about humans (thinking, willing, etc.) and the "flesh" as what is weak and fragile about them (their earthly and perishable elements). By sleeping the disciples have shown themselves to be ruled by the "flesh." Even though Jesus has persisted in meditation and prayer, he too runs the risk of being ruled by the flesh: "In the days of his flesh, Jesus offered up prayers and supplications, with loud cries and tears, to the one who was able to save him from death, and he was heard because of his reverent submission" (Heb 5:7).

39. *And again he went away and prayed:* The introductory phrase "and again" *(kai palin)* also appears in the next verse. This is part of a sequence in which Jesus goes off to pray three time and returns to find his disciples sleeping (though between 14:40 and 41 there is no mention of Jesus going off to pray).

saying the same words: This awkward participial phrase is omitted in many manuscripts, and there is some doubt about whether it belongs in Mark's text.

But Mark often uses *logos* ("word," translated as a plural here) to refer to Jesus' teaching (see 4:33; 8:32, 38; 9:10; 10:24).

40. *for their eyes were very heavy:* The passive participle *katabarynomenoi* ("were burdened, weighed down") illustrates the weakness of the flesh noted at the end of 14:38.

they did not know what they should answer him: The disciples' confusion here is reminiscent of Peter's immediate reaction to the transfiguration of Jesus ("for he did not know what to say," 9:6).

41. *he came a third time:* Jesus' third return is narrated without stating that he went away to pray. His three visits to Peter and the other disciples look back to his prophecy that Peter would deny him three times (14:30) and forward to the three denials by Peter (14:66-72).

Do you go on sleeping and taking your rest?: Although the sentence could be understood as an indicative ("you go on sleeping . . ."), it is best taken as a question. Having commanded the disciples to "be on watch" *(grēgoreite)* three times (see 14:34, 37, 38), Jesus finds them sleeping for the third time. To take it as an imperative (unless it is meant very ironically) conflicts with 14:42 ("Get up. Let us go").

He is being paid off: The verb *apechein* consists of the preposition *apo* ("from") and the verb *echein* ("have"). It usually has a commercial or financial meaning ("receive a sum in full"). For the problems associated with *apechei* here and the various solutions see Brown, *The Death of the Messiah* 1379–83. By opting for "the money is paid," Brown takes Judas as the implied subject, gives *apechein* its usual financial or commercial sense, and views *apechei* as a reference to the promise by the chief priests to give money to Judas in return for his betraying Jesus to them (see 14:11).

The hour has come: In light of 14:35 (and 13:32) the "hour" refers both to the historical moment of Jesus' death and to the eschatological "hour." Whereas Jesus prayed in 14:35 that "the hour might pass away *(parerchesthai)* from him," here in 14:41 he announces that "the hour has come *(erchesthai)*."

the Son of Man is being handed over into the hands of sinners: The title "Son of Man" and the verb *paradidonai* recall the language of the Passion predictions (see 8:31; 9:31; 10:33-34). The same terms appeared in Jesus' prophecy about his own fate in 14:21 ("the Son of Man is handed over"). The new element is "sinners" *(hamartōloi)* as the ones to whom the Son of Man is handed over. Compare 9:31 ("into the hands of humans") and 10:33 ("to the chief priests and scribes . . . to Gentiles"). There is here an ironic echo of Jesus' early description of his mission: "I did not come to call the just, but sinners *(hamartōloi)*" (2:17).

42. *Get up. Let us go:* The same command appears in Jesus' farewell discourse according to John (14:31). Despite the disciples' persistent weakness and failures Jesus invites them to accompany him as he moves forward to the cross. For other imperatives addressed to the disciples in 14:32-42 see 14:32 ("Sit here while I pray"), 14:34 ("Remain here and keep on watching"), and 14:38 ("Keep watching and praying").

the one who hands me over has come near: Here Judas is described as *ho paradidous me*, thus evoking the theme of Jesus being "handed over" and alluding back to the plot between Judas and the chief priests in 14:10-11. The verb *ēngiken* (from *engizein*) first appeared in Mark's opening summary of Jesus' preaching in 1:15: "the kingdom of God is at hand (or: has come near)." Its use here constitutes a subtle reminder of the eschatological dimension of the events described in the Gethsemane pericope.

INTERPRETATION

The episode about Jesus in Gethsemane functions as a bridge between his arrival at the Mount of Olives (14:26-31) after the Last Supper and his betrayal by Judas and subsequent arrest (14:43-52). It emphasizes the humanity and nobility of Jesus as well as the weakness of his disciples.

Jesus goes to Gethsemane to pray (14:32), and in 14:33-36 we learn about the content of his prayer. Mark twice supplies the content first in indirect discourse (14:33, 35) and then in direct discourse (14:34, 36). The first sequence brings out Jesus' personal distress and confusion with two emotional verbs ("distressed and troubled") and then with an echo of an OT lament psalm (Pss 42:5, 11; 43:5). The second sequence (14:35-36) concerns Jesus' struggle to accept the fate that seems to await him, first by praying that "the hour might pass away from him" and then by putting his life in the hands of his Father ("Abba, Father . . . not what I wish but what you wish").

In a structure that interlocks with the first part, Mark in 14:35-42 three times has Jesus go apart from the disciples to pray and return to them and find them sleeping (14:35-38, 39-40, 41a). The disciples serve as exemplars for the weakness of the flesh (14:38). Peter in particular is singled out for criticism (14:37). The one who earlier claimed that he would never betray Jesus (14:29, 31) is not strong enough to "watch one hour" with him. The threefold proof of Peter's weakness ("Simon, are you sleeping?") prepares for his threefold denial of Jesus in 14:66-72. Nevertheless, even though Jesus has proof of his disciples' weakness and has prayed that they may not "enter into testing" (14:38), he still asks them in 14:42 to accompany him as he faces the mystery of the cross ("Get up. Let us go").

There are also obvious links between the Gethsemane episode and the three Passion predictions in the journey narrative (8:31; 9:31; 10:33-34) as well as Jesus' Passion prediction at the Last Supper (14:21) with regard to the title "Son of Man" and the motif of Jesus being "handed over." There are less obvious but nonetheless important links with the transfiguration episode (9:2-8), especially in the presence of the three core apostles (Peter, James, and John) and their confusion about what to say (9:6 and 14:40). Whereas the transfiguration episode reveals the glorious and even divine aspects of Jesus' person, the Gethsemane episode shows forth the human and even fragile aspects of his person. The references to "the hour" (14:35, 37, 41) and the use of *ēngiken* ("has come near") help to link the present suffering of Jesus to the mystery of the coming kingdom of God (see 1:15 and 13:32) and provide an eschatological context.

The links of the Gethsemane episode to the Lord's Prayer have often been noted, even though Mark's Gospel does not contain the full text of that prayer (see Matt 6:9-13 and Luke 11:2-4). Jesus addresses God as "Abba, Father" in 14:36 (see Luke 11:2). He prays that God's will may be done in 14:36 (see Matt 6:10). And he asks that his disciples not "enter into testing" in 14:38 (see Matt 6:13). Since the Lord's Prayer is a prayer for the full coming of God's kingdom ("Thy kingdom come") these echoes contribute to the eschatological mood of the Gethsemane pericope. Moreover, they also help readers to make connections between the experience of Jesus as he moves toward the cross and the language they use in prayer.

The first part of Jesus' prayer in Mark 14:34 ("my soul is sorrowful" = *perilypos estin hē psychē mou*) is generally regarded as a quotation of (or at least an allusion to) the refrain in Pss 42[41]:5, 11; and 43[42]:5: "Why are you sorrowful, O my soul?" *(hina ti perilypos ei, psychē).* What has been numbered traditionally as two psalms in fact seems to have been one long psalm. Psalms 42–43 are classified as an individual lament and contain the elements that appear in individual laments: complaints (42:3: "people say . . . 'Where is your God?'"; 42:9: "Why have you forgotten me?"), confessions of faith (42:2: "My soul thirsts for God"; 42:5b-6, 11; 43:5: "Hope in God, for I shall again praise him, my help and my God"), petitions for divine help (42:11: "Vindicate me, O God, and defend my cause against an ungodly people"), and references to thanksgiving sacrifices (43:4: "Then I will go to the altar of God").

The most famous OT lament is Psalm 22. According to Mark 15:34 the first words of Psalm 22 are the last words of Jesus (see the Interpretation of 15:33-39). The laments constitute the largest category of OT psalms (see Psalms 3, 5, 6, 7, 13, 17, 22, 26, 27, 28, and so forth). Throughout Jewish and Christian history the biblical laments with their open and metaphorical language have given words and images to sufferers and so enabled them to express both their pain and their faith in God, and thus overcome the isolation and hopelessness that so often accompany suffering.

The references to Psalms 42–43 and 22 at key moments in Mark's narrative of Jesus' Passion and death (14:34 and 15:34) suggest a powerful connection between the biblical laments and Jesus as "the man of sorrows." One early Christian approach to the OT Psalms was to read them as "the book of Christ"—as if the speaker of the laments and other psalms was Jesus. This insight is rooted in the many NT uses of OT psalms as part of the words of Jesus.

Taking the OT laments as the background for the Gethsemane episode (and the crucifixion) helps to explain Jesus' expressions of genuine distress as well as his sentiments of trust in God and the petitions in them. The laments provide some of the language and images for Mark's descriptions of Jesus' sufferings. At the same time they link the suffering Jesus to the whole tradition of suffering encapsulated in the Psalms and to the sufferings of many people in our world today. Appreciation of the OT laments is essential for understanding Mark's christology and its ongoing theological significance.

As in many parts of the Markan Passion narratives, in 14:32-42 there is a contrast between the noble and heroic Jesus and the weak and cowardly disciples. The disciples, caught up in the drama of Jesus' Passion and witnessing his emotional prayers, nonetheless manage to fall asleep just when Jesus asks them to stay awake and pray. Still Jesus refuses to give up on the disciples. In fact, at the approach of his betrayer (one of the Twelve) he invites them to accompany him (14:42). In his *Death of the Messiah* Brown observes: "Mark writes his Gospel with the understanding that when the disciples finally came through their experience to comprehend what the suffering and death of Jesus meant, they responded obediently to this 'Let us go' by preaching the gospel and giving themselves to Jesus. Mark is inviting his readers to do likewise" (p. 214).

For Reference and Further Study

Barbour, Robert S. "Gethsemane in the Tradition of the Passion," *NTS* 16 (1969–70) 231–51.

Feldmeier, Reinhard. *Die Krisis des Gottessohnes. Die Gethsemaneerzählung als Schlüssel der Markuspassion.* Tübingen: J.C.B. Mohr [Paul Siebeck], 1987.

Holleran, J. W. *The Synoptic Gethsemane.* Rome: Gregorian University Press, 1973.

Kelber, Werner H. "Mark 14:32-42: Gethsemane," *ZNW* 63 (1972) 166–87.

Kiley, Mark. "'Lord Save My Life' (Ps 116:4) as a Generative Text for Jesus' Gethsemane Prayer (Mark 14:36a)," *CBQ* 48 (1986) 655–59.

Murphy-O'Connor, Jerome. "What Really Happened at Gethsemane?" *Bible Review* 14/2 (1998) 28–39, 52.

Saunderson, Barbara. "Gethsemane: The Missing Witness," *Bib* 70 (1989) 224–33.

Stanley, David M. *Jesus in Gethsemane.* New York: Paulist, 1980.

55. *The Arrest of Jesus* (14:43-52)

43. And just then while he was still speaking there arrived Judas, one of the Twelve, and with him a crowd with swords and wooden clubs from the chief priests and scribes and elders. 44. The betrayer had given them a signal, saying: "The one whom I kiss—he is the one. Seize him and lead him away securely." 45. And when he came, right away he approached him, and said: "Rabbi." And he kissed him warmly. 46. They laid hands on him and seized him. 47. One of the bystanders drew his sword, struck the slave of the high priest, and cut off his ear. 48. And in answer Jesus said to them: "Have you come out as against a bandit with swords and wooden clubs to arrest me? 49. Day by day I was with you in the Temple teaching, and you did not seize me. But let the Scriptures be fulfilled." 50. And they all left him and fled. 51. And a certain young man was following with him, clothed with a linen cloth on [his] naked [body]. And they seized him. 52. But he left behind the linen cloth, and he fled naked.

NOTES

43. *And just then:* Mark's signature phrase *kai euthys* links this episode with Jesus' statement in 14:42 that "the betrayer" was near. See also 14:45: *kai elthōn euthys.*

   Judas, one of the Twelve: According to 14:10-11 Judas had initiated the plot against Jesus. And according to 14:17-21 Jesus knew that one of the Twelve was betraying him. The designation of Judas as "one of the Twelve" previously appeared in 14:10 and 14:20, and serves as a reminder that one of Jesus' own closest disciples handed him over to his executioners.

   a crowd with swords and wooden clubs: Here the word *ochlos* ("crowd") is used negatively, though Vincent Taylor (*Mark* 558) may go too far in calling them "a hired rabble," since they have been sent by "the chief priests and scribes and elders"—the prime movers against Jesus in the Passion narrative. Their weapons are *machairai* ("long knives" or "short swords") and *xyla* (objects made of "wood"—clubs, staves, etc.).

44. *the betrayer had given them a signal:* The description of Judas as "the betrayer" *(ho paradidous)* not only evokes the earlier description of Judas (see 3:19; 14:42) but also is part of the "handing over" *(paradidonai)* motif that is prominent throughout the gospel with respect to John the Baptist (1:14), Jesus (3:19; 9:31; 10:33; 14:10-11, 41-42; 15:1, 10, 15), and disciples (13:11-12). By calling Judas "one of the Twelve" and "the betrayer" Mark makes his readers face the fact that one of those closest to Jesus set up the process that led to his death on the cross. The word *syssēmon* ("signal") appears only here in the NT; compare *sēmeion* in Matt 26:48.

   The one whom I kiss—he is the one: The "kiss" was used by rabbis and their pupils as a greeting and sign of respect. The action was most likely a "peck" on the cheeks, similar to greetings used in the Middle East today. The "holy kiss" *(philēma)* became a customary greeting and sign of affection in the early church (see Rom 16:16; 1 Cor 16:20; 2 Cor 13:12; 1 Thess 5:26; 1 Pet 5:14). Whether either of these practices illumines the kiss by Judas is debatable and not really important. The point is that Judas' kiss is a cynical device to insure that the "crowd" will arrest the right man: Jesus.

lead him away securely: The adverb *asphalōs*, translated here as "securely," most likely refers to efficiency and expeditiousness in arresting Jesus. His captors must make sure that the arrest goes without a "hitch." That Judas is expressing compassion and concern for Jesus ("safely") is dubious. It is too late for that.

45. *And when he came, right away he approached him:* Mark's pet phrase *kai euthys* is interrupted by one aorist participle *(elthōn,* "coming") and followed by another *(parelthōn,* "approaching"), thus producing an awkward but attention-getting introduction to Judas' act of betrayal.

"Rabbi": In Mark's time the term is probably still a sign of respect or honor ("my great one"), and not yet a proper title for designating a Jewish teacher (as in Matt 23:8). Thus far in Mark "Rabbi" has been used twice with reference to Jesus: by Peter at the transfiguration (9:5), and again by Peter with reference to the withered fig tree (11:21). Some manuscripts have "Rabbi, Rabbi," thus highlighting the hypocrisy of Judas.

he kissed him warmly: The compound Greek verb *katephilēsen* seems to heighten the intensity conveyed by *philēsō* in 14:44 and further emphasizes Judas' hypocrisy. What seems like a gesture of special respect and affection is in fact a clever way to make sure that Jesus is arrested.

46. *They laid hands on him and seized him:* The signal arranged by Judas and his execution of it work perfectly, and so Jesus is successfully arrested. Whereas elsewhere in Mark the "hand" *(cheir)* of Jesus brings healing (see 1:31; 5:23, 41; 6:5; 7:32; 8:23, 25; 9:27; 10:16), here Jesus is betrayed "into the hands of men" (9:31; see also 14:41). The word for "seize" *(kratein)* was used previously in Judas' instruction in 14:44.

47. *One of the bystanders:* Many commentators suggest that with this vague phrase Mark was deliberately concealing the identity of a disciple of Jesus (see Matt 26:51; Luke 22:49-50), the most likely suspect being Peter (see John 18:10-11). But the term used by Mark *(parestēkotōn,* "bystanders") never refers elsewhere (see 14:69, 70; 15:35, 39) to Jesus' disciples. Its occurrence here suggests that for Mark the deed was done by someone other than a disciple of Jesus (a member of the *ochlos* or some third party).

drew his sword, struck the slave of the high priest, and cut off his ear: The fact that the perpetrator has a sword *(machaira,* see 14:43) suggests that he was one of the *ochlos*. The description of the victim as "the slave of the high priest" reminds us about the source of the opposition to Jesus in Jerusalem and the nature of the *ochlos*. The use of the diminutive *ōtarion* for "ear" leads some commentators to argue that only the man's earlobe was cut; compare *ōtion* ("ear") in Matt 26:51, and *to ous autou to dexion* ("his right ear") in Luke 22:50.

48. *in answer Jesus said to them:* Jesus' complaint seems to be addressed to the "crowd" sent by the chief priests, scribes, and elders to arrest him (see 14:43).

    as against a bandit: The Greek word *lēstēs* can refer to bandits and robbers as well as to revolutionaries and "Robin Hood" types ("social bandits"). In either case *lēstai* are armed and dangerous. Jesus is complaining about the manner of his arrest—as if he were really an armed and dangerous man. In 11:17 the Temple officials were criticized for making the house of God into a "cave for robbers *(lēstai)*" (see Jer 7:11). The two men who are crucified along with Jesus are called *lēstai* in 15:27, as is Barabbas in John 18:40. The interpretive problem regarding *lēstēs* is deciding whether it means just a robber (which fits the relative quiet in Palestine during Jesus' time), or describes a social-political revolutionary (which fits better the time of the Jewish revolt of 66–73, when Mark's Gospel was being composed).

    to arrest me: The verb *syllabein* (only here in Mark) appears with reference to Jeremiah in the Septuagint (see Jer 43[36]:26; 44[37]:13), perhaps suggesting a link between two prophets who are arrested as a result of fidelity to their mission of proclaiming God's (unpopular) word.

49. *Day by day:* The problem is that Jesus, according to Mark's chronology, had been teaching in Jerusalem for only three days (see 11:11, 15, 27). Many scholars see the expression as proof of the superiority of John's chronology, which features several visits to Jerusalem on Jesus' part. Others suggest that *kath' hēmeran* be translated "by day"—as opposed to "by night" when Jesus was arrested.

    in the Temple teaching: The content of this teaching has been supplied in Mark 11–13. The setting is the large Temple complex, which had ample space for small gatherings such as those envisioned for Jesus and his disciples as well as their opponents.

    But let the Scriptures be fulfilled: For earlier references to the "Scriptures" see 12:10 *(graphē)* and 12:24 *(graphai)*. In this case the Scripture passage must be Zech 13:7, quoted in Mark 14:27: "I will strike the shepherd, and the sheep will be scattered." The arrest of Jesus constitutes the first blow against the shepherd. The appeal to God's will as revealed in the Scriptures also explains why Jesus, who throughout Mark's Gospel has manifested extraordinary power, puts up no resistance to his captors ("not what I wish, but what you wish," 14:36).

50. *they all left him and fled:* The flight by Jesus' disciples fulfills the second part of Zech 13:7: "and the sheep will be scattered." Those first disciples who "left" *(aphentes)* their homes and families to follow Jesus (see 1:18, 20) now leave *(aphentes)* Jesus at the beginning of his Passion.

51. *a certain young man was following with him:* The word *neaniskos* ("young man") appears again in 16:5, where it refers to the figure (probably an angel) who explains to the women why Jesus' body is not to be found in the tomb ("he is risen"). Even though "all" have fled (14:50), this young man is said to have been "following with him [Jesus]" *(synēkolouthei autō)*—the root *(akolouthein)* being the customary Markan verb for being a disciple. The young man's iden-

tity is a topic of longstanding dispute among scholars. Some regard him as a real historical figure, one of Jesus' own disciples (John the son of Zebedee, James the Lord's brother, or John Mark, understood to be the evangelist himself), or a curious neighbor aroused from sleep who gets swept up into the confusion surrounding the arrest. Others take the "young man" to be an angel (see 16:5), a symbol for Jesus himself, or even a symbol for the Christian undergoing baptismal initiation. The question of the young man's identity will probably never be resolved, but at least one can say with some confidence that he represents concretely the group of disciples whose flight was described in 14:50. Rather than symbolizing Jesus or the Christian, he stands for those who desert Jesus in times of trouble.

clothed with a linen cloth on [his] naked [body]: The "linen cloth" is a *sindōn*, the same word used in 15:46 for the burial cloth purchased by Joseph of Arimathea. The phrase *epi gymnou* ("on [his] naked [body]"—the words in brackets must be supplied) is strange enough that most scholars today argue for its inclusion in the text, even though it is absent from many manuscripts. Some argue that the young man had some clothing on underneath the *sindōn* ("underwear"), though that suggestion seems only to be softening the shame that the young man will experience.

52. *he left behind the linen cloth:* As in 14:50, someone who had left all things to follow Jesus now leaves Jesus.

he fled naked: In the Bible nakedness is a sign of shame. See, for example, Amos 2:16: "and those who are stout of heart among the mighty shall flee away naked in that day." In leaving behind his *sindōn* the young man chooses shame over fidelity to Jesus.

INTERPRETATION

According to Mark 14:43-46 the arrest of Jesus takes place as a result of Judas' betrayal of Jesus and the arrangement he worked out by which the "crowd" might arrest the one singled out by the signal of the "kiss." The main episode is followed by four shorter ones: the cutting of the ear of the chief priest's slave (14:47), Jesus' defense of himself (14:48-49), the desertion of him by his disciples (14:50), and the flight of the "young man" (14:51-52). The three short episodes are only loosely connected to the main episode, and in fact the next event (14:53-72) flows smoothly from 14:43-46.

The parallel Synoptic versions in Matt 26:47-56 and Luke 22:47-53 basically follow the Markan main episode, though Luke stresses Jesus' foreknowledge of the kiss as the signal of Judas' act of betrayal (Luke 22:48). Then both evangelists expand Mark 14:47 by specifying that the perpetrator was a disciple of Jesus (Matt 26:51; Luke 22:49-50). John (18:10) tells us that the disciple was Peter and the slave's name was Malchus. Matthew then has Jesus explain why this kind of violent action is unnecessary and that what is necessary is that the Scriptures (as the expression of God's will) must be fulfilled (Matt 26:52-54). Luke in 22:49 says that the disciples came equipped with swords (22:35-38), and notes in 22:51 that Jesus immediately healed the right ear of the chief priest's slave. Luke in 22:53 gives a theological interpretation to the arrest when he has Jesus say to his captors: "But this is your hour, and the power of darkness." Both Matthew and Luke omit the strange episode in Mark 14:51-52 about the young man who flees away naked.

As suggested in the Notes on 14:48, the term for "arrest" *(syllabein)* may indicate an analogy between Jeremiah and Jesus. At any rate, in the arrest narrative Jesus stands in the long line of biblical figures who suffer for their fidelity to their commission to proclaim the word of God (Jeremiah, the Suffering Servant of Second Isaiah, Ezekiel, and so on).

A striking OT parallel to the arrest of Jesus in the Synoptic Passion narratives comes in the passage in Wisdom of Solomon 1:16–2:24 about the plot by the "ungodly" against "the righteous man" (a text that reflects the influence of Isa 52:13–53:12). In this first-century Alexandrian Jewish text the "ungodly" enter into a conspiracy to snare the righteous man "because he opposes our actions . . . and calls himself a child of the Lord" (Wis 2:12-13). While it is doubtful that Mark used the book of Wisdom as a direct source, there are striking parallels between it and the Markan Passion narrative that help to illumine Mark's portrayal of Jesus as the suffering righteous one.

The various episodes that make up Mark 14:43-52 combine to present contrasting pictures of Jesus and his disciples in a concentric (A, B, A') pattern. (A) Many details in 14:43-46 (the arrest proper) bring out the treachery displayed by Judas: his arrival with an armed crowd, his prearranged signal, and the use of the kiss (normally a sign of respect and affection) as the signal. (B) By contrast, in 14:47-49 Jesus eschews violence and complains that there was no need to come after him as if he were a *lēstēs*. He goes on to explain why these terrible things are happening to him: "But let the Scriptures be fulfilled" (14:49). (A') Whereas the opening verses focused on the treachery of Judas, the closing verses describe the cowardly flight of all the disciples (14:50) and the flight of still one more hapless follower (14:51-52). Whereas these people once left all to follow Jesus, now they leave Jesus and flee from him.

For the Markan community that had already suffered persecution and faced the prospect of more suffering the account of Jesus' arrest in Mark 14:43-52 would have provided a powerful challenge. Will you follow the example of the noble and righteous Jesus? Or will you betray other believers (as Judas did Jesus) or flee at the first sign of conflict (as the rest of the disciples and the young man in particular did)? In the first century, throughout Christian history, and even today this passage provides guidance for Christians under pressure and a challenge to follow the example of Jesus the suffering righteous one and to reject the pattern of treachery and cowardice illustrated by Jesus' disciples.

FOR REFERENCE AND FURTHER STUDY

Haren, Michael J. "The Naked Young Man: A Historian's Hypothesis on Mark 14,51-52," *Bib* 79 (1998) 525–31.
Jackson, Howard M. "Why the Youth Shed His Cloak and Fled Naked: The Meaning and Purpose of Mark 14:51-52," *JBL* 116 (1997) 273–89.
Johnson, Steven R. "The Identity and Significance of the *Neaniskos* in Mark," *Forum* 8 (1992) 123–39.
Meyer, Marvin W. "The Youth in the Secret Gospel of Mark," *Semeia* 49 (1990) 129–53.
Viviano, Benedict T. "The High Priest's Servant's Ear: Mark 14:47," *RB* 96 (1989) 71–80.
Winter, Sara C. "The Arrest of Jesus. Mark 14:43-52 (par.) and John 18:2-12," *Forum* 1 (1998) 145–62.

56. *Jesus before the Sanhedrin and the Denial by Peter* (14:53-72)

53. And they led Jesus away to the chief priest, and all the chief priests and the elders and the scribes came together. 54. And Peter followed him from a distance right into the courtyard of the high priest, and he was sitting with the attendants and warming himself at the blazing fire. 55. The chief priests and the whole Sanhedrin were seeking testimony against Jesus in order to put him to death, and they were not finding it. 56. For many were bearing false witness against him, and their testimonies were not consistent. 57. And some were standing up and bearing false witness against him, saying: 58. "We heard him say, 'I will destroy this sanctuary made by hands, and within three days I will build another not made by hands.'" 59. And even so their testimony was not consistent. 60. And the chief priest stood up in their midst and asked Jesus, saying: "Have you nothing at all to answer what these men are witnessing against you?" 61. But he was silent and answered nothing at all. Again the chief priest asked him and said to him: "Are you the Messiah, the Son of the Blessed One?" 62. And Jesus said: "I am. And you will see the Son of Man seated at the right hand of the Power and coming with the clouds of heaven." 63. But the chief priest tore his garments and said: "Why do we still need witnesses? 64. You heard the blasphemy. What does it seem to you?" They all condemned him as deserving death. 65. And some

began to spit on him, and to cover his face and to strike him and to say to him: "Prophesy." And the attendants took hold of him with slaps.

66. And while Peter was down in the courtyard one of the servant women of the high priest came. 67. And she saw Peter warming himself and looked at him, and said: "You also were with the Nazarene Jesus." 68. But he denied it, saying: "I neither know nor understand what you are saying." And he went out into the forecourt, [and a cock crowed]. 69. And the servant woman saw him and began to say again to the by-standers: "This man is one of them." 70. But again he was denying it. And after a short while again the bystanders were saying to Peter: "Truly you are one of them, for you too are a Galilean." 71. And he began to curse and swear: "I do not know this man of whom you speak." 72. And immediately a cock crowed a second time. And Peter remembered the word as Jesus said (it) to him: "Before the cock crows twice, you will deny me three times." And he rushed out and wept.

NOTES

53. *they led Jesus away to the chief priest:* The narrative that left off in 14:46 ("they laid hands on him and seized him") is resumed here, and so "they" must be the "crowd with swords and wooden clubs" introduced in 14:43. Mark does not give the name of the high priest, but from biblical (see Matt 26:57) and other sources (especially Josephus) we know that his name was Caiaphas; he held the office from 18 to 36 C.E. It appears that the "trial" takes place at the house of Caiaphas (see 14:54, 66).

all the chief priests . . . came together: The idea that "all" assembled is probably another example of Mark's tendency to universalize (see the Note on 1:5). The three groups mentioned here have joined in opposing Jesus from his arrival in Jerusalem (see 11:18, 27; 14:1, 10, 43, 47; also 14:55, 60, 61, 63, 66; 15:1, 3, 10, 11, 31). The verb *synerchontai* is another example of the historical present tense.

54. *Peter followed him from a distance:* From 14:50 we are to assume that Peter was among those who left Jesus and fled. The one who once enthusiastically left everything to follow Jesus (1:16-18) now follows "from a distance" (*apo makrothen;* see 15:40, where the women observe Jesus' death "from a dis-tance").

right into the courtyard of the high priest: This confirms that the house of Caiaphas was the venue for the "trial" of Jesus. The courtyard *(aulē)* is mentioned again in 14:66 when the denial episode resumes.

sitting with the attendants: Whether the "attendants" were servants at the chief priest's household or servants of those who had come to the assembly (or both) cannot be determined. In either case they are "killing time" as they wait for the meeting to end (see 14:66-72 where this account continues).

at the blazing fire: The Greek term here is *phōs* ("light") rather than *pyr* ("fire"), and so the translation "blazing fire." Nights in Jerusalem around Passover time can be cold.

55. *The chief priests and the whole Sanhedrin:* The "trial" takes place inside the house of Caiaphas the high priest, while Peter and the attendants remain outside in the courtyard *(aulē).* "The whole Sanhedrin" presumably included members of the three groups mentioned in 14:53: chief priests, elders, and scribes. According to *m. Sanh.* 1.6 the "great Sanhedrin" consisted of seventy-one members. But since this number may not reflect pre-70 C.E. practice and the "whole Sanhedrin" may be a case of Markan universalizing (see the Note on 1:5) the Markan account probably should not be read through the eyes of the *Mishnah.*

    were seeking testimony against Jesus: Mark presents the proceedings as rigged against Jesus from the start. The verb "seek" *(zētein)* has already appeared several times (see 11:18; 12:12; 14:1, 11) in the context of the plot by the hostile Jewish leaders to put Jesus to death. Nevertheless, the "testimony" *(martyria)* is not yet sufficient for them to condemn Jesus if they hope to maintain the pretense of legality.

56. *many were bearing false witness:* The verb *pseudomartyrein* appeared in 10:19 in the context of a list taken from the Ten Commandments. The "trial" of Jesus is "illegal" at least in the sense that there are violations of the commandment about not bearing false witness (see Exod 20:16; Deut 5:20).

    their testimonies were not consistent: According to Deut 19:15 "only on the evidence of two or three witnesses shall a charge be sustained." Without the consistent testimony of two or three witnesses the pretense of legality could not be sustained in the case of Jesus.

57. *some . . . were bearing false witness against him:* This verse recapitulates what had already been said in 14:55-56, especially with the repetition of the verb *pseudomartyrein.* It also introduces the first of the specific charges made against Jesus in 14:58.

58. *We heard him say:* These witnesses claim to offer firsthand, not hearsay evidence against Jesus.

    I will destroy this sanctuary: The "I" *(egō)* adds emphasis to the saying. The verb *katalyein* ("destroy") appeared previously in the context of Jesus' prophecy of the destruction of the Temple *(hieron)* in 13:1 and will appear again in the taunting of Jesus on the cross in 15:29. The noun *naos* ("sanctuary") refers to the especially holy place, not to the whole Temple complex. *Naos* recurs also in 15:29, 38 (with respect to the rending of the veil of the sanctuary).

    made by hands . . . not made by hands: The opposition between *cheiropoiētos* ("made by hands"; see Acts 7:48; 17:24; Eph 2:11; Heb 9:11, 24) and *acheiropoiētos* ("not made by hands"; see 2 Cor 5:1; Col 2:11) is the difference between human agency and divine agency.

    within three days: While "three days" may simply be a synonym for a short period of time, it is hard to disregard some connection with the references to "after three days" in the Passion predictions (8:31; 9:31; 10:34) and so some association with the resurrected body of Christ (and perhaps also the church).

    I will build another: The adjective *acheiropoiētos* specifies the divine origin of the new sanctuary, but its precise nature is not clear. In the context of Jewish apocalyptic it refers most obviously to the perfect sanctuary that will replace the earthly Temple in Jerusalem. This tradition is rooted in the late OT writings (see Isaiah 40–66; Ezekiel 40–48) and expressed at great length in the Qumran *Temple Scroll* and other works roughly contemporary with the NT. But in the context of Mark's Gospel it more likely refers to the body of the risen Jesus (as in John 2:19-22) and/or to the Christian community as the place where God is now worshiped "in spirit and truth" (John 4:23).

59. *And even so their testimony was not consistent:* See the Note on 14:56b. Why their testimony was not consistent is problematic. The saying about destroying and building the sanctuary is to a large extent consistent with Jesus' prophetic entry into Jerusalem (11:1-11) and his prophetic actions in "cleansing" the Temple (11:15-19) and cursing the fig tree (11:12-14, 20-21) as well as his prophecy about the destruction of the Temple complex (13:1-2). In the crucifixion scene the charge is repeated by passersby (see 15:29). These Markan texts (plus their NT parallels in Matt 26:61 and Acts 6:13-14) suggest that there was some substance to the charge that Jesus did make such a prophecy. The problem comes in determining what he meant by it. Whereas his accusers at best seem to interpret it in the apocalyptic context of the divinely originated sanctuary to replace the Jerusalem Temple, Mark probably wants his readers to take it in the christological and ecclesiological senses.

60. *the chief priest stood up:* Since Mark interpreted the charges about the Temple saying as false (see 14:56, 57, 59), the chief priest is portrayed as trying to keep the "trial" on track. So he will move in 14:61 to the issue of claims about the identity of Jesus.

 Have you nothing at all to answer: This is an example of the double negative *(ouk . . . ouden)* construction, a favorite Markan technique. It is possible to take 14:60b as comprising two questions: "Have you nothing at all to answer? What (is it that) these men are witnessing against you?"

 against you: The prefix *kata* ("against") in the verb *katamartyrein* ("witnessing against") is part of the motif of hostility "against" Jesus in the trial narrative. See also 14:55 ("seeking testimony against Jesus") and 14:64 ("all condemned *[katekrinan]* him").

61. *he was silent:* For Jesus' silence at the trial before Pilate see 15:5. In both cases Jesus refuses to cooperate in an unjust procedure. In both there may also be an allusion to the silence of the Suffering Servant of Isa 53:7: "he did not open his mouth." See also Acts 8:32 and 1 Pet 2:21, 23.

 answered nothing at all: As in 14:60, Jesus' refusal to cooperate is highlighted by a double negative *(ouk . . . ouden).*

 Are you the Messiah, the Son of the Blessed One?: The chief priest's persistent *(palin,* "again") questioning moves into the topic of Jesus' identity. The term "Blessed One" *(eulogētos)* is here a synonym for God. Its use serves to create a "Jewish" atmosphere where pious people avoid using the divine name and so heightens the irony of the chief priest observing theological niceties while unjustly condemning Jesus to death. For the combination of Jesus as "Messiah" and "Son of God" see the very beginning of Mark's Gospel (1:1).

the Messiah: For Jesus as the *christos* ("anointed one" = Hebrew "Messiah") in Mark see 1:1; 8:29; 9:41; 12:35; and 15:32; 13:21-22 warns against "false messiahs." The most important texts are 1:1 (the opening of the gospel) and 8:29 (where Peter confesses Jesus to be the Messiah, but Jesus corrects his definition to include the mystery of the cross). For the OT background of the title and a discussion about whether Jesus was regarded as the Messiah during his lifetime see Brown, *Death of the Messiah* 473–80.

the Son of the Blessed One: As noted above, this is the equivalent of "Son of God." For Jesus as the "Son of God" in Mark see 1:1, 11; 3:11; 5:7; 9:7; 13:32; and 15:39. The most important texts are 1:1 (part of the gospel's opening); 1:11 and 9:7 (where the heavenly voice identifies Jesus as the Son of God); and 15:39 (where a centurion identifies Jesus as the Son of God). For the OT background and a discussion about when Jesus was regarded as the Son of God see Brown, *Death of the Messiah* 480–83.

62. *Jesus said: "I am":* Jesus' response to the chief priest's question constitutes an unambiguous affirmation that he is indeed "the Messiah, the Son of the Blessed One." Whereas throughout Mark's Gospel Jesus displays ambivalence toward his identification as the Messiah (the so-called Messianic Secret), here at the start of the Passion narrative he boldly accepts ("I am") the designation because he is now revealed as the suffering Messiah. At this moment he confirms what Mark (1:1), the demons (3:11; 5:7), Peter (8:29), and the heavenly voice (1:11; 9:7) have been saying about him.

and you will see: The verb *opsesthe* is in the second person plural form and suggests that all the members of the Sanhedrin will see the glorious Son of Man.

the Son of Man: The Markan "Son of Man" references to Jesus fall into three categories: as a self-reference (= "Son of Adam" or "I"), as part of the Passion predictions (8:31; 9:31; 10:33-34), and as a glorious figure to appear at the last judgment (8:38; 13:26). At the trial scene the three aspects of "Son of Man" come together. For two earlier sequences in which "Messiah," "Son of God," and "Son of Man" coalesce see 8:27–9:8 (8:29, 31, 38; 9:7) and 13:21-32 (13:21-22, 26-27, 32). For the OT background of "Son of Man" see Brown, *Death of the Messiah* 509–15.

seated at the right hand of the Power: The OT background is Ps 110:1: "Sit at my right hand" (see Mark 12:35-37). The NT reference is to the exaltation of Jesus at his resurrection. The term "Power" is a (somewhat unusual) synonym for God (see "Blessed One" in 14:61)

coming with the clouds of heaven: The OT background is Dan 7:13: "I saw one like a son of man coming with the clouds of heaven." The NT reference is to the parousia of Jesus as a glorious end-time figure (see the Notes on 8:38 and 13:26).

63. *the chief priest tore his garments:* In the OT tearing one's garments symbolizes grief, especially at the death of a loved one (see Gen 37:34; Josh 7:6; 2 Sam 1:11-12; 2 Kgs 2:12). The chief priest's action here suggests that his grief on hearing Jesus' response was as great as if he heard about the death of a loved one (or even greater). According to *m. Sanh.* 7:5 the judges at a trial for blasphemy "stand on their feet and tear their clothing and never sew them back up."

Why do we still need witnesses?: By his forthright confession ("I am") Jesus has effectively incriminated himself and so obviated the need for more witnesses against him.

64. *You heard the blasphemy:* The charge of blasphemy was raised against Jesus in 2:7 when he declared to the paralyzed man: "Your sins are forgiven." For other uses of *blasphēmein* and *blasphēmia* see 3:28-29; 7:22; and 15:29. Its use here need not be restricted to taking the divine name YHWH in vain (see Lev 24:11). Rather it must refer to a more general kind of offensive speech, which in the case of Jesus according to Mark must refer to his affirmation of his identity as the Messiah, Son of God, and Son of Man (and perhaps also to the suggestion that he would rebuild the Temple "not made by [human] hands" in 14:58). For the question of the charge of blasphemy against Jesus see Brown, *Death of the Messiah* 530–47.

What does it seem to you?: Although the chief priest has rigged the trial from the start, he still wants to involve the whole Sanhedrin in a legal verdict against Jesus.

They all condemned him as deserving death: The expression "they all" reminds the reader that the chief priests and "the whole Sanhedrin" (see 14:55) were seeking to execute Jesus. The verb *katakrinein* ("condemn") continues the motif of hostility against *(kata)* Jesus (see 14:55, 60). Thus part of the third Passion prediction is being fulfilled: "The Son of Man will be handed over to the chief priests and scribes, and they will condemn him to death." The Jewish punishment for blasphemy was death by stoning: "One who blasphemes the name of the Lord shall be put to death; the whole congregation shall stone the blasphemer" (Lev 24:16a). But the Jewish officials hand Jesus over to the Roman prefect Pontius Pilate for death by crucifixion in 15:1. For an explanation see John 18:31: "The Jews replied, 'We are not permitted to put anyone to death.'"

65. *some began to spit on him:* Mark most likely intends that "some" refers to members of the Sanhedrin. The construction "began" plus the infinitive is characteristic of Mark. The verb "spit" *(emptyein)* links this mockery of Jesus as a prophet to the Roman soldiers' mockery of him as "King of the Jews" in 15:16-20 (see 15:19).

to cover his face and to strike him and to say to him: "Prophesy": In the trial before the Sanhedrin Jesus was accused of prophesying the destruction of the sanctuary and did prophesy the glorious coming of the Son of Man. In this mockery Jesus is asked to play the prophet again and (while blindfolded) to identify the one who struck him.

the attendants tooks hold of him with slaps: The "attendants" were previously mentioned in 14:54. Their taking charge of Jesus "with slaps" recalls the Servant's words in Isa 50:6: "I gave my back to those who struck me, my cheeks to those who pulled out my beard; I did not hide my face from insult and spitting."

66. *while Peter was down in the courtyard:* The narrative resumes the story begun in 14:54, which had Peter sitting by the fire in the courtyard with the "attendants." We are probably to assume that the trial of Jesus and the denials by

Peter are taking place simultaneously. The statement that Peter was "down *(katō)* in the courtyard *(aulē)*" suggests that the trial was held on the second floor (or at least a raised part) of the high priest's house.

one of the servant women . . . came: The Greek word *paidiskē* is a diminutive of *pais* and refers to a woman of "the servant class" ("maid, female slave, servant girl"). The verb *erchetai* ("lit. "comes") is in the historical present tense as are several other verbs in the passage.

67. *she saw Peter . . . and looked at him:* The two verbs (participles) of seeing *(idousa . . . emblepsasa)* suggest first a sighting and then a closer look leading to a recognition of Peter.

You also were with the Nazarene Jesus: The assumption is that the servant woman had previously seen Jesus and Peter together. For other occurrences of *Nazarēnos* in Mark see 1:24; 10:47; and 16:6. Its position here before the name of Jesus gives it special emphasis and even contempt ("that Nazarene").

68. *he denied it:* The verb *arneisthai* ("deny") appears in Mark only here (in the aorist tense) and in 14:70 (in the imperfect tense).

I neither know nor understand what you are saying: It is possible to break up the sentence into two sentences: "I neither know. . . . What are you saying?" Peter's statement is not so much a direct denial as it is an expression of confusion on the part of someone who does not know what to say. There is a progression in Peter's denials from his claim not to understand (14:68) through his repeated denials (14:69) to his cursing and swearing against Jesus (14:71).

he went out into the forecourt: Peter tries to escape to the *proaulion* ("forecourt"), the vestibule between the courtyard and the gate of the house.

[and a cock crowed]: The manuscripts are divided over whether to include this sentence. One can argue that since according to 14:72 a cock crowed a second time, there must have been a first cockcrow to fulfill Jesus' prophecy in 14:30: "before the cock crows twice, you will deny me three times." But was Mark's original sentence carelessly omitted by a scribe? Or did a scribe supply what he regarded as missing from Mark's text?

69. *the servant woman saw him and began to say again to the bystanders:* We are probably to imagine the same servant woman as still in the courtyard and calling after Peter as he was trying to escape to the forecourt, thus calling him to the attention of the bystanders.

This man is one of them: The woman's second accusation is a variation of the first one in 14:67.

70. *again he was denying it:* The imperfect tense of *ērneito* indicates perduring and repeated denials on Peter's part. The effect is more damning even than the description of the first denial in the aorist tense ("he denied").

the bystanders: Whereas the bystanders were only the audience for the servant woman's second accusation, now they make the third accusation.

for you too are a Galilean: How the bystanders know that Peter is a Galilean is not stated. See Matt 26:73: "for your accent betrays you." Since the bystanders are at the house of the high priest they may assume some hostility on the part of a Galilean toward the officials of the Jerusalem Temple.

71. *he began to curse and swear:* The familiar Markan construction "he began" (*ērxato*) introduces two very strong infinitives: *anathematizein* ("curse") and *omnynai* ("swear"). Peter is willing to swear an oath that he does not know Jesus. Whether his cursing was directed at Jesus is not clear.

I do not know this man of whom you speak: Peter's third denial is by far the most direct and explicit (compare 14:68, 70).

72. *And immediately:* This verse and the next (15:1) contain the last two instances of *kai euthys,* one of Mark's favorite expressions.

a cock crowed a second time: Thus Jesus' prophecy in 14:30 comes to fulfillment. For the first cockcrow see the Notes on 14:68. We are to imagine here not the time period of cockcrow (12 to 3 A.M.) but rather the actual crowing of a cock in the hours before dawn.

Peter remembered the word as Jesus said (it) to him: The "word" (*rēma*) is the prophecy of 14:30. The Markan construction here ("as," *hōs*) is awkward.

he rushed out and wept: The participle *epibalōn* derives from the verb *epiballein* ("throw over, put on, throw oneself on"). Its meaning here, however, is far from clear. Brown, *Death of the Messiah* 609–10, lists nine different proposals, and "with great hesitation" chooses "having thrown (himself out), i.e., rushed outside." Other possibilities include "he broke down," "began," "thought," "put on (a garment)," "answered," and "beat himself." The verb *klaiein* ("weep") is a highly emotional word, and describes Peter's shock of recognition at the enormity of his denials of Jesus. See Mark 5:38-39, where people are "weeping" (*klaiein*) over what they regard as the death of Jairus' daughter.

INTERPRETATION

The opening verse (14:53) serves as a bridge between the description of Jesus' arrest and the two scenes that follow. The account of the "trial" of Jesus before the chief priest and the whole Sanhedrin (14:55-65) is intercalated or sandwiched between parts of the story of Peter's denial (14:54, 66-72). The effect of this concentric structure (A, B, A') is to highlight the contrast between the noble Jesus and the cowardly Peter.

Whether on historical grounds one should speak of the episode of Jesus before the Sanhedrin as a legal trial is a matter of longstanding debate among exegetes and historians (see Brown, *Death of the Messiah* 315–560). However, Mark does present the procedure in 14:55-65 as a real (though rigged) trial. The judges and jurors are the chief priests and the whole Sanhredrin (14:55). There is a search (however unsuccessful) for testimony against Jesus (14:56-57). The two charges that emerge as substantive concern Jesus' threat to destroy the sanctuary (14:58) and the claim that he is the Messiah and Son of God (14:61). The chief priest makes an effort to have Jesus defend himself (14:60) and finally elicits from him a confession ("I am") regarding his identity as the Messiah and Son of God (and even the Son of Man) in 14:61-62. The chief priest seizes upon Jesus' confession and brands it as "blasphemy" (14:63-64). He then places the charge before the whole Sanhedrin, and their verdict is that Jesus deserves to die (14:64b). Finally some of the "jurors" join in mocking Jesus as a false prophet (14:65).

While the procedure is presented as a real trial, Mark also makes clear that it was rigged. He tells us that the chief priest and the whole Sanhedrin were actively soliciting testimony against Jesus "in order to put him to death" (14:55), and that much of the testimony was patently false (14:56, 57, 59). When the first accusation—about destroying the sanctuary—seems to be losing ground (14:59), the chief priest apparently out of desperation moves to the charge concerning Jesus' identity as the Messiah and Son of God (14:61-62). At this point Jesus is willing to incriminate himself ("I am"). The verdict, which was already determined from the start, is then ratified by the whole Sanhedrin (14:64). The lack of impartiality on the jurors' part is illustrated by their abuse of Jesus after the verdict (14:65). The whole account is held together by the motif of hostility toward Jesus expressed by the prefix *kata* ("against"; see the Notes on 14:55, 60, 64).

While on the historical level the procedure described by Mark as a Jewish trial was probably more like an investigatory hearing or grand jury proceeding (see John 18:12-14, 19-24), Mark (or the tradition he follows) seems intent on heightening the responsibility of the Jewish leaders in Jerusalem for Jesus' death and playing down the responsibility of the Roman prefect Pontius Pilate (compare John 18:28–19:16).

While Mark dismisses the accusation concerning Jesus' threat to destroy the sanctuary as based on inconsistent testimony (14:59), there is probably some substance to the charge. It fits well with the critical stance shown by Jesus toward the Jerusalem Temple and its leadership ever since his arrival in Jerusalem (see 11:1-21) and with his explicit prophecy about the Temple's destruction (13:2). It also fits well with the attitude that a Galilean prophet of the kingdom of God might display toward the religious monopoly represented by the Jerusalem Temple. And many NT writers felt obliged to address it and explain it away as referring to what Jesus could have done if he wished ("I can destroy," Matt 27:61), to the resurrected body of Jesus ("he spoke of the temple of his body," John 2:21), or to the Torah ("the customs that Moses handed on to us," Acts 6:14). "Where there's smoke, there's fire" runs the proverb. On the historical level the Temple saying very likely figured in the condemnation and execution of Jesus.

Mark, however, rejects the charge about threatening to destroy the sanctuary as based on inconsistent testimony. He is far more interested in the charge concerning the identity of Jesus. In fact, the combination of the three great christological titles in 14:61-62—Messiah, Son of God, and Son of Man—means that Mark intends us to view the trial scene as the climax to the portrait of Jesus he has been constructing all through the gospel. Now as the mystery of the cross comes into focus it is possible to grasp what kind of Messiah, Son of God, and Son of Man Jesus really is. Only at this moment can Jesus boldly affirm ("I am") his identity—precisely because these three titles applied to Jesus previously in the gospel are now firmly linked to his Passion and death.

Other threads of Markan christology appear in the trial scene. Jesus the suffering righteous one (see the book of Wisdom) is the innocent victim of hostility *(kata)* and false testimony. Jesus the Suffering Servant (see Isaiah 40–55) maintains silence during an unjust legal procedure (14:61 = Isa 53:7) and endures spitting and slaps (14:65 = Isa 50:6). And Jesus the prophet is mocked as a false prophet in a kind of cruel "blind man's bluff" game (14:65). Throughout the trial narrative Jesus appears an an innocent victim and a noble hero.

Peter, by contrast, appears as cowardly and even pathetic. Having fled from the one he once followed enthusiastically (14:50), Peter now follows "from a distance" (14:54), and at the same time as Jesus is being tried, Peter denies Jesus three times (14:66-72). In Peter's three denials there are several progressions. The audience moves from one of the servant women (14:66) through the servant woman and some bystanders (14:69) to the bystanders as a group (14:70). The accusations move from Peter's being with "the Nazarene Jesus" (14:67) through his being "one of them" (14:69) to his being "one of them . . . a Galilean" (14:70). And Peter's responses move from his confused evasion (14:68) through his repeated denials (14:70) to his cursing and swearing "I do not know this man" (14:71). The second cockcrow brings a shock of recognition to Peter (and the reader) and what seems to be repentance on Peter's part ("he wept").

The figures of Jesus and Peter provided the Markan community (and many Christians throughout history and today) with a stark contrast and a choice. According to Tacitus *(Ann.* 15.46) "Nero had self-acknowledged Christians arrested. Then, on their information, large numbers of others were condemned—not so much for incendiarism as for their anti-social tendencies." This means that some Roman Christians had informed on their fellow Christians and so brought about their deaths. Tacitus goes on to describe the gruesome punishments the Roman Christians faced: "Dressed in wild animals' skins, they were torn to pieces by dogs, or crucified, or made into torches to be ignited after dark as substitutes for daylight."

The Markan Christians had been (and were still) confronted with a terrible choice: fidelity to truth leading to suffering (as Jesus exemplifies), or cowardice and apparent safety (as Peter illustrates). At the same time the Roman Christians' knowledge of Peter's subsequent career as an apostle and his fate as a martyr at Rome reminded them that repentance and forgiveness are still possible even after denial and betrayal. Peter emerges as both an example to be avoided and a source of consolation (the forgiven sinner).

FOR REFERENCE AND FURTHER STUDY

Beavis, Mary Ann. "The Trial before the Sanhedrin (Mark 14:53-65): Reader Response and Greco-Roman Readers," *CBQ* 49 (1987) 581–96.

Blinzler, Josef. *The Trial of Jesus. The Jewish and Roman Proceedings Against Jesus Christ Described and Assessed from the Oldest Accounts.* Westminster, Md.: Newman, 1959.

Borrell, Agusti. *The Good News of Peter's Denial. A Narrative and Rhetorical Reading of Mark 14:54.66-72.* Atlanta: Scholars, 1998.

Brandon, Samuel G. F. *The Trial of Jesus of Nazareth.* London: Batsford, 1968.

Chilton, Bruce D. "The So-Called Trial Before the Sanhedrin. Mark 14:53-72," *Forum* 1 (1998) 163-80.

Donahue, John R. *Are You the Christ? The Trial Narrative in the Gospel of Mark.* Missoula: Scholars 1973.

Juel, Donald. *Messiah and Temple: The Trial of Jesus in the Gospel of Mark.* Missoula: Scholars, 1977.

Marcus, Joel. "Mark 14:61: 'Are You the Messiah-Son-of-God?'" *NovT* 31 (1989) 125–41.

McEleney, Neil J. "Peter's Denials—How Many? To Whom?" *CBQ* 52 (1990) 467–72.

Perrin, Norman. "Mark XIV.62: The End Product of a Christian Pesher Tradition?" *NTS* 12 (1965–66) 150–55.

Rivkin, Ellis. *What Crucified Jesus? The Political Execution of a Charismatic.* Nashville: Abingdon, 1984.

Sherwin-White, Adrian N. *Roman Society and Roman Law in the New Testament.* Oxford: Clarendon Press, 1963.

57. *Jesus before Pilate* (15:1-20)

1. And as soon as it was morning the chief priests convened a council with the elders and scribes and the whole Sanhedrin; and they bound Jesus, led him away, and handed him over to Pilate. 2. And Pilate questioned him: "Are you the King of the Jews?" But he answered him and said: "You say so." 3. And the chief priests were accusing him of many

things. 4. But Pilate questioned him again, saying: "Don't you answer anything at all? See how many charges they bring against you." 5. But Jesus answered nothing more at all, so that Pilate wondered.

6. At the feast he used to release to them one prisoner whom they requested. 7. There was a man named Barabbas imprisoned with the rebels who had committed murder in the uprising. 8. And the crowd approached and began to ask (that he do) as he was accustomed to do for them. 9. But Pilate answered them, saying: "Do you want me to release to you the King of the Jews?" 10. For he recognized that the chief priests had handed him over out of envy. 11. But the chief priests stirred up the crowd in order that he might release Barabbas to them instead. 12. But Pilate in turn answered and said: "What then [do you wish] I should do with [the one whom you call] the King of the Jews?" 13. But they in turn shouted out: "Crucify him." 14. But Pilate kept saying to them: "What evil has he done?" But they shouted all the more: "Crucify him." 15. But Pilate, wishing to satisfy the crowd, released Barabbas to them. And he handed Jesus over, having had him flogged, to be crucified.

16. But the soldiers brought him inside the courtyard (that is, the praetorium), and they summoned the whole cohort. 17. And they clothed him in purple, and plaiting a crown of thorns they put it on him. 18. And they began to salute him: "Hail, King of the Jews!" 19. And they were striking his head with a reed, and were spitting on him, and were kneeling down in homage to him. 20. And when they had mocked him they took off the purple garment from him and put his own clothes on him. And they led him away to crucify him.

NOTES

1. *as soon as it was morning:* The adverb *euthys* ("immediately") is one of Mark's favorite ways of introducing a new unit. The term is especially prominent in the early chapters of the gospel (see 1:3, 10, 12, 18, 20, 21, 23, etc.). It is difficult to determine whether *proi* is used here generically to mean "early" or to refer specifically to the fourth watch of the night (3 to 6 A.M.) as in 13:35. In either case it was not unusual that such actions would take place very early in the day.

the chief priests . . . and the whole Sanhedrin: From Jesus' arrival in Jerusalem his major opponents have been the chief priests, elders, and scribes (see 11:18, 27, 12:12; etc.). Here the term "Sanhedrin" is used to refer to a tribunal or supreme court made up of local Jewish religious and political leaders in Jerusalem (see 14:55 as well as Acts 4–6 and 22–24).

convened a council: The expression *symboulion poiēsantes* can be rendered "convened a council," thus suggesting a second Jewish trial for Jesus, or it can mean "made a plan," thus stating their intention to dispose of Jesus. The textual variant *symboulion hetoimasantes* ("prepared a plan") takes the second interpretation and strengthens it. Raymond E. Brown (*The Death of the Messiah*

[New York: Doubleday, 1994] 629–32) proposes a resumptive or recapitulative interpretation ("having made their consultation"), according to which the phrase refers back to the decision already taken in 14:55-65.

they bound Jesus, led him away, and handed him over: In binding *(dēsantes)* Jesus the Jewish leaders now treat him as a convicted criminal. In leading him away *(apopherein)* they transfer Jesus to the Gentile authorities and thus fulfill the third Passion prediction: "they will condemn him to death and hand him over to the Gentiles" (10:33). In handing him over *(paradidonai)* to Pilate they move forward one of the gospel's major motifs—used with reference to the arrest of John the Baptist (1:14) and the treachery of Judas (3:19), in the Passion predictions (9:31; 10:33-34), and especially in the accounts of Jesus' arrest and trial (14:10, 11, 18, 21, 41, 42, 44). See also 15:10 and 15.

to Pilate: Pontius Pilate was the prefect of Judea from 26 to 36 C.E. Contemporary Jewish sources (see the Interpretation) describe him as cruel and obstinate, not exactly as Mark does. His headquarters were in Caesarea Maritima on the Mediterranean coast. Since Jewish pilgrimage feasts (and especially Passover with its theme of national liberation) attracted large crowds and had the potential to inspire riots and uprisings, it was wise policy for the Roman prefect to come to Jerusalem and work with the local Jewish leaders in order to keep the peace. Whether Pilate stayed at the Fortress Antonia on the northern edge of the Temple complex or (more likely) at Herod's Palace on the western side of the city is a matter of longstanding debate.

2. *And Pilate questioned him:* Mark presents Jesus' hearing before Pilate as a dialogue constructed out of alternating "and" *(kai)* and "but" *(de)* sentences.

   Are you the King of the Jews?: This is the Roman outsider's translation of the Jewish term "Messiah." Pilate is asking whether Jesus is another one of those Jewish messianic pretenders who cause so much trouble to both the Roman officials and the local Jewish community (see the Note on 13:22). The Roman policy was to deal with such figures quickly and brutally.

   "You say so": By his noncommittal response Jesus questions the political framework in which Pilate asks the question. In the Jewish trial scene Jesus showed no hesitation in saying "I am" when asked whether he was "the Christ, the Son of the Blessed One" (14:61-62). However, by not denying here that he is "the King of the Jews" and explaining his own position Jesus leaves himself open to the further charges along the political line.

3. *the chief priests were accusing him of many things:* As in ch. 14 (see 14:1, 10, 43, 47, 53, 54, 55, 60, 61, 63, 66), so also in ch. 15 the chief priests take the lead in pressing for Jesus' condemnation and death (see 15:1, 10, 11, 31). The use of the imperfect tense ("were accusing") conveys the idea of their continuing to make accusations against Jesus. The word *polla,* though it can be taken as an adverb ("often"), is more likely a neuter plural noun in the accusative case ("many things").

4. *But Pilate questioned him again:* The particle *de* ("but") continues the pattern of alternating "and" and "but" sentences. The imperfect verb *epērōta* (lit. "was questioning") picks up on the imperfect "were accusing" in the previous verse.

Don't you answer anything at all?: The double negative in Greek *(ouk . . . ouden)* heightens the sense of Pilate's impatience with his prisoner. He presumably would have expected a more serious defense from someone on trial for his life.

how many charges: According to 15:2 there was one charge ("King of the Jews"), whereas according to 15:3 there were many charges. In fact, whatever other charges there were against Jesus they all were connected to Jesus' identity as "King of the Jews."

5. *But Jesus answered nothing more at all:* Another use of *de* ("but") and another double negative *(ouketi ouden)* call further attention to the mystery of Jesus' silence. There may be an allusion to the Suffering Servant of Isa 53:7: "he did not open his mouth."

   Pilate wondered: Pilate makes repeated and unsuccessful efforts to get Jesus to defend himself (see 15:2 and 4); Jesus' refusal to do so meets with surprise on Pilate's part. The motif suggests that Pilate was trying to be a fair judge and was concerned with justice. The only other use of *thaumazein* ("wonder") in the Markan Passion narrative is also attributed to Pilate: "Pilate wondered if he had already died" (15:44).

6. *At the feast:* From 14:1 ("two days before the Passover") we know that this feast is Passover. That we are to imagine the release of a prisoner at every pilgrimage feast is unlikely. But a release at Passover, given its prominence in Jewish history and its theme of liberation, would have been appropriate.

   he used to release to them: Whether Pilate initiated the custom or merely went along with something that had become customary in Judea is not clear. There is no other biblical or extrabiblical evidence for this practice, but granting pardons or clemency at great holidays was not uncommon in antiquity (and today).

   one prisoner whom they requested: The use of imprisonment as a legal penalty was not common in the Greco-Roman world, so we are probably to imagine that the "prisoner" was still awaiting trial or (even more likely) had already been sentenced to death (as Jesus had been, according to Mark). Mark's narrative assumes that the initiative in choosing the prisoner to be released lay with the crowd (see 15:8-9).

7. *a man named Barabbas:* The proper name here consists of two Aramaic elements: *bar* meaning "son" and *ʾabbaʾ* meaning "father." The derivation from Bar-Rabban ("son of the master") is less likely. There were rabbis known as "Bar-Abba," and the practice of using *bar* plus the father's name is witnessed in the cases of Simon bar Jona (for Peter; see Matt 16:17) and Simeon Bar Kokhba (or Kosiba) around 132–135 c.e. Some manuscripts supply Barabbas with the first name "Jesus" in Matt 27:16. Since one would expect him to have a first name and since it is unlikely that early Christians would have created the name "Jesus" for him there may well be a historical basis for this tradition. In either case the choice presented to the crowd—between Jesus of Nazareth (the real "Son of the Father") and (Jesus) Barabbas—is rich in irony and in theological significance.

imprisoned with the rebels who had committed murder in the uprising: It is possible (though very unlikely) to read this text as conveying the idea that Barabbas had been wrongly imprisoned, having been swept up in a mass arrest. The term *stasiastēs* generally refers to a "rebel" or "revolutionary," though it is hard to know how organized and political their uprising was. It certainly reached the point where someone was killed, but whether that was a Roman soldier or an innocent bystander or a fellow rioter is not known. Mark's phrase "in the uprising" suggests that this *stasis* had achieved some notoriety and could be referred to in a way that his readers would immediately understand.

8. *the crowd approached:* This is the first mention of "the crowd" *(ho ochlos)* since chs. 11 and 12 (see 11:18, 32; 12:12, 37, 41) apart from the reference to "a crowd" that accompanied Judas in the arrest of Jesus (14:43). Is this the same "crowd" that welcomed Jesus to Jerusalem? Or was this *ochlos* assembled and manipulated by the chief priests (see 15:11)? The participle *anabas* (lit. "having gone up") can hardly be used to decide Pilate's location as the Fortress Antonia or Herod's Palace.

   began to ask (that he do) as he was accustomed to do for them: The construction "began to ask" is characteristically Markan. The crowd, perhaps under the direction of the chief priests, takes the initiative in approaching Pilate. The phrase in parentheses ("that he do") is lacking in Mark's elliptical sentence but needs to be supplied for the translation.

9. *Do you want me to release to you the King of the Jews:* Pilate persists in using the Roman outsider's term for "Messiah" (see 15:2). The suggestion that Jesus of Nazareth might in fact be the King of the Jews in either a political or a religious sense would have been offensive to the Jewish leaders at Jerusalem and to their supporters. Pilate's question gives the impression that he is trying to save Jesus, whom he apparently regards as an innocent victim. By offering to release Jesus with a question that should elicit an affirmative answer he seems to want to anticipate the crowd's choice of the prisoner.

10. *he recognized:* That Pilate grasped what was going on in the case of Jesus and still handed him over to his executioners (see 15:15) makes him into (at best) a weak character—reminiscent of Herod Antipas in the account of the death of John the Baptist (6:14-29).

    the chief priests had handed him over out of envy: For the initiative displayed by the chief priests in the Markan Passion narrative see the Note on 15:3. For the significance of the verb *paradidonai* ("hand over") see the Note on 15:1. The noun *phthonos* can mean both "zeal" and "envy." From the perspective of the chief priests their actions in getting rid of Jesus would constitute "zeal" because they would be preserving the peace of Jerusalem and allowing the Passover to be celebrated properly. From Pilate's perspective (which Mark wants his readers to take) their actions appear to be another in the long series of internal Jewish disputes in Jerusalem in which the chief priests saw their power and influence being threatened.

11. *But the chief priests stirred up the crowd:* The use of the adversative particle *de* ("but"), which is already prominent in ch. 15 (see vv. 2, 4, 5, 6, 7, 9), becomes

even more frequent in what follows (see vv. 11, 12, 13, 14 [twice], 15, 16). It serves to move along the interaction and dialogue between Pilate and the crowd. It is not clear whether the chief priests only now begin to manipulate "the crowd" or whether they had created the crowd for their own purposes (see the Notes on 15:8).

in order that he might release Barabbas: The sentence is either designedly elliptical or has suffered an omission, since the idea is that the chief priests stir up the crowd in order that they might request that Pilate release Barabbas to them (see 15:6).

12. *Pilate in turn:* The adverb *palin*, which is usually rendered "again," is better translated as "in turn" or "thereupon" here and in 15:13. As with *de*, it helps to move forward the action and dialogue.

What then [do you wish] I should do with [the one whom you call] the King of the Jews: The material in brackets appears in a longer reading found in many manuscripts. The longer reading is even more ironic in that Pilate seems insincere in placing himself at the crowd's will and suggests that "King of the Jews" is the crowd's title for Jesus. In fact Pilate soon capitulates to the crowd's will (see 15:15), and "King of the Jews" is his title for Jesus (whom he never calls by name).

13. *they in turn shouted out:* The last use of *krazein* ("shout out") described the enthusiastic response of "the crowd" to Jesus' entry into Jerusalem (see 11:9). Here the crowd's shout contains the first mention of crucifixion in Mark's Gospel. The three Passion predictions (8:31; 9:31; 10:33-34) referred to Jesus' death but did not specify its mode.

14. *Pilate kept saying:* The imperfect tense of the verb *elegen* indicates repeated efforts on Pilate's part to save Jesus from death.

What evil has he done?: Pilate's question amounts to his implicit "not guilty" finding in the case of Jesus. This point is made much more explicit in Matt 27:24-27 (where Pilate washes his hands) and Luke 23:22 (where Pilate says "I have found in him no crime deserving death"). There may also be an echo of Isa 53:9: "he had done no violence, and there was no deceit in his mouth."

they shouted out all the more: The second shout (again *krazein*) of the crowd is even stronger and suggests that Pilate is losing control of the situation.

15. *wishing to satisfy the crowd:* Mark presents Pilate as both weak and pragmatic. He is weak in that he recognizes Jesus' innocence and knows that the "envy" of the chief priests is behind the crowd's demand but nevertheless he caves in to popular pressure. He is pragmatic in that his goal is to prevent a riot in Jerusalem at Passover time and so he takes the easy way out.

he handed Jesus over, having had him flogged, to be crucified: For the Markan motif of "handing over" *(paradidonai)* see the Note on 15:1. Just as the chief priests had handed Jesus over to Pilate (see 15:1, 10), now Pilate hands Jesus over to the Roman soldiers (see 15:16-20). The flogging, carried out with whips studded with pieces of metal and bone, was intended to weaken the person being executed; this punishment may explain why Jesus dies so quickly on the cross (see 15:44). Crucifixion was practiced on rebels (the "King of the Jews") and slaves, and as a public action was meant to deter others from rebellion.

16. *the soldiers brought him:* The phrase answers the question raised by 15:15: To whom did Pilate hand Jesus over? It also suggests that the flogging may have been carried out in the presence of Pilate and the crowd. The solders *(stratiō-tai)*, though under Roman command, would have been recruited from the Gentile population of Syria and Palestine.

inside the courtyard (that is, the praetorium): The courtyard *(aulē)* refers to an open space inside the walls of Pilate's temporary headquarters in Jerusalem. The Latin loanword *praetorium* referred originally to the general's tent, and came to mean the (permanent or temporary) residence of a Roman governor or high official. We are more likely to imagine that it was Herod's Palace than the Fortress Antonia in this case.

they summoned the whole cohort: Mark begins to use the historical present (lit. "they summon") as a means of making the narrative more vivid. A cohort *(speira)* was one-tenth of a legion and normally consisted of six hundred men. Here the term is used loosely to refer to all the soldiers on duty at the praetorium at the time.

17. *they clothed him in purple:* Just as members of the Sanhedrin are said to have mocked Jesus as a prophet ("Prophesy!") and beaten him in 14:65, so here the soldiers mock Jesus as a king/messiah and beat him. The "purple" garment most likely signifies royalty. When Alexander Balas offers Jonathan Maccabeus the Jewish high priesthood and kingship he promises him the right to dress in purple (see 1 Macc 10:20, 62; 11:58). By clothing their condemned prisoner in this way the soldiers are mocking his identity as "King of the Jews." From the perspective of Mark's readers, however, Jesus really is King of the Jews, and so what the soldiers do in hailing Jesus as a king is correct (ironically) at the most profound level.

plaiting a crown of thorns: In the Markan context the "crown" was more a part of the mockery of Jesus as King of the Jews than an instrument of torture. There has been a long debate about the precise meaning of *akanthinos* here (see Brown, *Death of the Messiah* 866–67) in which much depends on whether the crown is taken as intended to inflict pain (thornbush) or to symbolize kingship ("rays" emanating from the king's head).

18. *they began to salute him:* This is another example of one of Mark's favorite constructions: "began" plus the infinitive.

"Hail, King of the Jews": The soldiers' mocking salutation deliberately echoes the Latin greeting to the Roman emperor, *Ave Caesar* ("Hail, Caesar"). For Mark's community Jesus really deserved to be hailed as a king, indeed as "King of kings and Lord of lords" (see Rev 19:16).

19. *they were striking his head with a reed:* At this point the soldiers' mockery turns into physical abuse of Jesus. The "reed" *(kalamos)* was a mock version of the scepter of the king and so a symbol of royal power: "The Lord sends out from Zion your mighty scepter" (Ps 110:2). By beating the King of the Jews with his

own "scepter" the soldiers show how weak and ineffectual this king really is. For early Christian readers, of course, the suffering of Jesus and the cross manifested the power and wisdom of God (see 1 Cor 1:18-25), but it was also "a stumbling block to Jews and foolishness to Gentiles" (1 Cor 1:24).

were spitting on him: One does not spit on a king, whether out of respect for the office or fear of the punishment the king might inflict. Here there may be an allusion to the Servant's words in Isa 50:6: "I did not hide my face from insult and spitting."

were kneeling down in homage to him: Bending the knee in worship *(proskynēsis)* was part of the ritual observed in royal courts in the Greco-Roman world. In the only other occurrence of *proskynein* in Mark, the Gerasene demoniac kneels before Jesus and hails him as "the Son of the Most High God" (see 5:6-7).

20. *when they had mocked him:* The *proskynēsis* by the soldiers marks the end of the mockery of the one who in the eyes of Mark's readers (ironically) deserved the worshipful attitude being parodied by the soldiers. The mockery episode makes an important theological contribution by reminding readers of the difference between appearance (Jesus as a weak Jewish messianic pretender) and reality viewed from the perspective of faith ("King of kings and Lord of lords").

they took off the purple garment: The removal of Jesus' "royal" garment ends the soldiers' mock ritual. Brown (*Death of the Messiah* 873–77) provides a catalogue of ancient parallels under four headings: historical incidents, games of mockery, theatrical mimes, and carnival festivals. He observes (p. 877) that "the parallels establish verisimilitude: The content of what is described in the Gospels about the Roman mockery is not implausible, whether historical or not."

they led him away to crucify him: The sentence picks up on 15:15: "And he handed Jesus over . . . to be crucified," but there is no need to regard 15:16-20 as an interpolation on the grounds of an otherwise smooth transition from 15:15 to 15:21.

INTERPRETATION

The narrative about Jesus before Pilate (15:1-20) consists of an encounter between Jesus and Pilate (15:1-5), an encounter between Pilate and the crowd over whether Pilate will release Jesus or Barabbas (15:6-15), and the mockery of Jesus by the soldiers (15:16-20). In the first two parts there is a large amount of dialogue in which the "back and forth" is moved along by repeated uses of the particles *kai* ("and") and *de* ("but"). The third part is entirely narrative apart from the soldiers' mock salutation, "Hail, King of the Jews!" in 15:18. While many take 15:16-20 as a separate incident or as the introduction to what follows, it does form a fitting conclusion to the story of the "trial" of Jesus before the Roman prefect

Pontius Pilate (just as the mockery in 14:65 concluded the trial before the Sanhedrin).

In what sense does 15:1-15 describe a trial? The accusers are the chief priests (15:3), who make charges against Jesus on the basis of what emerged at the "trial" before the Sanhedrin on the previous evening (see 14:55-65). Whether there was a second trial early the next morning (15:1-2) or whether that was only a strategy session or even a recapitulation of what had been already decided is not entirely clear. What is clear is that the Roman prefect (*praefectus* was Pilate's proper title according to an inscription found at Caesarea Maritima in the early 1960s) possessed the legal authority to have Jesus put to death by crucifixion. According to Mark the Jewish leaders (especially the chief priests) had decided that Jesus was "deserving death" (14:64) and handed Jesus over to Pilate so that he might ratify their decision and carry out his execution according to Roman procedures.

In Pilate's mental framework and terminology the charge against Jesus is "King of the Jews" (15:2, 9, 12). This political categorization of Jesus is also an outsider's translation of Jewish expectations about the Messiah. The Jewish accusers reject it because for them Jesus is not the King of the Jews. The Roman governor, however, uses it to classify Jesus of Nazareth as yet another in a long series of Jewish religious fanatics who stir up the people with their visions of the kingdom of God. From the Roman perspective, if the kingdom of the God of Israel ever appears, the Roman emperor and empire cease to rule. Jesus' proclamation of the kingdom of God did have political implications. Hence it is Pilate's duty as the emperor's representative in Judea to put an end to the movement that has developed around Jesus of Nazareth.

Still, Pilate's verdict on Jesus is strangely ambivalent. Jesus as the accused is not cooperative. When asked if he is the "King of the Jews" Jesus responds with the enigmatic "You say so" (15:2), thus refusing to accept the political framework in which Pilate questions him. After Pilate's repeated efforts to get Jesus to defend himself (15:3-5) Pilate tries to persuade the crowd to have him release Jesus—something that he presumably could have done on his own. When the crowd prefers Barabbas to Jesus, Pilate asks the crowd what he should do with Jesus. When they say "Crucify him!" (15:13) Pilate makes an implicit declaration of Jesus' innocence when he asks "What evil has he done?" (15:14). Nevertheless, Pilate quickly caves in to pressure from the crowd, releases Barabbas, has Jesus flogged, allows him to be mocked and physically abused by the soldiers, and hands him over to be executed (15:15-20).

Mark's portrayal of Pilate is strangely ambivalent. Pilate begins as a pragmatic politician by asking Jesus directly, "Are you the King of the Jews?" He also seems to want to be fair to his prisoner, and so he urges

Jesus to defend himself in the interests of justice. Next he tries to get the crowd to extricate him (and Jesus) from what has become a tense situation. But this strategy fails when the crowd at the urging of the chief priests calls for the release of Barabbas instead of Jesus. Then when he asks the crowd for direction about what to do with Jesus they shout out "Crucify him!" twice. Finally Pilate gives up any pretense of seeking justice and goes along with the wishes of the crowd and those who are manipulating them. Pilate comes off as weak and vacillating when put in a difficult position.

Does Mark's picture of Pilate correspond with what is said about Pilate in extrabiblical sources? The most famous and often-quoted description of Pilate comes from Philo of Alexandria in his *Embassy to Gaius:* "naturally inflexible, a blend of self-will and relentlessness" (*Legat.* 301). Philo goes on to say that Pilate's tenure as prefect of Judea was characterized by "briberies, insults, robberies, outrages and wanton injuries, executions without trial constantly repeated, and ceaseless and supremely grievous cruelty" (*Legat.* 302).

Some elements in Philo's extreme (some say tendentious) description of Pilate do fit with Mark 15:1-20. Pilate's self-will and desire for control lead him into finally condemning someone he apparently regards as innocent. There is no full airing of the charges, and Jesus never gets to defend himself on his own terms. This is in fact an execution without a real trial. And when Pilate has Jesus flogged (perhaps in public) and hands him over for further abuse at the hands of his soldiers before having him crucified he manifests a streak of cruelty.

But where does Mark's portrayal of Pilate as weak and vacillating fit? Brown (*Death of the Messiah* 698–705) provides an illuminating analysis of six incidents in which ancient sources describe Pilate's confrontations with crowds during his prefecture in Judea: the iconic standards (Josephus, *War* 2.169-74 and *Ant.* 18.55-59), coins with pagan cultic symbols, the aqueduct riot (Josephus, *War* 2.175-77 and *Ant.* 18.60-62), bloodied Galilean sacrifices (Luke 13:1-2), the golden shields (Philo, *Legat.* 299-305), and the Samaritan prophet (Josephus, *Ant.* 18.85-89). These episodes show the pattern of a person who naïvely and recklessly rushes into tense situations, proceeds to make matters worse by his stubbornness, and finally backs off when confronted by a crowd. In light of these six incidents Brown concludes that Pilate's conduct toward Jesus according to the Gospels is not entirely out of character.

All this information raises the question of the basic historicity of Mark 15:1-20. That Jesus "suffered under Pontius Pilate" can hardly be doubted. However, the ancient descriptions of Pilate's character and actions under pressure at best establish the basic verisimilitude of Mark's account. Moreover, as the Notes have repeatedly shown, the narrative shows many signs of Mark's editorial hand, including some of his favorite words (e.g., *euthys*) and constructions (e.g., "began" plus the infinitive). In addition, there are many echoes of OT texts, especially the Servant Songs from Isaiah 40–55 (see below).

Furthermore, one must acknowledge some tendency on Mark's part (understandable especially if Mark's Gospel was written in Rome) to pass over rather quickly the fact that from a legal perspective the Roman prefect Pontius Pilate must have passed sentence on Jesus and so was responsible for his death by crucifixion. (Jews would have stoned Jesus if they were in full control of his execution.) Yet it is not fair to Mark to say that he flatters Pilate and absolves him of guilt in the case of Jesus. Indeed, his picture of Pilate as weak and vacillating is reminiscent of his presentation of Herod Antipas in the execution of John the Baptist (see 6:15-29).

Mark divides the responsibilities for Jesus' condemnation and subsequent execution between the Jewish chief priests and other leaders on the one hand and the Roman prefect Pilate and the soldiers under him on the other hand. The Jewish leaders in Jerusalem (not the whole people!) put the process into motion, but the ultimate legal responsibility lay with Pilate and the Romans.

While the historical questions raised by Mark 15:1-20 are both fascinating and important, they should not detract from the theological contributions made by the passage, especially in the area of christology. In it Jesus appears as the Servant of God, the Son of God, the King of the Jews, and the Suffering Righteous One.

Although there are no direct quotations from the Servant Songs of Isaiah 40–55, there are some allusions to them or at least echoes of them. In 15:5 Jesus falls silent before Pilate; see Isa 53:7: "he did not open his mouth." In 15:14 Pilate admits that Jesus had done nothing wrong; see Isa 53:9: "he had done no violence, and there was no deceit in his mouth." In 15:19 the soldiers insult and spit on Jesus; see Isa 50:6: "I did not hide my face from insult and spitting." The echoes of these OT Servant passages remind Mark's readers that Jesus in his Passion suffers as the Servant of the Lord.

That Jesus is the Son of God is brought out especially in the choice Pilate places before the crowd: Do they want Jesus of Nazareth or Barabbas? From the perspective of Mark's readers and Christian faith the choice is really between the genuine Son of God (Jesus of Nazareth) and one who (ironically) bears the name that means "Son of the Father." By making the wrong choice for Barabbas the crowd serves to bring into even sharper focus Jesus' real identity as the Son of God.

Jesus' identity as King of the Jews (see 15:2, 9, 12) is ironically highlighted by the mock ritual undertaken by the soldiers in 15:16-20. In their parody of the royal or even imperial court, when viewed from the perspective of Christian faith, the soldiers mock and abuse the real King of the Jews (the Messiah) and in fact someone who is a king ("King of kings and Lord of lords") more powerful and glorious than the Roman emperor.

Running through all three parts of Mark 15:1-20 is the theme of Jesus as the Suffering Righteous One. This figure is drawn most fully in Wis 2:12-20, which is itself based on Isaiah 53. Since the Wisdom of Solomon was composed in Alexandria in the first century B.C.E. one cannot be sure that Mark knew or used this book directly, but there are some striking parallels at least. The wicked oppose "the righteous man" because he reproaches them "for sins against the law" (Wis 2:12), because he "professes to have knowledge of God and calls himself a child of the Lord" (2:13), and because he "boasts that God is his father" (2:17). The plan of the wicked is to "test him with insult and torture" and "condemn him to a shameful death" (2:19-20). Their ultimate goal is to "test what will happen at the end of his life" (2:17). For those who are familiar with Mark's Gospel it is practically impossible to read Wis 2:12-20 and not think of Jesus' Passion and death.

For Reference and Further Study

Bond, Helen K. *Pontius Pilate in History and Interpretation.* Cambridge and New York: Cambridge University Press, 1998.

Hagedorn, Anselm C., and Jerome H. Neyrey. "'It Was Out of Envy that They Handed Jesus Over' (Mark 15.10): The Anatomy of Envy and the Gospel of Mark," *JSNT* 69 (1998) 15–56.

Kinman, Brent. "Pilate's Assize and the Timing of Jesus' Trial," *Tyndale Bulletin* 42 (1991) 282–95.

McGing, Brian C. "Pontius Pilate and the Sources," *CBQ* 53 (1991) 416–38.

58. The Crucifixion of Jesus (15:21-32)

21. And they pressed into service a passerby, a certain Simon of Cyrene, coming in from the countryside, the father of Alexander and Rufus, to carry his cross. 22. And they brought him to the place called Golgotha (which means "place of the Skull"). 23. And they were giving him wine mixed with myrrh. But he did not take it. 24. And they crucified him. And they divided his garments among themselves, casting lots for them [to decide] who might take them. 25. It was the third hour when they crucified him. 26. And the inscription of the charge against him was inscribed "The King of the Jews." 27. And with him they crucified two bandits, one at his right and one at his left. 29. And those who were pass-

ing by were vilifying him, wagging their heads and saying: "Well, well! You who are destroying the sanctuary and building it in three days, 30. save yourself by coming down from the cross." 31. So too the chief priests were mocking him to each other along with the scribes, and were saying: "He saved others. Himself he cannot save. 32. Let the Messiah, the King of Israel, come down from the cross that we may see and believe." And those who were crucified with him were reviling him.

NOTES

21. *they pressed into service:* The verb *aggareuousin* and several other verbs in 15:21-27 appear in the "historical present" tense, a familiar Markan stylistic device for enhancing narrative vividness. As 15:16-20 suggests, those who impressed Simon were the soldiers to whom Pilate had handed Jesus over. Roman soldiers had the right to force subject civilians to perform tasks for them (see Matt 5:41: "If anyone forces *(aggareusei)* you to go one mile . . .").

Simon of Cyrene . . . the father of Alexander and Rufus: Cyrene was the capital of Cyrenaica, part of modern Libya. It is likely that Simon was a Jew who had either settled in Judea or was visiting there. The phrase "coming in from the countryside" suggests that Simon was coming to Jerusalem for the Passover festival and that the place of Jesus' crucifixion was near a road. There is no indication that Simon had known Jesus beforehand. However, the reference to him as "the father of Alexander and Rufus" is often taken to mean that Mark's readers (at Rome?) knew Simon and his sons (see Rom 16:13: "Greet Rufus, eminent in the Lord, also his mother and mine") as fellow Christians (at least in the case of the sons).

to carry his cross: It was customary that the condemned person carry the horizontal crossbeam *(patibulum)* to the place of execution (where the vertical beam was stationary). That Simon was impressed to carry the crossbeam is usually explained as the result of Jesus' weakened condition due to the flogging and abuse from the soldiers. The description of Simon's action ("carry *[arē]* his cross") echoes Jesus' challenge in Mark 8:34: "If anyone wishes to follow me . . . let him take up *(aratō)* his cross. . . ."

22. *brought him to the place:* The site for the crucifixion would have been outside the walls of Jerusalem in Jesus' time (see Lev 24:14; Num 15:35-36). Since crucifixion was a public execution and was intended to deter others, it is likely that it took place by a road leading to and from the city gates (see the Note on the preceding verse). Shortly after Jesus' death Herod Agrippa I built the "Third Wall," which incorporated the traditional site of Jesus' crucifixion (now the Church of the Holy Sepulchre) within the city walls.

Golgotha (which means "place of the Skull"): The word "Golgotha" reflects the Aramaic *(gulgultā')* and Hebrew *(gulgōlet)* words for "skull." Its use for the place where Jesus was crucified is generally explained in terms of its topography: "a rounded knoll, rising from the surrounding surface" (Brown, *Death of the Messiah* 937).

23. *wine mixed with myrrh:* The action evokes Prov 31:6: "Give strong drink to one who is perishing, and wine to those in bitter distress." The narrative suggests that the soldiers ("they") gave Jesus the wine. The wine itself (rather than the myrrh) was intended to have a narcotic effect. The inclusion of myrrh seems to have made the wine more fragrant and appealing (according to Brown, *Death of the Messiah* 941).

    But he did not take it: Jesus' refusal is generally attributed to his desire to enter as fully as possible into the experience of suffering (see Taylor, *Mark* 589: "willing to die with an unclouded mind"). Some interpreters point to the "vow" that Jesus made at the Last Supper (14:25) not to drink wine "until that day when I drink it new in the kingdom of God."

24. *And they crucified him:* The central event in Mark's Gospel is narrated in a very short sentence (see 15:25, 27). The shape of Jesus' cross was most likely the *crux immissa* (the traditional † depiction) or the *crux commissa* (a T-shaped cross). The victim was first affixed to the crossbeam *(patibulum)* with ropes and/or nails through the wrists or forearms. Then the crossbeam was fitted on the vertical beam and the victim was lifted up and set on a peg or "seat" on the vertical beam and perhaps also on a footrest. The idea was to prolong the agony, not to make the victim more comfortable.

    they divided his garments among themselves: The soldiers' action evokes Ps 22:18: "they divide my clothes among themselves, and for my clothing they cast lots." According to Mark 15:20 Jesus had been given back his own clothes. The soldiers' lottery certainly concerned Jesus' outer garments (see John 19:23-24). Whether Jesus was crucified naked (the usual Roman practice) or wearing a loincloth (as a concession to Jewish sensibilities about nakedness) cannot be determined.

25. *It was the third hour:* By Roman reckoning this was 9:00 A.M.; compare John 19:14 where Jesus is still before Pilate at the sixth hour (Noon). Mark's Passion account is divided into three-hour sequences: "early" = 6:00 A.M.: Jesus before Pilate (15:1); the third hour = 9:00 A.M.: the crucifixion (15:25); the sixth hour = Noon: darkness (15:33); the ninth hour = 3:00 P.M.: Jesus' death (15:34); and "late" = 6:00 P.M.: burial (15:42). It is difficult to harmonize all the details in the Markan and Johannine Passion chronologies.

26. *the inscription of the charge:* By making public the crucified man's crime the authorities hoped to deter others from doing the same thing. Whether a placard with Jesus' "crime" was placed at the head of the cross (see Luke 23:37) or elsewhere is not made explicit by Mark. The awkward expression "the inscription . . . was inscribed" is generally attributed to Mark's fondness for repetition; see also the repetition of "they crucified him" in 15:24, 25, 27.

    "The King of the Jews": For this charge see Mark 15:2, 9, 12. The inscription was meant to warn Jews against following other charismatic leaders with messianic pretensions and to tell them that this is what happens to such persons. But from the perspective of Mark and other early Christians the inscription told the absolute truth about Jesus (by way of irony).

27. *with him they crucified two bandits:* Those crucified with Jesus were called *lēstai* (see 14:48), a word that sometimes had sociopolitical connotations (social bandits or rebels of the "Robin Hood" type) but at other times simply referred to common thieves. It is hard to resist seeing an allusion to Isa 53:12: "he [the Servant of the Lord] poured himself out to death and was numbered with the transgressors." In fact some manuscripts add, probably under the influence of Luke 23:37, what has been traditionally counted as Mark 15:28: "And the scripture was fulfilled that says, 'And he was counted among the lawless.'" But this is not Mark's usual way of referring to Scripture, and the best manuscripts do not contain this verse.

    one at his right and one at his left: We are reminded of the request by James and John to sit at Jesus' right and left hands in his glory (see 10:37). Here the bandits are not named, and eventually they join in mocking Jesus (see 15:32b). The story of the "good thief" appears only in Luke 23:39-43.

29. *those who were passing by:* See the Notes on 15:21 and 22 for the place of crucifixion by the roadside. The assumption is that these passersby knew little about Jesus but nonetheless verbally abuse him because he is being crucified as "King of the Jews."

    were vilifying him: The verb *eblasphēmoun* does not carry the technical OT sense of misusing the divine name (see Lev 24:10-23). As elsewhere in Mark (see *blasphēmein* in 2:7; 3:28, 29, and *blasphēmia* in 3:28; 7:22; 14:64), "blasphemy" is used loosely to refer to inappropriate and offensive speech.

    wagging their heads: The image alludes to Ps 22:7: "All who see me mock at me . . . they shake their heads." See also Lam 2:15: "all who pass along the way . . . wag their heads at daughter Jerusalem."

    Well, well!: The precise meaning and translation of the interjection *oua* are debated. The explanations range from irony ("Well, well") to real or imagined wonder ("Aha!").

    you who are destroying the sanctuary and building it in three days: The passersby bring up the first charge raised against Jesus in the trial before the Sanhedrin (see 14:58). The word *naos* ("sanctuary") can denote the holiest part of the Temple but here probably stands for the whole complex.

30. *save yourself by coming down from the cross:* It is necessary (and should be comparatively easy) for the Messiah who claims to destroy and restore the Temple to save his own life. For the mockers the fact of Jesus' crucifixion was definitive proof that his prophecies about the Temple (see 11:15-17; 13:2; 14:58) were false.

31. *the chief priests were mocking him . . . with the scribes:* Along with the elders, these groups have been the prime movers in bringing about the execution of Jesus (see 11:18, 27; 14:1, 10, 43, 53, 54, 55, 60, 61, 63, 66; 15:1, 3, 10, 11).

    He saved others. Himself he cannot save: The many uses of *sōzein* ("save") in Mark (3:4; 5:23, 28, 34; 6:56; 8:35; 10:26, 52; 13:13, 20) culminate in its occurrences in 15:30 and 31. In Mark's Gospel and the NT the meanings range from "rescue" and "heal" in their physical senses to "save" in a spiritual sense ("salvation"). At the cross Jesus' opponents challenge the Savior (understood in all its senses) to save himself from death (see 5:23).

32. *the Messiah, the King of Israel:* Here the mockers bring back the second charge made against Jesus in the trial before the Sanhedrin: "Are you the Messiah, the Son of the Blessed One?" (14:61). They use the more correct "insider" title "King of Israel" rather than the "outsider" title "King of the Jews" (15:2, 9, 12, 18, 26).

that we may see and believe: The opponents' skepticism (see John 6:30) ironically prepares for the Easter appearances of the risen Jesus (see Mark 14:28; 16:7; 1 Cor 15:3-5).

those who were crucified with him: See the Note on 15:27. The term *synestaurō-menoi* is not used here in its Pauline theological sense (see Rom 6:6; Gal 2:20). As noted above, there is no "good thief" in Mark. Brown (*Death of the Messiah* 999) summarizes the scene as follows: "The force of the third mockery, thus, is the culmination of hostility: Not only the haphazard passersby and the determined Sanhedrin enemies of Jesus, but even the wretches that share his fate speak ill of him. On the cross Jesus has no friends; he is a solitary righteous man closely surrounded on all sides by enemies."

INTERPRETATION

The first part (15:21-27) of Mark's narrative of the crucifixion of Jesus tells how Jesus came to be crucified. The account is sparse and understated, giving only the essential facts. It answers basic questions: Who?—Simon, Jesus, the soldiers, and the bandits; Where?—Golgotha; When?—the third hour; Why?—the "King of the Jews"; and How?—from carrying the cross to the actual crucifixion. Even though everything in Mark's Gospel has been leading up to this moment, the event itself is described in a remarkably concise and objective style. The key phrase "and they crucified him" appears three times (15:24, 25, 27), without embellishment or emotional commentary.

The second part (15:29-32) portrays Jesus as abandoned by his friends and followers and opposed not only by the Jerusalem leadership but also by casual passersby and the two criminals who are crucified with him. The charges raised against Jesus at the trial before the Sanhedrin—that he threatened to destroy the Temple, and that he claimed to be the Messiah—are thrown back at him. The opponents are certain that the fact of Jesus' crucifixion would be enough to prove that he was just another false Messiah. By having the two charges repeated by the spectators Mark reminds his readers why Jesus was being crucified. The reviling by three groups in turn—the passersby (15:29-30), the chief priests and the scribes (15:31-32a), and the two criminals (15:32b)—underlines the lonely plight of Jesus the Suffering Righteous One.

This passage is another good example of Mark's skill as a writer. His account of the details surrounding Jesus' crucifixion is quite plausible in light of what is known about how crucifixion was administered in the Roman empire, and so he achieves verisimilitude at the very least. The narrative is spare, without unnecessary details, and yet it is also dramatically powerful despite (or perhaps because of) its cool and objective style. The climax ("and they crucified him") is stated concisely and repeatedly, and in 15:29-32 the horror of the scene is allowed to sink in through the repetition of the charges from the Sanhedrin trial and the reviling by the three different groups of mockers.

The most prominent biblical text in Mark's crucifixion narrative is Psalm 22, which is customarily classified as a lament. Its first part (22:1-21a) alternates between complaints about various sufferings and confessions of trust in God. The second part (22:21b-31) assumes a mood of vindication, thanksgiving, and celebration. According to Mark 15:34 Jesus' last words are a quotation of the first words of Psalm 22: "My God, my God, why have you forsaken me?" For the problems associated with the interpretation of the quotation, see the next unit.

Psalm 22 is the prayer of a righteous person who has suffered greatly but has been vindicated, all the while retaining and being sustained by trust in God's power and care. The psalm not only provides a model or even a script for the story of Jesus' Passion and death, but also supplies the words and images in specific places: "they divided his garments among them" (Mark 15:24 = Ps 22:18) and "wagging their heads" (Mark 15:27 = Ps 22:7). The allusions to Psalm 22 and to other OT texts (see the Notes) remind us that for Mark and other early Christians Jesus suffered and died "according to the Scriptures" (1 Cor 15:3). Recourse to the OT Scriptures allowed them to make sense out of the cruel and shameful death Jesus suffered on the cross.

That Jesus was put to death by crucifixion can hardly be doubted. It was a cruel and shameful death. The Roman orator Cicero referred to crucifixion as a "most cruel and disgusting penalty" and "the extreme and ultimate penalty for a slave" (*In Verrem* 2.5.64, 66). Josephus called it "the most pitiable of deaths" (*War* 7.203). Even Paul conceded that proclaiming Christ crucified was "a stumbling block to Jews and foolishness to Gentiles" (1 Cor 1:23), and the author of Hebrews celebrated Jesus as the one who "endured the cross, disregarding its shame" (Heb 12:2). That Jesus was crucified was not the kind of thing early Christians would have invented if they wanted to impress their contemporaries.

The physical sufferings of a crucified person were intense, and indeed gruesome. Perhaps Mark's literary strategy of spare and objective reporting along with understatement serves to make the point more effectively than a detailed and graphic description of Jesus' physical sufferings (exposure to the hot sun, pain from the nails, the difficulty encountered in trying to breathe, and so on) would have achieved. But Mark also helps us to move beyond the physical sufferings of Jesus to recognize what was perhaps an even greater suffering that Jesus endured: misunderstanding and rejection by practically everyone.

The theme of misunderstanding and rejection runs through Mark's Gospel: the plot initiated by the Pharisees and Herodians (3:6), the unbelief shown by the people of Jesus' home town (6:1-6), the misunderstanding and obtuseness displayed by his disciples (8:14-21, and throughout the journey narrative in 8:22–10:52), opposition from the leadership in Jerusalem (11:1–12:44), and the final abandonment by his own disciples (14:43-52). Brown's comment (see the Note on 15:32) on the scene bears repeating here: "On the cross Jesus has no friends; he is a solitary righteous man closely surrounded on all sides by enemies."

For Reference and Further Study

Bailey, Kenneth E. "The Fall of Jerusalem and Mark's Account of the Cross," *ExpTim* 102 (1991) 102–05.

Blount, Brian K. "A Socio-Rhetorical Analysis of Simon of Cyrene: Mark 15:21 and Its Parallels," *Semeia* 64 (1994) 171–98.

Fitzmyer, Joseph A. "Crucifixion in Ancient Palestine, Qumran Literature, and the New Testament," *CBQ* 40 (1979) 493–513.

Hengel, Martin. *Crucifixion in the Ancient World and the Folly of the Message of the Cross.* Philadelphia: Fortress, 1977.

Schmidt, Thomas E. "Mark 15.16-32: The Crucifixion Narrative and the Roman Triumphal Procession," *NTS* 41 (1995) 1–18.

59. *The Death of Jesus* (15:33-41)

33. And when the sixth hour came, there was darkness over the whole land until the ninth hour. 34. And in the ninth hour Jesus screamed in a loud voice: "Eloi, Eloi, lama sabachthani," which means, "My God, my God, why have you abandoned me?" 35. And some of the bystanders, when they heard, were saying: "See, he calls Elijah." 36. But someone ran, filled a sponge with vinegary wine, put it on a stick, and was giving him to drink, saying: "Let's see if Elijah comes to take him down." 37. But Jesus let out a loud cry and expired. 38. And the veil of the sanctuary was rent in two from top to bottom.

39. And when the centurion who had been standing there opposite him saw that he thus expired, he said: "Truly this man was the Son of

God." 40. And there were also women looking on from a distance; and among them were Mary Magdalene, and Mary the mother of James the Younger and Joses, and Salome, 41. who when he was in Galilee were following him and ministering to him, and also many other women who came up with him to Jerusalem.

NOTES

33. *the sixth hour . . . the ninth hour:* In Mark's chronology of the day of Jesus' death (see the Note on 15:25) the darkness lasted from noon to 3:00 P.M.

   there was darkness over the whole land: The extent of the darkness is much debated, with opinions ranging from only the land of Judea (or Israel) to the whole earth. The Greek word *gē* can be used in both senses. The cause of the darkness has been attributed to natural phenomena such as a sandstorm or an eclipse as well as to miraculous divine intervention. The Markan meaning of the darkness is greatly illuminated by OT passages, especially Amos 8:9-10: "On that day, says the LORD God, I will make the sun go down at noon and darken the earth in broad daylight . . . I will make it like the mourning for an only son, and the end of it like a bitter day." See also Gen 1:2-3; Exod 10:21-23; Jer 15:9; 33:19-21; Joel 2:2, 31; and Zeph 1:15. The point is that the cosmos itself joins in mourning the death of God's Son.

34. *in the ninth hour:* That is, 3:00 P.M. This is the time of Jesus' last words, not necessarily the time of his death (though that seems to follow shortly).

   Jesus screamed in a loud voice: The vivid verb *eboēsen* reflects the intense physical suffering of the crucified one and underlines the decisive character of this moment in Jesus' struggle against the power of evil (which began in 1:12-13).

   Eloi, Eloi . . . why have you abandoned me?: The quotation of Ps 22:1 appears first in Aramaic (with perhaps some elements of Hebrew mixed in) and then in Greek form (though not that of the LXX). Whether Jesus would have spoken this biblical verse in Hebrew (the sacred language) or in Aramaic (his native tongue) has been much debated. For other uses of Aramaic words in Mark see 5:41; 7:34; 11:9, 10; 14:36; 15:22. For the question of the meaning of Ps 22:1 as Jesus' last words, see the Interpretation.

35. *some of the bystanders . . . were saying: "See, he calls Elijah . . .":* The many learned efforts to determine how the names of God ("Eloi, Eloi") and Elijah could have been confused in Hebrew or in Aramaic have not yielded a totally satisfactory explanation. Perhaps Brown (*Death of the Messiah* 1062) puts us on the right track by suggesting that in the Markan context (historical and literary) a Greek speaker might have imagined that "Eloi" and "Elijah" sounded alike in a Semitic language. Modern readers suppose the same thing. According to Mal 4:5 the prophet Elijah was expected to return before the day of the Lord: "Lo, I will send you the prophet Elijah before the great and terrible day of the Lord comes" (see our treatment of Mark 9:9-13). In the Markan context the prophet Elijah has twice served as the forerunner of the Messiah (see 1:2;

9:9-13). Just as John the Baptist (an Elijah figure in Mark 9:9-13) met his death on account of his fidelity to God, so Jesus (the Messiah) meets his death on account of his fidelity to God.

36. *someone ran, filled a sponge with vinegary wine:* There is very likely an allusion to Ps 69:21 here: "They gave me poison for food, and for my thirst they gave me vinegar to drink." Beyond that the text poses many problems. Who gave Jesus the wine? Was it a soldier or a bystander? What was the intent? Was it hostile (*oxos* = "vinegary wine") or sympathetic (as in 15:23)? What relationship does this action have to the Elijah episode? Were they two separate traditions joined awkwardly or a literary unit from the beginning?

Let's see if Elijah comes to take him down: The tone of the statement depends to a large extent on how the (unanswerable?) questions raised above are answered. It can be taken as the sincere hope of a sympathetic bystander who had heard about Jesus and the messianic hopes surrounding him, or it can be interpreted as the cynical comment of someone who mocks Jesus and what he stands for. The latter approach seems more likely in view of Mark's emphasis on the hostility of the bystanders and his extensive use of irony in ch. 15.

37. *Jesus let out a loud cry:* We are not told what Jesus said. It may simply have been the last shout of someone in great physical pain. Brown (*Death of the Messiah* 1079) suggests that the phrase is a reference back to 15:34 (= Ps 22:1) and so is an example of Mark's technique of recapitulation (see the Note on 15:1): "having let out *that* loud cry."

and expired: The verb *exepneusen* means "breathe one's last breath" or "die." Again Mark's cool and objective style may well heighten the reader's sympathy for Jesus at the moment of his death. That Jesus gave over his "spirit" (*pneuma*) to his heavenly Father at this point is clear. Whether Mark intended a connection to Jesus' giving of the Holy Spirit (also *pneuma*; compare John 19:30; 20:22) is not clear.

38. *the veil of the sanctuary was rent:* The "veil" (*katapetasma*) may have been either the curtain before the Holy of Holies or the one leading into the "Holy Place" where the Holy of Holies stood. The word *naos* ("sanctuary") refers to an especially holy place. The term has been used only in the charge against Jesus at the Sanhedrin trial ("I will destroy this sanctuary made by hands," 14:58) and in the mockery of Jesus at the cross ("you who destroy the sanctuary and build it in three days," 15:29). The verb *eschisthē* ("was rent") describes vividly what happened to the veil of the sanctuary. The only previous use of *schizesthai* in Mark appeared in the account of Jesus' baptism (1:10) as part of a complex of images—the heavens torn asunder, the dove-like descent of the Holy Spirit, and the voice from heaven—that depict the removal of barriers between heaven and earth. For the meaning of this sign, see the Interpretation.

in two from top to bottom: The reduplication (one of Mark's favorite literary devices) suggests that the veil will not be repaired.

39. *the centurion who had been standing there opposite him:* Mark uses the Latin loanword *kentyriōn* to refer to someone who is in charge of a hundred (*centum*) soldiers. Since the centurion is standing in front of Jesus the implication is that

he is in charge of the execution. Since he is a Roman soldier he can be assumed to be a Gentile.

saw that he thus expired: The verb used to describe the death of Jesus is *exepneusen,* the same verb as in 15:37. The adverb *houtōs* ("thus") suggests that the centurion reacts not only to Jesus' death on the cross but also to the portent (the rendering of the sanctuary veil) that accompanied it.

Truly this man was the Son of God: The title *hyios theou* ("Son of God") has no article ("the"), but in the context of Mark's Gospel the absence of the definite article need not blunt the theological significance of the title. We take this to be a genuine confession of faith that echoes Mark 1:1 ("Jesus Christ, the Son of God") and constitutes the climax of the gospel. Only at his death on the cross is the true identity of Jesus as the suffering Messiah and as God's Son revealed. The objection that a Gentile Roman soldier could not have meant what Mark means misses the point, since Mark is writing for Christian readers around 70 C.E. and the Markan Passion narrative is full of literary ironies. It is indeed ironic that in Mark's narrative the human being who correctly identifies Jesus as the Son of God should be the Gentile Roman soldier presiding at Jesus' death on the cross.

40. *women looking on from a distance:* Whereas the centurion was close to Jesus ("opposite him"), the women are kept back as spectators in the crowd. Nevertheless, these women (who knew Jesus well; see 15:41) see him die, and they will see where he is buried (see 15:47).

   Mary Magdalene, and Mary the mother of James the Younger and Joses, and Salome: Mary of Magdala (a village near the Sea of Galilee) is the key figure, since she witnesses the death of Jesus (15:40) and his entombment (15:47), and at Easter she will find his tomb empty (16:1-8). Most commentators identify the mother of "James the Younger" as the mother of the member of the Twelve known as James the son of Alphaeus (3:18) rather than of James "the brother of the Lord" (Jas 1:1). However, it is tempting to identify Mary the "mother of James the Younger and Joses" as also the mother of Jesus (see John 19:25-27) on the basis of Mark 6:3 ("Is not this the carpenter, the son of Mary and brother of James and Joses . . . ?"), though one might expect that she would be referred to here more simply as "the mother of Jesus." The reference to James as *mikros* ("little," or "younger") differentiates him at least from James the son of Zebedee (see 1:19; 3:17). Salome was a fairly common Jewish woman's name, and this figure is otherwise unknown. Compare the lists of women's names in Mark 15:47 and 16:1.

41. *who when he was in Galilee were following and ministering to him:* The three women are singled out (for the first time in Mark's Gospel!) as having been closely associated with Jesus and his movement even back in Galilee. The use of the verb *akolouthein* ("follow") suggests that they can be called "disciples" of Jesus, since *akolouthein* is the usual Markan (and NT) word for discipleship (see Mark 1:18; 2:14, 15; 5:24; 6:1; 8:34; 9:38; 10:21, 28, 32, 52). Their ministry probably consisted mostly in what constituted "women's work" in first-century Mediterranean society. The imperfect tense of the two verbs indicates the

women's continuing performance of their tasks while the group was in Galilee and probably during the journey up to Jerusalem.

and also many other women: Again for the first time (!) Mark acknowledges the existence of a larger band of women travelers on the journey to Jerusalem than simply Jesus and the Twelve (compare Luke 8:1-3).

INTERPRETATION

The narrative of the death of Jesus, while told in Mark's spare and objective style, is a rich mixture of cosmic and earthly portents, reports about Jesus' last words and his death, and reactions from bystanders. After recounting the portent of darkness from noon to 3:00 P.M. (15:33), Mark tells us that Jesus cried out in the words of Ps 22:1 (15:34). When there is confusion about whether Jesus was calling for Elijah someone offers him vinegary wine (15:35-36). The death of Jesus is marked by a loud shout and last breath (15:37). At the moment of Jesus' death the veil of the sanctuary in the Temple is rent in two (15:38). The passage ends with a climactic reaction from the Roman centurion (15:39) and a surprising notice about women followers who witness Jesus' death from a distance (15:40-41).

The individual elements in the Markan account are familiar to most readers today—perhaps so familiar that they pass over the many interpretive problems they raise (see the Notes). Some commentators emphasize historical probability or at least verisimilitude while others stress the scriptural and symbolic dimensions. The hermeneutical debate is sometimes posed as "history remembered" versus "prophecy historicized." The critical problem, of course, is trying to distinguish between the two.

Our concern at this point, however, is not to argue about the historical facts behind Mark's account. This task has been taken up admirably by Raymond E. Brown in *The Death of the Messiah*. Rather, our focus here is the Markan meaning of the various elements in the passage, with particular attention to Markan style and OT backgrounds (see the Notes). Our remarks in this Interpretation chiefly concern how Mark 15:33-41 relates to the two great themes of Mark's Gospel: christology and discipleship.

According to Mark 15:34 the last words of Jesus are a quotation of Ps 22:1: "My God, my God, why have you abandoned me?" That these words are intended as a cry of despair on Jesus' part makes no sense at all. Why would Mark write a "gospel" ("good news") about a tragic figure whose life ends in total despair? Such a work might qualify as a tragedy or a pathetic biography, but hardly as a gospel.

That on the historical level Jesus may have felt abandoned in his final hour—when his closest followers had fled in fear and every powerful group among his own people opposed him—is not impossible. That he even imagined momentarily that his heavenly Father had abandoned him is conceivable. Brown (*Death of the Messiah* 1044–51) develops this point at length: "Jesus is portrayed as profoundly discouraged at the end of his long battle because God, to whose will Jesus committed himself at the beginning of his Passion (Mark 14:36; Matt 26:39, 42) has not intervened in the struggle and seemingly has left Jesus unsupported" (p. 1049). Brown concludes that there is "no persuasive argument against attributing to the Jesus of Mark/Matt the literal sentiment of feeling forsaken expressed in the psalm quote" (p. 1051).

Brown's remarks, of course, are made in the context of a historical investigation into the death of Jesus. A literary and theological investigation of Mark's account would rightly place more emphasis on Psalm 22 taken as a whole as the prayer of a suffering righteous person and an important element in Mark's christology.

In Mark 15:21-32 there were already allusions to Psalm 22 in the dividing of Jesus' garments and in the bystanders wagging their heads at the crucified Jesus. The first part of Psalm 22 (vv. 1-21a) consists of alternating laments over present sufferings (vv. 1-2, 6-8, 12-18) and expressions of trust in God (vv. 3-5, 9-11, 19-21a). We can assume that those who make Psalm 22 their own prayer are really suffering and find in the words of this psalm a way of expressing their experiences and feelings.

At the same time, Psalm 22 is a statement of confidence in God's power to act and to vindicate the suffering righteous speaker. That confidence is based on what God has done in Israel's history (vv. 3-5) and in the speaker's own life (vv. 9-11). The second part of Psalm 22 (vv. 21b-31) confirms that God has indeed acted: "He did not hide his face from me, but heard when I cried out to him" (22:24b). In fact, the second part of Psalm 22 constitutes an invitation to participate in a thanksgiving sacrifice and the celebration that accompanies it.

It is important to take Psalm 22:1—the last words of Jesus according to Mark 15:34—*both* as the first words of a psalm of lament over real sufferings as well as an expression of trust in God's power to rescue an innocent sufferer, *and* as expressing the sentiments that Mark (and his source) regarded as appropriate to Jesus at the moment of his death on the cross. Jesus makes the words of Psalm 22 his own, and the words of Psalm 22 express perfectly the deepest stirrings of his heart. The whole of Mark's Gospel has been leading up to this point. At the cross the "secret" of Jesus' messianic identity is revealed. His way is not that of military might or political power (compare *Psalms of Solomon* 17), but rather the way of redemptive suffering: "the Son of Man came . . . to give his life as a ransom for many" (10:45).

A second great theme of Mark 15:33-41 is the various responses to Jesus at the moment of his death ("discipleship"). The portent of darkness

(15:33) suggests that the whole universe joins in mourning the cruel death of the Son of God. The rending of the veil of the sanctuary (15:38) indicates that in Jesus' death God has opened definitively the way between heaven and earth through Jesus' death on the cross. See the baptism account (with the only other Markan use of *schizesthai*) and the transfiguration account where the heavenly voice declares Jesus to be "my beloved Son" (1:11; 9:7). The veil portent is probably also an expression of divine judgment upon the continuing efficacy of worship at the Jerusalem Temple. This has been a major theme since Jesus' entrance into Jerusalem in Mark 11, and it comes to a certain anticipatory fulfillment in the rending of the sanctuary veil. For Mark's readers around 70 C.E. the veil portent at Jesus' death would help to explain the (real or impending) destruction of the Jerusalem Temple.

Not only do nature (darkness) and God (the rending of the Temple veil) respond sympathetically to Jesus in his suffering and death, but so also do certain humans. Whether or not the intent of the person (15:35-36) who offers Jesus the vinegary wine and looks for Elijah to come and rescue Jesus is to be taken as hostile, at least at the literary level of irony this person shows some human compassion. Whatever a Roman centurion (15:39) at the cross of Jesus might have meant in calling Jesus "Son of God," in the Markan theological context his testimony is an accurate confession of who Jesus really is. And the women followers (15:40-41) who mysteriously appear as witnesses to Jesus' death, burial, and empty tomb are models of fidelity in contrast to the unbelief and cowardice shown by the Twelve. As Brown observes, Mark 15:33-41 shows that it "is not true" that "God has not intervened in the struggle and left Jesus unsupported" (p. 1049).

FOR REFERENCE AND FURTHER STUDY

Corley, Kathleen E. "Women and the Crucifixion and Burial of Jesus. 'He Was Buried: On the Third Day He Was Raised,'" *Forum* 1 (1998) 181–225.

Danove, Paul L. "The Characterization and Narrative Function of the Women at the Tomb (Mark 15,40-41.47; 16:1-8)," *Bib* 77 (1996) 375–97.

Johnson, Earl S. "Mark 15,39 and the So-Called Confession of the Roman Centurion," *Bib* 81 (2000) 406–13.

Kim, Tae Hun. "The Anarthrous *hyios theou* in Mark 15,39 and the Roman Imperial Cult," *Bib* 79 (1998) 221–41.

Pilch, John J. "Death with Honor: The Mediterranean Style Death of Jesus in Mark," *BTB* 25 (1995) 65–70.

Schmidt, Thomas E. "Cry of Dereliction or Cry of Judgment? Mark 15:34 in Context," *Bulletin of Biblical Research* 4 (1994) 145–53.

Shiner, Whitney T. "The Ambiguous Pronouncement of the Centurion and the Shrouding of Meaning in Mark," *JSNT* 78 (2000) 3–22.

Ulansey, David. "The Heavenly Veil Torn: Mark's Cosmic Inclusio," *JBL* 110 (1991) 123–25.

60. *The Burial of Jesus* (15:42-47)

42. And as it was already late, since it was the Preparation (that is, before the Sabbath), 43. Joseph from Arimathea, a respected councilor, who was also looking for the kingdom of God, took courage, came in before Pilate, and requested the body of Jesus. 44. But Pilate wondered if he had already died. And summoning the centurion, he questioned him if he was already dead. 45. And having learned from the centurion, he granted the corpse to Joseph. 46. And he bought a linen cloth, took him down, tied him up in the linen cloth, and placed him in the tomb that was hewn out of rock, and rolled a stone at the door of the tomb. 47. And Mary Magdalene and Mary (mother) of Joses were observing where he had been placed.

NOTES

42. *as it was already late:* The word *opsia* is generally translated "evening." But the point of the hasty proceedings described in this passage is to be sure that Jesus is buried before the Sabbath begins at sunset (around 6:00 P.M.). Since according to Mark 15:34 Jesus died after 3:00 P.M. we are to imagine a time around 4:00 on Friday afternoon.

the Preparation (that is, before the Sabbath): The "preparation" *(paraskeuē)* refers to the period for accomplishing tasks that were not permitted to be done on the Sabbath. The Sabbath begins at sunset, and so the events described in this passage take place late on Friday afternoon. Mark generally uses the explanatory phrase "that is" with Aramaic words (see 3:17; 5:41; 7:11, 34; 15:22, 34). He apparently believed that his readers needed an explanation of *paraskeuē* as the time of preparation for the Sabbath *(prosabbaton)*.

43. *Joseph from Arimathea:* In Mark's narrative it seems that Joseph is not a disciple of Jesus (compare Matt 27:57; John 19:38). Arimathea is usually identified as Ramathaim (see 1 Sam 1:1). Wherever Joseph came from, it appears that he was not a Galilean (which also suggests that he was not a disciple of Jesus in Mark's view).

a respected councilor: The noun *bouleutēs* indicates that Joseph was a member of the Sanhedrin, the group of Jewish officials that had earlier condemned Jesus to death (see 14:55). Mark had insisted that "the whole council" had assembled (14:55) and that "all condemned him as deserving death" (14:64; see 15:1). The implication of Mark's narrative is that Joseph had joined in condemning Jesus—or perhaps Mark had exaggerated the scope of the meeting and the unanimity of the verdict.

who was also looking for the kingdom of God: This description of Joseph puts him in the same class as the scribe who affirmed Jesus' teaching about the importance of the love commandment(s) and whom Jesus declared as "not far from the kingdom of God" (12:34). As an observant Jew, Joseph takes upon himself the observance of Deut 21:22-23: "When someone is convicted of a crime punishable by death and is executed, and you hang him on a tree, his corpse must not remain all night upon the tree; you shall bury him on that same day, for anyone hung on a tree is under a curse. You must not defile the land that the Lord your God is giving you for possession."

took courage, came in before Pilate, and requested the body of Jesus: If Joseph did not take the initiative it appears that Jesus' corpse would have been thrown into a common grave. It would take some courage for a respected member of the Jewish council to approach Pilate directly and request the corpse of one who had shortly before been executed as "King of the Jews." If the request came from a disciple of Jesus it is very unlikely that Pilate would accede to it. This too indicates that Joseph had not been part of Jesus' movement and that he was acting out of genuine Jewish piety and not out of some prior knowledge of and affiliation with Jesus.

44. *Pilate wondered if he had already died:* According to Mark, Jesus was on the cross for six hours: from the third hour (15:25) to the ninth hour (15:33). Those who were crucified could linger for a day or two depending on their physical condition and the punishments (e.g., flogging) already inflicted on them. Pilate's "wonder" (for previous uses of *thaumazein* see 5:20; 6:6; and especially 15:5 with reference to Pilate) about whether Jesus was "already" (*palai*—the only occurrence in Mark) dead stems from the assumption that the process should have taken longer. The episode narrated in Mark 15:44-45 has the function of confirming that Jesus was really dead and not simply in a coma or a blackout.

summoning the centurion: This is presumably the same centurion who presided over the execution of Jesus and proclaimed that "this man was the Son of God" (15:39). Better than anyone else, the centurion could confirm that Jesus had really died.

45. *he granted the corpse to Joseph:* The verb *edōrēsato* implies a gift or favor done on Pilate's part. The general Roman practice was not to grant an honorable burial to those who had been crucified, though exceptions could be made through bribes or the influence of a distinguished family. This Roman custom clashed with the OT commandment (Deut 21:22-23) about burying someone hanged on a tree "on that same day." By acceding to Joseph's request Pilate allows a Jewish councilor to fulfill an OT commandment and keeps the corpse of Jesus out of the hands of Jesus' closest followers. The word for "corpse" *(ptōma)* is the same as the term used in 6:29 (and only there in Mark) for the corpse of John the Baptist. Its appearance here in 15:45 links the fates of John the Baptist and Jesus.

46. *he bought a linen cloth . . . and placed him in the tomb:* The four verbs in rapid succession—two aorist participles ("having bought . . . having taken down") and two third-person aorist singulars ("tied . . . placed")—contribute to the mood of haste that Mark creates as he describes Joseph trying to get Jesus

buried "on that same day" and before the Sabbath. The "linen cloth" *(sindōn)* was probably just a large piece of cloth like a sheet; the only other appearance of *sindōn* in Mark refers to the garment worn by the young man *(neaniskos)* in 14:51-52. There is no mention of washing or anointing Jesus' corpse with perfumes and spices (see John 19:39-40). The verb *eneilēsen* means "roll up" or "wrap" something or someone. To tie up Jesus' corpse in a *sindōn* was "the absolute minimum one could do for the dead" (Brown, *Death of the Messiah* 1246). That we are to imagine Joseph doing all these actions by himself is unlikely; we are probably to envision him giving orders to his servants (and thus avoiding for himself ritual defilement from contact with a corpse).

the tomb that was hewn out of rock: Some manuscripts use *mnēma* here for "tomb" (see 5:3, 5), but most have *mnēmeion,* which is the usual term in this context (see 15:46; 16:2, 3, 4, 5; also 5:2; 6:29). Jerusalem has been described as a city surrounded by a gigantic cemetery. In Jesus' time it was customary to cut out burial caves from the soft limestone rock. The corpse of the newly deceased would be laid out on a kind of shelf and allowed to decompose for a year or so. Then the bones would be gathered and placed in a stone ossuary ("bone box") that often bore an inscription with the names of the deceased on it.

rolled a stone at the door of the tomb: The idea was to prevent tomb robbing. The stone was probably a large flat circular stone that could be rolled into a groove cut out of the rock. While Mark tells all the things Joseph was doing, he never says that Joseph owned the tomb (compare Matt 27:60).

47. *Mary Magdalene and Mary (mother) of Joses:* See the Note on 15:40. Mary of Magdala is mentioned in 15:40, 47; and 16:1, and so she is the great principle of continuity in the accounts about Jesus' death, burial, and empty tomb. Mary (mother) of Joses is presumably the same as "Mary the mother of James the Younger and Joses" in 15:40; see the different description in 16:1: "Mary the (mother) of James."

were observing where he had been placed: The use of the imperfect "were observing" *(etheōroun)* suggests that these women took in everything from start to finish. Having witnessed Jesus' death, they also witnessed his burial and so on Easter morning they did not go to the wrong tomb. Note that Mark does not portray the women as participating with Joseph in the burial of Jesus. Rather, they are again spectators at a distance (see 15:40). Their chief function is to serve as witnesses to the events and the places in which these events occurred.

INTERPRETATION

Mark's narrative of the burial of Jesus first establishes the time as late Friday afternoon, just before the start of the Sabbath (15:42). Next it introduces Joseph of Arimathea and describes his request to Pilate for Jesus' body (15:43). Then at the center of the passage is the account of how Pilate ascertained from the centurion that Jesus was really dead; only then did Pilate release the body to Joseph (15:44-45). Next it describes Joseph's many activities as he hurried to give Jesus a decent burial before the Sabbath in accord with Deut 21:22-23 (Mark 15:46). Finally it tells how at least two of the women who witnessed Jesus' death also witnessed his burial (15:47). Thus the passage is an example of Mark's "sandwich" technique in that the consultation between Pilate and the centurion in 15:44-45 interrupts the account about Joseph of Arimathea in 15:43 and 15:46 (as well as the notices about the women in 15:40-41 and 15:47).

The burial narrative provides the link between the accounts of the death of Jesus (15:33-41) and the discovery of the empty tomb (16:1-8). It confirms that Jesus had really died and that on Easter Sunday the women went to the right place. Thus it is a presupposition for the early Christian proclamation "that Christ died for our sins in accordance with the scriptures, and that he was buried, and that he was raised on the third day" (1 Cor 15:3-4). This Markan narrative tells how "he was buried."

At this point in Mark's Gospel Pilate, the centurion, and the women are familiar characters. Pilate wonders at Jesus' quick death and finally releases his corpse. The centurion confirms that Jesus really died. The women take no part in the burial rites but observe where Jesus is buried. They all act in ways that are consistent with their behavior in the previous pericopes.

The new character is Joseph of Arimathea. He comes out of nowhere to take charge of Jesus' burial. His non-Galilean origin, his membership in the Sanhedrin, his status as a "respected councilor," and his success in getting Jesus' corpse released to him by Pilate all indicate that he was not a disciple of Jesus, even though Matthew (27:57) and John (19:38) feel compelled to make him into one. Rather, the description of Joseph as "looking for the kingdom of God" (15:43) places him along with the scribe of 12:28-34 in the category of observant Jews who exemplify the best in Israel's religious tradition. From Mark we get the picture of Joseph as a man who takes the risk of seeing to the burial of someone who had been crucified as the "King of the Jews." What inspires Joseph is his devotion not so much to Jesus whom he barely seems to know but to the OT commandment to bury a fellow Jew on the day of his death. His action evokes the example given by Tobit in burying his kinsmen in the Diaspora (see Tob 1:17-18; 2:3-4, 7-8). In any assessment of Mark's attitudes toward Judaism the figure of Joseph of Arimathea needs to be taken into account.

For Reference and Further Study

Brown, Raymond E. "The Burial of Jesus (Mark 15:42-47)," *CBQ* 50 (1988) 233–45.
O'Collins, Gerald, and Daniel Kendall. "Did Joseph of Arimathea Exist?" *Bib* 75 (1994) 235–41.

61. The Empty Tomb (16:1-8)

1. And when the Sabbath was over, Mary Magdalene and Mary the (mother) of James and Salome bought spices in order to go and anoint him. 2. And very early on the first day of the week they came to the tomb just after sunrise. 3. And they were saying to each other: "Who will roll back the stone for us from the door of the tomb?" 4. And looking up, they observed that the stone had been rolled back. For it was very large. 5. And on entering the tomb they saw a young man seated on the right side, wearing a long white robe. And they were utterly amazed. 6. And he said to them: "Do not be amazed. You seek Jesus the Nazarene, the one who was crucified. He has been raised; he is not here. Look, (this is) the place where they laid him. 7. But go, tell his disciples and Peter that he goes before you into Galilee. There you will see him, as he told you." 8. And they went out and fled from the tomb, for trembling and bewilderment took hold of them. And they said nothing to anyone. For they were afraid.

NOTES

1. *when the Sabbath was over:* The Sabbath would have ended around 6:00 on Saturday evening. At this point shops might open and the women would be able to purchase the *arōmata* ("spices, aromatic oils or salves") to tend to the corpse of Jesus. The main purpose of applying these *arōmata* was to keep down the stench from the corpse.

   Mary Magdalene . . . Salome: These three women all witnessed the death of Jesus according to 15:40. The two Marys witnessed Jesus' burial according to 15:47. The second Mary ("the [mother] of James") is presumably the same as "the (mother) of Joses" in 15:47, though the alternation in names is peculiar.

   to go and anoint him: For the Jewish custom of anointing a corpse see *m. Shabb.* 23:5: "They prepare all that is needed for a corpse. They anoint it and rinse it. . . ." In Mark's narrative the anointing and washing of Jesus' corpse had not taken place due to the haste in burying Jesus before the Sabbath began (compare John 19:39-40), and so the action of the unnamed woman in anointing Jesus' head in 14:3-9 was interpreted as the anticipation and substitution: "She anointed my body beforehand for burial" (14:8).

2. *very early on the first day of the week . . . just after sunrise:* Since Mark is fond of duplicate expressions these two temporal indications are probably best taken as meaning the same thing; that is, about 6:00 on Sunday morning. The verb *erchontai* ("lit. "they come") is an example of the historical present, another favorite Markan construction that also occurs in 16:4 (lit. "they observe") and 16:6 (lit. "he says").

3. *Who will roll back the stone . . . ?:* Why this did not occur to the women beforehand is an obvious question, especially since according to 15:47 the two Marys had witnessed the burial and seen the stone. But for them to voice this problem

on their way to the tomb helps to prepare for the surprise they encounter when they finally get to the tomb. For the task involved in rolling back the stone see the Note on 15:46.

4. *the stone had been rolled back:* The women's dilemma had already been resolved. Who rolled the stone back, however, is not stated. Was it the "young man" of 16:5, the risen Christ, or God?

For it was very large: The "afterthought" would make more sense at the end of 16:3.

5. *on entering the tomb:* This description confirms that the tomb mentioned in 15:46 was a burial cave hewn out of the rock.

a young man . . . wearing a long white robe: Matthew understood this figure to be an angel (see Matt 28:5), and this is probably as Mark intended it, but Mark does call him a *neaniskos* ("young man"), the same term he used to describe the young man clothed only in a linen cloth *(sindōn)* in 14:51.

they were utterly amazed: For previous uses of *ekthambeisthai* in Mark see 9:15 (with regard to the crowd's amazement at Jesus' arrival on the scene) and 14:33 (for Jesus' distress in Gethsemane). The term connotes intense emotion. The women did not expect to discover the tomb opened, a living being (an angel?) in it, and the corpse of Jesus nowhere to be found.

6. *You seek Jesus the Nazarene, the one who was crucified:* Jesus had been designated "the Nazarene" three times previously in Mark's Gospel: by the unclean spirit in the synagogue at Capernaum (1:23), by blind Bartimaeus (10:47), and by the high priest's maid questioning Peter (14:67). The verb *stauroun* ("crucify") was very prominent in ch. 15 (see vv. 13, 14, 15, 20, 24, 25, 27). Here, however, its participial form ("the one who was crucified") has the ring of an early Christian confession of faith (see 1 Cor 1:23; 2:2; Gal 3:1).

He has been raised; he is not here: The young man's explanation for the empty tomb is that Jesus has been raised from the dead. The aorist passive *ēgerthē* ("he has been raised") is a theological or divine passive (that is, God raised Jesus from the dead). For earlier Markan uses of *ēgerthē* see 2:12; 6:14, 16.

Look, (this is) the place where they laid him: We are to assume that the "young man" shows the women the shelf or slab on which Jesus' corpse had been laid out (see 15:46-47).

7. *go, tell his disciples and Peter:* The women are commissioned (as in the other gospels) to convey the message of Jesus' resurrection to the Eleven (with special prominence given once more to Peter). But if 16:8 is the original ending of Mark's Gospel the women fail to carry out their task.

he goes before you into Galilee: The special message confided to the women recalls Jesus' prophecy about himself in 14:28: "But after I am raised I will go before you into Galilee." Note the use of the divine passive in the reference to Jesus' resurrection ("after I am raised"). The combination of 14:28 and 16:7 leads the reader to anticipate a report about an appearance of the risen Jesus to his disciples in Galilee (see Matt 28:16-20; John 21:1-23).

8. *went out and fled . . . trembling and bewilderment . . . they were afraid:* It is not clear whether Mark intended the women's reaction to be taken as sheer terror or as holy awe in the face of God's mysterious workings.

they said nothing to anyone: The double negative *oudeni ouden* ("to no one nothing") underscores the point; see the double negatives in 15:4, 5 with regard to Jesus' silence before Pilate. Does this mean that the women said nothing only to those whom they met along their way to Peter and the other disciples? Or does it mean that they failed to deliver the message at all?

For they were afraid: The verse closes with the particle *gar* ("for"), a curious but not impossible way to end a book (see P. W. van der Horst, "Can a Book End with *gar*?" *JTS* 23 [1972] 121–24). If this was indeed intended to be the end of Mark's Gospel it is what we today might call a "cliffhanger."

INTERPRETATION

Mark 16:1-8 tells how the women discovered Jesus' tomb empty on Easter Sunday morning. Having purchased the materials for anointing the corpse of Jesus at the end of the Sabbath (16:1), the women go to the tomb early on Sunday and are amazed to find it open (16:2-4). As they enter the tomb a "young man" *(neaniskos)* announces that Jesus has been raised from the dead and commissions the women to tell Jesus' disciples that he goes before them into Galilee (16:5-7). The women are frightened, and they flee without saying anything to anyone (16:8).

Even a conservative commentator like Vincent Taylor observes about Mark 16:1-8 that "almost wholly its language consists of common Markan words" *(Mark 603)*. Taylor suggests that Mark composed the empty tomb narrative on the basis of (1) the tradition that on Easter Sunday morning women visited Jesus' tomb and found it empty, and (2) the early Christian kerygma that Jesus was buried and was raised "on the third day" (see 1 Cor 15:4) or "after three days" (Mark 8:31; 9:31; 10:33-34). In Mark's chronology the three days consist of Friday before sunset (Day 1), the Sabbath or Saturday (Day 2), and Saturday evening and Sunday morning (Day 3). For the OT significance of the third day as the decisive day for national restoration or "resurrection" see Hos 6:2: "After two days he will revive us; on the third day he will raise us up, that we may live for him."

One must distinguish between the Markan empty tomb account (probably a Markan composition) and the empty tomb tradition (a necessary presupposition for the early Christian proclamation about Jesus' resurrection). Moreover, one must admit that the empty tomb by itself does not prove that Jesus was raised from the dead. The women might have gone to the wrong tomb, or Jesus' disciples could have stolen his body, or Jesus might not really have died at all. Of course, the evangelists all take pains to show that none of these explanations is true (see Matt 27:62-66; 28:11-15; Mark 15:44-45; etc.).

For Mark and other NT writers the interpretation given by the "young man" is the only valid explanation of the empty tomb: "He has been raised; he is not here" (16:6). The young man is saying what early Christians said: Jesus of Nazareth, who really died, has been miraculously restored to life. For the historical background of Jewish and early Christian belief in the resurrection of the dead, see our treatment of Mark 12:18-27.

What is exceptional and distinctive about the early Christian proclamation that Jesus has been raised is that this happens to an individual (and not to all the dead) within the course of human history (and not at the end-time). Or to put these points in a way that is consistent with Paul's reflection on Jesus' resurrection and our resurrection in 1 Corinthians 15, the resurrection of Jesus constitutes the decisive event in a sequence of eschatological events that will issue in the fullness of God's kingdom. Jesus, the risen one, anticipates the glorious state that awaits all who remain faithful to his teaching and example.

The text of Mark's Gospel seems to break off somewhat awkwardly at 16:8 ("For they were afraid"). The "endings" found in some manuscripts (see the next unit) are generally regarded as non-Markan additions to the main text. The sudden ending at 16:8 has been explained in various ways. It is possible (but not very likely) that the evangelist died or was otherwise prevented from finishing his work. A better possibility is that the last page (or pages) of Mark's Gospel was lost. This is suggested by the anticipation of the appearance of the risen Jesus to his disciples in Galilee that is mentioned in 14:28 and 16:7. A third possibility (and the one that most scholars embrace today) is that Mark deliberately broke off his narrative at 16:8 ("For they were afraid").

Proponents of the third explanation usually appeal to Mark's skill as a writer (though some have called him "clumsy") and especially to his literary genius in leaving the story of Jesus open-ended and demanding a decision from the reader. Since Mark wrote mainly (if not exclusively) for fellow Christians he could expect all his readers to know the early Christian proclamation about the resurrection of Jesus. Moreover, in each of the Passion predictions (8:31; 9:31; 10:33-34) there has been a reference to the resurrection of Jesus. To those who know about and believe in Jesus' resurrection Mark is effectively saying: Go back and read again the story of Jesus the wonderful teacher and healer who is the suffering but now vindicated Messiah and Son of God.

If Mark 16:8 was the original ending of the gospel, what does this mean for our understanding of the women disciples? In particular, what do we make out of Mark's very emphatic comment in 16:8: "they said nothing to anyone"? In this Markan context the women fail to carry out the commission given to them by the "young man" to go and tell Jesus' disciples about the appearances of the risen Jesus that they were to experience in Galilee (16:7). In a sense their failure matches the failure of the male disciples so richly documented in chs. 14 and 15. If this is so, then Mark is saying to his readers that the character most worthy of their imitation is Jesus, and that even his earliest male and female followers, whatever their merits may have been, are not as worthy of their imitation as Jesus is.

The gospel then ends as it began, with a message from God (1:3; 16:7) pointing to a meeting with Jesus the Messiah and Son of God. As the good news of Jesus was rooted in Isaiah (see Isa 40:3 in Mark 1:3), the final command of the "young man" also echoes Isaiah, with its rhythm of forgiveness and restoration after failure: "I will lead the blind by a road they do not know, by paths they have not known I will guide them. I will turn darkness before them into light" (Isa 42:16; see Sharyn Echols Dowd, *Reading Mark* 167–69). The blindness that characterized the disciples throughout (see 8:18) will be lifted, to be replaced by seeing the risen Jesus in Galilee.

FOR REFERENCE AND FURTHER STUDY

Aichele, George Jr. "Fantasy and Myth in the Death of Jesus," *Cross Currents* 44 (1994) 85–96.

Bode, Edward L. *The First Easter Morning: The Gospel Account of the Women's Visit to the Tomb of Jesus.* Rome: Biblical Institute Press, 1970.

Boomershine, Thomas E. "Mark 16:8 and the Apostolic Commission," *JBL* 100 (1981) 213–23.

_____, and Gilbert L. Bartholomew. "The Narrative Technique of Mark 16:8," *JBL* 100 (1981) 213–23.

Danove, Paul L. *The End of Mark's Story: A Methodological Story.* Leiden: Brill, 1993.

Dowd, Sharyn Echols. "Reading Mark Reading Isaiah," *Lexington Theological Quarterly* 30 (1995) 133–43.

Hester, J. David. "Dramatic Inconclusion: Irony and the Narrative Rhetoric of the Ending of Mark," *JSNT* 57 (1995) 61–86.

Horst, P. W. van der "Can a Book End with *gar*? A Note on Mark XVI, 8," *JTS* 23 (1972) 121–24.

Lincoln, Andrew T. "The Promise and the Failure: Mark 16:7, 8," *JBL* 108 (1989) 283–300.

Magness, J. Lee. *Sense and Absence: Structure and Suspension in the Ending of Mark's Gospel.* Atlanta: Scholars Press, 1986.

O'Collins, Gerald. "The Fearful Silence of the Three Women (Mark 16:8c)," *Gregorianum* 69 (1988) 489–503.

_____. "Mary Magdalene as Major Witness to Jesus' Resurrection," *TS* 48 (1987) 631–46.

Petersen, Norman R. "When Is the End Not the End? Literary Reflections on the Ending of Mark's Narrative," *Int* 34 (1980) 151–66.

Trompf, Garry W. "The First Resurrection Appearance and the Ending of Mark's Gospel," *NTS* 18 (1971–72) 308–20.

62. *Later Endings* (16:9-20)

Whether Mark intended his gospel to end at 16:8 ("For they were afraid") or the ending was lost or never written, there is ample evidence that some of his early readers were dissatisfied with a story that seemed to break off so awkwardly. Hence various endings were supplied in the manuscript tradition, but none of them can be attributed to Mark the Evangelist with any confidence. Their vocabulary, literary style, and content are very different from what is in the body of Mark's Gospel, and these endings are unevenly represented in the manuscript tradition taken as a whole. As Bruce Metzger states after a careful examination of all the evidence: "the earliest ascertainable form of the Gospel of Mark ended with 16.8" (*A Textual Commentary on the Greek New Testament* 126).

The Shorter Ending. In some Greek, Latin, Syriac, and Coptic manuscripts Mark 16:8 is followed by this short ending:

> All that had been commanded they proclaimed briefly to those about Peter. Afterward Jesus himself appeared to them, and from the East as far as the West he sent forth through them the sacred and incorruptible proclamation of eternal salvation. Amen.

According to this ending the women did transmit the young man's message to Peter and the others, and then the risen Christ appeared to them and sent them forth to make disciples "from East to West" (see Matt 28:16-20). The Shorter Ending has the effect of tying up some loose ends about the women and about the apostles. Its language (e.g., "the sacred and incorruptible proclamation of eternal salvation") is very different from what appears elsewhere in Mark's Gospel and was clearly not composed by the evangelist.

The Longer Ending. The passage known traditionally as Mark 16:9-20 appears at the end of Mark's Gospel in a large number of manuscripts, in some cases after the Shorter Ending, but it is not present in the best Greek manuscripts (Sinaiticus and Vaticanus) as well as some important manuscripts of the ancient versions. There is no indication that Clement of Alexandria or Origen knew it, and Eusebius and Jerome claimed that it was absent from almost all the Greek manuscripts known to them. Its language, style, and content are so different from what appears in the body of Mark's Gospel that it cannot be regarded as the original ending.

The Longer Ending seems to be a compendium or epitome of resurrection appearance accounts found in the other gospels. There are four sections: (1) the appearance to Mary Magdalene (16:9-11; see Luke 24:10-11; John 20:14-18); (2) the appearance to the two disciples on their way to Emmaus (16:12-13; see Luke 24:13-35); (3) the commission to the Eleven remaining apostles to proclaim the gospel to "every creature" or "all creation" (16:14-18; see Matt 28:16-20; Luke 24:36-49; John 20:26-29); and (4) the ascension of Jesus (16:19-20; see Luke 24:50-51; Acts 1:9-11).

Perhaps part of a longer work something like a gospel harmony, Mark 16:9-20 was very likely composed in the second century C.E. and was attached to Mark's Gospel by someone who thought the text needed a better ending, especially in light of the promises about a resurrection appearance in Galilee in Mark 14:28 and 16:7.

A major theme in the first part of the Longer Ending is the disbelief shown by the Eleven regarding the reports about appearances of the risen Jesus (see 16:11, 13, 14). The third section (16:14-18) is noteworthy for the risen Jesus' discourse about proclaiming the gospel to "every creature" (or, "all creation"), his insistence on faith and baptism as necessary for salvation, and the list of "signs" that will accompany those who believe: exorcisms (see Mark 6:7, 13), speaking in new tongues (Acts 2:6; 1 Cor 14:2-5), handling serpents (Acts 28:3-5), drinking poison without harm (Eusebius, *Hist. eccl.* 3.39), and healing through the imposition of hands (Mark 6:13; Jas 5:14-15). For a full-scale analysis of this text and its second-century context see James A. Kelhoffer, *Miracle and Mission.* The text of Mark 16:9-20 reads as follows:

> 9. When he arose, early on the first day of the week he appeared first to Mary Magdalene from whom he had cast out seven demons. 10. She went and reported to those who had been with him, who were mourning and weeping. 11. When they heard that he was alive and was seen by her, they did not believe it. 12. Afterwards he appeared in another form to two of them who were walking to the countryside. 13. They went back and reported to the others. But they did not believe them. 14. Later he appeared to the Eleven as they were at table. And he rebuked their unbelief and hardness of heart because they did not believe those who saw him after he had been raised. 15. And he said to them: "Go into the whole world and proclaim the gospel to every creature. 16. Whoever believes and is baptized will be saved; but whoever does not believe will be condemned. 17. And these signs will accompany those who believe: In my name they will cast out demons; they will speak in new tongues; 18. [and with their hands] they will pick up serpents; and if they drink anything poisonous, it will not harm them; on the sick they will lay hands, and they will be well." 19. Then the Lord Jesus, after he spoke with them, was taken up into heaven and took his seat at the right hand of God. 20. They went out and preached everywhere, while the Lord worked with them and confirmed the word through the signs accompanying them.

The Freer Logion. This passage appears in Codex W (Washington), also known as the Freer Codex, after 16:14 in the Longer Ending. It is generally regarded as a scribal gloss inserted to soften the risen Jesus' criticism of the Eleven in 16:14: "And he rebuked their unbelief and hardness of heart because they did not believe those who saw him after he had been raised." The gloss seeks to explain the apostles' unbelief as due to the age in which they lived ("under Satan") before Jesus' death and resurrection opened up the possibility of true belief and righteousness. The language and style are very different from what one finds in the body of Mark's Gospel. The full text reads as follows:

> And they defended themselves, saying: "This age of lawlessness and of unbelief is under Satan who does not allow the truth and power of God to prevail over the unclean things of the spirit. Therefore reveal your righteousness now." They were speaking to Christ. And Christ replied to them: "The term of the years of the authority of Satan has been fulfilled. But now other terrible things draw near, even for those sinners on whose behalf I was handed over to death that they might turn to the truth and sin no more, in order that they may inherit the spiritual and incorruptible glory of the righteousness that is in heaven."

For Reference and Further Study

Cox, Stephen L. *A History and Critique of Scholarship Concerning the Markan Endings.* Lewiston, N.Y.: Edwin Mellen, 1993.

Farmer, William R. *The Last Twelve Verses of Mark.* Cambridge and New York: Cambridge University Press, 1974.

Holmes, Michael W. "To Be Continued. . . . The Many Endings of the Gospel of Mark," *Bible Review* 17/4 (2001) 12–23, 48–50.

Hug, Joseph. *La finale de l'Évangile de Marc (Mc 16,9-20).* Paris: Gabalda, 1978.

Kelhoffer, James A. *Miracle and Mission. The Authentication of Missionaries and Their Message in the Longer Ending of Mark.* Tübingen: J.C.B. Mohr [Paul Siebeck], 2000.

_____. "The Witness of Eusebius *ad Marinum* and Other Christian Writings to Text-Critical Debates concerning the Original Conclusion to Mark's Gospel," *ZNW* 92 (2001) 78–112.

Metzger, Bruce M. *A Textual Commentary on the Greek New Testament.* London and New York: United Bible Societies, 1971, 122–26.

Taylor, Vincent. *The Gospel According to St. Mark.* 2nd. ed. London: Macmillan, 1966, 610–15.

INDEXES

1. PRINCIPAL ANCIENT PARALLELS

Old Testament

Genesis

1:1–2:3	294
1:2	65
1:27	294–96
1:31	241
2:2	110
2:4-25	294
2:24	294–96
3:18	141
4:7	94
5:2	294
5:22-24	196
6:5	224
7:1	248
8:2	65
8:21	225
9:4-7	245
14:18-20	165
16:1-6	180
17:15-17	177
18:10-15	177
18:14	305
22:2	65, 338
22:12, 16	65
29:34	101
30:1-8	180
30:36	244
37:20	339, 341
38	349

Exodus

3	274
3–4	77
3:6	38, 351–52
3:14	213
3:15-16	351–52
3:18	244
3:20	35
4:5	351, 352
4:11	240, 242
4:21	145
5:3	244
7–14	214
8:15	145
8:27	244
8:32	145
9:34	145
12:1-28	384
12:6	392
12:11	191, 393
16:1-36	208
16:13-21	206
17:1-17	208
18:25	206
19–24	396
19:3-6, 24	122, 212
19:16-25	122, 212
20:2-6	344, 346
20:4-6	345
20:8-11	110
20:12	222–23

20:12-17	222
20:13-15	225
20:16	421
20:17	303
21:10	303
21:17	222–23
23:20	61
24	274
24:4	33
24:5-8	399
24:15-17	268
29:4-7	386
30:11-16	327
31:12-17	110
31:15	111
32–34	33
33:1-14	204
33:19-23	213
34	274
34:6	213
34:21	111
35:2	111
40:34-38	270

Leviticus

1–18	228
2:1-14	223
2:13	288–89
4:1–5:13	95
11:20-23	63
11:44	80

Early Christian Writings

2. SUBJECTS

3. AUTHORS